UNLOCKING

CONSTITUTIONAL &
ADMINISTRATIVE LAW

2nd edition

Mark Ryan

with contributions from
Steve Foster

HODDER
EDUCATION
AN HACHETTE UK COMPANY

Orders, please contact Bookpoint Ltd, 130 Milton Park, Abingdon, Oxon OX14 4SB.
Telephone: (44) 01235 827720. Fax: (44) 01235 400454. Lines are open from 9.00–5.00,
Monday to Saturday, with a 24-hour message answering service.
You can also order through our website www.hoddereducation.co.uk

If you have any comments to make about this, or any of our other titles, please send them to
educationenquiries@hodder.co.uk

British Library Cataloguing in Publication Data
A catalogue record for this title is available from the British Library

ISBN: 978 1 444 10921 4

First Edition Published 2007
This Edition Published 2010

Impression number   10   9   8   7   6   5   4   3   2
Year   2012   2011

Cover photo © Vito Palmisano / Photographer's Choice / Getty Images
Typeset by Phoenix Photosetting, Chatham, Kent

Printed in Italy for Hodder Education, an Hachette UK Company,
338 Euston Road, London NW1 3BH

Contents

Acknowledgements		*xviii*
Preface		*xix*
Guide to the book		*xx*
Table of cases		*xxii*
Table of statutes		*xxxv*
Table of statutory instruments		*xli*
Table of international legislation		*xlii*

1 INTRODUCTORY CONCEPTS

1.1	**The distinction between public law and private law**	**1**
	1.1.1 Private law	1
	1.1.2 Private law involving other than private individuals	2
	1.1.3 Public law	2
	1.1.4 Public law and criminal law	3
	1.1.5 Public law and politics	3
	1.1.6 Public law and European Union law	4
1.2	**The distinction between constitutional and administrative law**	**4**
	1.2.1 Constitutional law	4
	1.2.2 Administrative law	5

2 CONSTITUTIONS

2.1	**Definition**	**6**
2.2	**The contents of a constitution**	**7**
	2.2.1 The establishment of the institutions of government together with their roles, powers and functions	7
	2.2.2 The establishment of the relationship between the different institutions of the state	8
	2.2.3 The establishment of the relationship between the state institutions and the individual	8
	2.2.4. The methods and procedures to change the constitution	9
2.3	**Entrenching constitutional law**	**9**
2.4	**The purpose of a constitution**	**10**
	2.4.1 To ensure stability and order	10
	2.4.2 To ensure that government operates by consent and has constitutional and moral legitimacy	11
	2.4.3 To represent a constitutional watershed	12
	2.4.4 A constitutional limit and control on governmental power	12
	2.4.5 To affirm particular values and goals	12
2.5	**Different types of constitutions**	**13**
	2.5.1 Written and unwritten constitutions/codified and uncodified constitutions	13
	2.5.2 Rigid and flexible constitutions	14
	2.5.3 Federal and unitary constitutions	14
2.6	**Constitutionalism and acting 'constitutionally'**	**15**
	2.6.1 Introduction	15
	2.6.2 The basic principles of constitutionalism	16

3 THE NATURE OF THE BRITISH CONSTITUTION

3.1	Introduction and terminology	18
3.2	**Does the United Kingdom have a constitution?**	18
	3.2.1 The absence of a codified constitutional document	18
	3.2.2 The factors which indicate a British constitution	19
	3.2.3 The five tenets of the British constitution	20
	3.2.4 A system of government rather than a constitution?	20
3.3	**The nature of the British constitution**	21
	3.3.1 An uncodified constitution	21
	3.3.2 Why does the United Kingdom not have a codified constitution?	21
	3.3.3 The incremental development of the British constitution	22
3.4	**The key features of the British constitution**	22
	3.4.1 An unwritten constitution?	22
	3.4.2 Law and convention as sources	23
	3.4.3 The legislative supremacy of Parliament	23
	3.4.4 No special legal and higher status	23
	3.4.5 A flexible constitution	24
	3.4.6 A unitary constitution	25
	3.4.7 A limited monarchy	25
	3.4.8 No strict separation of powers	26
	3.4.9 An independent and impartial judiciary	26
	3.4.10 A parliamentary executive	26
	3.4.11 Responsible and accountable government	27
	3.4.12 A bicameral legislature	27
	3.4.13 A representative democracy	27
	3.4.14 An acceptance of the rule of law and respect for human rights	27
3.5	**Conclusion**	28

4 THE SOURCES OF THE BRITISH CONSTITUTION

4.1	Introduction	30
4.2	**The difficulties associated with the sources in the United Kingdom**	30
	4.2.1 What is a constitutional issue?	30
	4.2.2 The lack of a clear demarcation between constitutional and ordinary laws	31
	4.2.3 A sub-division of constitutional law	31
	4.2.4 All statutes passed in essentially the same manner	32
	4.2.5 No definitive list of statutes of a constitutional nature	32
	4.2.6 No Constitutional or Supreme Court specifically to resolve issues of a constitutional nature	33
4.3	**The classification of the sources of the British constitution**	34
	4.3.1 The classification of legal and non-legal sources	34
4.4	**Domestic primary legislation**	34
	4.4.1 Acts of Parliament	34
	4.4.2 Acts of Parliament affecting the organs of the state	35
	4.4.3 Acts of Parliament conferring rights on the individual	37
	4.4.4 Acts of Parliament restricting the freedoms of the individual	38
	4.4.5 Laws LJ and Acts of Parliament with constitutional status	38
4.5	**Domestic delegated legislation**	39
	4.5.1 The nature of delegated legislation	39
	4.5.2 Examples of delegated legislation	39
4.6	**Domestic legislation of local authorities and the devolved institutions**	39
	4.6.1 Local authorities and delegated legislation	39
	4.6.2 Legislation and the devolved institutions	40
4.7	**Legislation of the European Union**	40
	4.7.1 Primary sources	40

	4.7.2	Secondary sources	40
4.8		**Domestic case law**	**41**
	4.8.1	The role of the courts	41
	4.8.2	The common law	42
	4.8.3	Statutory interpretation	43
	4.8.4	Statutory interpretation and the Human Rights Act 1998	44
4.9		**The royal prerogative**	**45**
4.10		**European case law**	**45**
	4.10.1	The European Court of Justice in Luxembourg	45
	4.10.2	The European Court of Human Rights in Strasbourg	46
4.11		**The law and custom of Parliament**	**47**
4.12		**Treaties and international law**	**47**
4.13		**Constitutional conventions**	**48**
	4.13.1	Definition of a constitutional convention	48
	4.13.2	Preliminary points to note about constitutional conventions	48
	4.13.3	Constitutional conventions in respect of Parliament	49
	4.13.4	Constitutional conventions in respect of the monarch/executive	49
	4.13.5	Constitutional conventions in respect of the judiciary	50
	4.13.6	The significance of constitutional conventions	50
	4.13.7	The purpose of constitutional conventions	50
	4.13.8	Why are constitutional conventions followed?	51
	4.13.9	The flexibility of constitutional conventions	51
	4.13.10	What are the origins of constitutional conventions?	51
	4.13.11	The distinction between laws and constitutional conventions	52
	4.13.12	The judicial recognition of constitutional conventions	52
	4.13.13	Converting constitutional conventions into laws	53
4.14		**Authoritative writers**	**55**
4.15		**Acting unconstitutionally in the United Kingdom**	**55**
	4.15.1	The difficulties associated with the term unconstitutional in the United Kingdom	55
	4.15.2	Examples of acting unconstitutionally in the United Kingdom	55

5 THE SEPARATION OF POWERS

5.1		**Introduction**	**60**
5.2		**Definition**	**60**
	5.2.1	Introduction	60
	5.2.2	A pure separation of powers	61
	5.2.3	A less than pure separation of powers	61
5.3		**The different powers of the state**	**62**
	5.3.1	The legislative function	62
	5.3.2	The executive function	62
	5.3.3	The judicial function	63
5.4		**The relationship between the three powers in the United Kingdom**	**63**
	5.4.1	The (imaginary) Crime Act 2013	63
	5.4.2	The (imaginary) Tax Act 2013	64
	5.4.3	The (imaginary) Public Order Act 2013	64
5.5		**What is the rationale behind the separation of powers?**	**64**
	5.5.1	To avoid a concentration of public power in one body/institution	65
	5.5.2	To provide a system of checks and balances between the branches of government	65
	5.5.3	To provide an efficient government	65
	5.5.4	To safeguard the independence of the judiciary	66
5.6		**The separation of powers in the United Kingdom**	**66**
	5.6.1	The separation of powers as part of the British constitution	66
	5.6.2	The separation of powers not being part of the British constitution	67

	5.6.3	Initial observations on the separation of powers and the British constitution	67
5.7	**Aspects of the British constitution not in accord with the separation of powers**		**67**
	5.7.1	The parliamentary executive	67
	5.7.2	Delegated legislation	69
	5.7.3	The Crown/monarch is formally involved in all three branches of government	71
	5.7.4	The Appellate Committee of the House of Lords	72
	5.7.5	Parliament exercises functions other than legislative	74
	5.7.6	Historically, the executive has exercised a judicial function	74
	5.7.7	The Privy Council	75
	5.7.8	The law officers	76
	5.7.9	The Lord Chancellor	77
	5.7.10	Judges as legislators	80
	5.7.11	Administrative tribunals	82
5.8	**Aspects of the British constitution in accord with the separation of powers**		**83**
	5.8.1	Introduction	83
	5.8.2	The existence of three state institutions	83
	5.8.3	The legislature and judiciary	84
	5.8.4	The judiciary and executive	87
	5.8.5	The executive and legislature	89
5.9	**Conclusion**		**89**

6 THE RULE OF LAW

6.1	**Definition**		**93**
6.2	**The rule of law as a legal principle**		**94**
	6.2.1	A legal principle and procedural mechanism	94
	6.2.2	The limitation of the procedural mechanism	95
6.3	**The rule of law as a political ideal/theory**		**96**
	6.3.1	A formal view of the rule of law	96
	6.3.2	Raz and the rule of law	96
6.4	**The rule of law as a substantive concept**		**98**
6.5	**The rule of law as the antithesis of anarchy and chaos**		**100**
6.6	**The rule of law in international terms**		**100**
	6.6.1	The rule of law and the Universal Declaration of Human Rights	100
	6.6.2	The rule of law and the European Convention on Human Rights	101
	6.6.3	The Declaration of Delhi	102
	6.6.4	The European Union	102
6.7	**The rule of law in the British constitution**		**102**
	6.7.1	Introduction to the rule of law in the United Kingdom	102
	6.7.2	Dicey and the rule of law	103
	6.7.3	Dicey's first aspect	103
	6.7.4	Critique of Dicey's first aspect (element 1)	104
	6.7.5	Critique of Dicey's first aspect (element 2)	106
	6.7.6	Dicey's second aspect	109
	6.7.7	Critique of Dicey's second aspect	111
	6.7.8	Dicey's third aspect	113
	6.7.9	Critique of Dicey's third aspect	114
	6.7.10	The role of the United Kingdom courts and the rule of law	116
	6.7.11	Excessive state power?	121
6.8	**Conclusion**		**122**

7 PARLIAMENTARY SOVEREIGNTY

| 7.1 | **Introduction** | | **126** |

7.2	**Terminology**	**127**
	7.2.1 Legal sovereignty	127
	7.2.2 Political sovereignty	127
7.3	**The meaning and scope of legal sovereignty**	**128**
	7.3.1 Introduction	128
	7.3.2 The origins of parliamentary sovereignty	128
	7.3.3 What constitutes an Act of Parliament?	129
7.4	**Dicey and parliamentary sovereignty**	**131**
7.5	**Principle 1: The Queen in Parliament legally can pass any law**	**131**
	7.5.1 Parliamentary sovereignty and the common law	132
	7.5.2 Parliamentary sovereignty and the law-making process	132
	7.5.3 Parliamentary sovereignty and the interpretation of legislation	133
	7.5.4 Parliamentary sovereignty and the constitution	134
	7.5.5 Parliamentary sovereignty and international law	135
	7.5.6 Parliamentary sovereignty and extra-territorial jurisdiction	136
	7.5.7 Parliamentary sovereignty and the conferring of powers onto the executive	136
7.6	**Non-legal restraints on Parliament**	**137**
	7.6.1 Political restraints	137
	7.6.2 Political entrenchment	138
	7.6.3 Practical restraints	138
	7.6.4 Constitutional conventions	139
7.7	**Is there a limitation on the laws that Parliament can pass?**	**140**
7.8	**Principle 2: The courts do not challenge the authority of an Act of Parliament**	**141**
	7.8.1 Introduction	141
	7.8.2 The courts may assume that Parliament did not intend to act unconstitutionally	143
	7.8.3 The surrender of parliamentary sovereignty?	144
7.9	**Principle 3: Parliament cannot bind its successors**	**145**
	7.9.1 Introduction	145
	7.9.2 Express repeal	146
	7.9.3 Implied repeal	146
7.10	**Is legal entrenchment possible?**	**148**
	7.10.1 Entrenchment in terms of subject-matter	148
	7.10.2 Entrenchment in terms of the manner and form of later legislation	150
	7.10.3 The *Jackson* case	153
7.11	**Parliamentary sovereignty and devolution**	**154**
7.12	**Parliamentary sovereignty and the Human Rights Act 1998**	**155**
7.13	**Parliamentary sovereignty and the rule of law**	**156**

8 PARLIAMENT I: NATURE, FUNCTIONS AND PRIVILEGE

8.1	**Introduction and terminology**	**160**
	8.1.1 Parliamentary terms	160
	8.1.2 A vote of no confidence	161
	8.1.3 The summoning of a Parliament	161
	8.1.4 Parliamentary sessions	161
	8.1.5 Prorogation	162
8.2	**A bicameral legislature**	**162**
	8.2.1 Bicameralism	162
	8.2.2 Arguments in favour of bicameralism	163
	8.2.3 Arguments in favour of unicameralism	163
8.3	**The Queen in Parliament**	**163**
8.4	**The functions of Parliament**	**164**
	8.4.1 A legislative function (examining and passing proposals for law)	164

8.4.2	A deliberative function (the scrutiny of executive policy and administration)	164
8.4.3	A forum for debate (debating the major issues of the day)	165
8.4.4	To provide for taxation/finance	165
8.4.5	To safeguard the rights of individuals	165
8.4.6	The examination of proposed European legislation	165
8.4.7	A judicial function	166
8.5	**Parliamentary privilege**	**166**
8.5.1	Definition and types of privilege	166
8.5.2	The origins, sources and constitutional rationale of parliamentary privilege	167
8.6	**Freedom of speech**	**168**
8.6.1	Article 9 of the Bill of Rights 1689	168
8.6.2	Section 13 of the Defamation Act 1996	169
8.6.3	What are 'proceedings' in Parliament?	170
8.6.4	Proceedings in Parliament ought not to be 'impeached or questioned in any court'	171
8.7	**Other privileges**	**172**
8.7.1	The right to determine their own composition	172
8.7.2	The right to regulate their own internal proceedings	172
8.7.3	The right to punish individuals for contempt	173
8.8	**Members' interests and standards**	**174**
8.8.1	The Register of Members' Financial Interests	174
8.8.2	Standards in Public Life	175
8.8.3	The Parliamentary Standards Act 2009	176

9 PARLIAMENT II: THE HOUSE OF COMMONS

9.1	**The functions of the House of Commons**	**179**
9.1.1	Bagehot and the functions of the House of Commons	179
9.1.2	Modern functions of the House of Commons	179
9.2	**The size and composition of the House of Commons**	**181**
9.2.1	The number of seats in the House of Commons	181
9.2.2	The House of Commons as a representative body?	182
9.3	**The Member of Parliament**	**183**
9.3.1	The role of a Member of Parliament (MP)	183
9.3.2	The qualifications required to be an MP	184
9.3.3	The factors which disqualify a person from becoming an MP	184
9.3.4	By-elections	186
9.4	**The electoral system**	**186**
9.4.1	The system of voting	186
9.4.2	Election turnouts	187
9.4.3	The advantages of the 'first past the post' electoral system	188
9.4.4	The disadvantages of the 'first past the post' electoral system	189
9.4.5	Parliamentary constituency boundaries	190
9.5	**The current political composition of the House of Commons**	**191**
9.6	**The electorate**	**193**
9.6.1	The constitutional significance of voting	193
9.6.2	Who can vote in parliamentary elections?	193
9.6.3	Who is disqualified from voting?	194
9.7	**The supervision and conduct of elections and political parties**	**196**
9.7.1	The Electoral Commission	196
9.7.2	Election broadcasts	196
9.8	**The constitutional significance of the electoral system**	**197**
9.9	**An overview of the main elements of the House of Commons – a snapshot at February 2010**	**198**

9.10	**Reform**	**199**
	9.10.1 The electoral system	199

10 PARLIAMENT III: THE HOUSE OF LORDS

10.1	**Introduction and size of the House of Lords**	**202**
10.2	**The composition of the House of Lords**	**203**
10.3	**Lords Spiritual**	**203**
10.4	**The Judicial peers**	**204**
10.5	**Life peers**	**204**
	10.5.1 The Life Peerages Act 1958	204
	10.5.2 The creation of life peerages	205
	10.5.3 The appointment of party political peers	205
	10.5.4 The appointment of non-party political peers (independent peers)	205
10.6	**Hereditary peers**	**207**
	10.6.1 The position before the House of Lords Act 1999	207
	10.6.2 The arguments for the removal of the hereditary peers	207
	10.6.3 The House of Lords Act 1999	208
	10.6.4 Renouncing a peerage	209
10.7	**The party political composition of the House**	**210**
	10.7.1 Political breakdown of the composition of the House of Lords	210
	10.7.2 Government ministers in the House of Lords	211
	10.7.3 Independent/crossbench peers	211
	10.7.4 Other key personnel of the House	212
10.8	**Disqualification of membership of the House of Lords**	**212**
10.9	**The functions of the House of Lords**	**213**
	10.9.1 The judicial role of the House	214
	10.9.2 A forum for debate	214
	10.9.3 The revision of public Bills brought from the House of Commons	214
	10.9.4 The initiation of public legislation	215
	10.9.5 The consideration of subordinate legislation	215
	10.9.6 The scrutiny of the activities of the executive	215
	10.9.7 The scrutiny of private legislation	216
	10.9.8 The scrutiny of proposed European legislation	216
	10.9.9 A guardian of the constitution and watchdog of civil liberties and human rights	216
10.10	**The legal powers of the House of Lords**	**217**
	10.10.1 Legal limitations	218
	10.10.2 The use of the Parliament Acts	218
	10.10.3 Is the Parliament Act 1949 legal?	219
10.11	**Limitations imposed by constitutional convention**	**220**
10.12	**The relationship between the House of Lords and the House of Commons**	**222**
10.13	**Reform**	**224**

11 THE EXECUTIVE

11.1	**Introduction and terminology**	**229**
	11.1.1 Definition of government	229
	11.1.2 The constitutional monarchy and the Crown	229
	11.1.3 The different forms of executive	230
11.2	**The political executive/Her Majesty's Government**	**231**
	11.2.1 The monarch	231
	11.2.2 The Prime Minister	231
	11.2.3 The Cabinet	231
	11.2.4 Junior ministers	233
	11.2.5 Central government departments headed by a government minister	233
	11.2.6 The Privy Council	234

11.3	**The non-political or bureaucratic executive**	**234**
	11.3.1 The Civil Service	234
	11.3.2 Executive agencies/the 'Next Step Agencies'	237
	11.3.3 Non-departmental public bodies	237
11.4	**The executive in practical terms**	**238**
11.5	**Other executive bodies in the British constitution**	**238**
11.6	**The statistical breakdown of government ministers**	**239**
	11.6.1 The parliamentary executive	239
	11.6.2 Government ministers in the House of Lords	239
	11.6.3 The executive and the separation of powers	240
11.7	**The functions of the executive**	**240**
11.8	**The powers of the executive**	**241**
	11.8.1 Statutory powers	241
	11.8.2 Common law powers	242
11.9	**The royal prerogative**	**242**
	11.9.1 Definition	242
	11.9.2 The context of recent reform proposals	243
	11.9.3 The Public Admininstration Select Committee classification	243
	11.9.4 The 2009 Review	247
	11.9.5 The constitutional relationship between Parliament and the royal prerogative	248
	11.9.6 The constitutional relationship between the judiciary and the royal prerogative	249
	11.9.7 The constitutional significance of the royal prerogative	251

12 EXECUTIVE/PARLIAMENTARY RELATIONS

12.1	**The constitutional convention of ministerial responsibility**	**255**
	12.1.1 Classification	255
	12.1.2 The *Ministerial Code*	256
12.2	**The constitutional convention of collective ministerial responsibility**	**256**
	12.2.1 The loss of confidence of the House of Commons	257
	12.2.2 The government speaks with one single voice	257
	12.2.3 Cabinet discussions remain secret	258
12.3	**The constitutional convention of individual ministerial responsibility**	**258**
	12.3.1 Constitutional responsibility for professional conduct and departmental activity	258
	12.3.2 Resignations due to ministerial decisions or actions made as a minister	259
	12.3.3 Resignations due to the actions of departmental officials	259
	12.3.4 Constitutional responsibility for conduct in a minister's private life	260
	12.3.5 Uncertain aspects of individual ministerial responsibility	262
12.4	**Parliamentary questions**	**263**
	12.4.1 Oral questions in the House of Commons	263
	12.4.2 Oral questions to the Prime Minister	264
	12.4.3 The advantages and disadvantages of PMQs	264
	12.4.4 Oral questions to other government ministers	265
	12.4.5 The advantages and disadvantages of oral questions to ministers	265
	12.4.6 Written questions in the House of Commons	265
	12.4.7 The advantages and disadvantages of written questions	266
	12.4.8 Oral and written questions in the House of Lords	266
	12.4.9 Urgent questions	267
12.5	**Parliamentary debates**	**267**
	12.5.1 Debates in the House of Commons	267
	12.5.2 Debates in the House of Lords	269
	12.5.3 The advantages and disadvantages of parliamentary debates	270

12.6	**The parliamentary committee system**	**271**
	12.6.1 Classification	271
	12.6.2 Departmental select committees	271
	12.6.3 The function of select committees	272
	12.6.4 The composition of select committees	273
	12.6.5 The powers of select committees	273
	12.6.6 Select committee reports	273
	12.6.7 Other select committees	274
	12.6.8 Joint committees	274
	12.6.9 Committees in the House of Lords	274
	12.6.10 The advantages and disadvantages of select committees	275
	12.6.11 Recent reforms	276
12.7	**Scrutiny during the legislative process**	**276**
	12.7.1 Draft legislation	277
	12.7.2 The second reading	277
	12.7.3 The committee and subsequent stages	277
	12.7.4 Procedural matters	279
	12.7.5 Delegated legislation	279
12.8	**Scrutiny in the context of finance**	**281**
12.9	**Scrutiny in the context of Europe**	**282**

13 THE JUDICIARY

13.1	**Introduction and definition**	**285**
13.2	**The constitutional dimension of the judiciary**	**285**
	13.2.1 The separation of powers	286
	13.2.2 Parliamentary sovereignty	287
	13.2.3 The rule of law and the protection of the individual	288
	13.2.4 Judicial review	288
13.3	**The appointment of the judiciary**	**289**
	13.3.1 Judicial appointments	289
	13.3.2 Arguments against executive involvement in judicial appointments	289
	13.3.3 Arguments in favour of executive involvement in judicial appointments	290
13.4	**The independence of the judiciary**	**290**
	13.4.1 Statutory protection	291
	13.4.2 Common law protection	292
	13.4.3 Parliamentary protection	295
	13.4.4 Protection through constitutional convention	295
13.5	**Judicial accountability**	**295**
13.6	**The perception of judicial independence, neutrality and impartiality**	**296**
	13.6.1 The composition of the judiciary	296
	13.6.2 Judges and civil liberties	297

14 THE DECENTRALISATION OF PUBLIC POWER

14.1	**Introduction**	**300**
14.2	**Local government**	**301**
	14.2.1 Introduction and structure	301
	14.2.2 The functions of local government	302
	14.2.3 The advantages of local government	303
	14.2.4 The disadvantages of local government	304
	14.2.5 The control of local government	305
	14.2.6 The relationship between central and local government	307
14.3	**Scottish devolution**	**308**
	14.3.1 History	308
	14.3.2 Arguments for and against Scottish devolution	309

14.3.3	The Scottish Parliament	310
14.3.4	The Scottish administration	311
14.3.5	Legislation	312
14.3.6	Devolved and reserved matters	313
14.3.7	Tax-varying powers	314
14.3.8	Legislative competence	314
14.3.9	Ensuring the Scottish Parliament legislates within its powers	315
14.3.10	Challenging the actions of the Scottish Executive	315
14.3.11	The European Convention and devolution	315
14.3.12	The relationship with Westminster	316
14.3.13	Parliamentary sovereignty and the Scottish Parliament	316
14.3.14	Further reform	317
14.4	**Northern Irish devolution**	**318**
14.4.1	History	318
14.4.2	The Northern Ireland Assembly	319
14.4.3	The Northern Ireland Executive Committee	320
14.4.4	Legislation and legislative competence	320
14.4.5	Reserved, excepted and transferred matters	321
14.4.6	Ensuring the Northern Ireland Assembly legislates within its powers	321
14.4.7	Challenging the actions of the Northern Ireland Executive Committee	321
14.4.8	The relationship with Westminster and parliamentary sovereignty	322
14.4.9	Other strands to the Belfast Agreement	323
14.5	**Welsh devolution**	**323**
14.5.1	History	323
14.5.2	The National Assembly for Wales	323
14.5.3	The Welsh Assembly Government	324
14.5.4	Powers and responsibilities	326
14.5.5	The competence of the institutions	326
14.5.6	The relationship with Westminster and parliamentary sovereignty	327
14.6	**The position of England**	**328**
14.6.1	No English Parliament	328
14.6.2	Regional Development Agencies	329
14.6.3	The London Mayor and Assembly	329

15 THE EUROPEAN UNION

15.1	**The Treaties**	**335**
15.1.1	A *de facto* constitution?	335
15.1.2	The European Constitution/Treaty of Lisbon	336
15.2	**The institutions**	**336**
15.2.1	An outline of the institutions	336
15.2.2	The separation of powers in Europe	337
15.2.3	Democracy and the European institutions	338
15.3	**Sources of law**	**339**
15.3.1	Primary sources	340
15.3.2	Secondary sources	340
15.4	**The European Court of Justice**	**340**
15.4.1	The distinctive nature of the court	340
15.4.2	The role of the European Court of Justice	341
15.5	**Individuals**	**342**
15.6	**European Union law and parliamentary sovereignty**	**343**
15.6.1	Introduction	343
15.6.2	The primacy of European law	343
15.6.3	The reception of European Union law in the British constitution	344
15.6.4	The *Factortame* litigation	346
15.6.5	The constitutional impact of *Factortame*	347

16 THE EUROPEAN CONVENTION ON HUMAN RIGHTS

16.1	**Introduction and background**	**351**
16.2	**The enforcement machinery**	**352**
16.3	**The European Court of Human Rights**	**353**
	16.3.1 The Composition of the European Court of Human Rights	353
	16.3.2 The Grand Chamber of the European Court	353
16.4	**The Role of the European Court of Human Rights**	**354**
	16.4.1 The effect of the European Court of Human Rights' judgments and their effect	354
	16.4.2 The power to award just satisfaction	354
16.5	**State and individual applications**	**355**
	16.5.1 Inter-state applications	355
	16.5.2 Individual applications	356
	16.5.3 The requirement to be a victim	356
	16.5.4 Admissibility of applications	356
	16.5.5 The admissibility criteria	356
	16.5.6 Friendly settlements and striking out	357
16.6	**Lawful and permissible interferences with Convention rights**	**358**
	16.6.1 Prescribed by law/in accordance with law	359
	16.6.2 Legitimate aims	360
	16.6.3 Necessary in a democratic society	360
	16.6.4 The doctrine of proportionality	361
	16.6.5 The margin of appreciation	361
16.7	**Derogations and reservations**	**363**
	16.7.1 Derogation in times of war or other public emergency	363
	16.7.2 Reservations	364
16.8	**The rights guaranteed under the European Convention on Human Rights**	**365**
	16.8.1 Absolute and conditional rights	365
16.9	**Article 2 – The Right to Life**	**366**
	16.9.1 The scope of Article 2	366
	16.9.2 The duty to carry out an effective investigation	367
	16.9.3 The exceptions under Article 2.2	367
	16.9.4 Article 2 and the death penalty	368
16.10	**Article 3 – Prohibition of torture and inhuman and degrading treatment and punishment**	**368**
	16.10.1 The scope of Article 3	368
	16.10.2 Definition of torture, inhuman and degrading treatment or punishment	369
	16.10.3 Article 3 and corporal punishment	369
	16.10.4 Article 3 and deportation and extradition	370
16.11	**Article 4 – Prohibition of slavery and forced labour**	**371**
	16.11.1 The prohibition of slavery and servitude	371
	16.11.2 Prohibition of forced or compulsory labour	371
16.12	**Article 5 – Liberty and security of the person**	**372**
	16.12.1 Scope of the article	372
	16.12.2 Lawful detention after conviction	372
	16.12.3 Lawful arrest or detention for non-compliance of a lawful court order	372
	16.12.4 Lawful detention following arrest	373
	16.12.5 Other lawful restrictions	373
	16.12.6 Right to be informed of reasons for arrest and charge	373
	16.12.7 The right to be brought promptly before a judge for trial or release	374
	16.12.8 Right to challenge lawfulness of detention	374
	16.12.9 Right to compensation for breach of Article 5	375
16.13	**Article 6 – The right to a fair and public hearing**	**375**
	16.13.1 The scope of Article 6	375

16.13.2	The right of access to the courts	375
16.13.3	The right to a public hearing before an impartial court or tribunal	376
16.13.4	The right to effective participation in the trial	377
16.13.5	The presumption of innocence and the rule against self-incrimination	377
16.13.6	The right to legal assistance	378
16.13.7	The right to call and question witnesses	378
16.14	**Article 7 – Prohibition of retrospective criminal law and penalties**	**378**
16.14.1	The scope of Article 7	379
16.14.2	The exceptions to Article 7	379
16.15	**Article 8 – Right to private and family life**	**380**
16.15.1	The scope of Article 8	380
16.15.2	The right to respect for private life	380
16.15.3	The right to respect for family life	380
16.15.4	The right to respect for the home	381
16.15.5	The right to respect for correspondence	381
16.16	**Article 9 – Freedom of thought, conscience and religion**	**382**
16.16.1	The scope of Article 9	382
16.16.2	Permissible restrictions	382
16.17	**Article 10 – Freedom of expression**	**383**
16.17.1	The scope of Article 10	383
16.17.2	Restrictions on freedom of expression – Article 10(2)	383
16.18	**Article 11 – Freedom of assembly and association**	**384**
16.18.1	The scope of Article 11	384
16.18.2	Freedom of association	384
16.18.3	Freedom of peaceful assembly	385
16.19	**Article 12 – The right to marry**	**385**
16.19.1	The scope of Article 12	385
16.19.2	Restrictions on the right to marry	386
16.20	**Article 1 of the First Protocol – the right to property**	**386**
16.20.1	The scope of the right to property	386
16.20.2	Lawful restrictions on the right to property	386
16.21	**Article 2 of the First Protocol – the right to education**	**387**
16.22	**Article 3 – the right to free elections**	**387**
16.22.1	The scope of the right to vote	388
16.22.2	Limitations on the right to vote	388
16.23	**Articles 13 and 14 – the right to an effective remedy and freedom from discrimination**	**388**
16.23.1	The right to an effective remedy – Article 13	388
16.23.2	Prohibition of Discrimination – Article 14	389
16.23.3	The scope of Article 14	389
16.23.4	Justifiable discrimination	389

17 THE HUMAN RIGHTS ACT 1998

17.1	**Introduction**	**393**
17.2	**Pre-Human Rights Act 1998 position**	**393**
17.2.1	The role of the courts in protecting civil liberties	394
17.2.2	The role of Parliament in protecting civil liberties	394
17.2.3	The criticisms of the traditional system	394
17.3	**The passing of the Human Rights Act 1998**	**395**
17.3.1	Central aims and provisions of the Act	395
17.3.2	Retrospective effect of the Act	396
17.3.3	The rights guaranteed under the Act	397
17.4	**Use of Convention case law by the domestic courts**	**398**
17.5	**The doctrine of proportionality**	**399**

17.6	**Interpreting statutory provisions in the light of the Convention**	**401**
	17.6.1 The scope of section 3	402
17.7	**Declarations of incompatibility**	**404**
	17.7.1 Declarations of incompatibility in practice	405
	17.7.2 Statements of compatibility	407
	17.7.3 Remedial action	408
17.8	**Liability of public authorities under the Act**	**409**
	17.8.1 Definition of 'public authority'	410
	17.8.2 The 'horizontal' effect of the Human Rights Act 1998	411
17.9	**Remedies under the Act**	**412**
	17.9.1 Victims of a Convention violation	412
	17.9.2 Power to award an appropriate remedy	413
	17.9.3 Damages and the Human Rights Act 1998	413
17.10	**Freedom of expression and freedom of religion**	**415**
17.11	**Derogations and reservations**	**416**
	17.11.1 Derogations	416
	17.11.2 Reservations	417

18 FREEDOM OF SPEECH

18.1	**The constitutional importance of free speech**	**420**
	18.1.1 Introduction	420
	18.1.2 The justification for the principle of free expression	421
18.2	**Freedom of expression in the British constitution**	**422**
	18.2.1 The residual liberty of expression	422
	18.2.2 The interplay of freedom of speech with other competing interests	423
	18.2.3 The Human Rights Act 1998	424
	18.2.4 Article 10	424
18.3	**Free speech and the criminal law**	**426**
	18.3.1 Protecting religious sensibilities	426
	18.3.2 Protecting the public from indecent material	427
	18.3.3 Controlling material which depraves and corrupts	427
	18.3.4 Protecting public order	428
	18.3.5 Protecting the administration of justice	428
	18.3.6 Protecting national security	428
18.4	**Free speech and the civil law**	**429**
	18.4.1 The protection of reputation	429
	18.4.2 The protection of confidential information	430

19 JUDICIAL REVIEW I (RATIONALE AND PROCEDURE)

19.1	**Administrative law**	**433**
	19.1.1 Introduction	433
	19.1.2 Political control	434
	19.1.3 Legal control	434
	19.1.4. Extra-judicial remedies	435
19.2	**Judicial review**	**435**
	19.2.1 Definition	435
	19.2.2 A review and not an appellate jurisdiction	436
	19.2.3 The constitutional dimension of judicial review	437
	19.2.4 The controversial nature of judicial review	438
	19.2.5 A special 'administrative court'?	441
	19.2.6 The mechanics of judicial review	442
19.3	**Bodies subject to judicial review**	**442**
	19.3.1 Government/public bodies	443
	19.3.2 Judicial bodies	443

	19.3.3 Non-governmental bodies	443
	19.3.4 Private bodies and administrative principles	445
19.4	**Standing in judicial review**	**445**
	19.4.1 Individuals	446
	19.4.2 Groups/organisations	446
	19.4.3 Local government	447
	19.4.4 When should standing be determined?	447
19.5	**A public law issue**	**448**
	19.5.1 Public law issues	448
	19.5.2 Exclusive proceedings	448
	19.5.3 Collateral cases	449
	19.5.4 The use of a public law issue in an individual's defence	450
	19.5.5 Consent	450
19.6	**Procedure**	**451**
	19.6.1 The Pre-action Protocol and claim	451
	19.6.2 Permission to apply for judicial review	451
	19.6.3 The time limit	451
	19.6.4 The substantive hearing	452

20 JUDICIAL REVIEW II (GROUNDS OF REVIEW AND REMEDIES)

20.1	**Grounds for judicial review**	**454**
20.2	**The ground of illegality**	**455**
	20.2.1 Definition and classification	455
	20.2.2 Simple *ultra vires*	456
	20.2.3 Wrongful delegation of power	458
	20.2.4 Improper purpose	460
	20.2.5 Abuse of discretion	462
	20.2.6 Excess of jurisdiction	464
	20.2.7 Breach of the European Convention on Human Rights	467
20.3	**The ground of irrationality**	**468**
	20.3.1 Origins and definition	468
	20.3.2 The controversial nature of irrationality	469
	20.3.3 Irrationality in practice	471
20.4	**The ground of proportionality**	**471**
	20.4.1 Origins and definition	471
	20.4.2 Proportionality and irrationality compared	472
	20.4.3 Proportionality pre-Human Rights Act?	473
	20.4.4 Proportionality and the Human Rights Act 1998	473
	20.4.5 The demise of irrationality?	474
20.5	**The ground of procedural impropriety**	**475**
	20.5.1 Definition	475
	20.5.2 Statutory requirements	476
	20.5.3 Common law requirements: *Nemo judex in re sua*	477
	20.5.4 Common law requirements: *Audi alteram partem*	480
20.6	**Remedies**	**486**
	20.6.1 The different remedies available	486
	20.6.2 The discretionary nature of remedies	487
20.7	**The effectiveness of judicial review**	**488**
	20.7.1 Factors which support its effectiveness	488
	20.7.2 Factors which question its effectiveness	488
20.8	**Judicial review checklist**	**489**

21 GRIEVANCE MECHANISMS

21.1	**Tribunals**	**491**
	21.1.1 Definition and history	491

	21.1.2 Types of tribunals	492
	21.1.3 The constitutional position of tribunals	492
	21.1.4 Advantages of tribunals	493
	21.1.5 Disadvantages of tribunals	494
	21.1.6 Reform	495
	21.1.7 The Tribunals, Courts and Enforcement Act 2007	496
21.2	**Inquiries**	**497**
	21.2.1 Land inquiries	497
	21.2.2 Inquiries into national events/scandals	498
	21.2.3 Statutory inquiries into national events	498
	21.2.4 Non-statutory inquiries into national events	499
21.3	**Ombudsmen**	**500**
	21.3.1 Origins	501
	21.3.2 Maladministration	501
	21.3.3 Jurisdiction	502
	21.3.4 The investigation process	503
	21.3.5 Ombudsman or Ombudsmouse?	506
	21.3.6 Accountability	507
	21.3.7 Other ombudsmen	508
Glossary		*512*
Index		*514*

Acknowledgements

The books in this series are a departure from traditional law texts and represent one view of a type of learning resource that we feel is particularly useful to students. The series editors would therefore like to thank the publishers for their support in making the project a reality. In particular we would also like to thank Alexia Chan for her continued faith in the project from its first conception.

Jacqueline Martin & Chris Turner

I would like to thank Gibson Fairnie (for his assistance in proof reading the text), Donna Walker, Vicki Mcgeown and Steve Foster, for their support during the writing of this text. Finally, I would like to thank Jasmin and Amber at Hodder for their support in producing this second edition.

This book is dedicated to my mother and my siblings (John, PJ, Gerard, Mandy, Caroline and Maureen) and my nieces and nephews (Jamie, Jonathan, Tara, Natacha, Jade, Sebastian, Celia, Bailey, Dulcie, Ned and Theo).

Mark Ryan

Preface

The Unlocking the Law series is an entirely new style of undergraduate law textbook. Many student texts are very prose dense and have little in the way of interactive materials to help a student feel his or her way through the course of study on a given module.

The purpose of this series, then, is to try to make learning each subject area more accessible by focusing on actual learning needs, and by providing a range of different supporting materials and features.

All topic areas are broken up into 'bite-size' sections, with a logical progression and extensive use of headings and numerous sub-headings. Each book in the series will also contain a variety of charts, diagrams and key facts summaries to reinforce the information in the body of the text. Diagrams and flow charts are particularly useful because they can provide a quick and easy understanding of the key points, especially when revising for examinations. Key facts charts not only provide a quick visual guide through the subject but are useful for revision purposes also.

Note also that for all incidental references to 'he', 'him', 'his', we invoke the Interpretation Act 1978 and its provisions that 'he' includes 'she' etc.

Chapters 1–15 and 18–21 were written by Mark Ryan, and Chapters 16–17 were written by Steve Foster.

The law is stated as we believe it to be on 1 January 2010, although where space permits some material has been added after this date (for example, the results of the 2010 general election).

Mark Ryan
Steve Foster

Guide to the book

In the Unlocking the Law books all the essential elements that make up the law are clearly defined to bring the law alive and make it memorable. In addition, the books are enhanced with learning features to reinforce learning and test your knowledge as you study. Follow this guide to make sure you get the most from reading this book.

AIMS AND OBJECTIVES

Defines what you will learn in each chapter.

definition
Find key legal terminology at-a-glance.

SECTION

Highlights sections from Acts.

ARTICLE

Defines Articles of the EC Treaty or of the European Convention on Human Rights or other Treaty.

tutor tip
Provides key ideas from lecturers on how to get ahead.

CLAUSE

Shows a Bill going through Parliament or a draft Bill proposed by the Law Commission.

CASE EXAMPLE

 Illustrates the law in action.

JUDGMENT

Provides extracts from judgments on cases.

Indicates that you will be able to test yourself further on this topic using the Key Questions and Answers section of this book on www.unlockingthelaw.co.uk.

QUOTATION

Encourages you to engage with primary sources.

ACTIVITY

Enables you to test yourself as you progress through the chapter.

student mentor tip

Offers advice from law graduates on the best way to achieve the results you want.

SAMPLE ESSAY QUESTIONS

Provide you with real-life sample essays and show you the best way to plan your answer.

SUMMARY

Concludes each chapter to reinforce learning.

Table of cases

Please note: this table was prepared by the Publishers, who take full responsibility for any errors therein.

A v United Kingdom (2003) 36 EHRR 51 ....168, 169

A v United Kingdom (2009) 49 EHRR 29 ....105, 353, 355, 364, 373, 375, 392, 399, 400, 417

A v United Kingdom (human rights: punishment of child) (Application 25599/94) (Case
    100/1997/884/1096) [1998] TLR, 1 October; [1998] 2 FLR 959; (1998) 27 EHRR 611 ...356, 369, 370

A and Others v Secretary of State for the Home Department [2004] UKHL 56; [2005] 2 AC 68;
    [2004] 3 WLR 87; [2005] 3 All ER 169 ....222, 288, 297, 364, 400, 401, 406, 416, 417, 473

A and Others v Secretary of State for the Home Department (No 2) [2005] UKHL 71;
    [2006] 1 All ER 575 ....121, 125, 297

ADT v United Kingdom (2001) 31 EHRR 33 389

AF v Secretary of State for the Home Department [2009] UKHL 28 399

AWG Group Ltd v Morrison [2006] EWCA Civ 6; [2006] 1 All ER 967; [2006] 1 WLR 1163 294

Abdulaziz, Cabales and Balkandali v United Kingdom (Applications 9214/80, 9473/81,
    9474/81) (1985) 7 EHRR 471 389

Agricultural Horticultural and Forestry Industry Training Board v Aylesbury Mushrooms Ltd
    [1972] 1 WLR 190 ....477, 486

Agricultural, Horticultural and Forestry Industry Training Board v Kent [1970] 1 All 340 477

Ahmed v HM Treasury [2010] UKSC 2 ....457, 394

Ahmed v United Kingdom (Application 8160/78) (1981) 4 EHRR 126, EComHR 382

Airey v Ireland (Application 6289/73) (1979) 2 EHRR 305, [1979] ECHR 6289/73.......................376

Akdivar v Turkey (Application 21893/93) (1996) 1 BHRC 137, 23 EHRR 143 ....357, 381

Al-Saadoon and Mufhdi v United Kingdom, *The Times*, 10th March, 2010................................368

Allason v Haines (1995) 145 NLJ Rep 1576; (1995) *The Times*, 25 July 169

Allingham and another v Minister of Agriculture and Fisheries [1948] 1 KB 780 458

Alvin Lee Sinclair v Her Majesty's Advocate [2005] UKPC D2...316

Amekrane v United Kingdom (1974) 44 CD 101 357

Anderson and Others v Scottish Ministers [2002] SC (PC) 1 315

Anderson and Taylor v Home Secretary, *See* R (on the application of Anderson) v Secretary of
    State for the Home Department; R (on the application of Taylor) v Same—

Anderson v Gorries [1895] 1 QB 668...112, 292, 298

Anisminic Ltd v Foreign Compensation Commission [1969] 2 AC 147; [1968] 2 QB 862;
    (1969) 85 LQR 198...440, 466, 468

Arlidge v Mayor, Aldermen and Councillors of the Metropolitan Borough of Islington [1909]
    2 KB 127...305

Arrowsmith v United Kingdom (1978) 3 EHRR 218 382

Ashbridge Investments Ltd v Minister of Housing and Local Government [1965] 3 All ER
    371...465, 468

Assenov v Bulgaria (1999) 28 EHRR 652...374

Associated Provincial Picture House Ltd v Wednesbury Corporation
    [1948] 1 KB 223..399, 400, 437, 468, 469, 471, 474, 475

Attorney General v Crayford Urban District Council [1962] 2 All ER 147 457

Attorney General v De Keyser's Royal Hotel Ltd [1920] AC 508....................................132, 248, 253

Attorney General v Fulham Corporation [1921] 1 Ch 440 ....456, 468

Attorney General v Jonathan Cape Ltd (the Crossman Diaries case) [1976] 1 QB 752 ....52, 258

Attorney General v Observer Ltd and others [1988] 3 WLR 776 (The Spycatcher case) 430, 432

Attorney General v Wilts United Dairies Ltd (1921) 37 TLR 884 44

Attorney General for New South Wales v Trethowan [1932] AC 526; (1931) 44 CLR 394 ....150, 152

Attorney General of Hong Kong v Ng Yuen Shiu [1983] 2 All ER 346................................482

B and L v United Kingdom (2006) 42 EHRR 11 386

BBC v Johns (Inspector of Taxes) [1965] Ch 32...249

Barnard and others v National Dock Labour Board and another [1953] 2 QB 18; [1953]
    1 All ER 1113..459

Barthold v Germany (1985) 7 EHRR 383...361, 365
Beets and others v United Kingdom (2005) *The Times*, 10 March.......................373
Belgian Linguistics Case (No 2), The (1968) 1 EHRR 252 ....387, 389
Bellinger v Bellinger [2003] UKHL 21; [2003] 2 All ER 593 ....44, 58, 403–405
Benham v United Kingdom (1996) 22 EHRR 293 373
Bertrand Russell Peace Foundation v United Kingdom 14 DR 117 (1978) 357
Blackburn v Attorney General [1971] 1 WLR 1037; [1971] 2 All ER 1380...........139, 158, 250
Boddington v British Transport Police [1999] 2 AC 143...............................449, 450
Bowles v Bank of England [1913] 1 Ch 57...130
Bradlaugh v Gossett (1884) 12 QBD 271...173
Brannigan and McBride v United Kingdom (1993) 17 EHRR 539; (1993) *The Times*,
    28 May..364, 365
Brennan v United Kingdom (2002) 34 EHRR 18..378
Bribery Commissioner v Pedrick Ranasinghe [1965] AC 172......................151, 158
British Coal Corporation v R [1935] AC 500...138
British Oxygen Co Ltd v Minister of Technology [1971] AC 610 ....462, 468
British Railways Board v Pickin *See* Pickin v British Railways Board—
Brogan v United Kingdom (1988) 11 EHRR 117.............................374, 375, 416
Bromley London Borough Council v Greater London Council [1983] 1 AC 768; [1982]
    2 WLR 62...463
Brown v Stott (Procurator Fiscal, Dunfermline) and another [2003] 1 AC 681; [2001]
    2 All ER 97 ....316, 407
Broziek v Italy (1989) 12 EHRR 371 377
Brutus v Cozens [1973] AC 854 466
Bryan v United Kingdom (1995) 21 EHRR 342 ....376, 406
Bubbins v United Kingdom (Application 50196/99) (2005) 41 EHRR 24; [2005] All ER (D)
    290 (Mar)...368
Buckley v United Kingdom (1996) 23 EHRR 101...381
Bugdaycay v Secretary of State for the Home Department [1987] 1 AC 514...................470
Bulmer v Bollinger [1974] Ch 401..334, 341
Burmah Oil Company v Lord Advocate [1965] AC 75 ....45, 47, 115, 132, 248

Caballero v United kingdom (2000) 30 EHRR 643 374
Campbell v Mirror Group Newspapers Ltd [2004] UKHL 22; [2004] 2 AC 457........412, 413, 418, 430
Campbell v United Kingdom (1992) 15 EHRR 137...376
Campbell and Cosans v United Kingdom (1982) 4 EHRR 293 ....370, 387
Carltona Ltd v Commissioners of Works and Others [1943] 2 All ER 560.....53, 59, 240, 259, 459, 468
Case of Proclamations (1611) 12 Co Rep 74 ....45, 58, 249
Castells v Spain (1992) 14 EHRR 445..421
Chaffers v Goldsmid [1894] 1 QB 186..173
Chahal v United Kingdom (1996) 23 EHRR 413; (1996) *The Times*, 28 November;
    1 BHRC 405, ECtHR 105, 368, 370, 373, 374, 390, 395, 416
Cheney v Conn [1968] 1 WLR 242; [1968] 1 All ER 779...........................129, 135
Chester v Bateson [1920] 1 KB 829.........................55, 70, 80, 108, 288, 457
Chief Constable of North Wales Police v Evans [1982] 1 WLR 1155............................436
Child Support Agency (2001–02) Case No C.1685/00 507
Chorherr v Austria (1993) 17 EHRR 358 385
Choudhury v United Kingdom (1991) 12 HR LJ 172 ....382, 389, 391
Clark v University of Lincolnshire and Humberside [2000] 1 WLR 1988......................450
Coleen Properties Ltd v Minister of Housing and Local Government [1971] 1 WLF 433 465
Commission v France (Case C-30/89) [1990] ECR I-691 102
Commission v French Republic (Case 167/73) [1974] ECR 359 344
Commissioners of Customs and Excise v Cure and Deeley Ltd [1962] 1 QB 340.............107, 118, 457
Condron v United Kingdom (2001) 31 EHRR 1; [2000] Crim LR 679; [2000] TLR, 9 May..............378
Congreve v Home Office [1976] QB 629; [1976] 1 All ER 697................460, 468, 503
Connolly and Havering LBC v Secretary of State for Communities and Local Government
    [2009] EWCA Civ 1059..465
Corporate Officer of the House of Commons v Information Commissioner [2008]
    EWHC 1084 (Admin)...24
Costa v ENEL (Case 6/64) [1964] ECR 585; CMLR 425 ....46, 58, 343, 348

Costello-Roberts v United Kingdom, Judgment 25 March 1993; (1993) 19 EHRR 112....................370
Council of Civil Service Unions v Minister of State for the Civil Service (the GCHQ case)
    [1985] 1 AC 374; [1984] 3 All ER 935 ....249, 250, 253, 454, 455, 468, 469, 471, 475, 482, 490
Council of Civil Service Unions v United Kingdom (1987) 50 DR 228...384
Countryside Alliance v UK (2010) 50 EHRR S E6...220, 401
Cream Holdings Ltd v Banerjee [2004] UKHL 44; [2004] 3 WLR 918...415, 425
Customs and Excise Comrs v Cure & Deeley Ltd [1962] 1 QB 340; [1961] 3 All ER 641;
    [1961] 3 WLR 798; 105 Sol Jo 708, QBD 108

D v United Kingdom (Case 146/1996/767/964) (1997) 24 EHRR 423; (1997) *The Times*,
    12 May...370
Davy v Spelthorn Borough Council [1984] 1 AC 262 2
De Becker v Belgium (Application 00214/56) (1962) 1 EHRR 43, 1962 (1963) YB (ECHR)
    320 (27 March 1962) (1979–80), ECtHR..356
De Wilde, Ooms and Versyp v Belgium (1971) 1 EHRR 373..374
Debt of Honour Case, *See* R (on the application of Association of British Civilian Internees Far
    Eastern Region) v Secretary of State for Defence—
Derbyshire County Council v Times Newspapers Ltd and Others [1993] AC 534;
    [1993] 1 All ER 1011 ....33, 42, 47, 429
Dickson v United Kingdom (2008) 46 EHRR 41 381
Dillon v Balfour (1887) 20 LR Ir 600..170
Dimes v The Proprietors of the Grand Junction Canal (1852) 3 HLC 759.........................293, 478, 486
Douglas and Others v Hello! Ltd and others [2001] 2 WLR 992; [2001] 2 All ER 289;
    (2000) 9 BHRC 543; [2002] 1 FCR 289...380, 411, 415
Dr Bonham's Case (1610) 8 Co Rep 114a; 77 ER 646; 2 Brown 255...143
Dubowska and Skup v Poland (1997) 24 EHRR CD 75 382
Dudgeon v United Kingdom (Application 7525/76) (1981) 4 EHRR 149, [1981] ECHR
    7525/76, ECtHR, referred from (1980) 3 EHRR 40, EComHR 46, 58, 356, 362, 380, 413
Duport Steels Ltd and Others v Sirs and Others [1980] 1 All ER 529; [1980]
    1 WLR 142...66, 81, 85, 128, 142, 287

E v Secretary of State for the Home Department [2004] EWCA Civ 49...465
E (A Child), *Re* [2008] UKHL 66 401
EB v France (2008) 47 EHRR 21 406
Edinburgh and Dalkeith Railway v Wauchope (1842) 8 Cl & F 710 ....130, 131
Edore v Secretary of State for the Home Department [2003] EWCA Civ 716....................................400
Edwards v United Kingdom (2002) 35 EHRR 19..367, 389
El Farargy v El Farargy [2007] EWCA Civ 1149 295
Ellen Street Estates Ltd v Minister of Health [1934] 1 KB 590 ....147, 158
Enderby Town Football Club Ltd v Football Association Ltd [1971] 1 Ch 591 484
Engel v Netherlands (1976) 1 EHRR 647..372, 375, 379
Entick v Carrington (1765) 19 St Tr 1030 ....33, 42, 47, 58, 110, 112, 113, 116, 117, 125, 288, 394, 418
Equal Opportunities Commission and another v Secretary of State for Employment,
    See R v Secretary of State for Employment *ex parte* Equal Opportunities Commission
    and Another (the EOC case)—
Ex parte Fire Brigades Union, *See* R v Secretary of State for the Home Department *ex parte*
    Fire Brigades Union and Others—
Ezeh and Connors v United Kingdom (2002) 35 EHRR 691 ....375, 484

F v Switzerland (1987) 10 EHRR 411 ....385, 386
Fairfield v United Kingdom (Application No 24790/04) 356
Findlay v United Kingdom (1997) 24 EHRR 221 376
Fox v Stirk [1970] 2 QB 463..193
Fox, Campbell and Hartley v United Kingdom (1990) 13 EHRR 157..373
Friend v United Kingdom; Countryside Alliance v United Kingdom (2010) 50 EHRR SE6...........357

Garland v British Rail Engineering Ltd (Case 12/81) [1983] 2 AC 751; [1982] ECR 359..........345, 347
Gay News Ltd and Lemon v United Kingdom (1982) 5 EHRR 123...426
George Strauss HC Vol 568, Col 814 170
Gibson v Lord Advocate [1975] 1 CMLR 563 149

Gillan v United Kingdom (Application No 4158/05) [2010] ECHR 4158/05; [2010] NLJR 104;
    (2010) *The Times*, 15 January; [2010] All ER (D) 40 (Jan), ECtHR 107, 109, 124, 360
Gillow v United Kingdom (1986) 11 EHRR 335 381
Godden v Hales (1686) 11 St Tr 1165 145
Golder v United Kingdom (1976) 1 EHRR 524 ....375, 381, 392, 418
Goodwin v United Kingdom (1996) 22 EHRR 123 361
Goodwin v United Kingdom: I v United Kingdom (2002) 35 EHRR 18 ....380, 381, 386, 392, 405
Gouriet v Union of Post Office Workers [1978] AC 435; [1977] 1 QB 729 94
Granger v United Kingdom (1990) 12 EHRR 469 378

HK (An Infant), *Re* [1967] 2 QB 617 480
HM Treasury v Mohammed Jabar Ahmed and others (No 2) [2010] UKSC 5, [2010]
    2 WLR 378, [2010] All ER (D) 40 (Feb) 122, 457
Halford v United Kingdom (1997) 24 EHRR 523 ....380, 381
Hamer v United Kingdom (1982) 4 EHRR 139 386
Hamilton (v *The Guardian*) Case 1995 169
Handyside v United Kingdom (1976) 1 EHRR 737 ....101, 102, 353, 357, 360, 361, 365, 383, 420, 428
Hannam v Bradford City Council [1970] 2 All ER 690 479
Harman v Secretary of State for the Home Department [1983] AC 280 423
Harris v The Minister of the Interior (1952) (2) SA 428 (South Africa) 151, 158
Hashman and Harrup v United Kingdom [1999] TLR, 1 December; [2000] Crim LR 185;
    (1999) 30 EHRR 241 360
Hatton v United Kingdom (2003) 37 EHRR 28 ....353, 381
Hazell v Hammersmith and Fulham London Borough Council [1992] 2 AC 1 458
Heather, Ward and Callin v Leonard Cheshire Foundatin [2002] EWCA Civ 366 410
Hirst v United Kingdom (No 2) Application No 00074025/01 (2006) 42 EHRR 41;
    (2005) 42 EHRR 849; (2005) *The Times*, 10 October; *affirming* (2004) 38 EHRR 825
    (ECtHR) 57, 194, 195, 361, 388, 392
Hopkins v Parole Board [2008] EWHC 2312 (Admin) 484
Huang v Secretary of State for the Home Department [2007] UKHL 1 400

Infolines Public Networks Ltd v Nottingham City Council [2009] EWCA Civ 708 305
Inland Revenue Commissioner v National Federation of Self-Employed and Small
    Businesses Ltd [1982] AC 617 447
Inland Revenue Commissioners and Another v Rossminster Ltd and others, *See* R v Inland
    Revenue Commissioners *ex parte* Rossminster Ltd and others—
International Transport Roth GmbH v Secretary of State for the Home Department [2002]
    EWCA Civ 158; [2002] 3 WLR 344; [2002] 1 CMLR 52; [2001] TLR, 11 December 405
Internationale Handelsgesellschaft mbH v EVGF (Case 11/70) [1970] ECR 1125; [1972]
    CMLR 255 344
Ireland v United Kingdom (1978) 2 EHRR 25 ....355, 357, 369

Jackson v Her Majesty's Attorney General, *See* R (on the application of Jackson and others) v
    Attorney General—
Jameel v Wall Street Journal Europe Sprl [2006] UKHL 44 429
James v United Kingdom (1986) 6 EHRR 123 386
Jasper and Fitt v United Kingdom (2000) 30 EHRR 97 377
Jeffs v New Zealand Dairy Production and Marketing Board [1967] AC 551 459
Jepson and Dyas-Elliott (applicants) v The Labour Party [1996] IRLR 116 182
Jersild v Denmark (1994) 19 EHRR 1 ....355, 383
Johansen v Norway 44 DR 155 (1985) 371
Johnston v Ireland (1986) 9 EHRR 203 385
Jordan and others v United Kingdom (2003) 37 EHRR 2 ....367, 390

K-F v Germany (1997) 26 EHRR 390 373
Kanda v Government of the Federation of Malaya [1962] AC 322 482
Kansal v United Kingdom (2004) 39 EHRR 31 397
Kay v Lambeth London Borough Council; Price v Leeds City Council [2006] UKHL 10, HL,
    affirming conjoined appeal [2004] EWCA Civ 926, CA 398
Keenan v United Kingdom (2001) 33 EHRR 38 367

Khan v United Kingdom (2001) 31 EHRR 45 ....377, 389
Khawaja v Secretary of State for the Home Department *See* R v Secretary of State for the
  Home Department *ex parte* Khawaja—
Klass v Federal Republic of Germany (1978) 2 EHRR 214 356

Laker Airways v Department of Trade and Industry [1977] 1 QB 643 249
Laskey, Jaggard and Brown v United Kingdom (1997) 24 EHRR 39 380
Lawal v Northern Spirit Ltd [2003] UKHL 35; [2004] 1 All ER 187....................................294
Lawless v Ireland (No 3) (1961) 1 EHRR 15..363
Leander v Sweden (1987) 9 EHRR 343 383
Lingens v Austria (1986) 8 EHRR 407..421
Lister and others v Forth Dry Dock and Engineering Co Ltd and Another [1990] 1 AC 546;
  [1989] 1 All ER 1134 ....345, 347
Liversidge v Anderson [1942] AC 206..53, 118, 119, 297
Lloyd v McMahon [1987] 1 AC 625; [1987] 2 WLR 821; [1987] 1 All ER 1118 481
Locabail (UK) Ltd v Bayfield Properties Ltd (Leave to Appeal); Locabail (UK) Ltd v Waldord
  Investment Corporation (Leave to Appeal); Timmins v Gormley; Williams v Inspector of
  Taxes; R v Bristol Betting and Gaming Licensing Committee *ex parte* Callaghan [2000]
  QB 451; (1999) 149 NLJ 1793; [2000] 1 All ER 65, CA...293
London and Clydesdale Estates Ltd v Aberdeen District Council [1980] 1 WLR 182; [1979]
  2 All ER 876 476
London County Council v Attorney General [1902] AC 165 457
Lopez Ostra v Spain (1994) 20 EHRR 277 355
Lustig-Prean v United Kingdom; Beckett v United Kingdom (1999) 29 EHRR 548.........472
Lyons v United Kingdom (2003) 37 EHRR 183, CD 354

M, *Re* (1994), *See* M v Home Office and Others—
M v Home Office and Others [1994] 1 AC 377; [1993] 3 WLR 433; [1992] 4 All ER 97;
  [1993] 3 All ER 537, HL...66, 110, 125, 297
M v United Kingdom 54 DR 214 (1987) 357
MB, *Re*, *See* Secretary of State for the Home Department v MB—
McC (a minor), *Re*; *sub nom* McC v Mullan [1985] AC 528, [1984] 3 All ER 908 292
McCann, Farrell and Savage v United Kingdom (1995) 21 EHRR 97 ....355, 356, 366, 368
McCarthy and Stone Ltd v Richmond upon Thames London Borough Council [1992]
  2 AC 48..458
Macarthys v Smith [1981] 1 QB 180; [1979] 3 All ER 325; [1980] 2 CMLR 205....................345
MacCormick v Lord Advocate (1953) SC 396..149, 317
McGinley and Egan v United Kingdom (1998) 27 EHRR 1..380
McGonnell v United Kingdom (2000) 30 EHRR 289 376
McInnes v Onslow Fane [1978] 1 WLR 1520 481
McMullan, *See* McC (a minor), *Re*; *sub nom* McC v Mullan—
McShane v United Kingdom, Application No 43290/98, (2002) 35 EHRR 23; [2002] TLR,
  3 June..356
Madzimbamuto v Lardner-Burke [1969] 1 AC 645...56, 139
Malone v Metropolitan Police Commissioner [1979] Ch 344; [1979]
  2 All ER 620 ....81, 112, 114, 242, 393–395, 422
Malone v United Kingdom (1984) 7 EHRR 14 ....354, 359, 365, 380, 388, 395, 418
Manuel and Others v Attorney General [1983] 1 Ch 77; [1982] 3 All ER 822;
  [1982] 3 WLR 821 ....153, 158
Marbury v Madison (1803) 5 US 1 Cranch 137 ....26, 41, 82, 287
Marckx v Belgium (1979) 2 EHRR 330...380
Markt Intern Velag GmbH and Klaus Beermann v Germany (1989) 12 EHRR 161.............383
Marshall v Southampton and South West Hampshire Area Health Authority (No 1)
  (Case 152/84) [1986] QB 401; 1 CMLR 688; [1986] ECR 723...343
Mathieu-Mohin and Clerfayt v Belgium (1988) 10 EHRR 1.......................................193, 388
Matthews v United Kingdom (1999) 28 EHRR 361 ....193, 388
Meerabux v Attorney General of Belize [2005] UKPC 12 ....76, 293
Mendoza v Ghaidan [2004] UKHL 40; [2002] EWCA Civ 1533; [2002] All ER 1162 403
Merkur Island Shipping Corporation v Laughton and Others [1983] 2 AC 570................97
Metropolitan Properties Co (FGC) v Lannon [1969] 1 QB 577.....................................479, 486

Mortensen v Peters (1906) 14 SLT 227 ....135, 136
Mr M (2008-09) 506
Murray (John) v United Kingdom (1996) 22 EHRR 29 378
Murray (Margaret) v United Kingdom (1994) 19 EHRR 193 374

N v United Kingdom (2008) 47 EHRR 39 370
Nagle v Feilden [1966] 2 QB 633 445
National Provincial Building Society v United Kingdom (1997) 25 EHRR 127 386
New York Times Co v Sullivan (1964) 376 US 254 47
Nicholls v Tavistock Urban District Council [1923] 2 Ch 18 305
Niemietz v Germany (1992) 16 EHRR 97 380
Nottinghamshire County Council v Secretary of State for the Environment
    [1986] 1 AC 240 ....307, 441, 447, 470, 475, 488

O'Halloran and Francis v United Kingdom (2008) 46 EHRR 21 407
O'Hara v United Kingdom (2002) 34 EHRR 32 373
O'Reilly v Mackman [1983] 2 AC 237 ....448, 449
Observer, The, The Guardian and The Sunday Times v United Kingdom (1991)
    14 EHRR 153 ....383, 430, 432
Oldham v United Kingdom (2001) 31 EHRR 34 375
Ollinger v Austria (2008) 46 EHRR 38 385
Osman v United Kingdom (2000) 29 EHRR 245 ....358, 366, 376, 390

P, C and S v United Kingdom (2002) 35 EHRR 31 377
P (adoption: unmarried couple), Re sub nom G (adoption: unmarried couple),
    Re [2008] UKHL 38, [2009] AC 173, HL, reversing [2007] NICA 20, NI CA 399, 406
PM v United Kingdom (2006) 42 EHRR 45 390
Pabla Ky v Finland (2006) 42 EHRR 34 73
Padfield v Minister of Agriculture Fisheries and Food [1968] AC 997 ....461, 487
Parochial Church Council of the Parish of Aston Cantlow and others v Wallbank
    [2003] UKHL 37 411
Pearlman v Keepers and Governors of Harrow School [1979] 1 QB 56 466
Peck v United Kingdom (2003) 36 EHRR 31 380
Pepper v Hart [1992] 2 WLR 1032; [1993] 1 All ER 42 171
Phillips v Eyre (1870–71) LR 6 QB 1 96
Pickin v British Railways Board [1974] AC 765 ....47, 58, 85, 130, 142, 143, 145, 150, 158, 172
Pickstone v Freemans plc [1989] AC 66; [1988] 2 All ER 803 345
Pickwell v Camden London Borough Council [1983] 1 All ER 602; [1983] 2 WLR 583 463
Platform Arzte fur dan Laeben v Astria (1988) 13 EHRR 204 385
Poplar Housing and Regeneration Community Association Limited v Donoghue
    [2001] EWCA Civ 595 ....85, 403, 410
Porter and another v Magill [2002] 2 AC 357; [2001] UKHL 67 ....294, 461, 480
Practice Statement [1966] 1 WLR 1234 81
Prebble v Television New Zealand Ltd [1995] 1 AC 321; [1994] 3 WLR 970; The Times, 14 July 169
Pretty v United Kingdom (2002) 35 EHRR 1; [2002] 2 FCR 97;
    [2002] 2 FLR 45 ....358, 366, 382, 390, 399, 407
Prohibitions del Roy (1607) 12 Co Rep 63 72
ProLife Alliance v BBC See R (on the application of ProLife Alliance) v British Broadcasting
    Corporation—
Purdy v Director of Public Prosecutions, See R (on the application of Purdy v Director of Public
    Prosecutions—
Pye (JA) (Oxford) Ltd v United Kingdom 44302/02 [2007] ECHR 5559 (30 August 2007) [2007]
    ECHR 5559, 23 BHRC 405, [2007] RVR 302, (2008) 46 EHRR 45, [2008] 1 EGLR 111 (Grand
    Chamber); (2006) 43 EHRR 3 387

R v A (Complainant's Sexual History) [2001] UKHL 25; [2001] TLR, 24 May,
    [2002] 1 AC 45 ....86, 133, 402, 404, 419
R v Army Board of the Defence Council ex parte Anderson [1992] 1 QB 169;
    [1991] 3 WLR 42 484
R v Attorney General ex parte Rushbridger and another [2003] UKHL 38 404

R v Barnsley Metropolitan Borough Council *ex parte* Hook [1976] 3 All ER 452;
[1976] 1 WLR 1052 ....473, 480

R v Boundary Commission for England *ex parte* Foot [1983] 1 QB 600 190

R v Bow Street Metropolitan Stipendiary Magistrate *ex parte* Pinochet Ugarte (No 2);
sub nom Re, Pinochet Ugarte; *Re*, R v Evans and Another *ex parte* Pinochet Ugarte (No 2);
R v Bartle *ex parte* Pinochet Urgarte (No 2) [2000] 1 AC 119; [1999] 2 WLR 272; [1999]
1 All ER 577; [1998] TLR, 3 November, HL; *overruled* R v Bow Street Stipendiary
Magistrate, *ex parte* Pinochet Ugarte (Amnesty International intervening)
[2000] 1 AC 61; [1998] 4 All ER 897; [1998] 3 WLR 1456................................43, 58, 293, 394, 479, 486

R v Bow Street Metropolitan Stipendiary Magistrate *ex parte* Pinochet Ugarte (No 3)
(Amnesty International intervening) [2000] 1 AC 147; [1999] 2 All ER 97 ....293, 479, 486

R v Camborne Justices *ex parte* Pearce [1955] 1 QB 41 478

R v Chief Constable of Sussex *ex parte* International Trader's Ferry Ltd [1999] 2 AC 418;
[1997] 2 All ER 65...473

R v Chief Metropolitan Stipendiary Magistrate *ex parte* Choudhury [1991] 1 QB 429;
[1991] 1 All ER 306..426

R v Chief Rabbi of the United Hebrew Congregations of Great Britain and the
Commonwealth *ex parte* Wachmann [1993] 2 All ER 249 444

R v Commissioner of Customs and Excise, *ex parte* Kay [1996] STC 1500 436

R v Coventry City Council *ex parte* Phoenix Aviation and others [1995] 3 All ER 37.....................464

R v Criminal Injuries Compensation Board *ex parte* Lain [1967] 2 QB 864 249

R v Davies [2008] UKHL 36 132

R v Director of Public Prosecution *ex parte* Kebilene and Others, *sub nom* R v DPP, *ex parte*
Kebeline [1999] 3 WLR 972, HL; *Reversing* [1999] 3 WLR 175, DC.....................................155

R v Director of Public Prosecution *ex parte* Pretty and another, *See* R (on the application of
Pretty) v Director of Public Prosecutions—

R v Disciplinary Committee of the Jockey Club *ex parte* Aga Khan [1993] 2 All ER 853;
[1993] 1 WLR 909 444

R v Ealing London Borough Council *ex parte* Times Newspapers Ltd and others [1986]
LGR 316..241, 443, 461

R v East Sussex County Council *ex parte* Tandy [1998] 2 All ER 769; [1998] 2 WLR 884................464

R v Evans and Another *ex parte* Pinochet Ugarte; R v Bartle *ex parte* Pinochet Urgarte;
In re Pinochet Ugarte [1999] 1 All ER 577; [1998] TLR, 3 November *See* R v Bow Street
Metropolitan Stipendiary Magistrate *ex parte* Pinochet Ugarte (No 2); sub nom Pinochet
Ugarte (No 2) *Re*, R v Evans and Another *ex parte* Pinochet Ugarte (No 2); R v Bartle
ex parte Pinochet Urgarte (No 2)—

R v Football Association Ltd *ex parte* Football League Ltd [1993] 2 All ER 833 444

R v Gibson and another [1991] 1 All ER 439..427

R v Gloucestershire County Council and Another *ex parte* Barry; R v Lancashire County
Council *ex parte* Royal Association for Disability and Rehabilitation and Another
[1997] AC 584; [1997] 2 All ER 1; (1996) *The Times*, 12 July...464

R v Governor of Brixton Prison *ex parte* Enahoro [1963] 2 QB 455......................................459

R v Greater Manchester Coroner, *ex parte* Tal [1985] 1 QB 67..443

R v Her Majesty's Treasury *ex parte* Smedley [1985] 1 QB 657; [1985] 1 All ER 589.........................66

R v Hereford Magistrates' Court, *ex parte* Rowlands [1998] 1 QB 110...............................443

R v Horseferry Road Magistrates' Court *ex parte* Bennett [1994] 1 AC 42 ....118, 121, 125

R v Hull Prison Board of Visitors *ex parte* St Germain and others (No 2) [1979] 3 All ER 545;
[1979] 1 WLR 1401 484

R v Immigration Appeal Tribunal, *ex parte* Singh [1986] 1 WLR 910.......................................463, 468

R v Inland Revenue Commissioners *ex parte* Rossminster Ltd and others
[1980] AC 952, HL..57, 106, 115, 118, 136, 394

R v Inspectorate of Pollution and another *ex parte* Greenpeace Ltd (No 2) [1994] 4 All ER 329;
[1994] 4 All ER 319, CO...447

R v Jordan [1967] Crim LR 483 ....142, 145, 158

R v Kansal [2001] UKHL 62..397

R v Lambert, Ali and Jordan [2002] 2 AC 545; [2002] QB 1112 (CA); [2001] UKHL 37; [2001]
3 WLR 206; [2001] TLR, 6 July, House of Lords 397

R v Lewisham London Borough Cuncil *ex parte* Shell UK Ltd [1988] 1 All ER 938.........................461

R v Liverpool Corporation *ex parte* Liverpool Taxi Fleet Operators' Association
[1972] 2 QB 299...302, 482, 487

R v Lord Chancellor *ex parte* Witham [1997] 2 All ER 779 ....39, 44, 108, 439, 457, 468

R v Lord President of the Privy Council *ex parte* Page [1992] 3 WLR 1112 466

R v Lyons and others [2002] UKHL 44 ....354, 397

R v Mental Health Tribunal *ex parte* H [2001] EWCA Civ 415 405

R v Ministry of Defence *ex parte* Smith; R v Admiralty Board of the Defence Council;
   ex parte Lustig-Prean [1996] QB 517; [1996] 1 All ER 257, CA; *Affirming* [1995]
   4 All ER 427, QBD...394, 399, 438, 470–473, 475

R v North and East Devon Health Authority *ex parte* Coughlan [2001] 1 QB 213 482

R v Offen and Others [2001] 2 All ER 154; [2001] 1 WLR 253 402

R v Panel on Take-overs and Mergers *ex parte* Datafin plc [1987] 1 QB 815 443–445

R v Parliamentary Commissioner for Administration *ex parte* Balchin [1997] COD 146;
   [1998] 1 PLR 1..507

R v Parliamentary Commissioner for Administration *ex parte* Balchin (No 2) [2000] JPL 267;
   [1999] EGCS 78...507

R v Parliamentary Commissioner for Administration *ex parte* Balchin (No 3) [2002]
   EWHC 1876 (Admin) 507

R v Parliamentary Commissioner for Administration *ex parte* Dyer [1994] 1 All ER 375 507

R v Parliamentary Commissioner for Standards, *ex parte* Al Fayed [1998] 1 All ER 93 173

R v Penguin Books [1961] Crim LR 176...428

R v Ponting [1985] Crim LR 318 236

R v R (Rape: Marital Exemption) [1992] 1 AC 599; [1991] 4 All ER 481; [1991] 3 WLR 767;
   Affirming [1991] 2 WLR 1065; [1991] 2 All ER 257 ....82, 379

R v Race Relations Board *ex parte* Selvarajan [1975] 1 WLR 1686..459

R v Secretary of State for Employment *ex parte* Equal Opportunities Commission and
   Another (the EOC case) [1995] 1 AC 1; [1994] 1 All ER 910...............................347, 447, 487

R v Secretary of State for Foreign and Commonwealth Affairs *ex parte* Everett [1989]
   QB 811; [1988] TLR, 1 November; The Independent, 26 October, CA.............................246

R v Secretary of State for Foreign and Commonwealth Affairs *ex parte* Rees-Mogg [1994]
   QB 552; [1994] 2 WLR 115; [1994] 1 All ER 457; (1993) *The Times*, 24 July 246, 446

R v Secretary of State for Foreign and Commonwealth Affairs *ex parte* World Development
   Movement (The EOC Case) [1995] 1 All ER 611; [1995] 1 WLR 386................................435

R v Secretary of State for Health *ex parte* United States Tobacco International Inc [1992]
   1 QB 353 ....436, 487

R v Secretary of State for the Environment *ex parte* Greenpeace Ltd (No 2) [1994] 4 All ER 352....412

R v Secretary of State for the Environment *ex parte* Norwich City Council [1982] 1 QB 808 305

R v Secretary of State for the Environment *ex parte* Ostler [1976] 1 QB 122; [1976] 3 All ER 90......440

R v Secretary of State for the Environment *ex parte* Rose Theatre Trust Company Ltd [1990]
   2 WLR 186; 1 All ER 754 ....441, 446, 447

R v Secretary of State for the Environment, Transport and the Regions, *See* R (on the application
   of Alconbury Developments Ltd) v Secretary of State for the Environment, Transport and
   the Regions—

R v Secretary of State for the Home Department *ex parte* Al Fayed [1997] 1 All ER 228; (1996)
   The Times, 13 March..485

R v Secretary of State for the Home Department *ex parte* Anderson, *See* R (on the application
   of Anderson) v Secretary of State for the Home Department; R (on the application of
   Taylor) v Same—

R v Secretary of State for the Home Department *ex parte* Bentley [1994] QB 349; [1993]
   4 All ER 442 ....247, 250

R v Secretary of State for the Home Department *ex parte* Brind [1991] 1 AC 696;
   1 All ER 720 ....393, 395, 399, 418, 423, 432, 471, 473

R v Secretary of State for the Home Department *ex parte* Cheblak [1991] 1 WLR 890;
   [1991] 2 All ER 319..483

R v Secretary of State for the Home Department *ex parte* Daly, *See* R (on the application of
   Daly) v Secretary of State for the Home Department—

R v Secretary of State for the Home Department *ex parte* Doody [1993] 3 WLR 154;
   [1994] 1 AC 531 ....483, 485

R v Secretary of State for the Home Department *ex parte* Farrakhan [2002] EWCA Civ 606 401

R v Secretary of State for the Home Department *ex parte* Fire Brigades Union and Others
   [1995] 2 WLR 1; [1995] 2 All ER 244; [1993] 3 WLR 433 ....117, 121, 125, 241, 248, 297

R v Secretary of State for the Home Department *ex parte* Hosenball [1977] 1 WLR 766;
[1977] 3 All ER 452..119, 297, 482

R v Secretary of State for the Home Department *ex parte* Jeyeanthan; Ravichandran v
Secretary of State for the Home Department [2000] 1 WLR 354; [1999] 3 All ER 231...........477, 486

R v Secretary of State for the Home Department *ex parte* Khawaja [1984] AC 74;
[1983] 1 All ER 765; 2 WLR 321...55, 121, 465

R v Secretary of State for the Home Department *ex parte* Leech [1993] 4 All ER 539 ....241, 456, 473

R v Secretary of State for the Home Department *ex parte* McQuillan [1995] 4 All ER 400...............470

R v Secretary of State for the Home Department *ex parte* Northumbria Police Authority
[1989] 1 QB 26; [1988] 1 All ER 556, CA..249

R v Secretary of State for the Home Department *ex parte* Oladehinde [1991] 1 AC 254;
[1990] 3 All ER 383...460

R v Secretary of State for the Home Department *ex parte* Pierson [1998] AC 539 120

R v Secretary of State for the Home Department *ex parte* Simms; Same v Same *ex parte*
O'Brien [1999] 3 All ER 400; [1999] TLR, 9 July..120, 121

R v Secretary of State for the Home Department, *ex parte* Taylor and Anderson [2001]
EWCA Civ 1698 398

R v Secretary of State for the Home Department *ex parte* Tarrant [1985] 1 QB 251...........................484

R v Secretary of State for the Home Department *ex parte* Venables; R v Same *ex parte*
Thompson [1997] 3 All ER 97; (1996) *The Times*, 7 August; (1997) *The Times*,
13 June...75, 297, 434, 443, 463, 468

R v Secretary of State for Transport *ex parte* Factortame (No 2) [1991] 1 AC 603;
[1991] 3 CMLR 769; [1991] 2 Lloyd's Rep 648.....................46, 158, 287, 346, 347–350, 487

R v Secretary of State for Transport *ex parte* Factortame (No 3) [1992] 1 QB 680 347–350

R v Secretary of State for Transport *ex parte* Factortame (No 5) [2000] 1 AC 524;
[1998] TLR, 28 April..347–350

R v Shayler [2002] UKHL 11...607, 429

R v Skinner [1968] 2 QB 700...460

R v Somerset County Council *ex parte* Fewings [1995] 3 All ER 20, CA; *Affirming* [1995]
1 All ER 513 463

R v Soneji [2005] UKHL 49..477

R v Thames Magistrates' Court *ex parte* Polemis [1974] 2 All ER 1219..483

R v Warwickshire CC, *ex parte* Collymore [1995] ELR 217 452

R v Wear Valley District Council, *ex parte* Binks [1985] 2 All ER 699 ....436, 446, 483, 487

R (on the application of A and Others) v Lord Saville of Newdigate [2001] EWCA Civ 408..........400

R (on the application of Alconbury Developments Ltd) v Secretary of State for the
Environment, Transport and the Regions, *ex parte* Holding and Barnes plc
(The Alconbury Case) [2001] UKHL 23, [2001] 2 WLR 1389......................................406, 498

R (on the application of Ali) v Secretary of State for the Home Department [2003] EWHC 899
(Admin)...488

R (on the application of Amin) v Secretary of State for the Home Department [2003]
UKHL 51 ....367, 412

R (on the application of Anderson) v Secretary of State for the Home Department;
R (on the application of Taylor) v Same [2002] UKHL 46; [2002] 4 All ER 1089; HL;
Reversing [2001] EWCA Civ 1698, [2002] 2 WLR 1143, CA 75, 286, 297, 406

R (on the application of Animal Defenders International) v Secretary of State for Culture and
Media and Sport [2008] UKHL 15, HL, *affirming* [2006] EWHC 3069 (Admin), DC....................407

R (on the application of Association of British Civilian Internees Far Eastern Region) v
Secretary of State for Defence [2003] EWCA Civ 473; [2003] QB 1397; HC 324 (July 2005)
(Debt of Honour Case)..474, 502, 504, 505, 510

R (on the application of Balchin) v Parliamentary Commissioner for Administration (No 3),
See R v Parliamentary Commissioner for Administration *ex parte* Balchin (No 3)—

R (on the application of Bancoult) v Secretary of State for Foreign and Commonwealth
Affairs [2008] UKHL 61 ....251, 482

R (on the application of Bernard and others) v Enfield LBC [2002] EWHC 2282 (Admin).............413

R (on the application of Bradley and others) v Secretary of State for Works and Pensions
[2008] EWCA Civ 36; [2007] EWHC 242 (Admin) 471, 505, 509

R (on the application of British American Tobacco and others) v Secretary of State for Health
[2004] EWHC 2493 (Admin) 400

R (on the application of Brooke) v Parole Board [2008] EWCA Civ 29 488

R (on the application of C) v Upper Tribunal [2009] EWHC 3052 (QB).............................467
R (on the application of Chester) v Secretary of State for Justice [2009] EWHC 2923
    (Admin)..195, 405
R (on the application of Countryside Alliance and others) v Attorney General [2007]
    UKHL 52; [2006] EWCA Civ 817...220, 385, 401
R (on the application of Cowl) v Plymouth City Council [2001] EWCA Civ 1935.........................451
R (on the application of Daly) v Secretary of State for the Home Department [2001]
    2 AC 532; [2001] UKHL 26; [2001] 2 WLR 1622..399, 419, 474
R (on the application of DPP) v South East Surrey Youth Centre [2005] EWHC 2929 (Admin).....436
R (on the application of Equitable Members Action Group) v HM Treasury [2009] EWHC
    2495 (Admin)..506
R (on the application of Feakins) v Secretary of State for the Environment, Food and Rural
    Affairs [2003] EWCA Civ 1546..446
R (on the application of Gentle) v Prime Minister [2008] UKHL 20...500
R (on the application of Gillan) v Metropolitan Police Commissioner [2006] UKHL12.............109
R (on the application of Greenfield) v Home Secretary [2005] UKHL 14.......................414, 415
R (on the application of Hasan) v Secretary of State for Trade and Industry (now Business,
    Enterprise and Regulatory Reform) [2008] EWCA Civ 1311...485
R (on the application of Hirst) v Parole Board [2002] EWHC 1592 (Admin) 412
R (on the application of Holub and another) v Secretary of State for the Home Department
    [2002] EWHC 2388..412
R (on the application of Hurst) v HM Coroner for Northern District Council [2007] UKHL 13....397
R (on the application of Jackson and others) v Attorney General
    [2006] PL 187; [2005] UKHL 56; [2005] 3 WLR 733 ....129, 130, 140, 153, 154, 158, 218, 219
R (on the application of Jones) v Chief Constable of Cheshire Constabulary, Police
    [2005] EWHC 2457 (Admin) 95, 124
R (on the application of KB) v Mental Health Review Tribunal [2003] EWHC 193 (Admin) 413
R (on the application of Lewis) v Persimmon Homes Teeside Ltd [2008] EWCA Civ 746.............480
R (on the application of Limbu) v Secretary of State for the Home Department [2008] EWHC
    2261 (Admin)..488
R (on the application of Maiden Outdoor Advertising) v Lambeth LBC [2004] JPL 820.............465
R (on the application of Mohamed) v Secretary of State for Foreign and Commonwealth
    Affairs [2010] EWCA Civ 65...122
R (on the application of Montpeliers and Trevors Association) and another v Westminster City
    Council [2005] EWHC 16 (Admin) 447
R (on the application of N) v Secretary of State for the Home Department; Anufrijeva v London
    Borough of Southwark [2003] EWCA Civ 1406 414
R (on the application of Nottingham Healthcare NHS Trust) v Mental Health Review Tribunal
    [2008] EWHC 2445 (Admin) 443
R (on the application of Pretty) v Director of Public Prosecutions [2002] 1 AC 800 [2001]
    UKHL 61; [2001] 3 WLR 1598 ....399, 407
R (on the application of ProLife Alliance) v British Broadcasting Corporation (2003) The Times,
    16 May; [2003] UKHL 23; [2003] 2 WLR 1403...197
R (on the application of Purdy v Director of Public Prosecutions
    [2009] UKHL 45...382, 399, 407, 467, 468
R (on the application of Rogers) v Swindon NHS Primary Care Trust [2006] EWCA Civ 392.......471
R (on the application of Shabina Begum) v Denbigh High School [2006] UKHL 15................383, 416
R (on the application of Shields) v Secretary of State for Justice [2008] EWHC 3102 (Admin) 247
R (on the application of Technoprint Plc and Another) v Leeds City Councl [2007] EWHC 638
    (Admin)...471
R (on the application of West) v Lloyd's of London [2004] EWCA Civ 506; [2004] 3 All ER 251 ...444
R (on the application of West) v Parole Board [2005] UKHL 1; [2005] 1 All ER 755 ....436, 483
R (on the application of Wheeler) v Office of the PM [2008] EWHC 1409 (Admin).........................336
R (on the application of Williamson) v Secretary of State for Employment [2005]
    UKHL 15 ....387, 416, 418
Racal Communication Ltd, Re [1981] AC 374..466
Rai, Allmond and Negotiate Now v United Kingdom (1995) 19 EHRR CD 93 385
Raymond v Honey [1984] AC 1..394
Reference Re Amendment of the Constitution of Canada (1982) 125 DLR (3d) 1 52
Refha Partsis Erbakan Kazan and Tekdal v Turkey (2003) 37 EHRR 1...384

Reynolds v Times Newspapers Ltd [2001] 2 AC 127; [1999] 4 All ER 609;
[1999] 3 WLR 1010; [1998] 3 WLR 862, HL..411, 423, 429
Ridge v Baldwin [1964] AC 40..394, 480
Ringeisen v Austria (1971) 1 EHRR 455 375
Robins v The United Kingdom (1997) 26 EHRR 527..376
Rowe and Davis v United Kingdom (2000) 30 EHRR 1...377
Roy v Kensington and Chelsea and Westminster Family Practitioner Committee
[1992] 1 AC 624; 1 All ER 705...449, 450
Rusbridger v Attorney General [2003] UKHL 38...412

S v United Kingdom (Application No 34407/02, 31 August 2004).............................405
S (A Child), Re [2005] UKHL 47..415, 418, 425
S (children: care plan), Re; Re W (children: care plan) [2002] UKHL 10, HL; reversing W and B
(Children: Care Plan), Re; Re W (Children: Care Plan) [2001] EWCA Civ 757, CA.............403, 405
SW v United Kingdom; CR v United Kingdom (Cases 47/1994/494/576; 8/1994/495/577)
(1995) 21 EHRR 404 379
Saadi v Italy (2009) 49 EHRR 30 370
Sahin v Turkey (2004) 41 EHRR 109; (2004) 19 BHRC 590.......................................382
Saidi v United Kingdom (1993) 17 EHRR 251..378
Sander v United Kingdom (2001) 31 EHRR 44 376
Saunders v United Kingdom (Case 43/1994/490/572) (1996) 23 EHRR 313............354, 377
Secretary of State for Defence v Guardian Newspapers [1985] 1 AC 339 424
Secretary of State for Education and Science v Tameside Metropolitan Borough Council
[1977] AC 1014; [1976] 3 WLR 641...307
Secretary of State for the Home Department v AF [2009] UKHL 28.................119, 122, 123, 125, 483
Secretary of State for the Home Department v AF (proceedings under the Prevention of
Terrorism Act 2005); Secretary of State for the Home Department v AE (proceedings
under the Prevention of Terrorism Act 2005) [2010] EWHC 42 (Admin); [2010] All ER
(D) 86 (Jan), Admin Ct 123
Secretary of State for the Home Department v JJ and Others [2007] UKHL 45, HL
affirming [2006] EWCA Civ 1141; [2007] QB 446; [2006] 3 WLR 866, CA 121, 125, 298, 372
Secretary of State for the Home Department v MB, Re [2007] UKHL 46, affirming
[2006] EWCA Civ 1140, CA; reversing [2006] EWHC 1000 (Admin) 406
Secretary of State for the Home Department v Wainwright and Another,
See Wainwright v Home Office—
Selmouni v France (1999) 29 EHRR 403 ....354, 369
Shaw v DPP [1962] AC 220..43
Sheldrake v Director of Public Prosecutions: Attorney-General's Reference (No 4)
[2004] UKHL 43; [2005] 1 AC 264...403
Short v Poole Corporation [1926] 1 Ch 66..471
Siliadin v France (2006) 43 EHRR 16 371
Silver v United Kingdom (1983) 5 EHRR 347...359, 381, 388, 391
Simmenthal SpA v Amministrazione delle Finanze dello Strata (Case 70/77)
[1978] ECR 1453 344
Sirros v Moore [1975] 1 QB 118..292, 298
Smith v Chief Constable of Sussex, See Van Colle v Chief Constable of Hertfordshire Police;
Smith v Chief Constable of Sussex Police—
Smith v East Elloe Rural District Council [1956] AC 736...440
Smith v United Kingdom; Grady v United Kingdom (Applications 33985/96
and 33986/96) (1999) 29 EHRR 493.................355, 362, 365, 380, 389, 395, 472
Soering v United Kingdom (1989) 11 EHRR 439..................356, 368, 370, 371, 390, 413
South Yorkshire Transport Ltd and another v Monopolies and Mergers Commission
and another [1993] 1 All ER 289 467
Spencer v United Kingdom [1998] EHRLR 348; (1998) 25 EHRR CD 105..................357
Sporrong and Lonnroth v Sweden (1982) 5 EHRR 35..386
Stafford v United Kingdom (2002) 35 EHRR 32..372, 374, 398, 406
Starrs v Ruxton 2000 SLT 42; 2000 JC 208..315
Steel and Morris v United Kingdom (2005) 41 EHRR 22..378
Steel and Others v United Kingdom (1998) 28 EHRR 603................................358, 372, 385
Stockdale v Hansard (1839) 9 Ad & El 1; (1839) 3 St Tr (NS) 723............................130, 171

Stoke-on-Trent City Council v B & Q [1991] Ch 48...349
Stourton v Stourton [1963] 1 All ER 606; [1963] P 302...167
Sunday Times v United Kingdom (1979) 2 EHRR 245.................136, 359, 361, 362, 383, 392,
395, 418, 425, 432
Sutherland v United Kingdom (2001) *The Times*, 13 April 357
Swedish Engine Drivers' Union v Sweden (1976) 1 EHRR 617.......................................384

Taylor v Lawrence [2002] EWCA Civ 90; [2002] 3 WLR 641; [2002] TLR, 8 February.......................294
Thoburn v Sunderland City Council [2002] 1 CMLR 50; [2002] EWHC 195
    (Admin)..23, 32, 38, 58, 155, 347
Thynne, Wilson and Gunnell v United Kingdom (1990) 13 EHRR 666..............................374
Tinnelly v United Kingdom (1998) 27 EHRR 249 375
Tsirlis and Kouloumpas v Greece (1997) 25 EHRR 198..372
Tyrer v United Kingdom (1978) 2 EHRR 1 ....369, 370

United Communist Party of Turkey v Turkey (1998) 26 EHRR 121..................................384

V & T v United Kingdom (2000) 30 EHRR 121 ....75, 376, 377
Van Colle v Chief Constable of Hertfordshire Police; Smith v Chief Constable of Sussex
    Police [2008] UKHL 50; [2009] AC 225, HL, *reversing conjoined appeal* [2007] EWCA Civ
    325, [2007] 3 All ER 122, CA, *affirming* [2006] EWHC 360 (QB); (2006) *The Times,*
    28 March, QBD..366, 376
Van Droogenbroek v Belgium (1982) 4 EHRR 443...372
Van Gend en Loos v Nederlandse administratie der belastingen (Case 26/62) [1963] ECR 1;
    [1963] CMLR 105 ....343, 348
Van Mechelen v The Netherlands (1997) 25 EHRR 647 378
Vauxhall Estates Ltd v Liverpool Corporation [1932] 1 KB 733 ....146, 147, 158
Venables and Thompson v Associated Newspapers [2001] 1 WLR 1038...............................411
VgT Verein gegen Tierfabriken v Switzerland (2002) 34 EHRR 4 407
Vilvarajah and Four Others v United Kingdom (1991) 14 EHRR 248...................................370
Vine v National Dock Labour Board [1957] AC 488...459, 468
Vo v France (2005) 40 EHRR 12 366
Von Hannover v Germany (2005) 40 EHRR 1 ....380, 384

W and B (Children: Care Plan), *Re*; *Re* W (Children: Care Plan), *See* S (children: care plan),
    Re; *Re* W (children: care plan) [2002] UKHL 10, HL; *Reversing* W and B (Children: Care
    Plan), *Re*; *Re* W (Children: Care Plan)—
Waddington v Miah [1974] 1 WLR 683; [1974] 2 All ER 377 ....43, 119, 121, 144, 145, 394, 401
Wainwright v Home Office [2003] UKHL 53 ....396, 412, 414
Wandsworth London Borough Council v Winder [1985] 1 AC 461 ....449, 450
Webb v Chief Constable of Merseyside Police [2000] 1 All ER 209......................................117
Welch v United Kingdom (1995) 20 EHRR 247 379
Wheeler v Leicester City Council [1985] 1 AC 1054 461
White and Collins v Minister of Health [1939] 2 KB 838 ....465, 468
Whitehouse v Lemon [1979] AC 617 426
Willis v United Kingdom (2002) 35 EHRR 21..390
Wilson and others v United Kingdom (2002) 35 EHRR 20..384
Wilson v First County Trust Ltd (No 2) [2003] UKHL 40; [2003] 3 WLR 568 .....171, 396, 402, 404, 405
Wingrove v United Kingdom (Case 19/1995) (1996) 24 EHRR 1; (1996) *The Times*,
    5 December..426
Winterwerp v Germany (1979) 2 EHRR 387..372–374
Wynne v United Kingdom (1995) 12 EHRR 333 398

X v Federal Republic of Germany (1974) 46 CD 22 371
X v Y [2004] EWCA Civ 662 411
X and Y v Netherlands (1985) 8 EHRR 235..381
X Ltd v Morgan-Grampian (Publishers) Ltd [1991] AC 1; [1990] 2 WLR 421; [1990]
    1 All ER 616 128
X, Y and Z v United Kingdom Appl 21830/93 (1997) 24 EHRR 143.....................................380

YL v Birmingham City Council [2007] UKHL 27..410
Young, Webster and James v United Kingdom (1982) 4 EHRR 38...384

Z and others v United Kingdom (2002) 34 EHRR 3 ....369, 376, 388

Table of statutes

Please note: this table was prepared by the Publishers, who take full responsibility for any errors therein.

Acquisition of Land (Assessment of
Compensation) Act 1919 147
  s 2 146
  s 7 146
Act of Settlement 1700 ..... 185, 213, 217, 292, 298
Act of Union with Ireland Act 1800, *See*
Union with Ireland Act 1800—
Act of Union with Scotland 1706 (English
Parliament), *See* Union with England
Act 1706—
Act of Union with Scotland 1707 (Scottish
Parliament), *See* Union with Scotland
Act 1707—
Act of Union with Wales 1536 (Laws in
Wales Act) 323
Agricultural Marketing Act 1958 461
Ancient Monuments and Archaeological
Areas Act 1979 446
Anti-Terrorism, Crime and Security Act
2001 .... 105, 121, 138, 223, 298
  Pt 4 105
  s 23 .... 105, 400, 416, 473
Appellate Jurisdiction Act 1876 .... 203, 227

Bail Act 1976 104
Bail, Judicial Appointments etc (Scotland)
Act 2000 316
Baths and Wash-houses Acts 1846–78 ... 456, 457
Bill of Rights 1689 (Statute of William III
and Mary II) 35, 39, 171, 242, 248
  Art 1 35
  Art 4 282
  Art 6 35
  Art 9 .... 35, 47, 112, 134, 168,
                            169, 171, 172, 178
Boundary Commissions Act 1992 190
Bribery Amendment Act 1958 (Ceylon/Sri
Lanka) 151
British Nationality Act 1981 .... 213, 485
  s 44 485
British Railways Act 1836 142
British Railways Act 1968 .... 47, 142, 172
  Preamble 142
  s 18 142
Broadcasting Act 1990 171

Canada Act 1982 153
Children Act 1989 403
Children Act 2004—
  s 58 369

Chronically Sick and Disabled Persons Act
1970 464
Colonial Laws Validity Act 1865 150
  s 5 150
Communications Act 2003—
  s 321(2) 407
Community Care and Health (Scotland)
Act 2002 313
Constitutional Reform Act 2005 .... 14, 19, 24, 26,
                31, 36, 54, 67, 72, 74, 78,
                80, 83, 85, 87–91, 122,
                212, 214, 217, 276, 286,
                290, 298, 496
  Pt 3 .... 204, 286
  Pt 4 292
  s 1 12
  s 2 .... 78, 79, 211, 212
  s 3 .... 72, 80, 87, 88
  s 3(1) 291
  s 7 286
  s 17 .... 79, 12
  s 18 24
  s 33 .... 227, 292
  s 45 81
  s 61 289
  s 62 508
  s 148(4) 241
  Sch 12 289
Constitutional Reform and Governance
Act 2010 .... 177, 209, 226, 235,
                236, 247, 253, 289
  Pt 1 247
  Pt 4 226
  s 5 235
  s 7 236
  s 26 177
  s 27 177
  s 29 177
  s 32 177
  s 33 178
  s 34 178
  Sch 3 177
  Sch 4 178
Consumer Credit Act 1974 396
Consumer Protection Act 1987 132
Contempt of Court Act 1981 .... 136, 292, 298,
                428, 431
Coroners Act 1988 397
Coroners and Justice Act 2009—
  s 71 371
Counter-Terrorism Act 2008 122

Courts Act 2003 292
Crime (Sentences) Act 1997........................... 412
   s 2.. 402
   s 29.. 286
Criminal Evidence (Witness Anonymity)
   Act 2008.. 132
Criminal Justice Act 1988 117
   s 171..117, 241, 242
   s 171(1)...117
Criminal Justice Act 1991—
   s 35..74, 75, 120
Criminal Justice Act 2003 .... 168, 220, 287
Criminal Justice and Courts Services Act
   2000—
   s 60.. 75
Criminal Justice and Immigration Act 2008—
   s 79.. 382, 426
Crown Proceedings Act 1947............................112

Data Protection Act 1984 394
Data Protection Act 1998 .... 40, 136, 394
Debtors Act 1869.. 167
Defamation Act 1952.. 171
Defamation Act 1996—
   s 13.. 134, 168–170
   s 15.. 171
Defence Act 1842 248
Defence of the Realm Consolidation Act
   1914.. 70, 71, 80, 457
   s 1.. 70
Dentists Act 1878.. 32
Diplomatic Privileges Act 1964—
   s 2(1)...112
Drug Trafficking Act 1986 379

Education Act 1944 307
Education Act 1993 464
Education Reform Act 1988 302
Electoral Administration Act 2006.......... 24, 183,
                                      185, 188, 196
   s 14.. 194
   s 18.. 185
   s 69.. 188
   s 73.. 194
Employment Protection (Consolidation)
   Act 1978... 347, 447
Enterprise Act 2002 213
   s 266.. 185
Equal Pay Act 1970—
   s 1.. 345
Equality Act 2010...................37, 38, 114, 183, 394
European Communities Act 1972 .... 4, 36, 37,
                                       39, 40, 158, 314,
                                       322, 334, 344–349,
                                       352
   s 2.. 241, 340, 352
   s 2(1).. 344, 347
   s 2(2)... 347
   s 2(4).. 344, 345, 347–349
   s 3... 341, 352

European Parliamentary Elections Act
   1999 .... 134, 187, 219
European Union (Amendment) Act 2008 336
Export Control Act 2002—
   s 1.. 137

Fair Trading Act 1973—
   s 64.. 467
Family Law Reform Act 1969 193
Finance Act 1964.. 129
Finance Act 2008—
   s 58(4).. 120
Finance (No 2) Act 1940........................... 107, 457
   s 33.. 107
Fiscal Responsibility Act 2010 240
Foreign Compensation Act 1950 466
   s 4.. 466
Forfeiture Act 1870 .... 185, 213
Freedom of Information Act 2000 .... 24, 165

Gender Recognition Act 2004 .... 44, 380, 404
Geneva Conventions Act 1957........................ 129
Government of Ireland Act 1914............. 218, 318
Government of Wales Act 1998 .... 36, 154, 155,
                                       323, 325, 326,
                                       328, 331
   s 1.. 323
Government of Wales Act 2006 .... 24, 323, 325,
                                        327, 328, 331
   Pt 3.. 326, 327
   Pt 4.. 326, 327
   s 1.. 323
   s 3.. 324
   s 5.. 324
   s 7.. 324
   s 25.. 324
   s 45.. 238, 324, 325
   s 48.. 325
   s 58.. 326
   s 80.. 327
   s 81.. 327
   s 82.. 327
   s 93(5)... 328
   s 94.. 327
   s 94(1)... 326
   s 94(2)... 326
   s 97.. 327
   s 99.. 327
   s 101.. 327
   Sch 5 326
   Sch 9 327
Greater London Authority Act 1999...... 329, 331
Greater London Authority Act 2007............. 330

Health Act 2006 136
Health and Social Care Act 2008—
   s 145.. 410
Herring Fishery (Scotland) Act 1889—
   s 7.. 135

House of Commons Disqualification Act
 1975 ....36, 89, 185, 240
 s 1 ....85, 89, 240, 286
 s 1(1)(a) 185
 s 1(1)(b) 236, 240
 s 1(1)(c) 240
 s 1(1)(d) 240
 s 1(1)(e) 185
 s 2 ....36, 68
 s 2(1) 240
House of Commons (Redistribution of
 Seats) Act 1949—
 Sch 2, r 5 ....190, 191
House of Commons (Redistribution of
 Seats) Act 1958—
 s 2 191
House of Commons (Removal of Clergy
 Disqualification) Act 2001 185
House of Lords Act 1999 ....24, 36, 134, 158,
 185, 194, 203, 207–209,
 224, 227
 s 1 208
 s 2 208
Housing Act 1925 ....146, 147
 s 46 ....146, 147
Housing Act 1957—
 s 111 457
Housing Act 1985—
 s 32 461
Human Rights Act 1998 ....3, 24, 26, 37, 39,
 44, 56, 58, 73, 86, 105,
 108, 115, 116, 124, 125,
 133, 135, 137, 138, 147,
 148, 155, 156, 165, 171,
 174, 195, 242, 251, 274,
 286–289, 307, 312, 314,
 322, 351, 352, 357, 358,
 360–362, 364, 367, 388,
 390–405, 408–420, 422,
 424–426, 429, 431, 437,
 438, 441, 442, 444, 454,
 455, 467, 470, 473–475,
 488
 s 1 ....365, 395
 s 1(1) 397
 ss 2–4 419
 s 2 ....133, 352–354, 395, 398,
 399, 401, 408, 417, 424,
 440
 s 3 ....44, 86, 115, 133, 395,
 401–404, 408, 417
 s 4 ....99, 133, 155, 287, 395,
 396, 404, 408, 410, 417
 s 5 404
 ss 6–8 419
 s 6 ....115, 305, 395–397,
 408–411, 418, 438, 444,
 467, 468
 s 6(1) 409
 s 6(3) 410

s 6(3)(b) 410
s 6(5) 410
s 6(6) 409
ss 7–9 395
s 7 ....396, 409, 415, 418, 467
s 7(1) 412
s 7(3) 412
s 7(5) 412
s 7(7) 412
s 8 ....355, 413, 414, 418
s 8(2) 413
s 8(3) 413
s 8(4) 413
s 9(1) 413
s 9(3) 375, 413
s 10 ....241, 242, 274, 280,
 395, 404, 408, 409,
 418, 419
s 10(3) 408
s 11 395
s 12 ....395, 415, 418, 425, 432
s 12(2) 415, 425
s 12(3) 415, 425
s 12(4) 415
s 13 ....395, 415, 418
s 14 ....398, 416, 417, 418
s 15 ....398, 417, 418
s 15(3) 417
s 16(1) 417
s 16(2) 417
s 19 ....395, 409, 419
s 19(1) 407
s 21 ....312, 320
s 21(1) 251
Sch 2, paras 2, 3(1), 4 408
Sch 3 ....364, 416
Hunting Act 2004 ....130, 219, 220, 313

Identity Cards Act 2006 240
Immigration Act 1971 ....43, 121, 144, 460,
 465, 482, 483
 s 3 119
 s 13(5) 460
Immigration and Asylum Act 1999—
 s 32 405
Indecent Displays (Control) Act 1981—
 s 1 427
Industrial Training Act 1964 477
Inquiries Act 2005 ....498–500, 509
 s 1 ....241, 242, 498, 499
 s 2 498
 s 15 499
 s 21 499
 s 35 499
 s 38 ....440, 452
 s 49(1) 146
 s 49(2) 146
 s 50 244
 Sch 3 146

Insolvency Act 1986 213
s 427..185
Interception of Communications Act
1985 354
Interpretation Act 1978—
s 6(a) 133
Irish Church Act 1869 149

Judicial Committee Act 1833 76
Judiciary and Courts (Scotland) Act
2008 314

Legislative and Regulatory Reform Act
2006 ....137, 280
Licensing Act 2003 220
Life Peerages Act 1958 .....203–205, 210, 214, 227
Limitation Act 1980.. 111
Local Democracy, Economic Development
and Construction Act 2009—
s 61 190
Local Government Act 1972—
s 111 ....457, 458
s 120(1)(b) 463
Local Government Act 1974.............................508
Local Government Act 1985....................134, 329
Local Government Act 1988.............................306
Local Government Act 1999.............................306
Local Government Act 2000.............................306
s 2(1) 302, 332
Local Government and Public
Involvement in Health Act 2007 ....301, 306
s 62 306
s 129 303
Local Government Finance Act 1988.............306
Local Government Finance Act 1992.............434
Local Government Planning and Land Act
1980 306

Magna Carta 1215 ....35, 38
Matrimonial Causes Act 1973.........................44
s 11..44
Meeting of Parliament Act 1694....................161
Mental Health Act 1983 ....185, 213
s 72..405
s 73..405
s 141..185
Mental Health (Public Safety and
Appeals) (Scotland) Act 1999—
s 1...315
Merchant Shipping Act 1988 ....46, 346–348,
350, 487
Pt II..346
Merchant Shipping (Registration) Act
1993 347
Ministerial and Other Salaries Act 1975........239
Ministers of the Crown Act 1975..............39, 233

National Health Service Reorganisation
Act 1973..508
Nigeria Independence Act 1960.....................139

Northern Ireland Act 1998 ....152, 154, 155,
319, 320, 322, 331
Pt III...238, 320
s 1...152, 322
s 1(1) 322
s 2..321
s 5..320
s 5(6)...322
s 6(1) 320
s 6(2) 321
s 6(2)(e) 321
s 9..321
s 10..321
s 11..321
s 13..321
s 14..321
s 18..320
s 24..321
s 25..322
s 26..322
s 68..323
Sch 2 321
Sch 3 321
Northern Ireland Act 2009 321
Northern Ireland Constitution Act 1973—
s 31..318
Northern Ireland (Elections) Act 1998...........319
Northern Ireland (Emergency Provisions)
Act 1978—
s 1..373
s 14..374
Northern Ireland (St Andrews Agreement)
Act 2006...319

Obscene Publications Act 1959..............101, 360,
424, 427, 428, 430
s 1..427
s 4..424, 427, 428
s 4(1)...427
Obscene Publications Act 1964.......101, 427, 430
Offences Against the Person Act 1861—
s 61..46
s 62..46
Official Secrets Act 1911..................................236
Official Secrets Act 1989 ....429, 431
s 1..407, 428, 429
s 4..407, 429
Overseas Development and Co-operation
Act 1980...436

Parliament Act 1911 ....23, 36, 53, 54, 58, 71,
120, 127, 132, 136,
152–154, 160, 162,
164, 208, 217–219,
222, 223, 227,
279
s 1..218
s 2...218, 219
s 2(1)...153, 154, 219
s 7..134, 160

Parliament Act 1949 ....23, 58, 71, 120, 127,
132, 136, 140, 152–154,
164, 217–219, 222, 223,
227, 279
Parliamentary Commissioner Act 1967 217,
501, 502, 505, 507, 509
s 1...501, 507
s 5...502, 503
s 7...503
s 8(2)...503
s 9...504
s 10...504
s 10(3)..504
Sch 2...502, 509
Sch 3...502, 509
Parliamentary Constituencies Act 1986 190
Parliamentary Elections Act 1695 185
Parliamentary Papers Act 1840—
s 1...171
s 2...171
s 3...171
Parliamentary Standards Act 2009 24,
175–177
s 1...171
s 3...176
s 4...176
s 5...176
s 6...176
s 8...176, 177
s 8(7), (8) 176
s 9...176, 177
s 10...177
Pedlars Act 1871 95
Peerage Act 1963...209
Perjury Act 1911......................................38, 431
s 1...428
Police Act 1996 500
s 49...498
Police and Criminal Evidence Act 1984 394
s 1...105
s 41...110
s 42...110
Political Parties and Elections Act
2009..193, 196
Political Parties, Elections and
Referendums Act 2000 ....190, 196
Prevention of Oil Pollution Act 1971.............483
Prevention of Terrorism Act 2005 ....38, 57, 99,
100, 105, 121, 138,
222, 298
s 2...123, 241
s 3...406
Prevention of Terrorism (Temporary
Provisions) Act 1984 364
Prison Act 1952—
s 47...242
s 47(1)..120, 241, 456
Public Authorities (Reform) Act (Northern
Ireland) 2009 320
Public Health (London) Act 1891...................305

Public Libraries and Museums Act 1964 461
s 7...241
Public Order Act 1986................38, 394, 428, 431
s 18...428
s 29J...428
Public Service Ombudsman (Wales) Act
2005..508

Race Relations Act 1965...................................142
Race Relations Act 1976....................................37
s 71...461
Racial and Religious Hatred Act 2006...........428
Regional Development Agencies Act 1998...329
Representation of the People Act 1983..........185
Representation of the People Act 1981..........185
Representation of the People Act 1983...........37,
193, 194, 405
s 3...194, 195
Representation of the People Act 1985.........194,
195
Representation of the People Act 2000.........193,
302
Road Traffic Act 1988......................................316
s 172(2)(a) 407
Road Traffic Regulations Act 1984..................39

Sale of Goods Act 1979 ....31, 32
School Standard and Framework Act
1998..370
Scotland Act 1978...308
Scotland Act 1998 ....31, 32, 39, 58, 76,
134, 138, 139, 152, 154,
155, 308, 312–315,
317, 331
Pt IV 314
s 1...310
s 1(3)..310
s 2...310
s 3...310
s 19...311
s 28...312
s 28(2)..312
s 28(7)..154, 317
s 29...312
s 29(1)...314
s 29(2)...314
s 31...315
s 32...315
s 33...315
s 35...315
s 37...149
s 44...238, 311
s 45...312
s 47...312
s 57...315
s 58...315
Sch 4 314
Sch 5 313
Scottish Parliament (Constituencies) Act
2004..316

Scottish Parliamentary Standards
    Commissioner Act 2002 .... 40, 311
Scottish Public Services Ombudsman Act
    2002 508
Senior Courts Act 1981 .... 217, 441, 451, 457
    s 11 292
    s 130 44
Separate Representation of Voters Act
    1951 (South Africa) 151
Septennial Act 1715 .... 134, 161
Sewel Convention of the Scottish
    Parliament 59, 139, 317
Sex Discrimination Act 1975 .... 37, 114, 182,
                            183, 343, 345, 347
    s 13 183
Sex Discrimination (Election Candidates)
    Act 2002 182
Sexual Offences (Amendment) Act
    2000 .... 219, 357
South Africa Act 1909—
    s 35 151
    s 152 151
Southern Rhodesia Act 1965 .... 56, 139
State Immunity Act 1978—
    s 20 112
Statute of Westminster 1931 ...... 54, 138, 139, 153
    s 4 .... 54, 138, 139, 153
Statutory Instruments Act 1946 279
Suicide Act 1961 .... 382, 407
    s 2 467
    s 2(1) 407
Sunday Entertainments Act 1932—
    s 1 469
Supreme Court Act 1981, See Senior
    Courts Act 1981—

Taxes Management Act 1970 .... 106, 115
    s 20C 57, 106, 115, 137
Terrorism Act 2000 .... 121, 394, 403, 416
    s 11(2) 403
    s 44 .... 107, 109, 360
    s 45 109
Terrorism Act 2006 .... 24, 107, 122, 215, 394
    s 1 .... 122, 240
    s 2 122

Terrorist Asset-Freezing (Temporary
    Provisions) Act 2010 .... 115, 122, 276, 457
Theft Act 1968 108
Trade Union and Labour Relations Act
    1974—
    s 13 .... 85, 86
Transport Act 1962 450
Treason Felony Act 1848—
    s 3 404
Tribunals and Inquiries Act 1958 492
Tribunals and Inquiries Act 1971 492
Tribunals and Inquiries Act 1992 492
Tribunals, Courts and Enforcement Act
    2007 .... 286, 435, 443,
                            493–496, 508
    Pt 2 297
    s 1 291
    s 18 496
Tribunals of Inquiry (Evidence) Act
    1921 .... 146, 498–500
Triennial Act 1694 134

United Nations Act 1946—
    s 1 .... 394, 457
Union with England Act 1707 308
Union with Ireland Act 1800 .... 35, 149, 318
    Art 5 149
Union with Scotland Act 1706 .... 32, 35, 39,
                            149, 308
Universities (Scotland) Act 1853 149

Wales Act 1978 323
War Crimes Act 1991 .... 120, 136, 158, 219
War Damage Act 1965 .... 57, 115, 132, 157,
                            158, 394
Weights and Measures Act 1985—
    s 1 347
Welsh Church Act 1914 218
Wireless Telegraphy Act 1949 461

Youth Justice and Criminal Evidence Act
    1999—
    s 41 .... 133, 402

Table of statutory instruments

Please note: this table was prepared by the Publishers, who take full responsibility for any errors therein.

Adoption (Northern Ireland) Order 1987
(SI 1997/2203) (NI 22)—
Art 14 406

Civil Procedure Rules 1998 (SI 1998/
3132) 412, 441, 450
Pre-action Protocol......................................451
Pt 54..448, 451
r 54.1(2)(a) 448
r 54.5(1)(a), (b)..451
r 54.19(2) 437
Constitutional Reform Act 2005
(Commencement No. 11) Order 2009
(SI 2009/1604)...241
Counter-Terrorism Act 2008 (Foreign
Travel Notification Requirements)
Regulations 2009 (SI 2009/2493) 281

Defence (General) Regulations 1939
(SI 1939/927)..53
Reg 18B 118
Defence of the Realm Regulations—
Reg 2A(2)..457
Dock Workers (Regulation of
Employment) Order 1947
(SI 1947/1189)...459

Homosexual Offences (Northern Ireland)
Order 1982 (SI 1982/1536).......................46
Human Rights Act (Amendment) Order
2001 (SI 2001/1216)...................................416
Human Rights Act 1998 (Amendment
No 2) Order 2001 (SI 2001/4032) 416
Human Rights Act 1998 (Designated
Derogation) Order 2001 (SI 2001/
3644)..105

Industrial Training Levy (Agricultural,
Horticultural and Forestry) Order
1967 (SI 1967/1747)...................................477

Mental Health Act 1983 (Remedial) Order
2001 (SI 2001/3712)...................................405
Merchant Shipping (Registration of
Fishing Vessels) Regulations 1988.........346

National Assembly for Wales (Legislative
Competence) (Social Welfare) Order
2008 (SI 2008/1785)...................................326

Oral Snuff (Safety) Regulations 1989
(SI 1989/2347 (quashed) 436

Prison Rules 1964 (SI 1964/388)—
r 33..120
r 33(3) 456
Purchase Tax Regulations 1945 (S R & O
1945/517)—
reg 12..107, 457

Regulatory Reform (Collaboration etc
between Ombudsmen) Order 2007
(SI 2007/1889)..508
Road Traffic (Permitted Parking Area and
Special Parking Area) (County of
Warwickshire) (Borough of Rugby)
Order 2006 (SI 2006/2356) 39
Rules of the Supreme Court 1965
(SI 1965/828)—
Ord 53 ....448, 451

Secretary of State for Constitutional
Affairs Order 2003 (SI 2003/1887)...........39
Supreme Court Fees (Amendment) Order
1996 (SI 1996/3191)...................................457
Art 3 44

Terrorism (United Nations Measures)
Order 2006 (SI 2006/2657) (quashed) ...457

Table of international legislation

Please note: this table was prepared by the Publishers, who take full responsibility for any errors therein.

European Legislation

Directives
Directive 76/207/EEC (Equal Treatment) 343
Directive 95/46/EC (Processing of
    Personal Data) 40

Regulations
Council Regulations 1365/75 (European
    Foundation for the improvement
    of living and working conditions of
    workers) 40

Decisions
Council Decision laying down the
    Procedures for the Exercise of
    Implementing Powers Conferred on
    the Commission 99/468 [1999] OJ
    L184/23 41

Treaties and Conventions
Declaration of Delhi 102

EC Charter of Fundamental Rights 2000 352
EC Treaty—
    Art 234 .... 45, 46
European Convention on the Protection
    of Human Rights and Fundamental
    Freedoms 1950 .... 3, 37, 44, 46, 56, 58,
        86, 101, 105, 108, 109,
        111, 115, 120, 124, 133,
        135, 136, 155, 156, 171,
        174, 193, 220, 241, 280,
        286, 288, 305, 314, 315,
        322, 327, 351–365, 383,
        385, 387–393, 395, 397–
        404, 407–418, 424, 425,
        438, 440–442, 455, 456,
        467, 472–474, 487, 489
    Pt 1 .... 390, 395, 398
    Art 1 .... 135, 352, 356, 361,
        364, 388, 391, 398
    Arts 2–14 .... 365, 390, 391
    Arts 2–12 417
    Art 2 .... 351, 359, 363–368, 370,
        371, 387, 390, 397, 407
    Art 2(1) 368
    Art 2(2) 366, 367
    Art 3 .... 105, 351, 355, 363,
        365, 368–371, 387, 390,
        395, 397, 401, 416

Art 4 .... 366, 371, 397
Art 4(1) 363, 365, 371
Art 4(2) 371
Art 4(3) 371
Art 5 .... 105, 298, 315, 351,
    358, 359, 363, 366, 372–
    375, 379, 390, 395, 397,
    400, 402, 403, 405, 412,
    414, 416, 488
Art 5(1) 372, 416
Art 5(1)(a) 372
Art 5(1)(b) 372
Art 5(1)(c) 372, 373
Art 5(1)(d) 372, 373
Art 5(1)(e) 372, 373
Art 5(1)(f) 372, 373
Art 5(2) 94, 373, 374
Art 5(3) 363, 364, 374
Art 5(4) 372, 374, 414
Art 5(5) 375, 413
Art 6 .... 73, 75, 123, 169, 174,
    286, 295, 315, 316, 351,
    354, 358, 372, 375–379,
    381, 390, 396–398, 405–
    407, 410, 412, 414, 467,
    480, 481, 484,
    485, 498
Art 6(1) 375–378, 406
Art 6(2) 377, 378
Art 6(3)(a) 377
Art 6(3)(c) 377, 378, 484
Art 6(3)(d) 378
Art 6(3)(e) 377
Art 7 .... 43, 96, 120, 144, 363,
    365, 378, 379,
    390, 397
Art 7(1) 378
Art 7(2) 366, 379
Arts 8–12 390
Arts 8–11 358–360
Art 8 .... 44, 46, 169, 351, 357,
    359, 377, 380–382, 384–
    387, 389, 393–397, 399,
    405, 407, 410–412,
    414, 430, 467,
    472
Art 8(1) 380
Art 8(2) 380, 381
Art 9 .... 359, 382–384, 387,
    389, 397, 415, 416
Art 9(1) 382

Art 10 ....101, 197, 351, 359,
360, 383, 390, 395, 397,
400, 404, 407, 424–427,
429–432
Art 10(1)....................................101, 383, 424, 431
Art 10(2)..............................101, 360, 383, 421,
425–431
Art 11......................................359, 384, 385, 397
Art 11(1)..384
Art 11(2)..384, 385
Art 12 ....44, 360, 380, 385, 386,
397, 405
Art 13 ....365, 367, 376, 388–391,
398
Art 14 ....105, 358, 360, 388–391,
395, 397, 400, 406, 411,
416, 417
Art 15 ....105, 361, 363, 365, 371,
400, 416, 418
Art 15(2)..363, 379
Art 16 ....416, 418
Art 17 385
Art 19 ....353, 364
Art 20 353
Art 27(1)..353
Art 27(2)..353
Art 27(3)..353
Art 28 353
Art 30 353
Art 31 353
Art 33 ....355, 364
Art 34 ....356, 364, 392, 412
Art 35 ....352, 356, 357, 365, 392
Art 38 ....357, 365
Art 40 357
Art 41 ....354, 355, 365, 413
Art 43 ....353, 365
Art 44 365
Art 45 354
Art 46 ....353, 354
Art 47 353
Art 57 ....363–365, 417
European Convention on the Protection
of Human Rights and Fundamental
Freedoms Protocol 1 417
Art 1 ....381, 386, 390, 391, 397,
405, 411
Art 2 ....364, 387, 390, 391,
397, 416
Art 3 ....56, 193, 195, 360, 390,
391, 397
European Convention on the Protection
of Human Rights and Fundamental
Freedoms Protocol 4...............................417
Art 2 372
European Convention on the Protection
of Human Rights and Fundamental
Freedoms Protocol 6........................368, 417
Art 1 397
Art 2 397

European Convention on the Protection
of Human Rights and Fundamental
Freedoms Protocol 11 ....353, 417
European Convention on the Protection
of Human Rights and Fundamental
Freedoms Protocol 12......................389, 417
European Convention on the Protection
of Human Rights and Fundamental
Freedoms Protocol 13......................368, 417
European Convention on the Protection
of Human Rights and Fundamental
Freedoms Protocol 14......................357, 417

Geneva Convention 129

International Covenant on Civil and
Political Rights 1966 47
Art 26 389

Single European Act 1986 ....40, 335, 340

Treaty Establishing the European
Constitution...9
Treaty of Amsterdam 1997 ....102, 335
Treaty of Lisbon 2007 ....336, 338, 344, 349
Treaty of Maastricht (Treaty on the
European Union) 1992 ....335, 342, 508
Treaty of Nice 2000 (Protocol on the
Enlargement of the European Union)...335
Treaty of Paris 1951 (European Coal and
Steel Community) (CS Treaty) 335
Treaty of Rome 1957................40, 46, 58, 82, 335,
336, 338, 340,
343–345, 349
Art 34 473
Art 36 473
Art 141 (Old Art 119) 345, 347
Treaty on The Functioning of The
European Union (TFEU).......................336
Art 157 ....345, 347
Art 258 ....335, 337, 341, 342
Art 259 ....341, 342
Art 263 ....335, 341, 342
Art 265 ....341, 342
Art 267 ....45, 46, 335, 337, 341, 342
Art 288 340

Universal Declaration on Human Rights
1948 ....47, 57, 58, 100, 124
Art 11..120

Other International Legislation
Australia
Constitution (1901)...14
Ch 8 14
Constitution Act (1902) (NSW).......................150
Constitution Act (1902) (Amendment) Act
1929 (NSW)—
s 7A..150, 151

Brazil

Constitution (1988)—

Art 1 11

Art 3 12

Finland

Act on Commercial Leases 1993 73

France

Fifth Republic Constitution (1958)—

Art 23 69

Art 89 9

Germany

Constitution (1949) 14

Art 67 8

Art 20 95

India

Constitution 13

Pt III 9

Pt III, Art 19 420

Japan

Constitution (1947) 12

Art 98 10

Malawi

Constitution (1966) 12

Republic of Ireland

Constitution (1937) 12

5th Amdt (1973) 12

Art 6, s 1 11

Art 15.2 .... 62, 71

Art 15.4 .... 126, 144

Art 15.10 .... 74, 168

Art 15.12 168

Art 26 65

Art 34 65

Art 34.1 63

South Africa

Constitution (1997)—

s 2 10

Spain

Constitution (1978) 12

Sri Lanka

Ceylon (Constitution) Order in Council 1946—

s 29(4) 151

Sweden

Constitution (1975) 12

Instrument of Government 1975—

Chapter 1 95

USA

Constitution (1789) 8, 12–14, 82

1st Amdt (Bill of Rights 1791) 8, 420

Art IV 8

22nd Amdt (1951) 9, 54

Art I 36, 62

Art I, s 4 49

Art I, s 7 8

Art I, s 8 .... 8, 245

Art II, s 2 8

Art III 63

Art VI 10

West Germany

Constitution (1949) 12

1

Introductory concepts

public law
the law regulating the powers of the institutions of the state, how they relate to each other and how they relate to individuals

private law
the law regulating the relationship between individuals

At the end of this chapter you should be able to:

■ distinguish between **public law** and **private law**
■ define and distinguish between constitutional and administrative law

1.1 The distinction between public law and private law

In general, the term 'law' can be broadly divided into two branches: public law and private law. Constitutional and administrative law form part of public law.

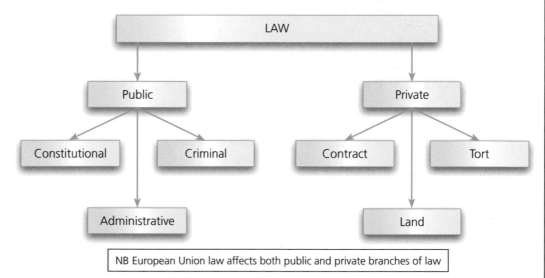

Figure 1.1 The distinction between public law and private law

1.1.1 Private law

In essence, private law is that branch of the law that is concerned with the relationship that individuals have with one another. For example:

■ An individual forms a legally binding contract with a work colleague when he agrees to purchase a three-piece settee from him (see further *Unlocking Contract Law*).

- An individual sues a neighbour in the law of defamation for making untrue slanderous accusations about his past (see further *Unlocking Torts*).
- Two adjoining land owners legally dispute the location of a boundary fence between their land (see further *Unlocking Land Law*).
- A pedestrian sues the driver of a car in the law of negligence after being badly injured in an accident caused by his careless driving (see further *Unlocking Torts*).

1.1.2 Private law involving other than private individuals

It is also worth noting at this point that it is possible for individuals to have private law transactions or legal relations with the state (in this context and for present purposes, the state means simply the government, public authorities, local authorities, etc). For example, an individual may form a legally binding contract with a local authority, or indeed may even sue that same body in the law of negligence if it has acted carelessly and caused harm. Although in one sense such relations would appear to form part of contract and tort law respectively (with the defendant in these cases being the state, rather than a private individual), such actions could also have a public law dimension. This is because as these actions in contract and negligence involve the state they will be governed by special rules and principles which have the effect of treating the state differently from an ordinary private individual defendant. This point serves to indicate at this early stage that in the United Kingdom the distinction between private and public law is not absolute and so it is not always easy to draw the line between them with complete precision. For example, in this context Lord Wilberforce in *Davy v Spelthorne Borough Council* [1984] 1 AC 262 commented:

JUDGMENT

'The expressions "private law" and "public law" have recently been imported into the law of England from countries which, unlike our own, have separate systems concerning public law and private law. No doubt they are convenient expressions for descriptive purposes. In this country they must be used with caution.'

For more on public law issues, see section 19.5.

1.1.3 Public law

Public law (which subsumes both constitutional and administrative law – see section 1.2) is that branch of the law that focuses on the power of the state. In essence, public lawyers are concerned with the location of state power, how that power is exercised and controlled, and how it impacts on the individual. At a very basic level, public law is concerned with the following questions:

- Who and what bodies/institutions/individuals exercise state/public power?
- What is the nature and extent of these powers?
- Why do these bodies/institutions exercise power?
- How do these bodies relate to each other?
- How is power used?
- How is the use of power regulated?
- How are these bodies/institutions/individuals made accountable?
- What protection is given to the individual from the power of the state?

In other words, the study of public law is concerned with the identification of public power, the institutions that exercise it and how these institutions relate to one another and to the individual. Most importantly, it is concerned with how the use of public power is regulated and controlled. Thus, the constitutional principle of the accountability of the state (whether it be in a legal or political form), is a major theme that underpins the subject of public law and consequently, therefore, this text.

In summary, in contrast to private law which is concerned essentially with individual/private legal relations, public law focuses on the structure and organisation of the state and how the individual relates to the state.

1.1.4 Public law and criminal law

human rights
rights and freedoms to which every human being is entitled

freedom of expression
a right set out in Article 10 of the European Convention on Human Rights and now part of UK law as a consequence of the Human Rights Act 1998

At this point, it is pertinent to note that the broad term public law also technically embraces criminal law, as crimes are termed as offences against the state, and so punishable by it. Although criminal law clearly has a public law dimension, historically the substantive subject of criminal law (eg offences against the person, theft, etc) has nevertheless been taught as a separate subject (see further *Unlocking Criminal Law*). Notwithstanding this, certain aspects of criminal law (for example the breadth and extent of police powers for arresting and detaining individuals) will necessarily be subsumed within the field of public law as they raise issues concerning basic **human rights** and civil liberties. In particular, the substantive criminal law offences which involve restricting **freedom of expression**, for example the laws of obscenity and indecency, will be considered as part of Chapter 18.

1.1.5 Public law and politics

constitution
the rules which govern the government which can be found in either a codified or uncodified form

constitutional convention
a binding political rule of the constitution

Public law, more so than any other substantive law subject, is intimately and inextricably linked with the disciplines of political science and government. As a consequence, it is an advantage to have a background interest in, and awareness of, general British politics when studying public law as the subject necessarily draws upon some of these principles. In fact, as we will see in Chapter 4, some of the sources of the British **constitution** are actually political practices (**constitutional conventions**).

For example, in the context of the government's relations with Parliament, government ministers are both collectively and individually responsible to Parliament for their actions and yet this accountability is not legal, but essentially political in nature, determined by predominately political factors. Furthermore, the connection and overlap between politics and constitutional law is evident in the context of civil liberties which involves the basic human rights and freedoms of the individual. These rights – which include, for example, the right to free speech – raise the issue of whether such rights should be enjoyed, and whether they are actually political/moral/religious questions which happen to be dressed up as legal questions which are determined by (unelected) judges in a courtroom (whether domestically or in Europe).

Public law is highly topical and an ever-changing and dynamic subject. In studying public law, therefore, it is advisable to keep abreast of recent developments through the daily broadsheet newspapers. Thus, every day there will be, invariably, something with a public law dimension and therefore of interest to public lawyers. Hypothetical examples could include the following:

- A government minister resigns over a scandal.
- A local authority acts illegally by abusing its powers.
- The European Court of Human Rights in Strasbourg makes a judgment against the United Kingdom for breaching the European Convention on Human Rights.
- The Queen approves the appointment of 10 new life peers to sit in the House of Lords.
- Parliament passes a law which restricts freedom of expression.
- The European Court of Justice in Luxembourg declares that the United Kingdom has failed to follow European Union law.

Administrative Court
that part of the High Court which processes judicial review cases

- The **Administrative Court** declares that the Home Secretary has breached the Human Rights Act 1998.

ACTIVITY

Applying the law

Read one week's issues of a national daily newspaper and try to identify articles which you think have relevance to the study of public law.

1.1.6 Public law and European Union law

As a result of the enactment of the European Communities Act 1972 (see Chapter 15), in recent decades both public law and private law have been significantly affected by, and subject to, European Union (EU) law. Although the main substantive subjects of EU law (eg the free movement of goods, workers, services, etc) are studied separately (see further *Unlocking EU Law*), certain aspects of it – such as the primacy of EU law – have had such a profound effect on the constitution of the United Kingdom that they have to be considered in any study of public law. In particular, the reception of EU law (which now has overriding legal effect) into the United Kingdom has resulted in, *inter alia*, the restriction of the power of the United Kingdom Parliament to pass any law that it chooses (see Chapter 7 in conjunction with section 15.6).

EU law
law and legal practices emanating from the European Union

KEY FACTS

Public law embraces both constitutional and administrative law and is essentially concerned with the organs of the state, together with how they relate to each other and to individuals. Public law is concerned with the use and regulation of public power.

1.2 The distinction between constitutional and administrative law

Although both constitutional and administrative law form part of the generic term public law, a distinction, albeit a fine one, can be made between them.

1.2.1 Constitutional law

At a very basic level constitutional law can be described simply as the law relating to the constitution. Although the term constitution will be considered in Chapter 2, for present purposes a constitution represents a set of basic rules and principles which govern the government/state.

A more detailed definition is provided by Barnett who defined constitutional law in the following terms:

QUOTATION

'Constitutional law is concerned with the role and powers of the institutions within the state and with the relationship between the citizen and the state.'

H Barnett, *Constitutional and Administrative Law* (7th edn, Routledge–Cavendish, 2009), p 3.

In other words, constitutional law concerns, among others, the following elements (all of which will be considered in this text):

parliament
composed of the House of Commons and the House of Lords

- The principal institutions of the state, *viz*, **Parliament** (see Chapters 8 to 10), the government (see Chapter 11), the courts (see Chapter 13) and devolved/decentralised state bodies (see Chapter 14).
- The specific roles and functions conferred on these institutions, together with the nature and extent of their powers (for example, see Chapter 11 on the powers of the executive).
- The procedures and mechanisms used to oversee, regulate and check these powers (for example, see Chapter 12 in relation to the parliamentary controls over the government).
- The ways in which these institutions relate to one another (for example, see Chapter 10 on how the House of Lords and Commons relate to one another).

■ The ways in which these institutions relate to the individual (for example, see Chapter 9 on parliamentary elections).

■ The basic and fundamental rights of the individual (for example, the right to life and free speech) and how – and to what extent – these rights and freedoms can be protected from infringement by the state (see Chapters 16 and 17 on human rights and Chapter 18 on freedom of speech).

1.2.2 Administrative law

In general terms, administrative law (in contrast to constitutional law above) is concerned with, simply, the law relating to the administration/government. Wade and Forsyth defined it in the following terms:

QUOTATION

'Administrative law may be said to be the body of general principles which govern the exercise of powers and duties by public authorities.'

H Wade and W Forsyth, *Administrative Law* (10th edn, Oxford University Press, 2009), p 5.

The government, its officers and agencies are invested with extensive powers to provide services (eg administering welfare benefits) and to carry out specific government functions (eg making regulations). Administrative law, therefore, is focused specifically on the various powers that the government exercises and how these powers are controlled and regulated to ensure that the administration acts strictly within its limits. This branch of the law is concerned with the control of the government through the mechanisms of **judicial review** (see Chapters 19 and 20), tribunals (see Chapter 21) and inquiries (see Chapter 21). In addition, it also embraces parliamentary/political controls in the form of the Parliamentary **Ombudsman** (see Chapter 21).

It is clear that in the United Kingdom the distinction between administrative law and constitutional law is not, necessarily, easy to draw. At a general level it could be said that whereas constitutional law tends to consider the whole apparatus of the state, administrative law, in contrast, is more specifically focused on how the executive/administration uses and misuses its powers. For practical purposes, this text considers each branch separately through a collection of various chapters: constitutional law is considered in Chapters 1–14 and 16–18 while administrative law is detailed in Chapters 19–21. In addition, a general introduction to European Union law is covered in Chapter 15. As such, it will be plain that constitutional law will form the major component of this book.

judicial review
the process whereby the courts review the legality of governmental actions

Ombudsman
an officer who investigates complaints of maladministration

KEY FACTS

Constitutional law is the law relating to the constitution, the state institutions, their powers, together with how they relate to the individual.

Administrative law is concerned specifically with the law relating to the administration/executive/government and its control.

ACTIVITY

Self-test question

How can one define and recognise constitutional law?

2

Constitutions

AIMS AND OBJECTIVES

At the end of this chapter you should be able to:

- Define a constitution
- Appreciate the nature and content of constitutions
- Appreciate the purpose of constitutions
- Distinguish between different types of constitution
- Understand the concept of constitutionalism

2.1 Definition

All organisations – whether a university chess club or a state – have a constitution of some description, as society requires rules in order to function and ensure order. These rules are simply known as the constitution (constitutional rules). Bradley and Ewing have noted that a constitution can be defined in two ways: with a narrow or a wide meaning. In a narrow sense they have described a constitution as:

QUOTATION

'a document having a special legal sanctity which sets out the framework and the principal functions of the organs of government within the state and declares the principles by which those organs must operate'.

A Bradley and K Ewing, *Constitutional and Administrative Law* (14th edn, Pearson/Longman, 2007), p 4.

In a broader sense of the term, they refer to, and quote, Wheare:

QUOTATION

'it is used to describe the whole system of government of a country, the collection of rules which establish and regulate or govern the government'.

K Wheare, *Modern Constitutions* (2nd edn, Oxford University Press, 1966), p 1.

In its first report in July 2001, the House of Lords Select Committee on the Constitution recognised the difficulty in defining the term constitution and put forward the following definition:

QUOTATION

'Our working definition of a constitution is that it is the set of laws, rules and practices that create the basic institutions of the state and its component and related parts, and stipulate the powers of those institutions and the relationship between the different institutions and between those institutions and the individual.'

First Report of Session 2001–02 of the House of Lords Select Committee on the Constitution, *Reviewing the constitution: Terms of reference and method of working* HL Paper 11 (2001), p 16.

For present purposes, therefore, we may conclude that a constitution is simply a set of rules and principles that govern the organisation and structure of the state which the governing institutions must, or should, adhere to. As will be indicated below, these constitutional rules almost invariably will be found in a single written document entitled 'The Constitution', although sometimes – as in the United Kingdom – these rules are located other than in a specific constitutional document (see Chapter 4 on the sources of the constitution of the United Kingdom).

ACTIVITY

Self-test question

Using the above definitions, how would you define a constitution in your own words?

2.2 The contents of a constitution

constitutionalism
the principle which requires a constitution to provide sufficient restraints on government/state power

What will a constitution contain? The exact contents of a state constitution will differ from state to state. It must be remembered that constitutions exist in both democratic and non-democratic countries, although by their nature, democratic constitutions should follow the principles of **constitutionalism** (see section 2.6.2).

As an introduction or foreword, a preamble is found in many state constitutions. It tends to be declaratory in nature and identifies the people as the constituent (sovereign) power from which the moral authority of the constitution derives. For example, in the Irish constitution (1937) it is stated at the outset that:

ARTICLE

We the people . . . do hereby adopt, enact and give to ourselves this constitution.

In general, the main text of a constitution will contain the following elements.

2.2.1 The establishment of the institutions of government together with their roles, powers and functions

A constitution will set out the basic ground rules of the state which will include the establishment of its institutions (and so their legitimacy – see section 2.4.2). In short, it will locate and establish the principal institutions of the state together with their roles/ functions:

Cabinet
the collection of the most senior government ministers

Supreme Court
the highest domestic court

- The law-making institution which passes legislation (Parliament/Congress/Assembly).
- The executive/government institution which enforces the law and makes policy decisions (Prime Minister/**Cabinet**/President).
- The judicial institution which interprets and declares the law (the courts/Constitutional Court/**Supreme Court**).

For example, the constitution of the United States of America (1789) states the following:

- Art I, s 1. All legislative powers herein granted shall be vested in a Congress of the United States, which shall consist of a Senate and House of Representatives.
- Art II, s 1. The executive power shall be vested in a President of the United States of America.
- Art III, s 1. The judicial power of the United States shall be vested in one Supreme Court, and such inferior courts as the Congress may from time to time ordain and establish.

In this way the constitution of the United States sets out the three key institutions of the state.

The constitution will also set out the specific powers of each institution. For example, again with reference to the constitution of the United States, Art II, s 2 states that the President shall have the power (with the consent of the Congress) to make Treaties and to nominate (also with congressional consent) the judges of the Supreme Court. Similarly, Art I, s 8 states that Congress shall have the power to lay and collect taxes and declare war. In short, a constitution will establish the key institutions of the state and allocate them constitutional roles and responsibilities and equip them with public powers.

2.2.2 The establishment of the relationship between the different institutions of the state

The constitution will also set out the constitutional relationship between the various institutions established under it. This relationship will necessarily involve the principle of the system of checks and balances between the institutions (see Chapter 5). For example, as seen above, the constitution of the United States stipulates that Congress is the body responsible for passing legislation; however, Art I, s 7 states that before a Bill becomes law it must be presented to the President for approval. If the latter rejects the Bill, it can still become law providing that Congress reconsiders it and both congressional chambers pass the Bill with a two-thirds majority. This therefore sets out the constitutional relationship between the President and Congress in the context of the passage of legislation.

In the German constitution (1949), Art 67 states that the Bundestag (the lower House of the German Parliament) can express a lack of confidence in the Federal Chancellor by electing (with a majority of its members) a successor to replace them. Thus, a major theme of public law is how the state institutions relate to and complement one another, and most importantly, how these institutions check and balance one another.

2.2.3 The establishment of the relationship between the state institutions and the individual

As noted above, constitutional law is partly concerned with how the individual relates to the state (ie what powers can the state exert over the individual?). For example, in what circumstances can the individual be arrested and detained or have their freedom of expression interfered with? A democratic constitution, however, will constitutionally ring-fence and safeguard certain basic rights of the individual with which the state institutions cannot interfere (or can only do so with compelling justification). In other words, this means that the rights of the individual are put beyond the reach of the state. In one sense, this can be seen as part of the social contract (see section 2.4.2) which the citizen makes with the state. This in turn confers legitimacy on the state institutions to rule.

One of the most famous declarations of basic and fundamental human rights is 'The **Bill of Rights'** containing the first 10 amendments of the constitution of the United States. As an example, Art IV of the Bill of Rights is set out below:

Bill of Rights
document containing a list of basic and fundamental human rights

> The right of the people to be secure in their persons, houses, papers, and effects, against unreasonable searches and seizures, shall not be violated, and no warrants shall issue, but upon probable cause, supported by oath or affirmation, and particularly describing the place to be searched, and the persons or things to be seized.

Similarly, Part III of the Indian constitution sets out the fundamental rights of the individual which include, among others:

- the right to equality
- the right to freedom of religion
- the right to freedom of speech, assembly, association, etc
- the right against exploitation.

By setting out the basic rights of the individual in the constitution in this way, these fundamental rights and freedoms are accorded special protection from infringement by the state.

2.2.4 The methods and procedures to change the constitution

Although constitutions are (generally) documents which embody the framework of the state, they are not necessarily meant to be documents which are incapable of amendment and improvement. Indeed, the contents of a state constitution which could not be altered in any way in order to adapt to changing times would make the citizens of that state a prisoner of their constitution, as their constitution may have been drafted decades, if not centuries, before. A constitution will typically, therefore, stipulate the method and procedures that must be complied with in order to alter its provisions.

For example, amendments to the constitution of the United States can be made provided two-thirds of both Houses of Congress, together with three-quarters of the state **legislatures**, approve such changes. In fact, there have been 27 such amendments made in the past two centuries – one notable example was the 22nd Amendment in 1951 when the constitution was altered to prevent a President being elected to serve more than two terms in office. Similarly, in France under Art 89 of the constitution of the Fifth Republic (1958), an amendment can be made when a proposal has passed – in identical terms – both Houses of the French Parliament and has subsequently been approved by the people in a referendum. In 2005 the French people, in a referendum, rejected the Treaty Establishing a Constitution for Europe.

legislature
the law-making body in a constitution

KEY FACTS

Key facts on the contents of a constitution

A constitution will contain the principal institutions of the state, their functions and powers.
A constitution will establish the relationship between each of the state institutions together with how these institutions relate to the citizen.
A constitution will also indicate how (or if) it can be altered and the process that must be undertaken to do so.

2.3 Entrenching constitutional law

Due to the nature of its subject-matter (establishing the structure and institutions of the state), a constitution and its laws ideally should be of a higher/fundamental status. In other words the law relating to the constitution (ie 'constitutional law') should in legal terms be superior and more fundamental than other 'ordinary' or 'non-constitutional' laws (eg private laws such as contract and trust law). Thus, as the constitution represents the basic framework of the government, it should necessarily have a greater legal and moral authority than other ordinary laws in the legal system. This reflects the comparative importance and significance of constitutional law. Indeed, it could be contended that in a jurisprudential sense, constitutional law is more significant and important than all other laws, which of course only exist because of the existence of a constitution and constitutional law.

Typically therefore the constitutional document embodying the constitutional law of the state will invariably be a form of law which is superior/higher than other laws in the legal system. For example, s 2 of the South African constitution of 1997 states that:

ARTICLE

This Constitution is the supreme law of the Republic; law or conduct inconsistent with it is invalid, and the obligations imposed by it must be fulfilled.

Similarly, Art 98 (Chapter X: *Supreme Law*) of the Japanese constitution (1947) states that:

ARTICLE

This Constitution shall be the supreme law of the nation and no law, ordinance, imperial rescript or other act of government, or part thereof, contrary to the provisions hereof, shall have legal force or validity.

In addition, see Art VI of the constitution of the United States.

As constitutional law will be accorded a higher and fundamental legal status, this means inevitably that it will be more difficult to alter than other 'ordinary' laws which can be amended, or even abolished, through the ordinary legislative process (see section 2.2.4 for the special procedures that may be necessary in order to amend a constitution).

The notion of constitutional law having a superior status will be reconsidered in Chapter 3 in the context of the United Kingdom's very unusual constitutional arrangements (see section 3.4.4).

KEY FACTS

 Key facts on constitutional law

Constitutional laws are typically given a higher and more fundamental legal status than other non-constitutional rules/laws (eg private laws governing the formation and enforcement of contracts made between private individuals – contract law).

2.4 The purpose of a constitution

Why do countries have constitutions? There are many reasons for creating a constitution and these are set out below.

2.4.1 To ensure stability and order

As noted above, all countries (and organisations) have a constitution of some description because all societies require rules and organisation in order to ensure stability. Without a set of basic rules there would be no structure or organisation and chaos would ensue. Constitutions, therefore, provide a set of basic ground rules and principles which establish and regulate the basic framework of the state. A constitution helps ensure that a state – or indeed even a social club – achieves its primary purpose and objectives.

For example, if one object of a people is to safeguard the basic rights of the individual in society (particularly vulnerable minorities), this can be achieved with a constitution setting up a mechanism such as a declaration of human rights, together with a Supreme/ Constitutional Court to safeguard and protect such rights from infringement.

2.4.2 To ensure that government operates by consent and has constitutional and moral legitimacy

Thomas Paine, writing in the eighteenth century, stated that:

QUOTATION

'A constitution is not the act of a government, but of a people constituting a government, and a government without a constitution is power without right … A constitution is a thing antecedent to a government; and a government is only the creature of a constitution.'

Rights of Man in *The Complete Works of Thomas Paine*, cited in M Allen and B Thompson, *Cases & Materials on Constitutional & Administrative Law* (9th edition, Oxford University Press, 2008) p 1.

What Paine meant was that a constitution ensures that the governing institutions (Congress/Parliament, President/government and courts) should have constitutional legitimacy and so govern with the consent of the people. In other words, by agreeing to and endorsing the constitution, the people confer legitimacy on it and the institutions created under it. For example, this was done in the Republic of Ireland where the constitution was approved by the people in a national referendum. Art 6, s 1 of the Irish constitution states specifically that:

ARTICLE

All powers of government, legislative, executive, and judicial, derive, under God, from the people, whose right it is to designate the rulers of the state.

This in turn conferred moral and constitutional authority on those institutions created under the Irish constitution to govern the state and regulate the lives of its citizens. As noted above, this can be likened to a social contract between the governed (the citizen) and the governing institutions (Parliament, government and the courts). As part of this constitutional bargain, the governing institutions are conferred with the constitutional and legal powers to rule and govern the people. In return, these institutions ensure stability and order in the state/society and are (largely) prevented from interfering with the basic human rights of the individual which are typically enshrined in a Bill/Charter of Rights.

A democratic constitution ensures (at least in theory) that government is with the consent of the people. For example, in Iraq in January 2005, the Iraqi people voted for a transitional National Assembly, which would draft a new constitution. This draft constitution was in turn approved by the people in a national referendum in October 2005, and subsequent to this the new democratically elected Iraqi government was formed. Having said this, the approval of the people can, in practice, be somewhat nominal as demonstrated by the Indian constitution. Although it was approved by a constitutent Assembly (representing the people), the terms of the constitution were not actually directly approved by the Indian people themselves.

In short, if the constitution – and as a consequence the state institutions created under it – has the consent of the people (nominal or otherwise), this means that its institutions have the constitutional legitimacy to carry out their prescribed functions and exercise their powers stipulated in the constitution. In other words, the constitution, the state apparatus and its institutions have a badge of legitimacy. In this context see Art 1 of the Brazilian constitution (1988):

All power emanates from the people, who exercise it by means of elected representatives or directly, as provided by this constitution.

2.4.3 To represent a constitutional watershed

A state constitution is generally founded to represent a break with the past and so represent a watershed in terms of the history, politics and institutional structure of that particular state. For example, the creation of a constitution may well follow:

- A revolution: the United States of America (1789)
- Independence following colonial rule: Malawi (1966)
- The removal of a dictatorship: Spain (1978)
- A war: West Germany (1949), Japan (1947).

The creation of a new constitution will enable that country to draw a clear line under its past and give it the opportunity to establish a new state apparatus with new institutions governed by principles which have the clear approval of the people. See for example, the new constitution of Iraq, which represents a clear break with its historical and authoritarian past.

2.4.4 A constitutional limit and control on governmental power

As a constitution establishes institutions and invests them with public powers and responsibilities, it is the hallmark of a democratic constitution that these institutions are controlled, regulated and checked by the constitution itself (which, of course, embodies the consent of the people, nominal or otherwise – see section 2.4.2). In other words, a constitution will set out the limitations of governmental power (this can be done in various ways, in particular see section 2.6.2 on the notion of constitutionalism). A constitution must therefore not only allocate and distribute public power, but must also ensure that the use of that power is checked; otherwise public power will be misused and abused at the expense of the citizen. For example, the Swedish constitution (the Instrument of Government of 1975 (Ch 1)) states boldly that:

Public power shall be exercised under law.

2.4.5 To affirm particular values and goals

All constitutions are by their nature man-made and so drafted with certain underlying principles and goals in mind. These could be, for example, the promotion of democratic values, open government, the welfare and public good of the citizen or the attainment of religious aims. For example, the Irish constitution of 1937 (as originally drafted) made specific reference to the special position of the Roman Catholic Church, thereby reflecting the importance attached to the church in society as a whole. It is of interest to note, however, that as a result of the divisive nature of this provision, in an amendment to the constitution in 1973 (the Fifth Amendment), the special position of the Catholic Church was removed. Similarly, the Brazilian constitution is not concerned solely with the organisation of the state institutions, but also extends to economic and social reforms in society as a whole. In particular, Art 3 sets out that one objective of the constitution is to eradicate poverty.

Key facts on the purpose of a constitution

The rationale behind a constitution is to ensure the following:

- order and stability
- the legitimacy of the governmental institutions
- to mark a watershed
- to limit governmental power
- to affirm specific goals considered important for that society.

ACTIVITY

Applying the law

In July 2013, a country obtains its independence after occupation by a foreign power for over 30 years. You are asked to advise the drafters of its new constitution as to how it should be drawn up. In particular,

- What needs to go into the constitution?
- What does not need to go into the constitution?
- How can you ensure that the constitution achieves both what (a) the citizens and (b) the envisaged governing institutions desire from the constitution?

2.5 Different types of constitutions

There are various types of constitutions in existence around the world and noted below are the principal ways in which they can be (very broadly) categorised and classified.

2.5.1 Written and unwritten constitutions/codified and uncodified constitutions

Historically, one major way of classifying and distinguishing between constitutions was through the labels of written and unwritten constitutions. A written constitution was one in which the rules of the constitution were located in a written document entitled 'The Constitution'. For example, the constitution of the United States can be found in the document called the 'United States Constitution', which contains seven Articles along with their various amendments. Similarly, the Indian constitution can be found in a document which comprises almost 400 Articles and nine accompanying schedules. In contrast, an unwritten constitution would be one in which the major constitutional rules of the state could not be found in a single written document – as in the United Kingdom.

Care, however, has to be taken with this particular method of classifying constitutions:

- Firstly, it is clear that not every single principle and rule relating to a constitution will be detailed in a single written constitutional document. For example, as constitutional rules are not necessarily self-explanatory or cover every constitutional eventuality, these rules have to be interpreted by the courts (Supreme/Constitutional or otherwise). As a consequence, these judgments interpreting the constitution will also form part of the constitutional rules which govern the country. In addition, the rules of a written constitution will be invariably supplemented by unwritten political practices and conventions which have grown up around it (on constitutional conventions see section 4.13).
- Secondly, even in the United Kingdom (which has historically been labelled as having an unwritten constitution in the absence of a single constitutional document called 'The United Kingdom Constitution'), it is nevertheless clear that many of its constitutional rules are actually written down: for example in parliamentary legislation.

As a consequence, in recent years it has become fashionable to classify constitutions on the basis of being codified or not, rather than on the basis of the written/unwritten dichotomy. In this way the constitution of the United States would be defined rightly as a codified constitution with its major rules being codified largely (but not exclusively) in its seven Articles and subsequent amendments. In contrast, the constitution of the United Kingdom can be described as uncodified in the sense that its constitutional rules and principles are located in a multitude of different sources which have not been brought together and codified in a single document (see further Chapter 4).

2.5.2 Rigid and flexible constitutions

Historically, constitutions have also been classified according to whether or not there is a special procedure which must be followed in order to change the constitutional text (and therefore constitutional law). In order to alter the content and provisions of a rigid constitution, a procedure is stipulated which requires specific legal/constitutional obstacles to be overcome. For example, a proposed amendment may require the approval of the people in a national referendum and/or the use of special majorities in the Parliament/ Assembly. By way of illustration, Chapter 8 of the 1901 'Constitution of Australia' stipulates that a proposed amendment to the provisions of the constitution must be initiated and approved in the Australian Parliament and thereafter approved by the Australian people in a referendum.

In contrast, a flexible constitution is one in which the content and principles of the constitution can be amended by the ordinary legislative process which is used to alter, or abolish, other 'ordinary' (ie non-constitutional) laws. Flexible constitutions are much less common than rigid constitutions because constitutional rules, by their very nature, are viewed as being fundamental, and so *should* be more difficult to change than other laws. Israel, New Zealand and the United Kingdom provide examples of flexible constitutions. An example of a recent change to the constitutional arrangements of the United Kingdom is illustrated by the enactment of the Constitutional Reform Act 2005 which created a separate Supreme Court which came into effect in 2009. This legislation was passed by the United Kingdom Parliament through the ordinary channels of the law-making process: the consent of both the House of Commons and the House of Lords, together with the **Royal Assent**. No special majority, or indeed referendum, was required.

Royal Assent
the consent conferred on a Bill by the monarch in order to convert into an Act of Parliament

It should be noted that just because a constitution is labelled as rigid (owing to its prescribed method of amendment), it does not necessarily follow that the constitution is never amended or that in practice it is *actually* very difficult to alter. In reality changes to a constitution are driven by, and dependent on, the political will in that particular state. As indicated above, the constitution of the United States has been altered on 27 occasions even though there are significant obstacles to be overcome in order to change it. In contrast, a flexible constitution may not necessarily be changed frequently in practice, even though it is possible to do so. Although the United Kingdom constitution has traditionally been labelled as flexible, there are certain aspects of it which have not actually been altered for generations. Two examples will suffice at this stage:

■ In Parliament, the House of Commons (as the elected House) has dominance over the House of Lords (see section 10.10).
■ The monarch will always confer her Assent to a Bill in order to make it law. This consent has not been refused for centuries (see section 11.9.3).

2.5.3 Federal and unitary constitutions

A federal constitution (such as in the United States, Australia and Germany) is one where the powers and responsibilities of the institutions of the state are constitutionally divided between the centre (federal institutions) and the regions/states/provinces. For example, in the United States the federal (national) Congress has specified powers and responsibilities under the constitution (eg in relation to national and international affairs). In contrast, the legislatures of the various states (eg Florida, California, etc) have powers and responsibilities which relate specifically to the regulation and government of that particular state. In essence the rationale behind a federal constitution is twofold:

- Firstly, to reduce further the power of the state (and so minimise the exercise of arbitrary power) by separating and dividing power and responsibilities between central and local institutions.
- Secondly, to safeguard and constitutionally ring-fence the powers of the local states/provinces/regions to enable them to determine their own local laws which are tailored to local needs.

local authorities
directly elected layer of government which administers functions at a local level and tailored to local needs

In a unitary constitution (found for example in the United Kingdom), power is focused in the main and central law-maker (in the United Kingdom this is Parliament). Although, as we shall see in Chapter 14, there exist a number of other decentralised bodies in the United Kingdom, namely **local authorities** and the Scottish Parliament, this does not however, make the United Kingdom a federal state, as these bodies are necessarily subordinate to, and ultimately dependent on, the United Kingdom Parliament in Westminster. For example, for five decades until the 1970s Northern Ireland had its own Parliament, but this was abolished by the Westminster Parliament which had established it in the first place. In short, these institutions do not have express constitutional protection, unlike the state/provincial/regional legislatures in a federal constitution.

ACTIVITY

Self-test question

Explain the main ways in which constitutions can be classified. Are these useful or definitive?

2.6 Constitutionalism and acting 'constitutionally'

2.6.1 Introduction

Although commentators appear to find it difficult to define the term constitutionalism, in essence it means government (or the institutions of the state) acting in accordance with the rules and principles enshrined in the constitution, thereby resulting in limited constitutional government. Generally anything allowed by a constitution would be considered as 'constitutional' (ie conforming to, and acting strictly within, the parameters permitted by the constitution). In countries which adhere to the ideas of limited government, however, constitutionalism would demand that there is sufficient control on the power of the government. In other words, a constitution should not be merely descriptive – simply describing the powers of the governing institutions – but must also control and check that power through the constitution. The rationale behind constitutionalism is to prevent an abuse of public power by the state institutions.

Consider the following imaginary constitution which details the following provision:

ARTICLE

Art X

The President may, if in his personal opinion he deems it appropriate to do so, order the arrest, detention, torture and execution of any citizens considered undesirable. This power, and the exercise of it, cannot be challenged in any court of law under any circumstances.

Suppose a President acted under this provision and used his conferred powers to torture 'undesirable' citizens of this state. In a very technical sense, the President could claim to be acting simply in accordance with what the constitution expressly permits him to do and, therefore, technically he could claim to be acting 'constitutionally' (at least in a bare legal sense). Public lawyers, however, would not regard the exercise of this power, and the content and nature of Art X itself, as following the basic precepts of constitutionalism. In short, this provision gratuitously – and unnecessarily – interferes with the basic and fundamental rights of the citizen. Moreover, Art X (and therefore the constitution) does not permit any effective regulation or legal check on the exercise of this arbitrary and exceptionally wide power which violates the basic human rights of the individual.

2.6.2 The basic principles of constitutionalism

The principles of constitutionalism (particularly in the context of the constitution of the United Kingdom) will be referred to continuously throughout this text, but for present purposes, it should be noted that in order to comply with constitutionalism, a constitution should control the use of public power in the following ways (as adapted from Barnett):

- The governing institutions should be separated in terms of personnel and functions (see Chapter 5 on the separation of powers).
- The basic rights of the individual should be safeguarded and protected (see Chapters 16 and 17).
- In exercising public power, state institutions must act strictly within their legal limits (see Chapter 6 on the rule of law together with Chapters 19 and 20 on judicial review).
- There must exist an independent court system staffed by impartial judges to check the use of public power (see Chapter 13 on the judiciary).
- Basic democratic and other principles and values must be adhered to (eg see Chapter 9 for democratic elections to the House of Commons).

In addition, owing to the unusual constitutional arrangements that exist in the United Kingdom, the terms acting 'constitutionally' and 'unconstitutionally' have specific meanings in our constitution (see section 4.15).

ACTIVITY

Essay writing

What government conduct or law would you consider to be (a) constitutional and (b) unconstitutional? Revisit this question after you have completed section 4.15 and again at the end of this text.

KEY FACTS

Key facts on the basic principles of constitutionalism

A constitution is a body of rules (usually enshrined in a formal document) which sets out the main framework of the state.
A constitution is a set of laws, rules and practices that create the basic institutions of the state, and its component and related parts, and stipulate the powers of those institutions and the relationship between the different institutions and between those institutions and the individual (working definition of the House of Lords Select Committee on the Constitution).
Constitutionalism is concerned with limiting governmental power through the rules and values of the constitution.
Acting constitutionally means acting in accordance with the rules of the constitution, whereas acting unconstitutionally means to breach and infringe these constitutional rules.

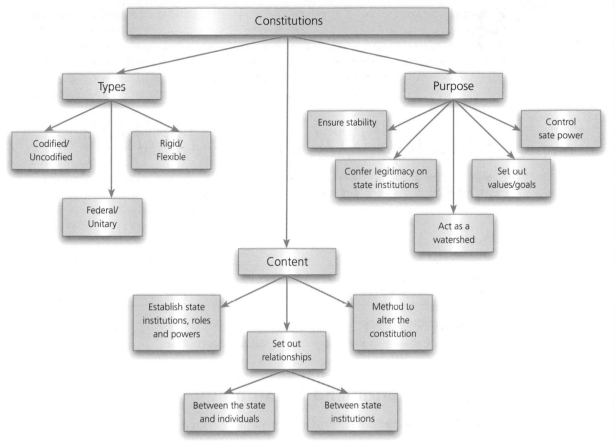

Figure 2.1 Constitutions

 SUMMARY

At the end of this chapter you should be able to:

■ Understand the nature and typical content of a constitution.
■ Appreciate why constitutions are created.
■ Identify and distinguish between different types of constitutions.
■ Understand the term 'constitution'.

Further reading

Books

Barendt, E, *An Introduction to Constitutional Law* (Oxford University Press, 1998), Chapter 1.

Barnett, H, *Constitutional and Administrative Law* (7th edn, Routledge–Cavendish, 2009), Chapter 1.

Bradley, A and Ewing, K, *Constitutional and Administrative Law* (14th edn, Pearson/ Longman 2007), Chapter 1.

Finer, S, Bogdanor, V and Rudden, B, *Comparing Constitutions* (Clarendon Press, 1995), Chapters 1 and 2.

Maddex, R, *Constitutions of the World* (2nd edn, CQ Press, 2001). This text sets out in very brief terms the main elements of one hundred constitutions of the world.

Wheare, K, *Modern Constitutions* (2nd edn, Oxford University Press, 1966), Chapters 1 to 4.

3

The nature of the British constitution

AIMS AND OBJECTIVES

At the end of this chapter you should be able to:

■ Explain what is meant by the term the British constitution
■ Identify and explain the main features of the British constitution

3.1 Introduction and terminology

The aim of this chapter is to provide a general overview of the main characteristics of the United Kingdom constitution. All of the features and themes detailed below will be developed, to a greater or lesser extent, throughout the rest of this text.

At this stage it is important to note that the United Kingdom is an unusual state in international law as it is composed of four distinct countries, namely:

■ England
■ Scotland
■ Wales and
■ Northern Ireland.

Moreover, there are three distinct legal jurisdictions and three systems of law, namely:

■ England and Wales (as a single jurisdictional entity)
■ Northern Ireland and
■ Scotland.

As there is a single constitutional framework which governs the whole of the United Kingdom, strictly speaking, it is correct to refer to *the United Kingdom constitution* (however, the exact constitutional arrangements pertaining to each jurisdiction may on occasions differ). In order to illustrate the workings of the constitution, throughout this text examples will be drawn from all three jurisdictions.

Furthermore, for ease of reference, hereafter in the text, the term *the United Kingdom constitution* will be replaced by the term *the British constitution*.

3.2 Does the United Kingdom have a constitution?

3.2.1 The absence of a codified constitutional document

Before considering the nature and sources of the British constitution, we must first consider the question of whether the United Kingdom has a constitution at all. This is because the United Kingdom lacks a formal codified document called 'The British

Constitution'. In short, there is no single document which has special legal status and which embodies the principal rules concerning the government of the country. If we refer to the definition of a constitution at section 2.1 it is clear that the United Kingdom does not possess a constitution in terms of the first definition (ie a constitutional document or code setting out the framework of the state with 'special legal sanctity' attached to it) as it lacks a single formal constitutional document. The United Kingdom does, however, have a constitution in the second sense of the term (ie 'a collection of rules' which govern the governing institutions) as it clearly has rules and practices (albeit derived from disparate sources) which govern the state. There are rules, for example, governing:

- How the various state institutions are composed.
- The scope of the powers exercised by the monarch.
- How the government is legally controlled.
- How legislation is passed.

Wheare has defined the United Kingdom constitution in the following terms:

QUOTATION

'The British Constitution is the collection of legal rules and non-legal rules which govern the government in Britain.'

K Wheare, *Modern Constitutions* (2nd edn, Oxford University Press, 1966), p 1.

3.2.2 The factors which indicate a British constitution

It could be argued that the following factors indicate (and presuppose) that the United Kingdom clearly has a constitution of some sort:

- If the United Kingdom had no constitution there would necessarily be no government, Prime Minister, Parliament or police force. Indeed, there would be no apparatus of the state of any kind.
- United Kingdom cases and statutes make specific reference to constitutional issues (an example of the latter is the Constitutional Reform Act 2005).
- Numerous books and papers have been written about 'The British Constitution' and the constitutional law of the United Kingdom.
- British commentators may on occasions speak of a 'constitutional crisis' (for example, commentators spoke of a constitutional crisis with the break up of the Prince of Wales' first marriage).
- There was (until 2007) a department called the Department for Constitutional Affairs headed by the Lord Chancellor and Secretary of State for Constitutional Affairs. In addition, the Cabinet has a sub-committee (a ministerial committee on the constitution).
- In 2001 the House of Lords established the House of Lords Select Committee on the Constitution with the specific remit to:
  (i) consider the constitutional implications of all public Bills, and
  (ii) to keep under review the operation of the constitution.

Although the United Kingdom may lack a single authoritative constitutional document, this does not mean that we do not have a constitution. The United Kingdom has a constitution in the broader sense of the term used above as it has rules and principles that regulate the government of the country. There is a clear framework of rules, both legal and political, from which we can identify:

- the key institutions of the state
- the composition and powers of these institutions
- how these institutions interrelate and check and balance one another
- how these institutions relate to the individual
- how the rights and freedoms enjoyed by the individual are safeguarded.

3.2.3 The five tenets of the British constitution

The United Kingdom, therefore, has a constitution, albeit different in form from other states that have a codified written document. It is highly pertinent to note that the House of Lords Select Committee on the constitution, in setting out its remit, identified five tenets of the British constitution which are as follows:

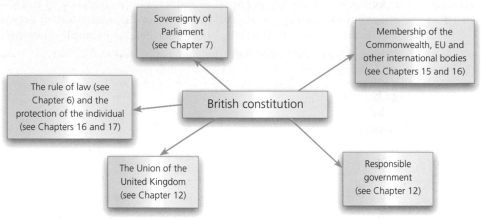

Figure 3.1 The five tenets of the British constitution

ACTIVITY

Applying the law

Can you think of any factors that might suggest that the United Kingdom has a constitution? Revisit this question after you have completed Chapter 3 and again at the end of this text.

3.2.4 A system of government rather than a constitution?

Some commentators such as Ridley, however, have questioned whether the United Kingdom has a constitution in any meaningful sense of the term given that it lacks the following characteristics of a constitution. These essential features as identified by Ridley are as follows:

■ 'It establishes, or constitutes, the system of government.' A constitution establishes (and so is necessarily prior to) the system of government and its institutions. In short, the constitution is a constituent act.

In the United Kingdom the system of government and state institutions have not been specifically created by a single authoritative constitutional document or code; instead, they have developed and evolved over the years. By way of example, the Scottish Parliament, a major institution of the state, was created only in 1998. It is of interest, however, to note that the legislation creating the Scottish Parliament was preceded by a national referendum in Scotland.

■ 'It therefore involves an authority outside and above the order it establishes.' A constituent power (namely the people) ratifies the constitution, thereby conferring it and the institutions established under it with constitutional legitimacy (see section 2.4.2).

In the United Kingdom the people in a referendum have never formally ratified the 'constitution'. Notwithstanding this, as we have a parliamentary democracy, the people do at least periodically elect the House of Commons which, in turn, gives democratic legitimacy to the laws that Parliament passes. Furthermore, these elections also confer legitimacy (albeit in an indirect sense) on the government to govern and determine major policy issues (see Chapter 11).

■ 'It is a form of law superior to other laws.' The laws of the constitution are supreme and a higher form of law in relation to other ordinary or non-constitutional laws.

In the United Kingdom, historically, the laws of the constitution have not assumed a higher legal status than other 'ordinary' laws. In this context, however, now see the comments of Laws LJ at section 4.4.5.

■ 'It is entrenched.' Owing to their content and importance, constitutional laws should be entrenched, thereby making it difficult (in some cases impossible) to repeal or alter them.

As a consequence of the principle of **parliamentary sovereignty**, historically, laws in the United Kingdom legally could not be entrenched and so protected from subsequent repeal or amendment. In this context, however, now see the comments of Laws LJ at section 4.4.5.

parliamentary sovereignty

the legal principle that the Crown in Parliament can pass any law it chooses

In the absence of these characteristics Ridley has argued that the United Kingdom does not have a constitution, but instead merely a system of government (F Ridley, 'There is no British Constitution: A Dangerous Case of the Emperor's Clothes' (1988) 41 Parliamentary Affairs 340).

ACTIVITY

Self-test question

Do you agree with Ridley's arguments that the United Kingdom does not have a constitution? Revisit this question after you have completed Chapter 3 and again at the end of this text.

3.3 The nature of the British constitution

3.3.1 An uncodified constitution

As noted above, the United Kingdom lacks a single authoritative constitutional text entitled 'The British Constitution'. Instead, the constitutional rules which regulate the government are located elsewhere in a variety of sources which include, *inter alia*, Acts of Parliament, case law and binding political practices (see Chapter 4).

In this sense, therefore, the United Kingdom has an uncodified constitution which sets it apart from most other states which have codified documents (eg the United States, France and the Republic of Ireland). As a result, the British constitution has been described by Finer, Bogdanor and Rudden as indistinct and indeterminate. In short, the exact boundaries of the British constitution are less easy to identify and pinpoint than in a state with a formal codified constitution. Indeed, even within the United Kingdom, academics and commentators may disagree over what is and what is not part of the constitution and even what is and what is not a constitutional issue (see section 4.2.2).

3.3.2 Why does the United Kingdom not have a codified constitution?

As noted in section 2.4.3, state constitutions are generally founded to represent a political watershed and a clear break with the past. The catalyst for this watershed could have been, for instance:

■ a political upheaval
■ an invasion
■ a revolution.

In simple terms, the United Kingdom/Britain (with the exception of the period of 1649–60 with Oliver Cromwell as Lord Protector overseeing a non-monarchial government under the 1653 Instrument of Government) has not experienced such momentous events as being invaded or colonised. As a consequence, it has not been felt necessary to create a new codified constitution to mark a watershed. In fact, it has been pointed out by the Institute for Public Policy Research that the reality is that very few constitutions are actually conceived as a result of a sober and measured reflection on the perceived short-comings of existing, functioning arrangements. Instead, they are drafted in the context of other factors such as political upheaval, independence, etc (R Blackburn (ed), *A Written Constitution for the United Kingdom* (Mansell Publishing Limited, 1993) p 5).

It is of interest to mention that in 1991 the Institute for Public Policy Research produced a draft '*Constitution for the United Kingdom*' and although this constitution has not been implemented, it does serve as a useful blueprint should there come a time when the United Kingdom decided that it required a written codified, entrenched constitution.

3.3.3 The incremental development of the British constitution

Most countries have a clear date indicating the origin of their constitution; for example, the Indian constitution was passed in 1949 and came fully into force in January 1950. In contrast, in the absence of a single constitutional text, the British constitution lacks a clear and single identifiable origin. Instead, the constitution has gradually developed over the centuries. In fact, one hallmark of the United Kingdom is that constitutional change has tended traditionally to be somewhat measured and incremental. As the British constitution has developed historically in an *ad hoc* fashion, it is clear that there has been no great and overall grand design behind it. Instead, it has grown organically to meet the needs required at the time and this is particularly the case in respect of, for example, the development of constitutional conventions (see section 4.13).

In recent years, however – since the election of the Labour government in 1997 – the form of our constitutional arrangements has been reshaped radically by the passage of a raft of constitutional statutes passed in very quick succession (see section 3.4.5). Indeed, in June 2009 the then Prime Minister, in a statement on constitutional renewal, announced a wide-ranging set of proposals for constitutional reform, including reform of the House of Lords, **devolution** and setting out the rights of the individual.

devolution

power which has been delegated to regional bodies in Scotland, Wales and Northern Ireland

KEY FACTS

Key facts on the nature of the British constitution

The United Kingdom, unlike most states, has an uncodified constitution. It lacks a single authoritative constitutional text/document in which the main rules and principles governing the framework and organisation of the state are set out.
Constitutions are established typically, for instance, in the aftermath of a war or gaining independence from a former colonial/foreign power. The United Kingdom historically has not experienced such momentous events, and therefore not found it necessary to mark a watershed by drafting a written codified document called 'The British Constitution'.
In the absence of a single constitutional text, the British constitution lacks a clear and single identifiable origin, and instead its constitutional rules and principles have developed incrementally over the centuries through, among other things, statute and common law.

3.4 The key features of the British constitution

The key features of the British constitution are set out below. By identifying and highlighting these features at this stage, students will be provided with a snapshot of the essential elements which make up the British constitution

3.4.1 An unwritten constitution?

As noted at section 2.5.1 above, constitutions historically, have been classified as either written or unwritten, with the United Kingdom traditionally falling within the latter category. Notwithstanding this, it must be remembered that many of the United

Kingdom's constitutional rules *are* written down and therefore are found in documentary form. For example, the legal and constitutional principle that parliamentary legislation (Acts of Parliament) can be enacted without the consent of the upper chamber is set out in the Parliament Acts of 1911 and 1949 (see section 10.10.1). The description of the British constitution as unwritten does not therefore appear to be strictly accurate. A more apposite label would be to describe the constitution as uncodified as the constitutional rules have not been brought together in one single authoritative document or constitutional code.

3.4.2 Law and convention as sources

The sources of the British constitution embrace both legal and non-legal sources.

The legal sources include, among others, Acts of Parliament, case law and international Treaties. The non-legal sources include binding political rules known as constitutional conventions.

It should be noted that the United Kingdom is not unique in having constitutional rules that are in effect political practices (for example, United Kingdom government ministers are constitutionally responsible to Parliament for their actions). Other countries also have political rules which supplement the legal rules detailed in their constitution. For example, in the United States of America, by convention congressional committees reflect the composition of Congress. What is significant in the United Kingdom, however, is the extent to which these political rules arguably play a more significant role in the context of our constitutional arrangements than they do in countries with a codified constitution.

See also Chapter 4.

3.4.3 The legislative supremacy of Parliament

In essence, the legislative supremacy of Parliament (parliamentary sovereignty) means that, in law, Parliament (technically the Queen in Parliament) can pass any law that it chooses. In short, historically there has been no legal limitation on the legislation that Parliament can pass. This feature is the foundation of, and underpins, the British constitution. This is in contrast to the vast majority of other constitutions. For example, the legislatures of the United States (Congress) and the Republic of Ireland (the Oireachtas) cannot pass any law that they choose. Instead, they are limited legally by their formal codified documentary constitutions.

As parliamentary sovereignty is the cornerstone of the British constitution it is considered in detail in Chapter 7. Moreover, as the United Kingdom's membership of the European Union has challenged the traditional conception of parliamentary sovereignty, the principle will be revisited in Chapter 15 in the context of the study of the European Union.

3.4.4 No special legal and higher status

As noted at section 2.3, constitutional laws (owing to their fundamental character and substance) typically, possess a higher and fundamental status in relation to other 'ordinary' or 'non-constitutional' laws such as contract or tort. In the United Kingdom, however, historically no clear and sharp distinction has been made between:

- constitutional (or fundamental) laws and
- ordinary or 'non-constitutional' laws.

In the United Kingdom, therefore, in historical terms, both laws have had equal legal standing. This point, however, has to be reconsidered in the context of the comments made by Laws LJ in *Thoburn v Sunderland City Council* [2002] EWHC 195 (Admin) where he drew a distinction between constitutional statutes and non-constitutional statutes (see section 4.4.5).

Historically, therefore, the United Kingdom has been characterised as having no special higher constitutional law and has lacked a clear hierarchy of laws which distinguishes constitutional laws from ordinary laws. As noted above, for commentators such as Ridley, one fundamental prerequisite of a constitution is that its constitutional laws should have a higher and superior legal status *vis a vis* other laws. The United Kingdom has historically lacked such a hierarchy of laws.

3.4.5 A flexible constitution

Following on from the fact that the United Kingdom has an uncodified constitution, together with the fact that its main characteristic is that Parliament can pass any law that it chooses, the British constitution is also described as being flexible (see section 2.5.2). In other words, unlike many other countries, there are no legally entrenched constitutional laws that cannot be repealed or are legally more difficult to repeal than ordinary non-constitutional laws. In essence, there is no aspect of the British constitution that cannot, in law, be altered. As Parliament theoretically can pass any law, this means that it can legally amend any legal rule or alter any aspect of our constitutional arrangements. For example:

- **The Constitutional Reform Act 2005**: s 18 of this Act created a separate Supreme Court to replace the Appellate Committee of the House of Lords, which was hitherto the highest domestic court which used to sit within Parliament (see section 5.7.4). The new Supreme Court, in contrast, is legally and constitutionally separate from Parliament.
- **The House of Lords Act 1999**: this Act reduced the number of hereditary **peers** (these were peers who assumed a place in the House of Lords by virtue of inheriting their seat) from 759 to 92. In effect, at a stroke, this Act reduced the size of the upper chamber by over one half (see section 10.6.3).

In short, the United Kingdom has been characterised as having a flexible constitution since its constitutional laws and rules can in theory be amended relatively easily (but note the point made at section 2.5.2). This is in contrast to other countries such as the United States whose constitution (Art V) stipulates a special procedure which must be complied with in order to amend the rules of the codified constitution.

As noted above, the flexibility of our constitution has been demonstrated graphically since the Labour government came to power in 1997 and proceeded to reshape radically the constitutional landscape of the United Kingdom. These changes include, among others:

- The **Human Rights Act 1998** conferring positive human rights on individuals.
- The Government of Wales Act 1998 which created the National Assembly for Wales.
- The House of Lords Act 1999 which removed the majority of hereditary peers from the House of Lords.
- The Freedom of Information Act 2000 which enabled individuals to have access to information held by public authorities. Interestingly, the disclosures made under the Freedom of Information Act as a result of the case of *Corporate Officer of the House of Commons v Information Commissioner* [2008] EWHC 1084 (Admin) led to the controversy over MPs' expenses (see section 8.8.3).
- The Constitutional Reform Act 2005 reformed the office of the Lord Chancellor and the system of judicial appointments.
- The Electoral Administration Act 2006 which reduced the minimum age of candidates to be elected to the House of Commons from 21 to 18 years.
- The Terrorism Act 2006 which created a criminal offence of encouraging terrorism (including statements which glorify the commission or preparation of acts of terrorism).
- The Parliamentary Standards Act 2009 which reformed the regulation of the expenses system of MPs.

peer
a person conferred with a peerage and a member of the upper chamber of Parliament, the House of Lords

Human Rights Act
legislation enacted in 1998 that brought the European Convention on Human Rights into domestic law for the whole of the UK on 2 October 2000

This collective raft of reforms represents arguably the most significant reshaping of the British constitution for centuries and demonstrates the highly flexible nature of our constitution. All this legislation, however, was passed through the ordinary parliamentary legislative process without the need for special majorities in either House (in this context see section 4.2.4) or the support of the people in a referendum. Although referenda were held in Scotland, Wales and Northern Ireland prior to the creation of the devolved institutions for these regions, such referenda were not strictly (ie legally) necessary in order to pass the relevant legislation (see Chapter 14).

ACTIVITY

Self-test questions

1. Why were the above reforms implemented?
2. Are you aware of any other constitutional reforms which have been made since the election of the Labour government in 1997?

3.4.6 A unitary constitution

The United Kingdom has a unitary constitution (as opposed to a federal one) in the sense that ultimate legal and political power is focused centrally in the Westminster Parliament. In essence, Parliament has the legal power in theory to enact laws for all parts and legal jurisdictions (ie Scotland, Northern Ireland, England and Wales) that make up the United Kingdom. Under Parliament there exist the following layers of decentralised government:

- Local authorities.
- The Scottish Parliament.
- The National Assembly for Wales.
- The London Assembly.
- The Northern Ireland Assembly.

These layers of decentralised/devolved government, however, only exist (and in fact are permitted to exist) by virtue of Parliament in Westminster. In other words, they are all creatures of statutes passed by the Westminster Parliament and could ultimately be legally abolished by a subsequent Act of Parliament. These tiers of government, therefore, lack the constitutional status and legal/constitutional protection that they would enjoy under a federal constitution.

As noted at section 2.5.3, in a federal system of government such as the United States, the federal constitution divides the power of the state horizontally between the centre (federal institutions; Congress, President, etc) and the local regions (state legislatures, eg the State Legislature of Florida). In contrast, in the United Kingdom, Parliament could in legal theory abolish any local authority or devolved institution. Moreover, this could be achieved through an ordinary Act of Parliament, thereby reinforcing the flexibility of the British constitution (see section 3.4.5).

3.4.7 A limited monarchy

The Head of State in the United Kingdom is the monarch, although her role in the constitution is typically ceremonial. In historic terms, the monarch formerly enjoyed extensive personal legal powers and even today the Queen, in legal theory, still has considerable legal power vested in her. For example, the monarch can legally:

- dissolve Parliament
- dispense the prerogative of mercy
- appoint Supreme Court Justices.

These powers are, however, exercised by the monarch strictly in accordance with constitutional convention: that is, she acts on the advice of her ministers. For example, although the monarch formally and legally dissolves Parliament, it is the Prime Minister of the day that seeks a general election who will request that she do so. In other words, although these powers continue to be vested legally in the monarch, they are in effect practically exercised by her government ministers. In this sense the powers of the monarchy are constitutionally limited (limited by constitutional convention: see section 4.13) and thus the United Kingdom is characterised as having a limited constitutional monarchy. See also section 11.1.2.

3.4.8 No strict separation of powers

The United Kingdom historically, has been characterised as failing to adhere to a strict separation of powers whereby the three organs of state, namely the legislature, executive and judiciary, are separate and distinct from each other in terms of their functions and personnel. Instead, owing to the various overlaps of personnel and functions, the United Kingdom has traditionally exhibited a weak separation of powers.

The Constitutional Reform Act 2005, however, provides a recent example of Parliament attempting to realign our constitutional arrangements so as to accord with a stricter concept of the separation of powers. This Act, *inter alia*, constrains the role of the executive in the appointment of the judiciary and created a Supreme Court separate from Parliament.

See also Chapter 5.

3.4.9 An independent and impartial judiciary

Although the United Kingdom does not have a strict separation of powers, historically, the judicial arm of the state has been largely separate from the other two organs. Indeed, in constitutional terms it is of paramount importance that the judges are independent of both the executive and the legislature and that they are protected from political pressure.

A related characteristic of the British constitution is the limited role of the judiciary. In the United Kingdom the judiciary is constitutionally limited in the sense that it does not exercise the constitutional power enjoyed by many of their judicial counterparts elsewhere in the democratic world. For example, in the United States the Supreme Court has the power to declare Acts of Congress 'unconstitutional', and invalidate them if they contravene the written, entrenched constitution (*Marbury v Madison* (1803) 1 Cranch 137). This principle is known as the constitutional or judicial review of legislation. In contrast, in the United Kingdom, historically the judiciary has consistently reiterated that it was not constitutionally empowered to strike down and challenge Acts of Parliament. This point will be revisited in the context of both European Union law (see Chapter 15) and the Human Rights Act 1998 (see Chapter 17).

The judiciary is discussed in more detail in Chapter 13.

3.4.10 A parliamentary executive (see sections 5.7.1 and 11.6.1)

parliamentary executive

the constitutional arrangement whereby the executive/ government is drawn from, and accountable to, the legislature/ Parliament

The United Kingdom has a **parliamentary executive** whereby the executive (the government) is drawn from the legislature (Parliament). Far from being separated as required by a strict doctrine of the separation of powers (see Chapter 5), the executive and legislature are actually fused. This can be contrasted with the presidential system of government in, for example, the United States, where the executive (President) is constitutionally and legally separate from the legislature (Congress). Parliamentary executives, however, are not uncommon. For example, the Republic of Ireland also has a parliamentary executive, but, unlike the United Kingdom, it has a codified constitution.

See sections 5.7.1 and 11.6.1.

3.4.11 Responsible and accountable government

electorate

individuals eligible to vote in an election

A constitutional principle associated with the parliamentary executive is that of responsible government. This principle entails the government being politically and constitutionally accountable to Parliament (and ultimately therefore to the **electorate**) for its actions and decisions. In recent decades, however, there has been concern that the balance between the executive and the legislature has shifted far too much in favour of the former, thereby undermining the principle of accountable government. In short, the modern executive is (typically) in a position to dominate and largely control the legislature amounting to what Lord Hailsham described as an 'elective dictatorship' (see section 9.8 and Chapter 12).

3.4.12 A bicameral legislature

Parliament (the legislature) is the principal law-making body within the constitution and is bicameral as it is composed of two houses:

■ The House of Commons.
■ The House of Lords.

This is common to many major democracies whose legislatures comprise two chambers (eg the United States, France, Germany, Spain, etc). In contrast, it is generally the case that smaller states have unicameral legislatures with only one chamber (eg Denmark, Sweden and New Zealand – the latter abolished their second chamber in 1950). In terms of the principle of constitutionalism, bicameral legislatures disperse power, though not necessarily equally, between two competing sources of power/chambers/Houses.

See also Chapters 8–10.

3.4.13 A representative democracy

The United Kingdom has a parliamentary democracy whereby the composition of the legislature (or at least the House of Commons) is determined by the people through periodic and free national elections. See also section 9.4.

3.4.14 An acceptance of the rule of law and respect for human rights

A major characteristic of the British constitution is the acceptance of the rule of law, which is a foundation of any democratic state (see Chapter 6). This is the constitutional principle that all organs, institutions and state officials are under the law. The rule of law is linked inextricably to an independent and impartial judiciary (see Chapter 13) as it is, in effect, the judiciary that legally enforces the principles underpinning it.

The United Kingdom is also hallmarked by its historic general respect for basic human rights and freedoms. In other words, certain underlying democratic values are inherent within our constitutional arrangements such as:

■ The freedom of political action (Chapters 16–17).
■ The right to vote (see section 9.6).
■ Freedom of expression (see Chapter 18).

ACTIVITY

Essay writing

Explain the nature of each of the characteristics of the British constitution.
• Which features do you consider to be particularly important?
• Which features set the United Kingdom apart from other countries?
Revisit this activity at the end of this text.

The principles of the British constitution
• An uncodified constitution (although it is largely collected from written sources).
• A largely flexible constitution.
• In legal theory Parliament can pass any law that it chooses (parliamentary sovereignty).
• The sources of the constitution are both legal (eg Acts of Parliament) and non-legal (eg constitutional conventions).
• Historically, constitutional law has not had a fundamental, higher legal status.
• There is no strict separation of powers.
• An acceptance of the rule of law and respect for human rights.

The principles of the constitution which affect particular state institutions	
Parliament	• Parliamentary sovereignty. • A representative democracy. • A bicameral legislature. • A unitary constitution.
The government/executive	• A parliamentary executive. • Responsible and accountable government. • A limited monarchy.
The judiciary	• An independent and impartial judiciary. • Upholds the rule of law and respect for human rights.

3.5 Conclusion

According to Barber:

QUOTATION

'Britain is one of a very few states which lack a written constitution, but this bare accident of history does not provide an argument for us to adopt one. Britain's constitution has, by and large, been a success. It has produced stable government and – in terms of democracy, transparency, human rights and the provision of social welfare – it compares reasonably favourably with many other constitutions.'

N Barber, 'Against a written constitution', [2008] PL 11.

Bogdanor and Vogenauer concluded that although the enactment of a written constitution was feasible:

QUOTATION

'The problems involved in this enterprise are, however, formidable. Some of the problems are similar to those that have been faced and successfully resolved by other countries seeking to enact a constitution; others, however, are more specific to Britain, in particular, the problems of enacting a constitution that has long been uncodified, and of confronting the doctrine of the Sovereignty of Parliament.'

V Bogdanor and S Vogenauer, 'Enacting a British Constitution: Some Problems', [2008] PL 38.

Finally, in the then Prime Minister's Statement on Constitutional Renewal in 2009 he made the following statement:

QUOTATION

'It is for many people extraordinary that Britain still has a largely unwritten constitution. I personally favour a written constitution. I recognise that this change would represent a historic shift in our constitution arrangements ...'

Hansard, HC, Vol 493, col 798.

At the time of writing, however, there were no proposals for a written codified constitution.

 # Further reading

Books

Barendt, E, *An Introduction to Constitutional Law* (Oxford University Press, 1998), Chapter 2.

Blackburn, R (ed), *A Written Constitution for the United Kingdom* (Mansell Publishing Limited, 1993). This book rather usefully sets out a proposed blueprint for a written codified constitution for the United Kingdom.

Bogdanor, V, *The New British Constitution* (Hart Publishing, 2009), Chapters 1 and 9.

Finer, S, Bogdanor, V and Rudden, B, *Comparing Constitutions* (Clarendon Press, 1995), Chapter 3.

Munro, C, *Studies in Constitutional Law* (2nd edn, Butterworths, 1999), Chapter 1.

Articles

Barber, N, 'Against a written constitution' [2008] PL 11.

Bindman, G, 'Time to write it all down?' (2009) 159 NLJ 1564.

Bogdanor, N and Vogenauer, S, 'Enacting a British constitution: some problems' [2008] PL 38.

Ridley, F, 'There is no British Constitution: A Dangerous Case of the Emperor's Clothes' (1988) 41 Parliamentary Affairs 340.

4

The sources of the British constitution

AIMS AND OBJECTIVES

At the end of this chapter you should be able to:

- Appreciate the difficulties in ascertaining the sources of the British constitution
- Identify and explain the different domestic legal sources that make up the British constitution
- Identify and explain the different international legal sources that make up the British constitution
- Identify and explain the different domestic non-legal sources that make up the British constitution

4.1 Introduction

In the United States and the Republic of Ireland, the laws of the constitution can be found in their respective documentary constitutions. In contrast, as the United Kingdom has no codified constitutional document entitled 'The British Constitution', this necessarily raises the question of where the laws and rules of the constitution are to be found. The answer is that these rules are gleaned from consulting a wide range of sources. As indicated in Chapter 3, these disparate sources embrace, among others, legislation, case law and international Treaties together with constitutional conventions.

Notwithstanding this, as noted at section 2.5.1, the point needs to be made that even in countries with a codified constitution, not all aspects of the constitution will be set out explicitly in that constitutional documentary text. The legal rules contained in the documentary constitution will have to be interpreted by a Supreme or Constitutional Court and therefore these judicial interpretations will also form part of the constitutional rules. Furthermore, the legal rules of the constitution will be supplemented by binding political rules and practices.

4.2 The difficulties associated with the sources in the United Kingdom

The United Kingdom has a constitution of multiple sources. There are a number of difficulties in locating these sources.

4.2.1 What is a constitutional issue?

In the British constitution it is not necessarily easy to determine what is, and what is not, a constitutional principle, rule or issue. In the Republic of Ireland, for example, the principal constitutional laws and rules are set out in its formal constitutional text. In contrast, in the United Kingdom, in the absence of such a document, the task of identifying a law of (or issue relating to) the constitution is inevitably more difficult. Instead of consulting an authoritative constitutional text, the main rules and laws of the British constitution are found by consulting, *inter alia*, various statutes and case law and deciding whether the statute or case in question encapsulates a constitutional principle or rule. Indeed, in terms of the former, Hazell has commented that:

QUOTATION

'There is no clear classification of what is a constitutional Bill and what is not, and with our unwritten constitution it is impossible to devise one.'

R Hazell, 'Time for a New Convention: Parliamentary Scrutiny of Constitutional Bills 1997–2005' [2006] PL 247.

4.2.2 The lack of a clear demarcation between constitutional and ordinary laws

The above difficulty is exacerbated by the fact that constitutional law in the United Kingdom has not assumed a legally higher or fundamental status (but see Laws LJ at section 4.4.5). In fact, constitutional law in the United Kingdom is not even clearly segregated so as to demarcate it from other 'ordinary' non-constitutional laws. Dicey noted that:

QUOTATION

'There is under the English constitution no marked or clear distinction between laws which are not fundamental or constitutional and laws which are fundamental or constitutional.' (*sic*)

A Dicey, *Introduction to the Study of the Law of the Constitution* (10th edn, Macmillan, 1959), p 89.

In this way, as indicated earlier, the British constitution is somewhat indeterminate, as its parameters are not necessarily clear. Indeed, in giving evidence before the House of Lords Select Committee on the Constitution, Lord Irvine (the then Lord Chancellor) stated that the government not only did not have a definition of the British constitution, but that it took a pragmatic view as to whether a Bill should be termed a constitutional Bill or not.

Accordingly, the student of the British constitution needs to consult various statutes and decide on an Act by Act basis whether the legislation expounds a rule of the constitution. Compare for example the following two statutes:

- **The Sale of Goods Act 1979**: this Act regulates the selling of goods, for example their quality and being fit for their purpose, etc.
- **The Scotland Act 1998**: this Act established the Scottish Parliament together with the Scottish Executive (see Chapter 14).

The Sale of Goods Act 1979 is a non-constitutional statute as it is part of the private law of contract and is essentially concerned with individual contractual relations (therefore, generally speaking, not of interest to a public/constitutional lawyer). In contrast, the Scotland Act 1998 is clearly a constitutional statute as it creates a major institution of the state: the Scottish Parliament, which has the power to pass legislation (Acts of the Scottish Parliament). Very occasionally an Act may actually refer to the constitution in its title as with the passing of the Constitutional Reform Act 2005.

4.2.3 A sub-division of constitutional law

A proposal was put to the House of Lords Select Committee on the Constitution that in terms of parliamentary scrutiny of constitutional legislation it was possible to divide such Bills into the following:

- Bills of major (first class) constitutional significance and
- Bills of less than first class constitutional significance (legislation which represents a minor amendment to the constitution).

The rationale behind the proposal was to enable Bills of first class constitutional importance to receive greater and more effective scrutiny. The Committee recognised the problems with such a division as although Bills such as the House of Lords Bill 1999 and European Communities Bill 1972 would clearly fall within the first category, it questioned which category legislation such as the Political Parties, Elections and Referendums Bill 2000 would fall into. As such it would prove impossible to provide a watertight definition of a first class constitutional Bill (Fourth Report of Session 2001–02 of the House of Lords Select Committee on the Constitution, *Changing the constitution: The process of constitutional change*, HL Paper 69 (2002), p 17).

4.2.4 All statutes passed in essentially the same manner

Constitutional statutes cannot be identified simply by how they were enacted by Parliament. In essence there is a single passage for legislation and therefore constitutional statutes are passed through Parliament in the same way as non-constitutional statutes. In other words, no special majority is needed in the two Houses of Parliament in order to enact a statute that alters an established constitutional principle or which abolishes a previous constitutional statute.

Moreover, historically, these statutes (such as the Scotland Act 1998) have the same legal standing as other ordinary/non-constitutional statutes (such as the Sale of Goods Act 1979) which do not raise constitutional issues. Even though the 1998 Act established a key institution of the state, historically in law this Act does not have higher legal status than the Sale of Goods Act 1979. In fact, Dicey asserted that Acts such as the Union with Scotland Act (which established the Parliament of Great Britain) were not supreme over a statute such as the Dentists Act 1878, as both could be repealed in the same way. In short, the Scotland Act 1998, legally, can be repealed and amended in the same way as the Sale of Goods Act 1979 in the sense that no special majority of votes in either House is required.

This general point above, however, now has to be revisited in the light of Laws LJ's comments in the *Thoburn* (2002) case in which he stated that constitutional statutes, unlike non-constitutional statutes, cannot be impliedly repealed (see section 4.4.5).

In any event, it is worth noting that even though there is a single passage for legislation, a constitutional convention exists in the House of Commons that Bills of constitutional importance (however these are determined) are considered in a Committee of the Whole of the House, rather than in a general committee (formerly known as a standing committee) (see section 12.7.3). A recent example is the Constitutional Reform and Governance Bill in January 2010.

4.2.5 No definitive list of statutes of a constitutional nature

What is clear is that there is no exhaustive list of statutes deemed to be of constitutional status as stated by the House of Lords Select Committee on the Constitution:

QUOTATION

'The constitution is said to be in flux, and the sense of what it is constantly evolving. The constitution is uncodified and although it is in part written there is no single, accepted and agreed list of statutes which form that part of the constitution which is indeed written down.'

First Report of Session 2001–02 of the House of Lords Select Committee on the Constitution, *Reviewing the constitution: Terms of reference and method of working*, HL Paper 11 (2001), p 8.

4.2.6 No Constitutional or Supreme Court specifically to resolve issues of a constitutional nature

In terms of constitutional case law, the student must consider, on a case by case basis, whether or not it raises a constitutional issue or expounds a particular constitutional rule. The difficulty in the United Kingdom is the lack of a special Constitutional or Supreme Court which has the responsibility to process constitutional cases *per se*, as for example, do the Irish and United States Supreme Courts. Such courts authoritatively and definitively interpret the documentary constitution and will necessarily process cases that raise constitutional issues. Instead, the United Kingdom extracts its constitutional principles from case law drawn from all courts (both criminal and civil jurisdictions). Indeed, a case which *prima facie* appears to deal with a matter of private law (eg the law of trespass) may also have a constitutional dimension to it by raising a constitutional issue. For example:

CASE EXAMPLE

Entick v Carrington (1765) 19 St Tr 1030 (for details see section 4.8.2)

At one level this case may appear to deal with the private law of trespass, namely the King's messengers trespassing on Entick's property. In fact, the case has a clear constitutional resonance as it is also concerned with protecting the individual from the state and restricting the powers of the executive.

CASE EXAMPLE

Derbyshire County Council v Times Newspapers Ltd and Others [1993] 1 All ER 1011 (for details see section 4.8.2)

This case dealt with the private law of defamation, but it necessarily raised the constitutional issues of free expression and the freedom to criticise state/governmental institutions (see also section 18.4.1).

It should be pointed out, however, that although the United Kingdom lacks a special Constitutional or Supreme Court which specifically resolves constitutional issues *per se*, cases that form part of the jurisdiction of the Administrative Court (part of the High Court) will necessarily raise constitutional issues. This court is specifically responsible for applying judicial review principles to public authorities/government bodies so as to ensure that they exercise their legal public powers strictly in accordance with the law (see Chapters 19 and 20).

In contrast, it is pertinent to remember that not all cases coming before the new Supreme Court, despite its title, will necessarily be of interest to public/constitutional lawyers. In short, the Supreme Court essentially functions as the House of Lords used to and so it will process appeals concerning all aspects of law including private law cases. In one respect at least, the new court will resolve 'specified' constitutional issues as its jurisdiction will involve processing 'devolution' issues which concern the actions of the devolved institutions (see Chapter 14).

ACTIVITY

Applying the law

Explain the difficulties in trying to locate the sources of the British constitution.
Using your knowledge gained from the first three chapters, how would you decide whether something was a constitutional issue?

4.3 The classification of the sources of the British constitution

4.3.1 The classification of legal and non-legal sources

The aim of this section is to identify the variety of sources that make up the British constitution. A number of examples will be given to illustrate each particular constitutional source.

With the difficulties identified at section 4.2 in mind, set out below are some of the main rules and principles of the constitution extracted from a wide variety of sources. These sources can be demonstrated by the following diagram:

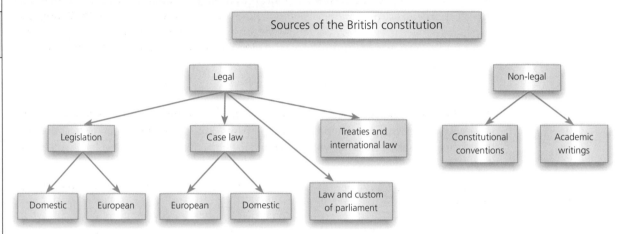

Figure 4.1 Sources of the British constitution

- Legal sources:
  - (a) Domestic primary legislation (see section 4.4)
  - (b) Domestic delegated legislation (see section 4.5)
  - (c) Domestic legislation of local authorities and the devolved institutions (see section 4.6)
  - (d) European Union legislation (see section 4.7)
  - (e) Domestic case law – the common law (see section 4.8.2)
  - (f) Domestic case law – interpreting statutes (see sections 4.8.3 and 4.8.4)
  - (g) Domestic case law – the royal prerogative (see section 4.9)
  - (h) European Union case law (see section 4.10.1)
  - (i) European Convention case law (see section 4.10.2)
  - (j) The law and custom of Parliament (see section 4.11)
  - (k) Treaties and international law (see section 4.12)
- Non-legal sources:
  - (a) Constitutional conventions (see section 4.13)
  - (b) Academic writings (see section 4.14)

4.4 Domestic primary legislation

4.4.1 Acts of Parliament

Domestic primary legislation is legislation passed by the Queen in Parliament. These Acts of Parliament will have passed through both the House of Commons and the House of Lords (unless the Parliament Acts apply – see section 10.10.1) and have received the

Royal Assent. These Acts are mostly piecemeal and *ad hoc* measures which have been passed over time to address a particular issue.

4.4.2 Acts of Parliament affecting the organs of the state

Primary legislation (as well as domestic delegated legislation) may have constitutional importance if it defines the powers of the state or government organs or regulates the procedure of those organs.

Below is a list of selected (but not exhaustive) statutes which illustrate a particular constitutional principle or rule.

The Magna Carta 1215 (affirmed as a statute in 1297)

This first authority concerns the limitation of an institution of the state, *viz*, the monarch. The historic document is of constitutional significance as it represented a legal limitation and curb on the power of the monarch. It also concerns the constitutional relationship between the individual and the state. In essence, the Magna Carta set out, among other things,

- the church's freedom;
- the protection of the liberties of 'freemen' not to be imprisoned:

> 'No freeman shall be taken or imprisoned, or be disseised of his freehold, or liberties, or free customs, or be outlawed, or exiled, or any otherwise destroyed; nor will we not pass upon him, nor condemn him, but by lawful judgment of his peers, or by the law of the land' (sic) (chapter 29).

In short, this is an embronic constitutional statement concerning an individual's right to a fair trial.

The Bill of Rights 1689

This statute concerns the constitutional relationship between two institutions of the state, namely, the monarch and Parliament. In brief, in historic terms the Bill of Rights sets out the conditions on which William of Orange (William III) ascended the throne as monarch. The Act altered the constitutional relationship between Parliament and the monarch, by expanding the power of the former at the expense of the latter. It included, among other things:

- Art 1 prohibiting the monarch from suspending laws without parliamentary consent (a constitutional limitation on the power of the monarch);
- Art 6 prohibiting the monarch from keeping a standing army without parliamentary consent (a constitutional limitation on the power of the monarch);
- Art 9 stated that 'the freedom of speech and debates or proceedings in Parliament ought not to be impeached or questioned in any court or place out of Parliament'. In essence, this meant that parliamentary members enjoyed legal immunity in respect of their words used in Parliament (see section 8.6.1).

The Union with Scotland Act 1706

One function of a constitution is to establish institutions of the state, as illustrated by this and the following statute. The Union with Scotland Act relates directly to the creation of the Parliament of Great Britain (the legislature which existed until 1800). Before this legislation, England (together with Wales) and Scotland had separate independent Parliaments and the effect of the Union legislation was to dissolve these and replace them with a single Parliament, namely, the Parliament of Great Britain.

The Union with Ireland Act 1800

This legislation provided for the unification of Great Britain and Ireland and created the Parliament of the United Kingdom of Great Britain and Ireland (replacing the Parliament of Great Britain above).

Parliament Act 1911 (as amended in 1949)

This Act set out the legal and constitutional relationship between two institutions of the state, the House of Commons and the House of Lords. It established the legal domination of the elected House of Commons over the unelected House of Lords. Prior to this Act a Bill required the consent of both Houses in order to become law. Thereafter, certain Bills technically required the consent of the House of Commons alone as the House of Lords could only delay the enactment of such legislation, but not veto it (see section 10.10.1).

The Act is also constitutionally significant as it reduced the maximum length of a Parliament from seven to five years. It is of interest to contrast this provision with other countries with codified constitutions. For instance, Art I of the United States constitution states that Senators serve for six years and members in the House of Representatives for two years.

The European Communities Act 1972

This Act is an example of Parliament formally incorporating international law obligations into the United Kingdom's domestic legal system. It is undoubtedly the most important statute passed in the past few hundred years. This Act legally incorporated European Community law (now called European Union law) and principles into the law and legal system of the United Kingdom. European law has had a profound effect on our uncodified constitutional arrangements. In particular, it has affected the classic doctrine of parliamentary sovereignty (as expounded by Dicey) as since 1973 Parliament cannot now simply pass any law that it chooses if that law will violate European Union law. It has affected the constitutional role of the judges in relation to legislation and has conferred European law rights on individuals that they can enforce in the domestic courts (see Chapter 15).

The House of Commons Disqualification Act 1975

This Act concerned the limitation of the power of the executive. It is concerned with the constitutional relationship and balance between the executive and the House of Commons. Section 2 specifies that only 95 government ministers (ministerial offices) can sit in the House of Commons, thereby ensuring (at least in constitutional theory) that the executive ministers, by virtue of their limited numbers, do not dominate the rest of the chamber (see section 11.6.3).

The Government of Wales Act 1998

This Act refers to the establishment of a new state institution. It devolved power to Wales by establishing a National Assembly for Wales. This legislation had been preceded by a referendum in Wales, which, albeit very narrowly, endorsed the creation of this Assembly. This demonstrates participatory democracy whereby the people who would be affected by the legislation were specifically consulted as to whether (or not) they approved of its proposals. As noted above, however, such a referendum was not technically legally necessary, but was considered politically appropriate (see section 14.5).

The House of Lords Act 1999

This Act altered the composition of an institution of the state, namely, the second chamber in Parliament. It removed the vast majority of hereditary peers from the House of Lords. The existence of hereditary peers (members who inherited their seats in the House of Lords) has always marked out the United Kingdom's constitutional arrangements as being very unusual in a democracy. The Act demonstrates graphically the power of Parliament to pass any law that it chooses. In short, the House of Lords Act 1999 effectively halved the size of the House of Lords (see section 10.6.3).

The Constitutional Reform Act 2005

This Act reformed various aspects of the constitution. As its title indicates, it is a quintessential constitutional measure. Its constitutional impact is as follows:

■ It made provision for a new Supreme Court (see section 5.7.4).

■ It reformed the way in which judges are appointed (see section 13.3.1 below).
■ It remodelled the historic role of the Lord Chancellor, who is a major official of state (see section 5.7.9).

ACTIVITY

Exercise

Select a number of the Acts of Parliament set out above and explain in each case why the statute is considered to be constitutionally significant. Find other Acts which relate to the organs of the state.

4.4.3 Acts of Parliament conferring rights on the individual

Legislation may also have constitutional importance if it contains provisions which directly or indirectly affect the rights and liberties of the individual. A statute may therefore have ramifications for human rights or fundamental freedoms either by conferring special rights on individuals, or by restricting their freedoms.

The following four Acts confer rights on individuals.

The Sex Discrimination Act 1975

This Act is an example of Parliament passing a law to protect individuals by providing them with legal redress and rights in the event of discrimination. In short, the Act makes it illegal to discriminate against men or women on the grounds of sex in the context of education, work, housing or providing goods or services. If an individual has been discriminated against he or she has the right to seek legal redress.

The Race Relations Act 1976

This Act relates to discrimination on the grounds of race (whether this is at work, renting accommodation, etc). If an individual has been racially discriminated against he or she has the right to seek legal redress. In both this statute and the one above, the state has recognised that one function of the state is to ensure that all individuals are treated with equal respect, providing them with a remedy if discrimination occurs.

NB At the time of going to print, the Equality Act 2010 had repealed and *restated* both the Sex Discrimination Act 1975 and the Race Relations Act 1976.

The Human Rights Act 1998

Along with the European Communities Act 1972, this statute is arguably the most constitutionally significant statute of the twentieth century. The Act gives further effect in domestic law to the fundamental rights and freedoms set out in the **European Convention on Human Rights**. This legislation represents a constitutional sea change in the way in which human rights are protected in the United Kingdom, as with the implementation of this Act individuals are permitted to raise alleged breaches of these rights directly before domestic courts (see Chapter 17).

European Convention on Human Rights
originally formulated in 1950, this document aims to protect the human rights of all people in the member states of the Council of Europe

The Representation of the People Act 1983

This Act consolidates earlier Representation of the People Acts, which conferred the legal right on individuals to vote in elections to the House of Commons. It is of constitutional importance as it relates directly to the foundation of (participatory) democracy and the constitutional relationship between the individual and the state: the right of the people to elect and determine the composition of the legislature, and indirectly, the executive.

It should be noted that under the doctrine of parliamentary sovereignty, all of the above statutes (even though they detail important principles underpinning our constitution) could be repealed or amended. No special procedure (or special majority in Parliament) is required to alter or repeal them. Notwithstanding this, these legislative measures contain fundamental constitutional principles which the courts will assume are not to be varied as they lie at the heart of the basis of our constitution. In short, they would not be amended without substantial constitutional upheaval.

NB: At the time of going to print, the Equality Act 2010 brought together, repealed and restated the various statutes concerning discrimination.

4.4.4 Acts of Parliament restricting the freedoms of the individual

It is important to note that Parliament will frequently pass statutes that will restrict the actions and freedoms of individuals. The following three Acts illustrate this.

The Perjury Act 1911

Under this Act it is a criminal offence for a person sworn in as a witness in court proceedings to make a statement which he knows to be false or does not believe to be true. This legislation protects the administration of justice.

The Public Order Act 1986

This legislation is concerned, *inter alia*, with the control and limitation of public processions and assemblies in order to protect public order.

The Prevention of Terrorism Act 2005

The objective of this Act is to prevent terrorism-related activity. The Act aims to achieve this by providing for the issuing of two types of 'control orders' which impose obligations on individuals who are suspected of being involved in terrorism-related activities. The obligations imposed would be tailored to the risk posed by the suspect concerned and could include, for example, restricting movement, prohibiting the possession of specified items or restricting communication and association. Owing to its draconian nature and restriction on human rights, the Act proved to be highly contentious but nevertheless passed expeditiously through Parliament.

ACTIVITY

Exercise

Select a number of the Acts of Parliament set out above and explain in each case what constitutional significance the statute has for the individual and individual rights. Find other Acts which have a constitutional impact on the individual.

4.4.5 Laws LJ and Acts of Parliament with constitutional status

As indicated above, historically the United Kingdom has been characterised as not having higher fundamental, entrenched laws. In recent years this orthodoxy has been questioned. For example, Laws LJ in *Thoburn v Sunderland City Council* [2002] EWHC 195 (Admin) (albeit *obiter*) argued that:

JUDGMENT

'We should recognise a hierarchy of Acts of Parliament: as it were "ordinary" statutes and "constitutional" statutes. The two categories must be distinguished on a principled basis.'

He added that these 'constitutional statutes' should embrace, among others, the following:

■ The Magna Carta.

- The Bill of Rights.
- The Union with Scotland Act.
- The Human Rights Act.
- The Scotland Act.
- The European Communities Act.

Furthermore, he commented that whereas ordinary statutes could be impliedly repealed by a later inconsistent Act, constitutional statutes such as the ones listed above are not subject to implied repeal.

ACTIVITY

Self-test question

What is the significance of Laws LJ's comments for our understanding of the sources of the British constitution?

4.5 Domestic delegated legislation

4.5.1 The nature of delegated legislation

delegated legislation
legislation made by the executive

Delegated legislation can also have constitutional significance. Delegated legislation is subordinate or secondary legislation made under the authority of a primary statute (the enabling Act of Parliament). This legislative power is conferred on the executive, for example a government minister. In doing so, it represents a clear breach of the separation of powers, but is justified constitutionally on the basis of practical necessity (see section 5.7.2).

4.5.2 Examples of delegated legislation

An example of the Prime Minister using a delegated legislative power is as follows:

The Secretary of State for Constitutional Affairs Order 2003 (SI 2003 No 1887)

This order transferred specified functions of the Lord Chancellor (whom at that point the government anticipated would be abolished under the impending Constitutional Reform Bill) to the newly created post of the Secretary of State for Constitutional Affairs. This order was passed under the aegis of the Ministers of the Crown Act 1975.

A further example, the Supreme Court Fees (Amendment) Order 1996, is detailed below in *R v Lord Chancellor, ex parte Witham* [1997] 2 All ER 779 (see section 4.8.3).

4.6 Domestic legislation of local authorities and the devolved institutions

4.6.1 Local authorities and delegated legislation

Local authorities enjoy a delegated legislative power. As local authorities technically form part of the executive, this is also a breach of the separation of powers, although this power is justified on the basis of practical necessity. An example is detailed below.

The Warwick District Council Off Street Parking Places Order 2006

Under the aegis of the Road Traffic Regulations Act 1984 (the primary/parent Act), Warwick District Council (part of Warwickshire County Council – an executive body) made the above delegated legislation which updated the existing charges for local council car parks.

4.6.2 Legislation and the devolved institutions

The devolved institutions also have the power to pass legislation (both secondary and primary in nature – see Chapter 14). For example, in the case of Scotland, the Scottish Parliament has the power to pass Acts of the Scottish Parliament, as illustrated by the following example.

The Scottish Parliamentary Standards Commissioner Act 2002

This Act established the office of a Parliamentary Standards Commissioner for the Scottish Parliament to investigate complaints concerning Members of the Scottish Parliament (MSPs) as to whether they had breached, for example, parliamentary Standing Orders or the Code of Conduct.

4.7 Legislation of the European Union

As a result of the European Communities Act 1972 European law (both primary and secondary) now forms an ever burgeoning and important part of the law of the United Kingdom (see Chapter 15). In broad terms there are two types of European Union law:

- primary sources and
- secondary sources.

4.7.1 Primary sources

These include the founding Treaty of Rome 1957 together with its subsequent amendment over the years (eg the Single European Act 1986 which, *inter alia*, extended the powers of the European Parliament).

4.7.2 Secondary sources

European Union legislation is passed by the European Union institutions and comes in a number of forms:

- Regulations
- Directives
- Decisions.

Regulations

The constitutional significance of regulations is that they are of general application and are self-executing as they do not require a Member State to formally implement them. In other words, the United Kingdom Parliament (or any other Parliament or Assembly in the Union) does not need to pass a law to incorporate the regulation as it will automatically form part of domestic law. An example of a regulation is detailed below:

Regulation 1365/75

This created a European Foundation for the improvement of living and working conditions of workers (which relates to individual social and economic rights).

Directives

In contrast to regulations above, directives do not have general application (instead they are addressed to particular Member States) and they require Member States to implement them through the passage of domestic legislation. In the United Kingdom directives can be implemented through either the passage of an Act of Parliament (see below) or by the means of delegated legislation in the form of a Statutory Instrument.

Council Directive 95/46/EC

The Data Protection Act 1998 was passed by the United Kingdom Parliament in order to implement the above European directive. This directive was aimed at protecting the rights of individuals in respect of personal data held about them. This issue relates directly to an individual's right to privacy.

Decisions

A decision does not have general application, but is addressed to particular parties (undertakings/companies) or Member States. Decisions can be used to implement a policy as illustrated by the example below:

Council Decision laying down the Procedures for the Exercise of Implementing Powers Conferred on the Commission 99/468 [1999] OJ L184/23

This Council decision, known as the 'Comitology decision', sets out the procedure to be followed when the Council confers a law-making power on the European Commission.

This delegation of legislative power is analogous to the United Kingdom Parliament (as the legislature) delegating a law-making power to the government (the executive) – see section 5.7.2.

Non-legally binding secondary sources

Opinions and recommendations are measures which do not have legally binding effect. For example, the European Commission can issue a 'reasoned opinion' in the context of enforcement proceedings against a Member State for violating European Union law. The opinion would set out the ways in which the Commission considered the Member State to have breached the law, for example by failing to implement a directive.

KEY FACTS

Key facts on legislation of the European Union
Legislation may have constitutional importance if it:
• establishes a state institution/organ of government;
• defines the powers of a state institution;
• regulates the functions of a state institution;
• regulates the procedure of a state institution;
• regulates the relationship between state institutions;
• regulates how the state relates to the individual by either conferring rights on the individual or by restricting their freedoms.

4.8 Domestic case law

4.8.1 The role of the courts

The courts play an important role in respect of constitutional rules. This is true also in countries where these rules are codified in a documentary constitutional text. This is because all constitutional rules (whether contained in a codified document, or not) need to be interpreted and clarified. As noted earlier, even in the United States the rules and principles set out in the constitution need to be interpreted, and this is performed by the United States Supreme Court (see *Marbury v Madison* (1803) 1 Cranch 137).

In the United Kingdom, in the absence of a single authoritative constitutional text, the courts play a particularly important role as many of our constitutional rules are to be found in court decisions (ie judicial decisions made in legal disputes brought before them for adjudication). For example, the most important principle of our constitution, namely, the legislative sovereignty of Parliament, is a court-based doctrine. This principle exists because the courts have declared it so in various decisions. Similarly, the separation of powers and the rule of law are underpinned by judicial decisions. Indeed, Dicey writing at the turn of the twentieth century referred to England as having a court-based constitution (a common law constitution). More recently it has been suggested that:

QUOTATION

'Our constitutional law remains a common law ocean dotted with islands of statutory provision.'

S Sedley, 'The Sound of Silence, Constitutional Law Without a Constitution'
[1994] 110 LQR 270.

It is certainly the case, however, that since the election of the Labour government in 1997, many statutes affecting the constitution have been enacted. In addition, it must be remembered that the courts are necessarily reactive as they must wait for a legal dispute to be brought before them in order to declare the law.

Not every court decision, of course, will illustrate or expound a constitutional principle or clarify a particular constitutional rule. Therefore it is necessary (as in the case of statutes), to examine each court decision on a case by case basis to ascertain whether the ruling has constitutional significance, and consequently whether it forms part of the constitutional law of the United Kingdom.

In the United Kingdom the courts may make decisions of constitutional importance either by:

- declaring the common law; or
- interpreting statutes in the light of certain constitutional principles.

4.8.2 The common law

Many of our constitutional rules are derived from the judiciary declaring the common law.

The following case declares that the government/state must act within the law:

CASE EXAMPLE

Entick v Carrington (1765) 19 St Tr 1030

Under a warrant issued by the Secretary of State, the defendants (the King's messengers) were required to search for John Entick and deliver him together with his papers before the Secretary of State. The allegation against Entick was that he was suspected of seditious libel. As the King's messengers broke into his house and seized his papers, Entick successfully sued them in the tort of trespass. As the trespass had not been justified by any legal authority (in other words by a valid warrant to enter Entick's premises), a tort had been committed. The case, though superficially concerned with the private law of trespass, has a clear constitutional dimension as it is concerned with the limitation of the power of the state, and protecting the individual from the exercise of arbitrary state power. In other words, in order for the state to enter a person's property, it must have appropriate legal authority or it will be deemed unlawful.

The following case concerns the protection of the constitutional principle of free expression and the freedom to express criticism of governmental institutions:

CASE EXAMPLE

Derbyshire CC v Times Newspapers Ltd and Others [1993] 1 All ER 1011

In this case Derbyshire County Council wished to sue *The Sunday Times*, its editor and two journalists in defamation for articles concerning alleged share dealings of the council. The House of Lords held that under the common law of defamation, Derbyshire County Council did not have the right to sue for damages as such a right would have been contrary to the public interest.

Although this case is in the context of the private law of defamation, it necessarily raises the constitutional issue of freedom of speech to criticise the government (see section 18.4.1).

The following case indicates that criminal offences (which restrict the freedom of the individual) can originate from the common law.

CASE EXAMPLE

Shaw v DPP [1962] AC 220

Shaw had been convicted, *inter alia*, of a common law conspiracy to corrupt public morals as he had conspired with advertisers and others to debauch and corrupt the morals of the youth and other subjects. Shaw had published a 'Ladies Directory' that contained the names and addresses of prostitutes. Shaw appealed and contended, *inter alia*, that there was no such offence. The House of Lords held that the courts had a residual power to supervise such offences that were prejudicial to public welfare. Viscount Simonds stated that:

JUDGMENT

'…there remains in the courts of law a residual power to enforce the supreme and fundamental purpose of the law, to conserve not only the safety and order but also the moral welfare of the State.'

The following case reaffirms the fundamental principle concerning the judicial arm of the state:

CASE EXAMPLE

R v Bow Street Metropolitan Stipendiary Magistrate, ex p Pinochet Ugarte (No 2) [2000] 1 AC 119 (for details see section 13.4.2)

In order to reiterate the fundamental importance of the principle of the independence of the judiciary and the right of individuals to a fair trial, the House of Lords set aside their previous decision in relation to a warrant for General Pinochet's extradition. The decision was set aside as one of the judges, Lord Hoffmann, had had a connection with Amnesty International who were seeking the extradition of Pinochet.

4.8.3 Statutory interpretation

The courts in interpreting statutes may do so in the light of certain constitutional principles. In particular, as the United Kingdom has historically lacked a Bill of Rights, the courts have used these principles in order to protect the individual. Accordingly, where a statute is unclear or ambiguous the courts can draw upon certain constitutional principles which include the assumption that surely Parliament would never have intended to:

■ legislate contrary to international law and Treaty obligations
■ legislate retrospectively
■ legislate so as to interfere with a person's right of access to the courts
■ create taxes in the absence of clear authority.

The following case illustrates the first two presumptions:

CASE EXAMPLE

Waddington v Miah [1974] 2 All ER 377

In this case the House of Lords interpreted the Immigration Act 1971 so that it did not have retrospective criminal effect. Lord Reid stated that 'it is hardly credible that any government department would promote or that Parliament would pass retrospective criminal legislation'. He also noted that Art 7 of the European Convention on Human Rights prohibited the imposition of retrospective criminal offences. In other words, the courts will assume that Parliament intended to legislate in accordance with the United Kingdom's international obligations.

The following case illustrates the third presumption:

CASE EXAMPLE

R v Lord Chancellor, ex parte Witham [1997] 2 All ER 779

Under the authority of s 130 of the Supreme Court Act 1981 (now known as the Senior Courts Act 1981) the Lord Chancellor made the following delegated legislative provision: the Supreme Court Fees (Amendment) Order 1996. Art 3 of this Order removed from litigants in person who received income support their (previously enjoyed) exemption from such fees. Witham, who was unemployed and on income support, was unable to institute proceedings in person for defamation as the exemption from paying fees had been removed by the 1996 Order. Witham sought judicial review of Art 3 of the Order as *ultra vires* and so beyond the legal powers of the Lord Chancellor.

It was held by the High Court that access to the courts was in effect a constitutional right recognised by the common law and that this right could only be restricted by clear and specific statutory authority. The court interpreted s 130 as not empowering the Lord Chancellor to issue Art 3, the effect of which had been to deny Witham access to the courts and legal redress (a common law constitutional right). This case demonstrates the courts protecting the rights of individuals to access the courts and thus seek justice.

The fourth presumption is demonstrated by *Attorney General v Wilts United Dairies Ltd* (1921) 37 TLR 884.

4.8.4 Statutory interpretation and the Human Rights Act 1998

In recent years the role of the courts in interpreting legislation has been heightened by the passage of the Human Rights Act 1998. The Act is in effect an interpretative one in that s 3 requires all courts and tribunals to interpret all legislation in accordance with the rights and freedoms enshrined in the European Convention on Human Rights. If the relevant statute cannot be read in line, the courts cannot strike down primary legislation; instead the higher courts can issue a **declaration of incompatibility** (see Chapter 17).

The following case is an example of the operation of the Human Rights Act:

CASE EXAMPLE

Bellinger v Bellinger [2003] UKHL 21

Mrs Bellinger was a transsexual who had been born male. In 1981 she went through a ceremony of marriage with a man. Section 11 of the Matrimonial Causes Act 1973 states that a marriage is valid only if the parties are male and female. Mrs Bellinger sought, and was denied, a declaration that her marriage was valid notwithstanding that she was born male. The House of Lords stated that the terms male and female in the Act were to be given their ordinary meaning and referred to the respective biological gender at birth. Accordingly, within the meaning of s 11, as the parties were not male and female, the marriage was not valid. The court did, however, issue a declaration of incompatibility that s 11 was incompatible with Art 8 of the European Convention on Human Rights (the right to respect for private and family life) and Art 12 (the right to marry). This did not mean that the 1973 Act was invalidated. However, in 2004 Parliament passed the Gender Recognition Act 2004 which recognised the reassigned gender of a person who has undergone gender reassignment.

For further examples see Chapter 17.

ultra vires
acting beyond specified legal powers

declaration of incompatibility
a declaration by the courts under the Human Rights Act 1998 that legislation is inconsistent with the European Convention

Self-test question

Why do you think decisions in the European Courts (the European Court of Justice and the European Court of Human Rights) are relevant to the study of the British constitution? Revisit this activity after completion of Chapters 15 to 17.

4.11 The law and custom of Parliament

Parliament (both the House of Commons and the House of Lords) regulates its own internal proceedings and determines its own standards of behaviour. This is done through laws and rules which are unique to it, known as the law and custom of Parliament (see section 8.5). These privileges (known as parliamentary privileges) are regarded as necessary in order to ensure that parliamentary members can carry out and discharge their constitutional functions. These laws/privileges comprise both:

▪ statutory sources (Art 9 of the Bill of Rights which guarantees freedom of speech in Parliament) and

▪ common law sources whereby the courts recognise that, for example, Parliament has the right to determine and regulate its own membership and proceedings. This includes how legislation proceeds through Parliament as demonstrated in the following case:

CASE EXAMPLE

British Railways Board v Pickin [1974] AC 765

Pickin sought to claim that Parliament had been fraudulently misled into passing the British Railways Act 1968. The House of Lords held that the role of the courts was merely to consider and apply enactments of Parliament and not to challenge the British Railways Act 1968. In essence, the courts would not question the internal proceedings within Parliament as to how the Bill came to be on the parliamentary roll (see sections 7.8.1 and 8.7.2).

KEY FACTS

Key facts on the law and custom of Parliament

Judicial decisions in case law may have constitutional importance if they:
- define the powers of a state institution (*Burmah Oil Company Ltd v Lord Advocate* (1965));
- regulate the relationship between state institutions; or
- regulate how the state relates to the individual by either conferring rights onto the individual (see *Entick v Carrington* (1765)) or by restricting their freedoms.

4.12 Treaties and international law

International Treaties such as:

▪ the Universal Declaration of Human Rights 1948 and

▪ the International Covenant on Civil and Political Rights 1966

also act as an indirect influence on the United Kingdom constitution. Moreover, case law from other national Supreme and Constitutional Courts may also prove to indirectly influence and shape our law. For example, in the *Derbyshire County Council* case (see sections 4.8.2 and 18.4.1) in the context of the importance attached to safeguarding freedom of speech, Lord Keith made reference to a decision issued by the United States Supreme Court (*New York Times Co v Sullivan* (1964) 376 US 254). This Supreme Court decision had endorsed the public policy interest in allowing a citizen to criticise an ineffectual or corrupt public official without fear of legal impediment.

4.13 Constitutional conventions

As noted above, the rules of the constitution can be divided into legal rules (above) and political rules, with the latter being constitutional conventions which are effectively binding political constitutional rules.

4.13.1 Definition of a constitutional convention

Dicey defined conventions in the following terms:

QUOTATION

'Conventions, understandings, habits or practices which, though they may regulate the conduct of the several members of the sovereign power, of the Ministry, or of other officials, are not in reality laws at all since they are not enforced by the courts. This portion of constitutional law may, for the sake of distinction, be termed the "conventions of the constitution", or constitutional morality.' (*sic*)

A Dicey, *Introduction to the Study of the Law of the Constitution* (10th edn, Macmillan, 1959), p 24.

More recently Barendt defined them as follows:

QUOTATION

'Constitutional conventions may be defined as principles of political or constitutional morality which are regarded as binding, but which are not legally enforceable.'

E Barendt, 'Fundamental Principles' in D Feldman (ed), *English Public Law* (Oxford University Press, 2004), p 14.

Furthermore, Barnett has provided a fuller definition:

QUOTATION

'A constitutional convention is a non-legal rule which imposes an obligation on those bound by the convention, breach or violation of which will give rise to legitimate criticism; and that criticism will generally take the form of an accusation of "unconstitutional conduct"'.

H Barnett, *Constitutional and Administrative Law* (7th edn, Routledge–Cavendish, 2009), p 36.

From these definitions we can see that constitutional rules can be distinguished between legal rules, which are enforced in a court of law, and political rules which are considered simply politically or morally binding. Barnett has contended that the breach or blatant disregard of a convention would be considered to be (morally) unconstitutional (see section 4.15.2).

4.13.2 Preliminary points to note about constitutional conventions

It should be noted that:

■ Firstly, constitutional conventions are not actually laws and yet they are studied as part of constitutional law. They are a very important part of the constitution and in fact may actually assume more constitutional significance than the legal rules that they supplement (see for example, the convention that the monarch will give her consent to a Bill presented to her – see section 4.13.6).

■ Secondly, constitutional conventions are not confined to the United Kingdom as they are also found in other countries such as the United States and Canada. These countries have codified constitutions and yet their constitutional text is supplemented by political conventional practices. For example, in Canada it is the practice that the federal Cabinet comprises representatives of all the Canadian provinces.

- Thirdly, constitutional conventions regulate key aspects of the British constitution and in particular, the government and the monarch. Some of the most important conventions are detailed below. It should be pointed out, however, that this is not an authoritative list (nor could it be, as inevitably there would be no universal agreement as to what it should include).

- Fourthly, in terms of their nature it should be noted that constitutional conventions are rules which are not necessarily prescribed with absolute precision (this gives them flexibility to develop and evolve) and there may be disagreement over their existence. It is important to remember that, unlike laws which are ultimately clarified in a court, there is no definitive authority or body which rules upon conventions. For example, although we are fairly clear in general terms about the rule governing the granting of the Royal Assent, other constitutional conventions are much less clear. For instance, in terms of ministerial responsibility, is it a modern day convention that ministers should resign for major mistakes in their government departments, as opposed to resigning for personal misadventures? (See section 12.3.5.)

4.13.3 Constitutional conventions in respect of Parliament

These include, *inter alia*, the following:

- Committees of the House of Commons should reflect the party political representation in the chamber (see section 12.6.4).
- Money Bills originate in the House of Commons.
- Parliament must meet at least once a year. It is of interest to compare this rule with the United States constitution, Art 1, s 4 of which states that, legally, Congress shall assemble at least once in every year.

4.13.4 Constitutional conventions in respect of the monarch/executive

These include, *inter alia*, the following:

- The monarch assents to a Bill passed by both Houses of Parliament (see section 11.9.3).
- Following a general election the monarch will appoint as Prime Minister the MP who is the leader of the political party who can command a majority of support in the House of Commons.
- Many of the legal powers formally vested in the monarch are in fact exercised in practice by the government of the day in the name of the Crown (see section 11.9.3).
- Government ministers are collectively responsible to Parliament for the overall operation of government policy (see section 12.2).
- Government ministers are individually responsible to Parliament for their actions and the policy and actions of their government department (see section 12.3).
- In the event of the government losing a motion of no confidence in the House of Commons, the Prime Minister must either recommend the dissolution of Parliament or offer his resignation with that of the government (see section 12.2.1).
- The Prime Minster should be drawn from, and sit in, the House of Commons (see section 11.2.2).
- Government ministers must sit in one of the Houses of Parliament (see section 11.6.1).
- Cabinet discussions should remain secret (see section 12.2.3).

4.13.5 Constitutional conventions in respect of the judiciary

These include, *inter alia*, the following:

- At least two of the twelve judges in the Supreme Court should be Scottish.
- The judiciary in general do not involve themselves in overtly party political issues (see section 13.4.4).

4.13.6 The significance of constitutional conventions

The importance of constitutional conventions, particularly in the British constitution, cannot be underestimated as these political rules and principles form a major aspect of our constitution. In fact, if we were to view the British constitution by simply examining the legal rules, then we would have a very jaundiced and imbalanced perception of the constitution. For example, in relation to the Royal Assent, although under the royal prerogative the monarch legally can refuse to give her consent to a Bill, in practice it has become a long-established convention that this assent is always granted on the advice of her ministers. If we were, however, to simply consider the legal rule concerning the Royal Assent in isolation without reference to the convention supplementing it, we would have a much distorted view of the realities of the modern monarch's powers and of the constitution.

4.13.7 The purpose of constitutional conventions

Sir Ivor Jennings stated that constitutional conventions:

QUOTATION

'provide the flesh which clothes the dry bones of the law; they make the legal constitution work; they keep it in touch with the growth of ideas'.

I Jennings, *The Law and the Constitution* (5th edn, Hodder and Stoughton, 1959) pp 81–82.

In short, constitutional conventions supplement the legal rules of the constitution. Their purpose is to ensure that the constitution can develop and adapt to ever changing contemporary principles and values. For example, the constitutional conventions regulating the legal powers of the monarch ensure that these powers are generally exercised by her government ministers on her behalf and in her name. This is consistent with democratic values as executive ministers are politically responsible to Parliament (through the convention of ministerial responsibility) whereas the monarch is unelected. It also illustrates the nature of the constitutional monarchy whereby the powers of the monarch are limited and controlled by binding political rules. Similarly, although the monarch formally undertakes the legal dissolution of Parliament, by convention she acts on the advice of the Prime Minister.

Constitutional conventions ensure that the constitution can develop on an incremental basis to address contemporary needs. For example, a constitutional convention (the Sewel Convention – named after Lord Sewel) has arisen as a result of the creation of the Scottish Parliament. In effect it states that the Westminster Parliament will not normally legislate in respect of 'devolved matters', except with the consent of the Scottish Parliament. This convention, therefore, regulates the constitutional and political relationship between the major institutions of the state (see section 14.3.13).

ACTIVITY

Self-test questions

1. How would you define a constitutional convention?
2. What constitutional purposes do they serve?

4.13.8 Why are constitutional conventions followed?

Constitutional conventions affect the main individuals and institutions in our constitution: the monarch, Prime Minister, Cabinet ministers, judges and members of the
House of Commons and Lords. Given that they are merely political rules, why are
they followed? Indeed, constitutional conventions are not *justiciable* (ie not suitable
for resolution before judicial proceedings) and so not enforced in a court. In fact,
according to the Joint Committee on Conventions, constitutional conventions, owing
to their nature, are 'unenforceable' (First Report of Session 2005–06 of the Joint
Committee on Conventions, *Conventions of the UK Parliament*, HL Paper 265-I, HC
1212-I (2006), para 279).

As political rules, constitutional conventions are considered by those bound by them
to be a constitutional and political obligation. In addition, political repercussions would
result from their breach which, as observed by Barnett, would involve allegations of
unconstitutional behaviour (ie acting contrary to the spirit and political principles underpinning the constitution – see section 4.15.2). For example, if the government were to lose
a vote of no confidence in the House of Commons and yet refused to resign and carried
on in office regardless, this would result in criticism. Furthermore, ministers will generally resign for major and embarrassing personal errors and misadventures (but less so
for departmental errors) because of the resulting criticism that would follow if they did
not (for examples, see section 12.3.4).

4.13.9 The flexibility of constitutional conventions

It should be noted that on occasions, owing to their flexible and non-legal nature, constitutional conventions can at times be set aside. For example, in the mid-1970s the convention of collective Cabinet responsibility was temporarily set aside in relation to the 1975
EEC national referendum. The Labour Cabinet at the time was divided over the issue of
the referendum, which concerned whether the United Kingdom should remain in the
EEC (as it was then known). The Labour Prime Minister at the time, Harold Wilson, set
aside this convention on this issue. It is also worth considering the current debate over
the relevance of the Salisbury-Addison/Government Bill Convention to the contemporary House of Lords (see section 10.11).

4.13.10 What are the origins of constitutional conventions?

The origins of the laws and legal rules of the constitution (whether it be in the form of a
statute or a constitutional principle extracted from a case) can be located relatively easily.
In contrast, the point at which a mere accepted practice has crystallised into a political constitutional rule with an obligation to follow it is much more problematic. This is
because constitutional conventions develop piecemeal over time on an *ad hoc* basis to
supplement the legal rules by adjusting and adapting the constitution to reflect contemporary political principles and needs.

In his work *The Law and the Constitution*, 1959, Sir Ivor Jennings suggested a three-part
test to determine the existence of a constitutional convention:

1. What are the precedents for the convention?
2. Do those connected with this rule believe that they ought to act in a certain constitutional way (ie follow this rule)?
3. Is there a constitutional reason for the rule?

It should be noted, however, that sometimes constitutional conventions can be created
by agreement. An example of this is the Sewel Convention in respect of the Scottish
Parliament (see section 14.3.13).

4.13.11 The distinction between laws and constitutional conventions

What is the difference between laws (legal rules) and constitutional conventions (non-legal/political rules)?

■ Firstly, in general, laws are enforced in a court, whereas constitutional conventions are not.

■ Secondly, as Alder has commented:

QUOTATION

'A law does not lapse if it becomes obsolete, yet a convention can disappear if it is not followed for a significant period, or if it is broken without objection.'

J Alder, *Constitutional and Administrative law* (7th edn, Palgrave/Macmillan, 2009), p 50.

In other words, Alder is making the point that, unlike a law, a convention depends upon regular and consistent use for its validation.

4.13.12 The judicial recognition of constitutional conventions

Although the courts do not enforce constitutional conventions, they have at times recognised their existence and made specific reference to them. An illustration of where a court made direct reference to the convention of collective responsibility is in the following case:

CASE EXAMPLE

Attorney-General v Jonathan Cape Ltd [1976] 1 QB 752

The Attorney-General sought an injunction to restrain publication of a book detailing the diaries of the late Richard Crossman, who died in 1974. The diaries detailed discussion in the Cabinet in the 1960s and the legal action was based on an alleged breach of confidence. The law of confidence concerns the situation where an individual has received information in circumstances that the information should remain confidential. Collective ministerial responsibility includes the rule that Cabinet discussions are secret, so as to allow ministers to discuss issues freely before a collective decision is agreed upon and thereafter defended publicly (see section 12.2.3).

The court held that under the law of confidence it could restrain the publication of politically confidential information where the public interest required restraint and here the convention was relevant to assessing the balance between the public interest and confidentiality. There was, however, a time limit after which the confidential nature of the information would lapse and on the facts, an injunction to restrain the publication in 1975 of discussion 10 years earlier (1964–66) was not justified.

Moreover, in the following case in the context of a Canadian constitutional convention, the Canadian Supreme Court recognised and acknowledged the convention's existence, but affirmed that as political rules, conventions cannot be enforced in a court of law:

CASE EXAMPLE

Reference Re Amendment of the Constitution of Canada (1982) 125 DLR (3d) 1

This case considered whether the consent of the Canadian provinces was necessary before the Canadian legislature requested the United Kingdom Parliament to amend the Canadian constitution in a way which affected the federal/provincial relationship. At this time, in order for the Canadian constitution to be altered, it required legislation from the Westminster Parliament in London. The Canadian Supreme Court held that as a matter of constitutional convention, the consent of the Canadian provinces was required, thereby recognising the existence of the convention. As a matter of law, however, such consent was not legally necessary. The court stated that in respect of the constitution's 'conventional rules':

JUDGMENT

'In contradistinction to the laws of the constitution, they are not enforced by the courts. One reason for this situation is that, unlike common law rules, conventions are not judge-made rules. They are not based on judicial precedents … Nor are they in the nature of statutory commands which it is the function and duty of the courts to obey and enforce. Furthermore, to enforce them would mean to administer some formal sanction when they are breached.'

In the following case, the Court of Appeal in determining the legal powers of a government minister made its decision in the context of the fact that the minister (under the convention of ministerial responsibility) was constitutionally, and politically, accountable to Parliament for his actions:

CASE EXAMPLE

Carltona Ltd v Commissioners of Works and Others [1943] 2 All ER 560

Carltona Ltd challenged the requisition of their factory by the Commissioners of Works. The power to requisition this property was made under the Defence (General) Regulations 1939. Carltona argued that the requisition was invalid as the decision had in practice been taken by a civil servant, (an Assistant Secretary) who was not a competent authority, instead of the Commissioners of Works. The Court of Appeal held that the order was valid, as it would not be practical for the minister to take every decision personally; accordingly, an official can make decisions on the authority of the minister so that the official acts in the name of the minister. Strictly speaking the official becomes the *alter ego* of the minister. Lord Greene MR stated that:

JUDGMENT

'Constitutionally, the decision of such an official is, of course, the decision of the minister. The minister is responsible. It is he who must answer before Parliament for anything that his officials have done under his authority, and if for an important matter he selected an official of such junior standing that he could not be expected competently to perform the work, the minister would have to answer for that in Parliament.'

Similarly, in the controversial (albeit historical) case of *Liversidge v Anderson* [1942] AC 206 the court was influenced by the convention of ministerial responsibility in reaching its decision concerning the exercise of the legal powers of a government minister to detain an individual during wartime (see section 6.7.10).

4.13.13 Converting constitutional conventions into laws

It is of course possible for a constitutional convention to be converted into statutory form, thereby making it a legal rule and so legally enforceable. In fact, this has already been achieved in the British constitution and is illustrated by the following two statutes.

■ **The Parliament Act 1911**: codification may be considered necessary if a constitutional convention is flagrantly breached. Before the Parliament Act 1911, it had been a convention that the House of Commons was the dominant chamber and that the House of Lords would ultimately give way to it. The constitutional convention was that the Lords would not oppose a money Bill passed by the Commons. The House of Commons was of course elected (although at this point it did not involve universal suffrage). In 1909 the Finance Bill containing Lloyd George's Budget was rejected by the House of Lords and this resulted in the passage of the 1911 Act, which effectively placed on a statutory basis the principle that the upper chamber was legally subordinate to the lower House (see section 10.10.1).

■ **The Statute of Westminster 1931**: s 4 of this Act codified (ie enacted in statutory form) the constitutional convention that the United Kingdom Parliament would not legislate for a Dominion (eg Canada, New Zealand and Australia) without their consent.

Moreover, during the passage of the Constitutional Reform Bill (which became the 2005 Act) an unsuccessful attempt was made to codify the historic constitutional convention that the Lord Chancellor must be both a peer in the House of Lords and a lawyer. It is of interest to remember that other countries have also enacted constitutional conventions in a legal form. For example, the 22nd Amendment to the constitution of the United States codified the convention that limited the President to two terms of office.

Although it is possible for constitutional conventions to be converted into legal rules, is this necessarily desirable? At least two basic objections can be raised:

■ Firstly, there would be inevitable debate over defining these conventions and their precise ambit.

■ Secondly, new constitutional conventions in any event would develop so as to supplement those conventions which had been codified.

Finally, it is pertinent to point out that in 2006 the Joint Committee on Conventions was established to consider the practicality of codifying the constitutional conventions which regulate the relationship between the House of Commons and the House of Lords. Its conclusions are set out at section 10.11, although for present purposes it is worth noting the following passage:

QUOTATION

'In our view the word "codification" is unhelpful, since to most people it implies rule-making, with definitions and enforcement mechanisms … It would raise issues of definition, reduce flexibility, and inhibit the capacity to evolve. It might create a need for adjudication, and the presence of an adjudicator, whether the courts or some new body, is incompatible with parliamentary sovereignty.'

First Report of Session 2005–06 of the Joint Committee on Conventions, *Conventions of the UK Parliament*, HL Paper 265-I, HC 1212-I (2006), para 279.

The Committee observed that codification of conventions in a broad sense could mean an authoritative statement of conventions, or in a narrower sense, the reduction of them 'to a literal code or system'. In any event, the Committee made it very clear that there was universal opposition to legislating on these matters (as this would, for example, affect their flexibility and inhibit their evolution). Furthermore, the courts should have no role in adjudicating on them.

KEY FACTS

Key facts on constitutional conventions

- 'Constitutional conventions may be defined as principles of political or constitutional morality which are regarded as binding, but which are not legally enforceable' (Barendt).
- Constitutional conventions regulate key aspects of the British constitution; in particular, the monarch and the government.
- They supplement the legal rules of the constitution and help to ensure that the constitution can develop and adapt to ever changing contemporary principles and values.
- Political repercussions would result from their breach which would lead to allegations of unconstitutional behaviour (acting in a morally unconstitutional way).

4.14 Authoritative writers

Historic writers on the British constitution include, for example, the works of Blackstone and Dicey. Indeed, Dicey's work (A Dicey, *Introduction to the Study of the Law of the Constitution* (10th edn, Macmillan 1959)), has informed our understanding of the constitutional principles of, *inter alia:*

■ the rule of law (Chapter 6)
■ constitutional conventions (see section 4.13)
■ parliamentary sovereignty (Chapter 7).

Today distinguished contemporary academics (eg the texts of Feldman *Civil Liberties and Human Rights in England and Wales* (2nd Edition, Oxford University Press, 2002) or Wade and Forsyth's *Administrative Law* (10th Edition, Oxford University Press, 2009)) will also be referred to in order to assist the court in applying the constitution.

It should also be remembered that senior judges, serving or otherwise, will write occasionally in legal academic journals and deliver extra-judicial speeches. For instance, in 2004 the then Lord Chief Justice, Lord Woolf, delivered a speech on the rule of law at Cambridge University (Lord Woolf, 'The rule of law and a change in the constitution' [2004] CLJ 317).

4.15 Acting unconstitutionally in the United Kingdom

4.15.1 The difficulties associated with the term unconstitutional in the United Kingdom

As observed at section 2.6, acting unconstitutionally means to act contrary to the constitutional rules, spirit and principles underpinning the constitution. In the United Kingdom in the absence of a codified document, the use of the term *unconstitutional* is problematic as the rules of the constitution have not been codified. In fact, these rules have not even been universally and definitively agreed upon and consequently, as indicated earlier at section 4.2, there is no universal agreement on what is, and what is not, a constitutional issue. In light of this, it is difficult to gain universal agreement on what is *unconstitutional*.

In addition, in the absence of a codified constitutional document which has fundamental status, the courts in the United Kingdom (unlike a number of Supreme or Constitutional Courts in other countries with a codified constitution) cannot declare Acts of Parliament to be legally unconstitutional. In other words, they cannot declare that an Act is invalid as being contrary to the principles set out in the constitution. This is because there is no fundamental, codified constitutional text and instead, owing to the principle of parliamentary sovereignty, Parliament legally can pass any law that it chooses as the courts are (traditionally at least) unable to challenge or question it (see Chapter 7). The impact of European Union law is dealt with at section 15.6.3.

4.15.2 Examples of acting unconstitutionally in the United Kingdom

In the United Kingdom we would consider the following to be unconstitutional:

■ A violation of the rule of law (see Chapter 6).
■ The arbitrary use of power without restraint (see Chapters 19 and 20).
■ The departure from and interference with fundamental principles including, for example, the right of access to the courts (see *Chester v Bateson* at section 5.7.2) or the presumption of innocence (*ex parte Khawaja* at section 6.7.10).
■ A breach or disregard of a constitutional convention (see section 4.13).
■ A breach of European Union law (see Chapter 15).

■ A breach of the European Convention (either through an adverse ruling of the European Court of Human Rights, or in the context a declaration of incompatibility made by the domestic courts under the Human Rights Act 1998 (see Chapters 16 and 17 respectively)).

Some more examples are detailed below.

Firstly, suppose the monarch refused to give the Royal Assent to a Bill, despite having been specifically requested to do so by the government. It is a constitutional convention that the monarch confers her assent to a Bill and, as indicated above, a breach of a constitutional convention leads to an accusation of unconstitutional conduct. The failure to give assent to the Bill would, however, not be illegal as the disregard of a constitutional convention is not enforced in a court of law. We could argue, therefore, that although this behaviour was *legally constitutional* (ie lawful), it would, nevertheless, be *morally unconstitutional* (as being contrary to the fundamental political principles underpinning the constitution).

Secondly, according to parliamentary sovereignty, Parliament legally can pass any law that it chooses and so the courts are unable to declare an Act of Parliament *legally unconstitutional* as being repugnant to the British constitution (but in this context see section 7.7). In theory, therefore, suppose Parliament chooses to pass the (imaginary) Elections Act 2013, s 1 of which deprives all individuals with an income of less than £5,000 a year of the right to vote in general elections. Commentators would undoubtedly consider this legislation to be unconstitutional, at least from a moral perspective (*morally unconstitutional*), as it interferes with basic democratic principles, namely participatory democracy and the right to vote. The Act, however, would in legal theory be technically enforceable and therefore *legally constitutional*, as Parliament under the British constitution legally can pass any Act that it chooses.

CASE EXAMPLE

Madzimbamuto v Lardner-Burke [1969] 1 AC 645

Lord Reid in the Privy Council made the point that under the principle of parliamentary sovereignty, Parliament can in legal theory pass any law (ie the Southern Rhodesia Act 1965), even if that statute contravened a well established constitutional principle (ie that the UK Parliament would not legislate for Southern Rhodesia without its consent). In this context he commented that:

JUDGMENT

'It is often said that it would be unconstitutional for the United Kingdom Parliament to do certain things, meaning that the moral, political and other reasons against doing them are so strong that most people would regard it as highly improper if Parliament did these things. But that does not mean that it is beyond the power of Parliament to do such things. If Parliament chose to do any of them the courts could not hold the Act of Parliament invalid.' (See also section 7.6.4.)

It is worth pointing out that the (imaginary) Elections Act 2013 would be inevitably challenged by aggrieved individuals under the European Convention on Human Rights:

■ Initially, in the domestic courts under the Human Rights Act 1998 by the seeking of a declaration that the Act contravenes Protocol 1, Art 3, in effect, the right to vote. Notwithstanding this, Parliament and the government could politically ignore any such declaration and the Act would remain in force (see Chapter 17).

■ Thereafter, aggrieved individuals could petition the European Court of Human Rights in Strasbourg. The European Court inevitably would declare that the (imaginary) Elections Act 2013 violated the European Convention and require that the United Kingdom remove this offending legislation. The United Kingdom Parliament could in legal theory ignore such a ruling, however, for political reasons it would implement the European Court's ruling. As an aside, in mid 2010 the British government had still not implemented the ruling of the European Court in *Hirst v UK* (2006) concerning the rights of prisoners to vote (see section 9.6.3).

Thirdly, an example of Parliament passing a statute which was arguably *morally unconstitutional* (but perfectly legal and enforceable) is the War Damage Act 1965 which, in effect, reversed a ruling of the House of Lords that proved to be financially inexpedient (see sections 6.7.9 and 7.5.1). It is a fundamental principle of the constitution that the role of the courts and the administration of justice is safeguarded. Similarly, it could conceivably be argued that s 20C of the Taxes Management Act 1970 was *morally unconstitutional* as it conferred exceptionally wide-sweeping powers on the executive at the expense of the individual (see *Rossminster Ltd and Others* at sections 6.7.5 and 6.7.9). Both statutes infringe major principles which are fundamental to the constitution.

Finally, as the term unconstitutional is necessarily a somewhat indistinct term, commentators inevitably will disagree over whether legislation or government action is *morally unconstitutional*. For example, is the Prevention of Terrorism Act 2005 *morally unconstitutional* as it interferes with the fundamental liberties of the individual, or is it a necessary response to an emergency, threatening the life and safety of the public?

ACTIVITY

Exercise

What is meant by acting unconstitutionally in the British constitution?

KEY FACTS

Key facts on the sources of the British constitution

Legal sources:

Domestic legislation
• Acts of Parliament
• Delegated legislation
• Legislation of local authorities and the devolved institutions

European Union legislation
• Primary sources
• Secondary sources

Domestic case law
• The common law
• Interpreting statutes
• The royal prerogative

European case law
• European Court of Justice
• European Court of Human Rights

The law and custom of Parliament
• Parliamentary privilege

Treaties and international law
• Universal Declaration of Human Rights 1948

Non-legal sources:

Constitutional conventions
Academic writings

SAMPLE ESSAY QUESTION

Essay: Where will you find the British constitution and what are the problems in locating its sources?

Introduction

UK is very unusual in lacking a written codified document setting out the principles of the constitution (contrast USA and Ireland).

As a result, UK constitutional rules are located in a wide range of different sources.

Problems in ascertaining sources

Whereas other countries typically distinguish between constitutional laws (fundamental/higher) and non-constitutional laws (ordinary), no such demarcation in UK (but see Laws LJ in *Thoburn* (2002)).

No special UK Supreme/Constitutional Court.

Domestic legal sources

Use examples of legislation which have established state institutions (eg Scotland Act 1998) and which have regulated the relationship between institutions (Parliament Acts 1911 and 1949).

Use examples of case law which have: limited the powers of institutions (*Proclamations* (1611)), set out the relationship between institutions (*Pickin* (1974)), between the individual and the state (*Entick* (1765)) and which set out fundamental principles (*Pinochet* (2000)).

International sources

European Union primary legislation (Treaty of Rome 1957 legislation) and secondary as amended (directives) as well as the case law of the European Court of Justice (*Costa* (1964)).

Articles of the European Convention on Human Rights, the case law of the European Court of Human Rights (*Dudgeon* (1981)) and its recent impact on domestic law via the Human Rights Act 1998 (*Bellinger* (2003)).

Universal Declaration of Human Rights 1948.

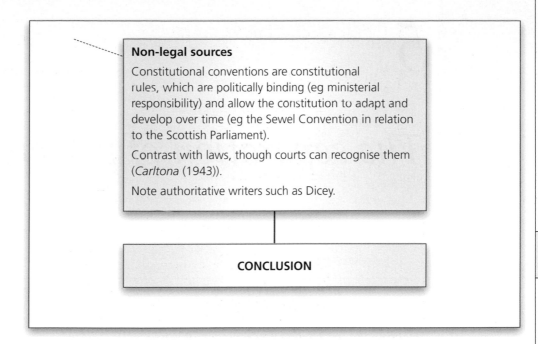

Non-legal sources

Constitutional conventions are constitutional rules, which are politically binding (eg ministerial responsibility) and allow the constitution to adapt and develop over time (eg the Sewel Convention in relation to the Scottish Parliament).

Contrast with laws, though courts can recognise them (*Carltona* (1943)).

Note authoritative writers such as Dicey.

CONCLUSION

 # Further reading

Books

Alder, J, *Constitutional and Administrative Law* (7th edn, Palgrave/Macmillan, 2009), Chapter 3.

Barnett, H, *Constitutional and Administrative Law* (7th edn, Routledge–Cavendish, 2009), Chapter 2.

Bradley, A and Ewing, K, *Constitutional and Administrative Law* (14th edn, Pearson/ Longman, 2007), Chapter 2.

Ellis, E, 'Sources of Law and the Hierarchy of Norms' in Feldman, D (ed), *English Public Law* (2nd edn, Oxford University Press, 2009), p 38.

Turpin, C, and Tomkins, A, *British Government and the Constitution* (6th edn, Cambridge University Press, 2007), Chapter 2, Pts 1 and 2.

5

The separation of powers

At the end of this chapter you should be able to:

■ Explain what is meant by the principle of the separation of powers
■ Identify and explain the aspects of the British constitution that violate the separation of powers
■ Identify and explain the aspects of the British constitution that accord with the separation of powers
■ Assess the overall significance of the separation of powers in the British constitution

5.1 Introduction

In the context of the chapter on constitutions we noted the importance of ensuring that state/governmental power is limited by a constitution. One way in which state power can be controlled is through the principle of the separation of powers. In essence, under this doctrine public/state power is divided and dispersed between separately constituted institutions, each with a distinct function to perform. This is in accord with the principle of constitutionalism, namely, that the power of the state should be limited. The aim of this chapter is to consider the constitutional doctrine of the separation of powers and examine its significance in the context of the British constitution.

5.2 Definition

5.2.1 Introduction

The separation of powers has been described in the following terms:

QUOTATION

'In a nation which has political liberty as the direct object of its constitution no one person or body of persons ought to be allowed to control the legislative, executive and judicial powers, or any two of them.'

　　Lord Lester and D Oliver (eds), *Constitutional Law and Human Rights* (Butterworths, 1997) p 21.

The doctrine of the separation of powers is typically associated with the French commentator Montesquieu writing in the eighteenth century. He was concerned with avoiding a concentration of state power and ensuring that this power was limited. Although the principle of dividing the various functions and powers of the state predates Montesquieu, his description of the three branches of government, namely the legislature, executive and judiciary, has a modern resonance.

In very general terms, the separation of powers denotes that in order to avoid an unnecessary concentration of state power, the following three state functions should be separate from one another:

- The legislative function (the law-making function).
- The executive function (the governmental function).
- The judicial function (the adjudicative and interpretative function).

In short, these functions should be separate and there should also be no overlap of personnel. The definition of the separation of powers, however, is a somewhat elastic concept which is subject to different interpretations. These range from a very strict separation of powers, through to gradations of the principle, whereby the functions and institutions interrelate and check and balance each other.

5.2.2 A pure separation of powers

A pure separation of powers would insist that the three organs of government be completely separate and constitutionally isolated from each other. This would entail the three elements of the state being institutionally separate from each other with each organ performing a specific and exclusive constitutional function. Furthermore, individuals should only form part of one organ. This therefore prohibits, for instance, a judge from sitting in the legislature as this would represent an overlap in terms of personnel. The three organs should be separated in terms of their functions so that each performs its own constitutional function and does not purport to exercise the specified function of another. This prohibits, for example, the courts making legislation and thereby performing a legislative function. Similarly, the legislature is prohibited from interfering with the courts' adjudicative and interpretative function.

In summary, under a pure separation of powers there should be no overlap in terms of:

- Functions (eg the judiciary should not exercise a legislative function or interfere with the executive function).
- Personnel (eg a judge should not form part of the executive body).
- Institutions (eg the executive body should not form part of another institution such as the legislature).

5.2.3 A less than pure separation of powers

In contrast to a pure separation of powers, there are various gradations of the doctrine whereby the functions/organs of government may be largely separate (to varying degrees), but interrelate and check and balance each other (eg the judiciary checks and balances the legislative power). This less than pure separation of powers – a weaker and partial separation – acknowledges the political reality that the machinery and practice of government require that state institutions have to work with one another. In fact, Barnett has argued that a pure separation of powers could prove to be unworkable in practice, as it could lead to constitutional deadlock between the institutions. Under a weaker version of the separation of powers, the tensions and checks and balances between the three state institutions aim to ensure that state power is not abused as it makes it necessarily more difficult for each branch of the state to carry out its particular function, as it is checked and balanced by the other branches.

ACTIVITY

Essay writing

Explain the difference between a pure separation of powers and a less strict version of the principle.

Key facts on the separation of powers

The separation of powers is an internal method of institutionally controlling state power.
Under the doctrine of the separation of powers, public/state power is divided and dispersed between separately constituted institutions, each with a distinct function to perform.
The separation of powers is an important aspect of constitutionalism.

5.3 The different powers of the state

The functions/powers of the state can, in effect, be divided into three. It should be noted, however, that this division into three clearly defined state functions is not without controversy. Some commentators have questioned whether it is really possible to definitively and clearly separate these functions/powers.

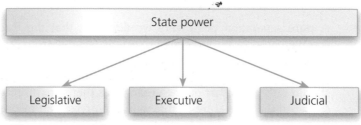

Figure 5.1 The different powers of the state

5.3.1 The legislative function

This function is performed by the legislature and it involves the enactment of general laws. In the United Kingdom the Queen in Parliament represents the law-maker (ie a Bill passes through both Houses of Parliament and receives Royal Assent in order to become an Act of Parliament). Similarly, in the Republic of Ireland the Oireachtas is the law-maker (Art 15.2 of the Irish constitution) and in the United States it is Congress (Art 1). We will see later, however, that in the United Kingdom (as in a number of other countries) the legislative role is not performed solely by the legislature.

5.3.2 The executive function

The executive (or governmental) function is performed by the government or administration. The executive administrates (carries out) the functions, powers and duties contained in general legislative provisions. The executive is the most difficult of all three organs to define, and it has been described simply as the residual functions/roles of the state that exist once the legislative and judicial functions have been outlined and demarcated (Lord Lester and D Oliver (eds), *Constitutional Law and Human Rights* (Butterworths, 1997), p 22).

In general terms, the executive executes the law as it carries out and implements it. In the United Kingdom not only does the executive initiate policy (including the drafting of parliamentary legislative proposals), but it also implements the resulting legislation. In addition, the executive determines and executes public policy in terms of both domestic and foreign affairs. In the United Kingdom the term executive can include the following bodies:

- The Sovereign as the nominal head of the executive (see section 11.1.2).
- Her Majesty's Government comprising the Prime Minister, Cabinet, junior government ministers (in effect the political executive), supported by government departments staffed by civil servants (see Chapter 11).

- Local authorities. It should be noted that it is possible for the two branches of the executive function (ie central and local government) to be of different political colours. For example, in the 1980s when central government (the political executive) was Conservative, and many local authorities were controlled by the Labour Party, this led to friction and litigation between the branches of the executive. This led to what has been described as the *juridification* of their constitutional relationship. This meant that the courts were used in order to demarcate the boundary between central and local government (see section 14.2).
- The armed forces and the police who carry out and implement the law on a practical basis (see section 11.4).

In the United States the political executive is the President and in the Republic of Ireland it is the government (ie Taoiseach and Cabinet).

5.3.3 The judicial function

The judicial function is performed by the judiciary and it involves the determination of the law laid down in statutes or in the common law in relation to disputes arising from that law. It is a forum for resolving legal conflicts. The judicial arm of the state, therefore, settles legal disputes by interpreting and applying the law to a particular case before it. In the United Kingdom this function is performed by an array of judges (both senior and junior, full-time and part-time, legally qualified and those lacking formal legal qualifications, ie magistrates). As we shall see later, however, the judicial function is not exclusively performed by the judiciary alone.

In the United States Art III of the constitution confers judicial power on the judges and the Supreme Court. In the Republic of Ireland Art 34.1 stipulates that the exclusive responsibility to administer justice is performed by the judiciary (including the Irish Supreme Court).

KEY FACTS

Key facts on the different powers of state

In general terms:
- The legislative function involves enacting law.
- The executive function involves the implementation of that law as well as making policy decisions.
- The judicial function involves settling legal disputes arising from the law.

5.4 The relationship between the three powers in the United Kingdom

In the United Kingdom the three functions of the state are not isolated and completely separate from one another. Instead, they interrelate with each other. This is illustrated in the context of the creation and enforcement of primary legislation. Detailed below are three examples of how the various state functions would combine with each other in the context of (imaginary) legislation.

5.4.1 The (imaginary) Crime Act 2013

The policy behind this legislation is that the government (the political executive) responded to a perceived public need for a new criminal offence to be introduced. After a White Paper on the policy had been issued, the government drafted the proposed new offence in The Crime Bill. This is an example of the executive formulating policy by initiating new legislative proposals in order to create a new criminal offence.

As part of the Queen's Speech in November 2012 (the beginning of the 2012–13 parliamentary session), the government presented the Crime Bill to Parliament for it to approve. Parliament as the legislature is responsible for enacting legislation and both Houses (House of Commons and the House of Lords) considered the measure, and the Bill was amended to remedy some minor drafting inaccuracies. Once the Crime Bill passed successfully through both Houses of Parliament it received the Royal Assent (as we saw at section 4.13.4, by constitutional convention, such assent is always given by the monarch) and it became the Crime Act 2013.

Once in force, the Crime Act 2013 would be enforced by the police (the executive in practical terms), who would bring before the Crown Prosecution Service (an independent body but a non-ministerial government department which is responsible for the prosecution of offenders) cases of individuals who are alleged to have committed the new criminal offence enshrined in the Act. In court the offender would be tried and the court process would determine whether the offence contained within the Crime Act 2013 had been breached and if so, decide what punishment would be appropriate (the parameters of the punishment available being stipulated in the Crime Act).

5.4.2 The (imaginary) Tax Act 2013

The government wanted to introduce a new tax and this policy was encapsulated in the Tax Bill. This Bill was then presented to Parliament (with the House of Commons having special responsibility for financial measures) for it to accept (with or without amendments) or reject. After Parliament approved the Tax Bill it was given the Royal Assent and it became the Tax Act 2013. This Act would then be enforced (ie the new tax would be collected by HM Revenue and Customs – a non-ministerial government department) and in the event of a dispute arising concerning the interpretation of this measure (ie what payment is due in law), ultimately the judicial arm of the state would adjudicate on this (although a tax tribunal – the Tax Chamber – would initially process the issue).

5.4.3 The (imaginary) Public Order Act 2013

In 2013 Parliament passed, and the Royal Assent was given to, the Public Order Bill making it the Public Order Act 2013. Section 1 of the Act stated that the Home Secretary may pass such regulations (in the form of a Statutory Instrument) as he thinks fit in order to protect public order. This is an example of Parliament delegating a legislative power to a government minister which would enable him/her to pass delegated/secondary legislation (see section 5.7.2).

In constitutional terms, the reality in this example is that the executive (which typically controls the House of Commons) has drafted a Bill which, after it has been made law, has conferred a legislative power back onto itself, that is onto a government minister: the Home Secretary.

ACTIVITY

Applying the law

Identify an Act of Parliament that has been passed recently by Parliament and consider how the three state institutions have interacted in the context of that legislation.

5.5 What is the rationale behind the separation of powers?

The separation of powers is central to a democratic constitution.

5.5.1 To avoid a concentration of public power in one body/institution

As noted above, Montesquieu argued that state power should be divided and separated in order to avoid a concentration of power which otherwise could lead to tyranny and oppression:

'When legislative power is united with executive power in a single person, or in a single body of the magistracy, there is no liberty … Nor is there liberty if the power of judging is not separate from legislative power and from executive power. If it were joined to legislative power, the power over the life and liberty of the citizens would be arbitrary, for the judge would be the legislator … All would be lost if the same man or the same body of principal men, either of nobles, or of the people, exercised these three powers: that of making the laws, that of executing public resolutions, and that of judging the crimes or the disputes of individuals.'

C Montesquieu, *The Spirit of the Laws* (1748), cited in A Bradley and K Ewing, *Constitutional and Administrative Law* (14th edn, Pearson/Longman 2007), pp 84–85.

Thus, if one person performed two or more state functions this would inevitably lead to oppression and tyranny. For example, if a person making the laws (a legislative role) also enforced and implemented these legislative provisions (an executive role) and then determined whether a person had violated that law in a case before them (a judicial role), this person would in effect enjoy excessive and tyrannical powers. If all state power was concentrated in one body, therefore, it would inevitably be abused.

5.5.2 To provide a system of checks and balances between the branches of government

Under a partial separation of powers the objective is to avoid a concentration of power. This is achieved not by an absolute separation and isolation of the three functions, but instead through the creation of a number of checks and balances between them. In other words, one institution may well interfere with the (constitutional) functions of another. For example, in the Republic of Ireland, the Oreachtas as the legislature is responsible for enacting laws. Under Art 34 of the Irish constitution, however, the Irish Supreme Court may declare legislation legally unconstitutional and therefore null and void. Moreover, under Art 26 the President of Ireland (a formal and typically ceremonial aspect of the executive) may refer a Bill that has not yet been signed (and so yet to become an Act) to the Supreme Court in order to determine whether or not it is unconstitutional. If the Bill, or any part of it, is deemed unconstitutional, the Bill cannot become law. This therefore frustrates the legislature in its function of law-making.

Similarly, the doctrine of the separation of powers is clearly evident in the United State's constitution as it is based on a subtle set of checks and balances. For instance, the President (executive) can, initially at least, check the legislature in the context of legislation by vetoing proposed legislation which has successfully passed through Congress. Ultimately, however, the latter can overturn the presidential veto by a two-thirds majority in each House. In addition, in terms of appointments to the Supreme Court, the Senate (the second chamber of Congress) must confirm a Presidential nomination (an executive decision) of a proposed Justice.

5.5.3 To provide an efficient government

At one level the doctrine of the separation of powers helps to achieve efficient government. In short, by specifically allocating definite functions to specific institutions staffed with particular expertise (eg judges who are expert at assessing evidence and judging), this necessarily provides efficient government.

5.5.4 To safeguard the independence of the judiciary

The separation of powers subsumes the fundamental notion that the judiciary should be constitutionally independent. In other words, in a democratic constitution it is of paramount importance that the judges – who form part of the court system – are independent, impartial and free from interference from the other branches of government (particularly the executive). The principle of the independence of the judiciary embraces, *inter alia*, the notion that the judiciary must be free to determine disputes before them strictly in accordance with the law (see Chapter 13).

KEY FACTS

The reasoning behind the separation of powers includes
• To avoid an abuse of state power by preventing a concentration of public power in one body/institution.   • To provide a system of checks and balances between the branches of government.   • To provide efficient government.   • To safeguard the independence of the judiciary.

5.6 The separation of powers in the United Kingdom

The question as to whether or not the United Kingdom adheres to the principles underpinning the separation of powers is somewhat controversial as there is no clear agreement on this point. It does depend, of course, in which sense the term is being used.

5.6.1 The separation of powers as part of the British constitution

For example, in *R v Her Majesty's Treasury, ex parte Smedley* [1985] 1 QB 657 Sir John Donaldson MR stated that:

JUDGMENT

'Although the United Kingdom has no written constitution, it is a constitutional convention of the highest importance that the legislature and the judicature are separate and independent of one another.'

Similarly, Lord Diplock in *Duport Steels Ltd and Others v Sirs and Others* [1980] 1 All ER 529 has commented that:

JUDGMENT

'It cannot be too strongly emphasised that the British constitution, though largely unwritten, is firmly based on the separation of powers: Parliament makes the laws, the judiciary interpret them.'

Further, Lord Templeman in *M v Home Office and others* [1994] 1 AC 377 has noted that:

JUDGMENT

'Parliament makes the law, the executive carry the law into effect and the judiciary enforce the law.'

5.6.2 The separation of powers not being part of the British constitution

In contrast, the academic writer de Smith writing in 1998 dismissed the separation of powers in the context of the United Kingdom by arguing that:

QUOTATION

'No writer of repute would claim that it is a central feature of the modern British constitution.'

S de Smith and R Brazier, *Constitutional and Administrative Law* (8th edn, Penguin, 1998), p 18.

NB Now, however, note the recent reforms made under the Constitutional Reform Act 2005 detailed later in this chapter.

5.6.3 Initial observations on the separation of powers and the British constitution

What is clear is that:

- Firstly, the British constitution does not follow a pure separation of powers with each branch of the state completely separated from each other in terms of functions and personnel. Instead, to the extent that it does adhere to the separation of powers, it follows a partial/modified version involving checks and balances.
- Secondly, even where the United Kingdom does depart from the doctrine of the separation of powers, these departures may well be driven by practical necessity. In any event, they may well be governed by constitutional conventions.

The issue of the separation of powers in the British constitution is inevitably less clear cut than in other countries. This is because in other democracies with a codified constitution the principle of the separation of powers has been specifically written into, and so is structurally part of, the constitutional text (eg France and the United States). In contrast, the British constitution has developed incrementally and organically over hundreds of years. It is perhaps worth remembering that the modern expression of the separation of powers is found in Montesquieu writing in the eighteenth century (and subsequently incorporated into the constitution of the United States). Yet a number of our constitutional rules and principles predate this; for instance, the office of the Prime Minister dates back to the first part of the eighteenth century. Finally, it is of interest to note that the institutional structure of the European Union does not exhibit a clear separation of powers (see section 15.2.2).

5.7 Aspects of the British constitution not in accord with the separation of powers

Detailed below at Figure 5.2 are the main ways in which the constitution does not follow the separation of powers (pure or otherwise). It must be remembered that some of the overlaps are now historical and have been subject to reform in recent years.

5.7.1 The parliamentary executive (an overlap of the legislature and the executive)

One of the main characteristics of the British constitution is that it has a parliamentary executive, as, by constitutional convention, the executive (the political executive) is drawn from the legislature (Parliament). In general, the political executive (the government) comprises over 100 members, most of whom are drawn from the elected House of Commons. The remainder are peers in the House of Lords (see section 11.6.2). For

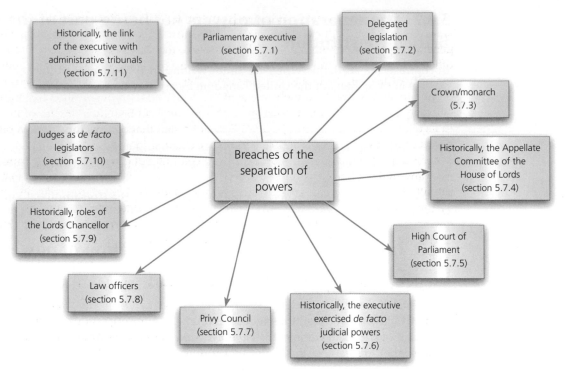

Figure 5.2 Aspects of the British constitution not In accord with the separation of powers

example, in February 2010 HM Government was listed as being comprised of 120 members, 96 of whom were MPs from the House of Commons and 24 peers from the House of Lords (see section 11.6.1).

In terms of personnel, therefore, it is clear there is an overlap between members of the executive and the legislature, with members of the government enjoying both executive and legislative functions. Indeed, Bagehot writing in the nineteenth century noted that:

QUOTATION

'The efficient secret of the English Constitution may be described as the close union, the nearly complete fusion of the executive and legislative powers.'

W Bagehot, *The English Constitution* (Oxford University Press, re-printed 2001), p 11.

The parliamentary executive and accountable government

One clear advantage of a parliamentary executive is that the government is directly accountable and responsible to Parliament, and in fact, this is a major principle of the constitution (see ministerial responsibility at section 12.1). As government ministers are drawn from within Parliament, this provides the opportunity for them to be accountable on a daily basis through the following parliamentary mechanisms:

- written and oral questions (see section 12.4);
- debates (see section 12.5);
- select committees (see section 12.6.2).

In addition, s 2 of the House of Commons Disqualification Act 1975 specifically limits the number of government ministers (ministerial offices) who can sit in the House of Commons to 95 MPs out of a total of 650 MPs. This, at least in constitutional theory, prevents the government from dominating the House of Commons.

Notwithstanding the above, it is certainly the case that in the last few decades the parliamentary executive has generally ensured dynamic government whereby the government has been able to influence heavily the parliamentary legislative programme. A widely perceived difficulty, however, is that due to the electoral system, the government generally speaking (though not at all times – note the May 2010 general election), secures office following a general election with the support of a clear (and sometimes substantial) majority of seats in the House of Commons. This in turn means that the government can dominate the Commons to such an extent that it has led to the suggestion that the balance between the executive and the legislature has swung too heavily in favour of the former. In fact, Lord Hailsham writing in the 1970s suggested that our electoral system produced a government which was akin to an 'elective dictatorship' (see section 9.8).

Although Parliament, in the context of the separation of powers, is the supreme legislative/law-making body, the question has to be asked as to whether in practice Parliament actually legislates or whether it merely legitimises and 'rubber stamps' the Bills initiated by the government of the day. Each year most Bills enacted as Acts of Parliament are government-sponsored Bills. Few Bills which become Acts have been drafted and initiated by members of Parliament themselves acting as parliamentarians (known as Private Members' Bills).

The parliamentary executive and the devolved institutions

It is also worth noting that the devolved institutions in Scotland, Wales and Northern Ireland exhibit a form of a parliamentary executive. For example, in Scotland the Scottish Executive/Government (effectively the Scottish Cabinet) is drawn from the Scottish Parliament (Members of the Scottish Parliament – MSPs).

The position in other countries

The feature of a parliamentary executive is not, of course, restricted to the United Kingdom. The Republic of Ireland with its written, entrenched codified constitution also has a parliamentary executive whereby the Irish government (comprising the Taoiseach and Cabinet ministers) is drawn from, and constitutionally accountable to, the Irish Parliament (the Oireachtas).

In contrast, in the United States the President does not form part of the legislature as it is a presidential system of government with the President sitting separately from Congress. In France, Cabinet ministers do not sit in the French Parliament as Art 23 of the French constitution (Fifth Republic) states that membership of government is incompatible with that of Parliament. Both the United States and France reflect a greater degree of separation of powers between the executive and legislature than the United Kingdom.

ACTIVITY

Self-test question

What do you think are the dangers of having a parliamentary executive, particularly in the context of the British constitution?

5.7.2 Delegated legislation (an overlap involving the executive performing a legislative function)

Introduction

Under the separation of powers, the constitutional function of the legislature is to enact law, and the role of the executive is to execute and apply it. The practice of delegated legislation, however, entrusts a law-making power onto a member of the executive (ie a government minister or a local authority). The process of delegated legislation involves Parliament passing an Act (the 'enabling' or 'parent' Act), which in turn confers a power on a minister to make delegated legislation (also known as secondary/subordinate legislation) which generally takes the form of a Statutory Instrument (see section 12.7.5).

The rationale behind delegated legislation

The rationale behind delegating a legislative power to the executive is partly one of practical necessity. In practice it would be impossible for Parliament to legislate all the details of all the laws that are necessary in a modern society. The general principle governing delegated legislation is that the enabling Act encapsulates the general principles/policies of the legislation, while the secondary legislation – made under the authority of that Act – supplements these general broad principles with detailed provisions. Thus, it fills in the fine details of legislation.

Delegated legislation also has practical uses, as it allows the law to be flexible and responsive, for example updating levels of fines. An example of a local authority enjoying a delegated legislative power to alter local car parking charges was illustrated at section 4.6.1.

Even though there is a widespread view endorsing the practical necessity for the continued use of delegated legislation (although not necessarily in the volume in which it is used), it still represents a violation of the separation of powers. It should also be remembered that the vast majority of domestic legislation which is passed each year is delegated, and so not primary Acts of Parliament.

There are, however, both political and legal controls over the use of this type of legislation.

Parliamentary control of delegated legislation

This is covered at section 12.7.5.

Legal control of delegated legislation

Delegated legislation is also subject to scrutiny and control by the courts. It is a general legal principle that a minister can only pass delegated legislation that is authorised and envisaged by the parent Act. The executive must, therefore, pass legislation which is *intra vires* (within the legal powers conferred by the Act). If the legislation made is outside the powers conferred, and so beyond the purpose for which the delegated power was given, it can be declared *ultra vires* by the courts and invalidated. In this way, the courts minimise the practice of delegated legislation being a violation of the separation of powers. The courts ensure that the executive uses its conferred delegated legislative powers strictly for its envisaged purpose so that it is not abused. It also ensures that parliamentary sovereignty is upheld by ensuring that Parliament's will is not thwarted, for example by a minister passing legislation which had not been specifically envisaged by Parliament. An example of the legal control exercised by the courts over the use of delegated legislation is illustrated by the following case:

CASE EXAMPLE

Chester v Bateson [1920] 1 KB 829

Section 1 of the Defence of the Realm Consolidation Act 1914 conferred the power on the Minister of Munitions to issue regulations (delegated legislation) to prevent the successful prosecution of the war being endangered. Under the Act, the minister issued reg 2A(2) which stated that 'no person shall, without the consent of the Minister of Munitions take ... any proceedings for the purpose of obtaining an order or decree for the recovery of possession of, or for the ejectment of a tenant of, any dwelling house' in which a munitions worker was living.

Chester (a landlord) served on Bateson (a tenant employed in a shell shop) notice of his intention to recover possession of his property as Bateson's tenancy had expired. Bateson challenged this by contending that Chester had not obtained the consent of the minister before commencing proceedings. Chester contended that the Regulation was *ultra vires* the Defence of the Realm Consolidation Act 1914 and the court agreed. The court held that the Regulation effectively prevented the landlord from having access to the courts in order to recover his property without first obtaining the consent of the minister. Avory J stated that:

'In my opinion there is not to be found in the statute [1914 Act] anything to authorise or justify a regulation having that result; and nothing less than express words in the statute taking away the right of the King's subjects of access to the Courts of Justice would authorise or justify it.'

Delegated legislation in other countries

The use of delegated legislation, of course, is not confined to the British constitution. In the Republic of Ireland, for example, although Art 15.2 of the constitution states that only the Oireachtas may create laws, the Irish Parliament does, however, regularly delegate a power to make ministerial orders on government ministers. These legislative instruments are also supervised by the courts.

5.7.3 The Crown/monarch is formally involved in all three branches of government (an overlap of the legislature, executive and judiciary)

In the United Kingdom the term Crown can denote either the government/executive or the monarch. As noted at section 3.4.7, the United Kingdom has a monarchical constitution and the monarch is constitutionally involved (to a greater or lesser extent) in all three functions of government.

The monarch and the legislative function

The Queen is formally part of the legislature (Parliament) and involved in the legislative process as a Bill requires the granting of the Royal Assent in order for it to become an Act of Parliament. In fact, the supreme legislative power in the United Kingdom is technically known as the Queen in Parliament. The role of the monarch is reflected in the enacting formula of a typical public Bill:

SECTION

BE IT ENACTED by the Queen's most Excellent Majesty, by and with the advice and consent of the Lords Spiritual and Temporal, and Commons, in this present Parliament assembled, and by the authority of the same, as follows …

A slightly revised version is used where the Parliament Acts of 1911 and 1949 have been used (see section 10.10.1).

In practical reality, the role of the monarch in the legislative process is a purely formal one as by constitutional convention the monarch will grant her assent to a Bill unless her government ministers advise her not to do so. Similarly, in the Republic of Ireland the Head of State (President of Ireland) signs Bills passed by the Oireachtas to give them the force of law. In the United States, the President signs Bills passed by Congress (although he approves them, he can also veto them).

In addition, as part of the legislature, the Queen opens each new parliamentary session and delivers the 'Queen's Speech' which details the government's proposed legislative programme for the ensuing parliamentary session. By constitutional convention, the speech is, of course, written by the government of the day and represents the Bills which they anticipate will become law.

The monarch and the executive function

The monarch is constitutionally part of the executive as she is the Head of State and the political executive is known as Her Majesty's Government. The monarch appoints the Prime Minister together with other government ministers, although these appointments are in practice a formal process, as they are governed by constitutional convention. Although the monarch will formally appoint government ministers, this is done on the recommendation of the Prime Minister of the day and so the political reality is that it is the latter who actually chooses which individuals will occupy which particular ministerial office. The monarch is also Head of the armed forces and is in fact technically the Commander-in-Chief of the armed forces (the executive in practical terms).

The monarch and the judicial function

The monarch is also formally part of the judiciary in the sense that she is the source and font of all justice (although she does not actually sit in court as a judge: *Prohibitions del Roy* (1607) 12 Co Rep 63). In fact, judicial appointments are made in the name of the Crown (hence 'Her Majesty's Judges' who operate and dispense justice in the 'Royal Courts of Justice'). Although the monarch formally makes these judicial appointments, by constitutional convention, she will act on the basis of ministerial advice. It is of constitutional interest to note that historically the judicial oath of allegiance sworn by judges is *not* to the British constitution or to the people, but instead to the Crown.

5.7.4 The Appellate Committee of the House of Lords

The historical constitutional function of the House of Lords

■ Firstly, the House comprises part of the legislature as it is the upper chamber in Parliament (see Chapter 10). Thus, it plays an integral part in the law-making process.

■ Secondly, the House, or more specifically a committee of the House known as the Appellate Committee of the House of Lords, acted historically as the highest domestic court in the United Kingdom. The judges in the Appellate Committee were technically known as the Lords of Appeal in Ordinary (more commonly referred to as the law lords). In legal theory the law lords could perform two different constitutional functions:

(i) A judicial function – they resolved legal disputes as part of the the Appellate Committee.

(ii) A legislative function – they could engage in debate and vote on proposed legislation during the passage of a Bill in the second chamber.

A new Supreme Court

Part 3 of the Constitutional Reform Act 2005 established a Supreme Court to replace the Appellate Committee of the House of Lords. The purpose of this Act was to bring the British constitution more into line with a stricter separation of powers as the Supreme Court is legally, constitutionally and physically separate from Parliament. The new court became operational in October 2009 and the law lords who were judicially active at this time were transferred to the new court and became Justices of the Supreme Court. These Justices exercise the same powers as the judges of the former Appellate Committee with the exception that they also process 'devolution' issues (see Chapter 14), a function which has been transferred from the Judicial Committee of the Privy Council (see section 5.7.7).

Three additional points should be noted. Firstly, those retired law lords who were not transferred to the new Supreme Court in 2009 still remain in the House of Lords and will continue to sit as crossbenchers (see section 10.7.3). As a result, in 2010 we *still* have judges (albeit retired ones) sitting in the House of Lords. Secondly, the judges that were transferred to the Supreme Court in 2009 can return to the House of Lords on their retirement from the Court. Thirdly, detailed below are the main arguments that were used for and against the removal of the law lords from Parliament and the setting up of a new Supreme Court:

The arguments for the removal of the law lords from Parliament

■ It was part of the government's drive to modernise a constitution which was antiquated in a number of ways.

■ It would realign the constitution in accordance with a purer separation of powers. As noted by the Lord Chancellor:

QUOTATION

'The Law Lords are judges and not legislators: the separation between those two roles should be made explicit. That principle of separation is already established in many other democracies.'
House of Lords Select Committee on the Constitutional Reform Bill, Constitutional Reform Bill (HL)
Volume 2: Evidence, HL Paper 125-II (2004), p 9.

- In this way, separating the judges from Parliament would enhance their independence.
- As a result of other constitutional reforms (in particular, the Human Rights Act 1998), it was important to separate clearly the law lords from Parliament.
- It would be consistent with Art 6 of the European Convention which prescribes a right to a fair trial.
- The self-denying ordinance of the law lords (whereby they would not participate in relation to matters with a 'strong element of party political controversy' (Lord Bingham, *Hansard*, HL Vol 614 Col 419) was no longer sustainable. A complete separation from the legislature would avoid law lords having to 'recuse' themselves from court cases in relation to legislation which they had previously had a role in scrutinising/passing.
- On a pragmatic and practical level, in terms of accommodation, the law lords could be better catered for in a new Supreme Court building specifically equipped for that purpose.

It should be noted that the proposal for a Supreme Court had significant support, including the then senior law lord, Lord Bingham, the Bar, the Law Society and a number of academics. There were, however, a number of arguments levelled against the creation of a new Supreme Court.

The arguments against removal

- As noted by Lord Norton, the law lords were already considered to be independent, therefore separation could hardly 'enhance' their independence (*Hansard*, HL Vol 657, col 1269).
- If the argument for a Supreme Court was based solely on the principle of the separation of powers, it foundered because according to a former law lord (Lord Lloyd): 'the separation of powers is not part of our constitution'. (*Hansard*, HL Vol 665, col 57).

Article 6 of the European Convention does not always require an institutional separation of powers as illustrated by the following case:

CASE EXAMPLE

Pabla Ky v Finland (2006) 42 EHRR 34

In 1997 an MP of the Finnish Parliament acted as an expert member of a panel of the Finnish Court of Appeal which rejected Pabla Ky's appeal concerning a rent contract. Pabla Ky contended that the dual constitutional function of the MP (ie as part of the legislature and the Court of Appeal) violated Art 6 of the European Convention protecting the right to a fair trial before an independent and impartial court.

A chamber of the European Court held by a majority that there had been no violation of Art 6 as the MP in the case had not previously participated in the passing of the legislation which was at issue (Act on Commercial Leases 1993) as he had not been part of Parliament at this time.

The Court stated that:

JUDGMENT

'The Court is not persuaded that the mere fact that the MP was a member of the legislature at the time when he sat on the applicant's appeal is sufficient to raise doubts as to the independence and impartiality of the Court of Appeal. While the applicant relies on the theory of separation of powers, this principle is not decisive in the abstract.' (*sic*)

■ No practical benefit would result from the separation. Instead, the new Supreme Court Justices could become constitutionally isolated without the protection of Parliament. Moreover, not only would the judges lose out on the benefit of working with parliamentarians (eg non-lawyers), but Parliament itself would lose the advantage of the input of their judicial wisdom. It should be noted, however, that both Houses already contain a number of lawyers.

■ The cost would not justify the reform.

It is not without significance that at the time of the 2005 Act, the law lords themselves were roughly divided on the issue (the then senior law lord, Lord Bingham in favour, the then second senior law lord, Lord Nicholls, against it). On the Supreme Court see: M Ryan, 'The House of Lords and the Shaping of the Supreme Court' [2005] 56 NILQ 135.

ACTIVITY

Self-test question

From a constitutional perspective, do you think that the new Supreme Court is necessary?

5.7.5 Parliament exercises functions other than legislative (an overlap involving the legislature performing a judicial function)

The nature of the law and custom of Parliament

Although Parliament is the legislature, it is also responsible for regulating, controlling and disciplining its members which is effectively a judicial function. These parliamentary privileges are unique to the two Houses of Parliament and its members, and are derived from the law and custom of Parliament.

These privileges are regulated by both Houses of Parliament. Each House exercises its own jurisdiction and can punish those individuals who disregard its rules or who commit a contempt of Parliament, for example obstructing Parliament in its functions. This can include interfering with a witness or a Member of Parliament.

The High Court of Parliament

In these circumstances each House of Parliament acts as a constituent part of the High Court of Parliament, thereby performing a judicial function. In 2003, for instance, the House of Commons temporarily suspended an **MP** for breaching parliamentary rules. In effect, Parliament acts as a self-regulating body and the 'ordinary' courts exercise no jurisdiction over these matters. More recently, in 2009, the House of Lords suspended two peers until the end of the parliamentary session.

MP
a member of Parliament, specifically in the House of Commons

Parliamentary law in other countries

The notion that the legislature regulates its own composition and proceedings is not confined to the United Kingdom. For example, in the Republic of Ireland, Art 15.10 of the constitution expressly authorises the two Houses of the Oireachtas to decide their own rules in terms of the rights of the Houses and their members. Further, if these rules are violated, each House may impose penalties.

5.7.6 Historically, the executive has exercised a judicial function (an overlap involving the executive performing a judicial function)

Ministers have, historically, been given powers which were, in effect, judicial in nature. For example, under s 35 of the Criminal Justice Act 1991 Parliament conferred a power on the Home Secretary to determine the period of imprisonment (the 'tariff') to be served by discretionary life prisoners. The constitutional rationale behind this power was that the Home Secretary had a general responsibility for public order and maintaining public confidence in the criminal justice system. The use of this power, however, was controlled legally by the courts in judicial review proceedings (see Chapters 19 and 20) as illustrated by the following case:

CASE EXAMPLE

R v Secretary of State for the Home Dept, ex parte Venables and Thompson [1997] 3 All ER 97

Venables and Thompson were convicted of the murder of two-year-old James Bulger. The trial judge stated that in his view the minimum period of detention necessary to satisfy retribution and deterrence was a tariff of eight years. The Lord Chief Justice advised a tariff of 10 years, but the Home Secretary, in exercising his powers under s 35 of the Criminal Justice Act 1991, imposed 15 years. In reaching this decision the Home Secretary indicated that he had had regard for the public concern regarding this case. A public petition including 278,300 signatures, over 5,000 letters and 20,000 'coupons' from a newspaper had demanded that Venables and Thompson should be detained for life.

Venables and Thompson challenged the use of the Home Secretary's discretion and the House of Lords held, *inter alia*, that he had acted unlawfully as he had misdirected himself by giving weight to irrelevant considerations (namely, the public protest directed to the detriment of these two particular individuals). Lord Steyn stated that:

JUDGMENT

'In fixing a tariff the Home Secretary is carrying out, contrary to the constitutional principle of the separation of powers, a classic judicial function … the power to fix a tariff is nevertheless equivalent to a judge's sentencing power. Parliament must be assumed to have entrusted the power to the Home Secretary on the supposition that, like a sentencing judge, the Home Secretary would not act contrary to fundamental principles governing the administration of justice.'

Thus, as the Home Secretary was exercising a sentencing power (a judicial function) he was required to remain detached from the pressures of public opinion. As a postscript to the *Venables* case, Venables and Thompson subsequently petitioned the European Court of Human Rights (*V & T v UK* (2000) 30 EHRR 121) and successfully contended that their right to a fair trial under Art 6 had been breached. In brief, the setting of the tariff (which was tantamount to a judicial sentence) had not been performed by an independent and impartial figure, as the Home Secretary was part of the executive. After this European ruling, Parliament enacted s 60 of the Criminal Justice and Courts Services Act 2000 which now requires that the tariff (now known as the minimum term) to be served by young offenders is to be determined by the trial judge. As a result, this realigned the British constitution more in accord with a stricter separation of powers. Similarly, see also *R (Anderson) v Secretary of State* (2002) at section 13.2.1, which resulted in further reforms of the *de facto* judicial powers of the Home Secretary.

5.7.7 The Privy Council (an overlap involving the executive performing legislative and judicial functions)

The Privy Council (which is part of central government and so part of the executive today) historically has acted as the chief advisory body to the monarch. Its importance, in modern times, however, has been superseded by the development of the Cabinet. In fact, the Privy Council has been described as:

> 'today little more than an organ for giving formal effect to certain acts done under prerogative or statutory powers'.
>
> O Hood Phillips, P Jackson and P Leopold, *Constitutional and Administrative Law*
> (8th edn, Sweet & Maxwell, 2001), p 334.

The Privy Council numbers over 500 members (ie Privy Councillors) who comprise individuals of high rank. It includes, among others, the following:

- The Prime Minister.
- Cabinet ministers.
- The Leader of the Opposition.
- Senior judges (both from the United Kingdom and the Commonwealth).
- Other senior public figures.

The Lord President of the Council is the ministerial head of the Privy Council Office. Meetings of the Privy Council normally comprise:

- Meetings involving the monarch together with (typically) four selected Cabinet ministers (Her Majesty in Council) at which formal validity will be given to instruments/orders previously agreed at a Cabinet meeting.
- Meetings without the monarch (a Committee of the Privy Council).

The role of the Privy Council is to advise the Queen in carrying out her responsibilities as monarch. These responsibilities and acts comprise Orders in Council or proclamations. The latter are used, for example, to dissolve Parliament prior to a general election.

The Privy Council can make orders, known as Orders in Council, which comprise:

- Statutory Orders in Council (a form of delegated legislation) – where the power to make the order has been delegated by statute onto Her Majesty. By constitutional convention she acts on the advice of her ministers.
- Non-statutory Orders in Council – derived from the common law royal prerogative. Such orders (historically) have been used to regulate the **Civil Service** (see the GCHQ case at section 11.9.6).

As pointed out by Hood Phillips, the nature of an Order in Council can be legislative, executive or judicial.

In addition to the above, one committee of the Privy Council has a judicial function: the Judicial Committee of the Privy Council. This was established under the Judicial Committee Act 1833 and acts as the final court of appeal for various Commonwealth countries (for example, in relation to Belize, see *Meerabux v Attorney General* (2005) at section 13.4.2), together with a domestic jurisdiction hearing appeals from Guernsey, Jersey and the Isle of Man. In addition, up until 2009 the Privy Council also heard 'internal' devolution cases (for example, whether the Scottish Parliament had exceeded its legal powers under the Scotland Act 1998 – see Chapter 14), but this responsibility has now been passed to the new Supreme Court. The judges staffing the Judicial Committee comprise the Justices of the new Supreme Court (although other senior judges may sit as well).

5.7.8 The law officers (an overlap involving members of the executive/government sitting in the legislature and performing a quasi-judicial function)

The Attorney General and Solicitor General are members of the government, but not the Cabinet (although the Attorney General can attend the Cabinet when the agenda contains their responsibilities).

Civil Service
the personnel who carry out and implement policies as determined by government ministers

The Solicitor General acts as the deputy to the Attorney General. These law officers are chosen from MPs or peers and so are part of the legislature (they therefore form part of the parliamentary executive). In February 2010, the Attorney General was drawn from the House of Lords (Baroness Scotland) and the Solicitor General from the House of Commons (Vera Baird). The Attorney General has three broad roles. Firstly, as a minister she is responsible for superintending a number of bodies which include the Crown Prosecution Service and Serious Fraud Office and in line with the convention of ministerial responsibility, she is accountable to Parliament for them. Secondly, she is the legal adviser to the Crown (ie the government) and sometimes Parliament itself and is the Crown's representative in court. Thirdly, as an independent officer of the Crown the Attorney General has the function of acting as the *guardian of the public interest*. In this context she should act *independently of the government* and not take instructions from it. In short, the Attorney General has a number of different responsibilities and as noted by Bradley and Ewing:

QUOTATION

'The law officers of the Crown (in particular the Attorney General in England and the Lord Advocate in Scotland) have duties of enforcing the criminal law which are sometimes described as 'quasi-judicial'; it must be emphasised that the law officers are members of the executive and are not judges.'

A Bradley and K Ewing, *Constitutional and Administrative Law*, (14th edn, Pearson/Longman, 2007) p 89.

In terms of recent reforms of the Attorney General, the government consulted on this issue (*A Consultation on the Role of the Attorney General*, Cm 7192 (2007)) and thereafter included some reform proposals as part of Pt 2 of the Draft Constitutional Renewal Bill (Cm 7342-II (2008)). However, in July 2009 the then Lord Chancellor, in a ministerial statement, made the following point:

QUOTATION

'In the event, the significant, necessary reforms to the role of Attorney General are being achieved without the need for legislation. For example, the Attorney has reached a new settlement with the Directors of Public Prosecutions, the Serious Fraud Office and Revenue and Customs Prosecutions to improve relationships, guarantee prosecutorial independence while ensuring an appropriate degree of accountability and to improve transparency about the relationship, as reflected in the new protocol setting out the respective responsibilities of the Attorney and the Directors. This builds on the Prime Minister's statement in July 2007, that the Attorney General has herself decided, except if the law or national security requires it, not to make key prosecution decisions in individual criminal cases. Furthermore, the new protocol makes it clear that the Attorney General will not be consulted in any case which concerns an MP or peer or where there is a personal or professional conflict of interest, other than where her decision is required by law. This protocol will be published by the Attorney very shortly. Furthermore, the Attorney General now only attends Cabinet when matters affecting her responsibilities are on the agenda.'

Hansard, HC Vol 496, col 106 WS.

5.7.9 The Lord Chancellor (historically, an overlap of the legislature, executive and judiciary)

The office of the Lord Chancellor has traditionally been cited as a classic example of the way in which the United Kingdom violates the separation of powers as he formed part of all three state institutions. His main historical responsibilities in relation to each institution are detailed below:

The legislature

The Lord Chancellor sat in the upper chamber as the impartial *ex officio* Speaker of the House of Lords and presided over the House. This role encompassed a number of ceremonial roles (eg the state opening of Parliament). He also exercised a limited power to keep order within the chamber and represented the House both domestically and internationally.

The executive

As a minister of the Crown, the Lord Chancellor was a senior member of the Cabinet and head of a major government department: the Lord Chancellor's Department. In June 2003 this department was replaced with the Department for Constitutional Affairs which had responsibility for, *inter alia*, the administration of legal aid. The Lord Chancellor was also a spokesman for the government in the House of Lords.

The judiciary

The Lord Chancellor could sit as a senior judge in the Court of Appeal, the Privy Council or the Appellate Committee of the House of Lords. This judicial function was governed and regulated by a constitutional convention that the Lord Chancellor would not sit in clearly political cases or those in which the government was a party. The Lord Chancellor was also Head of the Judiciary in England and Wales and President of the Supreme Court of Judicature (the historic collective term for the Court of Appeal, High Court and Crown Court and not to be confused with the new Supreme Court under the Constitutional Reform Act 2005). In respect of the judiciary, the Lord Chancellor was also involved in the appointment of a wide range of judicial posts. For example, in respect of the law lords, by constitutional convention the Prime Minister would consult him on suitable candidates (these appointments would then be formally appointed by the monarch). Further, the Lord Chancellor was responsible for processing complaints against judges and administering judicial discipline.

ACTIVITY

Self-test question

What do you think were the dangers of the Lord Chancellor exercising all three functions indicated above?

Changes to the office of the Lord Chancellor made by the Constitutional Reform Act 2005

In June 2003, in pursuance of modernising the constitution and realigning it with the separation of powers, the government announced the abolition of the office of the Lord Chancellor. Simultaneously, the post of Secretary of State for Constitutional Affairs was established which it was envisaged would eventually supersede the office of the Lord Chancellor. However, the Constitutional Reform Bill proved to be highly contentious in the House of Lords and was amended so as to retain, and so merely modify, the office of the Lord Chancellor, rather than abolish the post outright. This explained the subsequent adoption of the dual title of *Secretary of State for Constitutional Affairs and Lord Chancellor* (in 2010 now called *the Secretary of State for Justice and Lord Chancellor*). In essence, the changes effected by the Act in respect of the Lord Chancellor are as follows:

The legislature

■ The Speaker of the House of Lords

In the context of reforming the office of the Lord Chancellor, it was necessary to reform his position as Speaker of the House of Lords. For one thing, s 2 of the Constitutional Reform Act 2005 made it clear that a future Lord Chancellor may not even be a peer (it had been a longstanding constitutional convention that he sat in the upper chamber). In 2006 the House of Lords agreed to the Report of the Select Committee on the Speakership of the House (First Report, HL Paper 92 (2005)). This report recommended that the House elect a Speaker for five years to replace the Lord Chancellor. In July 2006 the House elected Baroness Hayman as Lord Speaker.

The Lord Chancellor as a peer

One issue raised by the Constitutional Reform Bill was whether a future Lord Chancellor/Secretary of State for Constitutional Affairs should continue to be drawn exclusively from the House of Lords. The House of Lords attempted to amend the Bill by codifying the constitutional convention that the Lord Chancellor should be a peer and therefore be unable to sit in the House of Commons. In the end, a compromise was reached between the government and the House of Lords with the effect that s 2 of the Act states that a person cannot be recommended for appointment by the Prime Minister as Lord Chancellor unless he was qualified by experience which could include, for example, experience as a member of either House. As a result, a future Lord Chancellor may not necessarily be drawn from the second chamber. Indeed, in June 2007 Jack Straw MP was appointed as Lord Chancellor and Secretary of State for Justice (in 2010 he was replaced by Kenneth Clarke MP).

The executive

The Lord Chancellor as a government minister

The Lord Chancellor/Secretary of State will continue to act as a minister and head a government department (in 2010 this was the Ministry of Justice which replaced, in 2007, the Department for Constitutional Affairs) with responsibility for, *inter alia*, the justice system. He will inevitably continue to form part of the Cabinet, however, with a dilution of his responsibilities it remains to be seen how senior a figure he will be viewed as in future. Indeed, his constitutional responsibilities within the Cabinet will continue to include protecting the independence of the judiciary and ensuring that the principles underpinning the rule of law are not infringed by the government's legislative proposals. In this context, s 17 of the Act sets out the oath to be sworn by the Lord Chancellor:

SECTION

'I will respect the rule of law, defend the independence of the judiciary and discharge my duty to ensure the provision of resources for the efficient and effective support of the courts for which I am responsible.'

The Lord Chancellor/Secretary of State's position as a government minister (and so part of the parliamentary executive) will therefore *still* represent a breach of the separation of powers.

The judiciary

The appointment of judges

In the event of a vacancy in England and Wales, since April 2006 the new statutory Judicial Appointments Commission (established under the Act) presents a candidate to the Lord Chancellor who can then accept, reject or require a reconsideration. Although the Act reduces the discretion of the Lord Chancellor in making judicial appointments, it still retains him as part of the process (on whether the executive should be involved in judicial appointments see section 13.3).

The Lord Chancellor as a judge

In terms of sitting as a judge, even before the Constitutional Reform Bill had been introduced into Parliament, the then Lord Chancellor, Lord Falconer, had already announced in the government's September 2003 consultation paper on the reform of the Lord Chancellor, that he did not intend to sit as a judge as:

QUOTATION

'It can no longer be appropriate for a senior judge to sit in Cabinet or for a Government Minister to be our country's senior judge. I have myself made it clear that I shall not sit judicially.'

Constitutional reform: reforming the office of the Lord Chancellor CP 13/03 (2003), pp 5–6.

The Act now prohibits the office-holder of the Lord Chancellor from holding judicial office.

■ The Head of the Judiciary

The Lord Chief Justice has now assumed the office of the President of the Courts of England and Wales and is the Head of the Judiciary of England and Wales. Notwithstanding this, under s 3 of the Act the Lord Chancellor has a statutory obligation to 'uphold the continued independence of the judiciary' (see section 13.4.1)

ACTIVITY

Essay writing

Compare and contrast the legislative, executive and judicial roles exercised by the Lord Chancellor before and after the enactment of the Constitutional Reform Act 2005.

5.7.10 Judges as legislators (an overlap involving the judiciary performing a legislative function)

In the British constitution the judicial function involves:

■ resolving legal disputes
■ determining the law laid down in (a) statutes and (b) the common law and
■ providing relevant remedies.

This necessarily raises the question of where the constitutional line exists between the act of interpreting and the act of legislating, and whether the courts ever exercise a *de facto* legislative function.

The interpretation of statutes

In interpreting statutes, the constitutional role of the courts is to ascertain the intention of Parliament when it passes legislation. The obvious difficulty is that words may have a variety of different possible meanings, and in order to circumscribe the role of the courts when determining the meaning of legislative provisions, the judiciary have developed a number of self-limiting principles of statutory interpretation which assist them. For example, the literal rule requires judges to give words their ordinary and natural meaning.

In addition, judges will construe unclear ambiguous legislation in the light of certain constitutional principles such as the right of access to the courts. These constitutional presumptions are, of course, judicial creations and determined by the judiciary themselves. For instance, in *Chester v Bateson* at section 5.7.2, Avory J made it clear that nothing less than express words in the Defence of the Realm Consolidation Act 1914 would justify a regulation passed under it which denied a person access to the courts and the administration of justice.

The common law

The common law involves the courts declaring points of law in the context of cases that come before them for their resolution. The gradual development of the common law (which is achieved by the courts making decisions in the context of case law) necessarily permits a degree of flexibility in allowing common law principles to develop and adapt to changing circumstances (social or moral). This is illustrated particularly in the context of the private law of negligence which has progressively developed during the twentieth century.

In *Duport Steels Ltd and Others v Sirs and Others* [1980] 1 All ER 529 Lord Scarman noted that in the context of the common law and equity, society had permitted the judges 'to formulate and develop the law'. Furthermore, in *Malone v Metropolitan Police Commissioner* [1979] Ch 344 Sir Robert Megarry VC made it clear that at times judges do legislate, albeit only interstitially, and he specifically distinguished between 'The extension of the existing laws and principles' and the creation of wholly new rights, for example in the instant case, a tort of privacy (see section 6.7.9). In short, it is Parliament's role to create such new rights.

In the context of judges and the legislative function, it is pertinent to repeat the point that Dicey made a century ago:

QUOTATION

'A large proportion of English law is in reality made by our judges … the adhesion by our judges to precedent, that is, their habit of deciding one case in accordance with the principle, or supposed principle, which governed a former case, leads inevitably to the gradual formation by the courts of fixed rules for decision, which are in effect laws.'

A Dicey, *Introduction to the Study of the Law of the Constitution* (10th edn, Macmillan, 1959), p 60.

Moreover in 1966 Lord Gardiner issued on behalf of the law lords the following seminal practice statement which enabled the House of Lords to depart from its previous decisions (*Practice Statement* [1966] 1 WLR 1234):

JUDGMENT

'Their Lordships nevertheless recognise that too rigid adherence to precedent may lead to injustice in a particular case and also unduly restrict the proper development of the law. They propose, therefore, to modify their present practice and, while treating former decisions of this House as normally binding, to depart from a previous decision when it appears right to do so.'

Also, some judges perform a legislative function when they make rules of procedure, practice rules and directions for the courts to follow. For example, s 45 of the Constitutional Reform Act 2005 confers a power on the President of the Supreme Court to make Supreme Court Rules which will govern the practice and procedure to be followed in court.

Do judges make law?
In general terms as to whether the judges perform a legislative/law-making function, Barnett has argued that:

QUOTATION

'It is artificial to deny that judges "make law". Every new meaning conferred on a word, every application of a rule to a new situation, whether by way of statutory interpretation or under common law, "creates" new law. Judges have themselves abandoned the fiction of the "declaratory theory" which asserts that they do not "make" law, but merely discover its true meaning. From the separation of powers perspective, judicial law-making should cause disquiet only if judges display overtly dynamic law-making tendencies.'

H Barnett, *Constitutional and Administrative Law* (7th edn, Routledge–Cavendish, 2009), p 89.

An interesting example of the judiciary effectively 'making' the law is illustrated by the following case.

CASE EXAMPLE

R v R [1992] 1 AC 599

In this case the House of Lords set aside the long-standing common law rule that a husband could not rape his wife. Even though this historic rule was viewed as anachronistic, the ruling nevertheless represents a *de facto* use of law making power. In constitutional terms, the process must necessarily be seen as *de facto* legislative, with the courts developing/creating the law.

Judicial law-making outside the United Kingdom

It should be noted that the notion that judges are *de facto* lawmakers is not confined to the British constitution. For example, it is also illustrated in the following judicial decision in the context of the United States constitution:

CASE EXAMPLE

Marbury v Madison (1803) 1 Cranch 137

In this case, the United States Supreme Court enunciated a major principle underpinning the American constitution by declaring that the Supreme Court had the constitutional power to declare an Act of Congress to be unconstitutional (and so invalid) where it was repugnant to the written constitution. This case illustrates the powerful position of the judiciary in relation to a constitution, as the power to declare congressional legislation legally unconstitutional had not been specifically and expressly stated in the text of the constitution, but instead had been deemed implicit by the Supreme Court.

Similarly, in the context of the European Union, the European Court of Justice in Luxembourg has developed fundamental principles of European law which have not been expressly or explicitly spelt out in the original 1957 Treaty of Rome. For example, neither of the following principles were expressly written in the text of the Treaty, but were nevertheless deemed implicit:

■ The principle of direct effect which conferred European Union law rights on individuals which could be enforced in the domestic courts of Member States.
■ The principle of the primacy of European Union law which required that where European law and domestic law were inconsistent, the former must prevail.

ACTIVITY

Essay writing

To what extent do judges ever perform a legislative function and what are the constitutional implications of this?

5.7.11 Administrative tribunals (historically having a link with the executive)

Many legal disputes that an individual will have with the state will be resolved not by the ordinary courts of law, but instead by an administrative tribunal. These tribunals act in a judicial manner and apply law to the facts before them. Historically, in terms of the principle of the separation of powers, there has been concern expressed that these bodies were effectively associated with the administration over which they were adjudicating. However, in 2006 the independence of tribunals was enhanced by removing them from their associated and sponsoring parent government department and transferring them to the new Tribunals Service (see section 21.1.3).

Aspects of the British constitution which infringe the separation of powers

The following aspects of the British constitution are infringements of the separation of powers:

- The parliamentary executive whereby the executive is drawn from the legislature. Although this allows government ministers to be accountable directly to Parliament, there has been concern that this overlap permits the executive to control the legislature.

- The practice of delegated legislation entrusts a law-making power onto a member of the executive. In constitutional theory it is controlled by both parliamentary and legal means.

- The monarch is constitutionally involved (albeit formally) in all three functions of government.

- Parliament exercises functions other than legislative as it can act as the High Court of Parliament.

- The Privy Council is an executive body which has legislative and judicial functions.

- The Attorney General is part of the government (ie the parliamentary executive) and has a quasi-judicial function.

- The judges inevitably perform a *de facto* legislative function in interpreting statutory provisions and developing common law principles.

Historically, the following aspects of the British Constitution were violations of the separation of powers but have now been subject to recent reform:

- The Appellate Committee of the House of Lords has been replaced by a new Supreme Court.

- Although historically the Home Secretary exercised *de facto* judicial powers in relation to sentencing, legislation has subsequently reformed this overlap.

- The Lord Chancellor historically has been involved in all three functions, but the Constitutional Reform Act 2005 has reformed this overlap (although the Lord Chancellor will *still* form part of the parliamentary executive – see above).

- Historically, concern has been expressed at the link between the executive and administrative tribunals; however, recent reforms have enhanced the independence of tribunals.

5.8 Aspects of the British constitution in accord with the separation of powers

5.8.1 Introduction

Although the above examples indicate the ways in which the United Kingdom infringes the doctrine of the separation of powers, these violations may be driven by practical considerations (eg delegated legislation and judges making practice rules). In any event, the breaches of the separation of powers may well be governed by constitutional conventions. For example we have already noted the following:

- The parliamentary executive (see section 5.7.1) – although government ministers are drawn from Parliament, they are governed by the conventions of collective and individual ministerial responsibility.
- The role of the monarch (see section 5.7.3) – although the monarch is involved in all three state institutions, these are largely formal overlaps as she is governed by convention (eg in respect of the Royal Assent).

The existence of these constitutional conventions, therefore, serves to mitigate the fact that there is a notional or apparent breach of the separation of powers.

5.8.2 The existence of three state institutions

It is also clear that (at least descriptively) it is possible to identify the three state institutions in the British constitution as follows:

- The legislature (the United Kingdom Parliament).
- The executive (the United Kingdom government comprising the Prime Minister, government ministers, government departments, civil servants together with local authorities).
- The judiciary (the judges in the various different jurisdictions of the United Kingdom).

It is also worth noting that in terms of dividing state power:

- The legislative branch is divided into two chambers (the House of Commons and the House of Lords). Parliament, therefore, does not necessarily act as a single cohesive force (see section 10.12).
- The executive branch is divided into central and local government. As indicated earlier, there can be tension and conflict between these two branches of the executive.

Both of the above divisions ensure that there are competing power sources within the legislative and executive state institutions.

- The judicial branch of state is divided into a formal hierarchical court structure and a system of tribunals.

The following examples illustrate how the British constitution, to varying degrees, respects the doctrine of the separation of powers (whether a pure or weaker version of the principle):

5.8.3 The legislature and judiciary

- **Historically there has been no judicial review of parliamentary legislation**
  Parliamentary sovereignty is the foundation of the British constitution with the result that the courts (at least historically) could not strike down an Act of Parliament. This respects the pure doctrine of the separation of powers with the courts recognising the constitutional function of Parliament which is to enact primary legislation (Parliament is, of course, democratically elected). The role of the courts, accordingly, is simply to interpret Acts of Parliament and not to question or challenge them (but now see the impact of European Union law at section 15.6).

  In countries such as the United States and the Republic of Ireland, however, their respective Supreme Courts can invalidate legislation passed by the legislature (as part of the checks and balances of the separation of powers and the constitution). In contrast, France exhibits a purer separation of powers as the French courts lack the constitutional authority to judicially review legislation passed by the French Parliament. However, the French Constitutional Council can consider the 'constitutionality' of legislation before it becomes law. If such a measure is declared 'unconstitutional' (as being contrary to the constitution) it cannot be promulgated.

- **The *sub judice* resolution**

  sub judice
  the principle that there should be no discussion of matters proceeding through the courts

  Parliament recognises the respective constitutional roles of the court and the legislature through the use of the *sub judice* resolution. This prohibits parliamentary members commenting on 'live' or pending cases before the courts. This rule protects the role of the judiciary in carrying out its judicial business free from interference (see section 13.4.3).

- **Parliamentary criticism of the judiciary**
  By parliamentary practice, parliamentary members refrain from criticism of individual judges except on a substantive motion supporting an address to remove them. This prevents interference with the judicial function.

- **Internal parliamentary proceedings**
  The judiciary will refrain from trespassing upon the constitutional province of Parliament in respect of the law and custom of Parliament. For example, they will refuse to

investigate the internal proceedings of Parliament, even if specifically invited to do so in litigation. In *British Railways Board v Pickin* [1974] AC 765 the House of Lords held that if it is alleged that Parliament had been 'deceived' into passing a particular piece of legislation, then this is a matter for Parliament to rectify, and not the courts (see sections 7.8.1 and 8.7.2).

■ Judicial appointments

There is a degree of separation between the legislature and the judiciary in that the former has no part to play in the appointment of judges, although Parliament can remove the senior judiciary (see section 13.4.1). In contrast, in the United States putative Justices of the Supreme Court have to undergo a congressional hearing before the Senate (the upper chamber in Congress), who are required to approve these appointments. For example, in 2009 the Senate confirmed the appointment of Justice Sotomayor.

■ Judicial disqualification

Section 1 of the House of Commons Disqualification Act 1975 prohibits full-time members of the judiciary from sitting in the House of Commons, thereby achieving a degree of separation between the judiciary and the legislature.

■ The new Supreme Court

As noted at section 5.7.4, historically the law lords formed part of the legislature; however, the Constitutional Reform Act 2005 transferred the serving law lords in 2009 to a new Supreme Court which is constitutionally, practically and legally separate from Parliament. This brought the British Constitution more into line with a stricter separation of powers.

■ Statutory interpretation

In terms of interpreting legislation, the courts have consistently reiterated the constitutional role of the judge in relation to statute law. This is illustrated by the House of Lords in the following case, where they effectively rebuked the Court of Appeal in terms of how they had interpreted a statutory provision:

CASE EXAMPLE

Duport Steels Ltd and Others v Sirs and Others [1980] 1 All ER 529

The case concerned the very restrictive interpretation which the Court of Appeal had given to s 13 of the Trade Union Labour Relations Acts 1974 (as amended in 1976) which, in effect, conferred an immunity in tort in respect of acts done by a person in contemplation or furtherance of a trade dispute.

On 2nd January 1980 the Iron and Steel Trades Confederation (ISTC) called a strike of its members employed by the British Steel Corporation with which it was in dispute concerning wage rates for 1980. In an effort to exert pressure on the government to provide British Steel with extra public funds so that it could make a more acceptable offer to ISTC, by 17th January the latter had resolved to extend the strike to its union members in the private sector of the steel industry.

Duport Steels Ltd together with other private companies sought injunctions against Sirs (general secretary of ISTC) and others against inducing private employees to break their contracts of employment and come out on strike. Although at first instance the injunctions were refused, they were granted by the Court of Appeal on the basis that the dispute on 17th January was a second dispute, this time involving the government, and therefore did not fall within a trade dispute (as the government was not an employer). The court also considered the injustice to employers and workers in the private sector and the economic consequences for the country as a whole of the extension of the strike.

The House of Lords, however, reversed this decision and stated that the test was subjective in that, provided Sirs and others honestly believed at the time that their action might help one of the parties to the trade dispute achieve their objectives, then they would be entitled to immunity in tort under s 13. The action of Sirs and others, therefore, had been taken in furtherance of the trade dispute with British Steel. Lord Diplock reaffirmed that the role of the courts in relation to statutory provisions was to give effect to the words that Parliament had approved:

JUDGMENT

'Where the meaning of the statutory words is plain and unambiguous it is not for the judges to invent fancied ambiguities as an excuse for failing to give effect to its plain meaning because they themselves consider that the consequences of doing so would be inexpedient, or even unjust or immoral. In controversial matters such as are involved in industrial relations there is room for differences of opinion as to what is expedient, what is just and what is morally justifiable. Under our Constitution it is Parliament's opinion on these matters that is paramount.'

Similarly, Lord Scarman noted that his criticism of the Court of Appeal was:

JUDGMENT

'... that in their desire to do justice the court failed to do justice according to law'.

More recently the retired judge Lord Carswell commented that:

QUOTATION

'The judges have had the job of trying to apply legislation conscientiously and, according to my own observations and practice, they have tried to observe that as faithfully as possible. The judges' own opinions of the legislation are irrelevant and are left out of account. They take the law as enacted by Parliament and apply it, whatever they think of it and whether they think it is good or bad.'

Hansard, HL Vol 716, col 1566.

It should also be pointed out that under s 3 of the Human Rights Act 1998, all courts and tribunals are now required to interpret all legislation in line with the rights detailed in the European Convention on Human Rights where it is possible to do so. It is clearly the case that this statutory obligation has inevitably given the judges a more dynamic approach to statutory interpretation. Nevertheless, Lord Woolf CJ in *Poplar Housing and Regeneration Community Association Ltd v Donoghue* [2001] EWCA Civ 595 made it very clear that the constitutional role of the judiciary in relation to the Human Rights Act 1998 (and the constitution in general) was to interpret legislation and not to legislate:

JUDGMENT

'It is difficult to overestimate the importance of s 3 ... When the court interprets legislation usually its primary task is to identify the intention of Parliament. Now, when s 3 applies, the courts have to adjust their traditional role in relation to interpretation so as to give effect to the direction contained in s 3 ... [but] ... s 3 does not entitle the court to *legislate* (its task is still one of *interpretation*, but interpretation in accordance with the direction in s 3).'

A case, however, in which the House of Lords arguably crossed the line between interpreting and legislating was in *R v A (Complainant's sexual history)* [2001] UKHL 25 (see section 17.6.1).

Aspects of the British constitution in accord with the separation of powers (legislature & judiciary)

The following aspects of the British constitution are in accord with the principles underpinning the separation of powers (a pure version or otherwise) in respect of the legislature and judiciary:

- The *sub judice* resolution ensures that Parliament does not interfere with the constitutional role of the court which is to resolve cases free from influence or interference.
- By parliamentary practice, parliamentary members refrain from criticising individual judges, as this could undermine their perceived independence.
- The courts do not interfere with the internal proceedings of Parliament.
- Parliament is not involved in the appointment of judges.
- Full-time judges are precluded from sitting in the House of Commons.
- In 2009 under the Constitutional Reform Act 2005, the judicially active law lords were removed from Parliament and reconstituted in a separate Supreme Court.
- The judges have consistently reiterated their limited constitutional role in respect of interpreting statutory provisions.

5.8.4 The judiciary and executive

◼ Judicial independence of the executive

It is a fundamental constitutional principle that the judiciary must remain independent of the executive. Indeed, s 3 of the Constitutional Reform Act 2005 specifically requires ministers of the Crown to uphold **judicial independence** and prohibits them from having special access to the judiciary. Moreover, the Act put on a statutory footing the *concordat* which had been agreed between the Lord Chief Justice and the Lord Chancellor. The *concordat* spelt out the constitutional relationship (and demarcated the boundaries) between the executive and the judicial arms of the state.

judicial independence
the principle that judges are independent of the other arms of the state

◼ Executive criticism of judges

By constitutional convention, members of the executive do not criticise decisions of judges. According to Sir Ivor Judge in his evidence to a Select Committee, in the event of a government minister's department receiving an adverse judgment in the Administrative Court:

QUOTATION

'… commenting on the judge seems to me to be completely unacceptable, but of course the Minister is allowed to say "we disagree with the judge's position and we intend to appeal"'.

House of Lords Select Committee on the Constitution, '*Relations Between the Executive, the Judiciary and Parliament*, HL Paper 115 (The Stationery Office, 2007), Q 284.

◼ The removal of senior judges

Senior judges are not removable by the government of the day, but instead by Parliament. This means that the executive cannot simply remove a judge who has proved to be troublesome for the government in court.

◼ Judicial review (adhering to the separation of powers?)

Judicial review involves the courts reviewing the actions of the executive to ensure that ministers/executive officials act lawfully and strictly with their legal powers when they, for example:

◼ Enact delegated legislation.
◼ Make a public law decision.
◼ Exercise a public law discretion.

In constitutional terms, on the one hand, judicial review could be seen as a violation of a pure separation of powers as the judiciary is effectively interfering with the actions of another state institution: the executive. Conversely, on the other hand, the process of judicial review could be viewed as part of a modified version of the separation of powers, with the courts checking and balancing the executive, thereby avoiding an abuse of executive power.

In the United Kingdom, the courts are conscious of their constitutional position in supervising the activities of the executive. For instance, in the context of an alleged abuse of power by a local authority in respect of how it exercised a particular public law discretion (eg in terms of the allocation of financial resources), the judges will act with restraint in ensuring that they do not substitute their judicial view of how a particular public law discretion should have been exercised with that of the local authority. Instead, they ensure that the discretion exercised was within the legal limits of the local authority. Judicial review is essentially a procedural mechanism which is aimed at the decision-making process, rather than the decision itself *per se* (see section 19.2.2).

In the context of the relationship between the separation of powers and judicial review, Craig has noted that the concept of the separation of powers:

QUOTATION

'operates as a source of judicial legitimacy, with the courts defending their role as the rightful interpreters of legislation, and of the legality of executive action. It serves also as the foundation for judicial restraint, with the courts being mindful of not substituting their view on matters of discretion for that of the body to whom Parliament has granted the power.'

P Craig 'Fundamental Principles of Administrative Law in Relation to Basic Principles of Constitutional Law' in D Feldman (ed), *English Public Law* (2nd edn, Oxford University Press, 2009), p 608.

■ The reform of the Lord Chancellor

As indicated earlier, under the Constitutional Reform Act 2005 the Lord Chancellor is no longer the Head of the judiciary in England and Wales and shares the administering of judicial discipline with the Lord Chief Justice (with the latter able to give, for example, a formal warning to a judicial holder – with the agreement of the Lord Chancellor). Moreover, the Lord Chancellor no longer sits as a judge, thereby making a clearer separation between the judiciary and the Lord Chancellor (who still remains a member of the political executive).

KEY FACTS

Aspects of the British constitution in accord with the separation of powers (executive & judiciary)
The following aspects of the British constitution are in accord with the principles underpinning the separation of powers (a pure version or otherwise) in respect of the executive and judiciary: • Section 3 of the Constitutional Reform Act 2005 specifically requires ministers of the Crown to uphold judicial independence and prohibits them from having special access to the judiciary. • By constitutional convention, members of the executive do not criticise decisions of judges. • The senior judiciary are protected from removal by the executive/government. • The process of judicial review could be viewed as part of a modified version of the separation of powers, with the courts checking and balancing the executive, thereby avoiding an abuse of executive power. • The Lord Chancellor's historic judicial functions have been reformed under the Constitutional Reform Act 2005. In particular, he is no longer the Head of the judiciary in England and Wales nor sits as a judge.

5.8.5 The executive and legislature

■ **The House of Commons Disqualification Act 1975**

Section 1 of the House of Commons Disqualification Act 1975 prohibits specified non-elected members of the executive (ie members of the armed forces, civil servants and the police) from sitting in the lower House, thereby achieving a degree of separation between the executive and the House of Commons. In addition, as indicated earlier, the Act specifically limits the number of government ministers who can sit in the House of Commons to 95 MPs thereby, in constitutional theory, preventing the government from dominating the House of Commons.

■ **Lord Chancellor**

As the Lord Chancellor is no longer the Speaker in the House of Lords, this has severed the historic connection between the Speaker and the government (although historically the Lord Chancellor, despite being a member of the executive, was of course supposed to act impartially when acting as Speaker). The newly elected Lord Speaker of the House of Lords (this was Baroness Hayman in February 2010) is not a member of the Cabinet and is politically impartial.

KEY FACTS

Aspects of the British constitution in accord with the separation of powers (executive & legislature)
The following aspects of the British constitution are in accord with the principles underpinning the separation of powers (a pure version or otherwise) in respect of the executive and legislature:
• The House of Commons Disqualification Act 1975 prohibits specified non-elected members of the executive from sitting in the House of Commons.
• The Speaker of the House of Lords is no longer a member of the Cabinet.

5.9 Conclusion

Even before the advent of the Constitutional Reform Act 2005, Munro had made the following concluding observation concerning the separation of powers in the British constitution:

QUOTATION

'In a variety of important ways, ideas of the separation of powers have shaped constitutional arrangements and influenced our constitutional thinking, and continue to do so. The separation in the British constitution, although not absolute, ought not to be lightly dismissed.'

C Munro, *Studies in Constitutional Law* (2nd edn, Butterworths, 1999), p 332.

Finally, the following point is worth noting:

QUOTATION

'Constructive relationships between the three arms of government – the executive, the legislature and the judiciary – are essential to the effective maintenance of the Constitution and the rule of law.'

Sixth Report of Session 2006–07 of the House of Lords Select Committee on the Constitution, *Relations Between the Executive, the Judiciary and Parliament*, HL Paper 115 (The Stationery Office, 2007), p 7.

The separation of powers in the British constitution in 2010			
	Legislature/ Legislative function	**Executive/ Executive function**	**Judiciary/ Judicial function**
Parliament	**Constitutional function to pass primary legislation**		• The High Court of Parliament – regulates its own proceedings
Executive	• Passes delegated legislation • Forms the parliamentary executive	**Constitutional function to determine and initiate policy. Implements and carries out the law**	• (Historically, it was given a judicial function in the context of sentencing)
Judiciary	• Develops the common law • Retired law lords still sit in Parliament (albeit as crossbenchers) (CRA 2005)		**Constitutional function to resolve legal disputes and interpret the law**
The monarch	• Queen in Parliament • Royal Assent	• Her Majesty's Government ministers	• Her Majesty's judges
The Lord Chancellor	• Part of the parliamentary executive	• Senior Cabinet minister and Head of a government department (Ministry of Justice) • Approves judicial appointments	• The Lord Chief Justice disciplines judicial holders with the agreement of the Lord Chancellor
The Privy Council	• Orders in Council	• Precursor to the Cabinet and advises the monarch	• Judicial Committee of the Privy Council

Table 5.1

SUMMARY

▨ The separation of powers is a key concept in any democratic state.
▨ The separation of powers divides state power into the following three functions:
  ● Legislative – enacting law.
  ● Executive – implementing the law and making policy decisions.
  ● Judicial – interpreting the law and settling legal disputes.
▨ The separation of powers can be interpreted in a very strict sense or in a looser sense involving a system of checks and balances.
▨ The separation of powers avoids a concentration of state power and ensures the judiciary are independent.
▨ The British constitution is not in accord with the separation of powers in the following ways:
  ● Parliamentary executive (including the Lord Chancellor and law officers).
  ● Delegated legislation.
  ● Crown formally involved in all three functions.
  ● High Court of Parliament.

- Privy Council.
- Judges performing a legislative function.
- The British constitution is in accord with the separation of powers in the following ways:
  - Courts do not review legislation passed by Parliament (except in the context of the EU).
  - Sub judice resolution.
  - Courts refuse to investigate the internal proceedings of Parliament.
  - Full-time judges and specified non-elected members of the executive are disqualified from the House of Commons.
  - By constitutional convention members of the executive do not criticise judicial decisions.
- The Constitutional Reform Act 2005 reformed the role of the Lord Chancellor and removed the law lords from the House of Lords.

SAMPLE ESSAY QUESTION

How does the British constitution violate the principle of the separation of powers?

Introduction:

Definition of the separation of powers (note the distinction between a pure and less than pure separation of powers). Briefly explain the nature of the British constitution

The parliamentary executive:

Executive drawn from Parliament

Note the constitutional advantage of this which enables the government to be held to account to the legislature

Consider whether the balance has shifted in favour of the executive

Note the parliamentary executive includes both the Lord Chancellor and the law officers

Delegated legislation:

Executive performing a legislative function in passing delegated/subordinate legislation

Note the practical rationale for it and the legal (ie courts) and parliamentary controls on its use

The Crown:

Monarch formally forms part of the executive, legislature and judiciary (note, however, this is a formal overlap in reality)

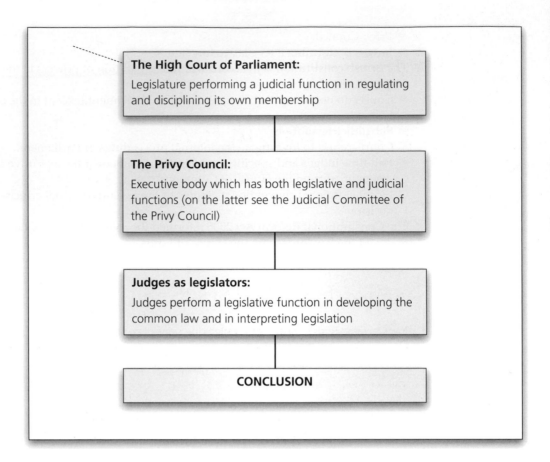

Further reading

Books

Alder, J, *Constitutional and Administrative Law* (7th edn, Palgrave/Macmillan, 2009), Chapter 5.

Bradley, A and Ewing, K, *Constitutional and Administrative Law* (14th edn, Pearson/Longman, 2007), Chapter 5.

Leyland, P, *The Constitution of the United Kingdom* (Hart Publishing, 2007), pp 53–63.

Munro, C, *Studies in Constitutional Law* (2nd edn, Butterworths, 1999), Chapter 9.

Articles

Barber, N, 'Prelude to the Separation of Powers' [2001] 61 CLJ 59.

Barendt, E, 'Separation of Powers and Constitutional Government' [1995] PL 599.

Bradley, A, 'Relations between Executive, Judiciary and Parliament: an Evolving Saga?' [2008] PL 470.

Munro, C, 'The Separation of Powers: Not such a Myth' [1981] PL 19.

6

The rule of law

AIMS AND OBJECTIVES

At the end of this chapter you should be able to:

- Explain what is meant by the rule of law
- Explain Dicey's conception of the rule of law
- Explain the criticism of Dicey's conception of the rule of law
- Assess the application of the rule of law to the British constitution

6.1 Definition

QUOTATION

'A "health warning" is in order for anyone venturing into this area … There is considerable diversity of opinion as to the meaning of the rule of law and the consequences that do and should follow from breach of this concept.'

Professor Craig, Sixth Report of Session 2006–07 of the House of Lords Select Committee on the Constitution, *Relations between the executive, the judiciary and parliament*, HL Paper 151 (2007) Appendix 5, p 97.

QUOTATION

'For my part two core meanings of the rule of law are essential to an understanding of our public law. The first is not a legal concept. The rule of law is a term of political philosophy or institutional morality. It conveys the idea of government not under men but under laws. It eschews the instrumentalist conception of law that enables an oppressive regime to attain its aims by the use of law, as happened in South Africa in the apartheid era. It addresses the moral dimension of public power …

In its second sense the rule of law is a general principle of constitutional law. Its central focus is to constrain the abuse of official power. It protects a citizen's right to legal certainty in respect of interference with his liberties. It guarantees access to justice. It ensures procedural fairness over much of the range of administrative decision-making by officials.'

Lord Steyn, *The Constitutionalisation of Public Law* (The Constitution Unit, 1999), p 4.

In essence, the rule of law means that government and its officials, together with private citizens, must act under the law. The rationale behind it is to control the exercise of public power by the state by ensuring that it is exercised strictly within legal limits. As such, the courts play a central role in upholding the rule of law and therefore, this principle is inextricably linked with the independence of the judiciary (see Chapter 13).

The rule of law does not have one clear fixed meaning, but instead has been subject to a number of different interpretations. It is a key component of the principle of constitutionalism, namely, that governmental action must be subject to limitation in order to avoid an abuse of power.

The rule of law is not a modern concept, but is of ancient origin as it was Aristotle (*The Politics* (Penguin, 1962), p 143) who stated that:

QUOTATION

'It is preferable that that law should rule rather than any single one of the citizens.'

In other words, under the rule of men, citizens are governed by men (or a group of individuals) who are capable of acting in an irrational, capricious and vindictive manner. In contrast, under the rule of law, citizens are governed by an overarching universal law. Moreover, 'the law', unlike the rule of men, is not applied in a capricious or irrational fashion and governs the actions of private individuals and state officials alike. In short, all are under the law. In this context, Lord Denning MR in the Court of Appeal in *Gouriet v Union of Post Office Workers* [1977] 1 QB 729 commented that:

JUDGMENT

'To every subject in this land, no matter how powerful, I would use Thomas Fuller's words over 300 years ago: "Be you ever so high, the law is above you".'

In the United Kingdom, in the absence of a written codified constitution legally restraining the actions of the government, the rule of law assumes a particularly important position.

In modern parlance, the rule of law can be interpreted in different ways. For example, Bradley and Ewing (*Constitutional and Administrative Law* (14th edn, Pearson/Longman, 2007), pp 99–103) identified the following three elements of the rule of law today that they consider to be particularly worth noting:

- Law and order are better than anarchy.
- There should be government according to the law.
- The rule of law as a political doctrine.

6.2 The rule of law as a legal principle

6.2.1 A legal principle and procedural mechanism

In this interpretation, the rule of law is seen as a procedural mechanism (Barnett referred to it as a procedural device) controlling and limiting the exercise of governmental/public power. The actions of state officials (eg government ministers or police officers) which impact on the individual should have a clear foundation in law. As noted by Bradley and Ewing this is the principle of legality.

For example, Art 5(2) of the European Convention on Human Rights states that:

ARTICLE

'Everyone who is arrested shall be informed promptly, in a language which he understands, of the reasons for his arrest and of any charge against him.'

These requirements ensure that an arrested person understands why, and on what grounds (ie legal basis), he has been arrested and detained by the state. It also makes state officials legally accountable for their actions, as when they interfere with individual freedoms they are required to justify legally their actions. The rule of law in this sense is a procedural mechanism (the principle of legality) which ensures that government and its officials act under the law. An interesting example of the principle of legality is illustrated by the following case.

CASE EXAMPLE

R (Jones) v Chief Constable of Cheshire Police [2005] EWHC 2457 (Admin)

Jones had been issued a pedlar's certificate under the Pedlars Act 1871, and when arrested and interviewed by the police on suspicion in relation to an offence of dishonesty (although he was never charged), his certificate was seized. The court granted a declaration (in judicial review proceedings) that the police had no lawful power to seize or revoke the certificate as the Pedlars Act 1871 had contained no provision to that effect.

In other countries, the principle that government action must be in accordance with the law will be specifically set out in the written codified constitutional text. For example, as noted at section 2.4.4, in Sweden Chapter 1 of the 1975 Instrument of Government states that 'Public power shall be exercised under law'. Similarly, Art 20 of the German constitution states that:

ARTICLE

'The executive and the judiciary are bound by the law.'

Thus, in the United Kingdom, in the absence of a written codified document legally and constitutionally restraining the power of government, the rule of law is of paramount importance. The judiciary uphold the constitutional principle that all individuals (both private and state officials) are under the law. In particular, they ensure that government and its officials are accountable to the law through the procedural mechanism of judicial review (see Chapters 19 and 20). In brief, the judiciary supervises the actions of the executive to ensure that it acts strictly within its legal powers.

6.2.2 The limitation of the procedural mechanism

As noted by Bradley and Ewing, the rule of law should not simply be confined to the consideration of the principle of legality. In other words, if the rule of law is viewed exclusively as a procedural mechanism which asks simply (and only) whether a government official possessed, for example, the requisite legal power to arrest an individual (ie had the state official followed the law?), then this in itself does not necessarily fully protect the individual (see the imaginary Detention Act 2013 detailed at section 6.4). This is because it is possible – in the British constitution at least – for exceptionally wide and extensive powers of arrest and detention to be conferred legally on state officials. Such powers could in effect be used almost at will and to the clear detriment of the individual. Notwithstanding their impact on individual freedoms, if these powers had a legal basis to them, under the principle of legality (which requires state action to have a legal foundation), the use of them would be lawful as these powers would necessarily be legitimised by the law. In strict procedural terms, therefore, these state officials would be acting 'according to the law'.

The rule of law, accordingly, may also embrace a broader meaning with a substantive content which would, among other things, critically evaluate laws that have been made in terms of their impact on human rights and other fundamental principles (see section 6.4).

Key facts on the rule of law as a legal principle

The rule of law as a legal principle ensures that government acts under the law.
In this sense it is a procedural mechanism which protects the individual from an unlawful use of state power as it requires state officials to justify their actions.

ACTIVITY

Essay writing

What is the difference between the rule of law and the rule of men?

6.3 The rule of law as a political ideal/theory

6.3.1 A formal view of the rule of law

This interpretation of the rule of law is concerned with the form that the law takes. In other words, once a law has been passed in the requisite constitutional manner (eg in the United Kingdom this would involve the Queen in Parliament passing an Act of Parliament), the law itself should exhibit particular characteristics.

6.3.2 Raz and the rule of law

Raz is a major exponent of a formal conception of the rule of law (J Raz, 'The Rule of Law and its Virtue' [1977] 93 LQR 195). In essence, he stated that the rule of law is a political ideal which means that individuals should be ruled by the law and that the law must be able to guide individuals if they are to obey the law. As a consequence, this allows individuals to plan their lives accordingly.

In particular Raz argued that the making of laws should be guided by, *inter alia*, the following principles:

QUOTATION

'(1) All laws should be prospective, open and clear.'

Prospective laws – Laws should be prospective so that laws look forward rather than punishing behaviour retrospectively. Such retrospective laws are objectionable because, of course, the individual has no control over their past conduct. Owing to their retrospective nature, they do not permit the law to guide and influence an individual's future behaviour. In this context, Willes J in *Phillips v Eyre* (1870–71) LR 6 QB 1 has noted:

JUDGMENT

'Retrospective laws are, no doubt, *prima facie* of questionable policy, and contrary to the general principle that legislation by which the conduct of mankind is to be regulated ought, when introduced for the first time, to deal with future acts and ought not to change the character of past transactions carried on upon the faith of the then existing law … Accordingly, the Court will not ascribe retrospective force to new laws affecting rights, unless by express words or necessary implication it appears that such was the intention of the legislature.'

Moreover, Art 7 of the European Convention on Human Rights specifically outlaws retrospective criminal offences:

ARTICLE

'No one shall be held guilty of any criminal offence on account of any act or omission which did not constitute a criminal offence under national or international law at the time when it was committed.'

Open laws – Laws should be open so that individuals are able to access them. Laws should not be secret or difficult to locate as this would not enable the individual to be guided by the law.

One result of secret laws is that as individuals will necessarily be unaware of them, they will inevitably be in a state of apprehension. For example, if an individual is unsure as to whether it is a criminal offence (punishable by a term of imprisonment) to hold a political demonstration, in order to err on the side of caution, he would in all likelihood not demonstrate in case the demonstration violated the law. Significantly, this demonstration could have been a protest about, for instance, the policies of the incumbent government.

Clear laws – Laws should be clear and intelligible so that the individual can understand them. Ambiguous, imprecise or unclear laws will inevitably confuse the individual and prevent the law guiding and influencing their actions.

In the context of open and clear laws, in *Merkur Island Shipping Corporation v Laughton and others* [1983] 2 AC 570 Sir John Donaldson MR in the Court of Appeal stated that:

JUDGMENT

'The efficacy and maintenance of the rule of law, which is the foundation of any parliamentary democracy, has at least two pre-requisites. First, people must understand that it is in their interests as well as in that of the community as a whole, that they should live their lives in accordance with the rules and all the rules. Second, they must know what those rules are. Both are equally important.'

In recent years the following developments have been made to make legislation clearer and thus more accessible:

- Explanatory notes – these notes which accompany Bills and Acts are prepared to make legislation more intelligible to individuals. These explanatory notes have been made available to the public since 1998. Furthermore, in 2006 the Coroner Reform: The Government's Draft Bill, Cm 6849 (DCA, 2006) was published which included detailed passages explaining each aspect/clause of the Bill in alternative pages. This was designed specifically to make the draft Bill as intelligible (and so accessible) to the public as possible.
- Explanatory memorandum – is now available in respect of Statutory Instruments. Such notes explain the purpose, objective and application of the measure.

Further, Lord Bingham has argued that the volume of modern legislation raises problems of accessibility, but that in addition:

QUOTATION

'... the length, complexity and sometimes prolixity of modern common law judgments, particularly at the highest level, raise problems of their own.'

'The Rule of Law' [2007] 66 CLJ 67.

QUOTATION

'(2) Laws should be relatively stable.'

Raz

Laws should remain relatively stable and not change too frequently as otherwise individuals could be fearful that the law may have changed in the intervening period, and so therefore they would be unable to plan their lives effectively for fear that the law had in fact changed.

QUOTATION

> '(3) The making of particular laws (particular legal orders) should be guided by open, stable, clear and general rules.'
>
> Raz

For example, particular laws of an ephemeral status (eg administrative law-making/delegated legislation) should be enacted in the context of 'detailed ground rules laid down in framework laws' (ie parent legislation).

Thus, Raz views the above characteristics as not in themselves concerned with the substance of the law itself (see section 6.4), but instead with the form of the law. Raz accepts that these characteristics (open, clear, stable, prospective laws) could, of course, be met by a non-democratic state. He also included within the principles underpinning the rule of law that the independence of the judiciary must be guaranteed. It is the courts that apply the law and they should do so free from external interference. The judiciary, in ensuring the correct application of the law should also apply the principles of **natural justice/the duty to act fairly** (see Chapter 20) and ensure that they are observed. In addition, the courts should be accessible to an aggrieved individual (so that the judiciary can provide an effective remedy), and the judges should have power of review over both primary and subordinate legislation and administrative action to ensure conformity with the principles underpinning the rule of law.

natural justice/ duty to act fairly
common law rules developed by the judiciary to ensure that public bodies exercise their powers and functions fairly

KEY FACTS

Raz states that the following principles comprise a formal conception of the rule of law:
Laws should possess the following characteristics in order to conform to a particular standard which should enable them to guide individual behaviour: • Open • Clear • Stable • Prospective.
The following principles concern the legal machinery for enforcing the rule of law: • The independence of the judiciary must be guaranteed as the judges ensure that the law is correctly applied and followed. In ensuring the correct application of the law they will apply the principles of natural justice/the duty to act fairly. • The courts should be accessible to individuals so that the judiciary can provide an effective remedy, and the judges should have power of review over legislation and administrative action to ensure conformity with the principles underpinning the rule of law.

6.4 The rule of law as a substantive concept

This interpretation of the rule of law is concerned in particular with the substantive content of laws. In essence, laws should encapsulate and contain certain fundamental values, for example, the respect for basic constitutional principles such as the protection of basic human rights.

In this context, consider the following imaginary statute:

The (Imaginary) Detention Act 2013

Section 1 permits a police officer to arrest, and detain for 10 days, any individual who criticises the economic policy of the incumbent government.

In February 2013, Gibson is arrested and detained for 10 days for criticising the Chancellor of the Exchequer's Budget proposals. In relation to the rule of law as a substantive concept, the questions are *not* simply:

■ Does the state official (ie police officer) possess the legal power to detain Gibson? (ie is Gibson's detention authorised by law/Act of Parliament?) – see the principle of legality at section 6.2.
and
■ Has this law (the (Imaginary) Detention Act 2013) been promulgated in the constitutionally correct manner by the appropriate body? (ie was it passed by the Queen in Parliament)?
and
■ Does this law exhibit certain characteristics? (ie is the (Imaginary) Detention Act 2013 open, clear, stable, general and prospective so as to be capable of guiding Gibson's behaviour?) – see the formal conception of the rule of law at section 6.3.2.

Rather, the rule of law as a substantive concept is concerned with the substance and moral character of the law and asks the following question:

■ *Should* state officials (the police) have been conferred with wide and extensive powers of detention in respect of individuals who merely criticise a government's economic policy? In other words, *should* Parliament have passed the (Imaginary) Detention Act 2013 in the first place?

In this sense the rule of law embraces a substantive concept as it evaluates laws made according to a set of fundamental constitutional principles which include the protection of individual freedoms. In this way, this interpretation of the rule of law effectively has a moral dimension which would question whether the state really required the (Imaginary) Detention Act 2013. This would be on the basis that it is draconian legislation which unnecessarily violated the principles underpinning the rule of law (ie it is an excessive interference with an individual's right to freedom of expression and the right of personal liberty). Ironically, therefore, the (Imaginary) Detention Act 2013 – although it was itself a law – would inevitably be considered to be a violation of the rule of law (as a substantive concept). Although such legislation would undoubtedly be considered *morally unconstitutional* (see section 4.15), owing to the doctrine of parliamentary sovereignty it would nevertheless be legally enforceable (though subject to a declaration of incompatibility by the courts under section 4 of the Human Rights Act 1998 – see section 17.7).

The inherent problem with the substantive conception of the rule of law is that the principles which underpin it (including the basic rights of the individual and the balancing of these rights against other competing interests such as public order/safety and national security, etc), are not universally agreed upon. For example, there is no universal agreement on the legitimate scope of police powers or on the morality of abortion and the respective rights of mother and unborn child. To some extent, therefore, the substantive conception of the rule of law is necessarily subjective and in essence depends upon a personal conception of human rights. In short, it depends to a great extent upon one's personal judgement of what is a 'good law' (morally right because it protects the rights *you* favour) and what is a 'bad law' (morally wrong because it infringes rights that *you* favour).

For example, returning to the example given at section 4.15.2, does the Prevention of Terrorism Act 2005 breach the rule of law because it interferes with the fundamental liberties of the individual? Or, is it consistent with the rule of law as an unfortunate, but necessary, response to an emergency threatening the life and safety of the public? In fact, is the Act aimed at actually protecting the rule of law itself by dealing with elements that threaten to undermine the existence of the state itself?

ACTIVITY

Applying the law

Distinguish between the rule of law as:
- A procedural mechanism.
- A political ideal.
- A substantive concept.

6.5 The rule of law as the antithesis of anarchy and chaos

This (rather basic) interpretation of the rule of law emphasises the need for social order within the state as apposed to anarchy and chaos. In other words, the rule of law requires an ordered state comprising, *inter alia*, a functioning legal system and independent judges through which citizens' disputes can be resolved and settled by peaceful and consensual means, as opposed to having to resort to armed force. This interpretation would be in contrast to a country which was, in effect, administered by state officials who acted arbitrarily and in a completely unregulated and capricious fashion. In short, a state governed by the rule of men.

An inextricable aspect of an ordered legal system is the principle of the independence of the judiciary and a court system. In order to hold the government to account, to ensure that legal disputes are resolved fairly and according to the law and that citizens will have confidence in the administration of justice, judges must be impartial and independent from the government and state officials.

6.6 The rule of law in international terms

As noted above, the concept of the rule of law is of some antiquity and is also used in an international context, although its meaning may differ.

6.6.1 The rule of law and the Universal Declaration of Human Rights

The preamble to the Universal Declaration of Human Rights (1948) adopted by the General Assembly of the United Nations confirms respect for fundamental human rights and states:

ARTICLE

'whereas it is essential, if man is not to be compelled to have recourse, as a last resort, to rebellion against tyranny and oppression, that human rights should be protected by the rule of law'.

In effect, this emphasises that the state should protect basic individual rights and not undermine them. Implicit within this is that should such rights be infringed by the state, then the individual should have access to legal machinery (ie the courts) in order to challenge it.

6.6.2 The rule of law and the European Convention on Human Rights

The European Convention sets out the basic rights and freedoms of the individual and seeks to ensure that these rights enjoyed by each individual are protected by their respective state and domestic legal system. The European Court of Human Rights, in interpreting the rights of the Convention, draws upon the concept of the rule of law. In fact, the preamble makes reference to the rule of law as being part of the common heritage of the signatory states.

Most of the rights (eg the right to freedom of expression) in the European Convention are conditional rights, rather than being absolute (see Chapter 16). In brief, conditional rights can be legitimately interfered with by the state for specified and limited purposes. For example, Art 10 confers on everyone the right to freedom of expression. This right is, however, conditional and can be legitimately interfered with in order to, *inter alia*, protect health or morals (see section 18.2.4). Moreover, any legitimate interference with the Convention rights has overtones of the terminology of the rule of law. This is illustrated by the following case:

CASE EXAMPLE

Handyside v United Kingdom (1976) 1 EHRR 737

Handyside was a publisher of the *Little Red Schoolbook* (a reference book aimed at children and adolescents aged 12–18 which had a section concerning sex, including topics on masturbation, contraceptives, pornography, etc). He was prosecuted under the Obscene Publications Act 1959 (as amended in 1964), as the book was adjudged to be obscene. Handyside argued (unsuccessfully) in the European Court of Human Rights that this criminal conviction and the destruction of his books violated Art 10 (the right to freedom of expression).

In essence, any interference with Art 10 had to be consistent with the main elements of the rule of law. In other words, the restriction/interference had to have a legitimate aim and be 'prescribed by law' which, in effect, concerned the form and nature of the law purporting to restrict the Convention right (ie the Obscene Publications Acts 1959 and 1964). The reasoning of the court in the case was as follows:

The court noted at the outset that the action taken against Handyside (ie his conviction and destruction of his books) was an interference with his right to freedom of expression under Art 10(1). However, the question was: could it be justified?

- Firstly, any interference with Handyside's right had to be 'prescribed by law'. In other words, the interference had to have a clear legal foundation in domestic law so that it was accessible and intelligible to Handyside. The court held that the Obscene Publications Acts 1959/1964 were clearly set out in domestic law.
- Secondly, any interference with Handyside's right to freedom of expression had to have a legitimate aim. Art 10(2) permits interference where the aim is to protect morals. In this case the court held that the interference with Handyside's right was in the interests of the protection of morals (ie the children who would be exposed to the book) and so had a legitimate purpose under Art 10(2).
- Thirdly, any interference with Handyside's right also needed to be proportionate and so not excessive, thereby ensuring that restrictions did not unnecessarily infringe the rights of the Convention. In this case the restriction on Handyside's right to freedom of expression had not been disproportionate and so was necessary in a democratic society.

In short, the European Court of Human Rights held that the interference with Handyside's right to freedom of expression under Art 10 was legitimate, prescribed by law and justified. The reasoning employed by the court clearly draws upon the various principles underpinning the rule of law.

ACTIVITY

Applying the law

Re-read the *Handyside* case example above and link the reasoning and tests employed by the European Court with the principles underpinning the rule of law that you have already covered in this chapter.

6.6.3 The Declaration of Delhi

In 1959 the Declaration of Delhi was issued by the International Commission of Jurists. Although the Declaration is not legally binding, it noted that the obligations imposed by the rule of law included, *inter alia*, the right to a representative government, an independent judiciary and a fair trial including due process.

6.6.4 The European Union

In the context of the European Union, the 1997 Treaty of Amsterdam made it clear that the Union itself was founded on respect for democratic principles, human rights and the rule of law. Furthermore, in performing its function of interpreting European Union law, the European Court of Justice uses a number of principles to assist it. One of these principles is that of legal certainty which is essentially based on the rule of law. For example, in reviewing the acts/legislation made by the political institutions (ie the Council/Commission/European Parliament/European Council), the European Court in *Commission v France* Case C–30/89 [1990] ECR 1-691 has noted that:

JUDGMENT

'It must be remembered that the Court has repeatedly held that certainty and forseeability are requirements which must be observed all the more strictly in the case of rules liable to entail financial consequences.'

KEY FACTS

Key facts on the rule of law in international terms

- The rule of law is a concept of some antiquity that has been subject to a number of different interpretations and meanings.
- In general terms it means that all are subject to the law, rather than being subject to the whims of man (the rule of men).
- It is a key element of constitutionalism which is aimed at ensuring that government and its officials act under the law and strictly within their legal powers.
- It can be interpreted as a principle of legality, a political ideal and as a substantive concept.
- At a basic level it emphasises the need for social order within the state as opposed to anarchy and chaos.
- The principle is also used in an international context.

6.7 The rule of law in the British constitution

6.7.1 Introduction to the rule of law in the United Kingdom

The rule of law is a central aspect of the British constitution. In fact, it assumes a particular significance in the absence of a written codified and entrenched document which legally and constitutionally sets out the limits of the government (particularly in the context of human rights). Jowell has noted that in countries with a written constitution, a Bill of Rights will typically disable the government and elected Parliament from abusing their power, while in the United Kingdom the rule of law as an unwritten principle of the constitution 'performs a similar disabling function' ('The Rule of Law and its underlying values' in J Jowell and D Oliver, *The Changing Constitution* (6th edn, Oxford University Press, 2007), p 17). It should be remembered, however, that the British courts have been traditionally unable to challenge primary legislation (see Chapter 7).

In the United Kingdom, therefore, the rule of law denoting the fundamental principle that government is under the law, takes on a particular significance. Indeed, Lord Woolf in a lecture on the rule of law reaffirmed the constitutional significance of the principle:

QUOTATION

'One of the most important of the judiciary's responsibilities is to uphold the rule of law, since it is the rule of law which prevents the Government of the day from abusing its powers.'

Lord Woolf, 'The rule of law and a change in the constitution' [2004] 64 CLJ 317.

In the United Kingdom, the rule of law (at least historically) has been closely associated with Dicey. This classic conception of the rule of law in his book *Introduction to the Study of the Law of the Constitution* represented an early attempt at explaining the rule of law in the context of the 'English' constitution (today Dicey would use the term the British constitution). In particular, Dicey argued that the constitution rested upon the twin pillars of parliamentary sovereignty and the rule of law.

Although Dicey's conception has been criticised (and these criticisms are considered below), his principles arguably still have resonance today.

6.7.2 Dicey and the rule of law

Dicey highlighted three aspects (or conceptions as he described them) of the rule of law:

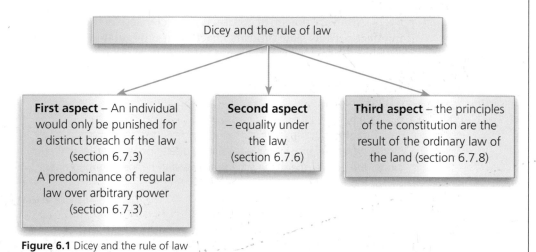

Dicey and the rule of law

First aspect – An individual would only be punished for a distinct breach of the law (section 6.7.3)

A predominance of regular law over arbitrary power (section 6.7.3)

Second aspect – equality under the law (section 6.7.6)

Third aspect – the principles of the constitution are the result of the ordinary law of the land (section 6.7.8)

Figure 6.1 Dicey and the rule of law

6.7.3 Dicey's first aspect

Dicey stated that the rule of law meant:

QUOTATION

'that no man is punishable or can be lawfully made to suffer in body or goods except for a distinct breach of law established in the ordinary legal manner before the ordinary courts of the land. In this sense the rule of law is contrasted with every system of government based on the exercise by persons in authority of wide, arbitrary, or discretionary powers of constraint.

It means, in the first place, the absolute supremacy or predominance of regular law as opposed to the influence of arbitrary power, and excludes the existence of arbitrariness, of prerogative, or even of wide discretionary authority on the part of the government. Englishmen are ruled by the law, and by the law alone; a man may with us be punished for a breach of the law, but he can be punished for nothing else.'

A Dicey, *Introduction to the Study of the Law of the Constitution* (10th edn, Macmillan, 1959), pp 188 and 202 respectively.

This first aspect effectively can be broadly broken down into two elements:

- An individual is only punished for a breach of the law.
- The predominance of regular law.

Element 1 – An individual is only punished for a breach of the law
In short, Dicey argued that a punishment would only be imposed on an individual if he violated the law as established in ordinary legal proceedings before a court. In other words, the individual was not subject to the whims of a state official.

Element 2 – The predominance of regular law
In essence, Dicey argued that the rule of law denoted the predominance of regular law as opposed to the exercise of arbitrary power. As regular law had a clear legal origin and was reasonably precise in its ambit, the use of regular law can be controlled. Regular law did not involve the granting of arbitrary or wide discretionary powers on state officials as such powers could be used to the detriment of the individual. As Dicey asserted 'wherever there is discretion there is room for arbitrariness'. Regular law, therefore, necessarily limited and controlled the use of state power.

In contrast to regular law (which has a clear legal origin and clear legal limits), wide discretionary powers on the other hand, lacked clear ascertainable legal parameters (the rule of men). As a consequence, it would be difficult for an individual to challenge government officials and contend that they had abused their wide discretionary powers. Arbitrary power, of course, is characterised by the lack of clear legal limits and it in effect permits state officials to act in an unregulated and effectively unchallengeable manner. This in turn makes it difficult to make these bodies legally accountable for their actions which adversely and unfairly affect the individual. As stated by Lord Bingham:

QUOTATION

'The broader and more loosely-textured a discretion is, whether conferred on an official or a judge, the greater the scope for subjectivity and hence for arbitrariness, which is the antithesis of the rule of law.'

'The Rule of Law' [2007] 66 CLJ 67.

Legal accountability, therefore, benefits the individual as it gives certainty in terms of the limits and parameters of state power. It has also been argued that from an administrative/governmental perspective, regular law (with the absence of wide discretionary powers) benefits state officials as it makes the use of their powers more efficient.

6.7.4 Critique of Dicey's first aspect (element 1)

In terms of the first element of Dicey's first aspect, it is worth noting the following examples which indicate that an individual could 'suffer in body or goods' without having violated a law as established before the ordinary courts.

- **Remand** – under the Bail Act 1976 an *unconvicted* defendant can be remanded in custody prior to his criminal trial. There are, of course, sound public policy reasons for the authorisation of the detention of such an individual, for example if the court is satisfied that if granted bail the defendant released on bail would abscond, commit an offence or interfere with witnesses. In the event of an individual subsequently being found not guilty at trial, he *has* suffered in body while waiting for the criminal trial to commence.

■ **Search powers** –s 1 of the Police and Criminal Evidence Act 1984 authorises a police officer to stop and search a person or vehicle for stolen or prohibited articles provided the officer has reasonable grounds for suspecting that he will find such articles. The officer may detain the person or vehicle in question for the purpose of the search. Suppose David is detained and searched in the street under this provision: provided the police officer had reasonable grounds for suspecting that he would find stolen/ prohibited articles on David's person, the detention and search would be lawful even though no such articles were actually found. David has suffered in body in the absence of a violation of the law.

■ **Indefinite detention of suspected international terrorists** – Below is an interesting example of how Parliament can pass a law which authorises the indefinite detention of non-United Kingdom nationals suspected of terrorism. In summary, foreign nationals were detained without either charge or trial and so were made to 'suffer in body' even though no charge was brought against them.

CASE EXAMPLE

A and others v Secretary of State for the Home Department [2004] UKHL 56

Section 23 (Pt 4) of the Anti-terrorism, Crime and Security Act 2001 authorised the indefinite detention without charge or trial (ie detention without trial) of foreign nationals suspected of being international terrorists, but who could not be deported (whether temporarily or indefinitely). These detainees could not be charged before a court as, *inter alia*, the exposure of the alleged evidence against these individuals could compromise the intelligence services who had gathered it. Further, these individuals could not be deported as under Art 3 of the European Convention, a state cannot deport an individual to a country where there is a real risk that the deportee will be subjected to torture or inhuman or degrading treatment (see section 16.10.4). As a consequence, the detainees were not prosecuted for any criminal offences, nor were they deported, which left the suspects detained indefinitely without charge or trial. These individuals could, however, leave the United Kingdom voluntarily to go to a country which would accept them.

Under Art 5 of the Convention deportation proceedings of individuals must be pursued with due diligence (*Chahal v UK* (1997) 23 EHRR 413) and so in 2001 the government made the Human Rights Act 1998 (Designated Derogation) Order in respect of this obligation (ie an official departure from Art 5). Such derogations are permissible under Art 15 in times of war or other public emergency threatening the life of the nation (eg the threat of terrorism).

Detainees held under the Act challenged this terrorism legislation and derogation Order under the Human Rights Act 1998. The House of Lords declared that s 23 of the Act was incompatible with Arts 5 (right to liberty and security of person) and 14 (right not to be discriminated against) and the derogation made by the government was quashed. In brief, the court held that s 23 of the Act was disproportionate and discriminatory against non-UK nationals. Lord Nicholls stated that: 'Indefinite imprisonment without charge or trial is an anathema in any country which observes the rule of law.'

It should be noted, however, that owing to the doctrine of parliamentary sovereignty, this decision of the court did not disapply the 2001 Act (see section 17.7); instead it merely alerted Parliament and the government that the Act violated the European Convention. In due course, the Prevention of Terrorism Act 2005 replaced the provisions for detention without trial under Pt 4 of the 2001 Act with 'control orders'. On powers to deal with terrorism, see section 6.7.11.

As a postscript to this case, in 2009 in *A v UK* (2009) 49 EHRR 29 the European Court of Human Rights held that there had been a violation of Art 5 of the European Convention.

■ **Compulsory purchase powers** – local authorities typically have powers of compulsory purchase which empowers them to compulsorily purchase private property, for example to make way for a new road. In these circumstances, the homeowner will suffer in goods without having breached a law.

6.7.5 Critique of Dicey's first aspect (element 2)

This aspect of Dicey's first conception has been subject to some criticism.

The first point to ask is are there any wide discretionary powers which are open to abuse in the modern British constitution? Although there are laws which are relatively precise, there are examples where exceptionally wide powers have been conferred on the executive by legislation. It should be remembered that under the principle of parliamentary sovereignty, Parliament can simply pass whichever law it chooses. For instance, the following case is a good example of Parliament passing a law which conferred an exceptionally wide power on state officials:

CASE EXAMPLE

Inland Revenue Commissioners and Another v Rossminster Ltd and others [1980] AC 952

Section 20C of the Taxes Management Act 1970 stated that a judicial authority could issue a warrant authorising Inland Revenue officers to enter and search premises if satisfied that 'there is reasonable ground for suspecting that an offence involving any form of fraud in connection with, or in relation to, tax has been committed and that evidence of it is to be found on premises specified in the information'.

A senior revenue officer suspected some tax fraud had been committed, and sought and obtained a warrant to search the premises of Rossminster Ltd, and to seize anything the officers had reasonable cause to believe as evidence of a tax fraud. The revenue officers (accompanied by the police) entered Rossminster Ltd's premises and seized anything believed to be evidence of a tax fraud. As Rossminster Ltd had not been informed of the specific offences suspected, or the person suspected of committing them, they sought judicial review to quash the search warrant as illegal.

The Court of Appeal granted such a declaration. In particular Lord Denning MR commented that 'The trouble is that the legislation is drawn so widely that in some hands it might be an instrument of oppression'. He noted further that an offence involving fraud in relation to tax could include a number of different kinds of offences and so in pursuance of the traditional role of the courts to protect the liberty of the individual, the warrant must particularise the specific offence.

The House of Lords, however, reversed the decision of the Court of Appeal and held that the warrants were lawful as they had been issued strictly in accordance within the legal authority of s 20C. Lord Scarman commented regrettably that even though the warrant had not been particularised, the requirements of the Act had nevertheless been complied with. He stated that although the provision was lawful, it represented 'a breath-taking inroad upon the individual's right of privacy and right of property'.

In this context, it is of course worth remembering that as a consequence of the parliamentary executive, it is invariably the case that it is the government which drafts the Bill which in turn confers a wide statutory power on the executive (see sections 5.7.1 and 5.4.3). Indeed, as indicated at section 4.15.2, it was suggested that the Taxes Management Act could well be construed by some commentators to be *morally unconstitutional*.

In addition, delegated legislation confers a law-making power on the executive to enact law, and there is inevitably an element of discretion in carrying out this function. The courts will, however, imply certain limits in respect of the use of this power (see in context of judicial review, Chapters 19 and 20) as illustrated by the following example:

CASE EXAMPLE

Commissioners of Customs and Excise v Cure & Deeley Ltd [1962] 1 QB 340

Section 33 of the Finance (No 2) Act 1940 conferred a power on the Commissioners of Customs and Excise to 'make regulations providing for any matter for which provision appears to them to be necessary for the purpose of giving effect to the provisions of this Part of this Act and enabling them to discharge their functions'. In pursuance of this power, the Commissioners made reg 12 of the Purchase Tax Regulations 1945 which, in essence, stated that if a person failed to return a tax return – or an incomplete one – the Commissioners may determine the amount of tax appearing to them to be due and demand this payment and that this shall be deemed the proper tax due.

The Queen's Bench Division held that reg 12 was *ultra vires* s 33 of the Finance Act. The court held that although s 33 (ie *appears to them to be necessary*) appeared to confer a discretion on the Commissioners, it did not necessarily make that body the sole judge of what its powers were, as well as to how it could exercise those powers.

The court held that reg 12 purported to confer on the Commissioners the powers of a judge and it tried to oust the jurisdiction of the court. The consequence of the regulation was to substitute the figure which the Commissioners *deemed* to be due, for the figure that was *lawfully and actually* due under the law. As Sachs J noted:

JUDGMENT

'In the result this attempt to substitute in one segment of the taxpayer's affairs the rule of tax collectors for the rule of law fails.'

A more recent example of Parliament (largely controlled, of course, by the government) proposing to confer wide discretionary powers on the state (in the form of the police) was the Terrorism Bill of 2005 (which became the Terrorism Act 2006). The Terrorism Act 2006 sought to permit the police to detain terrorist suspects for up to a maximum of 90 days without charge. It was argued that such a time limit was necessary in order to allow the prosecuting authorities to acquire and analyse the evidence against those detained under the legislation. In the event, at the Report stage of the Bill the House of Commons voted against the detention of up to 90 days and instead voted for the reduced period of 28 days. During the passage of the Bill, a number of commentators argued that the period of 90 days was excessive and contrary to the traditions of the rule of law. It must be remembered that the detention relates to the period before the detainee has even been charged with committing an offence.

Such was the criticism of the draconian and excessive nature of the proposed powers (which would have conferred extensive and wide-ranging powers on the police), that it represented the first defeat in the House of Commons for the Labour government since assuming office in 1997. The government subsequently tried again to extend the detention period as part of the 2008 Counter-Terrorism Bill (see section 6.7.11). In addition, see the stop and search powers authorised under s 44 of the Terrorism Act 2000 in circumstances where it is considered 'expedient for the prevention of acts of terrorism' (but now see *Gillan* (2010) below).

The advantages of state discretion

In terms of discretionary powers, it is clear that in a complex modern state, discretion is a necessary tool for the modern day administrator. In fact, far from adversely affecting the individual, discretionary power in the hands of a state official can be used for their advantage and benefit. In other words, if 'regular, clear and precise laws' are applied rigorously to all individuals at all times and in all circumstances, this in itself can cause injustice and unfairness to a particular individual. Accordingly, discretion can be used by an administrator to mitigate the rigidity and harshness of the law particularly, for example, in the context of providing welfare benefits.

Thus, far from being a disadvantage, discretion is a necessary and unavoidable tool as the following examples demonstrate:

■ Local authorities (an executive body) with limited and finite financial resources need the power to make decisions as to how best to deploy those limited resources. The use of the discretion is, however, controlled through the process of judicial review so that its exercise is legal, rational and procedurally fair (see Chapter 20). In this way, the use of the discretion is regulated in order to avoid an abuse of power.

■ The Crown Prosecution Service (which takes over prosecutions instigated by the police) has a discretion not to prosecute in an appropriate case. This decision is taken with consideration of *The Code for Crown Prosecutors* in mind.

■ The courts, in dispensing punishment to convicted offenders may have a degree of discretion, within specific parameters, as to which sentence to impose. This is determined according to the facts and circumstances of the particular case. In brief, it would be manifestly unfair to stipulate exactly the same penalty on all defendants convicted of the same offence (eg theft under the Theft Act 1968), as the circumstances, nature, impact and significance of the offence (together with the circumstances of the convicted defendant) will necessarily vary. Although judicial discretion is considered to be a central part of the practice of sentencing, there is inevitably a risk of disparity between sentences imposed. In effect, therefore, this discretion is to some extent 'structured' by the establishment of general sentencing principles (ie see the authoritative Guidelines produced by the Sentencing Guidelines Council which aims to encourage consistent sentencing in court).

The control of discretion

If discretion is considered a necessary tool, its use needs to be controlled and circumscribed, otherwise the unregulated use of a discretionary power could be tantamount to the use of arbitrary power. This regulation can be achieved through the courts via the process of judicial review (see Chapters 19 and 20). For example, a statute may confer a discretionary power on a government minister to:

1. 'act as he thinks fit'/'act when it appears to him to be necessary',
or
2. 'pass such regulations as he thinks fit', in order to achieve a particular public purpose.

The courts, however, will necessarily imply that the use of such power is not without its legal limits. Although Parliament has conferred a discretionary power, it is assumed that Parliament envisaged the minister exercising that discretion/power to use it:

■ Legally.
■ Rationally.
■ In a procedurally fair manner.
■ Consistently with the rights set out in the European Convention (now required under the Human Rights Act 1998).

In this way the courts can control and 'structure' the use of discretionary power. We saw that in *Cure & Deeley* (and previously in *Witham* at section 4.8.3 and *Chester v Bateson* at section 5.7.2) that the courts will make it plain that notwithstanding the power to enact delegated legislation which 'appears to them to be necessary', this is not an absolute power. As pointed out by Lord Bingham:

QUOTATION

'There is in truth no such thing as an unfettered discretion, judicial or official, and that is what the rule of law requires.'

'The Rule of Law', [2007] 66 CLJ 67.

Dicey specifically disapproved of, and referred to, 'wide discretionary authority'. Today in a modern-day complex state, discretion is inevitable and practically unavoidable.

Moreover, the principle of discretion can benefit the individual by mitigating the harshness of the law but that discretion must be exercised within clear legal parameters and subject to review by the courts to ensure that it is not abused or misused. Recently, in *Gillan v UK* (2010) (Application No 4158/05) the European Court of Human Rights held that the wide discretion of the police to stop and search individuals under the Terrorism Act 2000 violated Art 8 of the European Convention.

JUDGMENT

'In matters affecting fundamental rights it would be contrary to the rule of law, one of the basic principles of a democratic society enshrined in the Convention, for a legal discretion granted to the executive to be expressed in terms of an unfettered power. Consequently, the law must indicate with sufficient clarity the scope of any such discretion conferred on the competent authorities and the manner of its exercise …

In conclusion the Court considers the powers of authorisation and confirmation as well as those of the stop and search under section 44 and 45 of the 2000 Act are neither sufficiently circumscribed nor subject to adequate legal safeguards against abuse. They are not, therefore "in accordance with the law".'

It is of interest to point out that in *R (Gillan) v Metropolitan Police Commissioner* [2006] UKHL12, the House of Lords earlier had held that these provisions did *not* violate the convention.

ACTIVITY

Self-test question

What do you think are the advantages and disadvantages of the use of executive or other discretion?

KEY FACTS

Key facts on Dicey's first aspect of the rule of law

Dicey's first aspect is that a punishment would only be imposed on an individual if he violated the law as established in the ordinary legal proceedings before a court. It also denoted the predominance of regular law as opposed to the exercise of arbitrary power.
It is clear that at times individuals can suffer without breaking the law (eg remand, stop and search powers of the police etc).
Discretion is inevitable and necessary in a modern state and can be used to the advantage of the individual in order to mitigate the harshness of the 'regular' law. This discretion, however, has to be regulated.

6.7.6 Dicey's second aspect

In terms of equality before the law, Dicey stated that:

QUOTATION

'… with us no man is above the law, but (what is a different thing) that here every man, whatever be his rank or condition, is subject to the ordinary law of the realm … In England the idea of legal equality, or of the universal subjection of all classes to one law administered by the ordinary courts, has been pushed to its utmost limit. With us every official, from the Prime Minister down to a constable or a collector of taxes, is under the same responsibility for every act done without legal justification as any other citizen.

> … equality before the law, or the equal subjection of all classes to the ordinary law of the land administered by the ordinary law courts; the "rule of law" in this sense excludes the idea of any exemption of officials or others from the duty of obedience to the law which governs other citizens or from the jurisdiction of the ordinary tribunals'.
>
> A Dicey, *Introduction to the Study of the Law of the Constitution*
> (10th edn, Macmillan, 1959), pp 193 and 202–203 respectively.

Dicey argued that all individuals (both private citizens and state officials) are under the ordinary law. As a consequence, if a state official breached the law, he would be treated in the same way as an ordinary private individual would be if they had violated the same law: the same law would be applied to both before the ordinary courts. In other words, state officials did not enjoy special immunities from the law nor were they given special protection from the reaches of the 'ordinary' law.

In particular, Dicey contrasted our system with that which existed in France, whereby disputes with the government or state officials were processed in specific courts/tribunals (*tribunaux administratifs*). These tribunals processed administrative law (*droit administratif*), which was distinct from the ordinary court system. This meant that in France, there was a clear and separate system of administrative law which regulated the constitutional relationship between the individual and the state. Dicey perceived that these tribunals afforded the state and its officials a degree of protection which meant that these officials were not fully accountable as a private citizen would be before the ordinary court system. In fact, the *tribunaux administratifs* were staffed by specialists in public administration who were able to determine and assess the liability of public officials.

Dicey's principle of equality under the law is neatly illustrated by *Entick v Carrington* (1765) (see section 4.8.2). In this case, officials of the state were sued in the law of trespass for unlawfully entering Entick's property and seizing his papers. A private individual would have been sued in the same way had they entered and seized Entick's property. This illustrates the state being held to account by the ordinary law of the land before the ordinary court system.

A further example is demonstrated by the police exceeding their legal powers of detention:

SECTION

> Section 41 of PACE 1984 requires that a suspect may not be held in police detention beyond 24 hours without being charged (unless this has been extended under s 42 by a superintendent or above). If the police exceed this time limit without lawful authority, then they (typically the Chief Constable) are liable to be sued in the tort of false imprisonment in the same way that an individual would be if they detained another individual without lawful authority.

An interesting judicial affirmation of the principle that everyone is equal under the law, in particular government ministers, is illustrated by the following case:

CASE EXAMPLE

M v Home Office [1994] 1 AC 377

M, a citizen of Zaire, was unsuccessful in seeking political asylum in the United Kingdom. On the day he was to be removed from the country, he applied for leave to move for judicial review of this rejection. The judge in chambers thought M might have an arguable point and therefore required M's deportation to be postponed pending the application. The judge thought that counsel for the Secretary of State had, in effect, given an undertaking that M would not be removed pending the hearing of his case. In any event, M was removed from the United Kingdom to Paris bound for Zaire. Later that evening the judge issued a mandatory 'without notice' order which required the Home Secretary to return M to the jurisdiction of the court. The Home Secretary successfully challenged this order on the basis that the judge had had no jurisdiction to make it. Nevertheless, M's lawyers issued contempt proceedings against the Secretary of State for failing to comply with the court order while it was in force.

The House of Lords held, firstly that the court did have the jurisdiction to make coercive orders against ministers of the Crown (while they were acting in their official ministerial capacity). Secondly, if a government minister ignored an injunction made against him in his official capacity as a minister, the court possessed the jurisdiction to make a finding of contempt of court against him or his government department. Lord Templeman stated that:

JUDGMENT

'The argument that there is no power to enforce the law by injunction or contempt proceedings against a minister in his official capacity would, if upheld, establish the proposition that the executive obey the law as a matter of grace and not as a matter of necessity, a proposition which would reverse the result of the Civil War.'

6.7.7 Critique of Dicey's second aspect

The rule of law and judicial review

Although Dicey disapproved of the French administrative law system, in the last few decades it is arguable that the United Kingdom has developed a separate form of administrative law which in some ways is akin to the French system. In fact, judicial review proceedings, in which the courts supervise the actions of the executive to ensure that they act lawfully, are hallmarked by special features which are not present in the ordinary court system (see Chapter 19, and in particular section 19.2.5). For example:

- A claimant must seek permission to apply for judicial review (there is no right *per se*).
- A claimant must act promptly and not later than three months (in contrast, litigants suing in tort have six years – three if it involves personal injuries (Limitation Act 1980)).
- The claim must be made against a public body (or a body treated as such).
- The claim must also concern a public law issue (for example, how a public body misused its public law powers).
- The remedies which the court can issue are discretionary, and not automatic. As a consequence, even if the claimant can demonstrate that a public authority has acted unlawfully by misusing its public law powers, the court may take the view that it is not in the interest of public administration to grant relief.
- Judicial review proceedings are heard before specialist judges in the Administrative Court.
- These judges apply special public law principles (eg the public body must act rationally, in a procedurally fair way and respect the requirements of the European Convention on Human Rights).

In this way the state and its officials are not being treated in the same way as ordinary individuals. Instead, they are subject to a specialist court applying special public law principles. In this sense, in many ways the Administrative Court is not too dissimilar to the French administrative law system which Dicey disapproved of. In fairness to Dicey, however, the process of judicial review is an area of judicial activity which has only really exploded in the second half of the twentieth century.

The system of administrative tribunals

Today many disputes between the individual and the state (for example, in relation to the processing of welfare benefits and immigration) are resolved not through the ordinary courts, but instead by specialist tribunals (see section 21.1).

Main exceptions to the principle of equality

Although there should be general equality under the law, this does not mean that there should be no immunities at all or that all should be treated the same in all circumstances. There are a number of exceptions to the general principle of equality before the law and these include:

- Article 9 of the Bill of Rights 1689 states that the freedom of speech, debates or proceedings in Parliament ought not to be questioned in a court. The constitutional rationale behind this legal immunity for parliamentarians is to ensure that they can exercise their functions without fear of litigation. This immunity is regulated by Parliament itself so that if a member abuses this immunity (eg gratuitously defames a constituent), this will be investigated and punished by Parliament (see section 8.7.3).

- The Sovereign, together with foreign Heads of State/Sovereigns enjoy legal immunity from criminal liability: s 20 of the State Immunity Act 1978. However, following the passage of the Crown Proceedings Act 1947, Crown government departments could thereafter be sued in private law as of right.

- Diplomatic agents enjoy immunity under s 2(1) of the Diplomatic Privileges Act 1964.

- In relation to the courts, judges of the superior courts are not liable for anything said while carrying out their judicial function (*Anderson v Gorries* [1895] 1 QB 668) (see section 13.4.2). This is justified on the basis of the protection of judicial independence and the administration of justice so that judges can perform their constitutional functions of adjudication and apply the law independently, without fear of litigation. This benefits the wider public whose cases will be processed by the courts.

- For public policy reasons, specified classes of individuals are treated differently. For example, employers and employees as a group or class of individuals, have different obligations imposed upon them by the law which reflect the imbalance of power in their relationship. This is also the case in respect of landlords and tenants.

- In respect of equality it should be remembered that public authorities exercise particular functions that individuals do not. The exercise of these powers, therefore, has no real parallel in the private world of individuals. As a result, it is argued therefore that these bodies should be subject to *additional* legal controls.

The consequences of treating 'unequal' entities (ie state officials and private individuals) equally, is that it can give rise to constitutional difficulties as illustrated in *Malone v Metropolitan Police Commissioner* [1979] Ch 344. In brief, Malone alleged that the tapping of his telephone conversations in order to obtain evidence against him in criminal proceedings was unlawful. The court held, however, that there was no law against it. Sir Robert Megarry VC stated that:

JUDGMENT

'England, it may be said, is not a country where everything is forbidden except what is expressly permitted; it is a country where everything is permitted except what is expressly forbidden … if such tapping can be carried out without committing any breach of the law; it requires no authorisation by statute or common law; it can lawfully be done simply because there is nothing to make it unlawful.'

In this case the tapping of Malone's telephone took place on the premises of the Post Office and so no breach of the law of trespass had taken place (contrast *Entick* – see section 4.8.2). This case demonstrated the danger in treating constitutional unequals (here the police and a private individual – the latter would not have had access to Post Office premises) equally, as in these circumstances, in pursuance of protecting the individual, the actions of the police should be subject to *extra* controls and regulation.

ACTIVITY

Applying the law

Should the government be equally bound by the law? Can you think of reasons why the government should (a) be immune under the law and (b) have more duties under the law?

KEY FACTS

Key facts on Dicey's second aspect of the rule of law

Dicey contended that all individuals (both private individuals and state officials) are equal under the ordinary law. This meant that if a state official breached the law, he would be treated in the same way as an ordinary private individual. Under the principle of equality, state officials did not enjoy special immunities from the law.
It is clear that there are a number of exceptions to the principle of equality before the law: • The Sovereign, foreign Heads of State, diplomats and parliamentarians enjoy immunity from the law. • Judges of the superior courts are not liable for anything said while carrying out their judicial function. • In terms of their rights and responsibilities, certain classes of people, for instance landlords and tenants, will be treated differently under the law.

6.7.8 Dicey's third aspect

Dicey stated that:

QUOTATION

'We may say that the constitution is pervaded by the rule of law on the ground that the general principles of the constitution (as for example the right to personal liberty, or the right of public meeting) are with us the result of judicial decisions determining the rights of private persons in particular cases brought before the courts ... with us the law of the constitution, the rules which in foreign countries naturally form part of a constitutional code, are not the source but the consequence of the rights of individuals, as defined and enforced by the courts.'

A Dicey, *Introduction to the Study of the Law of the Constitution*
(10th edn, Macmillan, 1959), pp 195 and 203 respectively.

Dicey was making the point that Britain had a court-based constitution (in effect, a common law constitution) in the sense that the principles of the constitution, concerning the rights of the individual, were the direct consequence of decisions made by judges. In this way, Dicey contrasted the English (British) constitution with constitutional arrangements pertaining elsewhere, in which the rights and freedoms of the individual derived from a written codified constitutional document embracing a Bill or Charter of Rights.

For example, Entick (see section 4.8.2) successfully sued the King's messengers (state officials) in the ordinary law of trespass. Entick did not need to rely on a constitutional guarantee set out in a Bill of Rights. Instead, Entick relied on the common law to equip him with a practical remedy which could be enforced in the ordinary courts. For Dicey, these practical remedies gave the individual better protection than guarantees enshrined in a written constitution (typically in a Bill of Rights). As pointed out by Craig:

QUOTATION

'Dicey dealt in detail with the precarious protection of rights on the continent, where constitutions enshrining rights would often be abrogated at the stroke of the pen or the point of a sword. He felt that in the UK, where individual rights were the result of numerous judicial decisions indicating when the individual was at liberty to speak freely etc, it would be considerably more difficult for an authoritarian regime to sweep these rights aside.'

Sixth Report of Session 2006–07, *Relations between the executive, the judiciary and the Parliament*, HL Paper 151 (2007), Appendix 5, p 98.

ACTIVITY

Self-test questions

1. How did Dicey think that liberty should be protected?

2. Do you agree with him?

6.7.9 Critique of Dicey's third aspect

The courts have clearly fashioned a number of common law remedies for the individual which include the following:

- Trespass to person.
- Trespass to land.
- Trespass to property.
- False imprisonment.
- Assault.
- Battery.

These remedies, accordingly, can be used against state officials, as well as other individuals. For example, if an individual is unlawfully detained by the police they can sue in an action for false imprisonment. These remedies are in addition to any statutory rights and remedies which have been specifically conferred by an Act of Parliament (eg the right not to be discriminated against on the grounds of sex under the Sex Discrimination Act 1975 – at the time of going to print this has now been restated in the Equality Act 2010). The courts, however, can only protect the individual if *in fact* a particular right has been recognised either by the common law or by statute.

This point was neatly illustrated in the *Malone* case at section 6.7.7, as one of Malone's submissions against the Metropolitan Police Commissioner in respect of the tapping of his telephone was that it violated his right to privacy. Sir Robert Megarry VC countered this by indicating that no tort of privacy existed as Parliament had not legislated to create one and the courts in developing the common law had not fashioned one. In fact, in terms of the separation of powers, he noted that it was not the constitutional function of the judiciary to 'legislate in a new field' and create this new right of privacy:

JUDGMENT

'No new right in the law, fully-fledged with all the appropriate safeguards, can spring from the head of a judge deciding a particular case: only Parliament can create such a right.'

The courts, therefore, have been selective as to which tortious remedies an aggrieved individual can employ.

In any event, the capacity of the courts to protect the individual from the actions of the state are necessarily curtailed by the central element of the British constitution, namely, parliamentary sovereignty. Although Parliament can pass legislation conferring legal remedies on an individual (eg in the context of sexual and racial discrimination), it can conversely, pass laws which interfere excessively with the liberties and freedoms of the individual. In these circumstances, the courts are effectively rendered powerless if this excessive interference is expressly authorised and legitimised in the provisions of an Act.

For instance, it is worth recalling Lord Scarman's comments in *Rossminster Ltd* (1980) in relation to s 20C of the Taxes Management Act 1970 which conferred sweeping powers on Inland Revenue officers (see section 6.7.5). According to Lord Scarman although the Act represented a 'breath-taking inroad into the right of individual privacy', it was not the constitutional responsibility of the court to set it aside.

In fact, Parliament has on occasions passed retrospective law to negate and reverse the ruling of the courts. The most famous example being the enactment of the War Damage Act 1965 which in effect overruled the decision in the *Burmah Oil* case (see sections 4.9 and 7.5.1). This legislation was arguably *morally unconstitutional* (see section 4.15.2) as it interfered with the ruling of the highest court on the grounds of financial expediency. More recently, see the retrospective Terrorist Asset-Freezing (Temporary Provisions) Act 2010 at section 20.2.2.

In short, the courts:

- can develop the common law so as to provide practical remedies if an individual's (selected) freedoms have been violated, and
- will also interpret unclear legislative provisions in the light of constitutional principles which protect the individual (eg the presumption that Parliament did not intend to interfere with a person's right of access to the courts – see section 4.8.3).

Ultimately, however, Parliament can simply override the protection provided by the judges by passing legislation which clearly and explicitly authorises an interference with the freedoms of the individual. In contrast, under a codified constitution with an entrenched Bill of Rights, such legislation – all things being equal – would be rendered legally (and morally) unconstitutional and declared invalid by a Constitutional/Supreme Court.

For Dicey, however, as Parliament is elected by the people (or at least the dominant House of Commons is) it is answerable to the people and so this in itself necessarily restrains Parliament from passing draconian laws. In short, the constitutional theory is that parliamentarians will not pass laws which would unnecessarily and gratuitously infringe individual rights and freedoms, as the electorate have political sovereignty (see section 7.2.2). In other words, MPs must face the public at the time of re-election at a general election and so are ultimately answerable to the people for the laws that they have passed. The problem with this, of course, is that draconian legislation which only affects a certain section of society (eg prisoners, terrorist suspects and paedophiles) may in reality be popular with the public at large. This serves to illustrate that democracy should not be necessarily equated simply with majority rule as it may be necessary to ring-fence the rights of 'unpopular' individuals and protect them from the 'tyranny of the majority' (the relationship between the rule of law and parliamentary sovereignty will be considered at section 7.13).

Another point to note is that this element of Dicey's conception of the rule of law is now subject to the passage of the Human Rights Act 1998. This Act, in effect, gives further effect in the law of the United Kingdom to the rights enshrined in the European Convention on Human Rights. Under s 3 of the Act all courts and tribunals have the responsibility of interpreting all legislation consistently 'so far as it is possible to do so' in line with the rights of the European Convention. The effect of s 6 of the Act is that the courts and tribunals themselves, in effect, constitute a public authority for the purposes of the Act and so when interpreting or developing the law, they must act consistently with the European Convention. The Human Rights Act represents a significant shift in terms of 'rights protection' in the British constitution, and in some ways is akin to a Bill or Charter of positive rights (albeit a weak one) whereby positive and lawful justification is now needed for the state to interfere with the rights of the individual.

Although the Human Rights Act would appear to be at odds with Dicey's suspicions of written constitutional guarantees of rights, the articles of the Convention are enforced by individuals before the courts (in fact, any court or tribunal and not necessarily the Administrative Court). The role of the courts, therefore, will continue to remain central to the protection of individual rights. Under the Human Rights Act 1998 the function of the court is to uphold the protection afforded by these rights by construing all legislation in line with the Convention and ensuring that public authorities fully respect these rights and freedoms.

ACTIVITY

Self-test question

What impact do you think that the Human Rights Act 1998 has had on Dicey's third aspect of his conception of the rule law?

KEY FACTS

Key facts on Dicey's third aspect of the rule of law

Dicey contended that our constitution was in effect a court-based constitution in the sense that the rights and freedoms of the individual were the direct consequence of decisions made by judges.
In this way, Dicey contrasted the English (United Kingdom) constitution with the constitutional arrangements elsewhere, in which the rights and freedoms of the individual were derived from a written codified constitutional document embracing a Bill or Charter of Rights.
Dicey's third aspect now has to be re-evaluated in the light of the passage of the Human Rights Act 1998 which in effect represents a list of basic positive rights of the individual which can be enforced in the domestic courts.

6.7.10 The role of the United Kingdom courts and the rule of law

The following cases are examples where the principles underpinning the rule of law have been invoked in the courts.

The rule of law as a basis for the control of **de facto** *arbitrary powers*

In *Entick v Carrington* (see section 4.8.2) one of the arguments used by the defendants (ie the state) as a justification for the use of the warrant was that this power was essential to 'government and state necessity' and moreover that such warrants had been issued before and had not been questioned. Lord Camden CJ stated:

JUDGMENT

'This power, so claimed by the secretary of state, is not supported by one single citation from any law book extant … According to this reasoning, it is now incumbent upon the defendants to shew the law, by which this seizure is warranted. If that cannot be done, it is a trespass.' (*sic*)

The court also rejected the argument based on state necessity. In short, this case tells us that it is not the constitutional function of the judiciary to equip the government with new powers. If the government required these powers, then Parliament would need to pass the requisite legislation. In fact, the *Entick* case neatly demonstrates all three of Dicey's propositions:

- **The government/state must act within the law and not exercise arbitrary powers** – The state tried (unsuccessfully) to use a power in the form of a warrant which had no legal foundation or origin. As a result, the state could not 'trump' or lawfully negate the common law right (as expressed in the law of trespass) not to be trespassed against without lawful justification.
- **Equality under the law** – The state was held to account according to the ordinary law (trespass) before the ordinary courts.
- **A court-based constitution** – The ordinary courts provided Entick with a practical remedy against the state in the law of trespass.

More recently in *Webb v Chief Constable of Merseyside Police* [2000] 1 All ER 209 the Court of Appeal reiterated the principle that government is under the law. In this case the court made it clear that it was unlawful for a public authority (ie the police) to expropriate money or property from an individual without authorisation in a statute.

The House of Lords also reiterated the rule of law in the following ruling by refusing to countenance an abuse of public power by the executive:

CASE EXAMPLE

R v Secretary of State for the Home Department, ex parte Fire Brigades Union [1995] 2 All ER 244

The Criminal Injuries Compensation Scheme was established in 1964 under the royal prerogative to provide compensation to victims of crimes. In 1988 the Criminal Justice Act codified the scheme, but under s 171 it would not come into force until a day to be determined by the Secretary of State. This section therefore conferred a power on the minister to decide exactly when the statutory scheme should come into force. In December 1993 a government White Paper indicated that the compensation provisions of the Act would not be implemented, but would in due course be repealed. Instead, in March 1994 the government announced (under the royal prerogative) that a new tariff scheme would take effect from April 1994 (this flat-rate tariff scheme was in effect a cheaper scheme as it would compensate victims on the basis of the category that they fell into, rather than on an individual basis).

Trade Unions (whose members were susceptible to violent crime in their work) sought judicial review of the decision and sought a declaration, *inter alia*, that the Secretary of State had acted unlawfully by failing to bring into force the above provisions of the 1988 Act.

The House of Lords held that the Home Secretary had a power to act (as he had been conferred with a discretion as to when it was appropriate to bring the scheme into force) and that this was a matter for him to decide. Accordingly, it would not be constitutionally appropriate for the courts to interfere and require the Home Secretary to bring those provisions of the Act into effect. This statutory discretion, however, was not unlimited and the Home Secretary was required (while the sections were not in force) to keep under review the question of whether these provisions should be brought into force. It was, therefore, unlawful and an abuse of power to use royal prerogative power inconsistently with that responsibility. As a result, the Home Secretary's decision not to implement the provisions of the Act and that a tariff scheme would be implemented in its place, was unlawful. Lord Browne-Wilkinson stated that:

JUDGMENT

'It does not follow that, because the Secretary of State is not under any duty to bring the section into effect, he has an absolute and unfettered discretion whether or not to do so ... the Secretary of State comes under a clear duty to keep under consideration from time to time the question whether or not to bring the section (and therefore the statutory scheme) into force. In my judgment he cannot lawfully surrender or release the power contained in section 171(1) so as to purport to exclude its future exercise either by himself or by his successors.'

Similarly, in *Cure & Deeley* (1962) (see section 6.7.5) the courts demonstrated that they will limit the scope of wide discretionary powers conferred on executive authorities. The case below demonstrates the courts invoking the rule of law in overseeing executive action:

CASE EXAMPLE

R v Horseferry Road Magistrates' Court, ex parte Bennett [1994] 1 AC 42

Bennett was a New Zealand citizen who claimed that he had been kidnapped from South Africa and brought to England where he was arrested to face criminal charges. The Magistrates' Court refused his request to adjourn the committal of his case to the Crown Court. Bennett sought judicial review of the decision, but the High Court refused his application.

The House of Lords held that the courts should take cognisance of the circumstances which led a defendant to appear before the court. In this case, Bennett had been brought back to the United Kingdom without regard to the available extradition process and in violation of international law. The High Court could therefore inquire into the circumstances that led an individual to be brought before the court and could stay the prosecution (as an abuse of process) if it was satisfied that extradition proceedings had been disregarded. Lord Griffiths stated that:

JUDGMENT

'The judiciary accept a responsibility for the maintenance of the rule of law that embraces a willingness to oversee executive action and to refuse to countenance behaviour that threatens either basic human rights or the rule of law.'

Judicial deference

In contrast to the cases above, on occasions the courts have (albeit historically) adopted a 'hands off approach' in order to avoid trespassing on the constitutional role of the executive (eg to determine public policy or to make politically sensitive decisions). In this way judicial deference to executive decision-making avoids infringing the principle of the separation of powers as the executive has been charged with making these decisions. This in turn, however, gave the individual little legal protection from the exercise of state power, as illustrated in the following infamous and historic case:

CASE EXAMPLE

Liversidge v Anderson [1942] AC 206

Under reg 18B of the Defence (General) Regulations 1939, the Secretary of State could make an order to detain a person if he *had reasonable cause* to believe that the person was of hostile origin or associations.

The House of Lords held that under this emergency legislation (in the context of the Second World War) a court could not inquire as to whether in fact the minister had reasonable grounds for his belief that the person be of hostile associations. In other words, this was an issue of executive discretion for the minister concerned and the court could not require the minister to give the particulars of the grounds on which he had had reasonable cause to believe the detainee to be of hostile associations.

This is a highly controversial case as it effectively conferred a considerable power onto the executive. Indeed, as Lord Atkin said in his dissenting opinion, 'I protest, even if I do it alone, against a strained construction put on words with the effect of giving an uncontrolled power of imprisonment to the minister'.

In this case the court was aware that the minister was politically accountable for his actions to Parliament under the constitutional convention of ministerial responsibly (see section 4.13.12).

The controversial majority decision in this case was rejected in subsequent case law: see Lords Diplock and Scarman in *Inland Revenue Commissioners and Another v Rossminster Ltd and others* [1980] AC 952.

A more recent example than *Liversidge* of the courts adopting a 'hands-off approach' (where the source/nature of information against the individual was highly confidential) is the following case:

CASE EXAMPLE

R v Secretary of State for Home Affairs, ex parte Hosenball [1977] 1 WLR 766

Hosenball was an American journalist and in the interests of national security the Home Secretary had decided to make a deportation order against him under s 3 of the Immigration Act 1971. It was alleged that Hosenball had obtained for publication information harmful to the security of the United Kingdom. He was informed that he could make representations to an individual panel in respect of his deportation, but could not appeal. Despite a request by Hosenball's solicitors, the Secretary of State declined to provide further information (ie the relevant particulars of what was alleged against him).

The panel subsequently conducted a hearing at which Hosenball called witnesses and made representations. Shortly afterwards the Secretary of State made the deportation order which Hosenball sought to quash on the grounds that the rules of natural justice had been violated as he had been denied the particulars of the allegations made against him.

The Court of Appeal held that the principles underpinning natural justice were modified when issues of national security were involved. Here public policy necessitated the protection of the confidentiality of security information. On the facts of the case, the Secretary of State had considered personally Hosenball's request for further particulars of the allegations (but that this had been refused as it was not in the interests of national security to provide further information) and there was nothing to suggest that he had acted unfairly. The court also noted that under the convention of ministerial responsibility the Secretary of State was politically answerable to Parliament for his decision. Lord Denning MR observed that:

JUDGMENT

'There is a conflict here between the interests of national security on the one hand and the freedom of the individual on the other. The balance between these two is not for a court of law. It is for the Home Secretary, he is the person entrusted by Parliament with the task. In some parts of the world National Security has on occasions been used as an excuse for all kinds of infringements of individual liberties. But not in England.'

More recently, see *Secretary of State for the Home Department v AF* (2009) at section 6.8.

ACTIVITY

Self-test question

What is wrong with the (albeit rather historical) approach taken by the majority in *Liversidge* (1942)?

The rule of law in the defence of fundamental constitutional principles

As noted at section 4.8.3, in construing legislative provisions, the courts will do so in the light of certain constitutional principles and presumptions. In this way, the courts recognise and uphold the principles which underpin the rule of law.

Retrospective legislation

One constitutional principle is the presumption against retrospective legislation (see sections 4.8.3 and 6.3.2). In *Waddington v Miah* [1974] 2 All ER 377 the House of Lords construed the Immigration Act 1971 so as not to have retrospective criminal effect. Lord Reid drew upon the presumptions that surely Parliament would never pass retrospective criminal legislation or knowingly legislate contrary to international law/Treaties as he stated that:

JUDGMENT

'There has for a very long time been a strong feeling against making legislation, and particularly criminal legislation, retrospective.'

Lord Reid then referred to Art 11 of the Universal Declaration of Human Rights and Art 7 of the European Convention. In this light, he argued:

JUDGMENT

'So it is hardly credible that any government department would promote or that Parliament would pass retrospective criminal legislation'.

Similarly, the House of Lords in *R v Secretary of State for the Home Department, ex parte Pierson* [1998] AC 539 ensured that the Home Secretary's powers of reviewing a tariff to be served by a mandatory life sentence prisoner (s 35 of the Criminal Justice Act 1991), did not, in effect, retrospectively increase a sentence. Lord Steyn noted that:

JUDGMENT

'Unless there is the clearest provision to the contrary, Parliament must be presumed not to legislate contrary to the rule of law. And the rule of law enforces minimum standards of fairness, both substantive and procedural.'

These cases, of course, do not mean that Parliament cannot explicitly pass laws which are retrospective or even contrary to the European Convention. In terms of the former, in 1991 Parliament passed the War Crimes Act which is clearly retrospective legislation as it relates to atrocities committed during the Second World War in Germany or territories occupied by Germany. Moreover, it is of interest to note that this Act was enacted under the Parliament Acts of 1911 and 1949, as the House of Lords refused to pass it and therefore it was passed without their consent (see section 10.10.2). More recently see the retrospective effect of s 58(4) of the Finance Act 2008.

The principle of legality

In order to protect the individual, the courts use the doctrine of legality. This precludes statutory interference with the rights/freedoms of citizens unless this is expressly provided for with specific words (this means that general words will be insufficient to achieve this aim). This is illustrated in the following case:

CASE EXAMPLE

R v Secretary of State for the Home Department, ex parte Simms and another [1999] 3 All ER 400

O'Brien and Simms had been convicted of murder and claimed to have been the victims of a miscarriage of justice and they sought to reopen their cases through oral interviews with journalists. Under paras 37 and 37A of the Prison Service Standing Order 5A (made under s 47(1) of the Prison Act 1952 and r 33 of the Prison Rules 1964), the prison authorities refused to permit these interviews unless the journalists concerned signed an undertaking not to publish any part of the resulting interviews. The journalists refused to do so and O'Brien and Simms challenged the lawfulness of the above prison policy.

The House of Lords held that a blanket ban on interviews of prisoners by journalists was unlawful. The purpose of the interviews was, in effect, to enlist the investigative resources of the journalists to help the prisoners gain access to justice, with the eventual aim of demonstrating that there had been a miscarriage of justice. The court held that a blanket ban, therefore, deprived a prisoner of a basic and fundamental right, that of gaining access to justice. Paragraphs 37 and 37A were to be interpreted in line with the principle of legality, which meant that ambiguous or general words did not override fundamental rights such as the right to gain access to justice (which was in effect a constitutional right). Although the paragraphs themselves were not *ultra vires*, the above policy was unlawful. Lord Steyn stated that:

JUDGMENT

'The starting point is the right of freedom of expression. In a democracy it is the primary right: without it an effective rule of law is not possible … They wish to challenge the safety of their convictions. In principle it is not easy to conceive of a more important function which free speech might fulfil.'

The presumption of innocence

One constitutional principle underpinning the rule of law is the presumption of innocence (ie the burden/standard of proof). In *R v Secretary of State for the Home Department, ex parte Khawaja* [1984] 1 AC 74, the House of Lords stated that in relation to an application for judicial review of an order detaining an individual under the Immigration Act 1971, it was for the executive/state to prove to the court (on the balance of probabilities) the facts relied upon by an immigration officer as justifying determination that the person *was* an illegal entrant.

KEY FACTS

Key facts on the British courts and the rule of law

The constitutional function of the judiciary is to uphold the principles underpinning the rule of law.
The courts control the *de facto* use of arbitrary powers by the state (*ex parte Fire Brigades Union* (1995) and *ex parte Bennett* (1994)).
The courts also interpret law in light of certain constitutional principles: • Prospective legislation (*Waddington v Miah* (1974)). • The principle of legality (*ex parte Simms and another* (1999)). • The presumption of innocence/standard of proof (*ex parte Khawaja* (1984)).

6.7.11 Excessive state power?

The past few years have been punctuated by the successive passage of legislation designed to counter terrorism. These Acts have cumulatively increased the power of the state to interfere with the rights of the individual with the public policy intention of combating terrorism. For example:

■ The Terrorism Act 2000 – this Act, in effect, placed counter-terrorist powers on a permanent basis (ie not annually reviewed by Parliament).

■ The Anti-terrorism, Crime and Security Act 2001 (passed in the aftermath of the terrorist attacks of 9/11) – increased police stop and search powers and authorised the indefinite detention of individuals suspected of international terrorism. The latter was subsequently (and successfully) challenged in the House of Lords in *A and others v Secretary of State* (2004) (see section 6.7.4) which in turn led to the following Act:

■ The Prevention of Terrorism Act 2005 – the Act authorised control orders on individuals which could be used, for example, to restrict their movements (eg a curfew). These control orders were introduced as a result of the successful challenge (above) to the indefinite detention of suspects. The breadth of control orders made under the 2005 Act were then challenged successfully in *Secretary of State for the Home Department v*

JJ and others (2007). In addition, the failure to disclose sufficient evidence against an individual detained under a control order was challenged successfully in *Secretary for the Home Department v AF* (2009). See Section 6.8.

■ The Terrorism Act 2006 (passed in the aftermath of the bombings in London) – this Act, *inter alia*, extended the length of time that terrorist suspects could be held without charge from 14 to 28 days. As indicated earlier (see section 6.7.5), the government had originally sought a period of detention of 90 days, but the House of Commons refused to accept this. The Act also created an offence of encouraging terrorism (s 1) and one relating to the dissemination of terrorist publications (s 2), both of which raise issues of an interference with freedom of speech.

■ The Counter-Terrorism Act 2008 – this Act, *inter alia*, provided for the post-charge questioning of terrorist suspects. The Bill had originally sought powers to allow the detention and questioning of suspects for up to 42 days without charge, but this was abandoned after defeat in the House of Lords.

■ The Terrorist Asset-Freezing (Temporary Provisions) Act 2010 – this Act was passed in the context of the decision of the Supreme Court in *HM Treasury v Ahmed* (2010) – see section 20.2.2.

According to LIBERTY (an organisation dedicated to the protection of human rights), although a government has a responsibility to take steps to protect individuals from terrorism, this does not justify encroaching unnecessarily on individual rights and freedoms. The concern of LIBERTY is that legislative measures which confer excessive powers on the state are counterproductive as they risk alienating individuals (thereby acting as a 'recruiting sergeant' for terrorism) and in fact threaten the values which we should be striving as a society to protect. Finally, at the time of writing, a further case in which the rule of law was invoked by the courts was *R (Mohamed) v Secretary of State for Foreign and Commonwealth Affairs* [2010] EWCA Civ 65.

6.8 Conclusion

The rule of law is a central aspect of the British constitution as it is an essential element of constitutionalism, namely, the principle that government and state power must be limited, regulated and controlled. The rule of law is also inextricably linked with the independence of the judiciary as one of the constitutional responsibilities of the judiciary is to uphold the various principles underpinning the rule of law. In particular, a practical demonstration of the rule of law is illustrated each time a judge in judicial review proceedings in the Administrative Court holds the executive and public bodies legally to account for the misuse of their public law powers. This reaffirms the principle that all bodies, and in particular the government, are under the law.

In fact, the importance attached to the principle of the rule of law was recently given statutory recognition in s 1 of the Constitutional Reform Act 2005:

SECTION

1. This Act does not adversely affect –
(a) the existing constitutional principle of the rule of law , or
(b) the Lord Chancellor's existing constitutional role in relation to that principle.

For example, traditionally the Lord Chancellor would try to ensure that the principles underpinning the rule of law (eg safeguarding the presumption of innocence) were respected when, for example, draft legislative measures were being considered in Cabinet. In addition, s 17 of the Act details the oath to be taken by the Lord Chancellor, which specifies that the incumbent must respect the rule of law (see section 5.7.9). In 'The Rule of Law' [2007] 66 CLJ 67, Lord Bingham identified the following eight principles/rules:

- The law must be accessible, intelligible, clear and predictable.
- Questions of legal right and liability should be resolved (ordinarily) by the application of the law and not the exercise of discretion.
- Laws should apply equally.
- Law should afford adequate protection of (fundamental) human rights.
- Means should be provided for resolving civil disputes.
- Public officers and ministers must exercise their powers reasonably, in good faith, for their proper purpose and without exceeding their limits.
- State adjudicative proceedings should be fair.
- The State must comply with its obligations in international law.

The following is a recent case in which the rule of law was invoked.

CASE EXAMPLE

Secretary of State for the Home Department v AF [2009] UKHL 28

Under s 2 of the Prevention of Terrorism Act 2005 the Secretary of State made a non-derogating control order against AF (and others). The House of Lords held that in terms of Art 6 (the right to a fair trial) the 'controlled' individual had to be given sufficient information about the case/allegations against him.

Lord Hope said:

JUDGMENT

'If the rule of law is to mean anything, it is in cases such as these that the Court must stand by principle. It must insist that the person affected be told what is alleged against him.'

As a postscript to the case, in *Secretary of State for the Home Department v AF* [2010] EWHC 42 (Admin) the Administrative Court quashed AF's control order (with retrospective effect).

Finally, in considering the rule of law, the following comments of Lord Woolf are worth noting:

QUOTATION

'Ultimately, it is the rule of law which stops a democracy descending into an elected dictatorship.'
Lord Woolf, 'The rule of law and a change in the constitution' [2004] 63 CLJ 317.

SUMMARY

- The rule of law is a concept of some antiquity.
- The rule of law has been subject to a number of different interpretations ranging from a legal principle which ensures that government acts under the law to a political ideal/theory which focuses on a formal conception of the principle and the form that laws should take (Raz). The principle is also used in an international context.
- The rule of law is a key element of constitutionalism ensuring that government officials act strictly within their powers and the courts play a crucial role in holding the executive to account.
- The rule of law in the United Kingdom is closely associated with Dicey who expounded the following principles:
  - That no man was punishable except for a distinct breach of the law as established in ordinary legal proceedings before a court.

- The predominance of regular law over the exercise of arbitrary power (including wide discretionary power).
- No man is above the law – equality before the law.
- The United Kingdom has a court-based constitution in that the freedoms of the individual were the direct consequences of the decisions made by the judiciary.
■ Dicey's principles, though persuasive, have been subject to criticism:
  - Individuals can suffer without violating the law.
  - Discretion is necessary in a modern state (although it must be regulated by the courts).
  - There are exceptions to the principle of equality (eg parliamentarians) and the development of judicial review is akin to the French tribunaux administratifs.
  - The Human Rights Act 1998 has created positive rights (albeit they are enforced before the courts).

SAMPLE ESSAY QUESTION

What is meant by the rule of law in the context of constitutional law?

Introduction:

Note the rule of law as a concept with different meanings.

In essence, it means government acting under the law and that all are subject to the law.

The rule of law as a legal principle:

The principle is seen as a procedural mechanism checking the executive/state whereby the actions of public officials should have a foundation in law (*Jones* 2005).

Note the limitation of this principle (link to the substantive concept of the principle below).

The rule of law also ensures social order.

A formal view of the rule of law:

Raz's formal conception concerning the form that laws should take (prospective, clear, open, stable etc).

The rule of law as a substantive concept:

Link the rule of law with certain fundamental values and human rights (eg presumption of innocence).

The international dimension of the rule of law:

Universal Declaration of Human Rights

European Convention (see *Gillan* (2010))

The rule of law in the UK:

Dicey's three principles:

1. Predominance of regular law as opposed to arbitrary power (*A and others* (2004))

2. Equality under the law (*M v Home Office* (1994))

3. The rights of individuals are the consequence of judicial decisions (*Entick* (1765) but see Human Rights Act 1998

Note criticism of Dicey and the application/relevance of his principles today.

The courts and the rule of law:

Note the constitutional role of the judiciary to uphold the rule of law and limit executive power (*Bennett* (1994) and *Fire Brigades Union* (1995)).

Also see the recent cases involving powers of the state under terrorism legislation (*JJ* (2007) and *AF* (2009)).

CONCLUSION

 # Further reading

Books

Barnett, H, *Constitutional and Administrative Law* (7th edn, Routledge–Cavendish, 2009), Chapter 3.

Bradley, A and Ewing, K, *Constitutional and Administrative Law* (14th edn, Pearson/ Longman, 2007), Chapter 6.

Lord Bingham, *The Rule of Law* (Allen Lane, 2010).

Craig, P, 'Fundamental principles of administrative law in relation to basic principles of constitutional law' in Feldman, D, (ed), *English Public Law* (2nd edn Oxford University Press, 2009), p 600.

Jowell, J, 'The Rule of Law and its underlying values' in Jowell, J and Oliver, D, (eds) *The Changing Constitution* (6th edn, Oxford University Press, 2007), p 5.

Articles

Lord Bingham, 'Dicey Revisited' [2002] PL 39.

Lord Bingham, 'The rule of law' (2007) 66 CLJ 67.

Foster, S, 'The fight against terrorism, detention without trial and human rights' (2009) 14 Coventry Law Journal, 3 (available at www.westlaw.com).

Majid, A, 'Do we care about the rule of law?' (2005) 155 NLJ 1561.

Raz, J, 'The Rule of Law and its Virtue' (1977) 93 LQR 195.

Lord Steyn, 'Democracy, the Rule of Law and the Role of Judges' [2006] EHRLR 243.

Lord Woolf, 'Droit Public-English Style' [1995] PL 57.

7
Parliamentary sovereignty

AIMS AND OBJECTIVES

At the end of this chapter you should be able to:

- Define the term parliamentary sovereignty
- Identify and explain Dicey's conception of parliamentary sovereignty
- Identify and explain the different aspects of parliamentary sovereignty
- Explain how parliamentary sovereignty relates to other aspects of the British constitution
- Explain the constitutional importance of parliamentary sovereignty

7.1 Introduction

Parliamentary sovereignty is the central element of the British constitution and it is impossible to understand the nature and mechanics of the constitution without an appreciation of this principle. In fact, this doctrine sets the British constitution apart from the vast majority of other democratic states. For example, although the legislative bodies of the United States' Congress and the Republic of Ireland's Oireachtas are law-making bodies which pass primary legislation, these legislatures do not have unlimited law making powers as they are constitutionally and legally constrained by their written codified constitutions. For example, Art 15.4 of the Irish constitution states that the Oireachtas shall not enact legislation 'which is in any respect repugnant' to the constitution. In other words, if these bodies were to pass legislation which was inconsistent with the rules laid down in their codified constitutions, it would be subject to judicial review (constitutional review) by their respective Supreme Courts and declared illegal, that is to say legally unconstitutional (contrast with section 4.15) and so invalid.

In contrast, in the United Kingdom the Queen in Parliament (or Crown in Parliament) can in legal theory pass any law and the legislation which is enacted is not subject to judicial review by the courts. This is because Parliament has not historically been constrained by a higher set of legal rules enshrined in a written constitution. In other words, Acts of Parliament (unlike Acts of the United States Congress) could not be tested or questioned against an overriding codified constitution (however, the position in the context of European Union law will be considered at section 15.6). Indeed as Bogdanor has observed:

QUOTATION

'The British Constitution could thus be summed up in just eight words: "What the Queen in Parliament enacts is law".'

The New British Constitution (Hart Publishing, 2009) p 13.

Although in the United Kingdom the courts, historically, have not subjected Acts of Parliament to judicial review, they do review and invalidate delegated legislation made by the executive. This is because this type of legislation (eg Statutory Instruments) does not enjoy the sovereign status of primary legislation as it has not been passed by the legislature, but rather by the executive (see section 5.7.2). Finally, although the principle of a legislature with the legal power to make any law that it chooses is very unusual, it is not unique. New Zealand also has an uncodified constitution which contains a Parliament (a unicameral legislature comprising the House of Representatives) which possesses the constitutional characteristic of sovereignty and, as in the United Kingdom, it is able to pass any law that it chooses.

7.2 Terminology

The term parliamentary sovereignty (which denotes that the Queen in Parliament has unlimited legislative power) is arguably apt to mislead, because the term 'sovereignty' can have another meaning. For example, it is used in the context of international law, relations and politics to indicate that a state is independent and sovereign (for example, France or Italy). As a consequence, a number of legal academics prefer to use the term the legislative supremacy of Parliament. Notwithstanding this, as parliamentary sovereignty (at least in historic terms) is closely associated with Dicey, and as he used this term, this book will do likewise. This should not be problematic providing we understand the sense in which the term is being used, namely to denote the legal principle that Parliament can in theory pass any law that it chooses.

As indicated earlier, Dicey argued that the constitution was founded on the following twin pillars:

- The rule of law and
- Parliamentary sovereignty.

In respect of the term sovereignty, he specifically differentiated between:

- Legal sovereignty and
- Political sovereignty.

7.2.1 Legal sovereignty

In essence, legal sovereignty is concerned with the legislative power of the Queen in Parliament (the principle that any legislation can be made on any subject). Legal sovereignty is concerned with the constitutional relationship between the courts and the legislature (hence it is therefore necessarily an issue of constitutional significance). It is with legal sovereignty that this chapter is specifically concerned. Legal sovereignty relates to Bills which have been consented to (and therefore have become Acts of Parliament) by the following three constitutional elements:

- The House of Commons.
- The House of Lords (providing the Parliament Acts of 1911 and 1949 do not apply – see section 10.10.1 below).
- The monarch (The Royal Assent).

Legal sovereignty is not concerned with the political machinations within Parliament which led to the passing of an Act. It is not therefore concerned with the scenario, for example, whereby a highly controversial Bill only narrowly passed through both Houses.

7.2.2 Political sovereignty

In contrast, political sovereignty rests with the people (the electorate), for as Dicey noted, the electorate can 'always enforce their will'. By this he meant that politically, Parliament (or more specifically the House of Commons and so by extension, the government) is accountable directly to the people at every general election. In a sense, therefore, this is analogous to a social contract between the governed (specifically the electorate) and the state, whereby the people at a general election confer power and constitutional legitimacy on Parliament to legislate. Such authority can, of course, be revoked by the people at the next general election.

Logically therefore, as Parliament can pass legally any law it chooses, this could include a draconian law which breaches the basic rights and freedoms of the individual. Such legislation would, however, be unlikely to be passed as, ultimately, parliamentarians serving in the House of Commons would have to face the electorate at some point within the next five years. Political sovereignty, therefore, places external, political restraints on the legislation that the Queen in Parliament will actually enact in practice.

KEY FACTS

Key facts on the definition of sovereignty

- Legal sovereignty is concerned with the legal relationship between Parliament and the courts.
- Political sovereignty is concerned with the political relationship between Parliament (specifically the House of Commons and by extension the government) and the people (the electorate).

7.3 The meaning and scope of legal sovereignty

7.3.1 Introduction

Parliamentary sovereignty means simply that the Queen in Parliament legally can pass any law (with one exception – see section 7.9) as the courts do not have the constitutional power to invalidate laws and declare them to be legally unconstitutional (see section 4.15) or even illegal (but see in the context of European Union law at section 15.6).

In essence, as made clear by Lord Diplock in *Duport Steels Ltd and others v Sirs and others* [1980] 1 All ER 529: 'Parliament makes the laws, the judiciary interpret them'. In fact, this constitutional interaction between the two arms of the state has been described by Lord Bridge in *X Ltd v Morgan-Grampian (Publishers) Ltd* [1991] 1 AC 1 in terms of a 'twin sovereignty':

JUDGMENT

'In our society the rule of law rests upon twin foundations: the sovereignty of the Queen in Parliament in making the law and the sovereignty of the Queen's courts in interpreting and applying the law.'

7.3.2 The origins of parliamentary sovereignty

In view of the fact that parliamentary sovereignty is the key element of the British constitution, it is perhaps surprising that the exact origin of the principle is not clear. In other countries, citizens can date accurately the origin and promulgation of their written codified constitution (eg the Indian constitution was declared passed in November 1949 and came into force on 26th January 1950). What is clear is that parliamentary sovereignty is a common law doctrine. In other words, it is the courts that have for centuries in their judgments accepted that the Queen in Parliament can pass any law. In this context, Wade has made the following point:

QUOTATION

> 'The rule of judicial obedience is in one sense a rule of common law, but in another sense – which applies to no other rule of common law – it is the ultimate *political* fact upon which the whole system of legislation hangs. Legislation owes its authority to the rule: the rule does not owe its authority to legislation. To say that Parliament can change the rule, merely because it can change any other rule, is to put the cart before the horse.'
>
> H Wade, 'The basis of legal sovereignty' [1955] CLJ 172.

More recently, in terms of the origin of the principle of parliamentary sovereignty, Lord Steyn in *R (Jackson) v Attorney General* [2005] UKHL 56 reaffirmed that:

JUDGMENT

> 'It is a construct of the common law. The judges created this principle.' (But see his further comments at section 7.7).

In short, parliamentary sovereignty exists because judges have, for centuries, consistently stated that they do not have the constitutional power to review or question Acts of Parliament and that the judicial function is limited to interpreting legislation in order to ascertain the intention of Parliament in passing it. The case below illustrates the principle:

CASE EXAMPLE

Cheney v Conn [1968] 1 WLR 242

Cheney was assessed for income tax under the Finance Act 1964. Part of the receipts from those taxes for these years (1963–65) were allocated to the construction of nuclear weapons. Cheney challenged his tax assessments on the basis that part of the proposed use of the taxes (ie the construction of nuclear weapons) was contrary to international law: the Geneva Convention (scheduled to the Geneva Conventions Act 1957).

The High Court (Chancery Division) held that the charge to tax under the Act and the tax assessments were not invalidated. Even if there was a conflict between international law and statute, where the latter's provisions were clear and unambiguous, it would prevail. Ungoed-Thomas J stated that:

JUDGMENT

> 'If the purpose for which a statute may be used is an invalid purpose, then such remedy as there may be must be directed to dealing with that purpose and not to invalidating the statute itself. What the statute itself enacts cannot be unlawful, because what the statute says and provides is itself the law, and the highest form of law that is known to this country. It is the law which prevails over every other form of law, and it is not for the court to say that a parliamentary enactment, the highest law in this country, is illegal.'

ACTIVITY

Applying the law

Why do you think that it is logically impossible for the principle of parliamentary sovereignty to be established in an Act of Parliament?

7.3.3 What constitutes an Act of Parliament?

As the principle of parliamentary sovereignty necessitates that the courts obey and apply Acts of Parliament, this in turn begs the question as to what exactly is an Act of Parliament.

In identifying what constitutes an Act of Parliament, historically the courts have applied the 'enrolled Bill rule' as stated by Lord Campbell in the following case:

CASE EXAMPLE

Edinburgh and Dalkeith Railway Co v Wauchope (1842) 8 C1 & F 710

Wauchope unsuccessfuly argued that a statute (a private Act of Parliament) should be disapplied because the standing orders of the House of Commons had not been complied with. These orders had required that individuals affected by the proposed legislation were to be consulted. In terms of a Bill's passage through Parliament, Lord Campbell in the House of Lords noted (albeit *obiter*) that:

JUDGMENT

'All that a court of justice can look to is the parliamentary roll; they see that an Act has passed both Houses of Parliament, and that it has received the Royal Assent, and no court of justice can inquire into the manner in which it was introduced into Parliament, what was done previously to its being introduced, or what passed in Parliament during the various stages of its progress through both Houses of Parliament.'

Thus, the judges will simply look to the 'parliamentary roll' to ascertain whether or not a Bill had become an Act of Parliament. The judiciary will not be concerned with the internal process and passage of that Bill within Parliament as that would inevitably contravene parliamentary privilege which dictates that Parliament has the constitutional right to determine and monitor its own proceedings (see section 8.7.2). In referring to the parliamentary roll, the procedure historically adopted by the courts would be as follows:

The enrolled Bill rule

- Has the Bill received the consent of the House of Commons?
- Has the Bill received the consent of the House of Lords?
- Has the Bill been granted the Royal Assent?

If the answer to all three questions is yes, the Bill is treated as an Act of Parliament. The courts, therefore, are not concerned with how (or more pertinently, why) the Bill came to be on the parliamentary roll (on this point, see also *Pickin* at section 7.8.1). As noted by Bradley, however, today the courts do not need to consult the parliamentary roll as the words of enactment at the beginning of a statute will indicate this information (House of Lords Select Committee on the Constitution, Seventh Report of Session 2005–06, *Constitutional aspects of the challenge to the Hunting Act 2004*, HL 141 (2006), Appendix 3).

ACTIVITY

Self-test question

What constitutional problems (if any) would arise if the courts were to investigate how a Bill proceeded through Parliament?

As it is the Queen in Parliament who makes Acts of Parliament, it is clear that a 'mere' resolution of the House of Commons is not an Act of Parliament as it does not alter the law nor does it have sovereign status (*Stockdale v Hansard* (1839) 9 Ad & El 1; *Bowles v Bank of England* [1913] 1 Ch 57). Thus, it should be remembered that technically it is an Act of Parliament enacted by Parliament which is sovereign, rather than Parliament itself. In the context of what constitutes an Act of Parliament see the *Jackson* case at sections 7.10.3 and 10.10.3.

- Parliamentary sovereignty means that in legal theory the Queen in Parliament legally can pass any law.
- Parliamentary sovereignty is a construct of the common law.
- In determining what constitutes an Act of Parliament, historically the judges would look to the 'parliamentary roll' to ascertain whether or not a Bill had become an Act of Parliament. The judiciary would not be concerned with the internal process of the Bill through Parliament (*Edinburgh and Dalkeith Railway v Wauchope* (1842)).

7.4 Dicey and parliamentary sovereignty

Dicey viewed the principle of parliamentary sovereignty as the cornerstone of the constitution and described it in the following terms:

QUOTATION

'The principle of Parliamentary sovereignty means neither more nor less than this, namely, that Parliament thus defined has, under the English constitution, the right to make or unmake any law whatever; and, further, that no person or body is recognised by the law of England as having a right to override or set aside the legislation of Parliament.'

A Dicey, *Introduction to the Study of the Law of the Constitution*
(10th edn, Macmillan, 1959), pp 39–40.

Dicey viewed parliamentary sovereignty as having both positive and negative elements.

■ The positive aspect was that the Crown/Queen in Parliament legally can pass any law it chooses (with one exception – see principle 3 below).

■ The negative aspect was that no court or other body can question a statute.

Dicey's conception is considered below in the following three interconnected elements/principles:

Figure 7.1 Parliamentary sovereignty and the common law

7.5 Principle 1: The Queen in Parliament legally can pass any law

This in essence embodies the positive element of parliamentary sovereignty, namely, the Queen in Parliament can, in legal theory, pass any law (including the repeal or modification of any existing primary legislation). Parliament can pass any law it considers necessary because under the British constitution there is, legally, nothing to stop Parliament from doing so.

7.5.1 Parliamentary sovereignty and the common law

In the United Kingdom's three legal systems (see section 3.1) there is a hierarchy of laws as Acts of Parliament (statutory sources) are higher in legal status than the common law. In short, where the content of the common law and a statute are inconsistent, the latter will prevail. This means that should Parliament decide to do so, it can legislate to override (or codify) the common law as illustrated in the context of the law of tort, when in 1987 Parliament passed the Consumer Protection Act. In fact, the Act was passed in order to comply with a European Union directive, thereby also demonstrating the influence European law has had, and continues to have, on the British constitution (see Chapter 15).

Similarly, in the context of the royal prerogative (a power which the government derives from the common law – see section 11.9), Parliament can, if it chooses to do so, legislate in an area already covered by the royal prerogative. In these circumstances, the resulting statutory provisions will take precedence over the royal prerogative and thereafter the government would be required to act in accordance with the new statutory provision rather than the pre-existing royal prerogative. As Lord Dunedin stated in *Attorney-General v De Keyser's Royal Hotel Ltd* [1920] AC 508 (see section 11.9.5):

JUDGMENT

'If the whole ground of something which could be done by the prerogative is covered by the statute, it is the statute that rules.'

In addition, as noted at section 4.9, in *Burmah Oil Co Ltd* (1965) the House of Lords had determined that although the destruction of the oil installations in Burma during the Second World War was permissible under the royal prerogative, it nevertheless necessitated compensation for the damage caused. In direct response to this judgment, Parliament in 1965 passed the War Damage Act which in effect nullified the above decision of the House of Lords. In short, therefore, the common law can be overridden by an Act of Parliament at any time. This in itself raises an interesting constitutional issue, as, if the principle of parliamentary sovereignty is a 'construct' and rule of the common law, can Parliament legislate to change the common law rule espousing parliamentary sovereignty? (see section 7.10). More recently the Criminal Evidence (Witness Anonymity) Act 2008 abolished the restrictive common law rules on witness anonymity during a criminal trial as set out in the House of Lords' judgment in *R v Davies* [2008] UKHL 36.

7.5.2 Parliamentary sovereignty and the law-making process

Parliament has legislated to alter the law-making process for passing primary legislation, thereby changing the legal and constitutional relationship between the two Houses of Parliament. As will be explored in more detail at section 10.10.1, the combined effect of the Parliament Acts of 1911 and 1949 is that the House of Lords can delay the enactment of a Bill for approximately one year. As a result, after 1911 a Bill can become an Act of Parliament without the consent of one of the constituent elements of the 'Crown in Parliament': the House of Lords. The Parliament Acts, therefore, have altered the passage of primary legislation within Parliament and rendered the consent of the House of Lords theoretically unnecessary in respect of those Bills passed under its provisions.

In addition, through the Parliament Acts, Parliament has altered the judicial perception of what amounts to an Act of Parliament for when the Parliament Acts are involved (which in itself is rare), the consent that the courts require in order to be satisfied that a Bill has become an Act is simply that it has received the consent of the following two elements:

■ The House of Commons.

■ The monarch (via the granting of the Royal Assent).

7.5.3 Parliamentary sovereignty and the interpretation of legislation

One constitutional role of the judiciary is to interpret Acts of Parliament with a view to ascertaining the intention of Parliament. The judges have historically, developed certain judicial guidelines in construing legislative provisions. In addition, Parliament has given statutory guidance to the courts as to how to construe legislative provisions. For example, s 6(a) of the Interpretation Act 1978 states that unless the contrary intention is indicated in a statute: 'words importing the masculine gender include the feminine'.

More recently Parliament passed the Human Rights Act 1998 which, in effect, is an interpretation Act governing how all legislation (pre- and post-1998) should be interpreted. It expressly directs the judiciary to interpret wherever possible all legislation in line with the articles of the European Convention on Human Rights:

SECTION

Interpretation of legislation

s 3(1)

So far as it is possible to do so, primary legislation and subordinate legislation must be read and given effect in a way which is compatible with the Convention rights.

This mandatory provision imposes a new statutory obligation on the judiciary instructing them how to interpret legislation affecting human rights. In effect, it requires the judiciary to ensure that the interpretation of the legislation before them is consistent and compatible with the Articles of the European Convention (unless the words of the legislation cannot bear such a meaning and a declaration of incompatibility may be given under s 4 (see section 17.7)). As a consequence of this 'new' statutory instruction, the judiciary may have to depart from a previous judicial interpretation of a provision of an Act which had been made prior to the enforcement of the Human Rights Act 1998 (this former judicial interpretation would not, of course, have necessarily been made with the articles of the Convention in mind).

This raises the extent to which s 3 has affected the constitutional role of the judiciary, whereby judges have construed legislation in such a way as to blur the constitutional line between interpretation and legislation. For a case in which it is arguable that the judges may well have crossed this boundary and legislated, see s 41 of the Youth Justice and Criminal Evidence Act 1999 in *R v A (Complainant's sexual history)* [2001] UKHL 25 (see section 17.6.1).

Moreover, s 2 of the Human Rights Act 1998 states that a court in the context of applying a Convention right must take into account, *inter alia*, any judgment of the European Court of Human Rights. This provision, therefore, specifically directs the judiciary to consider the jurisprudence of the European Convention in Strasbourg when interpreting legislation.

The Human Rights Act 1998 has clearly altered the way in which the judiciary interpret United Kingdom legislation. Indeed, in *R v A* Lord Hope has described s 3 as:

JUDGMENT

'quite unlike any previous rule of statutory interpretation. There is no need to identify an ambiguity or absurdity. Compatibility with convention rights is the sole guiding principle ... But the rule is only a rule of interpretation. It does not entitle the judges to act as legislators.'

Parliament could, of course, also legally repeal this Act thereby relieving the judiciary of this statutory interpretative obligation. As indicated at section 7.12, however, it would appear that the Act could only be repealed on an express basis, and not on an implied one.

7.5.4 Parliamentary sovereignty and the constitution

As Parliament can, in law, pass any primary legislation that it chooses, this necessarily means that it can also pass any law which alters, whether incrementally or radically, the nature of the United Kingdom's uncodified constitution. As noted earlier at section 3.4.5, the United Kingdom has a flexible constitution. In other countries with a codified rigid constitution (eg the United States), in order for the constitution to be altered a special procedure stipulated in the constitution has to be complied with (see section 2.5.2).

In contrast, in the United Kingdom the rules of the constitution do not have special or entrenched legal status and can therefore be altered by Parliament at will. As a consequence, Parliament can simply amend the British constitution by passing a Bill through the ordinary parliamentary legislative process like any non-constitutional Bill (although by constitutional convention, constitutional Bills in the House of Commons are considered on the Floor of the House – see section 12.7.3). Even though a Bill may have profound, far-reaching constitutional implications, no special majority is needed within Parliament (nor does it need to be supported by the people in a referendum) for the Bill to become an Act. Moreover, even though the resulting Act may radically reshape the United Kingdom's constitutional arrangements, and no matter how politically controversial it is, the courts are, legally, disabled from challenging or invalidating the Act. In legal theory, therefore, Parliament can reform the constitution in any way it sees fit.

A few examples will suffice to demonstrate the principle that Parliament can alter any aspect of the British constitution and it is pertinent to note the comments in 2000 of the Royal Commission on the reform of the House of Lords which stated that, in relation to the 1997 Labour government's initial batch of constitutional reforms, such measures:

QUOTATION

'would have been impossible under the laborious systems required to amend the written constitutions of many other countries'.

A House for the Future Cm 4534 (The Stationery Office, 2000) para 5.2.

Some key constitutional changes since 1997:

- **The Scotland Act 1998** (this Act devolved power to Scotland – see section 14.3).
- **The House of Lords Act 1999** (this Act removed most of the hereditary peers from the House of Lords – see section 10.6.3).
- **The European Parliamentary Elections Act 1999** (this Act altered the electoral system used to elect MEPs to the European Parliament from the **'first past the post'** system to one in which elections took place on the basis of a proportional party list system).

'first past the post'
the electoral system used to elect MPs in which the candidate with the most votes in a constituency wins the seat

In effect, therefore, no aspect of the constitution is technically unalterable (but see section 7.7). In fact, in 1996 Parliament (rather controversially) amended Art 9 of the Bill of Rights Act 1689 by the enactment of s 13 of the Defamation Act 1996 (see section 8.6.2). A further example of a major constitutional change being effected by statute is The Local Government Act 1985 which abolished the Greater London Council (the GLC) and metropolitan councils in London. It demonstrated graphically that local government in the context of the British constitution does not enjoy 'constitutional status' in the sense that it does not have any special constitutional or legal protection from the legislature (see section 14.2.5).

In addition, Parliament can choose to lengthen or shorten the life of a Parliament. For example, the Septennial Act 1715 stipulated that the maximum length of a parliamentary term was seven years (it had previously been three years under the Triennial Act 1694). At the beginning of the twentieth century, s 7 of the Parliament Act 1911 reduced this period to five years. Although five years is the current maximum length of term for modern Parliaments, this period could be either shortened or lengthened by another Act of Parliament.

Thus, as Parliament can (at least in legal theory) seemingly alter any aspect of the British constitution, this begs the question as to whether parliamentary sovereignty is consistent with constitutionalism (see sections 7.6 and 7.13).

ACTIVITY

Self-test question

What are the advantages and disadvantages of Parliament being able to reform the constitution through the passage of a simple Act of Parliament?

7.5.5 Parliamentary sovereignty and international law

Parliament can pass legislation which breaches international law. This was illustrated earlier in *Cheney v Conn* (1968) (see section 7.3.2) and the following case illustrates the same point:

CASE EXAMPLE

by-law
subordinate legislation made by local authorities

Mortensen v Peters (1906) 14 SLT 227

A **by-law** was passed (by the Fishery Board for Scotland) under s 7 of the Herring Fishery (Scotland) Act 1889 which prohibited trawling within the Moray Firth (part of the Moray Firth is an area beyond British territorial waters). Mortensen (a Danish captain of a Norwegian trawler) was convicted in a Scottish Sheriff Court for violating the above by-law. Mortensen's appeal was based, *inter alia*, on international law which permits a state to regulate fishing within its territorial waters; however, Mortensen had been arrested in that part of the Moray Firth which was outside British territorial waters.

The High Court of Justiciary held that the intention of Parliament in the 1889 Act was to allow by-laws to be passed covering the Moray Firth even if this was contrary to the rules of international law as part of this area is in international waters. It should be recalled that there is a statutory presumption that Parliament does not intend to legislate contrary to international law (see section 4.8.3).

JUDGMENT

'For us an Act of Parliament duly passed by Lords and Commons and assented to by the King, is supreme, and we are bound to give effect to its terms.'

The Lord Justice-General

Even in the context of the European Convention on Human Rights, and irrespective of the Human Rights Act 1998, Parliament can in legal theory if it chooses to do so (though politically unlikely), legislate contrary to the articles enshrined in the European Convention.

Notwithstanding the general rule above, Parliament is constrained (in the context of international law) by the international Treaties which the United Kingdom has signed. For example, in respect of the European Convention, Art 1 states that:

ARTICLE

'The High Contracting Parties shall secure to everyone within their jurisdiction the rights and freedoms defined in Section I of this Convention.'

As a result, historically Parliament has tried to avoid passing legislation which violates the rights set out in the Convention, thereby honouring (in international law) the United Kingdom's international obligations in respect of this Treaty. Although in strict legal theory Parliament could deliberately and flagrantly legislate contrary to these articles (irrespective of its obligations in international law to protect such rights), the political consequences of such legislation would involve criticism of the United Kingdom in the Council of Europe together with possible expulsion (see section 4.15.2).

In addition, in terms of European Union law, Parliament could (in legal theory) pass legislation which clearly and expressly contravenes and repudiates European Union law principles (see section 15.6.5).

It is worth noting that although Parliament passes laws on its own volition (albeit invariably under the impetus and direction of the executive), it will also pass legislation in order to fulfill its international obligations. For example, when the European Court of Human Rights has declared that law in the United Kingdom is inconsistent with the Convention, Parliament will invariably introduce legislation in order to remedy this defect, as in international law it is required to fulfill the requirements set out by the court in Strasbourg. The Contempt of Court Act 1981 is an example of this. This legislation regulates freedom of expression (eg of the press) pending and during a court hearing. It was passed in response to a ruling of the European Court that the common law of contempt of court had unnecessarily infringed freedom of speech (*Sunday Times v UK* (1979) 2 EHRR 245).

In short, Parliament passed this legislation as a direct result of external pressure, namely the United Kingdom's international obligation to comply with a ruling of the European Court of Human Rights. Similarly, in the context of European Union law, Parliament will pass laws in response to European directives. For example, the Data Protection Act 1998 was enacted as a result of a directive.

7.5.6 Parliamentary sovereignty and extra-territorial jurisdiction

In legal theory, Parliament can enact legislation which purports to have extra-territorial effect. In other words, it could legislate outside the legal jurisdiction of the United Kingdom (see *Mortensen* (1906) at section 7.5.5). The classic example to illustrate this has been put forward by Sir Ivor Jennings (*The Law and the Constitution* (5th edn, Hodder and Stoughton, 1959), pp 170–171). He theorised that Parliament could, in legal theory, pass legislation banning smoking on the streets of Paris (interestingly, in the Health Act 2006 Parliament did legislate to ban smoking in United Kingdom public places). In fact, Parliament has legislated for territory outside of the United Kingdom. The War Crimes Act 1991. This Act has extra-territorial effect as it concerns murder, manslaughter or culpable homicide committed by a British citizen (or resident in the United Kingdom) in Germany or an area under German occupation between 1939–45. The Act was passed under the Parliament Acts 1911 and 1949 as the House of Lords refused to pass it. In particular, they were concerned that the Act had criminal retrospective effect (see section 6.3.2) and there were reservations about the reliability of evidence dating back 50 years.

ACTIVITY

Self-test question

Could the United Kingdom Parliament legislate for the Republic of Ireland?

7.5.7 Parliamentary sovereignty and the conferring of powers onto the executive

Parliament can legislate to confer wide discretionary powers on the executive. As noted earlier in *Inland Revenue Commissioners and another v Rossminster Ltd and others* [1980]

AC 952 (see section 6.7.5), s 20C of the Taxes Management Act 1970 conferred very wide powers on Inland Revenue officers to search premises. In this case Lord Scarman lamented that as the Act had been complied with:

JUDGMENT

'It is therefore with regret that I have to accept that, if the requirements of section 20C of the Taxes Management Act 1970 … are met, the power exists to enter, and search premises, and seize and remove things there found and that the prospect of an immediate judicial review of the exercise of the power is dim.'

Today such a provision may be challenged under the Human Rights Act 1998 (see Chapter 17).

In fact, Parliament often confers law-making powers on the executive in the form of an enabling Act. For example, s 1 of the Export Control Act 2002 conferred a power on the Secretary of State to make an order (delegated legislation in the form of a Statutory Instrument) in connection with imposing export controls in respect of goods. As indicated earlier (see section 5.7.2), therefore, Parliament can legislate to violate the separation of powers by conferring a discretionary law-making power on the executive.

The Legislative and Regulatory Reform Act 2006

Under this Act a government minister is empowered to legislate by making an order, known as a legislative reform order, to remove unnecessary red tape and regulation (ie to remove outdated legislation). The constitutional advantage levelled in favour of this legislation is that unnecessary legislative provisions can be efficiently removed without following the alternative long-winded route of a Bill. The disadvantages are that this measure permits primary legislation to be altered by means of a secondary legislation (known as an 'Henry VIII power/clause').

In the context of Parliament conferring duties and powers on the executive, it is pertinent to note that, at least in recent decades, the executive has to a large extent dominated the House of Commons. By extension, therefore, the executive has largely controlled Parliament as a whole (see Chapter 12), and determined the legislation that it passed.

7.6 Non-legal restraints on Parliament

7.6.1 Political restraints

Although Parliament can, in legal theory, pass any law that it chooses, this does not necessarily mean that Parliament *will* pass any such law. This is because although there may be an absence of legal limitations on Parliament, there are, of course, political restraints on it. As indicated earlier, political sovereignty rests with the people as the people elect Parliament and therefore the electorate act as a political restraint on the laws that Parliament passes.

In other words, if Parliament passed a highly controversial, objectionable and draconian law, at the following general election these parliamentarians (specifically the elected MPs) would have to face the wrath of the electorate as they sought to be re-elected. In short, as Dicey noted: 'The electors can in the long run always enforce their will' (A Dicey, *Introduction to the Study of the Law of the Constitution* (10th edn, Macmillan, 1959), p 73). As such, Parliament is limited politically as inevitably it will refrain from passing legislation which the electorate would find unacceptable.

One obvious difficulty with this analysis, of course, is that the draconian legislation in question may only affect, or be directed at, a minority of the population who, as a group may not necessarily be popular (eg prisoners). As a result, such legislation may in fact be acceptable to (and indeed popular with) the majority of the population who would be unaffected by its consequences. As Bogdanor has observed:

> 'New threats, and, in particular, the growth of terrorism, mean that neither public opinion nor Parliament can any longer necessarily be relied upon to protect the rights of unpopular minorities. The progress through Parliament of the 2001 Anti-terrorism, Crime and Security Act and of the 2005 Prevention of Terrorism Act shows that parliamentary scrutiny of legislation bearing on human rights can be somewhat perfunctory during a period of moral panic.'
>
> V Bogdanor, *The New British Constitution*, (Hart Publishing, 2009), pp 55–56.

That said, at least since the operation of the Human Rights Act 1998, all legislation must now be interpreted in light of the articles of the European Convention (see Chapter 17).

ACTIVITY

Self-test question

How effective do think political sovereignty is as a political restraint on the laws that Parliament passes?

7.6.2 Political entrenchment

Although according to Dicey legislation cannot be *legally entrenched* and protected from repeal, nevertheless, it may well be the case that certain Acts of Parliament (owing to their content and political importance) can become *politically entrenched* in the sense that Parliament may lack the political will (ie support of the electorate) to repeal them.

One example could be the Human Rights Act 1998. In strict legal terms, Parliament could expressly repeal this legislation (on implied repeal of this Act see sections 4.4.5 and 7.12). Politically, however, it may be very difficult for Parliament to muster the support from the electorate to repeal this legislation. In short, once the Human Rights Act conferred positive rights on individuals which they can enforce against the state in a court, it may prove to be very difficult *politically* (and *internationally*) to revoke them. In other countries the rights of the individual are contained in a Bill or Charter of Rights which will, typically, form part of a legally entrenched constitution. These rights, therefore, will be difficult to alter or abolish as they are legally entrenched in a codified constitution.

Similarly, the Scotland Act 1998 which established the Scottish Parliament in Edinburgh can in legal theory be expressly repealed (on implied repeal see sections 4.4.5 and 7.11), but in political terms it may prove to be very difficult to repeal. Indeed, the creation of the Scottish Parliament had been preceded by a referendum in Scotland in which the Scottish people endorsed the principle of a new Scottish Parliament.

7.6.3 Practical restraints

In respect of parliamentary sovereignty, it is important to distinguish between what is legally possible (which in legal theory is limitless) and what is *actually* possible in practice. For example, in 1931 Parliament passed the Statute of Westminster which stated in s 4, that no United Kingdom statute passed after the commencement of this Act shall extend to the law of a Dominion (in 1931 these Dominions included Australia, Canada, New Zealand, the Irish Free State and Newfoundland), unless the Dominion in question requested and consented to that legislation.

In strict legal theory, however, the United Kingdom Parliament could simply repeal this provision and proceed to legislate for one of the above Dominions against their consent. This point was made by Viscount Sankey LC in the Privy Council in *British Coal Corporation v The King* [1935] AC 500, who stated that:

JUDGMENT

'It is doubtless true that the power of the Imperial Parliament to pass on its own initiative any legislation that it thought fit extending to Canada remains in theory unimpaired: indeed, the Imperial Parliament could, as a matter of abstract law, repeal or disregard s 4 of the Statute. But that is theory and has no relation to realities.'

In addition, should Parliament legislate to repeal the grants of independence to former dependent territories (eg Nigeria Independence Act 1960) with the intention of revoking their independent status, the mere legal passage of such legislation would not, of course, affect the *actual* independence of that particular state.

As Lord Denning MR in *Blackburn v Attorney General* [1971] 2 All ER 1380, commented:

JUDGMENT

'Take the Statute of Westminster 1931, which takes away the power of Parliament to legislate for the dominions. Can anyone imagine that Parliament could or would reverse that statute? Take the Acts which have granted independence to the dominions and territories overseas. Can anyone imagine that Parliament could or would reverse those laws and take away their independence? Most clearly not. Freedom once given cannot be taken away. Legal theory must give way to practical politics.'

Moreover, to take the example used above concerning Parliament legislating to ban smoking on the streets of Paris (see section 7.5.6), Sir Ivor Jennings has pointed out that such a law would not be effective within Paris itself as it is outside the jurisdiction of the United Kingdom courts. In strict legal theory the legislation in question would be legally valid, but not practically enforceable in France.

7.6.4 Constitutional conventions

Parliament can choose to legislate contrary to a constitutional convention. For example, since the establishment of the Scotland Act 1998 a convention has been established to the effect that the United Kingdom Parliament will not legislate in the context of a devolved matter for Scotland without the consent of the Scottish Parliament (the Sewel Convention). As a constitutional convention, it is simply a political rule of the constitution and as such, in legal theory, Parliament could choose to ignore it and proceed to pass legislation for Scotland in the absence of the consent of the Scottish Parliament. The political ramifications of such action, however, would inevitably prevent Parliament from passing such legislation.

Constitutional conventions, therefore, do not legally bind Parliament and this point was reiterated by Lord Reid in the Privy Council in the following case:

CASE EXAMPLE

Madzimbamuto v Lardner-Burke [1969] 1 AC 645

In 1965 it was a well-established constitutional convention that the United Kingdom Parliament did not legislate for Southern Rhodesia (now Zimbabwe) without the consent of the government of the legislative Assembly of Southern Rhodesia. In 1965, however, the Prime Minister of Southern Rhodesia issued a declaration of independence to the effect that Southern Rhodesia was now an independent sovereign state and no longer a crown colony. The United Kingdom nevertheless passed legislation (Southern Rhodesia Act 1965) purporting to apply to Southern Rhodesia in contravention of the above convention.

Lord Reid noted that although the constitutional convention was an important principle, it had no legal effect which limited the legal powers of Parliament to pass legislation (see the full quotation at section 4.15.2). In fact, in reality the legislation in question did not have any impact on Southern Rhodesia and illustrates the practical limitations on Parliament (analogous to legislating to ban smoking on the streets of Paris).

ACTIVITY

Applying the law

Can the Queen in Parliament, legally, pass the following laws and if so, what would be their effect?

*   The House of Lords Bill (which proposes to reinstate the expelled hereditary peers).
*   The Mexico Bill (which proposes to make it a criminal offence for anyone to eat chewing gum on the streets of Mexico City).
*   The Elections Bill (which proposes to abolish elections to the House of Commons).
*   The Local Government Elections Bill (which proposes to exclude anyone earning less than £25,000 a year from voting in local government elections).
*   The Prime Minister Bill (which proposes to override the constitutional convention that the Prime Minister must be drawn from within Parliament).
*   The Courts Bill (which proposes to abolish jury trial for all criminal offences).

Revisit your answers after reading section 7.7.

7.7 Is there a limitation on the laws that Parliament can pass?

Dicey noted that there was one clear limitation on Parliament, namely that Parliament cannot bind its successor, or be bound by its predecessor (see section 7.9). In addition, the judiciary (both in a judicial and an extra judicial context) have suggested that there are in fact limits to Parliament's legislative power. For example, recently in the House of Lords Lord Steyn made the following (albeit *obiter*) observation in *R (Jackson) v Attorney General* [2005] UKHL 56 (for the facts see section 10.10.3):

JUDGMENT

'If the Attorney General is right the 1949 Act could also be used to introduce oppressive and wholly undemocratic legislation. For example, it could theoretically be used to abolish judicial review of flagrant abuse of power by a government or even the role of the ordinary courts in standing between the executive and citizens. This is where we may have to come back to the point about the supremacy of Parliament. We do not in the United Kingdom have an uncontrolled constitution as the Attorney General implausibly asserts... The classic account given by Dicey of the doctrine of the supremacy of Parliament, pure and absolute as it was, can now be seen to be out of place in the modern United Kingdom. Nevertheless, the supremacy of Parliament is still the *general* principle of our constitution. It is a construct of the common law. The judges created this principle. If that is so, it is not unthinkable that circumstances could arise where the courts may have to qualify a principle established on a different hypothesis of constitutionalism.

In exceptional circumstances involving an attempt to abolish judicial review or the ordinary role of the courts, the Appellate Committee of the House of Lords or a new Supreme Court may have to consider whether this is a constitutional fundamental which even a sovereign Parliament acting at the behest of a complaisant House of Commons cannot abolish.'

In other words, if Parliament passed legislation which abrogated certain fundamental principles of the constitution, then the courts, in applying the common law principle of parliamentary sovereignty, may decide that even Parliament (notwithstanding the sovereignty of Parliament) could not make such legislation. It is of interest to note that in his evidence to the House of Lords Select Committee on the Constitution in November 2005, the Lord Chancellor disagreed with Lord Steyn's comments that, aside from Europe, Parliament was prevented from legislating in respect of certain principles of the constitution. The Lord Chancellor considered himself to 'be on the side of the conventional constitutional thinkers' on this issue (Sixth Report of the House of Lords Select Committee on the Constitution, *Meeting with the Lord Chancellor,* HL Paper 84 (2005), Q15).

Similarly, Lord Woolf writing extra judicially in 1995 commented that there might be limits on Parliament's legislative powers as enforced by the courts if Parliament passed legislation fundamentally undermining the rule of law (in particular, by removing or substantially impairing the constitutional role of the courts in the context of judicial review):

QUOTATION

'If Parliament did the unthinkable, then I would say that the courts would also be required to act in a manner which would be without precedent. Some judges might choose to do so by saying that it was an unrebuttable presumption that Parliament could never intend such a result. I myself would consider there were advantages in making it clear that ultimately there are even limits on the supremacy of Parliament which it is the courts' inalienable responsibility to identify and uphold. They are limits of the most modest dimensions which I believe any democrat would accept. They are no more than are necessary to enable the rule of law to be preserved.'

Lord Woolf, 'Droit Public-English Style' [1995] PL 57.

The above examples are, of course, highly unlikely to occur in practice and so these potential limitations are somewhat theoretical.

ACTIVITY

Self-test question

What do the above judicial comments tell us about the constitutional relationship between the judiciary and the legislature?

KEY FACTS

Key facts on the limitations of Parliament in law-making
Parliament can in legal theory pass a law which:

- Abolishes or alters the common law.
- Infringes international law.
- Alters (either marginally or radically) the uncodified constitution.
- Has extra-territorial jurisdiction.
- Alters the law-making process or the judicial rules of statutory interpretation.
- Is retrospective in nature.
- Abrogates a constitutional convention.
- Confers wide discretionary powers on the executive.

There are, however, political and practical restraints on parliamentary sovereignty.

7.8 Principle 2: The courts do not challenge the authority of an Act of Parliament

7.8.1 Introduction

Dicey stated that:

QUOTATION

'No person or body is recognised by the law of England as having a right to override or set aside the legislation of Parliament.'

A Dicey, *Introduction to the Study of the Law of the Constitution* (10th edn, Macmillan, 1959), p 40.

This principle represents the negative side of parliamentary sovereignty, namely, that no body (court or otherwise) can challenge an Act of Parliament. This is, of course, inextricably linked to the first principle that the Crown in Parliament can in law pass any law that it chooses because once the legislation is enacted, no court can invalidate it. In essence, therefore, parliamentary sovereignty concerns the constitutional relationship between the United Kingdom's courts and the United Kingdom Parliament, with the former being legally subordinate to the latter. Thus, irrespective of the content of the statute, the courts' constitutional responsibility is simply to interpret and apply the legislation passed by Parliament.

CASE EXAMPLE

R v Jordan [1967] Crim LR 483

Jordan had been convicted and sentenced to imprisonment for offences committed under the Race Relations Act 1965. He contended that the Act was invalid on the basis that it curtailed freedom of expression and sought legal aid to apply for a writ of *habeas corpus* on this ground.

The Queen's Bench Division of the High Court held that the courts did not have the power to question the validity of primary legislation. Jordan's claim was dismissed as completely unarguable.

Similarly, in *Duport Steels Ltd and others v Sirs and others* [1980] 1 All ER 529 Lord Scarman reiterated that the constitutional relationship between the judge and parliamentary legislation was that the former:

JUDGMENT

'must not deny the statute. Unpalatable statute law may not be disregarded or rejected, merely because it is unpalatable.'

The following case illustrates a number of principles relating to sovereignty and the constitutional relationship between the courts and Parliament.

CASE EXAMPLE

British Railways Board v Pickin [1974] AC 765

In 1968 a private Act of Parliament (The British Railways Act 1968) was passed with the effect of nullifying the effect of an earlier private Act of 1836. The latter had established a railway line and provided that if such a line should be abandoned, the lands on which the line was built should vest in the owners of the adjoining lands. Instead, under s 18 of the later 1968 Act, such land would now vest in the British Railways Board.

Pickin owned land adjoining a track and instituted an action against the British Railways Board claiming ownership of the adjoining land to the centre line of the track. The Board argued that under the 1968 Act the land vested in the Board. In reply, Pickin alleged that the Board (in promoting the British Railways Bill) had misled Parliament by a false recital in the preamble to the 1968 legislation. It was argued accordingly that the Board could not rely on the 1968 Act to deprive Pickin of title to this land. The Court of Appeal reversed a decision to strike out Pickin's above argument and the Board appealed to the House of Lords which allowed its appeal.

The court held that the function of the court was to apply Acts of Parliament. It was not lawful to impugn the validity of legislation by seeking to establish that Parliament in passing such legislation had been misled by fraud.

JUDGMENT

'The idea that a court is entitled to disregard a provision in an Act of Parliament on any ground must seem strange and startling to anyone with any knowledge of the history and law of our constitution' (Lord Reid).

Further, Lord Morris noted:

JUDGMENT

'When an enactment is passed there is finality unless and until it is amended or repealed by Parliament. In the courts there may be argument as to the correct interpretation of the enactment: there must be none as to whether it should be on the Statute Book at all.'

The *Pickin* case illustrates the following principles concerning our constitution:

- Firstly, the court reiterated that the courts do not have the constitutional authority to impugn or challenge the validity of an Act. This applied whether the statute was a public or private Act of Parliament (the case concerned a private Act).
- Secondly, Lord Reid dismissed the notion that the modern courts could disregard an Act of Parliament on the basis that: 'it was contrary to the law of God or the law of nature or natural justice' as 'since the supremacy of Parliament was finally demonstrated by the revolution of 1688 any such idea has become obsolete'(*sic*). This was a clear reference to, and repudiation of, the earlier historic case of *Dr Bonham's Case* (1610) 8 Co Rep 114 in which Coke CJ had stated that the common law would control and adjudge to be void an Act of Parliament which was 'against common right and reason, or repugnant, or impossible to be performed'.

It should be remembered that although the courts will not impugn the validity of an Act of Parliament, this does not preclude them from questioning and invalidating secondary legislation. In fact, the courts regularly judicially review the content and exercise of delegated legislation by the executive and other bodies (see Chapters 19 and 20). Although the term judicial review is used in the British constitution, this is in relation to delegated legislation rather than primary legislation (but in the context of European Union law see section 15.6.4).

ACTIVITY

Applying the law

Can you envisage any circumstances in which Parliament passed an Act where it would be (a) morally, or (b) constitutionally appropriate for the courts to question it?

7.8.2 The courts may assume that Parliament did not intend to act unconstitutionally

Although the courts do not question an Act of Parliament, it is pertinent to point out that it is in fact the judiciary who interpret statutes and extract and apply their meaning. As Dicey noted:

QUOTATION

'Parliament is supreme legislator, but from the moment Parliament has uttered its will as lawgiver, that will becomes subject to the interpretation put upon it by the judges of the land.' (*sic*)

A Dicey, *Introduction to the Study of the Law of the Constitution*
(10th edn, Macmillan, 1959), p 413.

Moreover, as indicated earlier at section 4.8.3, in construing legislation the courts have developed a number of principles as aids to their construction. For example, one historic constitutional role of the United Kingdom judges is to safeguard the freedom of the individual. As a result, where legislation appears to be ambiguous or capable of a number of interpretations, the courts will apply certain constitutional fundamentals in interpreting that legislation.

These 'constitutional presumptions' include, *inter alia*, that surely Parliament would never have intended the following results:

- An interference with the human rights and liberties of the individual.
- A restriction of an individual's access to the courts.
- To legislate contrary to an international Treaty or international obligations.

These presumptions are justified on the constitutional basis that if Parliament had intended to achieve any of the outcomes indicated above, it would have made this very clear in the relevant statutory provision. As pointed out at section 4.8.3, the last presumption was demonstrated in *Waddington v Miah* [1974] 2 All ER 377 where the House of Lords interpreted the Immigration Act 1971 in line with Art 7 of the European Convention (which outlaws the imposition of retrospective criminal legislation). In other words, the courts assume that Parliament intends to act consistently, and so legislate in line with its international obligations, unless the statute clearly indicates this not to be the case (in the context of European Union law see section 15.6.5).

In the Republic of Ireland, the Irish constitution also uses an analogous presumption, namely, the *presumption of constitutionality*. Article 15.4 of the Irish constitution states that the Oireachtas shall not pass legislation inconsistent with the written codified constitution. As a result of this, unless the contrary is proved, the courts will assume that legislation passed by the Oireachtas is 'constitutional', and so in accordance with the constitution.

Dicey summarised the first two principles underpinning parliamentary sovereignty in the following way:

QUOTATION

'Parliamentary sovereignty is therefore an undoubted legal fact. It is complete both on its positive and on its negative side. Parliament can legally legislate on any topic whatever which, in the judgment of Parliament, is a fit subject for legislation. There is no power which, under the English constitution, can come into rivalry with the legislative sovereignty of Parliament.'

A Dicey, *Introduction to the Study of the Law of the Constitution* (10th edn, Macmillan, 1959), pp 68–70.

7.8.3 The surrender of parliamentary sovereignty?

Although there are no limits on the laws that it can pass, this does not mean that Parliament cannot, ultimately, surrender its sovereignty forever. In other words, Parliament could in legal theory simply dissolve itself. On this point Dicey has argued that Parliament:

QUOTATION

'may simply put an end to its own existence. Parliament could extinguish itself by legally dissolving itself and leaving no means whereby a subsequent parliament could be legally summoned.'

A Dicey, *Introduction to the Study of the Law of the Constitution* (10th edn, Macmillan, 1959), p 69.

In this sense, Parliament could legally terminate itself – which is likened to a suicide, and which is, of course, irreversible.

In the albeit unlikely event of the United Kingdom adopting a codified entrenched constitution containing constitutional laws which had a higher special legal status, Parliament would need to divest itself of the principle of parliamentary sovereignty. This is because the United Kingdom could not have a legally entrenched codified constitution (which would legally control the laws which the new legislature could pass), while simultaneously retaining the principle of parliamentary sovereignty.

Key facts on Courts challenging Acts of Parliament

- Historically, the courts cannot question Acts of Parliament (*R v Jordan* (1967), *British Railways Board v Pickin* (1974)). This is in contrast, for example, to the Supreme Court in the United States or the Republic of Ireland.

- The constitutional function of the judiciary is limited simply to interpreting and ascertaining the meaning of an Act of Parliament. In construing legislation, however, the courts will apply certain constitutional fundamentals and assume that Parliament did not intend to legislate 'unconstitutionally' (*Waddington v Miah* (1974)).

7.9 Principle 3: Parliament cannot bind its successors

7.9.1 Introduction

The third aspect of parliamentary sovereignty involves the following two interrelated principles:

■ Parliament cannot bind its successors. For example, the Parliament in 2013 cannot restrict the laws that could be passed by the Parliament of 2014.

■ Parliament cannot be bound by its predecessor. For example, the Parliament of 2014 cannot be bound or restricted by the 2013 Parliament.

In summary, it has been argued that traditionally Parliament cannot entrench legislation. Dicey stated that on the occasions that language had been used in an Act of Parliament purporting to imply that a particular statute could not be altered or repealed by a subsequent Parliament, 'the endeavour has always ended in failure'. Thus, one Parliament cannot be bound by its predecessors.

This principle ensures that each new Parliament retains its sovereign power to pass whatever legislation is deemed necessary at the time. If one Parliament could tie the hands of its successor, the later Parliament would not enjoy full legislative power to pass any legislation that it chooses, as it would be restrained by this former Parliament. Today this principle can be justified on the basis that each new Parliament should enjoy full sovereign legislative power as each new Parliament represents the latest will of the people as reflected in the latest general election (see political sovereignty at section 7.2.2). It also means that laws can adapt to new developments and that one Parliament does not become a prisoner of the views (as embodied in legislation) of a previous Parliament (perhaps of centuries before).

This principle means that in the United Kingdom, Acts of Parliament cannot be legally (as opposed to being politically) entrenched, that is to say that they cannot legally be protected from repeal by a subsequent Parliament at a later date. As Herbert CJ noted centuries ago in *Godden v Hales* (1686) 11 St Tr 1165:

'If an Act of Parliament had a clause in it that it should never be repealed, yet without question, the same power that made it may repeal it.'

Indeed, this would even apply to two Acts passed within the same parliamentary term, whereby an Act passed in the first session of a Parliament could be repealed by a later Act in the second session of the same Parliament, although this would be highly unlikely to happen in practice.

Self-test question

How would you distinguish between the legal and political entrenchment of legislation?

The principle that Parliament cannot bind its successors is achieved through the twin doctrines of:

- Express repeal.
- Implied repeal.

7.9.2 Express repeal

This is the principle that a later Act of Parliament expressly and explicitly repeals an earlier inconsistent Act (or section of it). Parliament can *unmake* any law that it chooses. In fact, an Act of Parliament will detail in its Schedule the legislation (or provisions of such) that is to be specifically repealed. For example, s 49(1) of the Inquiries Act 2005 expressly repealed the Tribunals of Inquiry (Evidence) Act 1921 and s 49(2) made reference to Sched 3 which detailed the extent of other provisions of statutes which were repealed or revoked. The doctrine of express repeal means that even if, as Herbert CJ indicated above, an Act stated that it was exempt from repeal, it could nevertheless be expressly repealed by a later Act (see further section 7.10.1).

7.9.3 Implied repeal

The doctrine of implied repeal comes into operation when two Acts of Parliament dealing with the same subject-matter are inconsistent with each other, but the later Act does not expressly repeal the earlier one. In these circumstances the doctrine of implied repeal would ensure that the provisions of the later Act prevailed, by impliedly repealing the earlier Act to the extent that it was inconsistent. In short, this means that two inconsistent Acts stating two different things on the same subject-matter cannot stand together. In this way, the courts give effect to the latest will of Parliament (as reflected at the last general election). The doctrine is illustrated by the following two cases:

CASE EXAMPLE

Vauxhall Estates Limited v Liverpool Corporation [1932] 1 KB 733

Section 2 of the Acquisition of Land (Assessment of Compensation) Act 1919 provided for the assessment of compensation in respect of land acquired compulsorily by a government department or local authority. Section 7 of the Act provided that: 'The provisions of the Act or order by which the land is authorised to be acquired, or of any Act incorporated therewith, shall, in relation to the matters dealt with in this Act, have effect subject to this Act, and so far as inconsistent with this Act those provisions shall cease to have or shall not have effect'.

In 1925 s 46 of the Housing Act provided for the assessment of such compensation for land acquired compulsorily on a less generous basis. The Corporation of Liverpool proposed a scheme under the 1925 Act for the improvement of Liverpool which included lands owned by Vauxhall Estates Ltd who contended that the amount of compensation should be assessed under s 2 of the 1919 Act. This was because the assessment of compensation under the 1925 Act differed materially from the 1919 Act and so s 7 of this Act rendered the later Act of no effect. Counsel for Vauxhall had argued that s 7 of the 1919 Act purported, in effect, to prevent the implied repeal of its provisions (thereby purporting to tie the hands of a successor Parliament).

The Divisional Court held that the 1925 Act repealed by implication (ie impliedly repealed) the earlier Act of 1919, to the extent that it was inconsistent. The court held that even if the 1919 Act had purported to apply to future Acts, s 46 of the 1925 Act would prevail. On the facts, Avory J concluded that on its true construction, s 7 applied only to existing Acts in 1919 and not to future Acts (the other two judges did not decide this issue).

JUDGMENT

'Speaking for myself, I should certainly hold, until the contrary were decided, that no Act of Parliament can effectively provide that no future Act shall interfere with its provisions.' (Avory J)

CASE EXAMPLE

Ellen Street Estates Limited v Minister of Health [1934] 1 KB 590

In this case the Court of Appeal approved of, and followed, the decision in *Vauxhall Estates* (see above). It is of interest to note that counsel for Vauxhall appeared for Ellen Street Estates and submitted that the Divisional Court decision in *Vauxhall Estates* had been wrongly decided and that it was possible for Parliament to state that an Act could be repealed in express terms only, and not by implication. Since s 46 of the 1925 Act was inconsistent with the 1919 Act, and the 1925 Act had not expressly repealed it, accordingly, this later provision (s 46 of the 1925 Act) should have no legal effect. The Court of Appeal rejected this contention in the following terms by Maugham LJ:

JUDGMENT

'The Legislature cannot, according to our constitution, bind itself as to the form of subsequent legislation, and it is impossible for Parliament to enact that in a subsequent statute dealing with the same subject-matter there can be no implied repeal. If in a subsequent Act Parliament chooses to make it plain that the earlier statute is being to some extent repealed, effect must be given to that intention just because it is the will of the Legislature.'

Thus, even if a Parliament in 2013 stated in an Act that it could not be repealed, according to the above doctrines a later Parliament could either:

■ expressly repeal this legislation with an Act of Parliament specifically stating this (express repeal); or

■ impliedly repeal this legislation by passing an Act of Parliament which was plainly inconsistent with the provisions of the earlier Act (implied repeal), but without expressly repealing (or even referring to) the earlier 2013 Act.

Notwithstanding the points made above, the doctrine of implied repeal needs to be reconsidered in the context of the following:

■ European Union law (see section 15.6).
■ The Human Rights Act 1998 (see section 7.12).
■ Other constitutional statutes (see Laws LJ at section 4.4.5).

KEY FACTS

Key facts on binding Parliamentary successors

Parliament cannot bind its successors or be bound by its predecessors. This is achieved through the following doctrines:

● Express repeal is the principle that a later Act of Parliament expressly and explicitly repeals an earlier inconsistent Act (or section of it).

● Implied repeal is the principle that when two Acts of Parliament dealing with the same subject-matter are inconsistent with each other (but the later Act does not expressly repeal the earlier one), the later Act impliedly repeals the earlier one to the extent that it is inconsistent (*Vauxhall Estates Limited v Liverpool Corporation* (1932) and *Ellen Street Estates Limited v Minister of Health* (1934)).

These doctrines taken together indicate that Parliament cannot entrench legislation against subsequent repeal by a later Parliament.

7.10 Is legal entrenchment possible?

Is it at all possible for Parliament to bind its successors and legally entrench legislation?

In essence, academic commentators traditionally have distinguished between two types of entrenchment:

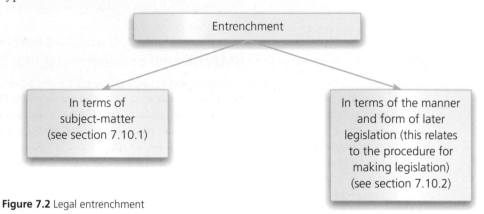

Figure 7.2 Legal entrenchment

One argument typically levelled in favour of entrenchment is that since the principle of parliamentary sovereignty is a common law rule, and since statutes have a superior status to the common law, logically therefore, why cannot Parliament simply legislate to alter this common law rule relating to sovereignty and entrenchment? According to Wade, however, as indicated at section 7.3.2 although the rule of judicial obedience to statutes is in one sense a rule of the common law, in another sense it is a political fact.

QUOTATION

'What Salmond calls the "ultimate legal principle" is therefore a rule which is unique in being unchangeable by Parliament – it is changed by revolution, not by legislation; it lies in the keeping of the courts, and no Act of Parliament can take it from them.'

H Wade, 'The basis of legal sovereignty' [1955] CLJ 172.

(In the terms of a 'revolution' see the European Union at section 15.6.5.)

7.10.1 Entrenchment in terms of subject-matter

Democratic constitutions generally protect certain subject-matters (such as fundamental basic human rights or other fundamental principles) from legal infringement or revocation by later legislation. Thus, such rights are typically 'constitutionally ring-fenced' in a Bill or Charter of Rights and are thereby placed out of the reach of the legislature and the 'ordinary' legislative process.

In contrast, in the United Kingdom as a result of parliamentary sovereignty, even if such basic rights were embodied in statutory form which stated that owing to their nature they could never be repealed (eg an entrenched British Charter of Rights), a future Parliament could simply legislate to revoke them at a later date (on the Human Rights Act 1998 see section 7.12). Indeed, Lord Scarman in 1974 commented that:

QUOTATION

'It is the helplessness of the law in face of the legislative sovereignty of Parliament which makes it difficult for the legal system to accommodate the concept of fundamental and inviolable human rights'.

Lord Scarman, *English Law: The New Dimension* (1974), p 15.

Dicey's theory is known as the continuing theory of sovereignty, whereby each Parliament has full legislative sovereignty.

Acts of Union

It is commonly suggested, however, that owing to their content and fundamental importance, one category of statutes – the Union Acts – cannot subsequently be repealed. The two Union Acts are:

- The Union with Scotland Act 1706 – which united England and Wales with Scotland to form the Parliament of Great Britain; and
- The Union with Ireland Act 1800 – which united England, Wales and Scotland with Ireland to form the Parliament of the United Kingdom.

The argument is that these Acts have a special legal status. In other words, they are legally entrenched against repeal and the Acts themselves indicate as much. In fact, Dicey made specific reference to the Union Acts. In respect of the 1706 Act which had enacted, *inter alia*, that Scottish university professors should acknowledge, profess and subscribe to the Confession of Faith (a protestant doctrine), he noted that the Act 'in substance enacts that this provision shall be a fundamental and essential condition of the treaty of union in all time coming'. Notwithstanding this, as he pointed out, this provision was subsequently partly repealed by the Universities (Scotland) Act 1853. Furthermore, more recently s 37 of the Scotland Act 1998 stated that the Union with Scotland Act 1706 has effect subject to this later Act.

Similarly, Art 5 of the Union with Ireland Act 1800 stated:

SECTION

'that the Doctrine, Worship, Discipline, and Government of the said United Church (United Church of England and Ireland) shall be, and shall remain in full force for ever … [and] … that the Continuance and Preservation of the said United Church, as the established Church of England and Ireland, shall be deemed and taken to be an essential and fundamental Part of the Union.'

The Irish Church Act 1869 subsequently disestablished the Irish Church. In summary, Dicey stated that:

QUOTATION

'The history of legislation in respect of these very Acts affords the strongest proof of the futility inherent in every attempt of one sovereign legislature to restrain the action of another equally sovereign body.'

A Dicey, *Introduction to the Study of the Law of the Constitution* (10th edn, Macmillan, 1959), p 65.

These examples indicate that even if an Act stated that because of its subject-matter, its provisions are 'fundamental and unalterable', they could, nevertheless, be repealed by a subsequent Parliament.

Notwithstanding the above, in the context of the Union with Scotland Act 1706, see the *obiter* comments of Lord Cooper in *MacCormick v Lord Advocate* (1953) SC 396 and Lord Keith in *Gibson v Lord Advocate* [1975] 1 CMLR 563.

ACTIVITY

Self-test question

What would be the constitutional advantages and disadvantages of Parliament being able to entrench the subject-matter of legislation against subsequent repeal by a later Parliament?

7.10.2 Entrenchment in terms of the manner and form of later legislation

This type of entrenchment refers to entrenching legislation in terms of the manner and form of later legislation (that is to say the procedure for making legislation). In other words, it is concerned with the following type of scenario:

The (imaginary) British Charter of Rights Act 2013

Section 1: the rights detailed in this Act can only be repealed by a future Parliament with the support of 80 per cent of both Houses of Parliament.

The above Act purports to entrench the human rights detailed in it by providing that these rights cannot be repealed by a later Parliament unless it has the support of 80 per cent of both Houses of Parliament. Unlike the first type of entrenchment (see section 7.10.1), this Act is not stating that its provisions can *never* be repealed under any circumstances in the future. Rather, by stipulating that 80 per cent support of both Houses is required, it is purporting to make it *difficult* for a subsequent Parliament to repeal its provisions. In other words, it is purporting to entrench those rights by requiring a specified 'manner and form' of later legislation in order to repeal them (the manner and form here being the support of 80 per cent of both Houses of Parliament).

The question is what would happen if a 2014 Parliament passed an Act revoking the human rights that were enshrined in the British Charter of Rights Act 2013, but it did so through the ordinary parliamentary process (ie the Bill passed through with a simple majority vote in both chambers and not the 80 per cent as stipulated in the Act). Would the 2014 Act be legal?

There is no absolute answer to this question. Under the traditional conception of parliamentary sovereignty the 2014 Act would prevail, notwithstanding that it had not complied with the manner and form provision stipulated in s 1 of the 2013 Act. Indeed, if we recall the enrolled Bill rule (see section 7.3.3), the courts would simply look to see if the 2014 Bill was on the parliamentary roll and as stated in *Pickin* (1974), the courts would not investigate the internal proceedings of Parliament (as this risks breaching the separation of powers). On this traditional basis, therefore, it could be argued that provided the 2014 Bill was on the parliamentary roll having obtained the consent of both Houses, the courts would not investigate further as to whether the Bill had obtained the support of 80 per cent of both Houses.

There is, however, some support for the proposition that legislation (for example the above 2014 Act) would not be enforced – or even constitute an Act – where a previous Act (for example the above 2013 Act) had, in effect, entrenched its provisions by specifically stipulating the 'manner and form' that had to be followed by later legislation in order to repeal it. Three standard cases are used to support this argument (the so-called 'self-embracing theory of sovereignty'):

CASE EXAMPLE

Attorney General for New South Wales v Trethowan [1932] AC 526

The Colonial Laws Validity Act 1865 (a United Kingdom statute) conferred power on the New South Wales legislature to make laws in respect of the constitution of that state. Section 5 of the Act stated that every representative legislature shall have full power to make laws respecting the constitution providing such laws 'shall have been passed in such manner and form as may from time to time be required by any Act of Parliament'.

The Constitution Act 1902 as amended in 1929 (s 7A) stated that no Bill abolishing the Legislative Council of New South Wales (the upper chamber) should be presented to the Governor (for royal consent) until it had been approved by a majority of the electors. The same procedure was needed to repeal s 7A.

In 1930 both Houses of the New South Wales legislature passed two bills (to abolish the Legislative Council and repeal s 7A), however, neither Bill had been approved by the electorate. Two members of the Legislative Council (which was purportedly being abolished) sought a declaration that the two Bills could not be presented to the Governor for assent until approved by the electors, together with an injunction to prevent the Bills being presented for assent.

The Privy Council (on an appeal from the High Court of Australia) confirmed that the Bills needed to comply with the 'manner and form' as stipulated in s 7A. Thus the Bills required the support of the electors before they could lawfully be presented to the Governor.

NB See the redefinition theory below.

CASE EXAMPLE

Harris v The Minister of the Interior (1952) (2) SA 428

Section 152 of the South Africa Act 1909 stipulated that a Bill which amended section 35 of the Act (concerning the de-registering of individuals for voting purposes on the basis of their colour), required the consent of two-thirds of both Houses (sitting together) of the South African Parliament.

The Supreme Court of South Africa held that in order to pass the 1951 Separate Representation of Voters Act (which had been passed by the two Houses separately and so not sitting together), the 'manner and form' stipulated by s 152 of the South Africa Act 1909 had to be followed. As a consequence the 1951 Act was null and void.

CASE EXAMPLE

The Bribery Commissioner v Pedrick Ranasinghe [1965] AC 172

Section 29(4) of the Ceylon (Constitution) Order in Council 1946 stated that the Ceylon Parliament may amend or repeal any of the provisions in this Order, but that no Bill be presented for Royal Assent unless it had endorsed on it a certificate stating that it had been passed by not less than two-thirds of the House of Representatives.

The Privy Council affirmed the judgment of the Supreme Court of Ceylon that as the Bribery Amendment Act 1958 (which in effect altered the constitution) had no such certificate, the orders made by the Bribery Tribunal (under the 1958 Act) against Ranasinghe were null and inoperative. In short, in amending the Ceylon constitution, the Speaker's certificate was a necessary part of the legislative process and so any Bill not complying with s 29(4) was invalid and *ultra vires*. The Bribery Amendment Bill, therefore had to follow the 'manner and form' set out in s 29(4).

Although these cases demonstrate that in each case the legislature was required to follow the stipulated 'manner and form' for later legislation, as Commonwealth authorities they are not strictly analogous with the sovereign United Kingdom Parliament. As Barnett has commented, the cases indicate that:

QUOTATION

'Legislative bodies do not necessarily enjoy full sovereign power, and that some form of "higher law" may control their powers. In each of these cases, the powers of the legislatures of New South Wales, South Africa and Ceylon (as it then was) had been established under an Act of the sovereign United Kingdom Parliament. That being so, the legislative bodies had to comply with the constitutional laws in force.'

H Barnett, *Constitutional and Administrative Law* (7th edn, Routledge–Cavendish, 2009), p 158.

In fact, Dicey clearly distinguished between sovereign legislatures (eg the United Kingdom Parliament) and non-sovereign law-making bodies (subordinate legislatures). In particular, judicial persons would have the 'authority to pronounce upon the validity or constitutionality of laws' which had been passed by non-sovereign law-making bodies.

What is clear, therefore, is that although as a constitutional principle, all legislatures pass laws, this does not mean that they are all sovereign. For example, the Scottish Parliament is a legislature with the power to pass Acts of the Scottish Parliament (see section 14.3); however, it is necessarily a limited legislature with limited law-making powers as it is governed, and legally controlled, by the legislation which established it: the Scotland Act 1998. In this way the Scottish Parliament should be contrasted with the sovereign United Kingdom Parliament in Westminster which has neither been established, nor had its powers delegated or controlled, by a prior constitutional document.

The redefinition theory

A variant of the manner and form argument in favour of entrenching legislation is the so-called redefinition theory of sovereignty. In general an Act of Parliament is passed by a combination of all of the following:

- The House of Commons.
- The House of Lords.
- The monarch (in the form of the Royal Assent).

Under the redefinition theory it is possible for legislation to, in effect, be entrenched by specifying an additional element to the above constituent parts in order to amend or repeal specified (important) legislation. In this way Parliament is redefining itself in relation to certain legislation, making it more difficult to repeal, as an *extra* element has been added to the legislative process (see the *Trethowan* case above). This extra element will typically be the support of the people in a referendum.

Consider the following provision of the Northern Ireland Act 1998 which states that:

SECTION

s 1

It is hereby declared that Northern Ireland in its entirety remains part of the United Kingdom and shall not cease to be so without the consent of a majority of the people of Northern Ireland voting in a poll held for the purposes of this section.

What is the legal meaning of this provision? Could a later Parliament simply legislate to sever Northern Ireland from the rest of the United Kingdom without the consent of the people in the province? A traditional view of sovereignty would be that a later Act, following the enrolled Bill principle, could sever Northern Ireland without the consent of the people as stated in s 1 of the 1998 Act. In other words, the courts would not look beyond the parliamentary roll to ascertain whether an additional element had been satisfied (ie the consent of the people of Northern Ireland).

In contrast, one theory is that s 1 of the 1998 Act has redefined Parliament for the purposes of the future status of Northern Ireland. In other words, any Bill attempting to sever the province would require the consent of the following elements in order to be a valid Act:

- The House of Commons.
- The House of Lords (though technically not needed if the Parliament Acts of 1911 and 1949 are used).
- *The consent of the people of Northern Ireland voting in a poll.*
- The monarch (in the form of the Royal Assent).

It is certainly true that Parliament has already redefined how it passes legislation which is accepted and recognised by the courts. As we shall see (section 10.10.1) under the Parliament Acts of 1911 and 1949 the consent of the House of Lords is no longer needed – all that is required is for the Speaker of the Commons to indicate that a Bill has passed under the Parliament Acts. Accordingly, why is it not possible to add an extra element (eg the consent of the people in a referendum)? In this context, consider the following case:

Manuel v Attorney General [1983] 1 Ch 77

Canadian Indian Chiefs sought a declaration that the Canada Act 1982 was *ultra vires* as it was inconsistent with the safeguards provided by the Statute of Westminster Act 1931. Section 4 of the 1931 Act stated that no statute shall extend to a Dominion (eg Canada) without its express consent (the argument was that the Indian peoples had not given their consent). The Court of Appeal refused the declaration on the basis that the Canada Act 1982 was valid as its preamble stated that Canada had expressly requested and consented to this legislation, thereby satisfying s 4 of the 1931 Act.

The court did, however, state *obiter* (making it clear that they were *not* purporting to decide the issue) that it was content to assume that the following proposition was correct: 'that Parliament can effectively tie the hands of its successors, if it passes a statute which provides that any future legislation on a specified subject shall be enacted only with certain specified consents' (Slade LJ).

According to Ellis this case:

QUOTATION

'contains a tiny judicial hint that English courts might consider a future UK Parliament bound by a stipulation as to manner and form, although under what conditions this might be so it is difficult to predict'.

'The Legislative Supremacy of Parliament and its Limits' in D Feldman (ed),
English Public Law (2nd edn Oxford University Press, 2009), p 132.

7.10.3 The *Jackson* case

It is worth noting the recent House of Lords decision in *R (Jackson and Others) v Attorney General* [2005] UKHL 56 – for the facts of this case see section 10.10.3. For present purposes, the case concerned the 1911 Parliament Act (as amended in 1949) which allows legislation to be passed without the consent of the House of Lords. Section 2(1) of the 1911 Act, however, expressly excludes from its ambit a Bill purporting to extend the life of Parliament. According to the Act therefore, legislation proposing to extend the life of Parliament required the express consent of the House of Lords.

According to Young:

■ Seven of their Lordships held that were future legislation to be passed extending the maximum duration of Parliament beyond five years – but without the consent of the Upper House – the courts would not recognise this legislation as a valid Act of Parliament. In other words, a future Parliament (consisting *only* of the House of Commons and the Monarch) could not legislate contrary to s 2(1) (ie extend the life of Parliament without the consent of the Lords).

■ By a majority, five of their Lordships considered that the Parliament Acts *themselves* could not be used to delete the exception set out in s 2(1). In other words, they were of the opinion that a Bill purporting to delete the requirement in s 2(1) (ie that a Bill to extend the life of Parliament was excluded from the Parliament Acts), could not *itself* be pushed through under the Parliament Acts. Instead, it would need the express consent of the House of Lords. Conversely, it is noteworthy that the then senior law lord, Lord Bingham, indicated that the special procedure under the Act theoretically could be used to delete this exception in s 2(1). See A Young, 'Hunting sovereignty: *Jackson v Her Majesty's Attorney-General*' [2006] PL 187.

Finally in relation to this case, Turpin and Tomkins have noted that although a number of their Lordships made reference to the 'manner and form' argument (eg see Lord Steyn), nevertheless:

QUOTATION

'All such comments were *obiter*, and none resolves the matter definitively. Even after *Jackson* there can be no certainty as to whether the manner and form argument is, or is not, part of the law governing the Westminster Parliament.'

C Turpin & A Tomkins, *British Government and the Constitution*, (6th edition, Cambridge, 2007), p 60.

Conclusion

Notwithstanding the continuing debate concerning *legal entrenchment*, it is undoubtedly the case that a number of legislative enactments (particularly those which confer rights and remedies) are in fact *politically entrenched* in the sense that although legally these Acts could be repealed, the practical reality is that the political will to do so would be lacking. As a result, even if the traditional and orthodox view of parliamentary sovereignty is taken that legal entrenchment is not possible, political entrenchment of certain legislation is possible. Thus, the practical distinction between legal and political entrenchment becomes less important.

ACTIVITY

Exercise

Do you think that Parliament can entrench legislation in terms of the manner and form of later legislation? What would be the constitutional advantages and disadvantages of being able to do so?

KEY FACTS

Key facts on entrenchment

It is traditionally stated that in terms of subject-matter Parliament cannot entrench legislation against subsequent repeal.

There is disagreement over whether Parliament can entrench itself in terms of the manner and form of later legislation:

- The orthodox view (Dicey's continuing theory of sovereignty) is that one Parliament cannot bind another in terms of the manner and form of later legislation.
- A more modern view is that it is possible for one Parliament to bind itself in this way.
- A variant of the manner and form argument is the *redefinition theory of sovereignty* which states that Parliament can redefine its constituent elements to include an extra element such as the consent of the people (or a section of it) in a referendum.
- The majority (*obiter*) view in *Jackson* (2005) was that s 2(1) of the Parliament Act 1911 could not be removed without the consent of the House of Lords.

7.11 Parliamentary sovereignty and devolution

In 1998 Parliament passed three devolution Acts which delegated powers to the following regions:

- Scotland (Scotland Act 1998).
- Wales (Government of Wales Act 1998).
- Northern Ireland (Northern Ireland Act 1998).

These bodies have been established by the Westminster Parliament and so are legally subordinate to it. For example, s 28(7) of the Scotland Act 1998 states that the Westminster Parliament can still legislate for Scotland:

> 28A
> This section does not affect the power of the Parliament of the United Kingdom to make laws for Scotland.

Strictly speaking, of course, in legal theory such a provision is not necessary as Parliament can in any event pass any law that it chooses, including legislating for Scotland.

In legal theory, these devolved bodies could be simply extinguished by the Westminster Parliament passing legislation expressly repealing the above devolution Acts. Indeed, in the early 1970s Parliament revoked the Northern Irish Parliament which had operated for 50 years (see section 14.4.1). In terms of the implied repeal of this legislation, however, in *Thoburn v Sunderland City Council* (2002), Laws LJ indicated that the above devolution Acts fell within the definition of 'constitutional statutes', and as such, would not be susceptible to implied repeal (see section 4.4.5). In any event, as indicated earlier, in political terms it might prove difficult to repeal these Acts (this is certainly the case in respect of the Scotland Act 1998 (see section 14.3.13)).

7.12 Parliamentary sovereignty and the Human Rights Act 1998

In terms of the link between parliamentary sovereignty and the Human Rights Act, two points need to be made.

Firstly, the Human Rights Act 1998 does not enable the courts to invalidate Acts of Parliament which are plainly inconsistent with articles of the European Convention. Although s 4 of the 1998 Act enables the higher courts to issue a declaration of incompatibility in such circumstances, such a declaration *in itself* does not invalidate the offending legislation. The Act, therefore, maintains parliamentary sovereignty. The government's White Paper which preceded the Human Rights Act 1998, made it plain that under the Act the judiciary would not have the power to strike down Acts of Parliament as this would be likely to bring the courts into constitutional conflict with the legislature. Furthermore, it was noted there was no evidence that such constitutional power was sought either by the judges themselves or by the public (Rights Brought Home: The Human Rights Bill, Cm 3782, Home Office (1997), para 2.13).

In short, as noted by Lord Steyn in *R v DPP exp Kebilene and others* [1999] 3 WLR 972:

JUDGMENT

'It is crystal clear that the carefully and subtly drafted Human Rights Act 1998 preserves the principle of Parliamentary sovereignty.'

The Human Rights Act, therefore, is unlike Charters or Bills of Rights in other countries which typically have fundamental legal status. Indeed, the Act was passed through the ordinary parliamentary legislative process and can in fact (at least in legal theory), be expressly repealed at anytime by a future Parliament. It can be argued, however, that the Act is at least politically entrenched as it would prove difficult to revoke the Act and remove these positive individual rights (see section 7.6.2).

Secondly, the Human Rights Act in one respect is not an 'ordinary statute' as it is, in effect, an 'interpretative Act' setting out how the judiciary are to interpret legislation. As such, it is clear that the rule of implied repeal does not apply to the Act in the sense that:

■ The Human Rights Act 1998 does *not* impliedly repeal any Act (or provision of it) passed before 1998 which is inconsistent with one of the articles of the European Convention (given further effect by the 1998 Act). On this point the White Paper stated that the Act was 'intended to provide a new basis for judicial interpretation of all legislation, not a basis for striking down any part of it' (para 2.14).

■ The Human Rights Act 1998 itself is not *impliedly* repealed by legislation passed after 1998 which is inconsistent with the articles of the European Convention. During the parliamentary passage of the Bill the Lord Chancellor – who introduced the Bill – made it clear that the doctrine of implied repeal could have no application to the Act (*Hansard* HL Vol 583, col 509). It should be remembered that Laws LJ (see section 4.4.5) has argued that the Human Rights Act, together with the devolution Acts above, are 'constitutional statutes', and so not subject to implied repeal.

Finally, it is of interest to have regard to the observations of Ellis who has suggested that although the consequences of the Human Rights Act will take some years to pan out:

QUOTATION

'If the invariable reaction to a declaration of incompatibility proves to be an immediate remedial order, it might be concluded that the authority of Parliament has in fact been considerably diminished and its supremacy relinquished to the Convention and the courts. The effect of such a position would, in practice, be only slightly different from a power of judicial review over primary legislation.'

'The Legislative Supremacy of Parliament and its Limits', in D Feldman (ed), *English Public Law* (2nd Edition, Oxford University Press, 2009), p 134.

7.13 Parliamentary sovereignty and the rule of law

Dicey noted that parliamentary sovereignty and the rule of law pervaded the whole of the constitution, and that parliamentary sovereignty favoured the supremacy of the law of the land. He also pointed out that the independent position of the judiciary under the constitution (which of course uphold the rule of law) was secured by Parliament (it should be remembered that senior judges are not removable by the executive (see section 13.4.1)).

Although Parliament can pass any law it chooses, the courts will construe legislation in the light of the political/moral precepts underpinning the rule of law which respect basic constitutional principles (the protection of rights, access to the courts, etc). Writing extra-judicially, Lord Woolf noted that our parliamentary democracy is based on the rule of law:

QUOTATION

'As both Parliament and the courts derive their authority from the rule of law so both are subject to it and cannot act in a manner which involves its repudiation. The respective roles do not give rise to conflict because the courts and Parliament each respects the role of the other.'

Lord Woolf, 'Droit Public-English Style' [1995] PL 57.

This raises the issue of constitutionalism and parliamentary sovereignty. As defined earlier (see sections 2.6 and 4.15), constitutionalism is the principle that state power is effectively limited by constitutional rules (typically contained in a written codified constitutional document). Under the principle of parliamentary sovereignty, however, there are no legal limits restraining the laws that Parliament can pass, as there is no codified constitution constraining it as in other countries. Is parliamentary sovereignty, therefore, consistent with constitutionalism?

One response to this is that although in legal theory Parliament can pass any law that it chooses, in reality it does not. It is an unwritten maxim of the British constitution generally that those in power (parliamentarians and ministers) do not use their full powers to the maximum. In other words, Parliament is restrained politically and morally by the precepts underpinning the rule of law, and generally does not legislate contrary to them.

This is not to say that Parliament has not legislated in breach of the rule of law, as demonstrated by the War Damage Act 1965 which overruled a judicial ruling of the House of Lords for economic expediency (see sections 4.9, 6.7.9 and 7.5.1). Although the British constitution is based on the twin pillars of parliamentary sovereignty and the rule of law, morally, the latter will typically restrain the former. In legal terms, however, ultimately, they are unequal pillars as Parliament can (if it so chooses) legislate to undermine the principles underpinning the rule of law. It is also pertinent to remember that owing to the electoral system, as the government of the day typically has dominance over the House of Commons, this has led to the argument that in practice we have 'executive sovereignty' rather than parliamentary sovereignty (see section 9.8).

In the final analysis, it is of interest to note that recently the then Lord Chancellor commented that we must trust Parliament to understand the basis of our constitution so as not to violate the rule of law (Sixth Report of Session 2005–06 of the House of Lords Select Committee on the Constitution *Meeting with the Lord Chancellor* HL Paper 84 (2005), Q20).

ACTIVITY

Exercise

Revisit Chapter 6 and explain how the rule of law relates to, and restrains, parliamentary sovereignty.

SUMMARY

- Parliamentary sovereignty is the key principle which underpins the British constitution.
- Parliamentary sovereignty is concerned with the legal relationship between the courts and the legislature/Parliament.
- Parliamentary sovereignty has been closely associated with Dicey who viewed it as having positive and negative elements.
- The positive element was that the Crown/Queen in Parliament legally can pass any law. This is because in the British constitution (unlike in other countries) there is no codified document to stop it from doing so. Parliament can therefore alter any aspect of the constitution or alter any law that it chooses.
- Dicey identified one legal exception to the above which was that Parliament could not bind its successors. This is achieved through the twin doctrines of express and implied repeal.
- Although there may be an absence of legal limitations on Parliament, there are nevertheless political and practical restraints on the laws that Parliament can pass.
- The negative element of parliamentary sovereignty was that no court/body can question a statute. This means that the courts obey and apply Acts of Parliament (historically applying the 'enrolled Bill rule' to ascertain whether a Bill had become an Act).
- In recent years Dicey's principle that Parliament cannot bind its successors has been questioned.
- Today the principle of parliamentary sovereignty must be considered in the context of EU law (Chapter 15).

What is meant by the term parliamentary sovereignty?

Introduction:

Definition: Crown in Parliament can pass any law

Distinguish between legal and political sovereignty

Parliamentary sovereignty is central to the British constitution in the absence of a codified constitutional document (Dicey's conception of the principle is highly influential)

Crown in Parliament can pass any law:

To alter the common law (War Damage Act 1965), to change the constitution (House of Lords Act 1999), to legislate extra-territorially (War Crimes Act 1991) and to interfere with human rights (Anti-terrorism, Crime and Security Act 2001).

Notwithstanding the above, note the practical restraints on Parliament (Denning MR in *Blackburn* (1971)) and those imposed by constitutional convention (Sewel Convention).

Note the recent comments of Lord Steyn in *Jackson* (2005).

No court can question an Act of Parliament:

See *Jordan* (1967) and *Pickin* (1974).

Parliament cannot bind its successors:

See the traditional Diceyan view in *Vauxhall* (1932) and *Ellen Street Estates* (1934).

Other views on binding Parliament in terms of manner and form *Minister of the Interior* (1952), *Bribery Commissioner* (1965) and *Manuel* (1983). Also see the obiter comments in *Jackson* (2005).

The relevance of parliamentary sovereignty today:

Now subject to European Union law – see European Communities Act 1972 and *Factortame* (1991) at section 15.6.

CONCLUSION

Further reading

Books

Barnett, H, *Constitutional and Administrative Law* (7th edn, Routledge–Cavendish 2009), Chapter 6.

Bradley, A, 'The Sovereignty of Parliament – Form or Substance?' in Jowell, J and Oliver, D, *The Changing Constitution* (6th edn, Oxford University Press, 2007), p 25.

Leyland, P, *The Constitution of the United Kingdom* (Hart Publishing, 2007) pp 37–48.

Articles

Allan, T, 'Parliamentary sovereignty: law, politics, and revolution', [1997] 113 LQR 443.

Bingham, Lord, 'Dicey Revisited' [2002] PL 39.

Burns, S, 'When is an Act of Parliament not an Act of Parliament?' (2006) 156 NLJ 191.

Jowell, J, 'Parliamentary Sovereignty under the New Constitutional Hypothesis' [2006] PL 562.

Wade, HWR, 'The basis of legal sovereignty' [1955] CLJ 172.

Young, A, 'Hunting sovereignty: *Jackson v Her Majesty's Attorney-General*' [2006] PL 187.

8

Parliament I: Nature, functions and privilege

AIMS AND OBJECTIVES

At the end of this chapter you should be able to:
- Identify and explain the different functions of Parliament
- Explain the nature and significance of parliamentary privilege

8.1 Introduction and terminology

The United Kingdom Westminster Parliament is bicameral as it is composed of two Houses. It is also tripartite as it is composed of three constituent elements. These elements are as follows:

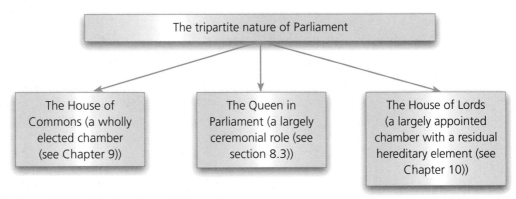

Figure 8.1 The tripartite nature of Parliament

8.1.1 Parliamentary terms

A parliamentary term is the period which exists between national general elections. Each Parliament lasts for a term which is divided up into a number of sessions. The United Kingdom Parliament, unlike some other legislatures such as the Scottish Parliament, does not have a fixed parliamentary term as it is variable and can last up to five years. Section 7 of the Parliament Act 1911 states that the current maximum length of a parliamentary term is five years.

In fact, even the maximum length of a parliamentary term (which in other countries will be specifically stipulated in its written codified constitutional document) can be altered by statute. For example, the Parliament Act 1911 reduced the maximum length of a parliamentary term to five years (the previous Septennial Act 1715 had set the length at seven years). Moreover, since 1911 the length of the parliamentary term has, out of practical necessity, been extended during both World Wars; for example, the 1911 Parliament was extended to after the First World War and the 1935 Parliament to 1945.

In contrast to other countries with fixed-term Parliaments where the date of a general election has been stipulated by the constitution, in the United Kingdom it is effectively the executive (specifically the Prime Minister) that determines the length of the parliamentary term by deciding when to call a national general election for the House of Commons. In essence, an election will be called when it is most advantageous to the executive (ie when they are most likely to win it). The United Kingdom is not unique in this sense, as in the Republic of Ireland, the Taoiseach (the Irish Prime Minister) also determines the timing of the next general election.

A parliamentary term ends when Parliament is dissolved by a proclamation issued by the Crown (the monarch) under the royal prerogative. By constitutional convention this power to dissolve Parliament will be exercised on the advice of the Prime Minister. In this way the latter determines the length of a parliamentary term and when a general election will be called (on suggested reform in this area, see section 11.9.3). In general, parliamentary terms in modern times tend to be around four years. The dissolution of one Parliament leads to the summoning of the next one which will be established after the general election.

8.1.2 A vote of no confidence

Although in general it is the Prime Minister that effectively determines the timing of a general election, there is, however, one circumstance when this will be decided for him. In the event of a government losing a vote of no confidence in the House of Commons, in general terms the constitutional convention is that the Prime Minister should request a dissolution of Parliament from the monarch, thereby precipitating a general election. This is somewhat rare, although in 1979 the Labour Prime Minister James Callaghan lost a vote of no confidence by one vote, as a result of which he requested a dissolution. Mrs Thatcher won the resulting general election and became Prime Minister in May 1979 (see further section 12.2.1).

8.1.3 The summoning of a Parliament

After a general election, the Crown (the monarch), under the royal prerogative, summons a new Parliament. Following the general election of 2010 a new Parliament was summoned and it became the 55th Parliament (each Parliament is numbered). Directly after a general election the monarch will appoint the Prime Minister and by constitutional convention she will appoint the person who commands the support of the majority of MPs in the House of Commons. As a consequence of our electoral system, this is, in general terms, a mere formality. When a Prime Minister has won a second or third successive general election victory (as with Tony Blair in 2001 and 2005), the monarch does not appoint the Prime Minister as he is *still* the Prime Minister and by constitutional convention he will be asked to form the next government.

Under the Meeting of Parliament Act 1694, Parliament, by law, must be summoned to meet at least once in every three years. The practical reality is that after a general election, the next Parliament will be summoned quickly. This is because in practice, Parliament will be held annually as the machinery of government necessitates this (for example, income tax for the following year needs to be authorised by Parliament).

8.1.4 Parliamentary sessions

Every parliamentary term is subdivided into parliamentary sessions consisting of approximately one year each. Each parliamentary session (which typically begins in November and ends the following October) will be opened by the State Opening of

Parliament and the Queen's Speech. The Queen's Speech is written by the government of the day and outlines its proposed legislative programme for the ensuing session.

Parliamentary sessions tend to be approximately one year. This is because of constitutional convention and not because of any legal statutory requirement. These sessions can, however, be longer immediately following a general election. For example, the general election of 2005 meant that the first session of the new Parliament ran from June 2005 to October 2006 (a period of almost 18 months). A typical Parliament will comprise four sessions before the Prime Minster calls a general election, although under the Parliament Act 1911, it could run to five sessions.

8.1.5 Prorogation

At the end of each parliamentary session Parliament is prorogued (ie suspended). The effect of this is that if a Bill introduced in one parliamentary session has not passed through Parliament and received the Royal Assent by the end of that session, it is lost and the Bill would have to be re-introduced (as a new Bill) in the following session. In recent years, however, it has been possible to 'carry over' Bills from one parliamentary session to the next. For example, the Constitutional Reform Bill 2003–04 was carried over in the House of Lords (where it had not completed its stages owing partly to the fact that very unusually, it was sent to a select committee for detailed consideration) to the 2004–05 parliamentary session. In fact, this arrangement in respect of the Constitutional Reform Bill was specifically referred to in the Queen's Speech of November 2004.

During the prorogation of Parliament all business in both Houses ceases (including work in parliamentary committees).

KEY FACTS

Parliamentary terminology
• The period between Parliaments is known as a term and each term is subdivided into a maximum of five sessions.
• Each session is approximately one year and at the end of each session, Parliament is suspended (prorogued).
• Before a general election Parliament is dissolved by the monarch and after each general election each new Parliament is summoned by the monarch.

8.2 A bicameral legislature

8.2.1 Bicameralism

bicameralism
a legislature
composed of two
chambers

The United Kingdom Parliament is **bicameral** consisting of two chambers (namely, the elected House of Commons and the non-elected House of Lords). The majority of legislatures/assemblies in the world are, however, unicameral consisting of only one chamber. For example:

- New Zealand (House of Representatives).
- Denmark (Folketing).
- Sweden (Riksdag).

Unicameral legislatures tend to be found in smaller states (with one clear exception being China) with relatively homogenous populations. In contrast, the United Kingdom, together with most large democracies such as the United States, Canada, France, Italy and Spain, has two chambers. Indeed, a bicameral system tends to be found particularly in federal states such as Australia and the USA where the upper House can represent the interests of the various different regions and peoples. Moreover, most lower chambers tend to be more powerful than their corresponding upper chambers (one exception is the United States Senate).

8.2.2 Arguments in favour of bicameralism

■ Two chambers disperse the power to make law between two (rival) power centres. By dispersing and dividing the power to make legislation, it is necessarily constitutionally limited.
■ Two chambers can ensure that legislative proposals are examined and scrutinised more effectively than in a unicameral legislature, as legislation must (generally speaking) pass through both chambers in order to become law. In particular, a second chamber can look afresh at, and revise, legislative proposals which have passed through the lower House.
■ A second chamber can act as a constitutional safeguard and protector of the constitution from the wishes of the (more generally powerful) lower chamber.

8.2.3 Arguments in favour of unicameralism

■ Unicameral legislatures tend to be more decisive.
■ Unicameral systems avoid inter-chamber constitutional conflict which is necessarily inherent in a bicameral system where two chambers compete with each other.

In any event, in respect of recent attempts at reforming the House of Lords (see section 10.13), in March 2007 the House of Commons voted to retain a bicameral system by 416 votes to 163. As a result, it is clear that any future reform of the House of Lords will necessarily involve retaining the second chamber. Historically, some countries such as Denmark and New Zealand have abolished their second chambers (1953 and 1950 respectively), although in both cases, the populations are comparatively small (5 and 4 million respectively).

ACTIVITY

Self-test question

Do you think that the United Kingdom should have a bicameral legislature? Revisit this question after you have completed Chapter 10 (the House of Lords).

8.3 The Queen in Parliament

It is the Queen in Parliament (Crown in Parliament) which passes primary legislation, and so the monarch is a constituent element of Parliament. Her main constitutional roles include:

■ Summoning Parliament after a general election.
■ Proroguing Parliament at the end of a parliamentary session.
■ Dissolving Parliament prior to a general election.
■ Opening each parliamentary session with the State Opening and the delivery of the Queen's Speech.
■ Granting assent to a Bill in order for it to become an Act of Parliament.
■ Appointing the Prime Minister who is drawn from Parliament.
■ Appointing government ministers who are drawn from Parliament.

The above constitutional duties are performed by the monarch but, generally speaking, in accordance with constitutional convention she acts on the advice of her government ministers.

The monarch is not allowed in the House of Commons to observe debates (a consequence of the English Civil War), which is why Members of Parliament (MPs) go to the House of Lords to hear the delivery of the Queen's Speech. The monarch is, however, permitted to listen to debates in the Lords. The monarch will be considered again at section 11.1.2.

8.4 The functions of Parliament

The principal functions of Parliament are set out below, but they do, of course, necessarily blend with the individual constitutional functions of the two Houses. Although Parliament is the legislature, it will be noted that its constitutional responsibilities are not confined to simply passing legislation. In 2006 the parliamentary website (www.parliament.uk) identified the following functions of Parliament.

8.4.1 A legislative function (examining and passing proposals for law)

The passing of legislation is the principal constitutional function of a legislature. In the United Kingdom the Queen in Parliament is the supreme domestic law-making body. As Parliament is elected by the people and composed of elected representatives (at least in terms of the House of Commons), the resulting laws made, represent the will of the people.

Although in constitutional theory it is the Queen in Parliament who passes the law, the practical reality is that Parliament to a large extent passes laws which have been drafted and initiated by the government of the day. Indeed, such is this dominance, it could be argued that, generally speaking, Parliament merely rubberstamps or legitimises the legislative proposals sought by the government. One of the constitutional functions of the executive in the British constitution is that of developing policy and initiating proposed legislation (eg the Legislative and Regulatory Reform Bill, the Prevention of Terrorism Bill and the Identity Card Bill).

Notwithstanding the above, some legislative proposals are initiated by parliamentary members in the form of Private Members' Bills. These can be initiated by members in either House, but the likely success of these measures becoming law are, to a large extent, dependent on support from the government, as it dominates the parliamentary timetable. During the session of 2008–09 out of 27 public Bills which obtained the Royal Assent, 23 were government Bills and four were Private Members' Bills (Factsheet L2, *'Private Members' Bills Procedure'*, (House of Commons Parliamentary Copyright, 2010), p 2). In addition to the above public Bills, Parliament also processes private Bills (sponsored by, for example, local authorities) and hybrid Bills (a mixture of public and private elements).

In general terms, Bills require the consent of both Houses of Parliament in order to become law. In exceptional cases, however, only the consent of the House of Commons is necessary in the event of the Parliament Acts 1911 and 1949 being used (see section 10.10.1).

8.4.2 A deliberative function (the scrutiny of executive policy and administration)

Parliament acts as a constitutional check on the exercise of executive power. In short, Parliament scrutinises executive policy, administration and actions thereby ensuring that the government of the day is constitutionally accountable and responsible to Parliament (which, of course, represents the people). In constitutional theory, accountability is secured through the following parliamentary mechanisms:

- The scrutiny of legislative proposals.
- Debates.
- Questions.
- Select committees.

For a detailed consideration of the nature and effectiveness of these mechanisms, see Chapter 12. As John Stuart Mill noted in the nineteenth century:

QUOTATION

The constitutional function of Parliament (particularly in the context of a parliamentary executive), therefore, is to hold the government to account: make it explain and justify its policies and actions/decisions. In doing so, Parliament acts as a constitutional restraint on the executive and may influence its actions. In this way Parliament acts as a forum for influencing executive policy. By scrutinising the actions of the executive, Parliament confers constitutional legitimacy on executive actions.

Both Houses scrutinise the actions of the executive, and it is particularly important in the absence of a written entrenched codified constitution that the executive is effectively scrutinised by Parliament. Effective and meaningful scrutiny, of course, necessarily depends upon the government providing accurate and full information. In the United States of America Freedom of Information provisions have permitted access to government information and in the United Kingdom in 2000 Parliament passed the Freedom of Information Act which (subject to certain conditions and exceptions) equips individuals with access to governmental information and records.

8.4.3 A forum for debate (debating the major issues of the day)

Both Houses of Parliament act as forums for debate on matters of public importance and interest. One interesting development which has taken place in recent years is the use of a parallel chamber known as Westminster Hall. Due to the congested nature of the timetable in the House of Commons, debates can now take place in this 'parallel' chamber. Such debates might otherwise have found little space on the Floor of the House of Commons.

8.4.4 To provide for taxation/finance

By voting for taxation, Parliament enables the administration of government to be carried out. In order for the government of the day to raise money it must have the express permission of Parliament. In particular, it is the House of Commons (which is directly elected by the people) which has control over such financial matters (ie scrutinising expenditure and authorising spending as well as taxation; on taxation, see the annual Budget – the Finance Bill).

8.4.5 To safeguard the rights of individuals

This is a function performed by both Houses. In particular, every MP in the House of Commons has a specific constituency with a responsibility to help redress constituents' grievances (see section 9.3.1). In terms of protecting the rights of the individual, the House of Lords has a particular role to act as a constitutional safeguard and watchdog of civil liberties when considering legislative proposals which threaten to undermine the basic rights of the individual (see section 10.9.9). In addition, Parliament has established the Joint Committee on Human Rights to consider matters relating to human rights and to consider remedial orders made under the Human Rights Act 1998 (see Chapter 17).

8.4.6 The examination of proposed European legislation

As a member of the European Union, laws can be made in Europe (principally in the Council which is the Union's legislature), which directly affect the United Kingdom.

In fact, these laws can override the domestic law (including Acts of Parliament) of the United Kingdom (see section 15.6). Parliament, through committees in both Houses, supervises proposed legislative measures in Europe (see section 12.9).

8.4.7 A judicial function

In 2006 although the parliamentary website listed the hearing of judicial appeals by the Appellate Committee as a function, in October 2009 this function was transferred to the new Supreme Court. Notwithstanding this, both Houses perform a judicial function in the context of enforcing parliamentary privilege and disciplining members who act in contempt of either House (see section 8.5).

In addition to those already mentioned, the following functions could be added:

■ **The recruitment of the government**

As the United Kingdom has a parliamentary executive, the executive is necessarily drawn from Parliament. By constitutional convention, members of the government must sit in either House of Parliament (except the Prime Minster who must sit in the Commons). Parliament, therefore, provides the pool from which the government is drawn. Although ministers are drawn from both Houses, they predominately come from the House of Commons (see section 11.6.1).

■ **The removal of specified personnel**

Both Houses of Parliament acting in concert with each other are constitutionally responsible for removing key personnel, for example senior judges (see section 13.4.1) and the Parliamentary Commissioner for Administration (see section 21.3.6).

KEY FACTS

The functions of Parliament	Performed by
Legislative	Both Houses, although ultimately the House of Commons is dominant.
The control of finance	The House of Commons (exclusively).
Safeguarding rights	Both Houses, although the House of Lords has a particular responsibility for this.
Scrutiny of the executive	Both Houses, although the House of Commons is typically dominated by the government of the day.
Scrutiny of European legislation	Both Houses.
Debate	Both Houses.
Recruitment of the government	Both Houses, though largely from the House of Commons.
Representative	The House of Commons as it is elected, although life peers in the Lords can to some extent reflect society at large.
Judicial	Both Houses enforce parliamentary privilege.

8.5 Parliamentary privilege

8.5.1 Definition and types of privilege

Erskine May defined the privileges of Parliament in the following way:

QUOTATION

'Parliamentary privilege is the sum of the peculiar rights enjoyed by each House collectively as a constituent part of the High Court of Parliament, and by Members of each House individually, without which they could not discharge their functions, and which exceed those possessed by other bodies or individuals. Thus privilege, though part of the law of the land, is to a certain extent an exemption from the general law.'

E May, *Parliamentary Practice* (23rd edn, LexisNexis Butterworths, 2004), p 75.

According to Erskine May, at the commencement of each new Parliament, the Speaker of the House of Commons lays claim to the following rights/privileges known as the four petitions (it is taken that similar privileges also apply in the Lords):

■ **Freedom of speech**
(see section 8.6).

■ **Freedom from arrest**
The freedom of members not to be arrested within Parliament was established at a very early date and the constitutional rationale behind it was to enable members to attend the chamber so that they could perform their constitutional functions as part of Parliament. This privilege was confined to arrest in the context of civil matters (not criminal ones) and, as noted by the Joint Committee on Parliamentary Privilege (see below), since the almost practical abolition of imprisonment for debt (Debtors Act 1869), it seems to have little modern relevance (with the exception of an immunity from arrest for disobeying a court order in civil proceedings – *Stourton v Stourton* [1963] 1 All ER 606). In 1999 the Joint Committee recommended its abolition (Joint Committee on Parliamentary Privilege, *Report, Volume 1 – Report and Proceedings of the Committee*, HL Paper 43-I HC 214-I (1999), p 85).

■ **Free access to the monarch**
Both Houses have access to the Sovereign (although peers have access as individuals) and MPs attend the Lords to hear the Queen's Speech.

■ **The most favourable construction be placed upon the proceedings in the House.**
According to Erskine May, today this is simply 'a formal courtesy'.

In addition to the above, Parliament also enjoys, *inter alia:*
– the right to determine and regulate its own membership and internal proceedings (see sections 8.7.1 and 8.7.2)
– the right to administer punishments in the event of a privilege being breached (see section 8.7.3).

NB Following the search in November 2008 of the MP Damian Green's parliamentary office by the police, the Committee on Issue of Privilege (Police Searches on the Parliamentary Estate) was established by the House of Commons. Its remit was to 'review the internal processes of the House administration for granting permission for such action, to consider any matter relating to privilege arising from the police operation, and to make recommendations for the future'. At the time of going to print the Committee had just issued its report (*Police Searches on the Parliamentary Estate*, First Report, HC 62 (The Stationary Office, 2010)).

8.5.2 The origins, sources and constitutional rationale of parliamentary privilege

Parliamentary privilege forms part of the law and custom of Parliament. The sources of privilege are found in Acts of Parliament (eg Art 9 of the Bill of Rights 1689), practices within Parliament and court decisions which have identified the existence of privileges and rights. Parliament, through the enactment of a statute can:

■ Create new privileges.
■ Amend or modify an existing privilege. For example, see s 13 of the Defamation Act 1996 (see section 8.6.2).
■ Abolish a privilege. For example, the Criminal Justice Act 2003 abolished the immunity and privilege of members to be excused *as of right* from jury service.

The constitutional reason that parliamentary members enjoy these privileges, immunities and rights is to ensure that they can carry out their constitutional functions as part of Parliament. Members need to be able to air grievances and call to account the government. Moreover, Parliament itself must be able to regulate its own composition and affairs without interference from either the ordinary courts or the government. In this way, Parliament enjoys independence.

Parliamentary privileges and immunities (in particular freedom of speech), are not unique to the United Kingdom. For example, Art 15.10 of the Irish Republic's constitution permits both chambers of the Oireachtas to make their own internal rules and standing orders regulating each House. These internal rules and procedures cannot be challenged by the Irish courts.

8.6 Freedom of speech

8.6.1 Article 9 of the Bill of Rights 1689

Members of Parliament in both Houses enjoy an absolute immunity in respect of freedom of speech within Parliament:

SECTION

Article 9, the Bill of Rights 1689
'The freedom of speech and debates or proceedings in Parliament ought not to be impeached or questioned in any court or place out of Parliament.'

The constitutional rationale behind this is to enable parliamentary members to have freedom of speech so as to be able to discuss whatever subject they choose ('freedom of speech and debates'). The legal immunity is absolute and includes immunity from both civil and criminal liability as proceedings 'ought not to be impeached or questioned'. This enables members freely to perform their parliamentary functions and duties (raising issues of public concern, etc) without the fear of legal repercussions. In *A v United Kingdom* (2003) (see below) the European Court of Human Rights accepted that the justification for this absolute immunity was twofold:

■ Firstly, it permitted free debate.
■ Secondly, it ensured a constitutional separation between the judiciary and the legislature, as the former could not interfere with debates and speeches in the latter.

Similarly, in the Republic of Ireland, Art 15.12 of the constitution protects members of both Houses of the Oireachtas in respect of what they say in the legislature, with all official reports and 'utterances' being privileged.

As Art 9 confers an absolute immunity on members this would appear to contravene one of the principles underpinning the rule of law, namely, equality under the law with no immunities from its ambit (see section 6.7.6). As a result, it is imperative that parliamentary members use this right/immunity in a responsible way and do not abuse it. In the event of abuse, as recognised by the European Court in *A v United Kingdom* (2003), one safeguard is that internal parliamentary disciplinary proceedings can be taken against the member involved (see section 8.7.3).

Parliamentary privilege does not apply where an MP repeats outside Parliament words which he has used in a speech made earlier in the House of Commons. This explains why MPs may be willing to make comments within Parliament which they will not repeat outside the chamber for fear of legal repercussions.

8.6.4 'Proceedings in Parliament ought not to be impeached or questioned in any court'

Under the Bill of Rights the courts cannot question proceedings in Parliament. However, since the *Pepper v Hart* (1993) decision (below) the courts can make reference to parliamentary materials as an aid to the construction of legislation.

CASE EXAMPLE

Pepper v Hart [1993] 1 All ER 42

The House of Lords held that in order to give effect to the true intention of Parliament in interpreting legislation, the court could refer to parliamentary materials where the legislation in question was:
- ambiguous, obscure or absurd;
- the material relied on consisted of statements made by the minister or promoter of the Bill together (if needed) with other such parliamentary material necessary to understand these statements, and that these statements were clear.

The court made it clear that this reference to parliamentary material would not infringe Art 9 of the Bill of Rights as it was not 'questioning' the freedom of speech within Parliament, rather the court was merely trying to give effect to the intention of Parliament.

In the context of the Human Rights Act 1998 the House of Lords has held that in evaluating the compatibility of Acts of Parliament with European Convention rights, the court if necessary could have regard to relevant background material (ie explanatory departmental notes and ministerial statements when the Bill was progressing through its parliamentary stages), but not to debates in order to identify the policy objective of the legislation (*Wilson v First County Trust Ltd (No 2)* [2003] UKHL 40).

It should be pointed out that s 1 of the Parliamentary Standards Act 2009 makes it plain that nothing in the Act affected Art 9 of the Bill of Rights 1689. Clause 10 of the original Bill had provided that parliamentary privilege would be set aside to enable evidence to be adduced in court against an MP in relation to a criminal offence under the original incarnation of the Bill (eg the offence of paid advocacy).

Publication of proceedings outside Parliament

Section 1 of the Parliamentary Papers Act 1840 conferred an absolute privilege on a person who publishes a paper/report printed by order of, or under the authority of Parliament (correct copies were covered by s 2). This Act had been passed in the context of (and in response to) litigation involving Stockdale suing Hansard for defamation for publishing a report ordered by the House of Commons (*Stockdale v Hansard* (1839) 9 Ad & E1). In this case, although Lord Chief Justice Denman accepted that the House had exclusive jurisdiction over its proceedings, it could not by resolution simply declare the material to be privileged.

Under s 3 of the 1840 Act, extracts from or abstracts of the above parliamentary papers attract qualified privilege, and in terms of broadcasting s 3 was subsequently amended by the:

- Defamation Act 1952 (in respect of radio).
- Broadcasting Act 1990 (in respect of television).

In terms of reporting parliamentary proceedings, s 15 of the Defamation Act 1996 gives qualified privilege to a fair and accurate report of these proceedings.

NB In October 2009, a court order (albeit temporarily) prevented the *Guardian* reporting certain proceedings in Parliament (ie concerning a parliamentary question) – see G Slapper, 'Parliamentary supremacy, suing witnesses for the prosecution, legal aid not Cinderella, how a litigant can change the law' (sic) (2010) 59 *Student Law Review* 18.

KEY FACTS

Art 9 of the Bill of Rights 1689
Article 9 of the Bill of Rights 1689 protects parliamentary members from civil and criminal liability from things said in Parliament.
It protects proceedings in Parliament which would include, *inter alia*: • Debates and proceedings on Bills. • Questions. • Proceedings within committees. • Parliamentary votes.
From a constitutional perspective Art 9: • Permits free debate and enables parliamentary members to discuss whatever subject they choose without the fear of legal ramifications. • Ensures a clear constitutional separation between the judiciary and the legislature.

8.7 Other privileges

Other privileges enjoyed by both Houses are:

■ The right to determine their own composition.
■ The right to regulate their own internal proceedings.
■ The right to punish individuals for contempt or breach of privilege.

8.7.1 The right to determine their own composition

by-election
an election which takes place in a constituency when an MP's seat becomes vacant

The House of Commons will, for example, determine who is qualified to be a member of the House and decide if a person is unfit to serve. The House will also determine the timing of **by-elections**.

8.7.2 The right to regulate their own internal proceedings

As pointed out by Evans (*Handbook of House of Commons Procedure* (7th edn, Dods, 2009), p 33), this is known as the 'exclusive cognisance' of its proceedings. Each House will make standing orders to regulate its proceedings including in relation to the passage of legislation. As indicated earlier (see section 7.3.3), the courts will not look beyond the parliamentary roll and question the manner of parliamentary proceedings as this would violate the separation of powers between the judiciary and the legislature. As a consequence, Parliament will determine its own internal proceedings and decide if these proceedings have been interfered with. As pointed out by Lord Reid:

JUDGMENT

'The court has no concern with the manner in which Parliament or its officers carrying out its Standing Orders perform these functions. Any attempt to prove that they were misled by fraud or otherwise would necessarily involve an inquiry into the manner in which they had performed their functions in dealing with the Bill which became the British Railways Act 1968.'

British Railways Board v Pickin [1974] AC 765.

In this case, Lord Morris added that it would be both undesirable and impracticable for the courts to embark upon such an inquiry. In fact, as illustrated by the following two cases, the courts have made it very clear that the internal administration of the House of Commons is not subject to control by the courts.

CASE EXAMPLE

Bradlaugh v Gossett (1884) 12 QBD 271

The House of Commons passed a resolution excluding Bradlaugh from the chamber (even though he had been elected to the House of Commons) 'until he shall engage not further to disturb the proceedings of the House'. Bradlaugh unsuccessfully sought a declaration that this order was void together with an order restraining the Serjeant-at-Arms from preventing him from entering the House. The court held that it could not inquire into the propriety of a resolution of the House (this was a matter relating to the internal proceedings of the House).

CASE EXAMPLE

Chaffers v Goldsmid [1894] 1 QB 186

The court stated that no action would lie in the event of a member of the House of Commons refusing to present a petition (to redress certain grievances) to the chamber presented to him by a constituent.

More recently the Court of Appeal has made it clear that as the activities of the Parliamentary Commissioner for Standards (see section 8.8.2) were in essence concerned with the proceedings of the House, they were beyond the supervisory powers of the courts to control what the officer did in relation to an investigation (*R v Parliamentary Commissioner for Standards, ex parte Al Fayed* [1998] 1 All ER 93).

In regulating its own proceedings, the Houses can, for example:

■ Exclude disorderly strangers.
■ Resolve to sit in a secret session.
■ Debate any matter it chooses (subject to the *sub judice* resolution – see section 13.4.3).

8.7.3 The right to punish individuals for contempt

Erskine May defined contempt of Parliament as:

QUOTATION

'generally speaking, any act or omission which obstructs or impedes either House of Parliament in the performance of its functions, or which obstructs or impedes any Member or officer of such House in the discharge of his duty, or which has a tendency, directly or indirectly, to produce such results'.

E May, *Parliamentary Practice* (23rd edn, LexisNexis Butterworths, 2004), p 128.

Erskine May points out that contempt covers, *inter alia,* the following:

■ Misconduct in the presence of the House or a committee.
■ Disobeying a rule or order.
■ Misconduct of members (eg an MP accepting a bribe).
■ Premature disclosure of committee proceedings.
■ Obstructing or molesting members.
■ Obstructing officers of the House or witnesses.

The procedure in respect of contempt or a breach of privilege (by a member)

A member will raise the issue with the Speaker who will decide if it takes precedence over business. If so, the member can table a motion for the next day proposing that the matter is referred to the Select Committee on Standards and Privileges. The Committee in considering the matter has the power to send for persons, records and papers. Unlike in ordinary criminal or civil cases, the accused member is (generally) not allowed representation by counsel. If the Committee decides that a breach has occurred, a debate on the Committee's report will ensue. The House then decides whether or not to accept the report and recommendations of the Committee (on occasions it may not), and will determine the punishment. In the upper chamber, the House of Lords Committee for Privileges investigates if a breach of privilege or contempt has taken place and reports to the House, who in turn, will determine what action (if any) to take.

Both Houses have their own penal jurisdiction and punishments which are separate from the ordinary courts. These are as follows:

- Imprisonment (although it has not been used for some time).
- Fines (seemingly lapsed in the House of Commons although an MP's salary can be suspended).
- Expulsion (historically, the House of Lords does not have the power to expel permanently a member, but see recent proposed reforms at section 10.13).
- Suspension.
- A formal reprimand or admonishment.

In this context, it is pertinent to note that Parliament is specifically excluded from the ambit of the Human Rights Act 1998 as under it, Parliament does not have to follow legally the requirements of the European Convention (including Art 6 – the right to a fair trial). Notwithstanding this, as pointed out by the Joint Committee on Parliamentary Privilege, Parliament in exercising its internal disciplinary powers could theoretically be challenged under Art 6 of the Convention before the European Court of Human Rights in Strasbourg if its proceedings are not fair. As a result, it indicated that Parliament should adopt (at least) minimum requirements of fairness in its internal disciplinary procedures (Joint Committee on Parliamentary Privilege, *Report, Volume 1 – Report and Proceedings of the Committee*, HL Paper 43-I HC 214-I (1999), para 284). The Joint Committee also recommended the enactment of a Parliamentary Privileges Act which would codify parliamentary privileges.

ACTIVITY

Self-test question

Do you think that the way in which Parliament disciplines those who commit contempt or a breach of privilege is consistent with the right to a fair trial under Art 6 of the European Convention? Revisit this question after having completed Chapter 16 on the European Convention.

KEY FACTS

The main privileges of Parliament
• Freedom of speech.
• Freedom from arrest.
• Free access to the monarch.
• The most favourable construction to be placed upon the proceedings in the House.
• The right to determine and regulate its own membership.
• The right to determine its internal proceedings.
• The right to administer punishments for contempt or breach of privilege.

8.8 Members' interests and standards

8.8.1 The Register of Members' Financial Interests

In the mid-1970s, the House of Commons established a compulsory Register of Members' Interests (renamed in 2009 as the Register of Members' Financial Interests) which required

MPs to declare their financial interests with the outside world (ie payments, remunerated directorships or trades, etc). In addition, MPs should declare interests when participating in debates. The House of Lords also has a Register of Lords' Interests in respect of consultancies, remunerated directorships, etc.

8.8.2 Standards in Public Life

As a result of the 'cash for questions' affair in 1994, the then Prime Minister established the Committee on Standards in Public Life 'To examine current concerns about standards of conduct of all holders of public office'. This committee (the Nolan Committee) issued its report in 1995 (First Report of the Committee on Standards in Public Life, *Standards in Public Life, Volume 1: Report*, Cm 2850-I (1995)) and led to:

- **The creation of the Select Committee on Standards and Privileges** (to replace the Committee of Privileges).
  Its responsibilities involve considering matters of privilege and contempt, overseeing the Parliamentary Commissioner for Standards (see below) and considering breaches of the Code of Conduct (see below).

- **The establishment of a Parliamentary Commissioner for Standards**.
  The functions of this officer, *inter alia*, are to:
  - Oversee the operation of the Register of Members' Financial Interests.
  - Advise MPs as to the interpretation of the Code of Conduct (see below) and monitor its operation.
  - Investigate complaints against MPs in breach of the Code and Rules, and report the conclusions to the Select Committee on Standards and Privileges (which produces its own report). It is the House, however, which will determine any penalty to be imposed.
  - Monitor and investigate complaints in respect of other registers (eg the Register of All-party Groups).

However, the remit of the Commissioner has now been complicated by the arrangements set out in the Parliamentary Standards Act 2009 (see section 8.8.3).

- **The establishment of the Code of Conduct for Members of Parliament**

QUOTATION

'1. The purpose of this Code of Conduct is to assist Members in the discharge of their obligations to the House, their constituents and the public at large by:
a) Providing guidance on the standards of conduct expected of Members in discharging their parliamentary and public duties, and in so doing
b) Providing the openness and accountability necessary to reinforce public confidence in the way in which Members perform those duties.
2. The Code applies to Members in all aspects of their public life.
…
7. In carrying out their parliamentary and public duties, Members will be expected to observe the following general principles of conduct identified by the Committee on Standards in Public Life in its First Report as applying to holders of public office.'

The Code of Conduct together with the Guide to the Rules relating to the conduct of Members,
HC 735 (The Stationery Office, 2009), p 3.

NB The Code and Guide to the rules have been periodically amended over time.

QUOTATION

'The seven principles of conduct
- Selflessness
- Integrity

- Objectivity
- Accountability
- Openness
- Honesty
- Leadership.'

First Report of the Committee on Standards in Public Life, *Standards in Public Life,*
Volume 1: Report, Cm 2850-I (1995), p 14.

Among other things, the Code of Conduct states that:

■ Members shall fulfil conscientiously, the requirements in relation to the registration of their interests.
■ Members shall not act as paid advocates.
■ Members should not accept a bribe to influence their conduct (as being contrary to the law of Parliament).

The House of Lords by way of a resolution in 2001 adopted the House of Lords Code of Conduct which set out the rules on Lords' interests (a new code was agreed in November 2009). It should be made clear that the Parliamentary Commissioner for Standards does not operate in the House of Lords. However, at the time of going to print, a House of Lords Commissioner for Standards was appointed to investigate alleged breaches of the new code discussed above.

8.8.3 The Parliamentary Standards Act 2009

QUOTATION

'"The public are sullen, some even mutinous."

(Sir Robert Worcester, June 2009)

1. We have been set up at a time when the House of Commons is going through a crisis of confidence not experienced in our lifetimes. This is largely, but not exclusively, because of the revelations about Members' expenses, bringing with it a storm of public disapproval and contempt. Public confidence in the House and in Members as a whole has been low for some time, but not as low as now. It is not too much to say that the institution is in crisis.'

House of Commons Reform Committee, *Rebuilding the House,*
First Report of Session 2008–09, HC 1117 (The Stationery Office, 2009), para 1.

In response to the furore over MPs' claims and expenses the Parliamentary Standards Act 2009 was passed (rather expeditiously). Section 3 of the Act established the following:

■ The Independent Parliamentary Standards Authority (IPSA) which represented a move away from self-regulation to an independent regulator.
■ The Commissioner for Parliamentary Investigations.
■ The Speaker's Committee for IPSA.

The Act stated that IPSA was to pay the salaries of MPs (s 4) and their allowances (in accordance with the MPs' allowances scheme to be prepared by IPSA (s 5)).

Under s 6 MPs would submit their allowances claim to IPSA who would determine whether or not to allow it. The IPSA is required by s 8 to produce an MPs' *code of conduct relating to financial interests* which 'must require members to register specified information about specified financial interests in a register maintained by the IPSA' (s 8(7)). The code must prohibit an MP from paid advocacy (s 8(8)). The code is subject to approval by the House of Commons.

Under s 9, the Commissioner for Parliamentary Investigations can undertake an investigation if he has reason to believe an MP may have been paid an allowance which he should not have been allowed or may have failed to comply with the requirement concerning the registering of information about specified financial interests (see above).

In the event of the Commissioner finding an allowance payment that should not have been paid or a failure to register a financial interest, he must (though not in every case) refer his findings to the House of Commons Committee on Standards and Privileges. Section 9 provides MPs with a safeguard as the above procedures must be fair, including the opportunity to make representations to the Commissioner, to be heard in person and, where appropriate, to call witnesses (in effect, these are the principles underpinning natural justice – see section 20.5.4).

Finally, s 10 made it a criminal offence to make an allowance claim with information which the MP knows to be false or misleading.

In this context, see also the following:

- In November 2009 the Committee on Standards in Public Life (chaired by Sir Christopher Kelly) published its report on its review of MPs' expenses (*MPs' expenses and allowances*, 12th Report of the Committee on Standards in Public Life, Cm 7724 (Crown Copyright, 2009)). It made a number of recommendations (eg rec 3 stated that 'MPs should no longer be reimbursed for the cost of mortgage interest payments or any other costs associated with the purchase of a property.').

- In December 2009 the Leader of the House set out the changes that would be made in view of the various recommendations made in the report above. In particular, these included:
  - 'Responsibility for maintaining the register of financial interests and the associated code of conduct should be removed from the independent regulator and returned to the House of Commons' (Kelly's rec 42). The government, therefore, proposed to repeal s 8 of the 2009 Act.
  - The independent regulator should be given statutory responsibility for setting the level of pay for MPs (Kelly's rec 43). The government proposed to bring forward legislation to enable IPSA to set the pay system of MPs.
  - The independent regulator should have responsibility for investigating allegations concerning breaches of the rules on expenses and appoint its own compliance officer (Kelly's rec 44). The government proposed to amend the 2009 Act to provide for a compliance officer to be appointed by the IPSA (in other words, to replace the Commissioner under the Act).
  - The enforcement regime of the regulator should be strengthened (Kelly's rec 45). The government proposed to provide the new compliance officer with the power to impose sanctions.
- In January 2010 IPSA launched a consultation on MPs' expenses which will inform the content of the MPs' expenses scheme. At the time of writing, IPSA was scheduled to be in operation in April 2010.

In February 2010 Sir Thomas Legg published his report on payments of the ACA (Additional Costs Allowance – ie the second home allowance) made to MPs between 2004 and 2009, together with any recommended repayments that individual MPs should make (House of Commons Estimate Committee, *Review of past ACA payments*, First Report of Session 2009–10, HC 348 (The Stationary Office, 2010)).

NB At the time of going to print, the Constitutional Reform and Governance Act 2010 had been passed which made the following changes to the Parliamentary Standards Act 2009:

- It replaces the Commissioner for Parliamentary Investigations with a Compliance Officer for the IPSA (s 26) and appointed by it (sch 3)
- It adds three lay members to the Speaker's Committee for the IPSA (s 27)
- It provides for the IPSA to determine the amounts of MPs' salaries (s 29) (under the 2009 Act, this was determined in accordance with House of Commons resolutions)
- Section 32 repeals s 8 of the 2009 Act which required the IPSA to produce an MPs' Code of Conduct in relation to financial interests

- Section 33 replaces s 9 of the 2009 Act (which concerned investigations by the Commissioner) with provisions concerning an investigation by the Compliance Officer and s 34 and sch 4 concern the Compliance Officer's enforcement powers

SUMMARY

- The United Kingdom has a bicameral legislature which disperses power between two chambers.
- The functions of Parliament involve:
  - A legislative function – passing law as the legislature.
  - A forum for debate.
  - Representing the will of the people and safeguarding the rights of individuals.
  - Disciplining and regulating its membership.
- Parliamentary privilege are those rights and immunities enjoyed by each House.
- Under Art 9 Bill of Rights 1689 parliamentary members enjoy the protection from legal liability for things said in Parliament as proceedings in Parliament should not be questioned in any court.
- Parliamentary privilege also embraces:
  - The right to determine their own composition.
  - The rights to regulate their own internal proceedings.
  - The right to punish individuals for contempt or breach of privilege.
- Each House has a *Code of Conduct* which governs its members. In the House of Commons a Parliamentary Commissioner for Standards has historically investigated complaints against MPs in breach of their Code.
- As a consequence of the controversy over MPs' claims and expenses, major reforms have taken place with a move from self-regulation to an independent regulator (Parliamentary Standards Authority).

Further reading

Books

Alder, J, *Constitutional and Administrative Law* (7th edn, Palgrave Macmillan, 2009), Chapter 11.

Carroll, A, *Constitutional and Administrative Law* (5th edn, Pearson/Longman, 2009), Chapter 10.

Loveland, I, *Constitutional Law, Administrative Law, and Human Rights* (5th edn, Oxford University Press, 2009), Chapter 8.

Oliver, D, 'The Powers and Privileges of Parliament' in Feldman, D, (ed), *English Public Law* (2nd edn, Oxford University Press, 2009).

Articles

Leyland, P, 'Freedom of information and the 2009 parliamentary expenses scandal' [2009] PL 675.

Parpworth, N, 'Nothing to declare?' (2009) 159 NLJ 1236.

Papers

Kelly, R and Gay, O, 'The establishment of the Independent Parliamentary Standards Authority' SN/PC/05167 (House of Commons, 2009).

Factsheet G06 'Disciplinary and Penal Powers of the House of Commons' (House of Commons, Parliamentary Copyright, 2003).

First Report of the Committee on Standards in Public Life, *Standards in Public Life, Volume 1: Report*, Cm 2850-I (1995).

Joint Committee on Parliamentary Privilege, *Report Volume I – Report and Proceedings of the Committee*, HL Paper 43-I, HC 214-I (1999).

Internet links

www.parliament.uk

9

Parliament II: The House of Commons

At the end of this chapter you should be able to:

- Identify and explain the different functions of the House of Commons
- Explain the composition of the House of Commons
- Explain the nature and significance of the electoral system

9.1 The functions of the House of Commons

The House of Commons is the lower, but pre-eminent chamber of Parliament. This is in common with other bicameral legislatures where the lower chamber is dominant (a clear exception to this is the House of Representatives in the United States which in some respects is not as powerful as the upper chamber: the Senate).

9.1.1 Bagehot and the functions of the House of Commons

The specific functions of the House of Commons overlap and blend with those of Parliament as a whole, and these are considered in brief below. Before considering them, it is of interest to set out the functions of the Commons as identified by Bagehot in the nineteenth century (W Bagehot, *The English Constitution* (Oxford University Press, 2001), Chapter 6). He set out the following five roles:

- **An elective function (the electoral chamber).**
- **An expressive function.**
- **A teaching function.**
- **An informing function.**
- **A legislative function.**

These will be referred to in the context of a modern formulation of the functions of the House of Commons below.

9.1.2 Modern functions of the House of Commons

Today the functions of the House of Commons can be defined as follows:

A representative role to represent and reflect the will of the people

As each MP is directly elected by his own constituents, the House of Commons performs a representative function reflecting the will of the people. How accurately that will is reflected is determined by the electoral system (see section 9.4). In the context of the representative function, in 2004 the Select Committee on Modernisation of the House of Commons issued a report entitled: 'Connecting Parliament with the Public'. It opened its report in the following manner:

QUOTATION

'The legitimacy of the House of Commons, as the principal representative body in British democracy, rests upon the support and engagement of the electorate. The decline in political participation and engagement in recent years, as well as in levels of trust in politicians, political parties and the institutions of State should be of concern to every citizen. But it should be of particular concern to the House of Commons.'

First Report of Session 2003–04, *Connecting Parliament with the Public*, HC 368 (2004), p 9.

In particular, the report set out recommendations to:

- Make the building more accessible to people.
- Make greater effort to engage young people.
- Encourage better use of information and communication technology, in order to re-connect the public with Parliament.

MPs also try to resolve the grievances of their constituents.

Bagehot commented that the House of Commons can 'express the mind' of the people on issues before it (the expressive function). In other words, the chamber reflects and expresses the will of the people and is the sounding board of the nation.

To make laws

In particular, the House of Commons has a dominant role in the passage of legislation as the most important Bills are usually commenced there and the consent of the House of Lords is not always necessary (see section 10.10.1). Bagehot subsumed within the legislative function the financial function (ie the authorisation of finance).

To provide the personnel of the government

It is the House of Commons that is largely responsible for providing government ministers (this is also the case in other parliamentary executives). In fact, it is the House of Commons which chooses the government as it is periodically elected and represents the will of the people. In effect, the government is determined by the outcome of the general election, as the leader of the political party that secures the majority of seats in the House of Commons will, by constitutional convention, be appointed Prime Minister by the monarch. For example, in May 1997 Tony Blair's Labour Party secured the majority of seats in the House of Commons and he was appointed Prime Minister. Bagehot described this function as the elective function with the House of Commons as the 'electoral chamber'.

To provide the Official Opposition

The House of Commons also (largely) provides the opposition to the government (known as Her Majesty's Official Opposition). The main Official Opposition in the February 2010 Parliament was the Conservative Party as they had the second largest number of seats in the Commons (193). They act as the 'government in waiting' and their responsibility is to scrutinise and examine government actions and policy.

To scrutinise the executive

In constitutional terms, a major role of the House of Commons is to hold the government to account to the elected representatives of the people.

To maintain the government

As noted at section 5.3.2, it is the constitutional function of the government to govern. The role of the House of Commons is somewhat contradictory as it should constitutionally sustain the government (while the government has the support and confidence of the lower House), allowing it to govern and carry on the business of government. At the same time, the House simultaneously must scrutinise the actions and policy of the government and withdraw support from it if it loses confidence in it (in other words, if the government has lost the confidence of the people). On rare occasions, such as in 1979, the government has lost a vote of no confidence, thereby symbolically losing the support of the people as represented in the House of Commons (see section 12.2.1).

To legitimise government actions

The House of Commons effectively legitimises government actions if they pass scrutiny. This could be in the form of a particular government policy or in a Bill drafted by the government. In this context it is important to bear in mind the political composition of the House of Commons which is dictated by the nature of the electoral system (see section 9.5).

A judicial function

The House of Commons also performs, in effect, a judicial function when it enforces parliamentary privilege (see section 8.7.3).

In addition, according to Bagehot the teaching function of the House of Commons involved it teaching 'the nation what it does not know' (arguably this could occur, for example, in the context of a debate). The informing function involved the House making 'us hear what otherwise we should not' (it could be argued that this function would be performed in the context of questions to government ministers and also in the course of debates).

KEY FACTS

The key functions of the House of Commons
Representative Each MP is elected and collectively they express the will of the nation.
Recruitment of government The government is drawn largely from the lower chamber.
To maintain the government and legitimise its actions The chamber sustains and maintains the government. The latter needs the support of the chamber to survive.
To redress grievances and scrutinise the executive MPs try to resolve the grievances of their constituents and the chamber as a whole holds the government to account (which can include a vote of no confidence in it).
Legislative Bills pass through both chambers with the most important Bills usually beginning in the lower chamber.
Judicial The House enforces parliamentary privilege and disciplines members.

9.2 The size and composition of the House of Commons

9.2.1 The number of seats in the House of Commons

The size of the last four House of Commons is set out below:

- 1992/1997 – 651 MPs
- 1997/2001 – 659 MPs
- 2001/2005 – 659 MPs
- 2005/2010 – 646 MPs
- After the 2010 general election the House contained 650 MPs.

In comparison to other democracies, with 650 MPs the House of Commons is a large lower chamber in relation to its population. In contrast, for example, the United States has 435 members in the House of Representatives.

9.2.2 The House of Commons as a representative body?

The regions

The House of Commons is part of the United Kingdom Parliament and so MPs represent all parts of the state as indicated below:

The 2005–2010 Parliament

England	–	529 MPs (533 after the 2010 general election)
Wales	–	40 MPs
Scotland	–	59 MPs
Northern Ireland	–	<u>18 MPs</u>
		646 MPs (650 after the 2010 general election)

Source: www.parliament.uk

Ethnic minorities

In the 2005 general election 15 black and minority ethnic MPs (standing for mainstream political parties) were elected. The Electoral Commission has pointed out that proportionately:

QUOTATION

'While this figure still falls well short of the total required for the House of Commons to mirror the UK population (51), it is more than twice that in 1992 and nearly four times that in 1987.'

Election 2005: turnout. How many, who and why? (Electoral Commission, 2005), p 18.

Women

The number of female MPs in the past five Parliaments is as follows:

Women MPs

1987 Parliament	–	41 MPs
1992 Parliament	–	60 MPs
1997 Parliament	–	120 MPs
2001 Parliament	–	118 MPs
2005 Parliament	–	128 MPs

Factsheet M4 'Women in the House of Commons' (Parliamentary Copyright, 2009), p 7.

Even though 128 female MPs were returned in 2005, proportionately this is still less than 20 per cent of all MPs in the House of Commons. The longstanding concern about the under-representation of women in the House of Commons led to the passage of the Sex Discrimination (Election Candidates) Act 2002. This Act enabled political parties to take positive action to encourage the election of female MPs by permitting political parties to draw up an 'all-female shortlist' for the selection of their official parliamentary constituency candidate for a general election. This legislation amended the Sex Discrimination Act 1975 as detailed in the following case:

CASE EXAMPLE

Jepson and Dyas-Elliott (applicants) v The Labour Party [1996] IRLR 116

Jepson and Dyas-Elliott were not considered for selection as Labour Party candidates in parliamentary constituencies because these particular constituencies were required to have all-women shortlists. The policy behind this was to increase the number of women elected to Parliament.

Jepson and Dyas-Elliott contended that they had been unlawfully discriminated against on the grounds of their sex (they were male and so prevented from forming part of the shortlist) contrary to s 13 of the Sex Discrimination Act 1975.

The tribunal upheld their complaints that the policy of all-women shortlists contravened the Sex Discrimination Act. This was because the endorsement of a prospective parliamentary candidate was an 'authorisation' under the Act which facilitated 'engagement in a particular profession', that is the public office of an MP.

At the time of going to print, the Equality Act 2010 (which brought together and restated the various laws on discrimination) has extended the use of women-only shortlists until 2030.

Age

MPs tend to be middle-aged, although the 2005 Parliament included three MPs under 30 years of age. It should be pointed out that although individuals can vote at 18, until the passing of the Electoral Administration Act 2006 they could not become MPs until 21 years of age to ensure that MPs had a minimum of experience. The 2006 Act reduced the minimum age to 18. On the age, gender, occupation, ethnicity, education and parliamentary experience of MPs, see R Cracknell, 'Social background of MPs' (House of Commons Library, 2009).

ACTIVITY

Exercise

Do you think that the House of Commons is sufficiently representative of the population? In terms of its constitutional legitimacy, does this matter?

9.3 The Member of Parliament

9.3.1 The role of a Member of Parliament (MP)

The United Kingdom has a representative democracy. Although MPs are elected representatives of the people, this does not mean that they are simply their delegates who mechanically act on instructions from the electorate. MPs clearly serve their constituents, represent their concerns and redress their grievances, but they also exercise independent mature judgement by themselves.

Carroll (*Constitutional and Administrative Law* (5th edn, Pearson/Longman, 2009), p 132) has identified five competing factors ('constituencies') which a modern MP has to consider, namely:

■ The political party

The overwhelming majority of MPs are members of an organised political party with official policies. Political parties ensure discipline through a 'whip' system which compels MPs within that party to vote for the official party line. As a consequence, MPs can be ultimately deselected as the parliamentary candidate for their constituency in a future general election if they behave (and vote) in a way which is detrimental to the official party line and interests.

■ The constituency

A constituency MP has to be sensitive to the needs of his constituents. (Para 6 of *The Code of Conduct for Members of Parliament* – see section 8.8.2 – states that MPs have a 'special duty to their constituents'.) MPs will typically have surgeries to meet constituents and will also receive written correspondence from them. According to the House of Commons Information Office, an MP has a number of different methods of resolving grievances which include writing to the relevant department or minster and/or making an appointment to meet the minister in person (Factsheet M1 'You and Your MP' (Parliamentary Copyright, 2009), p 5). In addition, an MP may refer the issue to the parliamentary Ombudsman (see section 21.3).

In fact, an MP may have a constituency which has particular circumstances (eg a government proposal to site a chemical plant there) which will require the MP to articulate and raise in Parliament in the interests of his constituents (whether or not this happens to be against the official party political line).

■ An MP's own conscience

As indicated by Edmund Burke writing in the eighteenth century, MPs are not mere delegates of the people, but are also charged with exercising their personal judgement on a matter. Indeed, some issues which come before Parliament are defined as 'free vote issues' which are above party political divisions. These will typically be on moral issues such as the death penalty. Interestingly, the debate and votes in February 2003 and March 2007 on the future reform of the House of Lords were officially on the basis of a free vote, free from party political pressure.

■ An interest group

An MP may have a close relationship with certain interest groups, for example a trade union or a charity/business organisation. Under the Register of Members' Financial Interests (see section 8.8.1) MPs have to declare their financial interests with the outside world.

■ Acting in the public interest

An MP is a parliamentarian and as such one of his constitutional roles is to hold the government to account. It would appear that MPs perform this role most effectively when they sit in select committees scrutinising government departments. Select committee reports tend to produce a cross-party consensus and it seems that MPs in this context act in a less partisan way than they do when they return to the Floor of the House (see section 12.6.6). Moreover, para 6 of *The Code of Conduct for Members of Parliament* states that 'Members have a general duty to act in the interests of the nation as a whole'.

9.3.2 The qualifications required to be an MP

In essence any individual is eligible to become an MP provided:

- they are 18 years of age or older; and
- are a citizen of the United Kingdom, the Commonwealth or the Irish Republic.

The vast majority of MPs belong to a recognised political party with very few independent MPs being elected. Accordingly, the practical reality is that in order to become an MP, a person will need to be selected by a political party as its prospective parliamentary candidate for a constituency.

Prospective parliamentary candidates need to provide a deposit of £500 in order to take part in an election which is lost in the event of a candidate securing less than 5 per cent of the total votes cast in a constituency. The rationale behind the deposit is to prevent frivolous candidates standing for election. From a constitutional perspective, however, it could be argued that the use of the deposit actively discourages individuals from standing for election (putting oneself up for election is part of a participatory democracy). It may also impact adversely on smaller parties who may wish to field candidates in all or most constituencies.

9.3.3 The factors which disqualify a person from becoming an MP

Erskine May (*Parliamentary Practice* (23rd edn, LexisNexis Butterworths, 2004), Ch 3) identified, *inter alia*, the following factors which disqualify a person from becoming an MP and sitting in the House of Commons:

■ Under age

Although individuals can vote at 18 years of age (see section 9.6.2), historically they could not stand for parliamentary elections until they were 21 (Parliamentary Elections Act 1695). Under the Electoral Administration Act 2006, the age has now been reduced to 18. In contrast, in the House of Lords, peers must be at least 21 years of age to take their seat.

■ Aliens

Aliens under the Act of Settlement 1700 are disqualified from membership of either House. The British Nationality Act 1981 states that this does not apply to individuals who are Commonwealth citizens or from the Republic of Ireland. However, s 18 of the Electoral Admininstration Act 2006 limited the rights of the former to stand for election to those with a right of abode or indefinite leave to remain.

■ Peers

Members of the House of Lords cannot sit in both parliamentary chambers. It is pertinent to point out, however, that those hereditary peers removed from the House of Lords under the House of Lords Act 1999 (see section 10.6.3) are eligible to be elected as MPs. Indeed, in 2001 one hereditary peer (Viscount Thurso), who formerly sat in the House of Lords until 1999, was elected as an MP (John Thurso). He was re-elected at the 2005 general election.

■ Those suffering from mental illness

Those detained under mental health legislation (ie Mental Health Act 1983) will be disqualified. Under s 141 of the 1983 Act there is a procedure to vacate the seat of an MP who is of 'unsound mind' and the seat will become vacant.

■ Treason

Those convicted of treason under the Forfeiture Act 1870 until pardoned or the term of imprisonment has expired are disqualified.

■ Bankruptcy

In relation to England and Wales, an individual who has a bankruptcy restrictions order in effect against them is disqualified (s 266 of the Enterprise Act 2002). In Northern Ireland it is where they are declared bankrupt and in Scotland against whom a sequestration of estate is awarded (s 427 of the Insolvency Act 1986).

■ Those convicted of crimes

Under the Representation of the People Act 1981, an individual serving a prison sentence of more than a year for any offence is disqualified. This was passed in the context of the election of Bobby Sands as a Westminster MP (who at the time was a prisoner on hunger strike in Northern Ireland).

■ Corrupt/illegal practices

Under the Representation of the People Act 1983 (as amended) an individual convicted of a corrupt practice at an election is disqualified for five years. Those convicted of illegal practices are disqualified for three years.

■ Religious representation

In recent years a disqualification in relation to the clergy has been removed. The House of Commons (Removal of Clergy Disqualification) Act 2001 provides that no ministers of any religious denomination are disqualified from membership of the House of Commons. The exceptions to this are the Archbishops and Bishops in the House of Lords (see section 10.3).

■ The House of Commons Disqualification Act 1975

This Act constitutionally and legally prohibits certain elements of the executive (civil servants, police officers, etc) from sitting in the House of Commons as part of the legislature (see section 11.6.3). It is interesting to note that s 1(1)(a) of the Act excludes judges from sitting in the House of Commons (including now of course the serving Supreme Court Justices). This preserves a degree of separation between the judiciary and the legislature; however, Justices of the Peace are eligible to sit as MPs.

■ Other legislatures

In addition, s 1(1)(e) of the House of Commons Disqualification Act 1975 disqualifies members of other legislatures outside the Commonwealth (except the Republic of Ireland). In contrast, MPs can be members of, for example, the Scottish Parliament,

National Assembly for Wales or the Northern Ireland Assembly. Indeed, in 2009 Alex Salmond, the leader of the Scottish National Party had a dual mandate in that he was a member of both the House of Commons and the Scottish Parliament (in terms of the latter, he was the First Minister).

9.3.4 By-elections

In the event of an MP dying (or being disqualified) his seat becomes vacant and a by-election will ensue. For example, when the Labour MP Robin Cook died in August 2005, a by-election was held in that constituency in September 2005. On this occasion another Labour MP was elected in his place, although it is not always the case that the same political party will win back the seat. For example, when Rachel Squire, a Labour MP, died in January 2006, at the ensuing by-election in February 2006, her seat was taken by a Liberal Democrat candidate.

KEY FACTS

The Role of the MP
An MP has to consider the following competing interests: • party political pressure from the political party to which he belongs; • his constituents who elect (and re-elect) him into office as a constituency MP; • his own conscience on moral matters (eg on the death penalty); • an interest group with which he has a close relationship (eg a trade union); • acting as a parliamentarian in the public interest.

9.4 The electoral system

9.4.1 The system of voting

The United Kingdom uses a single member constituency, simple majority system. It is commonly referred to as the 'first past the post' system. The mechanics of the system are detailed below:

- The whole of the United Kingdom is divided up into single member constituencies (for the 2010 general election there were 650 parliamentary constituencies).
- In each constituency political parties will put forward one candidate as a prospective MP. Political parties do not, however, have to contest each seat. For example, in Northern Ireland the main political parties have not traditionally put up candidates owing to the historically idiosyncratic political make-up of the province.
- Each registered voter who chooses to vote (many choose not to vote) puts a cross on the ballot paper next to the chosen candidate.
- Once polling has closed, all the votes cast will be counted. The winning candidate (and so the elected Member of Parliament for that constituency) will be the person who has secured more votes than any other candidate. For example:

Constituency of Birmingham Erdington general election 2005		
Electorate of 64,951 – 48.9% turnout (31,746 voted)		
Party candidate	**Votes cast in favour**	**% of vote**
Labour (elected as MP)	16,810 (a majority of 9, 575)	53%
Conservative	7,235	23%
Liberal Democrat	5,027	16%

Table 9.1

It is imperative to point out that this does not mean that the winning candidate has to obtain 51 per cent of votes cast. In fact, in most cases the winning candidate will not do so.

It is in this way that the United Kingdom's electoral system has been described as the 'first past the post' system as it has been likened to a horse race. In short, the horse that crosses the line first – irrespective of how wide or narrow the margin – is declared the winner. In this sense, the only horse (or candidate) that matters is the winner.

◾ As the United Kingdom Parliament has single member constituencies, each constituency returns one MP. In some other countries, constituencies are multi-member constituencies whereby a number of representatives are returned for a particular constituency. This scenario is not totally unfamiliar to the United Kingdom as, for example, large multi-member constituencies are used when electing United Kingdom Members of the European Parliament under the European Parliamentary Elections Act 1999.

Although only one MP is returned for each constituency, that MP represents the whole of the constituency irrespective of whether a particular constituent voted for them or not (or even if that constituent was ineligible to vote, eg he was under 18 years of age at the time of the election). Moreover, by constitutional convention one MP will not act for the constituent of another MP unless he is unwilling or unable to act.

◾ All constituencies return their MP (either a newly elected MP or an MP who has been re-elected) to the House of Commons. By constitutional convention, the leader of the party with the majority of seats in the House of Commons will be formally appointed Prime Minister by the monarch and asked to form Her Majesty's Government.

9.4.2 Election turnouts

The turnout of the population eligible to vote at the last five general elections is indicated below:

Election turnouts 1987–2005
1987 – 75.3% (of those registered to vote)
1992 – 77.7%
1997 – 71.4%
2001 – 59.4%
2005 – 61.4%

Table 9.2
Source: *Election 2005: turnout. How many, who and why?*
(Electoral Commission, 2005), p 20.

It is in this context that the 2004 report of the Select Committee on Modernisation of the House of Commons (see section 9.1.2) should be seen. In short, the 2001 general election turnout (ie 59.4 per cent) by those registered to vote was the lowest since 1918. The general decline in voting necessarily means a reduction in participatory democracy, whereby voters are disconnected with the electoral and parliamentary process.

Although the percentage of voters who voted in the 2005 election was a marginal improvement on the 2001 election, the Electoral Commission indicated that 17 million people who were registered to vote did not cast a vote. It identified the following factors which contributed to people not voting in the 2005 general election:

◾ A general disillusionment with politics.
◾ An ignorance about politics.
◾ A perception that voting made no real difference.
◾ The difficulty in deciding which political party to vote for.
◾ The nature of the election campaign.

In terms of the constitutional and political significance of elections, the Commission made the following comment:

QUOTATION

'Elections underpin our democracy, ensuring that our representative institutions are both accountable to public opinion and legitimised by it. They provide an opportunity for politicians and political parties to outline their ideas and to defend their performance. Elections can interest, inform and empower people and, by doing so, can help to build political engagement.'

Election 2005: turnout. How many, who and why? (Electoral Commission, 2005), p 53.

One highly revealing statistic concerning the 2005 general election is that nationally the Labour Party polled less votes (9,552,436) than those electors who were registered to vote, but chose not to exercise their franchise (17 million).

In recent years in order to address voter apathy, there have been attempts to engage with voters by using different forms of voting methods. For example, local government elections have experimented with polling booths located in supermarkets as well as universal postal votes. The Electoral Administration Act 2006 is particularly concerned with increasing the highest possible turnout at elections. For example, in order to encourage public participation in elections, s 69 requires that:

SECTION

'A local electorate officer must take such steps as he thinks appropriate to encourage the participation by electors in the electoral process in the area for which he acts.'

ACTIVITY

Self-test questions

Why do you think there is a relatively poor turnout for general elections? In terms of the legitimacy of the House of Commons, does this matter?

9.4.3 The advantages of the 'first past the post' electoral system

The United Kingdom's electoral system is somewhat controversial in certain aspects (see section 9.4.4), but it has a number of distinct advantages:

■ Simplicity

In contrast to other systems available (and in particular to the one recommended by the Jenkins Commission in 1998 – see section 9.10.1), the current electoral system is comparatively simple. It is relatively straightforward for the public to understand as only one box on the ballot paper needs to be crossed. In contrast, in some other systems such as the Single Transferable Vote, candidates are ranked in order of preference. Our system is also straightforward to administer and provides an efficient method of voting and of forming a parliamentary chamber. It is also a relatively inexpensive system of voting because it is easy to administer.

■ Single member constituencies

The system uses single member constituencies, which has the advantage that every constituency in the United Kingdom has one single, identifiable Member of Parliament who represents the interests of that particular constituency. In this way it constitutionally links each MP with one specific geographical area of the state.

■ Produces strong government

In general terms, and certainly in the last few decades, the electoral system produces an electoral result which confers one political party (historically either Labour or Conservative) with a majority of seats in the House of Commons. In fact, in six out of seven general elections held between 1979 and 2005 (the exception being 1992), the electoral system has produced a government with a substantial working majority of seats. For example, in 1983 the Conservative government had a majority of 144 seats, while in 1997 the Labour government enjoyed a majority of 179 seats. It is argued that such majorities allow the government to be decisive and to govern by translating its legislative programme as set out in its general election manifesto, into laws. Moreover, a strong decisive government is an advantage in a crisis (international or domestic) and is generally regarded as preferable to an inherently weaker government typically found in coalition governments consisting of an amalgamation of rival and competing political parties.

In this context it is pertinent to note that although Italy has historically been hallmarked by its coalition and unstable governments, in the 1990s they reformed their electoral system from a proportional one to a mainly 'first past the post' system. This appeared to usher in a period of more stable government. In 2006, however, the system was reformed, reverting back to a proportional system which in turn resulted in the general election of April 2006 producing a somewhat inconclusive result.

9.4.4 The disadvantages of the 'first past the post' electoral system

There are at least four major problems with the system as detailed below:

▣ A disproportionate system

One clear difficulty with the electoral system is that it is possible for an MP to be elected on a minority of the votes. The following example from the 2005 general election makes this point:

Birmingham Sparkbrook and Small Heath constituency 2005	
Electorate 73,721 – 51.8% turnout (38,192 voted)	
Party candidate	**Votes cast in favour**
Respect	10,498
Conservative	3,480
Labour	13,787
Liberal Democrat	7,727

Table 9.3

Source: http://news.bbc.co.uk

This example shows that the Labour candidate who won this constituency to become its MP did so with less than 50 per cent of the total votes cast (in fact on the basis of only 36 per cent). Indeed, more people voted against the Labour candidate, than in favour of him. This illustrates the nature of the 'first past the post' system: in order to become an MP, all that has to be achieved is to secure more votes than any other candidate. In fact, in 2005 in Crawley the Labour candidate won with 39.1 per cent of the votes cast (16,411) which represented only 37 more votes than her nearest (Conservative) rival who came second (16,374 votes/39.01 per cent) (*The Times*, 7th May 2005, p 72).

If the above scenario is replicated in many constituencies across the United Kingdom, then it is possible to see how a government can become elected with a majority of seats in the House of Commons, but with only a minority of the votes cast nationwide in their favour. At the 2005 general election the Labour Party secured 55 per cent of the seats in the House of Commons and yet secured only 35.2 per cent of the total votes cast nationwide. In contrast, the Conservative Party polled 32.4 per cent of the votes cast and secured only 198 seats, representing just over 30 per cent of the House of Commons. This in turn raises the question of whether a government elected on this basis has political legitimacy. Indeed, in the second half of the twentieth century, no government (Labour or Conservative) assumed office with over 50 per cent of all votes cast.

■ Voter apathy

One possible reason for poor turnouts at general elections (as pointed out by the Electoral Commission) is the perception that voting 'makes no difference'. In fact, a number of constituencies in the United Kingdom are considered 'safe seats' in the sense that one particular political party traditionally has always won the seat. As a result of this, voting for a candidate of a different political party in such a 'safe' constituency would appear to be fruitless. It must be remembered that under the electoral system the 'winner takes all' and the votes cast for the losing candidates are disregarded. These votes are, in effect, wasted votes.

■ Variations in constituencies

As the United Kingdom uses the single member constituency system, this inevitably results in some regional variations. The average size of the electorate in a constituency is around 68,500 (Factsheet M1 'You and Your MP' (Parliamentary Copyright, 2009), p 3). Some constituencies, however, such as the Isle of Wight had an electorate of 109,046 at the 2005 general election whereas, in contrast, the constituency of Na h-Eileanan an Iar in Scotland had an electorate of only 21,576. In other words, the value of a vote cast in the latter constituency will have more significance (in terms of determining who wins the seat) than in the former, much larger constituency. In essence, a vote in a smaller constituency – in proportionate terms – is more significant than a vote in a larger constituency. This necessarily raises the issue of whether all votes have equal value.

■ Third parties

One clear disadvantage of the 'first past the post' system is that it is essentially designed to accommodate a two-party system and so smaller third parties are penalised. For example, at the 2005 election, although the Liberal Democrats polled 5,985,454 votes nationally (roughly two-thirds of the votes polled for the Conservative Party), they obtained only about one-third of the number of parliamentary seats as the Conservatives (see section 9.5).

9.4.5 Parliamentary constituency boundaries

The review of constituency boundaries due to population movement is carried out by four Boundary Commissions, one for each of the countries of the United Kingdom, and they are governed by the Parliamentary Constituencies Act 1986 (as amended by the Boundary Commissions Act 1992). On receipt of a report of a Boundary Commission, a government minister would lay a draft order before Parliament for it to approve, giving effect to the Commission's recommendations. Under the Political Parties, Elections and Referendums Act 2000 the functions of the Boundary Commissions were scheduled to be transferred to the Electoral Commission; however, s 61 of the Local Democracy, Economic Development and Construction Act 2009 now provides that this transfer will not take place.

The redrawing of constituency boundaries inevitably has an impact on one or more political parties (ie they either gain or lose potential seats). The redrawing of such constituencies can, therefore, be controversial and in the early 1980s the Leader of the Labour Party sought to challenge one of these proposed changes:

CASE EXAMPLE

R v Boundary Commission for England, ex parte Foot [1983] 1 QB 600

Michael Foot, the leader of the Labour Party and Leader of the Opposition, unsuccessfully sought in judicial review to prohibit the Boundary Commission for England from submitting to the Home Secretary its revised parliamentary constituencies. The Court of Appeal noted that the Commission's duty did include giving effect to, *inter alia*, r 5 (Sched 2 to the House of Commons (Redistribution of Seats) Act 1949), which provided that 'The electorate of any constituency shall be as near the electoral quota as is practicable' (this was designed to ensure the principle of equal representation for electors). It was held, however, that the rule (as a result of s 2 of the House of Commons (Redistribution of Seats) Act 1958), had the status of a guideline and that Foot had failed to discharge the heavy onus of showing that the recommendations of the Boundary Commission were conclusions which no reasonable Commission could have come to.

Constituency boundaries are reviewed and re-adjusted periodically (every 8 to 12 years). For example, in 2007 the Boundary Commission for England issued its Fifth Report (Boundary Commission for England, Fifth Periodical Report, Cm 7032 (The Stationary Office, 2007)). As a result of the most recent revision of boundaries, the Parliament following the 2010 general election contains four more English MPs.

KEY FACTS

Key facts on the electoral system

- The United Kingdom uses the 'first past the post' system which comprises single member constituencies (following the 2010 general election there will be 650 MPs).
- Political parties put forward one candidate as a prospective MP for each constituency.
- The elected Member of Parliament for each constituency will be the person who has secured more votes than any other candidate.
- The leader of the political party that gains the majority of seats in the House of Commons will become Prime Minister.

9.5 The current political composition of the House of Commons

The main political parties polled the following votes at the 2005 general election:

Party	Votes cast	% of votes
Labour	9,552,436	35.2 %
Conservative	8,784,915	32.4%
Liberal Democrat	5,985,454	22%

Source: *Election 2005: turnout. How many, who and why?* (Electoral Commission, 2005), p 17.

The political breakdown of the House of Commons immediately following the 2005 general election was as follows (it should be noted that although at the time of going to print it was possible to add the results of the 2010 general election which resulted in a hung Parliament and a Conservative–Liberal Democratic coalition government, this Chapter was written before the 2010 results were available):

2005 general election		2010 general election	
Party	Seats	Party	Seats
Labour	355	Labour	258
Conservative	198	Conservative	306
Liberal Democrat	62	Liberal Democrat	57
Scottish National Party	6	Scottish National Party	6
Democratic Unionist	9	Democratic Unionist	8

2005 general election ctd		2010 general election ctd	
Sinn Fein (historically do not take their seats for political reasons)	5	Sinn Fein	5
Social Democratic Labour Party	3	Social Democratic Labour Party	3
Ulster Unionist	1	Alliance	1
Plaid Cymru	3	Plaid Cymru	3
Others • Respect Party – G Galloway • Independent – P Law • Independent Kidderminster Hospital and Health Concern – R Taylor	3	Others • Green • Independent	2
Speaker	1		1
TOTAL	646 MPs		650 MPs

Table 9.4

Source: *Election 2005: turnout. How many, who and why?* (Electoral Commission, 2005), p 17.
The *Times* guide to the House of Commons 2010 (Harper Collins Publishers, 2010), p. 9.

On the basis of these figures, after the 2005 general election the Labour majority was 65 (if the Speaker is not considered) which meant that the Labour Party (and so by logical extension, the Labour government – see section 9.9) had 65 more MPs than all of the other political parties put together.

Three points are worth remembering about the political composition of the House of Commons.

■ Firstly, the House of Commons is not one single entity that acts as a single unit. Instead, it is composed of a variety of different political parties vying with each other (although it tends to be dominated by one political party).

■ Secondly, the overwhelming majority of MPs are members of political parties and therefore very few independent MPs are elected. In 2005, excluding the Speaker of the House, only two independent MPs were elected (see 'Others' in the 2005 column of the table above). In this way the House of Commons differs from the House of Lords which is composed of a number of independent peers known as crossbenchers (see section 10.7.3).

■ Thirdly, the political composition of the House of Commons will change inevitably (albeit marginally) over the course of a parliamentary term. This necessarily has an impact on a government's majority (which may be highly significant if its majority is slim). There are two main reasons for this:

(i) By-elections will be held in the wake of the death of an MP. By-elections are not rare events; for example, in the 1992–97 parliamentary session, there were 18 by-elections which resulted in nine seats changing political hands (Factsheet M 14 'By-election results: 1992–97' (Parliamentary Copyright, 2003), p 2).

(ii) Change of allegiance – it is possible for an MP to change political party. For example, in 1999 Shaun Woodward changed parties from Conservative to Labour. This is known as 'Crossing the Floor' of the Commons.

ACTIVITY

Problem solving

Compare the votes cast for each main political party at the 2005 general election and correlate this with the number of seats that they obtained in the House of Commons. What does this tell us about the electoral system?

9.6 The electorate

9.6.1 The constitutional significance of voting

In a representative democracy it is a prerequisite that democracy is a participatory democracy. This means that, *inter alia*, citizens regularly determine who should represent them in Parliament and who should govern the country. In the United Kingdom the people do not *directly* elect the government/executive, rather they elect representatives (MPs) from whom the government is drawn (see Bagehot's elective function, see section 9.1.2).

The constitutional significance of the electorate voting in elections has been clearly recognised by Art 3, Protocol No 1 of the European Convention:

ARTICLE

'The High Contracting Parties undertake to hold free elections at reasonable intervals by secret ballot, under conditions which will ensure the free expression of the opinion of the people in the choice of the legislature.'

The European Court in *Mathieu-Mohin and Clerfayt v Belgium* (1988) 10 EHRR 1 regarded this provision as a very important free-standing right as well as a prerequisite for the enjoyment and protection of other European Convention rights:

JUDGMENT

'Since it enshrines a characteristic principle of democracy, Article 3 of Protocol No. 1 is accordingly of prime importance in the Convention system.'

In the case of *Matthews v UK* (1999) 28 EHRR 361, the European Court of Human Rights declared that the United Kingdom had violated Art 3, Protocol No 1 when Matthews (a British citizen) resident in Gibraltar (which was not part of the United Kingdom, but a dependent territory), had been denied the right to vote in elections to the European Parliament. As Gibraltar had not been included in the franchise for European parliamentary elections, Matthews had been denied any opportunity to express her opinion as to who should be elected as an MEP.

9.6.2 Who can vote in parliamentary elections?

This is set out in the Representation of the People Act 1983 (as amended). A person can vote who is:

- Of voting age: 18 years or over on polling day (the Family Law Reform Act 1969 reduced the voting age from 21 years of age to 18).
- Registered in the register of parliamentary elections for that particular constituency. Electoral registration officers have a responsibility to produce an electoral register which is compiled on the basis of returns made by householders (the Political Parties and Elections Act 2009 provides for the introduction of individual electoral registration). Students are permitted to vote in either their permanent constituency address or in their university constituency (*Fox v Stirk* [1970] 2 QB 463). In recent years the electoral register has been reformed with the effect that it is now a 'rolling register' which is amended continuously. In addition the term 'residency' has been amended so as to include the homeless, allowing them to vote (as amended by the Representation of the People Act 2000).
- Not disqualified from voting (see section 9.6.3).
- A British, Irish or qualifying Commonwealth citizen who is resident in the United Kingdom (the last two are explained by our historical ties).

■ A person who is a British citizen resident outside the United Kingdom and qualified as an overseas elector (Representation of the People Act 1985 as amended).

A general election will be held on one day so that all the polls are held simultaneously. An individual can vote only once in one single constituency and so cannot vote in more than one constituency in a parliamentary election. It is possible to vote by post (eg if a voter is overseas) or proxy (eg if the voter has a physical disability). In an attempt to combat fraud s 14 of the Electoral Administration Act 2006 requires postal and proxy voters to provide their signature and date of birth on their application form.

Voting is by secret ballot, although voting is not compulsory as in some countries such as Australia. This necessarily has an impact on electorate turnouts at general elections, and in 2005 the then Leader of the House of Commons put forward the suggestion of introducing compulsory voting in order to increase turnout.

9.6.3 Who is disqualified from voting?

The following factors disenfranchise a person from voting at general elections as set out in the Representation of the People Act 1983 (as amended):

■ Peers in the House of Lords (however, members of the House of Lords who were removed under the House of Lords Act 1999 are eligible to vote).
■ Persons under the age of 18 years on the day of the election – on this point it is worth noting that the electorate for each constituency does not equate to the population of that constituency, as it necessarily excludes anyone under 18.
■ Historically there was a common law rule of incapacity to vote by reason of a person's mental state; however, s 73 of the Electoral Administration Act 2006 abolished any common law rule which provided that a person was subject to a legal incapacity to vote by reason of his mental state (thus illustrating how Parliament can override common law – see section 7.5.1).
■ Persons guilty of corrupt or illegal practices at elections (within the past five years).
■ Citizens of the European Union and other countries (except citizens from the Republic of Ireland or those qualifying from the Commonwealth).
■ Those detained in mental hospitals (as a result of criminal activity) as authorised by statute. It should be noted that the consultation process which followed the *Hirst* case below, also embraced the position of certain people detained in mental hospitals.
■ Convicted prisoners during the term of their detention. Section 3 of the Representation of the People Act 1983 states that:

SECTION

A convicted person during the time that he is detained in a penal institution in pursuance of his sentence … is legally incapable of voting at any parliamentary or local government election.

This is a blanket exclusion on prisoners from voting which means that even if the prisoner was scheduled for release a week after polling day at a general election, legally they would still be precluded from voting at it. The Act, however, does not apply to:

■ persons imprisoned for contempt of court, s 3(2)
■ those imprisoned for default in paying a fine, s 3(2)
■ prisoners on remand and unconvicted mental patients (as amended by the Representation of the People Act 2000).

In the *Hirst* case (see below) in the European Court of Human Rights, the government tried to justify the disenfranchisement of prisoners on the basis that it pursued the following legitimate aims, namely 'of preventing crime and punishing offenders and enhancing civic responsibility and respect for the rule of law, by depriving those who have breached the basic rules of society of the right to have a say in the way such rules are made for the duration of their sentence' (para 33). The blanket disenfranchisement of United Kingdom prisoners to vote was tested in this case.

CASE EXAMPLE

Hirst v United Kingdom (No 2) (2004) 38 EHRR 40

Hirst had been serving a sentence of life imprisonment and as a convicted prisoner was legally disqualified from voting (s 3 Representation of the People Act 1983). In the United Kingdom domestic courts he unsuccessfully sought a declaration under the Human Rights Act 1998 that such a provision violated Art 3, Protocol No 1 (the right to free elections). He subsequently petitioned the European Court of Human Rights.

A chamber of the European Court held that there had been a breach of Art 3 of Protocol No 1. The court reaffirmed that elections were the foundation of an effective democracy. Although the right to vote was not absolute, any limitations had to be proportionate. The court held that as the ban applied automatically to convicted prisoners while in prison and irrespective of the length of sentence or the offence committed, it amounted to a disproportionate restriction of Art 3 of Protocol No 1.

JUDGMENT

'The applicant in the present case lost his right to vote as the result of the imposition of an automatic and blanket restriction on convicted prisoners' franchise and may therefore claim to be a victim of the measure.'

This decision was subsequently upheld by the Grand Chamber (by 12 to 5 votes) (*Hirst v United Kingdom (No 2)* (2006) 42 EHRR 41).

The United Kingdom was left to decide on the choice of means for securing the above right which had been infringed and in December 2006 the government initiated a consultation process on the issue. The second stage of this process concluded in September 2009 (*Voting Rights of Convicted Prisoners Detained Within the United Kingdom* CP96/09 (2009)). The government had made it clear in the consultation process that it did not propose to give all prisoners the right to vote (in particular, the most serious and dangerous prisoners would not be able to vote). In the context of prisoners being unable to vote, see the case of *R (Chester) v Secretary of State for Justice* [2009] EWHC 2923 (Admin).

KEY FACTS

Voting at general elections
Voters must be:
• 18 years or over at the date of the poll.
• Registered in the register of parliamentary elections for that particular constituency. An electoral register is compiled on the basis of returns made by householders.
• A British, Irish or qualifying Commonwealth citizen (the latter two must be resident in the United Kingdom). Note: a person who is a British citizen resident outside the United Kingdom can qualify as an overseas elector (Representation of the People Act 1985 as amended).
Those currently disqualified from voting at general elections are:
• Peers in the House of Lords.
• Persons under the age of 18 years.
• Persons guilty of corrupt or illegal practices at elections.
• Citizens of the European Union and other countries (except citizens from the Republic of Ireland or those qualifying from the Commonwealth).
• Those detained in mental hospitals (owing to criminal activity) as authorised by statute.
• Convicted prisoners during the term of their detention (but reforms to alter this are currently under consideration).

Self-test question

What is the democratic importance of elections? In particular, do you think that prisoners should vote in elections?

9.7 The supervision and conduct of elections and political parties

9.7.1 The Electoral Commission

The Electoral Commission is an independent body established under the Political Parties, Elections and Referendums Act 2000. According to its website, the aim of the Commission:

QUOTATION

'We are an independent body set up by the UK Parliament. Our aim is integrity and public confidence in the democratic process.
We work to:

- register political parties
- make sure people understand and follow the rules on party and election finance
- publish details of where parties and candidates get money from and how they spend it
- set the standards for running elections and report on how well this is done
- make sure people understand it is important to register to vote, and know how to vote'

http://www.electoralcommission.org.uk/about-us

Under the 2000 Act the Electoral Commission has, among others, the following wide-ranging functions:

- It is required to report on the administration of elections (Parliamentary, European and devolved) and referendums.
- It keeps under review and reports on various electoral and political issues.
- It is empowered to provide assistance and advice.
- It provides advice to broadcasters on political broadcasts.
- It supervises the registration of political parties as, in order to contest an election, a political party needs to be registered with the Electoral Commission.
- It supervises the finances of political parties including the publication of financial information (statements of accounts). In short, political parties are subject to audit requirements and they must record donations received and campaign expenditure incurred. The Electoral Administration Act 2006 now provides for the regulation of loans and credit facilities.

The Political Parties and Elections Act 2009 made further changes. For example, the regulatory role of the Electoral Commission was enhanced by conferring on it a broader range of investigatory powers, together with new 'Civil Sanctions' (eg to impose a monetary penalty). In relation to donations to political parties, the Act set out new arrangements in order to improve transparency. The 2009 Act followed on from the government White Paper (*Party Finance and Expenditure in the United Kingdom, the Government's Proposals*, Cm 7329 (The Stationary Office, 2008)).

9.7.2 Election broadcasts

During general elections political parties are able to broadcast party political broadcasts in pursuance of persuading the electorate to vote for their prospective parliamentary candidates. This does not mean that all broadcasts will be screened as illustrated by the following case.

CASE EXAMPLE

R (ProLife Alliance) v British Broadcasting Corporation [2003] UKHL 23

ProLife Alliance was a political party (opposed to abortion) which was entitled to a party election television broadcast at the 2001 general election. The BBC, however, refused to transmit its election broadcast video on the grounds of taste and decency (they had a duty under their Charter to preserve good taste and decency), as it depicted the abortion process (although the video had been an honest and unsensationalised account). The party sought judicial review of this decision.

The House of Lords held that the principles underpinning freedom of speech under Art 10 of the European Convention on Human Rights required that access to a public medium of communication (ie a television broadcast) should not be refused on an unreasonable, arbitrary or discriminatory basis. The BBC had to justify restricting the content of a programme produced by a political party promoting its aims, but it was for the broadcasters and not the court to apply the appropriate standard. The court held that there was nothing in the reasoning or the overall decision of the BBC to suggest that they had used an inappropriate standard in determining whether the transmitting of ProLife's pictures was likely to be offensive to public opinion. It is of interest to note that in the Court of Appeal (whose decision was reversed by the Lords) Laws LJ had particularly emphasised the constitutional importance of free speech at election times.

9.8 The constitutional significance of the electoral system

The 'first past the post' electoral system has had a profound impact on the British constitution. As noted earlier, the system generally (at least in recent decades) results in one political party having a clear majority of seats in the House of Commons, thereby allowing it to form a government. In some cases, it can equip a party with an overwhelming and almost insuperable majority; for example, after the 1997 general election the Labour government enjoyed a commanding majority of 179 seats. It must be reiterated that most of the dominant political party's MPs will not formally be part of the government, but through a combination of party loyalty and the whip system, they will generally support its policies and legislative proposals.

The constitutional consequences of the electoral system include the following:

- It alters the constitutional balance between the executive and the House of Commons in favour of the former at the expense of the latter. In particular, with a commanding majority of seats in its favour, it would be very unlikely for a government to be defeated on its proposed legislation.
- Similarly, it would be very unlikely that a government would suffer the defeat of a vote of no confidence. Although in constitutional theory the motion of no confidence is the key parliamentary mechanism to remove a government during a parliamentary term, it is rarely successful. The last occasion when it was successful was in 1979, which triggered the 1979 general election (see section 12.2.1).
- It affects the composition of committees in the House of Commons as by constitutional convention, such committees reflect the party composition of the chamber. As a result, the governing party will necessarily have a majority of MPs of the same political persuasion serving in these committees.
- Lord Hailsham has argued that our electoral system results in what he termed 'an elective dictatorship' (Elective dictatorship, *Listener*, 21st October 1976, pp 496–500). In short, a government with the comfortable support of a majority of MPs in the House of Commons can, in effect, push through whatever legislation it deems necessary. In this way the House of Commons merely legitimises the wishes of the government, who in turn have generally been elected on the basis of a minority of the votes cast. According to Bogdanor:

'The legal doctrine of the sovereignty of Parliament has thus come to legitimize a political doctrine, the doctrine that a government enjoying an overall majority in the House of Commons should enjoy virtually unlimited power. What the governing party enacts thus becomes, *ipso facto*, constitutional.'

V Bogdanor, *The New British Constitution*, (Hart Publishing, 2009), p 15.

■ Finally, as an adjunct to the above point made by Lord Halisham, it raises the issue of whether such a government is truly politically legitimate with the moral right to carry out its electoral mandate. Indeed, in the second half of the twentieth century and the first part of the twenty-first, no government has secured more than half of the votes cast in a general election (although in 1955 Anthony Eden's Conservative Party secured 49.6 per cent of the votes cast). All of these administrations, therefore, were acting on the basis of the wishes of a minority of the electorate. In this sense it could be argued that the electoral system – to some extent – distorts the will of the electorate by, generally speaking, conferring an inordinate amount of power on one political party that forms the government. NB At the time of going to print, the 2010 general election had resulted in a hung Parliament which in turn led to the formation of a Conservative–Liberal Democrat government.

In fact, as a result of the Labour Party securing only 35 per cent of the votes cast at the 2005 election (and yet securing 55 per cent of the seats in the Commons in 2005), in the House of Lords the Liberal Democrats have questioned the relevance of the Salisbury-Addison/Government Bill Convention (see section 10.11). This convention dictates that the House should not oppose at second reading a government Bill which has been foreshadowed in the governing party's most recent general election manifesto.

9.9 An overview of the main elements of the House of Commons – a snapshot at February 2010

In brief, the House of Commons in February 2010 contained the following elements:

■ **Her Majesty's Government**
This consisted officially of 96 Labour MPs. A minority of these MPs sat in the Cabinet (20), but most ministers were outside it. These ministers were also supplemented by a number of unpaid members. All of Her Majesty's Government ministers were supported (at least in theory) by the remainder of the Labour MPs (government backbenchers).

■ **Her Majesty's Official Opposition**
The main Official Opposition was the Conservative Party (the second largest party with 193 MPs) headed by the Leader of the Opposition. The Liberal Democrats with 63 MPs acted as the second main Opposition. The remaining MPs from other parties (other than Labour), together with the independent MPs, also constituted part of the Opposition.

■ **Government front and backbenchers**
The Labour Party's frontbenchers were government ministers, whereas their backbenchers (known as government backbenchers) were not technically in the government *per se*, but being of the same political party as the government, generally speaking, supported the government.

■ **The Official Opposition's frontbenchers**
These were composed of shadow spokespersons of government departments collectively known as the shadow Cabinet. For example, the Conservative Shadow Home Secretary shadowed and opposed the Home Secretary. The Conservative Party's backbenchers were Conservative MPs who were not in the shadow Cabinet. Similarly, the Liberal Democrats had shadow spokespersons as frontbenchers, with backbenchers not being in their shadow Cabinet.

■ **Party whips**

Each political party had party whips to ensure discipline within the ranks of the party and ensure that MPs voted in accordance with official party allegiance and interests. Party whips also helped to keep their respective MPs informed about the parliamentary timetable and business.

■ **The Speaker of the House of Commons**

The Speaker of the House was elected by MPs in June 2009 (following Michael Martin's resignation) and as Speaker he put aside party loyalty and acted with complete impartiality and integrity. His constitutional roles included, among others:

- ■ To chair debates and proceedings (including calling members to speak).
- ■ To deal with the administration of the House.
- ■ To call members to order and keep order within the chamber.
- ■ To act as the representative of the House of Commons in state events.

The Speaker was assisted by three Deputy Speakers.

■ **The Leader of the House**

This was a member of the government who sat in the Cabinet. The responsibilities of this post included arranging and supervising government business in the chamber (in particular, the legislative programme).

9.10 Reform

9.10.1 The electoral system

The 1997 Labour Party manifesto committed the incoming government to establish an independent commission on the voting system for the House of Commons and thereafter to hold a referendum on the system. As indicated earlier, one of the perceived difficulties with the present 'first past the post' system (see section 9.4.4) is that it can distort the wishes of the electorate. In 1998 the Jenkins Commission delivered its report (*The Report of the Independent Commission on the Voting System*, Cm 4090-I (1998)) which recommended a highly convoluted system.

More recently the 2005 Labour Party manifesto proposed to review 'the experience of the new electoral systems' introduced since 1997. In 2008 the government issued its review (*Review of Voting Systems: the Experience of New Voting Systems in the United Kingdom Since 1997*, Cm 7304 (The Stationary Office, 2008)). This review was designed to inform the debate on electoral reform for Parliament. In February 2010 the Constitutional Reform and Governance Bill was amended in the Commons to provide for a national referendum on the electoral system (*Hansard*, HC Debates, Vol 505, col 790ff). This amendment provided that 'A referendum is to be held, not later than 31 October 2011, on the voting system for Parliamentary elections'. The question to be asked would involve a choice between the existing 'first past the post' system and the alternative vote system. This provision was removed when the Bill became an Act.

SUMMARY

- ■ The House of Commons is the lower chamber of Parliament and is wholly elected with 650 MPs. Its functions are as follows:
  - ● Legislative – to pass legislation as part of the legislature.
  - ● Representative – to reflect the will of the people at the latest general election and help resolve their grievances.
  - ● To recruit, maintain and hold the government to account.
  - ● To discipline its members.
- ■ An MP has a number of competing factors to consider ranging from following his political party to acting in the public interest.

■ There are a number of factors which disqualify a person from becoming an MP (eg serving a prison sentence of more than one year).

■ In terms of composition, concern has been expressed as to the extent to which the House accurately reflects society as a whole.

■ The electoral system used to elect MPs is the 'first past the post' using 650 single member constituencies.

■ There are a number of factors which disqualify a person from voting at a general election (eg convicted prisoners during their term of detention).

■ In terms of political composition, very few independent MPs are elected and so the three main political parties dominate the composition of the House.

■ The leader of the political party that secures the overall majority of seats after a general election will become the Prime Minister.

■ The Electoral Commission oversees the electoral process.

SAMPLE ESSAY QUESTION

Explain the electoral system used for electing MPs and consider whether the system should be reformed.

Introduction:

The House of Commons uses the 'first past the post' electoral system.

First past the post system:

Simple majority system

UK divided into single member constituencies

Winning candidate needs to obtain the most votes

Following an election, the leader of the party with the most seats (typically) becomes Prime Minster

Arguments for reform:

A disproportionate system which distorts the wishes of the electorate

Candidates can become MPs with less than 51% of the votes cast in a constituency

Governments can be formed with less than 51% of the votes cast nationwide

Disadvantages smaller third parties

Only the votes cast for the winning candidate count

Problem of safe seats

Arguments for retaining the system:

Simple system to operate (which encourages people to participate)

Produces (typically) a clear-cut election result

Produces (typically) strong government (which can act decisively)

Single member constituencies ensure a direct link between MP and constituents

Recent events:

The Jenkins Commission

The 2008 Ministry of Justice paper (*Review of Voting Systems*)

The amendment to the 2010 Constitutional Reform and Governance Bill requiring a referendum be held by 2011

NB The 2010 general election which produced (for the first time in almost four decades) a hung Parliament.

CONCLUSION

 # Further reading

Books

Barnett, H, *Constitutional and Administrative Law* (7th edn, Routledge–Cavendish, 2009), Chapters 12 and 13.

Carroll, A, *Constitutional and Administrative Law* (5th edn, Pearson/Longman, 2009), Chapters 6 to 8.

Loveland, I, *Constitutional Law, Administrative Law, and Human Rights* (5th edn, Oxford University Press, 2009), Chapter 7.

Papers

Cracknell, R, 'Social background of MPs' (House of Commons Library, 2009).

Election 2005: Turnout. How many, who and why? (The Electoral Commission, 2005).

Factsheet M1 'You and your MP' (Parliamentary Copyright, 2009).

Factsheet M7 'Parliamentary elections' (Parliamentary Copyright, 2008).

Sear, C, 'Electoral franchise: who can vote?' (House of Commons Library, 2005).

Internet links:

www.parliament.uk

www.electoralcommission.org.uk

10

Parliament III: The House of Lords

AIMS AND OBJECTIVES

At the end of this chapter you should be able to:

- Identify and explain the different types of membership of the House of Lords
- Explain the political composition of the chamber
- Identify and explain the various different functions of the House of Lords
- Identify and explain the legal and political powers of the House of Lords

10.1 Introduction and size of the House of Lords

The House of Lords has evolved over many hundreds of years and, in fact, pre-dates the House of Commons. It is the second chamber of Parliament and is, by both law and constitutional convention, subordinate to the House of Commons. The House of Lords is an unusual and distinctive House in a number of ways. For example:

- There is no legal or constitutional cap on the size of its membership. In fact, the size of the House is ultimately in the hands of the executive (specifically the Prime Minister).
- The composition of the House is very different to that of the House of Commons, as not only do a number of independent members sit in the upper House, but unique in a democracy, it comprises a number of individuals who have inherited their seat.

The House of Lords, historically, has been an exceptionally large House in comparison with other upper chambers. Indeed, before it was reformed in 1999, its membership was almost twice the size of the House of Commons. It is generally the case that where states have bicameral legislatures, the upper House will be smaller than the lower chamber. According to research undertaken by Russell, the second chamber of other states tends on average to be 60 per cent of the size of the lower one (M Russell, *Second Chambers Overseas: A Summary* (The Constitution Unit, 1999), p 3). Before the enactment of the House of Lords Act 1999, the House of Lords comprised almost 1,300 members, although not all regularly attended the House. In contrast, the House of Commons had 659 MPs (the 1997–2001 Parliament).

The size of upper chambers in other democracies is comparatively smaller. For example, the United States Senate has 100 members and Canada's Senate has 104. Moreover, there is no legal cap on the size of the House of Lords (although there is a statutory cap in respect of the House of Commons, this can be altered). This is not unique, however, as there is no fixed number of members in respect of, for example, Spain's Senato or Belgium's Sénat. In this respect, therefore, the size of the House of Lords constantly fluctuates as peers die and new **life peers** are created.

life peers

persons appointed to the upper chamber of Parliament

10.2 The composition of the House of Lords

The following diagram indicates the composition of the House of Lords in February 2010:

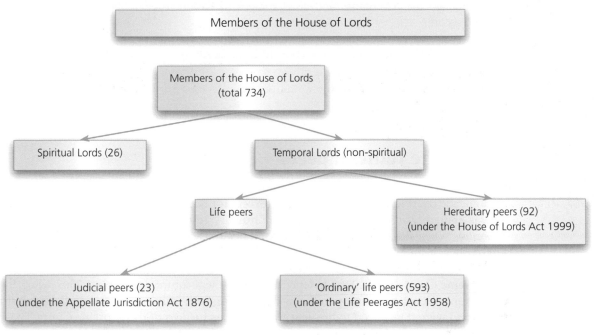

Figure 10.1 The composition of the House of Lords
Source www.parliament.co.uk

The House of Lords and gender

In February 2010, only 147 members of the House of Lords were female. The overwhelming majority of female members have been appointed there as life peers. As one-fifth of the House is female this is comparable to the elected House of Commons where, after the 2005 general election, 128 MPs out of 646 were female.

In broad terms, members of the House can be divided into Lords Spiritual and Lords Temporal.

10.3 Lords Spiritual

The Lords Spiritual are, technically speaking, not peers at all, but Lords of Parliament. They are further subdivided into 24 Bishops and two Archbishops of the established church: the Church of England. They represent the link between the church and State – the sovereign is, of course, the Supreme Governor of the Church of England and swears an oath on coronation as monarch to preserve the church. The spiritual members sit as 'independents' as they are independent of any political party (they sit on the *Bishops' Benches)*. They are *ex-officio* members of the House and when they retire from their religious office they leave the House (although it is possible for them subsequently to be appointed as life peers). The United Kingdom is in fact the only democracy in Europe that specifically reserves spiritual seats in its law-making body. Nevertheless, the 2000 Royal Commission on the Reform of the House of Lords (*A House for the Future*, Cm 4534 (The Stationery Office, 2000), Ch 15) specifically recommended the retention of such explicit religious representation. It further recommended that the designated religious element of any reformed House should be broadened to include other Christian denominations together with other non-Christian faiths (eg Islam, Judaism, etc). The Royal Commission noted the contribution the current Spiritual Lords made in the House. In addition, a number of members of both parliamentary chambers have a religious affiliation to various different faiths and are therefore able to contribute to debates with a religious dimension.

ACTIVITY

Self-test question

What are the advantages and disadvantages of having religious representation in the legislature?

As indicated by the diagram at section 10.2, the Lords Temporal are sub-divided into the following elements:

- Judicial peers.
- 'Ordinary' life peers.
- Hereditary peers.

10.4 The Judicial peers

Until October 2009, the Appellate Committee of the House of Lords was the highest domestic court in the United Kingdom (except for Scottish criminal matters). The Court was staffed by the Lords of Appeal in Ordinary (more commonly known as the law lords). When the law lords retired from judicial office, they remained in the House as crossbench members (see section 10.7.3). As indicated at section 5.7.4, under Pt 3 of the Constitutional Reform Act 2005, the Appellate Committee was replaced by a new Supreme Court outside and independent of the legislature. In October 2009 when the Supreme Court became operational the existing judicially active law lords (eg Lord Mance) were transferred to the new court to act as Justices of the Supreme Court. Those law lords who had already retired from judicial office remained in the House (eg Lord Carswell) and continued to sit as crossbench members. In due course, they will be joined by those judges who transferred from Parliament to the new Supreme Court when they retire from judicial office as Supreme Court Justices.

In short, in 2010 despite the creation of a new Supreme Court which is separate from Parliament, the House of Lords *still* contains judicial peers (albeit retired judges) who sit as crossbench members and can engage in the proceedings of the chamber. For example, see the following point made by Lord Carswell in the context of a debate on constitutional reform in 2010:

QUOTATION

'My Lords, I have had the privilege of being a Member of this House for a little over six years, but I have not until now had occasion to address your Lordships in debate. The reason is simple: I was, until my fairly recent retirement, a member of the Appellate Committee and sat as a Lord of Appeal in Ordinary. We all observed, rightly or wrongly, the self-imposed abstinence from participation in debates. But I am now released from that Trappist-type vow of silence and I hope to be able to make a modest contribution from time to time to the proceedings of the House.'

Hansard, HL Vol 716, col 1565.

ACTIVITY

Self-test question

What are the advantages and disadvantages of having the retired law lords in the legislature?

10.5 Life peers

10.5.1 The Life Peerages Act 1958

Under the Life Peerages Act 1958 the Crown (for practical purposes, the Prime Minister) is conferred with the power to award life peerages to individuals so that they can sit in the House of Lords. They now represent the largest single category of peers. There are at least three clear advantages to the creation of life peerages:

- Firstly, it means that distinguished individuals in different fields (such as medicine, commerce, academia, journalism, etc) can bring their particular skills, expertise and experience to bear in the workings of the House. This is particularly useful in the context of a debate or when scrutinising legislative proposals in these fields.

  The 2000 Royal Commission recognised the importance of this experience in respect of the workings of the House as 'Many can offer expertise and experience outside politics. Many are men and women of distinction in their own right'. Indeed, the Royal Commission noted that these characteristics were ones which they envisaged should ideally exist in any reformed second chamber.
- Secondly, as life peerages by their nature only exist for the life of the recipient, this means the awarding of life peerages does not permanently enlarge the size of the chamber.
- Thirdly, the creation of life peerages ensures that the House can be more representative of society. In particular, it specifically allows women and individuals from ethnic minorities to be appointed to the House. In fact, the vast majority of women sitting in the House of Lords have been appointed there under the Life Peerages Act 1958.

10.5.2 The creation of life peerages

The Life Peerages Act 1958 permits the Prime Minister of the day to create new life peers and is therefore a form of patronage. In theory, under the Act, the Prime Minister could technically recommend to the monarch that hundreds of new life peers of the same political colour as the governing party be appointed. This scenario raises an interesting issue as to whether it would be constitutional for the monarch to refuse to approve these peerages (see section 4.15). In any event, it is the Prime Minister who determines the size of the upper chamber as he decides how many life peerages to create. By constitutional convention, however, this power of the Prime Minister is not abused. Indeed, the Labour government's justification for creating a significant number of Labour life peers since 1997 was on the basis of ensuring a level of parity with the Conservative Party in the chamber.

10.5.3 The appointment of party political peers

The position is that the Prime Minister will determine the overall number of life peerages that are to be created and how many each party should receive, for example:

- 10 for Party A,
- 12 for Party B,
- 4 for Party C, etc.

Although the Prime Minister will determine the list of names for his own political party, the respective leaders of the other parties will decide their own list of names. These names would in due course be placed before the monarch to approve, and, by constitutional convention, she would act on the advice of the Prime Minister.

10.5.4 The appointment of non-party political peers (independent peers)

In terms of the appointment of non-party political peers (ie independent peers who sit as crossbenchers – see 10.7.3), it is the Prime Minister who will determine how many crossbench peers should be created. In 1999, the government announced in its White Paper (*Modernising Parliament, Reforming the House of Lords*, Cm 1183 (1999)) that in the transitional phase of reforming the House it would establish a non-statutory body to make these non-party political appointments. In essence, this independent body would determine the names of the non-party political peers. The Prime Minister would, however, still determine the number of crossbench peers required.

The House of Lords Appointments Commission

The House of Lords Appointments Commission is a non-statutory public body and was established in 2000. In 2010 it comprised the following:

- a chairperson (Lord Jay of Ewelme)
- three non-party political members
- three members who have been nominated from the three main political parties (Labour, Conservative and Liberal Democrats).

The Appointments Commission has two principal functions:

- Firstly, it determines the individuals who are to be recommended for nomination as non-party political peers. The Commission submits the required number of peers sought by the Prime Minister. On receipt of the nominations from the Appointments Commission, the Prime Minister will then put forward these recommendations to the monarch for approval.
- Secondly, it scrutinises all nominations for life peerages before they are appointed. This applies to both non-party political peers as well as to the party political peers submitted by the leaders of the political parties through the conduit of the Prime Minister.

According to the Commission:

QUOTATION

'The Commission must be assured that those recommended for political or non-party political peerages meet the highest standards of propriety. Nominations put forward by the political parties will include a statement as to any donations made to the Party concerned by an individual nominee'.

House of Lords Appointments Commission Information Pack,
Nominations for non-party political members of the House of Lords, para 28.

This function of the Appointments Commission's work did not prove to be controversial until 2006 when it declined to approve a handful of nominations for party political peerages. This in turn led to an investigation into the nomination of putative peerages (House of Commons Public Administration Select Committee, Second Report of Session 2007–08, *Propriety and Peerages*, HC 153 (2007)).

The Appointments Commission set out the assessment criteria that it would use in selecting non-party political peers to be as follows:

- An outstanding record of personal success and achievement in a person's chosen field.
- Integrity and independence.
- A commitment to the highest standards of public life.
- The ability to contribute effectively to the work of the House.

House of Lords Appointments Commission Information Pack,
Nominations for non-party political members of the House of Lords, para 6.

The Commission stated that all appointments would be on the basis of individual merit and that they wished to attract as wide a range of nominees as possible from all parts of the state. In 2009 the Commission revised its criteria so that nominees 'are willing to commit the time necessary to make an effective contribution', together with the requirements to confirm that they intend to remain independent of a political party and remain resident here for tax purposes.

In total, by February 2010 the Appointments Commission had appointed 55 peers which hitherto would have been, formerly, effectively within the power of the Prime Minister.

ACTIVITY

Essay writing

What are the advantages and disadvantages of having appointed life peers in the legislature? How do they differ from elected MPs in the House of Commons?

10.6 Hereditary peers

10.6.1 The position before the House of Lords Act 1999

Prior to the enactment of the House of Lords Act 1999, there were 759 hereditary peers and peeresses who inherited their seat in the Lords. This did not, however, mean that they all necessarily attended (the same point can also be made in respect of appointed life peers).

10.6.2 The arguments for the removal of the hereditary peers

In 1997 the Labour government was elected on a manifesto commitment to remove the right of hereditary peers to sit and vote in the House of Lords. In its subsequent White Paper of 1999 the government asserted that:

QUOTATION

'The right of hereditary peers to sit and vote in the House of Lords is a significant factor in the lack of political effectiveness and balance of the House. We believe no individuals should have the right to be Members of Parliament solely on the basis of the actions or position of their ancestors. A place in the legislature should be reserved for those who achieve it on their own merits. The continuing right of the whole hereditary peerage to sit and vote has been accepted as an anomaly for most of this century.'

Modernising Parliament, Reforming the House of Lords,
Cm 4183 (The Stationery Office, 1999) p 8.

The government, in its 1999 White Paper, identified the following reasons for their removal:

- Hereditary membership of a legislature was an anachronism – particularly in a democracy. It is of interest to note that, according to Russell (*Second Chambers Overseas: A Summary*, p 5), only one country in the world, Lesotho in Africa, uses the hereditary principle as the main basis for determining its second chamber.
- The hereditary element was unrepresentative of society (for example, only 16 of the hereditaries were female).
- Almost half of the hereditary peers (excluding those on leave or without a writ of summons to enter the House) were identified with the Conservative Party. The result of this was that – as a whole – the Conservative Party had an 'in-built party bias in the House of Lords'.

In due course the Labour government introduced legislation to remove the hereditary element from the House: The House of Lords Bill (which became the House of Lords Act 1999).

ACTIVITY

Self-test question

Can you think of any arguments in favour of retaining the hereditary principle in the House of Lords?

10.6.3 The House of Lords Act 1999

This legislation ended the right of hereditary peers to sit and vote in the House of Lords.

SECTION

s 1 of the House of Lords Act 1999
'No-one shall be a member of the House of Lords by virtue of a hereditary peerage.'

While the House of Lords Bill was being considered in the upper chamber, an amendment was made to it (the Weatherill amendment named after Lord Weatherill) which enabled 92 (approximately 10 per cent of the total) of the existing hereditary peers to remain in the chamber.

The government was prepared to accede to this compromise for two main reasons:

■ Firstly, it meant that the Bill would pass through the House of Lords and that at least the majority of hereditary peers (the other 667) would be removed. These individuals would thereafter be entitled to become MPs. In fact, in 2001 an ex-peer, Viscount Thurso (Liberal Democrat), was elected as an MP.

■ Secondly, the retention of a rump of hereditary peers was only ever meant to be a temporary arrangement pending long-term full reform of the House, at which point they would ultimately be removed.

The removal of the remaining hereditary peers?

In terms of long-term reform, the hereditary element is *still* present in the House. Although the Labour government's 2001 general election manifesto reaffirmed the commitment to remove the remaining hereditaries, a House of Lords Bill scheduled in the Queen's Speech in 2003 was subsequently abandoned. In fact, the Bill was never published. The 2005 Labour Party general election manifesto reaffirmed its commitment to Lords reform:

QUOTATION

'As part of the process of modernisation, we will remove the remaining hereditary peers.'
Britain *forward* not back, The Labour Party Manifesto 2005 (The Labour Party, 2005), p 110.

It is inevitable that full reform of the Lords will continue to be a protracted business. Indeed, although the House of Lords Act 1999 was supposed to be an interim measure pending long-term reform of the House, it is worth remembering that the 1911 Parliament Act was also supposed to be a temporary measure pending future reform being implemented. It is pertinent to note that in March 2007 the House of Commons voted in principle to remove the remaining hereditary peers by 391 votes to 111.

The remaining hereditary peers

Section 2 of the House of Lords Act 1999 retained 92 hereditary peers as follows:

■ 2 holding hereditary Great Offices of State (Lord Great Chamberlain – the Queen's representative, and the Earl Marshall – responsible for ceremonies).

■ 75 (in total) elected by each respective political party or group. The number of peers each party received was in direct proportion to the number of hereditary peers each party had at the time of the Act. As the Conservatives had the most hereditaries, they elected the most hereditary peers. The results were as follows:

42   Conservative
2   Labour
3   Liberal Democrat
28   crossbench (independent peers)

- 15 office holders (for example, Deputy Speakers and Committee Chairs) elected by the whole of the House of Lords.

Source: House of Lords Briefing, *Reform and Proposals for Reform since 1900* (Parliamentary Copyright, House of Lords, 2006) p 8.

Overall, 92 hereditary peers were retained, 3 of whom were female. As a result of the House of Lords Act 1999 we have the rather paradoxical situation in which the remaining peers – by virtue of their election – could in one sense claim to be more constitutionally legitimate than their life peer counterparts who have been simply appointed. The point, however, must be made that the electorate was very limited: the 15 office holders were elected by the whole House and the 75 party and crossbench peers were elected by their respective members. In any event, they were not elected by people outside the House.

The death of an (elected) hereditary peer

The House of Lords Act 1999 was meant to represent a staging post on the way to full long-term reform of the chamber. Full reform of the House has to date not been realised and consequently the 'transitional' House has had to deal with the situation when one of the remaining hereditary peers dies. From the end of 2001–02 parliamentary session, vacancies due to death have been filled by a by-election. Candidates for the by-election are filled, in essence, by peers expelled in 1999 (Standing Order No 10). It should be pointed out that the 2010 Constitutional Reform and Governance Bill proposed to abolish these by-elections in order to allow the hereditary element to eventually die out (see section 10.13). However, by the time this measure became the Constitutional Reform and Governance Act 2010, the above provision had been removed.

ACTIVITY

Self-test question

What are the advantages and disadvantages of having 'elected' hereditary peers in the House of Lords?

10.6.4 Renouncing a peerage

Under the Peerage Act 1963 it has been possible for hereditary peers to renounce their peerages. This represented an irrevocable renunciation for the duration of their lifetime, although their successors would not be affected by it. Under this legislation two major political figures renounced their hereditary peerages:

- Tony Benn – on the death of his father in 1960 he automatically succeeded to the hereditary peerage of the Viscountcy of Stansgate with an entitlement to sit in the House of Lords. At the time he was an MP and he wanted to renounce this peerage and continue to serve in the House of Commons. As an individual cannot sit in both Houses, his Bristol seat became vacant and a by-election was held. Although Benn won the by-election, the Election Court disbarred him from assuming his seat in the House of Commons. After the passing of the Peerage Act 1963, Benn renounced his peerage and was thereafter elected as an MP.
- In October 1963 Harold Macmillan resigned as Prime Minister. This resulted in the Earl of Home disclaiming his hereditary peerage under the 1963 Act to succeed Macmillan as Prime Minister (he became Sir Alec Douglas-Home). This was necessary as by constitutional convention a Prime Minister must be a member of the House of Commons (see section 4.13.4), thereby being directly accountable to the elected representatives of the people.

ACTIVITY

Essay writing

Compare and contrast the different types of members in the House of Lords.

Key facts on hereditary peers

Spiritual Lords	**Archbishops and Bishops** – they represent the link between the established church and the state. They provide a religious/moral dimension to the chamber. A very unusual category of members in a democratic legislature.
Temporal Lords	**Hereditary peers** – originally they inherited their seat in the chamber, although after the 1999 reforms they were 'elected' by their counterparts. A unique category of members in a democratic legislature.
	Life peers: • **Judicial peers** – members of the judiciary who have retired from judicial office. • **'Ordinary' life peers** – appointed under the Life Peerages Act 1958. They provide the chamber with expertise and specialism. A number of legislatures, including Canada, have appointed members.

10.7 The party political composition of the House

10.7.1 Political breakdown of the composition of the House of Lords

In common with the House of Commons, members in the House of Lords are organised into political parties and take a party whip. The House of Lords, however, is a less partisan chamber and members are more likely to defy their party whips and official political party largely on the basis that they are not subject to re-election. The main political parties are, therefore, represented in the Lords, although in contrast to the Commons, they are supplemented by a significant independent element.

In February 2010 the political breakdown of the House was as follows:

Political composition of the House of Lords 2010	
Party	**Number of peers**
Conservative	189
Labour	211
Liberal Democrat	72
Crossbenchers	182
Others	25

Table 10.1
These figures exclude members on leave of absence from the chamber, the Bishops, those disqualified as senior judges and an MEP.
Source: Parliament website: www.parliament.uk.

The above figures indicate that no one political party controls the House of Lords as the two main political parties now have approximate parity with each other. This has been achieved by two factors:

■ The removal of the hereditary peers expelled a significant number of peers who identified themselves with the Conservative Party.

■ A number of Labour life peers have been created since the election of the Labour government in 1997.

Before the 1999 reforms, the Conservative Party was the clear dominant grouping within the House. In February 2010 the Labour Party was the largest party in the House. It is pertinent to note that Russell and Sciara have argued in light of the distribution of seats between the main parties that:

QUOTATION

'Despite being unelected, the notion that the House of Lords is now a "representative" chamber – perhaps even more representative than the House of Commons – has thus grown in currency.'

M Russell and M Sciara, *The House of Lords in 2005: A More Representative and Assertive Chamber?*
(The Constitution Unit, 2006), p 8.

ACTIVITY

Problem solving

Compare and contrast the party political composition in the two Houses of Parliament.

10.7.2 Government ministers in the House of Lords

As will be considered at section 11.6.2, a number of government ministers, including a few Cabinet ministers, sit in the House of Lords. In February 2010 the government contained three cabinet ministers, four ministers and two law officers from the Lords. The most prominent figure historically was of course the Lord Chancellor; however, as stated in s 2 of the Constitutional Reform Act 2005, a future Lord Chancellor may be drawn from either chamber. Until the passage of this Act, by constitutional convention, the Lord Chancellor had traditionally resided in the upper chamber. In 2007, Jack Straw (an MP) became Lord Chancellor and in 2010 Kenneth Clarke assumed this office.

The constitutional advantage of ministers sitting in the House of Lords is that it ensures that the government has representatives in the upper chamber to act as spokespersons and to pilot Bills through it.

10.7.3 Independent/crossbench peers

The House of Lords is hallmarked in terms of its composition by virtue of the fact that a significant number of its members are classed as independents (crossbenchers – they sit on the crossbenches in the chamber between the benches of the government and the opposition). In essence cross benchers can be defined as those peers who do not take a party political whip and have no specific allegiance to one of the three main political parties. Crossbenchers sit as individual members and do not constitute a party. They do, however, regularly meet under the aegis of the Convener of crossbench peers where issues of common interest are raised and discussed. Crossbenchers are noted for their independent, non-party political stance on matters.

The importance of having an independent (non-politically aligned) element in the second chamber was emphasised strongly by the 2000 Royal Commission. In particular, it recommended that a fully reformed House should contain a strong crossbench element amounting to around 20 per cent of the total membership of the House. In terms of House of Lords reform, therefore, one of the consequences of the widely supported proposal of a wholly elected chamber, inevitably, would be the loss of this independent element. In short, elected members will invariably be associated with one of the major political parties. As we saw in respect of the House of Commons, very few politicians are elected as an 'Independent'.

In 2002 the Joint Committee on House of Lords Reform underlined the importance of the existing independent element of the House:

'The role of Crossbenchers is often particularly significant in relation to participation in debates and committees and the quality they bring to these deliberations.'

House of Lords Reform: First Report, HL Paper 17, HC 171 (2002), p 17.

The other advantage of having a sizeable independent, non-party political element is that it helps to ensure that, in terms of numbers, no one political party dominates the second chamber (see the following table).

Breakdown of the composition of the political and non-political elements in February 2010				
	Conservative	Labour	Liberal Democrats	Crossbencher
Life peers	141	207	67	149
Hereditary peers	48	4	5	33
Total	189	211	72	182

Table 10.2

Figures adapted from www.parliament.uk and do not include the Bishops, those peers on leave of absence, those disqualified as senior judges and an MEP.

10.7.4 Other key personnel of the House

The Speaker of the House

Traditionally the Speaker of the House of Lords has been the Lord Chancellor; however, following the Constitutional Reform Act 2005 which radically reformed the nature of this office, the House has had to make alternative arrangements in respect of the post of Speaker. Under s 2 of the Act a future Lord Chancellor may sit in either House and so therefore may not necessarily be a peer. As indicated at section 5.7.9, it is in this context that the chamber resolved to elect a Speaker for five years. They would be known as the Lord Speaker and would be expected to give up party politics and occupy the Woolsack (the seat on which, historically, the Speaker of the House sits). In July 2006 the House of Lords elected Baroness Hayman to act as Lord Speaker.

The Office of the Speaker of the Lords is not an exact parallel of the Speaker of the House of Commons, as the former has fewer responsibilities and is less powerful than her counterpart in the House of Commons. In fact, although she presides over proceedings, her role is in practice a symbolic one.

■ As the House of Lords is a self-regulating body (by virtue of its unelected status, the atmosphere is less partisan or politically charged), the responsibility for maintaining order rests not with the Speaker, but with the House collectively.
■ The Speaker does not call members to speak and neither does she curtail debate in the chamber.

In common with the House of Commons, however, the Speaker is assisted by a number of Deputy Speakers. Moreover, the Speakers in both Houses represent each respective House abroad and on ceremonial occasions.

The Leader of the House

The Leader of the House is a member of the Cabinet and is responsible for the conduct of government business in the chamber – this is a similar function to the Leader of the House of Commons.

10.8 Disqualification of membership of the House of Lords

There are a number of factors which disqualify individuals from membership of the House of Lords and to some extent these parallel those relating to the House of Commons (see section 9.3.3). According to Erskine May (*Parliamentary Practice* (23rd edn, Lexis-Nexis Butterworths, 2004), Chapter 3) the following are disqualified from membership:

■ Individuals under 21 years

(Standing Order No 2, 1685). This partly explains why historically some peers have been absent from the chamber as when they inherited their seat, they may have been too young to enter the House.

■ Aliens

Act of Settlement 1700 (as amended by the British Nationality Act 1981 which excludes Commonwealth and Republic of Ireland citizens from the 1700 Act).

■ Bankrupts

In England and Wales disqualification will apply if a bankruptcy restrictions order has been issued (the Insolvency Act 1986, as amended by the Enterprise Act 2002). In Scotland it applies where the member's estate is sequestered.

■ Treason

Those convicted of treason under the Forfeiture Act 1870 (until pardoned or the term of imprisonment has expired) are disqualified.

■ Mental health

Unlike the House of Commons, the Mental Health Act 1983 does not specifically apply to the Lords. The House of Lords Committee for Privileges (HL 254, 1983–84) has recommended that in order to resolve this issue, future legislation should make it clear that such mental health provisions applied to members of the House.

In terms of misconduct, it is important to point out that in 2009 the House of Lords Committee for Privileges concluded that the House could not expel permanently a member and could only suspend a member for a defined period (*The powers of the House of Lords in respect of its members*, 1st Report of Session 2008–09, HL Paper 87 (2009), Para 8) (see further section 10.13).

10.9 The functions of the House of Lords

In the absence of a written codified constitutional text there is no authoritative and constitutionally definitive statement which sets out the powers of the House of Lords (or for that matter, the House of Commons). In 1968, however, the government White Paper on House of Lords reform identified the following functions:

Functions of the House of Lords
Apart from providing the Supreme Court of Appeal, the House of Lords at present performs the following main functions:

(a) the provision of a forum for full and free debate on matters of public interest;
(b) the revision of public Bills brought from the House of Commons;
(c) the initiation of public legislation, including in particular those government Bills which are less controversial in party political terms and private members' Bills;
(d) the consideration of subordinate legislation;
(e) the scrutiny of the activities of the executive; and
(f) the scrutiny of private legislation.

House of Lords Reform, Cmnd 3799 (1968), para 8.

More recently the House of Lords Information Office has effectively subsumed these functions into four:

■ Making laws.
■ Holding the government to account.
■ Investigating policy issues.
■ The UK's highest court (now of course superseded by the operation of the Supreme Court in 2009).

The Work of the House of Lords 2007–08 (Parliamentary Copyright House of Lords, 2009), p 1.

In addition, it provided a useful breakdown of the time typically spent by the House of Lords on its various functions:

Breakdown of the workload of the House of Lords (at p 37 of the above).
- 60 per cent legislation (55 per cent Bills, 5 per cent Statutory Instruments)
- 40 per cent scrutiny (28 per cent Debates
                                7 per cent Questions
                                5 per cent Statements)

10.9.1 The judicial role of the House

It should be remembered that in a very general sense the House – as a whole – performs a judicial function when it regulates and enforces the internal rules of parliamentary privilege (see Chapter 8). For example, in terms of self-regulation, in 2009 the House of Lords suspended two peers until the end of the parliamentary session (see also section 10.13).

In addition, as indicated earlier at section 10.4, historically until 2009 the Appellate Committee of the House of Lords was the highest domestic court. As a result, the law lords formed part of both the legislature and the judiciary and so violated a pure interpretation of the separation of powers (see sections 5.2.2 and 5.7.4). The Constitutional Reform Act 2005, however, created a new separate free-standing Supreme Court which became operational in October 2009.

10.9.2 A forum for debate

The House of Lords is a debating chamber in which matters of public interest are examined and considered. As in the House of Commons, debates can take place either:

- in the context of the passage of legislation by debating the principles and details of a Bill; or
- as free-standing general debates.

Although both parliamentary chambers hold debates, it is generally argued that debates in the House of Lords are qualitatively better than in the House of Commons for three reasons:

- Firstly, there is a broader range of experience and expertise in the upper chamber which arguably allows debates to be richer and more informed than in the Commons. Much of this experience and knowledge has been appointed under the Life Peerages Act 1958, but some of it is drawn from the ranks of the hereditaries. It must also be remembered that peers are unsalaried and (if working) can continue with their careers in parallel with their duties in the House. Rogers and Walters have noted: 'the fact remains that the House of Lords as currently composed is a knowledgeable place in a way that distinguishes it from most other parliamentary assemblies in the world' (R Rogers and R Walters, *How Parliament works* (5th edn, Pearson/Longman, 2004), p 280).
- Secondly, the atmosphere of the chamber is less partisan. The 2000 Royal Commission made particular reference to the non-polemic style of the House.
- Thirdly, as an adjunct to the point above, a significant number of peers are crossbenchers in any event, and so are not aligned to the major political parties.

10.9.3 The revision of public Bills brought from the House of Commons

The House of Lords spends over half of its time examining legislative proposals. This indicates that a major constitutional function of the House of Lords is to act as a 'revising chamber'. Most important Bills, as well as controversial ones, tend to begin in the House of Commons where the government is dominant.

In considering and scrutinising public Bills which have passed through the Commons, the House of Lords can revise, propose and make amendments (with the exception of money/financial Bills – see section 10.10.1). Such amendments can be:

■ technical drafting amendments to remedy unclear, imprecise or sloppily drafted provisions, or
■ policy amendments based on aspects or provisions of the Bill considered objectionable, unsatisfactory, unnecessary, etc. For example, in 2001 the Anti-terrorism, Crime and Security Bill was amended by the Lords in order to provide individuals with an appellate mechanism against deportation. Similarly, the detention of terrorist suspects for up to 28 days under the Terrorism Act 2006 has the safeguard that it is subject to periodic review by Parliament (a safeguard added by the Lords).

Although the procedure and nature of passing legislation is largely similar for both Houses, there are some key differences and these are considered at section 12.7.4.

10.9.4 The initiation of public legislation

In order to spread the legislative workload between the two parliamentary chambers, Bills can begin in either House. In fact, this practice is consistent with other countries such as France and the Republic of Ireland. Two examples of highly significant constitutional Bills which commenced in the House of Lords are as follows:

■ The Human Rights Bill (introduced in 1997).
■ The Constitutional Reform Bill (introduced in 2003).

In each case the Lord Chancellor, as a government minister, was responsible for piloting the Bill through the House.

In contrast to the above, money Bills must begin in the House of Commons as it is the pre-eminent chamber. Similarly, in Australia financial legislation must also be introduced in the lower House (the House of Representatives).

10.9.5 The consideration of subordinate legislation

As indicated at section 5.7.2, subordinate legislation is a clear violation of the separation of powers as it involves the executive performing a legislative function: making legislation (albeit subordinate legislation). In view of this breach, from a constitutional perspective it is imperative that subordinate legislation is subject to adequate scrutiny. As we shall see at section 12.7.5, it is generally agreed that parliamentary supervision of this type of legislation is insufficient; however, the House of Lords performs a useful role in providing some supervision of it. It does so through the following committees:

■ The House of Lords Select Committee on Delegated Powers and Regulatory Reform.
■ As part of the Joint Committee on Statutory Instruments.
■ The House of Lords Select Committee on the Merits of Statutory Instruments.

10.9.6 The scrutiny of the activities of the executive

As Parliament as a whole is constitutionally responsible for supervising the actions of the executive, this means that it is the responsibility of both the House of Commons and the House of Lords to hold the government to account (this is considered in Chapter 12). It should be remembered that the House of Lords contains a number of ministers who can be questioned and scrutinised directly by peers. Russell (*Second Chambers Overseas: A Summary* (The Constitution Unit, 1999), p 11) has noted that it is generally the case that upper chambers have less power in holding the government to account than lower Houses. In this respect, therefore, the House of Lords is comparable with other legislatures.

In essence, the House of Lords will scrutinise the actions and policy of the executive in the following ways:

- general debates
- debates on legislative proposals
- questions
- debates on government statements
- the committee system.

The 2000 Royal Commission argued that the second chamber needed to be authoritative because, together with the Commons, it must scrutinise effectively the work of the government. After all, a 'more accountable Government is better Government' (*A House for the Future*, Cm 4534 (The Stationery Office, 2000), p 80).

The importance of the House of Lords supervising and checking the actions of the government has been heightened in recent decades in light of the executive's general dominance in, and control over, the lower chamber (see section 9.8).

10.9.7 The scrutiny of private legislation

Private Bills affect particular groups or individuals, rather than having general application as do public Bills. Both Houses scrutinise and process private legislation.

In addition to the functions listed above, two other functions should be mentioned – the scrutiny of proposed European legislation and the role of guardian and protector of the constitution.

10.9.8 The scrutiny of proposed European legislation

One function not referred to in the 1968 White Paper (owing to the fact that the United Kingdom did not join the EEC until 1973 – now the EU) is the useful role that the modern House plays in respect of proposed European Union legislation. This consists of the House of Lords European Union Select Committee examining EU documents/matters before decisions are taken in respect of them by the British government in Europe.

10.9.9 A guardian of the constitution and watchdog of civil liberties and human rights

One function commonly attributed to the House of Lords is that of the guardian and protector of the constitution: a constitutional long-stop. It has been commented that this is a classic function performed by second chambers:

QUOTATION

'The origins of second chambers, either as a representative of "establishment" interests or as a representative of regional territories in a federal system, has made them natural bulwarks against impulsive or politically-motivated action taken by the lower house.'

A Reidy and M Russell, *Second Chambers as Constitutional Guardians & Protectors of Human Rights* (The Constitution Unit, 1999), p 2.

Such a role (ie acting as a 'natural bulwark') is particularly important in the context of the United Kingdom which lacks an entrenched codified constitution which acts as a restraint on the government, or indeed Parliament itself (on this point, see Chapter 7). As specifically pointed out by the 2000 Royal Commission:

QUOTATION

'The risk, however, is that a Government with a secure majority in the House of Commons, even if based on the votes of a minority of the electorate, could in principle bring about controversial and ill-considered changes to the constitution without the need to secure consensus support for them.'

A House for the Future, Cm 4534 (The Stationery Office, 2000), p 48.

In other constitutions, the upper House will typically have special legal powers in respect of legislation altering the constitution. In France, for example, the upper chamber (Senat) has a veto over constitutional amendments as they must pass both Houses. It is interesting to point out that the Royal Commission specifically refused to recommend that a reformed second chamber should have extra powers over 'constitutional legislation'. For one thing, it would be very difficult to definitively identify a 'constitutional Bill' (as noted at section 4.2).

In the following circumstances, however, various statutes have specifically recognised the constitutional role of the House of Lords as a 'constitutional long-stop'. The consent of the House is expressly required in order to:

■ Extend the life of Parliament (Parliament Act 1911).
■ Remove senior judges (Act of Settlement 1700 as amended by the Senior Courts Act 1981 – formerly the Supreme Court Act – and the Constitutional Reform Act 2005).
■ Remove the Parliamentary Ombudsman – see section 21.3.6 (The Parliamentary Commissioner Act 1967).

In addition, the recently created House of Lords Select Committee on the Constitution has the following remit:

QUOTATION

'To examine the constitutional implications of all public bills coming before the House; and to keep under review the operation of the constitution'.

> First Report of the House of Lords Select Committee on the Constitution,
> *Reviewing the constitution: Terms of reference and method of working*
> HL Paper 11 (2001), p 5.

KEY FACTS

Functions	
Judicial	• The House as a whole enforces parliamentary privilege.
Legislative	• Can initiate and revise private Bills. • Can initiate and revise public Bills – except money Bills. • Examines subordinate legislation. • Examines proposed European legislation
Scrutiny of the executive	• Debates. • Questions. • Committee work. • Legislation (see above, except private Bills).
Debating chamber	• General forum for debate on matters of public interest (see also in the context of the scrutiny of the executive).
Protector of the uncodified constitution	• Acts as a constitutional long-stop and watchdog of civil liberties.

10.10 The legal powers of the House of Lords

The powers of the upper chamber are limited by both law (Parliament Acts – see section 10.10.1) and constitutional convention (see section 10.11).

10.10.1 Legal limitations

Before the Parliament Act 1911, historically the two Houses of Parliament had equal legal power over legislation. In essence, the House of Lords could block/veto Bills passed by the Commons. A constitutional convention, however, had developed to the effect that on financial matters (ie money Bills) the upper House would not oppose such Bills passed by the Commons. Notwithstanding this, in 1909 the House of Lords rejected the government's finance Bill (the Budget) which the House had the power to do in law, but not by constitutional convention. This eventually led to the passage of the Parliament Act 1911 which legally limited the powers of the House of Lords.

The Parliament Act 1911 achieved the following things:

■ The House of Lords lost the legal power to reject money Bills (as certified by the Speaker in the House of Commons) which have passed through the Commons. After no more than a month in the Lords, if a money Bill has not been approved (ie passed) it proceeds to the Royal Assent without the consent of the Upper House (s 1).

■ Any public Bill passed by the House of Commons in three successive parliamentary sessions with at least two years between the second reading in the Commons in the first session and the third reading in the Commons in the third session, could become law without the consent of the Lords (s 2). In short, this meant that in future, the House of Lords could only delay legislation (effectively for two years). It thereafter had a temporary 'suspensive veto' over proposed legislation. In summary, although it could reject and oppose legislation, *ultimately* it could not stop it from becoming law.

The following were excluded from the ambit of the Parliament Act 1911:

■ A Bill proposing to extend the life of Parliament beyond five years.
■ A public Bill commenced in the House of Lords.
■ A public Bill sent to the House of Lords less than a month before the end of the session.
■ A private Bill.

In addition, it does not apply to Statutory Instruments (ie delegated legislation).

Source: House of Lords Briefing: *Work, Role, Function and Powers*
(Parliamentary Copyright, House of Lords 2009), p 5.

Although legally the House of Lords could have refused to pass the 1911 Parliament Bill, it seems clear that if they had done so the Prime Minister would have (in effect via the monarch) created sufficient new peers to ensure its passage. Indeed, in 1949 the 1911 Parliament Act was amended so as to reduce further the delaying power of the House of Lords. In fact, the Labour government of the day used the Parliament Act of 1911 itself to force through the Parliament Bill of 1949 against the wishes of the House of Lords (see the challenge to this in *Jackson* (2005) at section 10.10.3).

The change introduced by the Parliament Act 1949 was, in effect, to reduce the delaying power of the Lords to one year (ie the three successive sessions were reduced to two and the minimum period in the Commons reduced from two years to one).

As Russell has commented, it is relatively common for upper chambers to have the constitutional and legal power to delay legislation passed by the lower House (the 'suspensive veto'), although ultimately, as in the United Kingdom, generally speaking the lower chamber has the final decisive say (M Russell, *Resolving Disputes between the Chambers* (The Constitution Unit, 1999), p 3).

10.10.2 The use of the Parliament Acts

The Parliament Acts, historically, have been invoked rarely; however, the Labour government has used them three times since 1997. In total the use of the Acts has been as follows:

■ Welsh Church Act 1914 (disestablishment of the Church in Wales).
■ The Government of Ireland Act 1914 (Irish home rule).

- Parliament Act 1949 (to reduce further the legal powers of the House of Lords).
- War Crimes Act 1991 (concerned with atrocities committed in Germany and German-occupied territories during the Second World War).
- European Parliamentary Elections Act 1999 (established a 'closed party' list for candidates for elections to the European Parliament).
- Sexual Offences (Amendment) Act 2000 (reduced the homosexual age of consent to 16).
- Hunting Act 2004 (banned fox hunting – see section 10.10.3)

The provisions in relation to money Bills have not been invoked.

10.10.3 Is the Parliament Act 1949 legal?

In 2005, in one of the most important constitutional cases in recent times, the Appellate Committee of the House of Lords had to determine whether the Hunting Act 2004 and the Parliament Act 1949 had been lawfully passed as Acts of Parliament.

CASE EXAMPLE

R (Jackson and Others) v Attorney-General [2005] UKHL 56

The Hunting Act 2004 made the hunting of wild animals with dogs (ie fox hunting) illegal. This Act had been passed without the consent of the House of Lords under the Parliament Acts of 1911 and 1949. Jackson sought, unsuccessfully (in both the Divisional Court and the Court of Appeal), a declaration that:

- the Parliament Act 1949 was of no legal effect as it had been passed without the consent of the House of Lords; and
- as a consequence, the Hunting Act 2004 was of no legal effect and not an Act of Parliament.

The House of Lords dismissed Jackson's appeal and affirmed that the Parliament Act 1949 had been lawfully passed under the Parliament Act 1911 (notwithstanding the lack of consent from the Lords). As a result, the Hunting Act 2004 was a lawful Act of Parliament with full legal effect.

The House of Lords noted that after 1911 there were two routes to passing legislation:

- with the consent of the House of Lords; and
- without the consent of the House of Lords (under the Parliament Act).

As a matter of statutory construction, the 1911 Act did not preclude the use of the s 2 procedure (ie rendering the consent of the upper House unnecessary) to amend itself (ie to create the 1949 Act). Logically, therefore, on the basis of this judgment, it would appear that the Parliament Acts could be amended to reduce further the power of the House to delay legislation, for example to only six months.

One of the arguments advanced in favour of Jackson was that the 1949 and 2004 Acts were, in effect, *delegated legislation* as they were derivative of the 1911 Act. In short, they owed their validity to a prior enactment (the 1911 Act) and consequently with the status of delegated, rather than primary legislation, they could be reviewed by the court. The court dismissed this argument. As pointed out by Lord Bingham, the 1911 Act referred to legislation complying with the provisions of this Act becoming 'an Act of Parliament on the Royal Assent being signified thereto' (s 2(1)). This clearly denoted primary (and not delegated) legislation. As Lord Bingham stated:

JUDGMENT

'The 1911 Act did, of course, effect an important constitutional change, but the change lay not in authorising a new form of sub-primary parliamentary legislation but in creating a new way of enacting primary legislation.'

As a postscript to this case, in *R (Countryside Alliance and others) v Attorney General and another* [2007] UKHL 52, the House of Lords dismissed an appeal by the claimants who had argued that the Hunting Act breached both European Union and European Convention law (the latter was upheld by the European Court of Human Rights in *Countryside Alliance v UK* (2010) 50 EHRR S E6).

10.11 Limitations imposed by constitutional conventions

Quite apart from the legal limitations outlined above, the House of Lords traditionally has recognised that the House of Commons, as the elected House to which the government is directly accountable, is the pre-eminent chamber in Parliament. As a consequence, it adheres to the following three constitutional conventions in its dealings with the House of Commons. By convention the House of Lords:

▪ Should accord a second reading to a government Bill which has passed through the House of Commons and which has been foreshadowed in the governing party's most recent general election manifesto (the Salisbury-Addison/Government Bill Convention). This is on the basis that if a government has been elected on specified manifesto commitments, it would be constitutionally inappropriate and essentially undemocratic for the Lords to thwart the will of the people as expressed and represented in the House of Commons. In recent times the relevance of this convention has been questioned by the Liberal Democrats in the House. In the debate on the 2005 Queen's Speech, the Leader of the Liberal Democrats, Lord McNally, argued that: 'I do not believe that a convention drawn up 60 years ago on relations between a wholly hereditary Conservative-dominated House and a Labour Government who had 48 per cent of the vote should apply in the same way to the position in which we find ourselves today' (*Hansard*, HL Vol 672, cols 20–21).

The point that was effectively being made was that the Labour Party's share of the vote at the 2005 general election was 35 per cent of the votes cast and yet the party (from whom the government was drawn) obtained 55 per cent of the seats in the House of Commons (see section 9.5).

▪ Should consider government business within a reasonable time. It was on this basis that Lord Carter objected to the Constitutional Reform Bill being sent to a special Select Committee for detailed consideration (*Hansard*, HL Vol 658, col 999).

▪ Does not reject Statutory Instruments – although in law they are entitled to. Russell and Sciara (*The House of Lords in 2005: A More Representative and Assertive Chamber?* (The Constitution Unit, 2006), p 14) have pointed out, however, that in 2005 there was considerable tension between the government and the House of Lords over two delegated orders under the aegis of:

1. The Licensing Act 2003 (the Lords voted on a motion to condemn an order expanding drinking hours, though they did not defeat the order itself).

2. The Criminal Justice Act 2003 (an order – subsequently dropped – to restrict a defendant's right to jury trial in complex fraud trials).

Finally, regard should be had to the 2006 report of the Joint Committee on Conventions which had been established to examine the practicality of codifying the constitutional conventions which regulate the relationship between the two Houses. Its report (Joint Committee on Conventions, First Report of Session 2005–06, *Conventions of the UK Parliament*, HL Paper 265-I, HC 1212-I (2006)) concluded that the term codification was unhelpful as it implied rule-making and an enforcement mechanism, whereas by their nature, constitutional conventions were unenforceable. As a consequence, to codify a constitutional convention was a contradiction in terms:

QUOTATION

'Far from reducing the risk of conflict, codification might actually damage the relationship between the two Houses, making it more confrontational and less capable of moderation through the usual channels. This would benefit neither the Government nor Parliament (para 279) … However, we offer certain formulations for one or both Houses to adopt by resolution. In our view, both the debates on such resolutions, and the resolutions themselves, would improve the shared understanding which the Government seek (para 280) … all recommendations for the formulation or codification of conventions are subject to the current understanding that conventions as such are flexible and unenforceable, particularly in the self-regulating environment of the House of Lords (para 281).'

Joint Committee on Conventions, First Report of Session 2005–06, Conventions of the UK Parliament, HL Paper 265-I, HC 1212-I (2006).

The formulation suggested by the Committee included the following:

- The primacy of the House of Commons over the House of Lords was a fact which did not require codification.
- The convention that a manifesto Bill should be accorded a second reading by the House of Lords (the Salisbury–Addison Convention – see above) should be described as a *Government Bill Convention*. The House of Lords could debate and set out the terms of this convention for the Commons subsequently to debate and note.
- The existing convention that the government should have its business considered in a reasonable time in the upper chamber could be adopted by the House of Lords by way of a resolution. In addition, a new symbol could appear on the Lords' order paper indicating a Bill which had spent more than a certain period in the upper chamber (a period of 80 days was suggested).
- Although neither House rejects secondary legislation (Statutory Instruments) on a regular basis, in exceptional circumstances this may be appropriate and a statement to this effect could be adopted by both Houses (or either House):

QUOTATION

'There are situations in which it is consistent both with the Lords' role in Parliament as a revising chamber, and with Parliament's role in relation to delegated legislation, for the Lords to threaten to defeat an S.I.'

Joint Committee on Conventions, First Report of Session 2005–06, Conventions of the UK Parliament, HL Paper 265-I, HC 1212-I (2006), para 229.

- It was universally recognised that there was no need to *legislate* on these matters.
- It was made very clear that the courts should have no role in relation to determining whether a parliamentary convention has been breached.

In December 2006 the government issued its Formal Reply to this report in which it accepted the Committee's conclusions and recommendations (*Government Response to the Joint Committee on Conventions' Report of Session 2005–06: Conventions of the UK Parliament*, Cm 6997 (Crown Copyright, 2006)). In January 2007 both Houses (in separate resolutions) approved the Joint Committee's report.

ACTIVITY

Exercise

Compare and contrast the legal and political powers of the House of Lords.

Legal powers	

Parliament Acts 1911 and 1949	• No power to reject money Bills.
	• Only has the power to delay a public Bill for approximately one year.
	• Retains full legal power to veto:
	  (a) secondary legislation
	  (b) a public Bill initiated in the House of Lords
	  (c) a public Bill designed to extend the life of Parliament
	  (d) a private Bill.

Political powers	
Constitutional conventions	• The Salisbury–Addison/Government Bill Convention. • Government business to be considered within a reasonable time. • Does not veto secondary legislation.

10.12 The relationship between the House of Lords and the House of Commons

In general, the two Houses of Parliament co-operate with each other efficiently; otherwise parliamentary business would become unworkable. Indeed, in respect of Lords' amendments made to legislative proposals, in many cases these are accepted by the House of Commons (or, more specifically the government). For its part, the House of Lords has traditionally accepted that it is the subordinate chamber, although on occasions it will force the Commons to reconsider issues/policies, thereby acting as a watchdog and protector of the constitution.

Since its election in 1997, the Labour government has suffered only a handful of defeats on a government Bill in the House of Commons (for an example see section 6.7.5) whereas, in contrast, it has suffered a significant number of defeats in the Lords (see 'Government defeats in the House of Lords' SN/PC/03252 (House of Commons Library, 2009)). Whether this indicates the dominance that the executive typically has in the Commons, or whether it indicates a more forceful Lords (or whether it is probably both), is an interesting point. What does appear to be the case is that since the removal of most of the hereditary peers in 1999, the House of Lords now sees itself as more constitutionally legitimate than before, and so appears more willing to challenge the wishes of the lower chamber (which is largely controlled by the government). In fact, the calendar year of 2005 appears to have been a watershed in terms of executive/House of Lords relations:

QUOTATION

'2005 witnessed the biggest row between the government and the peers since the start of the twentieth century, leading to the biggest defeats in the Lords since Labour came to power … These and other events suggested that the chamber was growing increasingly assertive.'

M Russell and M Sciara, *The House of Lords in 2005: A More Representative and Assertive Chamber?*
(The Constitution Unit, 2006), p 5.

The authors are referring to the major controversy of that year which was the passage of the Prevention of Terrorism Act 2005. The Bill had been introduced as a response to a ruling of the Appellate Committee of the House of Lords (*A and Others v Secretary of*

State for the Home Department [2004] UKHL 56, see section 6.7.4) which had declared that it was unlawful to detain terrorist suspects under the Anti-terrorism, Crime and Security Act 2001.

In respect of the Bill, as noted by Russell and Sciara, two particularly significant developments occurred due to the scrutiny in the House of Lords, as a result of which:

QUOTATION

'The final outcome was a compromise, whereby there was some judicial involvement in issuing all control orders, and the government promised to review the law within a year and bring in a more considered bill. Whilst not being written into the bill this was seen as a victory for its opponents.'

M Russell and M Sciara, *The House of Lords in 2005: A More Representative and Assertive Chamber?*
(The Constitution Unit, 2006), p 10.

More recently in the context of further terrorism legislation, the Lords defeated an attempt in the 2008 Counter-Terrorism Bill to extend the detention of terrorist suspects to 42 days. Although the government could have resorted to the Parliament Acts, this would, of course, have delayed the introduction of the legislation.

ACTIVITY

Self-test questions

What is the constitutional relationship between the House of Lords and the House of Commons? Do you think that the House of Lords should ever obstruct the wishes of the lower (elected) chamber?

The differences between the House of Commons and the House of Lords		
	House of Commons	**House of Lords**
Composition	• Exclusively elected with constituency responsibilities.	• Unelected – although there are, in a technical sense, 'elected' hereditary peers. • No constituents.
Type of Member	• Elected politicians. • Few independents.	• Appointed and hereditary politicians. • Sizeable element of independents.
Expertise	• Full-time politicians.	• A wide range of experience and expertise. • Life peers specifically appointed for their expertise and experience. • Retired law lords possess legal expertise. • Bishops can provide expertise on religious matters.
Payment	• Salaried.	• Unpaid except ministers and Bishops (but peers can claim expenses).
Size of Chamber	• Statutorily capped at 650 MPs	• No fixed cap.

continued overleaf

Legislative Procedure	• Committee stage taken in general (public Bill) committees. • Use of guillotine. • (Largely) party political/partisan atmosphere.	• Committee stage on the Floor of the House. • No guillotine. • To some extent a less partisan and polemic atmosphere.
Relations with the Government	• Responsible for both maintaining and removing the government (vote of no confidence).	• No direct responsibility for maintaining or removing a government.

Table 10.3

10.13 Reform

The 1997 Labour Party manifesto gave a commitment to reform the House of Lords by removing the hereditary peers and establishing a joint parliamentary committee to consider long-term reform. As indicated earlier (see section 10.6.3) the House of Lords Act 1999 removed all but 92 of the hereditary peers. In tandem with the introduction of the 1999 House of Lords Bill, the government issued a White Paper (*Modernising Parliament, Reforming the House of Lords* Cm 4183 (The Stationery Office 1999)). This set out the various options for long-term reform to be considered by a Royal Commission, and the government's proposals for an independent Appointments Commission to select non-party political peers (a power previously exercised by the Prime Minister). This Appointments Commission was established in 2000 (see section 10.5.4) and has been operational ever since.

In January 2000 the Royal Commission under Lord Wakeham issued its report on future reform of the upper chamber (*A House for the Future* Cm 4534 (The Stationery Office, 2000)). In short, it recommended a mixed House with a largely appointed membership with a minority of members (65, 87 or 195) being elected as regional members.

In 2001 the government issued another White Paper on Lords reform (*The House of Lords – Completing the Reform*, Cm 5291 (2001)). This paper reaffirmed the government's commitment to removing the remaining hereditary peers and in terms of composition proposed a House of 600 members:

▨ One fifth elected.
▨ One fifth independents.
▨ The remainder being nominated by political parties.
▨ The law lords and Bishops to remain.

This proposal proved unpopular and in 2002 in order to achieve parliamentary consensus on a reformed composition, a Joint Committee on House of Lords Reform was established. In 2003 both Houses voted on the different options put forward by the Committee:

▨ Wholly elected chamber.
▨ Wholly appointed.
▨ 80% appointed.
▨ 80% elected.
▨ 60% appointed.
▨ 60% elected.
▨ 50% appointed/50% elected.

The Commons did not approve any of the options, although they came closest (281 votes in favour to 284 against) to endorsing the option which proposed an 80 per cent elected House. The House of Lords, rather predictably, approved the fully appointed option. In addition to the above options, the House of Commons voted on, and rejected (by 390 to 172 votes), a further option of the abolition of the House of Lords thereby leading to a unicameral Parliament. For an analysis of these votes see: M Ryan, 'Parliament and the Joint Committee on House of Lords Reform' (2003) 37 Law Teacher 310.

In September 2003 the government issued a consultation paper (*Constitutional reform: next steps for the House of Lords* – CP 14/03 (DCA, 2003)) in which it stated that in the absence of consensus on composition it nevertheless proposed to:

- Remove the remaining hereditary peers.
- Place the Appointments Commission on a statutory basis.

In 2005 an all-party group of MPs published a paper in which it tried to show that party political consensus was possible and recommended a 70 per cent elected House (K Clarke, R Cook, P Tyler, T Wright and G Young, *Reforming the House of Lords: Breaking the deadlock* (Constitution Unit, 2005)). Thereafter, the 2005 Labour Party general election manifesto stated that it would:

- Remove the remaining hereditary peers.
- Legislate to place reasonable limits on the time the House of Lords could delay legislation.
- Seek agreement on codifying the conventions between the two Houses following a review.

In June 2006 a Cross-Party Working Group on Lords Reform, consisting of members from both Houses and the main political parties, began the first of a number of meetings to discuss the future of reform.

In the 2006 Queen's Speech the government stated that it would work towards cross-party consensus on Lords reform and remove the remaining hereditary peers and in February 2007 another White Paper was issued (*The House of Lords: Reform*, Cm 7027 (The Stationery Office, 2007)). For its part, the government in the White Paper suggested that the reformed House should be a partly elected/partly appointed chamber containing 540 members. Moreover, no political party should have a majority of party political members and at least 20 per cent of the chamber's membership should be made up of non-party political members. It also recommended retention of the spiritual element. In essence, the White Paper paved the way for the following debates and votes to take place in the House of Commons in March 2007:

- The retention of a bicameral Parliament (Yes 416 votes, No 163 votes).
- No 1 – wholly appointed chamber (Yes 196, No 375).
- No 2 – 20% elected/80% appointed no vote.
- No 3 – 40% elected/60% appointed no vote.
- No 4 – 50% elected/50% appointed (Yes 155, No 418).
- No 5 – 60% elected/40% appointed (Yes 178, No 392).
- No 6 – 80% elected/20% appointed (Yes 305, No 267).
- No 7 – wholly elected chamber (Yes 337, No 224).
- The removal of the remaining hereditary peers (Yes 391, No 111).

R Cracknell, 'Commons divisions on House of Lords Reform: March 2007', SN/SG/4279
(House of Commons Library, 2007), p 2.

The overall result, therefore, was that the Commons supported the principle of retaining a second chamber, removing the remaining hereditary peers and having an upper House which was either fully or overwhelming elected (the former having the support of a majority of 113 MPs and the latter 38). One week later, informed by the votes taken in the Commons, the House of Lords voted overwhelmingly in favour of (rather unsurprisingly) a fully appointed House by 361 votes to 121. The other options were rejected with the 50 per cent elected House being decisively dismissed by 409 votes to 46 (see *Hansard*, HL Vol 690, cols 741–759). On these votes, see M Ryan, 'A consensus on the reform of the House of Lords?', [2009] 60 NILQ 325.

In July 2008 the government issued a White Paper aimed at completing the reform of the House of Lords (*An Elected Second Chamber: Further reform of the House of Lords* Cm 7438 (2008)). Following the votes in the Commons in March 2007, the White Paper confined the reform of the House of Lords to two options only: an 80 per cent or 100 per cent elected House. The paper left open which electoral system should be used. On this paper, see M Ryan 'The house that Jack built', (2008) 158 NLJ 1197.

In July 2009 the government unveiled the Constitutional Reform and Governance Bill which proposed the following:

- To abolish hereditary by-elections.
- To enable members to be removed (eg those convicted of serious criminal offences).
- To provide for the House to make Standing Orders whereby a member could be expelled/suspended.
- To allow a peer to resign from the House.
- To allow a member to disclaim their life peerage.

However, all of the above elements were removed from the Bill before the measure became the Constitutional Reform and Governance Act 2010. Part 4 of this Act made provision for members of the House of Lords to be deemed resident and domiciled in the UK for tax purposes. Section 42 enabled peers unwilling to be subject to the above to leave the House.

SUMMARY

- The House of Lords is the upper chamber of Parliament.
- Most of its members are appointed life peers who are appointed for life.
- The House is unusual in containing the following categories of members:
    - Spiritual Lords – Bishops and Archbishops of the Church of England.
    - Judicial peers – retired law lords.
    - Hereditary peers – the rump of hereditary peers left after the major reforms of 1999.
- In terms of political composition no one political party controls the House. In addition, the chamber contains a significant number of crossbenchers.
- There are a number of factors which disqualify individuals from membership of the House (eg under 21 years of age).
- The functions of the House include:
    - Making laws as part of the legislature.
    - Investigating policy issues.
    - Providing a forum for debate.
    - A protector of the constitution.
    - Disciplining its own membership.
- Its legal powers mean that it can delay a public Bill for approximately one year.
- Its political powers constrain it further by requiring that, for example, government business is considered in a reasonable time.
- The House of Lords has been subject to reform in recent years and there continues to be a lively political debate as to how this reform should be completed.

SAMPLE ESSAY QUESTION

What function does the House of Lords serve and what is its importance to the British constitution?

Introduction:

House of Lords is the second chamber in the UK bicameral Parliament

This historic chamber (it predates the Commons) has proved controversial owing to its distinct membership (see below)

Membership:

Note the different categories of members:

Spiritual Lords – Bishops and Archbishops of the Church of England

Life peers – Appointed under the Life Peerages Act 1958

Hereditary peers – Now governed by the House of Lords Act 1999 (hereditary peers are a controversial element in a democratic chamber)

Judicial peers – Retired senior judges under the Appellate Jurisdiction Act 1876

Functions:

These blend with Parliament as a whole –

Part of the legislative process by introducing Bills and revising those brought from the Commons (also involved in examining delegated as well as European legislation)

Scrutinises the government (debates, questions and in the context of the above)

A guardian of the Constitution (including the Select Committee on the Constitution)

Powers:

Legal powers – regulated by the Parliament Acts 1911 and 1949

Political powers – regulated by constitutional convention (eg the Salisbury–Addison/Government Bill Convention)

Constitutional significance:

It disperses power within Parliament between two chambers

It acts as a check on the executive/House of Commons

It improves legislation

It provides expert opinions on a wide range of issues and is a debating chamber

It is a constitutional safeguard (eg s 33 of the Constitutional Reform Act 2005 requires the consent of the Lords to remove Supreme Court Justices)

CONCLUSION

Further reading

Books

Carroll, A, *Constitutional and Administrative Law* (5th edn, Pearson/Longman, 2009), Chapter 9.

Loveland, I, *Constitutional Law, Administrative Law, and Human Rights* (5th edn, Oxford University Press, 2009), Chapter 6.

Russell, M, and Sciara, M, *The House of Lords in 2005: A More Representative and Assertive Chamber?* (The Constitution Unit, 2006).

Articles

Lord Bingham, 'The House of Lords: its future?' [2010] PL 261.

Ryan, M 'A consensus on the reform of the House of Lords?' [2009] 60 NILQ 325.

Ryan, M 'The house that Jack built' (2008) 158 NLJ 1197.

Papers

House of Lords Select Committee on the Constitution, 7th Report of Session 2005–06, *Constitutional aspects of the challenge to the Hunting Act 2004*, HL Paper 141 (2006), Appendix 3.

House of Lords Briefing, *Work, Role, Function and Powers* (Parliamentary Copyright House of Lords, 2009).

Royal Commission on the Reform of the House of Lords, *A House for the Future*, Cm 4534 (The Stationery Office, 2000).

The Work of the House of Lords 2007–08 (Parliamentary Copyright House of Lords, 2009).

Internet links

www.parliament.uk

11

The executive

AIMS AND OBJECTIVES

At the end of this chapter you should be able to:

- Define the term executive
- Identify the different types of executive
- Explain the composition of the executive
- Identify the different functions of the executive
- Identify and explain the statutory and common law powers of the executive

11.1 Introduction and terminology

11.1.1 Definition of government

As indicated earlier (see section 5.3.2), the executive or governmental function is performed by 'Her Majesty's Government' or the administration. It is important to realise that the term 'government' can be used in the following senses:

- Firstly, government can be used in a very broad sense to indicate that an individual is being 'governed' (ie controlled and regulated) by the state and its whole apparatus including, for example, Parliament, the police, the armed forces and the courts.
- Secondly, government can be used in a much narrower sense to indicate government administration, namely, Her Majesty's Government – the government.
- Thirdly, government can be used to denote local government whereby local authorities deliver services (such as housing and libraries) at a local level.

It is with the second definition that we will be particularly concerned.

11.1.2 The constitutional monarchy and the Crown

The United Kingdom has a constitutional monarchy with an unelected, hereditary sovereign as its Head of State. Republican countries such as the United States and the Republic of Ireland have elected Presidents to act as Head of State. The Queen's role is to a large extent symbolic, comprising ceremonial and formal responsibilities (however, the monarch does have some important residual constitutional powers – see section 11.9.3).

In the British constitution the executive is known as Her Majesty's Government as in constitutional theory the monarch appoints and dismisses government ministers. In addition, civil servants are employed and dismissed by the Crown. Further, in terms of the executive in practice, in a technical sense, the Queen is the Commander in Chief of the armed forces.

At this point the term 'Crown' needs to be explained as in the British constitution it can be separated into two elements:

■ Firstly, the Crown can be used to signify the monarch herself (the Sovereign),
■ Secondly, the Crown can be used to refer to the government of the day or the administration.

In modern parlance, the Crown is typically used in the second sense in order to distinguish between the personal constitutional role of the monarch (who has a largely formal role) from her political government ministers (who make political and executive decisions). This distinction is important because we have a constitutional monarchy – the monarch and her constitutional role is constrained by the uncodified constitution. The reality is that although in strict law the Sovereign enjoys considerable historic constitutional and legal powers, in practice these are either:

■ regulated by constitutional convention, or
■ are exercised by the Queen's ministers acting on her behalf in the name of the Crown/ monarch.

Thus, in a modern democracy it would be considered undemocratic (not to say morally unconstitutional – see section 4.15) for a monarch to exercise personally those powers legally vested in her as her predecessors would have done centuries before (eg to declare war).

11.1.3 The different forms of executive

The term executive embraces a number of elements and refers to those who administer and execute the law. A general distinction can be drawn between the following types of executive (drawing upon the terminology used by Heywood, *Politics* (Macmillan, 1997), Ch 16):

■ The political executive (Her Majesty's Government – see section 11.2).
■ The non-political or bureaucratic executive (the Civil Service – see section 11.3).
■ The executive in practical terms (the armed forces and various police forces – see section 11.4).
■ Other executives (local authorities, the Scottish Executive/Government, the Northern Ireland Executive Committee, the Welsh Assembly Government, executive power in the European Union – see section 11.5).
■ Public authorities/bodies. This is a public law term which we will return to in the context of judicial review (see section 19.3), but for present purposes it essentially refers to a public body performing public functions. It would include, for example, the following:
  1. Government ministers.
  2. Central government departments.
  3. Executive agencies and quangos.
  4. Local authorities.
  5. Devolved institutions.

In addition, the term would also include non-governmental bodies which perform a public function (eg the Panel on Take-overs and Mergers – see section 19.3.3).

ACTIVITY

Quick quiz

What do the following terms mean?

- The Crown.
- The government.
- The executive.

11.2 The political executive/Her Majesty's Government

11.2.1 The monarch

The political executive is constitutionally Her Majesty's Government and ministers swear an oath of allegiance to the Crown. In practice, the monarch's role is largely formal (see also sections 8.3 and 11.1.2).

11.2.2 The Prime Minister

Although the monarch is the Head of State and titular head of the executive, the Prime Minister is the effective Head of Government (contrast this with the position in the United States where the elected President is both Head of State and Head of Government). The constitutional office of the Prime Minister has developed historically by constitutional convention (contrast most other Prime Ministers/Presidents who owe their creation to a codified constitutional document) and is the head of the Cabinet (*primus inter pares* – first among equals). By constitutional convention the Prime Minister must be drawn from the House of Commons (see section 4.13.4) so that he can be held directly accountable to the elected representatives of the people (MPs).

The Prime Minister has *inter alia* the following constitutional functions:

- To preside over Cabinet meetings (see section 11.2.3).
- To act as a conduit between the monarch and the government (in this way the Prime Minster can keep the monarch informed of ongoing political developments).
- To act as the Minister for the Civil Service (he also has the title of First Lord of the Treasury, although in practice the Chancellor of the Exchequer is the acting head of government finance).
- To determine certain appointments. For example, these include the appointment of government ministers as well as determining the number of non-party political peers to be appointed to the House of Lords (see section 10.5.4).
- To co-ordinate government policy.
- To request a dissolution of Parliament prior to a general election.
- To establish certain non-statutory bodies (eg the House of Lords Appointments Commission in 2000 – see section 10.5.4).
- To issue and revise the *Ministerial Code* (Cabinet Office, revised July 2007), which is given to ministers on assuming office and details their responsibilities and expected standard of conduct. It is of interest to note that if the United Kingdom were to adopt a codified constitution, the rules set out in this Code would inevitably form part of it.

Ministerial Code
a code of conduct issued by the Prime Minister which government ministers are required to follow

The Prime Minister is given advice by the Policy Unit and specialist advisers.

11.2.3 The Cabinet

This body, like that of the office of the Prime Minister, owes its existence to constitutional convention. In constitutional theory, the Cabinet is the most significant political decision-making body in the constitution. The Cabinet comprises the most senior ministers in the government (the head of each government department) who discuss, debate and collectively agree on government policy (eg in relation to prisons or pensions, etc). In this way, the British constitution is hallmarked by *Cabinet government* with collective decision-making on major state and policy issues being made by a number of senior government ministers. In recent decades, however, the dominance of the office and personality of the Prime Minister has prompted the question as to whether we have '*Prime Ministerial government*' instead, whereby the Prime Minister dominates and overshadows the Cabinet. After all, it is the Prime Minister who determines and co-ordinates Cabinet discussion, and 'sums up' Cabinet opinion by determining the Cabinet view on a matter.

Moreover, he determines who will be a minister and the government portfolio that they will hold (for example, consider the major Cabinet reshuffle in May 2006). Ultimately, however, the Prime Minister needs the support and confidence of his Cabinet in order to maintain his position. Margaret Thatcher lost the full support of her Cabinet (and party) at the end of her tenure as Prime Minister and resigned thereafter.

The Cabinet is supported by the Cabinet Office (a Department of State). In addition, the Cabinet Secretariat serves to ensure that Cabinet business is co-ordinated and efficient. It supports and serves both Cabinet ministers (chairing committees) as well as the Prime Minister.

The Cabinet is regulated by the following conventions:

- As a general rule it is composed of around 20 ministers – the exact size of the Cabinet will vary over time as, for example, government departments are not static and will merge with each other from time to time (as determined by the Prime Minister).
- Its discussions remain secret (see section 12.2.3).
- Decisions are made collectively and once a decision has been reached all members of the Cabinet (together with the junior ministers) are bound, publicly, to support and endorse this policy. This is known as the constitutional convention of collective responsibility. In this way the Cabinet, together with the rest of the government ministers, present a united front to Parliament and the public (see section 12.2.2).

The Cabinet is supplemented by a number of specialist sub-Cabinet meetings which comprise a number of ministers. According to para 6.4 of the July 2005 version of the *Ministerial Code* 'they relieve the pressure on the Cabinet itself by settling as much business as possible at a lower level' and also underpin the convention of collective responsibility by making sure that:

QUOTATION

'Even though an important question may never reach the Cabinet itself, the decision will be fully considered and the final judgment will be sufficiently authoritative to ensure that the Government as a whole can be properly expected to accept responsibility for it.'

Ministerial Code, A Code of Ethics and Procedural Guidance for Ministers (Cabinet Office, revised July 2005).

Ministerial Committees of the Cabinet are established by the Prime Minister and in 2010 they included, for example, committees on:

- The constitution.
- Democratic Renewal Council.
- Domestic Affairs.

According to Weir and Beetham:

QUOTATION

'The fact is that the cabinet is now the creature of its own cabinet committees. The cabinet committee structure is now the real "engine-house" of government policy-making and decision-making. It is there if anywhere, and not in Cabinet, that long-term strategies and policy changes, such as the poll tax, are developed.'

Political Power and Democratic Control in Britain (Routledge, 1999) p 128.

ACTIVITY

Self-test question

What is the constitutional difference between Cabinet government as opposed to Prime Ministerial government?

11.2.4 Junior ministers

The Cabinet comprises the most senior type of government ministers who head government departments (eg the Secretary of State). Most ministers, however, are junior ministers (Ministers of State or Parliamentary Under-Secretaries of State) and do not form part of the Cabinet, although they are still bound by the convention of collective responsibility.

It is important to note that Her Majesty's Government is supported by a number of parliamentary private secretaries who are not formally part of the government *per se*, but who are each attached to, and support, a particular minister. The 2007 *Ministerial Code* states that they: 'are expected to support the Government in important divisions in the House' (*Ministerial Code* (Cabinet Office, revised July 2007), para 3.8).

ACTIVITY

Exercise

What is the distinction between a Secretary of State and a junior minister? Find out some examples to illustrate this distinction.

11.2.5 Central government departments headed by a government minister

Central government comprises a number of departments of state, each with a separate and specialist policy responsibility. In February 2010 there were over 20 departments of state which included, for example:

■ The Department for Work and Pensions.
■ The Ministry of Justice.
■ The Foreign and Commonwealth Office.
■ HM Treasury.

Each department is headed by a senior government minister (typically a Secretary of State) who will be supported by a number of junior ministers. For example, in February 2010 the Home Office comprised the following ministerial hierarchy:

Ministerial hierarchy in the Home Office
Secretary of State for the Home Department
2 Ministers of State: • Minister of State (Borders and Immigration)   • Minister of State (Crime and Policing)
3 Parliamentary Under-Secretaries of State.

Table 11.1

Source: www.parliament.uk

As indicated above, government departments are not static institutions, and ministerial policy responsibilities are subject to change, as the Ministers of the Crown Act 1975 enables (in effect) the Prime Minister to:

■ Transfer policy responsibilities between ministers. In 2003 specified functions of the Lord Chancellor were transferred to the newly created post of Secretary of State for Constitutional Affairs – this was the case even though the same person held both offices – The Secretary of State for Constitutional Affairs Order 2003 (SI 2003 No 1887).
■ Dissolve a government department and transfer its responsibilities to another minister.

This is achieved through the passage of a (statutory) Order in Council under the aegis of the (above) 1975 Act.

Central government departments can also be sub-divided into the following two elements:

■ **The political element (the temporary government ministers)** – most of whom will be elected politicians, but some will be peers, who will determine the political direction of the department and the policies that it will administer.

■ **The non-political element (the permanent civil servants)** – who carry out and implement the policies as formulated by their government ministers (see section 11.3). It should be noted that, since the 1990s, aspects of government departments have been separated and reconstituted as 'Next Step Agencies', and these are considered at section 11.3.2.

ACTIVITY

Exercise

Explain the different aspects of a central government department. Identify one government department and explain what it does.

11.2.6 The Privy Council

The Privy Council was the precursor to the modern Cabinet and today the Council's executive responsibilities have been eclipsed by it. It does, however, enable the government of the day to pass Orders in Council.

KEY FACTS

Key facts on the political executive

The political executive is also known as Her Majesty's Government and consists of the following:

• The monarch, who is the titular Head of HM Government. In practice, the monarch's role is largely formal.

• The Prime Minister is the practical Head of Government and of the Cabinet.

• The Cabinet is composed of Cabinet ministers who are senior government ministers who each head a particular government department of state. In theory it is the most important decision-making body in the constitution.

• Junior ministers (eg Ministers of State or Parliamentary Under-Secretaries of State) sit outside the Cabinet.

• Government departments each have a separate and specialist policy responsibility and are typically headed by a Secretary of State. They are staffed by politically impartial civil servants who carry out and implement the policies as formulated by their government minister – see section 11.3.1 below.

11.3 The non-political or bureaucratic executive

11.3.1 The Civil Service

The *Civil Service Code* (as amended in 2006) states that:

QUOTATION

'1. The Civil Service is an integral and key part of the government of the United Kingdom. It supports the Government of the day in developing and implementing its policies, and in delivering public services. Civil servants are accountable to Ministers, who in turn are accountable to Parliament.

2. As a civil servant, you are appointed on merit on the basis of fair and open competition … and are expected to carry out your role with dedication and a commitment to the Civil Service and its core values: integrity, honesty, objectivity and impartiality.'

Source: www.civilservice.gov.uk.

NB At the time of going to print, the Constitutional Reform and Governance Act 2010 has been passed, s 5 of which requires the Minister for the Civil Service to publish a Code of Conduct for the Civil Service.

Civil servants can be broadly divided into two distinct groups:

■ **Senior civil servants** – They have been described as 'Whitehall mandarins' (see Weir and Beetham below) with the most senior civil servant in a department being the Permanent Secretary (not to be confused with political parliamentary private secretaries – see section 11.2.4). Senior civil servants provide information to their respective government minister (their political master) and offer expert advice on policy matters. Civil servants do not control public policy – that is the responsibility of government ministers who are constitutionally accountable to Parliament. Civil servants account directly to their ministerial head and not to Parliament. Instead, it is the minister (as the public face and head of the department) who accounts to Parliament for the actions and policies of his department and officials (this is by virtue of the constitutional convention of individual ministerial responsibility – see para 1.2 of the *Ministerial Code*). It should be remembered that it is the case that the courts have sanctioned the practice whereby appropriately qualified civil servants can make decisions on behalf of their ministers (see sections 4.13.12 and 20.2.3).

In terms of determining policy, however, the dividing line between the senior graded civil servants and ministers is a fine one, as the latter necessarily make their policy judgments based (largely) on the information and advice provided by the former. Moreover, it should be pointed out that newly appointed Secretaries of State will inevitably lack experience and knowledge of the area of administration that they have been assigned. This is in contrast to the permanent, professional and seasoned senior civil servant. In this way, although it is a partnership between the minister and civil servant, it is inevitable that the former will be heavily reliant on the advice and information provided by the latter. It should also be remembered that in addition to their ministerial duties, most government ministers are also elected MPs and will have constituency matters to attend to.

According to Weir and Beetham, the dynamics of the relationship between minister and civil servant is that:

QUOTATION

'It is the officials who draft the papers ministers see, who filter the information they receive, who define many of the problems, who suggest most of the solutions, who draft the legislation and who ultimately take the great majority of decisions.'

S Weir and D Beetham, *Political Power and Democratic Control in Britain* (Routledge, 1999), p 170.

Senior civil servants must be distinguished from 'special advisers'. In addition to the advice proffered by senior civil servants, ministers may also be given advice by appointed special advisers who are technically temporary civil servants, but who provide advice on a partisan and political basis. In this way they can provide a useful counterpoint to the advice of the senior civil servants. They are appointed by Cabinet ministers, having been sanctioned by the Prime Minister, and are governed by a code of conduct (*Code of Conduct for Special Advisers*). The Constitutional Reform and Governance Act 2010 requires the Minister for the Civil Service to publish a Code of Conduct for Special Advisors. According to para 3.3 of the *Ministerial Code*, ministers are responsible for the conduct of their special adviser. The number of special advisers has grown in the past decade from 38 in 1995/96 to 78 in 2005/06 (O Gay and P Fawcett, 'Special Advisers' (House of Commons Library, 2005), p 8).

■ **Lower-ranking civil servants** (the vast majority of the Civil Service) who implement government policy and administration on a daily basis.

The constitutional characteristics of the Civil Service

Civil servants, historically, have been hallmarked by the following principles:

■ **Permanence** – In the British constitution government ministers are temporary, whereas civil servants are permanent appointments. This means that a change in government after a general election does not result in a change in the composition of the Civil Service. Civil servants will serve and owe allegiance to the government of the day irrespective of its political colour.

■ **Impartiality** – Civil servants are politically impartial in the sense that they must serve all governments equally well (Civil Service Code, para 2 – now see s 7 of the Constitutional Reform and Governance Act 2010). This means that whatever their own personal political beliefs, civil servants must serve a government irrespective of its political persuasion (para 13). In addition, in terms of objectivity, para 10 states that civil servants must not 'frustrate the implementation of policies once decisions are taken by declining to take, or abstaining from, action which flows from those decisions' (now see s 7 of the Constitutional Reform and Governance Act 2010). Moreover, s 1(1)(b) of the House of Commons Disqualification Act 1975 bars civil servants from becoming MPs. Furthermore, in light of their responsibilities to provide advice etc, the senior grades of the profession are barred from political activity at a national level. There are two categories below this politically restricted category: those who may engage in national and local political activity with permission and those in the lowest category who are free to be involved in such activities.

In terms of integrity, civil servants must not disclose official information without the requisite authorisation (*Civil Service Code*, para 6 – s 7 of the 2010 Act also makes reference to integrity). In the 1980s a senior civil servant disclosed to an opposition MP information pertaining to the sinking of the Argentine ship the *General Belgrano*. He was subsequently prosecuted under the Official Secrets Act 1911, although at his trial he was acquitted by the jury (*R v Ponting* [1985] Crim LR 318).

Civil servants' appointments have been historically overseen by the Civil Service Commissioners and are selected on merit. Finally, it is pertinent to point out that the *Ministerial Code* imposes a duty on ministers to uphold the political impartiality of the Civil Service (*Ministerial Code*, para 5.1).

■ **Anonymity** – As indicated above, government ministers must account to Parliament for the performance and actions of their department, thereby taking constitutional responsibility for their departmental civil servants. In this way the head of the government department (together with his junior ministers) represents the public face of the department with his permanent civil servants remaining anonymous. This in turn allows civil servants to give advice in confidence and enables them to serve successive different governments. The principle of anonymity has, however, been partly eroded by the fact that civil servants can appear before select committees to represent their minister (having been appropriately briefed in accordance with the 'Osmotherly Rules' – see section 12.6.5).

The management of the Civil Service

The minister responsible for the Civil Service (ie Minister for the Civil Service) is the Prime Minister and the employment terms and conditions of civil servants have been historically regulated by Orders in Council (legislation made under the royal prerogative – see *GCHQ* (1985) at section 11.9.6). In recent years, however, there has been a call for a Civil Service Act to be enacted which would regulate civil servants on a statutory basis. In 2008 the government produced the Draft Constitutional Renewal Bill (Cm 7342-II) which proposed to place the Civil Service on a statutory footing. This was followed by the Constitutional Reform and Governance Act 2010 which provides for:

■ a statutory basis for the Minister for the Civil Service to manage the Civil Service

■ the creation of a statutory Civil Service Commission. The Commission has a role in relation to the selection of civil servant appointments and in dealing with conduct that breaches the Civil Service Code of Conduct

- a requirement that the Minister publish a Civil Service Code of Conduct (which incorporates the core values of the Civil Service) as well as a code for special advisers
- the setting out in statute that selections to the Civil Service 'must be on merit on the basis of fair and open competition'.

ACTIVITY

Self-test question

What do civil servants do? What is their constitutional significance?

11.3.2 Executive agencies/the 'Next Step Agencies'

It is important to note that today the vast majority of civil servants work not in central government departments *per se*, but in executive agencies. The 'Next Step Agencies' (so called because they were named after a Cabinet paper: *Improving Management in Government: the Next Steps* (Cabinet Office, February 1988)) were established in the 1990s in an attempt to make government administration more efficient. In essence, this meant that certain aspects of a government department were separated and reconstituted under a specified agency headed by a Chief Executive. The objectives to be obtained by the agency (thereby in theory ensuring administrative efficiency) would be determined by the relevant government minister. Two examples of executive agencies in 2009 will suffice:

- The HM Prison Service (with a Director-General) under the aegis of the Ministry of Justice – this agency is concerned with keeping in custody those sentenced by the courts.
- The Driving Standards Agency (with a Chief Executive) under the aegis of the Department for Transport – this agency is responsible for promoting road safety by improving driving standards, which includes the testing of putative drivers.

The Tribunals Service is an executive agency under the umbrella of the Ministry of Justice (see section 21.1.6).

The parent government departmental minister remains constitutionally responsible for these *hived off* agencies (*Ministerial Code*, para 1.2). There has nevertheless been some constitutional disquiet as to whether ministers in practice take political responsibility for the operation of them (they are, of course, each headed by a Chief Executive who is a specified office holder), leading to a gap in constitutional accountability. For example, in the mid-1990s when prisoners escaped from Parkhurst Prison, the Home Secretary argued that there was a distinction between operational responsibility (ie being responsible for the day-to-day security of prisons) and the responsibility for overall general policy. The escapees were considered an operational matter and subsequently the Home Secretary announced that the Director-General (Chief Executive) of the Prison Service Agency had left his office.

It is pertinent to mention, in the context of the drive for efficiency in government, that the development of the *Citzens' Charter* in the 1990s was designed to specify standards in administration.

11.3.3 Non-departmental public bodies

In respect of 'national government' there exists a considerable number of non-departmental public bodies (NDPB), also variously called *Quangos* (quasi-autonomous non-governmental organisations). The Cabinet Office described them as follows:

QUOTATION

'An NDPB is defined as a "body which has a role in the process of national Government, but is not a Government Department or part of one, and which accordingly operates to a greater or lesser extent at arm's length from Ministers".'

Public bodies 2008. Making government work better, (Cabinet Office, 2008), p 3.

For example, in 2008 the Parole Board was an Executive NDPB under the sponsorship of the Ministry of Justice.

KEY FACTS

The non-political or bureaucratic executive
(1) The Civil Service, which can be broadly divided into two distinct groups: • Senior civil servants who provide information to their respective government minister and offer expert advice on policy matters. • Lower-ranking civil servants who simply implement government policy and administration. Civil servants account directly to their ministerial head and not to Parliament. The Civil Service is characterised by the following principles: • Impartiality and permanence – civil servants will serve and owe allegiance to the government of the day irrespective of its political colour. • Anonymity – as the departmental ministerial head represents the public face of the department, the permanent civil servants remain anonymous. (2) Executive agencies are aspects of a government department which, in order to promote efficiency, have been separated and reconstituted under a specified agency headed by a Chief Executive (eg the Driving Standards Agency). (3) Non-departmental public bodies (eg the Parole Board).

11.4 The executive in practical terms

Both the armed forces and the various police forces (one for each area of the country) form part of the executive in a very general and practical sense. The police, for example, practically enforce the criminal law against those individuals who, *prima facie*, violate it. In short, they carry out and implement the law on a practical basis. They are barred from membership of the House of Commons (see section 11.6.3).

11.5 Other executive bodies in the British constitution

There are other executive bodies in the British constitution:

Local authorities

From a constitutional perspective, local authorities, technically, form part of the executive. Local councillors are elected by local residents and the political composition of local authorities will, in various parts of the country, be different to that of central government. Local authorities possess both legislative and executive powers (see section 14.2).

Devolution

As part of the devolved settlements, the following executives were established:

- **Scotland** – s 44 of the Scotland Act 1998 established a Scottish Executive/Government (in effect, a Cabinet drawn from the Scottish Parliament). This section further provides that an individual cannot hold national ministerial office at Whitehall while being a member of the Scottish Executive.
- **Northern Ireland** – Pt III of the Northern Ireland Act 1998 provided for the establishment of an Executive Committee (analogous to the Scottish Executive).
- **Wales** – s 45 of the Government of Wales Act 2006 established a Welsh Assembly Government.

On all of the above executives see Chapter 14.

The European Union

Although there is no clear separation of powers between the European institutions, historically the European Commission has been regarded as the executive and the Civil

Service of Europe. However, both the Council and the European Council also perform executive functions by making executive decisions (see section 15.2.2).

11.6 The statistical breakdown of government ministers

11.6.1 The parliamentary executive

As the United Kingdom has a parliamentary executive system of government, government ministers are necessarily drawn from Parliament. The parliamentary executive in February 2010 can be illustrated by the following figure:

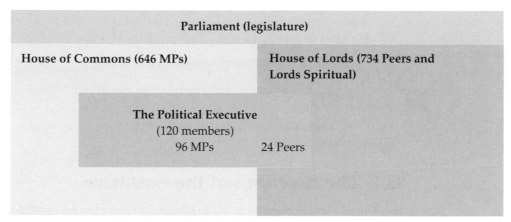

Source: www.parliament.uk

Figure 11.1 The parliamentary executive in February 2010

In terms of the statistical breakdown of the government in February 2010, of these 120 members, 23 were Cabinet ministers (including 3 peers), 33 were Ministers of State (including 4 peers) and 3 were law officers (2 of whom were peers). The remaining members of the government comprised Under Secretaries of State, parliamentary secretaries and government whips. (Source: figures extrapolated from www.parliament.uk.)

It is of interest to point out that in February 2010 almost one third of the government was female (36 out of 120) which included 4 female Cabinet ministers (out of 23). The United Kingdom Cabinet is smaller than in either Canada (36) or Australia (30), but larger than Ireland (15) (S King, *Regulating the Behaviour of Ministers, Special Advisers and Civil Servants* (The Constitution Unit, 2003), p 10). In addition, it should be pointed out that no more than 20 Cabinet salaries, other than the Prime Minister and Lord Chancellor, are payable (Ministerial and other Salaries Act 1975 as amended). In 2010 a report examined the number of ministers in modern government: House of Commons Public Administration Select Committee, *Too Many Ministers?* Ninth Report of Session 2009–10, HC 457 (The Stationary Office, 2010).

11.6.2 Government ministers in the House of Lords

As is clear from the figure above, the vast majority of ministers are MPs; however, a substantial minority (approximately one fifth) are peers in the House of Lords. In fact, historically, the majority of Cabinet members in the nineteenth century were peers. Although in some countries ministers cannot form part of the upper chamber, the advantages of it are that:

■ It ensures that the government has some representation in the upper House.
■ The upper House has the opportunity to scrutinise directly some government ministers.
■ Government ministers can pilot Bills through the upper House.

11.6.3 The executive and the separation of powers

The House of Commons Disqualification Act 1975 ensures that there is a degree of constitutional separation between certain elements of the executive and the House of Commons.

- Firstly, s 2(1) stipulates that no more than 95 persons can hold ministerial office in the House of Commons at any one time.
- Secondly, s 1 disqualifies the following members of the executive from membership of the House of Commons:

SECTION

s 1(1)(b) – those employed in the Civil Service
(c) – members of the regular armed forces
(d) – members of any police force.

ACTIVITY

Problem solving

Explain the statistical breakdown of the parliamentary executive. What is the constitutional significance of such data?

11.7 The functions of the executive

The constitutional functions of the executive comprise the following:

- **To formulate domestic public policy.** In short, the constitutional function of the government is to govern the state. The essence of Cabinet government is that a group of senior ministers collectively debate, determine and co-ordinate policies (for example how to address the issues of youth crime or pensions). These policies would thereafter be publicly supported by the government as a whole both in, and outside, Parliament.
- **To formulate and implement foreign policy.** This would include the deployment of troops overseas and responding to an international crisis.
- **To initiate legislative proposals.** Although Parliament is the legislature, it is the government of the day which drafts and introduces most Bills which are laid before Parliament to approve. Government ministers will have the constitutional responsibility to pilot these Bills through Parliament. These Bills will invariably embody certain government policy aims. For example:
  - (a) The Terrorism Act 2006 (s 1 made it a criminal offence to encourage acts of terrorism).
  - (b) The Identity Cards Act 2006 (provided the framework for a National Identity Register for the registration of individuals and the issue of identity cards).
- **To implement the law (and policy).** The executive 'executes' and carries out the law. Civil servants will implement the laws in relation to their respective government department. As illustrated in the *Carltona* case (1943) (see section 4.13.12), some senior civil servants will exercise legal powers on behalf of their minister thereby acting as their *alter ego*. The United Kingdom executive, therefore, can both initiate and execute the law. In practical terms, the implementation and enforcement of the law is performed by the police and in emergencies, by the armed forces (thereby ensuring public order).
- **To provide political leadership.** This is performed by the government as a whole, but in recent years has typically focused on the Prime Minister (for example, in the context of summits of the European Council – see section 15.2.1).
- **To make appointments.** For example, the Lord Chancellor will (ultimately) determine the appointments in respect of a range of judicial posts.

NB The recently passed Fiscal Responsibility Act 2010 imposes duties on the Treasury to secure sound public finances.

Essay writing

Consider the different functions of the executive. Are some more important than others?

11.8 The powers of the executive

In order to perform its responsibilities, the executive enjoys both statutory and common law powers.

11.8.1 Statutory powers

Most powers which government exercises are statutory. For example, an Act may:

Confer a power on a minister to pass delegated legislation in order to achieve specified aims:

■ Section 47(1) of the Prison Act 1952 empowers the Secretary of State to make rules in order to regulate and manage prisons (see *ex parte Leech* (1993) at section 20.2.2).

In addition, local authorities can pass delegated legislation in the form of by-laws in order to regulate local matters (eg local parks, or the banning of the consumption of alcohol in specified areas).

Confer a power on a minister to achieve specified purposes:

■ Section 1 of the Inquiries Act 2005 empowers a minister to establish a statutory inquiry (see section 21.2.3).
■ Section 2 of the Prevention of Terrorism Act 2005 empowers a minister to make a control order in respect of a person who is suspected of being involved in terrorism-related activity. A control order may, for example, restrict their movements within the United Kingdom.

Confer a power on a minister to determine when primary legislative provisions should be brought into force:

■ Section 148(4) of the Constitutional Reform Act 2005 authorised the Lord Chancellor to bring into operation the new Supreme Court (see the Constitutional Reform Act 2005 (Commencement No 11) Order 2009 which brought the new Supreme Court into effect in October 2009).
■ Section 171 of the Criminal Justice Act 1988 gave the Home Secretary a power to decide when to bring the statutory Criminal Injuries Compensation Scheme into effect (*R v Secretary of State for the Home Department, ex parte Fire Brigades Union* [1995] 2 All ER 244 at section 6.7.10).

Confer a power on a minister to pass delegated legislation which has the effect of amending primary legislation (known as an Henry VIII clause):

■ Section 10 of the Human Rights Act 1998 authorises ministers to pass remedial orders in order to render a provision of primary legislation compatible with the European Convention (see section 17.7.3).
■ Section 2 of the European Communities Act 1972 empowers a minister to transpose a European directive into domestic law through secondary legislation.

Impose a duty to achieve a specified purpose:

■ Section 7 of the Public Libraries and Museums Act 1964 imposes a statutory duty on all library authorities (in effect local authorities) to provide a comprehensive and efficient library service (see *ex parte Times Newspapers Ltd* (1986) at section 20.2.4).

Key facts on HM Government's statutory powers

HM Government possesses a number of statutory powers to do the following:

- To pass delegated legislation in order to achieve specified aims (eg s 47 of the Prison Act 1952).
- To achieve specified purposes (eg s 1 of the Inquiries Act 2005).
- To determine when primary legislative provisions should be brought into force (eg s 171 of the Criminal Justice Act 1988).
- To pass delegated legislation which has the effect of amending primary legislation (eg s 10 of the Human Rights Act 1998).

11.8.2 Common law powers

In addition to statute, government also draws powers from the common law:

- **A residual power to act** – There is a conception that public authorities enjoy a residual freedom to act as evidenced by *Malone v Metropolitan Police Commissioner* (1979) (see section 6.7.7) whereby Sir Robert Megarry VC made it clear that: 'England ... is a country where everything is permitted except what is expressly forbidden'. As a result, Malone's telephone line could be tapped because there was no 'positive' law to forbid it (although now see the Human Rights Act 1998 – Chapter 17). According to Le Sueur, however, this residual freedom of action would not apply to public authorities established by statute (eg local authorities) whose specific powers would be stipulated in legislation ('The Nature, Powers and Accountability of Central Government' in D Feldman (ed), *English Public Law* (2nd edn, Oxford University Press, 2009), p 187).
- **The royal prerogative** – (see directly below) this is an invaluable power which the government derives from the common law. A number of prerogative powers were abolished as part of the constitutional settlement which led to the Bill of Rights 1689, but a number still remain today.

11.9 The royal prerogative

11.9.1 Definition

QUOTATION

'A distinguishing feature of the British constitution is the extent to which government continues to exercise a number of powers which were not granted to it by a written constitution, nor by Parliament, but are, rather, ancient prerogatives of the Crown.'

The Governance of Britain, Cm 7170 (2007), p 16.

In its evidence to the House of Commons Public Administration Select Committee, the Treasury Solicitor's Department provided the following definition of the royal prerogative:

QUOTATION

'There is no single accepted definition of the prerogative. It is sometimes defined to mean all the common law, ie non-statutory powers, of the Crown. An alternative definition is that the prerogative consists of those common law powers and immunities which are peculiar to the Crown and go beyond the powers of a private individual eg the power to declare war as opposed to the normal common law power to enter a contract ... Whichever definition is used there is no exhaustive list of prerogative powers.'

Fourth Report of Session 2003–04, *Taming the Prerogative: Strengthening Ministerial Accountability to Parliament*, HC 422 (2004), Ev 13.

What is clear is that royal prerogative powers, historically, were exercised by successive monarchs over the centuries, but today with a constitutional monarchy those powers have in effect passed in practice to the government of the day (the vast majority of which will have been elected, although some ministers do sit in the House of Lords). Indeed, it would be considered (with some exceptions) undemocratic for an hereditary and unelected monarch to exercise personally the executive powers listed below.

11.9.2 The context of recent reform proposals

■ **The 2007 Green Paper** (*The Governance of Britain*, Cm 7170 (2007)) – in the context of limiting executive powers the government argued: '… in general the prerogative powers should be put onto a statutory basis and brought under stronger parliamentary scrutiny and control' (para 24). In addition, the government proposed specified reforms (eg to the Civil Service) and 'to undertake a wider review of the remaining prerogative, executive powers' (see section 11.9.4). The Green Paper resulted in a number of consultation exercises.

■ **The 2008 White Paper** (*The Governance of Britain – Constitutional Renewal*, Cm 7342–I (Crown Copyright, 2008)) – which set out the government's proposals for constitutional reform on, among other things, Treaties and war powers. The paper was published in conjunction with the following Bill (below).

■ **The 2008 Draft Constitutional Renewal Bill** (*The Governance of Britain – Draft Constitutional Renewal Bill*, Cm 7342–II (Crown Copyright, 2008)) – this Bill set out proposed legislative reforms on, among other things, the Civil Service and Treaties.

■ **The 2009 review of prerogative powers by the government** (see section 11.9.4).

11.9.3 The Public Administration Select Committee classification

The House of Commons Public Administration Select Committee (see 11.9.1) divided the royal prerogative powers into three broad types:

■ 'The Queen's constitutional prerogatives' (para 5).
■ 'The legal prerogatives of the Crown' (para 7).
■ 'Prerogative executive powers' (para 8). *concerned with*

In addition it is also possible to divide broadly, the prerogative powers between:

■ Those powers in the domestic sphere (eg the dissolution of Parliament, Royal Assent, mercy, etc)
■ Those powers relating to foreign affairs (eg ratifying Treaties, declaring war, deploying armed forces abroad, etc).

The Queen's constitutional prerogatives

The Public Administration Select Committee described these as 'the personal discretionary powers which remain in the Sovereign's hands' and would include the following:

To dissolve Parliament – Parliament must be dissolved prior to a general election and as we do not have fixed-term Parliaments, the Prime Minister of the day decides when to request a dissolution (see section 8.1.1). The dissolution is a prerogative act technically performed by the monarch, but by constitutional convention she will accede to such a request, thereby acting on the advice of her Prime Minister. The 2007 Green Paper (see above) argued that the Prime Minister should seek the approval of the House of Commons *before* asking for a dissolution. At the time of writing, the Select Committee on Modernisation of the House of Commons was undertaking an examination of the role of the Commons in the context of a decision to recall the House or to dissolve Parliament.

To appoint the Prime Minister – Although under the prerogative it is the monarch who formally appoints the Prime Minister, the practical reality is that following constitutional convention, she will appoint the party leader that has secured the majority of seats in the House of Commons (in other words, he who commands the support of the House). Problems could occur, however, following a general election when no one party has an overall majority of seats in a 'hung Parliament'.

NB At the time of going to print, the 2010 general election had resulted in a hung Parliament which in turn led to a Conservative–Liberal Democratic government.

To appoint government ministers – Although the monarch formally appoints government ministers (it is Her Majesty's Government), by constitutional convention she will act on the advice of her Prime Minister who will determine these appointments (eg after a reshuffle in the Cabinet).

To grant the Royal Assent – By constitutional convention the monarch will act on the advice of her ministers and grant Royal Assent to Bills. Such consent has not been refused for three centuries. In modern times the granting of the Royal Assent has not proved controversial.

The right to encourage, warn and advise her government ministers – Bagehot, writing in the nineteenth century, noted that a monarch had the constitutional right to encourage and warn her government ministers (by giving her opinion) as well as to be consulted by them, for example prior to the Budget (W Bagehot, *The English Constitution*, (Oxford University Press, 2001), p 64). Indeed, the current monarch has considerable experience, particularly in relation to the Commonwealth, as she has been Sovereign for over 50 years and has formally appointed a number of different Prime Ministers and numerous ministers over this time.

As noted by the Select Committee, although in normal circumstances the monarch would act on the advice of her ministers in terms of how these powers should be exercised, she also has the power: '(in grave constitutional crisis) to act contrary to or without Ministerial advice' (para 5).

ACTIVITY

Problem solving

Do you think that it would be the monarch's constitutional duty to refuse to grant the Royal Assent (ignoring the advice of her ministers) to the (imaginary) 2013 Abolition of Elections Bill which proposed to abolish parliamentary elections for 30 years? (On acting constitutionally and unconstitutionally – see section 4.15).

The legal prerogatives of the Crown

As noted by the Select Committee these include, for example:

- '... the principle that the Crown (or the state) can do no wrong' – the monarch cannot be sued in her own courts (she is, of course, the font of all justice as implemented by Her Majesty's judges).
- The Crown is only bound by Acts of Parliament through the use of express words or by necessary implication. For example, s 50 of the Inquiries Act 2005 states that the provisions of the Act bind the Crown.

ACTIVITY

Exercise

Compare and contrast the Queen's constitutional prerogatives with the legal prerogatives of the Crown.

Prerogative executive powers

The Select Committee suggested that the third type of prerogative power should be described as 'ministerial executive' power, as in practice it is government ministers who exercise these powers in the name of the Crown (as detailed below).

Government ministers' main powers

The Select Committee identified the main 'royal prerogative, or ministerial executive, powers exercised by ministers' to be as follows:

- **A declaration of war** – The decision to go to war is taken not by Parliament but by the government of the day (in effect, the Prime Minister) purporting to do so in the name of the Crown. In contrast, in the United States, Art 1, s 8 of the constitution states that it is Congress which declares war. In 2005 Clare Short MP introduced (albeit ultimately unsuccessfully) a Private Members' Bill: the Armed Forces (Parliamentary Approval for Participation in Armed Conflict) Bill, clause 7 of which would have required that no declaration of war on behalf of the United Kingdom should be made unless the proposal had been laid before each House of Parliament and approved by them.

- **The deployment and use of UK armed forces abroad** – Although the monarch is the titular Commander-in-Chief of the armed forces, as with the declaration of war, it is the government which in effect determines the disposition of troops overseas. In 2003 the Prime Minister allowed a vote in Parliament before the transfer of troops to Iraq, and this has in turn led to the question as to whether this is now a constitutional convention which must be followed in the future. It is clear that acting under the prerogative, the Prime Minister could have ignored an adverse parliamentary vote in 2003; however, this would no doubt have raised the issue of whether such conduct would have been construed as *morally* unconstitutional (see section 4.15).

Clare Short's 2005 Armed Forces Bill (noted directly above) also proposed that parliamentary approval would be required for Her Majesty's armed forces to participate in armed conflict. In support of her Bill, she argued that the rationale behind it was that:

- It was democratically appropriate that Parliament should approve a declaration of war and the deployment of troops in an armed conflict.

- It would help to ensure that such decisions were more effectively scrutinised and informed (*Hansard*, HC Vol 437, cols 1085–90).

Similarly, clause 3 of Lord Lester's 2006 Constitutional Reform (Prerogative Powers and Civil Service etc) Bill would have enabled Parliament to approve the commitment of the armed forces to armed conflict or war. Although neither Bill became law, in 2006 the House of Lords Select Committee on the Constitution issued a report on its review of the government's powers in this context and it concluded that:

QUOTATION

'The exercise of the Royal Prerogative by the Government to deploy armed force overseas is outdated and should not be allowed to continue as the basis for legitimate war-making in our 21st century democracy. Parliament's ability to challenge the executive must be protected and strengthened.'

House of Lords Select Committee on the Constitution, 15th Report of Session 2005–06
Waging war: Parliament's role and responsibility, HL Paper 236-I (2006), para 103.

It recommended that a constitutional convention should be developed which would require the government to seek parliamentary approval (except in emergency situations) prior to the deployment of troops in an armed conflict outside the United Kingdom.

In December 2006 another Private Members' Bill on this issue was published: Waging War (Parliament's Role and Responsibility) Bill. The Bill was sponsored by Michael Meacher MP and would have required the Secretary of State to lay before the House of Commons a mechanism to obtain the approval of the Commons for the deployment of

British troops for armed conflict. The then government's 2007 Green Paper (see section 11.9.2) argued that the power of the government under the prerogative to deploy the armed forces for conflict overseas in the absence of any formal parliamentary agreement was 'an outdated state of affairs in a modern democracy' (para 26). The subsequent 2008 White Paper *Constitutional Renewal* (see section 11.9.2) proposed that the best way forward was for the creation of a House of Commons resolution which would set out the parliamentary process which should be followed in order to approve the commitment of the armed forces to an armed conflict.

■ **The deployment of the armed forces domestically** – As noted by the Select Committee this could involve maintaining the peace of the realm (an executive function) by supporting the police.

■ **The ratification of international treaties** – Treaties are typically signed by the Secretary of State for Foreign and Commonwealth Affairs or sometimes by the Prime Minister. Historically, there has been a constitutional convention (the 'Ponsonby rule') whereby the government lays the Treaty before Parliament for at least 21 days before ratification, thereby enabling Parliament to be informed and for the content of the Treaty to be scrutinised. At the time of going to print, the Constitutional Reform and Governance Act 2010 has been passed, Part 2 of which placed the scrutiny of Treaties by Parliament on a statutory footing. In essence, s 20 provides that Treaties should be laid before Parliament before ratification and if the Commons resolved that a Treaty should not be ratified, the government could *not* proceed to ratify it. Section 22 provides for s 20 not to apply in exceptional cases.

Historically, the act of treaty-making is a function of the executive and is not susceptible to review by the courts:

JUDGMENT

'The treaty-making power of this country rests not in the courts, but in the Crown; that is, Her Majesty acting on the advice of her Ministers. When her Ministers negotiate and sign a treaty … they act on behalf of the country as a whole. They exercise the prerogative of the Crown. Their action in so doing cannot be challenged or questioned in these courts.'

Lord Denning MR in *Blackburn v Attorney General* [1971] 2 All ER 1380.

Similarly, the court dismissed Lord Rees-Mogg's judicial review application regarding the Secretary of State for Foreign and Commonwealth Affairs' decision to ratify the Maastricht Treaty (*R v Secretary of State for Foreign and Commonwealth Affairs, ex parte Rees-Mogg* [1994] QB 552).

■ **The issuing and revocation of passports** – this is determined by a government minister and has important constitutional implications as it affects an individual's freedom of movement. It is subject to legal supervision by the court:

CASE EXAMPLE

R v Secretary of State for Foreign and Commonwealth Affairs, ex parte Everett [1989] 1 QB 811

Everett, a British citizen in Spain, sought a new passport, but was refused one in pursuance of the Secretary of State's policy that passports were not issued where a warrant for arrest in the United Kingdom had been issued (Everett had not been given details of the warrant for his arrest). He sought judicial review of this refusal.

The Court of Appeal held that the judicial review of powers under the royal prerogative depended upon its subject-matter. A decision in relation to whether or not a passport should be issued was an administrative one which affected the rights of an individual and was unlikely to have implications for foreign policy and so was reviewable by the courts. On the facts, however, Everett had suffered no injustice or prejudice (he had been given before the court hearing the information which should have been provided, eg the details of the warrant) and there was no suggestion that there were any special circumstances to justify an exception to the policy to issue him a passport.

In its 2009 review of prerogative powers (see section 11.9.4), the government indicated that in due course it would introduce legislation in respect of the procedure for issuing passports.

■ **The granting of pardons (the royal prerogative of mercy)** – This involves the Crown pardoning criminals or reducing their criminal sentences. The Home Secretary advised the monarch historically, but today it is the Secretary of State for Justice that does so. The exercise of this power is, to some extent, subject to review by the courts:

CASE EXAMPLE

R v Secretary of State for the Home Department, ex parte Bentley [1994] QB 349

The Divisional Court held that the failure of the Home Secretary to appreciate that the royal prerogative of mercy (which 'was a broad and flexible constitutional safeguard against mistakes') could be exercised other than by the issuing of a free pardon (ie a posthumous conditional pardon) was subject to review by the courts. The Home Secretary was, accordingly, required to consider afresh whether it was just to use his prerogative powers so as to recognise the commonly accepted view that Bentley's brother (Derek Bentley – who had been executed in 1953) should have been reprieved.

The court stated that decisions taken under the royal prerogative were subject to judicial review where the nature and subject-matter of the particular prerogative were amenable to judicial adjudication (ie where it did not necessitate the court reviewing questions of policy).

See more recently *R (Shields) v Secretary of State for Justice* [2008] EWHC 3102 (Admin).

■ **The regulation of the Civil Service** – At the time of going to print, Pt 1 of the Constitutional Reform and Governance Act 2010 placed the power to manage the Civil Service on a statutory basis (see section 11.3.1).
■ **The recommendations for honours** (by the defence and foreign secretaries).
■ **The Prime Minister's ability to make appointments**
■ **The governance of territories (British) abroad**.
■ **Diplomatic matters.**

11.9.4 The 2009 Review

In October 2009 the government published its report on its survey of prerogative powers (*Review of the Executive Royal Prerogative Powers: Final Report* (Crown Copyright, 2009)). The review identified four main categories (see annex):

(a) 'prerogative powers exercised by Ministers'
For example, these included:
■ the Civil Service (eg the regulation of civil servants – but now see the Constitutional Reform and Governance Act 2010)
■ the justice system (eg mercy)
■ foreign affairs (eg sending ambassadors)
■ war, times of emergency and the armed forces (eg deploying forces abroad)
■ miscellaneous (power to hold non-statutory inquiries).

(b) 'executive constitutional/personal prerogative powers exercised by the Sovereign'
For example:
■ the Royal Assent

- the granting of honours
- the power to dismiss the government
- the appointment and removal of ministers
- to summon and dissolve Parliament.

(c) 'legal prerogatives of the Crown'

For example:
- Crown immunities
- the Crown as a preferred creditor.

(d) 'archaic prerogative powers'

For example
- the right to sturgeon, (wild and unmarked) swans and whales
- to mine precious metals.

11.9.5 The constitutional relationship between Parliament and the royal prerogative

In the hierarchy of legal sources, as statute law has a higher status than common law, Parliament can pass Acts of Parliament which eclipse powers under the royal prerogative (see section 7.5.1). In fact, Parliament can:

- expressly limit or abolish prerogative powers (Bill of Rights 1689); or
- pass laws which supersede these powers.

CASE EXAMPLE

Attorney-General v De Keyser's Royal Hotel Limited [1920] AC 508

In 1916 the Crown took possession of De Keyser's Hotel to accommodate the headquarters personnel of the Royal Flying Corps. De Keyser sought compensation for this use and occupation of the hotel. The government argued that the occupation had been exercised under the royal prerogative (the defence of the realm) and so no compensation was payable. De Keyser argued that it was occupied in accordance with the Defence Act 1842 which made provision for compensation.

The House of Lords held that the government occupation of the hotel was under the terms of the Act (and so the powers under the royal prerogative were not available to the government) which necessitated compensation. In summary, the Crown could not purport to act under the royal prerogative where the power had been superseded by legislation. (The issue concerning compensation for taking property under the prerogative was decided later in *Burmah Oil* (1965), at section 4.9).

More recently, Lord Browne-Wilkinson, in *R v Secretary of State for the Home Department, ex parte Fire Brigades Union and others* [1995] 2 All ER 244, noted that royal prerogative powers continue:

JUDGMENT

'in existence to the extent that Parliament has not expressly or by implication extinguished them'.

In addition to displacing prerogative powers through legislation, Parliament can ensure through the convention of ministerial responsibility that ministers are constitutionally and politically accountable for the use of these powers. With respect to parliamentary questions, generally speaking they can be asked about the prerogative except, for example:

- The advice the Prime Minister had given to the Sovereign in respect of honours.
- The dissolution of Parliament.
- The prerogative of mercy.

Reforms have been suggested to increase parliamentary control over the use of these powers.

- In March 2004 the House of Commons Public Administration Select Committee attached a draft Bill (supplied by Professor Brazier) to its report to ensure greater scrutiny of the prerogative. Clause 3 of the proposed Ministers of the Crown (Executive Powers) Bill would have imposed a duty on 'The Secretary of State' to lay a statement before Parliament setting out the nature, extent and safeguards in respect of all executive (royal prerogative) powers. Thereafter a joint select committee would review these powers and indicate whether reforms (in the form of draft legislation) should be made for Parliament to consider (Fourth Report of Session 2003–04, *Taming the Prerogative: Strengthening Ministerial Accountability to Parliament* HC 422, (2004) App 1). The then Labour government, however, in response to this report remained unpersuaded 'that the Committee's proposal to replace prerogative powers with a statutory framework would improve the present position' (*Government Response to the Public Administration Select Committee's Fourth Report of the 2003–04 Session*, 2004). NB But now see the recent reform proposals at section 11.9.2.
- Lord Lester's (albeit unsuccessful) 2006 Constitutional Reform (Prerogative Powers and Civil Service etc) Bill would have placed executive (prerogative) powers under the authority of Parliament. Clause 4 of the Bill would have established a Joint Committee of both Houses of Parliament to keep under review, and report to Parliament, the circumstances in which executive prerogative powers were exercised.

11.9.6 The constitutional relationship between the judiciary and the royal prerogative

It is clear that owing to their residual nature, new royal prerogative powers cannot be created, as noted by Diplock LJ in *BBC v Johns (Inspector of Taxes)* [1965] 1 CH 32:

JUDGMENT

'it is 350 years and a civil war too late for the Queen's courts to broaden the prerogative. The limits within which the executive government may impose obligations or restraints upon citizens of the United Kingdom without any statutory authority are now well settled and incapable of extension.'

Pre-existing prerogative powers such as keeping the Queen's peace can, however, adapt to the contemporary system of preserving the peace through modern day police forces (*R v Secretary for the Home Department, ex parte Northumbria Police Authority* [1989] 1 QB 26).

In historic terms, the courts supervision of prerogative powers amounted to recognising and demarcating their scope and existence (*The Case of Proclamations* (1611) 12 Co Rep 74), rather than investigating the manner in which they were used. The *GCHQ* case (1985) (see below), however, made it clear that the courts could legally supervise executive use of the royal prerogative in the same way that they reviewed the manner in which statutory powers were exercised. The *GCHQ* decision followed the earlier cases of *R v Criminal Injuries Compensation Board, ex parte Lain* [1967] 2 QB 864 and *Laker Airways Ltd v Department of Trade and Industry* [1977] 1 QB 643.

CASE EXAMPLE

Council of Civil Service Unions v Minister for the Civil Service [1985] 1 AC 374

This case is commonly known as the *GCHQ* case. In 1983 the Prime Minister (Minister for the Civil Service) issued an instruction pursuant to the Civil Service Order in Council 1982 that staff at Government Communications Headquarters (GCHQ) would no longer be permitted to be members of trade unions. No prior consultation had taken place before the instruction was issued and the workers' trade union sought judicial review of the Prime Minister's instruction on the basis that she had a duty to consult those affected by it before issuing it (ie the duty to act fairly).

The House of Lords held that government action was not immune from the jurisdiction of the courts merely because it derived from the royal prerogative. On the facts the claimants would have had a legitimate expectation of being consulted prior to the issuing of the instruction, however, this was trumped by national security considerations (ie, the risk of industrial unrest had prior consultation taken place). It was for the executive and not the judiciary to decide whether on the facts of the case the requirements of national security outweighed those of fairness.

non-justiciable
an issue not suitable for resolution by the courts

The *GCHQ* case (1985) represents a watershed in terms of the prerogative as the House of Lords made it clear that the manner in which these common law powers were used was, depending on the subject-matter, subject to supervision by the courts. Thus, some uses of the prerogative would be *'justiciable'* (reviewable) while, according to Lord Roskill, others would be **'non-justiciable'**. For example the latter would include:

- The dissolution of Parliament.
- Ministerial appointments.
- Making Treaties (see *Blackburn v Attorney-General* (1971) at section 11.9.4).
- The defence of the realm.
- The granting of honours.
- Mercy (but now see *ex parte Bentley* (1994) at section 11.9.3).

The category of *'non-justiciable'* prerogatives attempts to ensure a constitutional demarcation between the separate roles of the judge and the politician as the exercise of the above (sensitive) powers are considered unsuitable for judicial/legal adjudication. The political and parliamentary supervision in respect of the use of these powers may, however, be considered insufficient.

Finally, the government in its recent 2009 review stated that the scope of prerogative power was 'notoriously difficult to determine', as although the courts decide (ultimately) whether such a power exists:

QUOTATION

'The difficulty is that there are many prerogative powers for which there is no recent judicial authority and sometimes no judicial authority at all.'

Review of the Executive Royal Prerogative Powers: Final Report, (Crown Copyright, 2009), p 7.

KEY FACTS

Key facts on the royal prerogative

Historically, the courts confined themselves to demarcating the scope and existence of royal prerogative powers.
In the *GCHQ* case (1985) the House of Lords made it clear that the courts could supervise the manner of the use of royal prerogative powers providing the subject-matter was *justiciable* (ie reviewable by the courts).
According to Lord Roskill some uses of the prerogative such as the dissolution of Parliament were not amenable to judicial adjudication.

11.9.7 The constitutional significance of the royal prerogative

It is clear that government needs powers which are analogous to the royal prerogative (eg to deploy troops quickly, to respond to international crises, etc). The question is whether there is sufficient constitutional control (legal or parliamentary) over the use of these powers. Royal prerogative powers raise the following issues:

■ **The rule of law** – Brazier (the specialist adviser to the Public Administration Select Committee) has stated that:

QUOTATION

'Governments should not have imprecise powers. As a matter of basic constitutional principle the user of a power should be able – and if asked should be obliged – to identify the source of that power and to describe its nature and extent. Ministers should be required to do just that.'

Fourth Report of Session 2003–04, *Taming the Prerogative: Strengthening Ministerial Accountability to Parliament*, HC 422, (2004) p 24.

Historically, the constitutional concern in relation to the royal prerogative has been that there was no definitive list of these powers and their precise extent was not always clear (but now see the 2009 review at section 11.9.4).

■ **Democracy** – The government of the day can make major political and constitutional decisions (eg declaring war) without (in law) approval from the democratically elected House of Commons.
■ **Legal accountability** – Although the courts will review the manner in which prerogative powers are used, this is subject to the proviso that such powers are *justiciable* matters and so suitable for judicial supervision (ie they do not involve issues of political policy). Moreover, as pointed out by the Public Administration Select Committee, challenges in court necessarily come *after* the event, namely, after the prerogative has been used. Furthermore, s 21(1) of the Human Rights Act 1998 prescribes that an Order in Council made in exercise of Her Majesty's royal prerogative is treated as primary legislation and so cannot be invalidated by the courts under the Act. However, the House of Lords in *R (Bancoult) v Secretary of State for Foreign and Commonwealth Affairs* [2008] UKHL 61 held that prerogative legislation is subject to judicial review on the three traditional grounds. (On the grounds for judicial review, see Chapter 20.)
■ **The separation of powers** – The principle of *justiciabilty* is a judicial construction. It ensures that the judges act in a self-restrained manner and do not trespass onto the function of the executive who have been constitutionally charged with the responsibility for administering public policy and making executive/political decisions. *Justiciabilty*, therefore, on the one hand preserves the separation of powers between the executive and the judiciary, but on the other hand it leaves certain uses of the prerogative legally unaccountable to the courts.
■ **Political accountability** – Although ministers can be asked to account for the use of the royal prerogative, some aspects are exempt, for example the dissolution of Parliament. In addition, as with legal challenges, the Public Administration Select Committee has pointed out that accountability to Parliament will come *after* the event as ministers are not legally required to inform Parliament before such powers are exercised. The then Labour government's response to the Select Committee's report made the point that government ministers were accountable to Parliament for the use of prerogative powers, in particular through departmental select committees and the Prime Minister appearing before the Liaison Committee (see section 12.6.7). It also noted that the Select Committee had itself recognised that Parliament could overrule a prerogative power with legislation and so 'Parliament is by no means powerless in the face of the prerogative' (*Government Response to the Public Administration Select Committee's Fourth*

Report of the 2003–04 Session, (2004)). More recently, however, the 2007 Green Paper emphasised the importance of putting prerogative powers on a statutory basis (see section 11.9.2).

SUMMARY

- ◼ The executive refers to those who administer and execute the law. In the British constitution it embraces the following:
  - ● The political executive (HM Government) – including the Prime Minister, Cabinet and junior ministers.
  - ● The non-political/bureaucratic executive (the Civil Service) – civil servants implement the policies of their respective government ministers.
  - ● The executive in practical terms – the armed forces and various police forces.
  - ● Other executives – local authorities and executive bodies in the devolution settlements.
- ◼ The British constitution is hallmarked by a parliamentary executive whereby the executive is drawn from the legislature.
- ◼ The functions of the executive include:
  - ● To formulate and implement policies.
  - ● To implement and carry out the law.
  - ● To make specified appointments.
- ◼ The executive enjoys statutory powers to, for example, pass delegated legislation or bring primary legislation into force.
- ◼ The executive enjoys powers under the common law known as the royal prerogative.
- ◼ Parliament can limit prerogative power and the courts can supervise the manner in which they are used providing these powers are considered *justiciable*.

SAMPLE ESSAY QUESTION

What is the royal prerogative and what is its significance to the British constitution?

> **Introduction:**
> Definition – common law (non-statutory) powers enjoyed by the Crown

> **Types and nature:**
> - Queen's constitutional prerogatives (eg to dissolve Parliament)
> - Legal prerogatives of the Crown (eg the Crown can do no wrong)
> - Prerogative executive powers (eg the deployment of the armed forces)
> - Also note the general distinction between prerogative powers in the domestic sphere (eg Royal Assent) and those relating to foreign affairs (eg declaration of war)
> - See the recent 2009 classification by the government

> **The constitutional relationship between the prerogative and Parliament:**
>
> - Parliament can pass laws which limit, abolish or supersede prerogative powers (*De Keyser's Royal Hotel* (1920))
>
> - Recent reforms to give Parliament more control and scrutiny over prerogative powers (*The Governance of Britain* (2007) and the Constitutional Reform and Governance Act 2010)

> **The constitutional relationship between the prerogative and the courts:**
>
> - Historically the courts could recognise the existence and scope of prerogative powers
>
> - The *GCHQ* (1985) case made it clear that the courts could legally supervise the exercise of prerogative powers (though there were some *non-justiciable* areas)

> **The royal prerogative and constitutional principles:**
>
> - The rule of law (consider whether these powers are sufficiently clear and precise)
>
> - Democracy and political accountability (governmental decisions made without the approval of the elected House of Commons)
>
> - Legal accountability (note some powers are *non-justiciable*
>
> - The separation of powers (consider the constitutional relationship between the executive and the judiciary)

> **CONCLUSION**

Further reading

Books

Barnett, H, *Britain Unwrapped* (Penguin, 2002), Chapter 2.

Benn, A, 'How Democratic is Britain?' in Sutherland, K (ed), *The Rape of the Constitution?* (Imprint Academic, 2000), p 33.

Bradley, A and Ewing, K, *Constitutional and Administrative Law* (14th edn, Pearson/ Longman, 2007), Chapters 12 and 13.

Drewry, G, 'The Executive: Towards Accountable Government and Effective Governance?' in Jowell, J and Oliver, D, *The Changing Constitution* (6th edn, Oxford University Press, 2007), p 185.

Nolan, Lord, 'The Executive' in Lord Nolan and Sedley, S, *The Making and Remaking of the British Constitution* (Blackstone Press Limited, 1997), p 33.

Parpworth, N, *Constitutional and Administrative law* (5th edn, Oxford University Press, 2008) Chapter 4.

Weir, S and Beetham, D, *Political Power and Democratic Control in Britain* (Routledge, 1999), Chapters 6–8.

Articles

Ryan, M 'Sum of constituent parts' (2008) 158 NLJ 739.

Samiloff, J 'Who should declare war?'(2008) 158 NLJ 565.

Papers

Fourth Report of Session 2003–04, *Taming the Prerogative: Strengthening Ministerial Accountability to Parliament*, HC 422 (2004).

Eighth Report of Session 2008–09, *Good Government*, HC 97-1 (2009).

Maer, L and Gay, O, *The Royal Prerogative* (House of Commons Library, 2008).

Internet links

www.cabinetoffice.gov.uk

www.civilservice.gov.uk

12

Executive/parliamentary relations

AIMS AND OBJECTIVES

At the end of this chapter you should be able to:

■ Understand the nature and constitutional significance of the constitutional convention of ministerial responsibility

■ Understand the role and effectiveness of parliamentary scrutiny of the executive through questioning, debates and committees

Introduction

One of the central constitutional relationships in the British constitution is that between the executive/government and the legislature. As we have a parliamentary executive, one of the constitutional functions of Parliament is to scrutinise government ministers in respect of their policy, administration and actions (whether individually or collectively). In constitutional theory, therefore, ministers are both collectively and individually responsible to Parliament. Government accountability to both Houses of Parliament is secured through various parliamentary mechanisms such as questioning, debates and select committees, all of which are considered below. In short, Parliament acts as a constitutional check on the executive and this is particularly important in the absence of a codified constitution constraining the activities of the executive. The balance between Parliament and the government has been described in the following way by Charles Kennedy MP:

QUOTATION

'An effective Parliament should be neither excessively obstructive nor excessively subservient.'

Hansard, HC Vol 353, col 1109.

12.1 The constitutional convention of ministerial responsibility

12.1.1 Classification

The convention of ministerial responsibility is, arguably, the most important convention in our uncodified constitution, as it purports to hold the government accountable to Parliament (on constitutional conventions in general see section 4.13). In broad terms, the convention can be divided into:

■ The convention of *collective* ministerial responsibility.
■ The convention of *individual* ministerial responsibility.

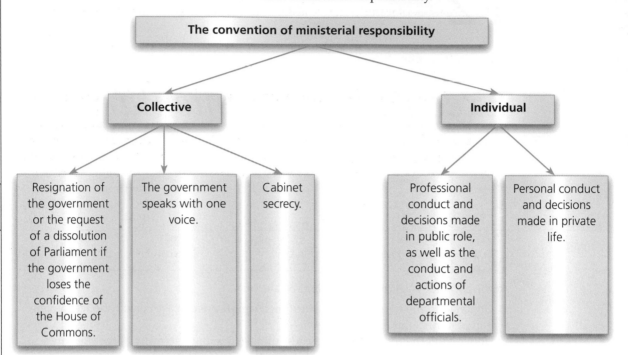

Figure 12.1 The convention of ministerial responsibility

12.1.2 The *Ministerial Code*

The *Ministerial Code* sets out clearly the constitutional responsibility of government ministers in relation to the convention of ministerial responsibility:

QUOTATION

■ 'Ministers have a duty to Parliament to account, and be held to account, for the policies, decisions and actions of their departments and agencies;
■ It is of paramount importance that Ministers give accurate and truthful information to Parliament, correcting any inadvertent error at the earliest opportunity. Ministers who knowingly mislead Parliament will be expected to offer their resignation to the Prime Minister;
■ Ministers should be as open as possible with Parliament and the public, refusing to provide information only when disclosure would not be in the public interest ...'

Ministerial Code (Cabinet Office, revised July 2007), para 1.2.
Source: www.cabinetoffice.gov.uk

The convention of ministerial responsibility should be seen in the context of the parliamentary mechanisms for holding the government to account (see sections 12.4 to 12.9).

It is worth noting that the convention of ministerial responsibility also applies to the devolved institutions. For example, in Scotland the Scottish Executive/Government is both collectively and individually responsible to the Scottish Parliament.

12.2 The constitutional convention of collective ministerial responsibility

Geoffrey Marshall (*Constitutional Conventions* (Clarendon Press, 1986), pp 55–61) has noted that in essence this convention is composed of the following three elements:

- The government must resign or advise a dissolution of Parliament if the confidence of the House of Commons is lost (the confidence rule).
- The government is united and speaks with one single voice on policy (the unanimity rule).
- The discussions (and disagreements) within Cabinet should remain secret (the confidentiality rule).

12.2.1 The loss of confidence of the House of Commons

If the government loses a motion of no confidence, then by constitutional convention, the Prime Minister should either recommend dissolution of Parliament in order that a general election could take place (which could, for example, result in a different government taking office as in 1979), or offer his resignation with that of the government. If this were to happen, it might be possible for an alternative government to be cobbled together from the other existing parties in the House without the need for an election. The vote of no confidence is the only parliamentary mechanism for removing an unpopular government mid-term between general elections.

As indicated above, however, the practical reality of the convention is that the motion of no confidence is rarely successful. In fact, in the past 100 years it has been successful only three times:

- 1979 Labour government.
- 1924 (January) Conservative government.
- 1924 (November) Labour government (the very first Labour government).

Three factors can explain why the vote of no confidence is rarely successful:

- The electoral system generally speaking (though not always) will provide the government of the day with the support of the majority of seats in the House of Commons.
- Recalcitrant government backbenchers may vote against their government on various legislative proposals, but would invariably be reluctant to vote against the government on a vote of no confidence leading to the fall of that government.
- As an adjunct to the above point, on a very cynical, but practical, point it is arguable that government backbench MPs may not wish to trigger a general election mid-term, as there is no guarantee that they would be re-elected.

12.2.2 The government speaks with one single voice

It is important that a government is seen to be confident and united over government policy. In contrast, a divided government which is split over major policies will be viewed as weak and lacking clear focus and direction. This principle, therefore, enhances the accountability of the government to Parliament because it avoids ministers disassociating themselves with policies with which they disagree or which have subsequently become deeply unpopular. Speaking with one voice (and voting the same way), therefore, requires individual ministers to defend publicly each others' broad departmental policies, as well as the overall strategy of governmental policy. Paragraph 1.2 of the *Ministerial Code* specifically requires ministers to uphold the principle of collective responsibility.

The convention of presenting a united front raises the following issues:

- Although major governmental decisions will be taken in Cabinet, junior ministers not party to these decisions will still be expected to defend them publicly. Further, even Cabinet ministers themselves who were not party to a decision made in a Cabinet sub-committee (see section 11.2.3) will also be expected to support it.
- If a government minister disagrees personally with the policy adopted by the government, he must either:
  (i) resign from office – thereby allowing him to criticise that policy subsequently from the backbenches. In 2003 Robin Cook MP resigned from the government over foreign policy in respect of Iraq; or

(ii) accept the nature of collective Cabinet decision-making (ie that not all collective decisions made will have universal and total support) and support that policy publicly, even though he has private reservations about it.

■ Historically, the principle has been departed from in exceptional circumstances. For example, in 1932 it was set aside in respect of a coalition government over the question of the issue of tariffs. More recently, the convention was departed from in 1975 when the Labour government was split over its attitude towards continuing membership of the European Economic Community (which the previous Conservative government had managed to secure). As a result, the incumbent Labour Prime Minister decided to set the convention aside for the purposes of an impending national referendum in 1975 on whether the United Kingdom should remain a member of the EEC. His justification was that this was a unique issue which divided the country as a whole (*Hansard*, HC Vol 884, col 1750). In addition to the above 'agreements to differ', ministers do not have to speak (or vote) the same way on free votes, for example on moral matters such as the death penalty.

ACTIVITY

Exercise

Do you think that the Labour government acted unconstitutionally in departing from the convention in 1975, or does it just demonstrate that constitutional conventions can adapt to exceptional circumstances?

12.2.3 Cabinet discussions remain secret

It is a general principal that discussions within Cabinet remain secret. This buttresses the point made at section 11.2.3, as it enables all shades of opinion within Cabinet to be put forward freely (and without prejudice), safe in the knowledge that the nature and content of this discussion will not subsequently be disclosed publicly. The *Ministerial Code* is quite explicit on this point:

QUOTATION

'Collective responsibility requires that Ministers should be able to express their views frankly in the expectation that they can argue freely in private while maintaining a united front when decisions have been reached. This in turn requires that the privacy of opinions expressed in Cabinet and Ministerial Committees … should be maintained.'

Ministerial Code (Cabinet Office, revised July 2007), para 2.1.
Source: www.cabinetoffice.gov.uk

On the secrecy of Cabinet discussions see *Attorney General v Jonathan Cape Ltd* (1976) at section 4.13.12.

12.3 The constitutional convention of individual ministerial responsibility

In essence this is composed of two elements:

■ Responsibility for conduct in a minister's public role as a minister of the Crown and the actions of his departmental officials.
■ Responsibility for conduct in a minister's private life.

12.3.1 Constitutional responsibility for professional conduct and departmental activity

Each Secretary of State will be head of a specific government department. As such, he will represent and defend that department in Parliament. Together with his ministerial team, he will answer questions during ministerial question time (see section 12.4.4) about the operation, policies and decisions made in respect of that department. In this way the Secretary of State will take the blame for errors or mismanagement that occur within his department, and protect the anonymity of his officials (see section 11.3.1). Government ministers, therefore, are not only responsible for their own decisions and actions made as a minister, but also for the actions of their departmental officials (also see *Carltona Ltd* (1943) at section 4.13.12 and 20.2.3).

12.3.2 Resignations due to ministerial decisions or actions made as a minister

Government ministers have to make executive and professional decisions for which they are responsible:

EXAMPLE

In 2002 Estelle Morris MP resigned from office as the Secretary of State for Education. She had previously, and publicly, committed herself to resigning if the government did not reach its literacy and numeracy targets by 2002. In addition, Morris also admitted that she was not as good a Secretary of State as she had been as an Under Secretary of State.

In addition to the above:

- In 1988 the Minister of Health (Edwina Currie MP) resigned after her comments concerning salmonella in eggs.
- In 1990 the Secretary of State for Trade and Industry (Nicholas Ridley MP) resigned for inappropriate remarks made about Germany.
- In 1986 the Secretary of State for Trade and Industry (Leon Brittan MP) resigned following the leaking of a confidential letter from the Solicitor General.

12.3.3 Resignations due to the actions of departmental officials

The classic example traditionally cited in this context is the famous *Crichel Down* Affair:

EXAMPLE

In 1954 Sir Thomas Dugdale MP resigned from office as the Minister of Agriculture. The issue concerned land ('Crichel Down') which had been acquired by the Air Ministry and then transferred to the Ministry of Agriculture (with the Crown Lands Commissioners subsequently administering it). Thereafter, a former landowner was refused permission to buy back the land and other landowners were not permitted to seek tenancies of it. An inquiry was established which criticised the handling by civil servants of this matter.

Dugdale subsequently resigned stating:

QUOTATION

'I, as Minister, must accept full responsibility to Parliament for any mistakes and inefficiency of officials in my Department, just as, when my officials bring off any successes on my behalf, I take full credit for them. Any departure from this long-established rule is bound to bring the Civil Service right into the political arena, and that we should all, on both sides of the House, deprecate most vigorously.'

Hansard, HC Vol 530, col 1186.

Immediately following Dugdale's resignation, the Home Secretary (Sir David Maxwell Fyfe MP) reviewed the convention, which he stated comprised four categories:

■ Firstly, a minister must protect a civil servant who has carried out an explicit order.
■ Secondly, a minister must protect and defend a civil servant who has acted properly in accordance with a policy which has been set down by the minister.
■ Thirdly: 'Where an official makes a mistake or causes some delay, but not on an important issue of policy and not where a claim to individual rights is seriously involved, the Minister acknowledges the mistake and he accepts the responsibility, although he is not personally involved. He states that he will take corrective action in the Department ... he would not, in those circumstances, expose the official to public criticism.'
■ Fourthly, where a civil servant engages in actions which are reprehensible (of which the minister disapproves and had no prior knowledge), the minister is not obliged to defend what he believes to be wrong, or the errors of his officials. The minister is, however, still constitutionally required to 'account' (ie explain) to Parliament what had transpired 'and render an account of his stewardship'.

Hansard, HC Vol 530, cols 1286–1287.

Crichel Down, historically at least (although it has been subject to different interpretations), is regarded as the seminal case illustrating government ministers being responsible for the actions of their officials, although there have been few examples since of ministers resigning in such circumstances. For example:

■ In 1983 James Prior MP the Secretary of State for Northern Ireland did not resign in respect of a break-out of prisoners from the Maze Prison in Ulster.
■ In 1982 William Whitelaw MP (the Home Secretary) did not resign when an individual managed to evade palace security and access the Queen's bedroom.

12.3.4 Constitutional responsibility for conduct in a minister's private life

Government ministers are individually responsible to Parliament for personal conduct in their private lives (eg of a financial nature). As noted by the Nolan Committee:

QUOTATION

'The public is entitled to expect very high standards of behaviour from Ministers, as they have profound influence over the daily lives of us all ... Financial misbehaviour in particular matters to us all, because it strikes at the very heart of that confidence which people must have in Ministers and the motives behind their decisions. The same cannot normally be said of sexual misconduct. It is true that the private lives of Ministers may occasionally be relevant to the performance of their public duties, for example when their private conduct runs directly counter to some public policy, gives rise to embarrassing publicity, or involves a security risk.'

First Report of the Committee on Standards in Public Life,
Standards in Public Life, Vol 1: Report, Cm 2850-I, (1995), pp 47–48.

Following on from the Nolan Committee, the *Ministerial Code* states the following:

QUOTATION

■ 'Ministers must ensure that no conflict arises, or appears to arise, between their public duties and their private interests;
■ Ministers should not accept any gift or hospitality which might, or might reasonably appear to, compromise their judgement or place them under an improper obligation.'

Ministerial Code (Cabinet Office, revised July 2007), para 1.2.

It could be argued that government ministers as individuals should enjoy absolute privacy in their private lives and that private activity should never be subject to public scrutiny. However, it can be argued more persuasively that a government minister's private affairs will be of public interest where these activities have an impact on his public role as a government minister.

Over the years there are a number of examples of government ministers resigning their office owing to their actions in their private life. Below are two examples:

In the context of financial activity

EXAMPLE

In December 1998 the following two ministers resigned:

- Peter Mandelson MP as Secretary of State for Trade and Industry.
- Geoffrey Robinson MP as Paymaster General (Treasury).

The latter had loaned the former money to help support the buying of a house. Mandelson later stated to the Committee on Standards and Privileges that the existence of the loan, which he had registered late, should have been made known to his Permanent Secretary 'so as to avoid the appearance of a conflict of interest' – which is why he resigned. Although he also argued that the House of Commons Register was not the only way to inform his Permanent Secretary (and others) of the loan.

In the context of sexual activity

EXAMPLE

In October 1983 Cecil Parkinson MP, the Secretary of State for Trade and Industry (he was also Conservative Party Chairman) resigned after it became known that he had made his secretary pregnant. Parkinson was a married man.

ACTIVITY

Self-test question

Do you think that a minister's private life should always remain private?

KEY FACTS

Key facts on ministerial responsibility

Collective responsibility	• Governmental resignation (or the request of a dissolution of Parliament) if the confidence of the House of Commons is lost (eg 1979). This is very unlikely in practice. • The government is united and speaks with one voice on policy. • Cabinet discussions should remain secret.
Individual responsibility for professional and actions of officials	• Actions as a minister (Estelle Morris). • Actions of officials (Sir Thomas Dugdale), but few resignations since.
Individual responsibility for private life	• In the context of financial activity (Peter Mandelson). • In the context of sexual activity (Cecil Parkinson).

12.3.5 Uncertain aspects of individual ministerial responsibility

The following four aspects of the convention are unclear:

■ **The reality of modern government**

It is uncertain whether, practically, it is possible for government ministers to be fully aware of what is going on inside their departments. Consider, for example:

● The size of modern government departments and complexity of modern day administration.

● Frequent Cabinet reshuffles. Ministers tend to be transient as they will inevitably occupy their ministerial posts for relatively short periods before being moved elsewhere (either in or out of government).

■ **Next Step Agencies**

The chain of accountability between government ministers and Parliament has in recent years been undermined somewhat by the emergence of Next Step Agencies (see section 11.3.2), which are aspects of a department (like the Prison Service) which have been separated and reconstituted as an executive agency. These agencies have their own Chief Executives and are semi-autonomous in their affairs. In strict constitutional theory, however, according to para 1.2 of the *Ministerial Code,* ministers are to be held to account for the actions of their respective Next Step Agencies.

■ **Resignation**

When should a minister resign? Paragraph 1.2 of the *Ministerial Code* (and the parliamentary resolution which the Code incorporates) makes it clear that a minister who knowingly misleads Parliament should offer his resignation to the Prime Minister. In what other circumstances, however, is it an obligation?

Today this issue is not clear and it has been complicated by the distinctions made below in relation to accountability and responsibility. It seems from the pattern of resignations in recent years that resignations tend to be concerned with personal misconduct in a minister's private sexual or financial life. In any event, the reality is that resignations are ultimately determined by extraneous factors: (the unpopularity of the minister, the lack of support from the party and/or Prime Minister, etc), rather than the actual event/decision/policy in question.

In fact, it is worth remarking that no ministers resigned in respect of the *Arms to Iraq Affair* (which in turn led to the Scott Report). In short, this episode concerned the relaxation in the late 1980s of government restrictions in respect of export controls concerning the selling of equipment (which was indirectly militarily useful) to Iraq. Parliament, however, had not been informed of this change in policy by the government and the Scott Report concluded that Parliament had therefore been misled. In addition, the whole episode illustrated the limitations of parliamentary mechanisms of scrutiny as, for example, the House of Commons Trade and Industry Select Committee had had difficulty in getting full information from ministers.

In the wake of the *Arms to Iraq Affair*, in 1997 the House of Commons passed a resolution (now incorporated within the *Ministerial Code*) setting out the responsibility of ministers to account fully to Parliament.

Two final points to note in relation to resignations are that:

■ A minister may be reshuffled to another department before it becomes necessary to seek his resignation.

■ Even if a minister does resign from government he may rejoin it at a later date. For example, although Peter Mandelson MP resigned in December 1998 (see section 12.3.4), less than a year later he returned to the Cabinet as Secretary of State for Northern Ireland.

■ **A distinction between accountable and responsibility?**

In modern times the following distinction has been drawn (by ministers) between accountability and responsibility:

- Constitutional responsibility concerns ministers being personally at fault and culpable in some way (thereby being constitutionally *responsible* to Parliament).
- Constitutional accountability, in contrast, concerns ministers not being personally responsible (personally culpable), but remaining constitutionally *accountable* to Parliament to account for what has happened (known as explanatory accountability). In terms of explanatory accountability, in November 2007 the Chancellor of the Exchequer made a statement to the House of Commons concerning the breach of procedures which resulted in personal data concerning child benefit from HM Revenue and Customs (a non-ministerial government department) going missing. He also apologised for the anxiety caused (*Hansard* HC Vol 467 col 1101).

Similarly, in recent years a distinction has also been drawn by ministers between:
- Being constitutionally responsible for general policy decisions.
- Not being constitutionally responsible (ie culpable) for their *operation* (ie the carrying out of that policy in a defective way).

For example, in 1984 James Prior MP drew a distinction between being responsible for policy, but not its implementation and so declined to resign for operational failures. Also, over a decade later, Michael Howard MP as Home Secretary did not resign over prison escapes as these were considered operational matters in the Prison Service (see section 11.3.2).

This latter distinction is particularly controversial as it begs the question as to who is constitutionally responsible in such circumstances. It leads, arguably, to a gap in constitutional responsibility with the relevant minister merely accounting to Parliament as to what has gone wrong.

ACTIVITY

Quick quiz

1. What is the difference between collective and individual responsibility?
2. What is the difference between individual responsibility for a minister's private life and individual responsibility for a minister's professional decisions?
3. In what circumstances is a minister responsible for the actions of his officials?
4. What factors mitigate against the operation of the convention (both collective and individual responsibility)?

12.4 Parliamentary questions

Introduction

Government ministers are asked parliamentary questions in both Houses and these questions can be either in written form (the overwhelming majority) or asked orally in either chamber:

QUOTATION

'The purpose of a question is to obtain information or press for action.'

E May, *Parliamentary Practice* (23rd edn, LexisNexis Butterworths, 2004), p 345.

12.4.1 Oral questions in the House of Commons

Oral questions are questions set down for an oral answer on the Floor of the chamber. In essence, there are two types of oral questions:

- Oral questions to the Prime Minister.
- Oral questions to other government ministers.

12.4.2 Oral questions to the Prime Minister

Prime Minister's Question Time (PMQs) is the most visible and widely published manifestation of Parliament holding the government to account (whether it is actually successful is a moot point). It takes place each Wednesday for 30 minutes. The procedure at PMQs is that MPs can ask the Prime Minister an *open question* (eg 'If he will list his official engagements for that Wednesday'), but the real question is the *supplementary question*. For example, Charles Kennedy MP asked the following supplementary question:

EXAMPLE

'The Prime Minister acknowledged that the state of the railways today is worse than when he became Prime Minister. Will he address the obvious question: why is it that, five years after the shambles of privatisation, a Labour Government have not done more to redress the situation?'

Hansard, HC Vol 385, col 768.

Questions about specific aspects of government departments (as opposed to the general tenor of government policy) should be directed to the relevant Secretary of State, rather than the Prime Minister. In a typical PMQ session only a limited number of questions can be asked in 30 minutes. For example, on 1st July 2009 a total number of 26 questions were asked (*Hansard*, HC Vol 495, col 292). Moreover, six of these were from the Leader of the Opposition and two from the leader of the second party of opposition (the Liberal Democrats).

12.4.3 The advantages and disadvantages of PMQs

Advantages

■ Although the open questions have to be tabled a few days in advance, the supplementary questions do not require notice. In this way PMQs can be highly topical. In the absence of notice, a Prime Minister will be tested on his competence over a wide range of different governmental issues.

■ On average the Prime Minister is questioned for two hours a month, in contrast to other government ministers who are questioned on a rota for around one hour every five weeks.

■ PMQs are a well-attended televised gladiatorial set-piece at which the Prime Minister is visibly held to account by parliamentarians.

■ A very poor performance by a Prime Minister in PMQs could affect his standing and perceived competence to govern both in and out of Parliament.

Disadvantages

■ PMQs may be seen simply as a party point-scoring exercise where political comments are exchanged between party politicians. In this light they do not really achieve anything.

■ The length of time available for questions is too short; the questions asked are too general; and the answers are too brief (in contrast to written questions below).

■ Sympathetic questions can be asked which draw attention to a positive aspect of government policy or achievements:

EXAMPLE

Siân C James (Labour): 'Will the Prime Minister join me in congratulating the Swansea division of the South Wales police on its excellent recent crime figures? ... I am sure that he will agree that those figures are worth celebrating.'

Tony Blair: 'I am very happy to congratulate the police in my hon. friend's constituency.'

Hansard, HC Vol 446, col 1477.

- Riddel (*Parliament under Blair* (Politico's, 2000), p 91) has suggested that the consolidation of two PMQ sessions to one (one of the first reforms undertaken by Tony Blair as Prime Minister) has resulted in a reduction in accountability. This is because the Leader of the Opposition can attack the Prime Minister only once a week as opposed to twice (the overall time allocated, however, is still the same as previously).
- The Prime Minister will be fully briefed and informed by civil servants regarding possible and probable supplementary questions which may arise (eg an MP's particular interest).

ACTIVITY

Self-test question

Do you think that PMQs is an effective way of holding the Prime Minister to account?

12.4.4 Oral questions to other government ministers

All heads of government departments will be subjected to an oral question time session on a rota basis. For example, see the questioning of the Home Secretary on 6th July 2009 (*Hansard*, HC Vol 495, col 675). Oral answers can be shared between the team of ministers in the department (as in the above example). All government departments will be subjected to oral parliamentary questions approximately once every five weeks.

The procedure for asking oral questions is to submit them at least three days in advance. These are then shuffled and a number will be randomly selected to be asked. The answers to the main questions will be drafted by civil servants for ministers to approve. The Speaker of the House of Commons plays a pivotal role in oral questions as he determines the pace and the number of supplementary questions (which must be linked to the main one) that can be asked (and by whom). In 2007, a part of question time was added allowing topical questions to be asked without notice of the subject (see the questions on 6th July above).

12.4.5 The advantages and disadvantages of oral questions to ministers

Advantages

- It ensures that each government department (and so the government collectively) is publicly held to account for their actions or omissions approximately every five weeks. It is a direct way of holding the government to account as answers must be given.
- It enforces accountability as government ministers must demonstrate knowledge and competence in respect of their particular department and policies.
- Each oral answer (as with PMQs) is printed in *Hansard* and so is a printed public record which can be referred to in the future.

Disadvantages

- Ministers will be well briefed by their civil servants in respect of the main as well as the anticipated supplementary questions.
- Questions which are not sufficiently connected with the main question can be ruled out of order (also if they are *sub judice*, etc).
- There is a lack of publicity concerning oral Question Time other than PMQs.
- Answers can be shared within a team of ministers and the rota ensures that they do not answer questions every week.

12.4.6 Written questions in the House of Commons

The vast majority of parliamentary questions are written rather than oral. This is due to the pressure of time on the parliamentary timetable as it would not be practical to expect ministers to provide oral answers to all, or even most, of the questions asked by MPs. The answers to written questions are printed in *Hansard*.

12.4.7 The advantages and disadvantages of written questions

Advantages

- MPs can be more persistent about a particular issue as MPs are permitted to ask more written questions than oral questions.
- Written answers to questions will tend to be more detailed, focused and informative (and arguably less elusive) than terse and somewhat general oral answers. For example, consider the highly detailed table of information provided on supply teachers to MP Sarah Teather's written question: (*Hansard*, HC Vol 447, cols 2005W–2012W).
- It is arguable that written questions are more about seeking information than simply party point-scoring.
- Rogers and Walters (*How Parliament Works* (5th edn, Pearson/Longman, 2004), p 302) have noted that one advantage of written questions is that it permits MPs to ensure that a substantial amount of information (which we would not otherwise be aware of) is put into the public domain. In this way a valuable bank of public information is created. On this point it is worth recalling one of Parliament's functions as identified by Bagehot, that of educating and informing the public (see section 9.1.1).
- Government departments are monitored by Parliament to ensure that questions are answered within a reasonable time and if not, they can be named and shamed.

Disadvantages

- Although answers are printed in *Hansard*, most people will be simply unaware of their existence.
- There are a number of ways in which an answer can be legitimately refused, for example if it concerns national security, commercial confidentiality or is simply too expensive to answer:

EXAMPLE

Chris Ruane MP: 'To ask the Minister of State, Department for Constitutional Affairs how many Orders in Council were passed in each of the past 30 years'.
Harriet Harman (The Minister): 'The information requested can only be provided at disproportionate cost.'

Hansard, HC Vol 443, col 1368W.

Similarly, in the House of Lords see the government's refusal to answer Lord Lester's written question concerning the pattern of compensation awards under the Human Rights Act 1998: *Hansard*, HL Vol 664, col WA191.

12.4.8 Oral and written questions in the House of Lords

As a number of government ministers sit in the Lords, questioning also takes place in the upper chamber. In this way the government is held to account in both parliamentary chambers. Questions in the Lords are as follows:

- Oral questions – these consist of a minister answering oral questions together with supplementaries at the start of the day. Slots are reserved for 'topical questions'.
- Questions for short debate – this is in practice a mixture of a question and debate session whereby a minister answers the question in a speech. A pertinent example is where Lord Patten asked whether the government considered that Britain needed a written constitution (*Hansard*, HL Vol 664, col 1242). This was followed by an hour-long

debate between members and was concluded by the Parliamentary Under-Secretary of State, Department for Constitutional Affairs.

■ Written questions – as in the Commons, members of the Lords can request written answers to their questions. Members can ask up to six written questions per day and the answers are published in *Hansard*.

12.4.9 Urgent questions

Both Houses have procedures to enable urgent questions to be asked in exceptional circumstances on matters of public importance such as a major international incident. In the House of Commons the Speaker may allow such a question to be asked. For example, in March 2005 an urgent question was allowed regarding the nature of the Attorney General's legal advice to the government concerning military action in Iraq in 2003 – this resulted in the Foreign Secretary being asked a series of questions on this issue (*Hansard*, HC, Vol 432, col 1003).

Urgent questions can also be asked in the House of Lords (known as a Private Notice Question).

KEY FACTS

Questions		
Type	**House of Commons**	**House of Lords**
Oral questions	• Oral questions to the Prime Minister (30 minutes/weekly). • Oral questions to other government ministers (on a rota). • Urgent questions.	• Oral questions. • Private Notice questions. • Questions for short debate.
Written questions	• Answers published in *Hansard*.	• Answers published in *Hansard*.

ACTIVITY

Essay writing

Do you think parliamentary questions are effective in holding the government to account? Are written questions more effective than oral ones?

12.5 Parliamentary debates

Introduction

Debates concerning government policy, decisions and future intentions are a major way in which the executive is held to account by Parliament. The two Houses are, after all, debating chambers. In constitutional theory, debates allow members to probe and expose weaknesses in government policy as well as highlighting alternative policies. Ultimately, it forces the government to justify and explain itself in a more detailed way than through parliamentary questions.

12.5.1 Debates in the House of Commons

There are various ways in which debates can take place on government policy:

■ **Debate on a vote of no confidence** (see also section 12.2.1)

It is a key principle in our uncodified constitution that the government of the day must retain the confidence of the House of Commons. After all, elected MPs represent the people.

If a motion of no confidence in the government (a confidence motion) is set down it will be accompanied by a debate. Owing to the electoral system, which typically confers a government with the support of a majority of seats in the Commons (together with the party machinery which ultimately demands loyalty of MPs), such motions are rarely successful. If a government loses the vote, a general election will generally be expected to follow as the House (as a conduit of the people) has declared that it no longer has confidence in the government to govern the country. Not only would the government morally have lost the constitutional right to govern, but in practical terms it would be impossible to govern as it would be unable to secure passage for essential measures such as the Budget.

The last government to fall losing a vote of no confidence was a Labour government in March 1979 (311 votes to 310 – *Hansard*, HC Vol 965, cols 461–590). This resulted in the May 1979 general election and the election of the Conservative government under Mrs Thatcher (who had tabled the motion as the Leader of the Opposition). Generally speaking, however, even though the vote of no confidence is one of the most important constitutional checks on the government – as it can remove a government during their term of office – it is rarely successful.

Three other points are also worth noting:

■ Firstly, a defeat on a major Bill (eg the Finance Bill encapsulating the Budget) may be considered to be a *de facto* vote of no confidence in the government.

■ Secondly, following on from the point above, ironically, a Prime Minister may use the issue of confidence *against* his own backbenchers in order to ensure that they support government proposals. In other words, the Prime Minister could warn that a defeat on a specific Bill/policy would be tantamount to a declaration of a vote of no confidence in the government which would result in the fall of the government. For example, in July 1993 the Prime Minister proposed a motion (which was carried) that the House had confidence in the government's policy on the adoption of the Protocol on Social Policy (*Hansard*, HC Vol 229, col 625).

■ Thirdly, a motion of no confidence can be directed at a single minister (though very unusual) rather than the government collectively. It is highly likely, however, that a minister warranting such attention would have resigned (or been sacked by the Prime Minster) before this became necessary. For a recent example of an (unsuccessful) motion directed at an individual minister (the Chancellor of the Exchequer) see *Hansard*, HC Vol 459, col 165.

■ **Set piece debates on the Queen's Speech and the Budget**

The Queen's Speech heralds the start of a new parliamentary session and it will set out the government's proposed legislative programme. This will be followed by a debate of a few days in which the government's proposals in general (the precise details will generally not be available at this point) will be debated. Thereafter a vote will take place on the government's intentions and if this were to be lost it would represent a crisis of confidence in the government. The House of Lords also debates the Queen's Speech, but no vote is taken.

In the context of the Budget (ie the tax proposals for the ensuing year) the Finance Bill will be debated and voted on (as any other Bill) and if the government were to be defeated on this it would be akin to a vote of no confidence as a government cannot govern without tax-raising powers.

■ **Opposition day debates**

Each parliamentary session, Her Majesty's Opposition is allocated 20 opposition days (these were previously known as Supply days) in which it can select the topic of government policy for debate. In this way the Opposition can dictate the government areas to be scrutinised and they are useful in exposing weaknesses in government policy. A highly pertinent use of one of these days was on 13th July 2000 (*Hansard*, HC Vol 353, col 1084) when the Opposition motion called for the introduction of reforms to re-assert the authority of the House of Commons and reverse the undermining of Parliament. This echoes a prevalent theme in public law that in recent decades the constitutional balance between the executive and legislature has shifted far too much in favour of the former at the expense of Parliament (whose function is to supervise the government of the day). A more recent example is the ninth allocated opposition day devoted to a debate on an Iraq War Inquiry (*Hansard*, HC Vol 490, col 312).

■ Debates in the context of an Early Day Motion

Early Day Motions (EDMs) enable a number of like-minded MPs to publicise and canvass support for specific issues. For example, in November 2008 they embraced such topics as urging the government to introduce early voting procedures to increase turnout and arouse voter engagement (Number 2478).

The parliamentary reality of EDMs is that they will not in general be debated, but merely serve as a mechanism for expressing the views of groups of MPs of varying sizes (who may sign up to the EDMs) on a particular subject.

■ Other debates in the House of Commons

- General debates (including topical debates).
- Adjournment debates.
- Debates on a substantive motion.
- Emergency debates.
- Debates in the context of the scrutiny of legislation – see section 12.7.

(On debates in general see *Dod's Handbook of House of Commons Procedure* (7th edn, Dod's, 2009) Chapter 9.)

12.5.2 Debates in the House of Lords

Debates also take place in the House of Lords and it is often assumed that the quality and standard of these debates is higher than in the House of Commons owing to the existence of a wide range of (unelected) experts on various subjects. In addition, debates tend to be less partisan in the Lords because the party whips have less influence in the second chamber.

Debates in the House of Lords are as follows:

■ Questions for short debates (see section 12.4.8)

■ Motions for general debates (in effect in three types – on debates in general, see *Handbook of the House of Lords Procedure* (2nd edn, Dod's 2006), Chapter 9):

    (i)   A motion to resolve (ie to obtain the view of the House on a particular subject).

    (ii)   A motion for papers (where a decision of the House on a subject is not required).

    (iii) A motion to 'take note' – for example, of the publication of a report:

EXAMPLE

> Lord Holme of Cheltenham: 'That this House takes note of the report of the Select Committee on the Constitution on Parliament and the Legislative Process'.
>
> *Hansard*, HL Vol 672, col 728.

Thereafter a two-and-half-hour debate followed on the report which was concerned with improving the legislative process.

■ Debates in the context of the scrutiny of legislation.

■ Set piece debates on the Queen's Speech, etc.

12.5.3 The advantages and disadvantages of parliamentary debates

Advantages

■ They make the government justify their policies and explain their strategies, thereby enabling weaknesses to be exposed. They also provide backbenchers with the opportunity to challenge government ministers directly.

■ Government ministers must retain the confidence of Parliament by demonstrating competence in their departmental area.

■ They allow the Opposition to raise and explain alternative policies and provide an opportunity to influence government thinking or strategy.

■ Debates become a matter of public record (they are printed in *Hansard*) and can inform and educate the public (see Bagehot at section 9.1.1).

Disadvantages

■ Where a debate is followed by a vote (eg in the context of legislation, the Queen's Speech or a vote of no confidence), owing to the typical dominance of the government in the House of Commons, it will inevitably win that vote. In this sense it could be argued that debates change nothing as although the Opposition may 'morally' win a debate, they will invariably lose the subsequent vote.

■ A number of debates, for example adjournment debates, may be sparsely attended. Although all debates will be printed verbatim in *Hansard*, many debates will not be widely reported by the media.

■ In terms of information and resources, there is a clear imbalance of power between members (of either House) and government ministers. The latter have civil servants working for them providing them with invaluable information.

■ There is limited time within the parliamentary timetable for full debates to take place (less so in the House of Lords, and the use of Westminster Hall has relieved some of the pressure in the Commons). Moreover, in the Commons the length of debate can be curtailed. For example, a guillotine motion can be applied to the time which can be spent discussing and debating a Bill (see section 12.7.4).

■ The question remains as to how influential parliamentary debates can be when it is arguable that the only political debate that really matters is the one in Cabinet (or more probably in a Cabinet committee) where government policy is being crystallised.

■ Debates, particularly in the House of Commons, can assume a partisan party point-scoring exercise.

ACTIVITY

Exercise

Do you think parliamentary debates are effective in scrutinising the government?

KEY FACTS

Debates	
House of Commons	**House of Lords**
• Debate in context of legislation.	• Debate in context of legislation.
• Debate on a vote of no confidence.	• Questions for a short debates.
• Set piece debates on the Queen's Speech and the Budget, etc.	• Debates on the Queen's Speech, etc.

• Opposition day debates.	• Motions for general debates.
• EDMs.	
• Other debates in the House of Commons.	

12.6 The parliamentary committee system

12.6.1 Classification

Parliamentary committees are the key way in which Parliament can hold the executive to account. They can be divided into general and select committees. In broad terms, public Bill committees (a type of general committee) scrutinise legislative proposals, whereas select committees are more investigative bodies which produce reports. It should be noted that from the 2006–07 parliamentary session, standing committees were renamed as general committees (with those standing committees scrutinising Bills being renamed public Bill committees).

Figure 12.2 The committee system in the House of Commons

12.6.2 Departmental select committees

Each government department is shadowed by a departmental select committee. In 2009 there were 19 such committees. In this way the range of government departments can be supervised:

An example of Government departments and related select committees	
Government department	**Departmental select committee**
Ministry of Defence	House of Commons Defence Committee
Home Office	House of Commons Home Affairs Committee
Department of Health	House of Commons Health Committee

Table 12.1

12.6.3 The function of select committees

QUOTATION

'Select committees shall be appointed to examine the expenditure, administration and policy of the principal government departments.'

Standing Order No 152. Source: www.publications.parliament.uk.

Select committees investigate issues (including collating evidence) and then issue reports on their findings. Their purpose is to supervise the activities, policies and decisions of their designated government department. In 2002 the Liaison Committee set out the following core tasks which select committees should seek to undertake (*Annual Report for 2002*, HC 558 (2003), p 9):

Core tasks of select committees

Task 1: To examine policy proposals from the UK Government and the European Commission in Green Papers, draft Guidance etc, and to inquire further where the Committee considers it appropriate.

Task 2: To identify and examine areas of emerging policy, or where existing policy is deficient, and make proposals.

Task 3: To conduct scrutiny of any published draft Bill within the Committee's responsibilities.

Task 4: To examine specific output from the department expressed in documents or other decisions.

Task 5: To examine the expenditure plans and out-turn of the department, its agencies and principal NDPBs.

Task 6: To examine the department's Public Service Agreements, the associated targets and the statistical measurements employed, and report if appropriate.

Task 7: To monitor the work of the department's executive agencies, NDPBs, regulators and other associated public bodies.

Task 8: To scrutinise major appointments made by the department.

Task 9: To examine the implementation of legislation and major policy initiatives.

Task 10: To produce Reports which are suitable for debate in the House, including Westminster Hall, or debating committees.

But now see section 12.6.11.

QUOTATION

'The overall effect of the core tasks has been to encourage select committees to carry out the full range of activities currently open to them'.

L Maer and M Sandford, *Select Committees under Scrutiny* (The Constitution Unit, 2004), para 22.

12.6.4 The composition of select committees

By constitutional convention membership is restricted to backbenchers who were historically proposed by a Committee of Selection; however, now see the recent reforms at section 12.6.11. As with public Bill committees, select committees will, by constitutional convention, mirror the composition of the Floor of the House. As a result, the governing party will invariably have a majority of supporters on them. Each committee has historically elected its own Chair and over the range of different select committees these positions will be held by members of the main political parties (but now see the recent reforms at section 12.6.11).

12.6.5 The powers of select committees

- **Specialist support** – Standing orders empower select committees 'to appoint specialist advisers to supply information which is not readily available or to elucidate matters of complexity'.
- **Accessing information** (persons and documents)
  In order to assist them in their work, standing orders enable select committees 'to send for persons, papers and records'. In essence, they have extensive powers of investigation to:
  (i) Request the attendance of a witness to provide evidence directly to the committee.
  (ii) Request that documentary evidence is provided.

Although select committees can summon a witness to attend and give evidence (it would be contempt of Parliament to fail to do so), they cannot compel government ministers (or members of either House of Parliament for that matter) to attend. In essence, whether they attend is really a matter for Parliament as a whole to decide. Moreover, a government minister will determine whether a civil servant will appear, and even then, they will be governed by the 'Osmotherly Rules' whereby:

QUOTATION

'Civil servants who give evidence to Select Committees do so on behalf of their Ministers and under their directions.'

Rule 40, Osmotherly Rules.
Source: www.cabinetoffice.gov.uk.

Furthermore, paragraph 41 reminds us that civil servants are directly accountable to ministers, and not to Parliament.

In general select committees tend to obtain the evidence (orally or in writing) that they seek. Two notable exceptions, however, include:

- Edwina Currie MP – she was initially reluctant to attend the Select Committee on Agriculture to explain her comments concerning the 'salmonella in eggs' issue. Although she did attend eventually, her attendance proved to be of little value.
- The Maxwell brothers refused to give evidence to the Social Services Select Committee in respect of the alleged mismanagement of pensions by their late father.

12.6.6 Select committee reports

Standing orders permit select committees 'to report from time to time'. The report is the essence of the select committee as it critically analyses the evidence before it and makes appropriate recommendations. These reports can be highly critical of government departments and by constitutional convention government should reply to them within two months. There have been concerns identified by the Liaison Committee about the timeliness of government replies to such reports (First Report, *Shifting the balance: Unfinished Business*, HC 321 (2001), paras 108–117).

In spite of the party political composition of select committees, it appears that most reports are unanimous. This makes a critical report of a government department all the more damaging as:

■ It has been made on a cross-party basis.
■ It is critical of the government notwithstanding that the governing party will ordinarily have a majority of support on the committee.

One problem with reports is that most are not debated on the Floor of the House. This is due to the pressure on the parliamentary timetable: a problem which is common to the other parliamentary mechanisms which aim to scrutinise the government (ie there is not enough time for debates, to ask oral questions, or to consider government legislative proposals in sufficient detail). In each session a few days are set aside to debate select committee reports on the Floor of the House, while the rest of the debates take place in Westminster Hall. In 2007 there were 23 debates in the Hall on 25 reports from 14 select committees (Factsheet P2, 'Departmental Select Committees' (Parliamentary Copyright 2009), p 5).

12.6.7 Other select committees

There are a number of specialised select committees.

■ **Liaison Committee** – this comprises the Chairs of the other select committees who meet to consider the work of other select committees. In recent years (since 2002) the Prime Minister has agreed to attend this committee and answer questions twice a year.
■ **Public Accounts Committee** – (see section 12.8).
■ **European Scrutiny Committee** – (see section 12.9).
■ **Public Administration Select Committee** – this considers, *inter alia*, reports of the Parliamentary Ombudsman (see section 21.3.4) and issues concerning the Civil Service.
■ **Regional Committees** – in 2009 eight regional committees were established, initially until the 2010 general election, to examine regional strategies and regional bodies.

12.6.8 Joint committees

There are also a number of joint committees which involve members from both Houses of Parliament. For example:

■ **Joint Committee on Human Rights** – this considers, *inter alia*, remedial orders made by ministers under s 10 of the Human Rights Act 1998. In addition, it examines the nature and content of Bills with a view to highlighting any issues of human rights which its provisions raise (on the Human Rights Act 1998 see Chapter 17).
■ **Joint Committee on Statutory Instruments** – this considers Statutory Instruments (see section 12.7.5).

12.6.9 Committees in the House of Lords

The House of Lords has its own separate system of committees. For the purpose of scrutinising the government the following are particularly important:

■ **House of Lords Select Committee on the Constitution** – This committee is charged with the function of examining the constitutional implications of all public Bills (including, therefore, government Bills).
■ **European Union Select Committee** – This committee considers European documents and other European Union matters (see section 12.9).
■ **House of Lords Select Committee on the Merits of Statutory Instruments** – (see section 12.7.5).

12.6.10 The advantages and disadvantages of select committees

Advantages

- They allow focused and in-depth examination of government departmental policy and activity in a way that is not possible through parliamentary questions or debates.
- As select committees are appointed for the duration of the parliamentary term (contrast, *ad hoc* public Bill committees), it enables their members to develop specialist knowledge in a specific area of government administration.
- They have discretion as to what they will investigate and how they will do so. Indeed, they can be very useful in investigating topical issues. For example, in August 2006 the Defence Committee issued a report on the situation in Iraq (13th Report of 2005–06, *UK Operations in Iraq*, HC 1241 (2006)).
- Select committees give backbenchers an enhanced role in holding the government to account and they tend to work on a non-partisan basis so that MPs of all political colours will work together as 'parliamentarians'. The cross-party political consensus of a report can prove particularly embarrassing for a government.
- Their reports, which contain written and oral evidence, provide useful public records of information on aspects of government policy (and other issues) which would otherwise not have been publicised.
- The reports of select committees can be used in the context of the legislative process to help inform and influence debate on the provisions of a Bill. For example, the House of Commons Public Administration Select Committee produced a useful and informative report on the Legislative and Regulatory Reform Bill as it was proceeding through Parliament (Third Report of Session 2005–06, *Legislative and Regulatory Reform Bill*, HC 1033 (2006)).
- Their reports can inform and influence current political debate concerning, *inter alia*, the exercise of governmental powers and draw media attention to them. For example, in July 2006 the House of Lords Select Committee on the Constitution issued a report reviewing the government's use of the royal prerogative in times of war and put forward a number of recommendations (15th Report of Session 2005–06, *Waging War: Parliament's role and responsibility* HL Paper 236-I (2006)). Also see the criticism of the government made by the Public Administration Select Committee for resisting the findings of the Ombudsman (see section 21.3.4).
- Governments, by constitutional convention, are expected to respond to reports, thereby forcing a government to explain itself in the wake of a highly critical report.
- Finally, according to the Select Committee on Modernisation of the House of Commons:

QUOTATION

'Our conclusion is that the select committees have served Parliament and the public well. They have enabled Members of Parliament to hold the Executive to account through more rigorous scrutiny than is possible on the floor of the House and they have brought before the public matters which otherwise might have remained concealed.'

First Report of Session 2001–02, HC 224 (2002), para 59.

Disadvantages

- In terms of their powers, select committees are the poor relation to the United States' Congressional Committees (Appropriation Committees) which can in effect withhold money from the administration if dissatisfied with departmental performance.
- On occasions select committees do not get access to the information that they seek. The *Arms to Iraq Affair* illustrated the limitations of the select committee system to obtain information (see section 12.3.5).

- Its reports are mere recommendations which a very confident government may be able to ignore. Select committees lack teeth because they cannot enforce their findings. Moreover, many select committee reports are not even debated which results in a lack of publicity for their work.
- Although they are empowered to appoint specialist staff, it is arguable that select committees need more resources to assist them in their deliberations. In contrast, government ministers have the full support of their departments. In May 2002, however, the House of Commons did approve a resolution including extra resources for select committees (*Hansard*, HC Vol 385, col 648ff).

12.6.11 Recent reforms

In November 2009 the House of Commons Reform Committee published its report: *Rebuilding the House*, First Report of Session 2008–09, HC 1117 (The Stationery Office 2009). This in turn led the House of Commons, in February and March 2010, to agree to the following reforms:

- To provide for a reduction in the size of select committees to a standard maximum of 11 to make them more effective.
- To review the role, resources and tasks of select committees.
- To allow Parliament to vote on September sittings.
- To engage the public more in relation to draft laws.
- To reform the petitioning system.
- To provide for the Chair (no longer Chairman) of select committees to be elected by the House.
- To provide for members of select committees to be elected (within their party groupings).
- To provide for a Backbench Business Committee to schedule non-ministerial business.

ACTIVITY

Quick quiz

1. What do select committees do?
2. What powers do select committees have?
3. What are the advantages and disadvantages of select committees in terms of holding the government to account?

12.7 Scrutiny during the legislative process

Introduction

The vast majority of Bills introduced in Parliament (which ultimately become law) are initiated by the executive (government Bills) and during the course of their various stages they will be subject to scrutiny by both Houses of Parliament. The examination and scrutiny of a government Bill, therefore, necessarily involves examining and scrutinising government policy as encapsulated within that Bill. Below is an overview of how the government is scrutinised during the law-making process.

It is worth noting at the outset that one of the criticisms made of primary legislation in recent years is not just the number of Bills which Parliament passes each year, but the cumulative volume of these Bills. For example, the Constitutional Reform Act 2005 is over 300 pages long and contains 149 sections together with 18 Schedules. In addition, legislation can be passed expeditiously, see the Terrorist Asset-Freezing (Temporary Provisions) Act 2010 which passed *all* its stages through both Houses in just five days.

12.7.1 Draft legislation

In recent years the government has produced a number of Bills in draft in order that they can be subject to pre-legislative scrutiny (although draft Bills have been published since the early 1990s, this practice of publishing Bills in draft has been slightly accelerated since 1997). It is argued that this produces better legislation as controversial or technical issues can be identified and discussed at this stage prior to the Bill being formally introduced into Parliament. In fact, it offers a real opportunity to influence the government's stance on a Bill in draft before it takes final shape. One criticism levelled against the Constitutional Reform Bill in 2003 was that this highly significant Bill had not been subjected to pre-legislative scrutiny. In contrast, parts of the July 2009 Constitutional Reform and Governance Bill had been issued previously in draft form (*Draft Constitutional Renewal Bill*, Cm 7342–II (2008)). In addition to producing some Bills in draft, in July 2007 the government started to publish a *Draft Legislative Programme* (DLP) setting out the Bills which it intended to include within the ensuing Queen's Speech.

12.7.2 The second reading

This permits the first opportunity for Parliament to reject a Bill with its general principles being debated and voted on (the first reading being a mere formality). Owing to executive dominance in the House of Commons, in general it is highly unlikely that a government would lose the vote at second reading. One prominent exception was the Conservative government's defeat on the 1986 Shops Bill concerning Sunday trading. At this time Mrs Thatcher as Prime Minister had a commanding majority of support in the House and her defeat was due to a significant number of her own backbenchers failing to vote in favour of the legislation. This illustrates that no matter the number of seats a government has supporting it, ultimately, it is the government's backbenchers who can break a government. This is the constitutional antidote to the 'elective dictatorship'.

12.7.3 The committee and subsequent stages

The committee stage

In the House of Commons the committee stage will typically take place in a public Bill committee which is composed of a small number of MPs (16–50 MPs). From the start of the 2006–07 parliamentary session the type of committees which were formerly known as standing committees were renamed 'general committees'. In particular, standing committees which were used to consider public Bills are now called 'public Bill committees' named after the Bill they are considering (eg the 2009 Equality Bill Committee considered the Equality Bill). The government minister sponsoring the Bill will be expected to defend it as it is considered in detail at this stage; however, a number of factors favour him:

- Firstly, by constitutional convention the committee will reflect the composition of the Floor of the House, inevitably therefore, providing the governing party with a numerical advantage when voting takes place.
- Secondly, the imbalance of power between the executive and the MP is illustrated by the fact that the minister will have a supporting team of civil servants to provide information. Indeed, historically such committees, in contrast to select committees, were not ordinarily evidence-taking committees:

QUOTATION

'Consideration of a bill is confined to the words in the bill and members who wish to draw on the services of informed and affected bodies do so on a personal basis.'

14th Report of Session 2003–04, *Parliament and the Legislative Process*,
Vol 1 Report, HL Paper 173-1 (2004), para 125.
NB But now see recent reforms below.

- Thirdly, unlike their departmental select committee counterparts, public Bill committees are selected on an *ad hoc* basis and not for the duration of a parliamentary term.
- Fourthly, only members of the public Bill committee can make amendments at this stage.

As noted by the Select Committee on Modernisation of the House of Commons, standing committees (now public Bill committees) have historically been one of the most criticised aspects of the parliamentary law-making process. Indeed, in its written evidence to the above Committee, the Hansard Society stated that many people argue that standing committees:

QUOTATION

'... fall badly between several stools: they fail to deliver genuine and analytical scrutiny of the provisions involved, their political functions are neutered, dominated almost exclusively by government ... they fail to engage with the public and the media (in contrast to select committees) and they do not adequately utilise the evidence of experts or interested parties'.

First Report of Session 2005–06, *The Legislative Process* HC 1097 (2006), Ev 108.

It should be noted that in recent years the House of Commons standing orders were amended with the effect that a public Bill committee to which a Bill has been committed by virtue of a programme order/motion, 'shall have the power to send for persons, papers and records' (ie take oral and written evidence) Standing Order No 84A – this is analogous to the powers of a select committee, see section 12.6.5.

In the House of Lords, the committee stage takes place on the Floor of the House allowing all peers to be involved in scrutinising the Bill.

The committee stage and constitutional Bills

By constitutional convention, in the House of Commons a Bill of *first class* constitutional importance would be committed to a Committee of the Whole House, rather than to a smaller public Bill committee. Hazell ('Time for a New Convention: Parliamentary Scrutiny of Constitutional Bills 1997–2005' [2006] PL 247) identified and examined the legislative process for 55 Bills considered to be of constitutional importance between 1997 and 2005 (a period of dramatic reform of the constitution). He noted that there was a strong presumption that Bills of first class constitutional importance (eg those dealing with devolution, referendums, Europe, Parliament and human rights) would be considered on the Floor of the chamber. In contrast, those Bills not counting as first class (eg immigration, the court system, freedom of information, etc) would be referred to standing committees. A second (intermediate) group of Bills (some first class and some not) involving subjects such as elections, emergencies and Northern Ireland, would be considered by a mixture of standing committees and Committees of the Whole House (with urgent Bills on these matters being taken on the Floor of the House).

As pointed out by Hazell, the advantages of consideration by a Committee of the Whole House is that it allows more members (and a greater range of them) to contribute to the examination of the Bill. However, committee stages on the Floor tend to be shorter than those in a standing (now called public Bill) committee and as a result there is a limited number of amendments that can be moved and debated.

Report stage

This provides another opportunity to scrutinise the Bill and influence it by proposing amendments.

Third reading

This is typically a short session (although in the House of Lords amendments can be made).

12.7.4 Procedural matters

The following factors favour the government in the legislative process:

- It controls the parliamentary timetable and the scheduling of Bills. In the House of Commons the government can use, for example, the guillotine motion (an allocation of time motion) to restrict debate and scrutiny of a Bill by providing that proceedings on the Bill end once a stated time has been reached. In the last decade, however, the guillotine has been overtaken by the introduction of 'programme motions' which are (theoretically) a more consensual and effective use of parliamentary time which formalises the agreement on the timetable of a Bill between the frontbenches.
- As noted at section 10.10.1, under the Parliament Acts 1911 and 1949 the House of Commons (controlled by the executive) can in any event ultimately reject amendments made by the House of Lords.
- A Bill which does not pass the requisite legislative stages within a parliamentary session will 'fall'. This has been mitigated in the past decade by the 'carry-over procedure' which allows a Bill to be carried over between parliamentary sessions, thus saving the Bill from abandonment. The Constitutional Reform Bill was a high profile Bill which was carried over (from the 2003–04 to the 2004–05 session).

There are some procedural differences in the way that the two Houses process legislation and these are indicated below:

- The committee stage in the House of Lords is taken on the 'Floor of the House', whereas in the Commons it usually takes place in a smaller public Bill committee.
- The government has control over the legislative timetable in the Commons.
- Unlike the Commons, in the Lords all amendments can be (in theory and practice) scrutinised.
- Unlike the Commons, in the Lords debates are not subject to the guillotine.

Overall, it would appear that the balance between the government of the day wishing to see its proposals enacted as law, and Parliament, whose role is to subject them to rigorous and detailed scrutiny, still clearly favours the executive. In short, if a government is determined enough, it can ensure that its proposals become law irrespective of the criticism levelled at it.

12.7.5 Delegated legislation

As indicated at section 5.7.2, when government ministers exercise a power to make delegated legislation they violate the principle of the separation of powers. As a consequence of this, there are a number of parliamentary controls over its use. Delegated legislation will typically be made in the form of a Statutory Instrument and so will be governed by the Statutory Instruments Act 1946. It should be pointed out that Statutory Instruments are now accompanied by an explanatory note to explain their nature and aid understanding. This should be seen in the context of the rule of law at section 6.3.2, which requires that laws should be accessible and clear.

The enabling Act itself will indicate the type of scrutiny the delegated measure is to receive from Parliament. In essence, the Act may state that the instrument:

- Is simply laid before Parliament. This means that Parliament's attention is simply drawn to it. Alternatively, the instrument may not have to be laid before Parliament at all.
- Is subject to a negative resolution which means that it is laid before Parliament and is subject to annulment by it within 40 days. In other words, the instrument will become law *unless* Parliament positively objects to it.

- Is subject to an affirmative resolution which means that it is laid before Parliament, but will not come into force unless it is assented to. In other words, Parliament has to approve it in order for it to come into effect. A variant on this is that it is laid and comes into effect immediately, but requires positive approval (eg within 28 days) in order to carry on in force.
- Is laid in draft form (with a positive or negative resolution).
- Is subject to what has been termed a 'super affirmative' procedure (involving 60 day periods). For example, see the remedial orders made under s 10 of the Human Rights Act 1998 used in order to remedy an incompatibility with the European Convention on Human Rights (see section 17.7.3).

In addition, the following committees have a role to play in the scrutiny of delegated legislation:

The Joint Committee on Statutory Instruments

This joint committee comprising members of both Houses is responsible for scrutinising all Statutory Instruments. Under Standing Order 151 it can draw Parliament's attention to an instrument which, *inter alia*:

- Imposes a charge/tax.
- Purports to have a retrospective effect.
- Appears to be *ultra vires*.
- Exhibits defective drafting.

Those instruments which only have to be laid before the House of Commons are scrutinised by the House of Commons Select Committee on Statutory Instruments.

The House of Lords Select Committee on the Merits of Statutory Instruments

This was established in 2003 and it draws the attention of the House of Lords to a Statutory Instrument (subject to a positive or negative resolution) laid which, *inter alia,* raises issues of public policy or does not perfectly achieve its policy objectives.

The House of Lords Select Committee on Delegated Powers and Regulatory Reform

This committee considers whether:

- any enabling Bill proposes to delegate legislative power inappropriately or
- the proposed parliamentary scrutiny of the delegated legislation to be made under the Act is inappropriate (ie it is insufficient). The Committee also reports on draft orders laid before Parliament under the aegis of the Legislative and Regulatory Reform Act 2006 (see section 7.5.7). The Commons has a similar Committee (the Regulatory Reform Committee).

The constitutional issues raised by delegated legislation

Firstly, each year Statutory Instruments statistically outnumber Acts of Parliament. For example, in 2006, 55 Public Acts gained Royal Assent in contrast to 3,509 Statutory Instruments which were made (R Cracknell, 'Acts and Statutory Instruments: Volume of UK legislation 1950 to 2007', SN/SG/2911 (House of Commons Library, 2008), p 3). Most domestic legislation, therefore, is not primary and so is not directly made by the legislature (Parliament).

Secondly, it must be remembered that it is the government of the day which will draft the enabling Bill. This means that (unless the Bill is amended), it will determine the degree of parliamentary control and supervision that is to be exercised over government ministers making Statutory Instruments under the enabling legislation. It is, therefore, not surprising that only around one tenth of Statutory Instruments subject to parliamentary supervision are the subject of a positive resolution.

Thirdly, parliamentary time is limited and negative resolutions rely on the willingness of parliamentarians to examine instruments subject to this procedure. This is another reason why positive resolutions are not used often.

Fourthly, debates in the Commons on Statutory Instruments may take place on the Floor of the House or much more likely, in a delegated legislation committee – a type of general committee (formerly known as a standing committee). For an example of such a committee, see the 2009 Fifth Delegated Legislation Committee which considered the Draft Counter-Terrorism Act 2008 (Foreign Travel Notification Requirements) Regulations 2009.

Finally, as observed by the Select Committee on Modernisation of the House of Commons:

QUOTATION

'To the extent that currently few SIs take up any Parliamentary time and that those that do are generally taken in standing committee, in a debate which may last up to one and a half hours, they have little bearing on Parliament's capacity to consider legislation.'

First Report of Session 2005–06, *The Legislative Process*, HC 1097 (2006), p 8.

Indeed, in the 2006–07 parliamentary session, whereas 1,380 Statutory Instruments were laid before the House of Commons, only 12 were considered in the House and 202 in committee (R Cracknell, 'Acts and Statutory Instruments: Volume of UK legislation 1950 to 2007', SN/SG/2911 (House of Commons Library, 2008), p 7).

KEY FACTS

Committees	
Departmental select committees	Appointed for each parliamentary term to supervise the activities, policies and decisions of their designated government department.
	Investigate issues, collate evidence and issue reports on their findings.
Public Bill committees	Appointed on an *ad hoc* basis to examine in detail the contents of proposed legislation.
Joint committees	Comprising members of both Houses to consider specific issues (eg the Joint Committee on Statutory Instruments).

ACTIVITY

Essay writing

Compare and contrast how primary and delegated legislation is scrutinised by Parliament. How effective is that scrutiny?

12.8 Scrutiny in the context of finance

Below is a very brief outline of how government is scrutinised in financial matters. It should be noted that financial matters are in essence determined by the House of Commons as it contains elected representatives.

Past expenditure

In terms of public money spent, government departments are monitored by the most important select committee in the House of Commons: the Public Accounts Committee. It scrutinises government expenditure (in terms of value for money) through the examination of audits made by the Comptroller and Auditor-General of the National Audit Office. This scrutiny involves assessing the efficiency of government spending and whether it has been used for the purposes authorised by Parliament. Each session Parliament will set aside a day to debate the reports made by the Public Accounts Committee.

Future taxation/expenditure

In particular, this will involve the raising of taxes to pay for government spending in the form of the annual Budget (the Finance Bill) which will be debated and voted on in one of the major set piece debates in the parliamentary calendar. It should be remembered that under Art 4 of the Bill of Rights 1689, Parliament must authorise the raising of taxation. In addition, the government will supply estimates (requests for specified money) and these are approved annually by Parliament via an Appropriation Act (and on an interim basis via a Consolidated Fund Act).

12.9 Scrutiny in the context of Europe

Government ministers attend meetings of the Council (Council of Ministers – which is the legislature of the European Union) and can commit the United Kingdom to European legislative proposals. Parliament provides extensive provision for the consideration of European law and proposals. In brief, two parliamentary committees perform this function:

- **The House of Commons European Scrutiny Committee** – which considers, *inter alia*, the legal significance of European documents and monitors the activities of British ministers in the Council. There are three European Committees A–C (types of general committees) which consider European documents recommended by the European Scrutiny Committee for debate. For example, Committee C considers education matters.
- **The House of Lords European Union Select Committee** – which scrutinises European legislative proposals and the reaction of the British government to them. The Committee has a number of sub-committees for example, Sub-Committee E considers law and institutions.

These two committees complement one another with the House of Lords Committee being more selective and detailed in its treatment of European documents than its more wide-ranging counterpart in the Commons.

As noted by the Wakeham Commission:

QUOTATION

'The United Kingdom Parliament already has one of the most highly developed systems in the EU for considering proposed European legislation and other proposals and for ensuring that Ministers are aware of the balance of opinion within Parliament before they commit the United Kingdom to any significant new position.'

A House for the Future, Cm 4534 (2000), p 83.

In particular, the House of Commons European Scrutiny Committee will scrutinise government ministers (largely through written reports) before and after they attend sessions of the Council (Council of Ministers – see section 15.2). In the Council, ministers are able to commit the United Kingdom to legislative proposals and so it is imperative that government ministers are scrutinised effectively. The House of Commons' 1998 *scrutiny reserve resolution* constrains a government minister from committing the United Kingdom in the Council, if the matter has *not* cleared scrutiny by the European Scrutiny Committee (or it is awaiting consideration by the Commons).

SUMMARY

- One of the central relationships in the British constitution is that between the executive and the legislature.

- The government is held to account by Parliament by the conventions of individual and collective responsibility.
- Collective responsibility involves:
  - The government offering its resignation (or requesting a dissolution of Parliament) in the event of the support of the House of Commons being lost.
  - The government speaks with one voice.
  - Cabinet discussions remain secret.
- Individual responsibility involves:
  - A minister being responsible for his public role/decisions and the actions of his officials.
  - A minister being responsible for his private life.
- Government is held to account through the following parliamentary mechanisms:
  - Ministers are asked parliamentary questions in both Houses with the most famous type of questioning being Prime Minister's Question Time.
  - Debates are held in both Houses concerning government policy and decisions.
  - Departmental select committees shadow government departments and examine their actions, policies and decisions.
  - During the legislative process both Houses scrutinise Bills.
  - Scrutiny of financial (performed by the Commons) and European matters.

SAMPLE ESSAY QUESTION

How does the legislature hold the executive to account?

Introduction:
- Constitutional function of the legislature is to supervise the actions of, and hold to account, the executive/government
- Link with the convention of ministerial responsibility

Legislation:
Primary (debates and votes during the various parliamentary stages in both Houses – though note the typical government dominance in the Commons and control of the timetable)

Secondary (note the important committee work, eg the Joint Committee on Statutory Instruments)

Parliamentary committees:
- Departmental select committees attached to each government department and responsible for examining its administration and policies
- Specialist committees (eg Public Accounts Committee which examines government expenditure)
- Public Bill committees examine legislation

Parliamentary debates and questions:

Set piece (eg on the Budget or the Queen's Speech)

Opposition days

Debates in the House of Lords

Vote of no confidence (link with the convention of collective responsibility and see the fall of the Labour government in 1979)

Parliamentary questions (both oral and written)

CONCLUSION

 # Further reading

Books

Marshall, G, *Constitutional Conventions*, (Oxford, Clarendon Press, 1986), Chapters 4, 6, 13 and 14.

Weir, S and Beetham, D, *Political Power and Democratic Control in Britain* (Routledge, 1999), Chapters 12–14.

Articles

Lord Hailsham, 'Elective dictatorship', *The Listener* (1976) 21st October, p 496.

Hazell, R, 'Time for a New Convention: Parliamentary Scrutiny of Constitutional Bills 1997–2005' [2006] PL 247.

Papers

Gay, O and Powell, T, 'Individual ministerial responsibility – issues and examples', 04/31 (House of Commons Library, 2004).

Gay, O, and Powell, T, 'The collective responsibility of Ministers – an outline of the issues', 04/82 (House of Commons Library, 2004).

Maer, L and Sandford, M, *Select Committees under Scrutiny* (The Constitution Unit, 2004).

Maer, L, Gay, O and Kelly, R, 'The Departmental Select Committee System', 09/55 (House of Commons Library, 2009).

Winetrobe, B, 'Shifting control? Aspects of the executive–parliamentary relationship', 00/92, (House of Commons Library, 2000).

Factsheet P1, 'Parliamentary Questions' (House of Commons Parliamentary Copyright, 2008).

Factsheet P2, 'Departmental Select Committees' (House of Commons Parliamentary Copyright, 2009).

Factsheet L1, 'Parliamentary Stages of a Government Bill' (House of Commons Parliamentary Copyright, 2008).

Factsheet L6, 'General Committees' (House of Commons Parliamentary Copyright, 2009).

Factsheet L7, 'Statutory Instruments' (House of Commons Parliamentary Copyright, 2008).

Internet links

www.parliament.uk

13

The judiciary

AIMS AND OBJECTIVES

At the end of this chapter you should be able to:

■ Understand the principle of judicial independence and impartiality
■ Appreciate the constitutional position of the judiciary

13.1 Introduction and definition

QUOTATION

'The public must have confidence in the impartiality, fairness and independence of the judiciary; otherwise they will be less likely to observe the law.'

Lord Woolf, *Shaping the Future*, www.dca.gov.uk 13th October 2004.

The independence and impartiality of the judiciary is a central element of any democratic constitution and, as noted at section 3.4.9, it is a key characteristic of Britain's uncodified constitution. The constitutional function of the judiciary is to provide for the resolution of constitutional/legal disputes and determine the law laid down in both statutory and common law sources. Although there is a close connection between the two terms and the two are often used synonymously, it is common to draw a technical distinction between judicial independence and judicial impartiality:

■ Judicial independence means that the judiciary is structurally separate from both the legislature and executive. In this way they can perform their judicial function strictly in accordance with the law free from any extraneous pressures (executive or legislative) to determine a case before them in a particular way.
■ Judicial impartiality means that judges perform their judicial function in a strictly impartial manner without any preconceptions or prejudgement based on class, sex, education, etc.

In this way judges can make independent and impartial decisions.

13.2 The constitutional dimension of the judiciary

The independence and impartiality of the judiciary must be viewed in the light of the following constitutional principles/concepts:

13.2.1 The separation of powers

As indicated in Chapter 5, the British constitution does not follow a strict separation of powers. In terms of personnel, however, there has been a general separation between the judiciary on the one hand and the executive/legislative arms of the state on the other (s 1 of the House of Commons Disqualification Act 1975 prohibits full-time judges sitting in the House of Commons). Historically, however, there have been two prominent exceptions:

■ **The Lord Chancellor** (an overlap of the judiciary, executive and legislature).

Before 2003 the Lord Chancellor sat as a senior judge, was a member of the Cabinet as a senior ranking government minister and (by constitutional convention) was a member of the upper House in Parliament where he performed the functions of both Speaker and a senior government spokesperson. As indicated at section 5.7.9, the Constitutional Reform Act 2005 has now reformed the office so that the Lord Chancellor no longer:

i) acts as a senior judge (in 2003 Lord Falconer indicated that he would no longer sit as a judge); and

ii) acts as the Head of the Judiciary of England and Wales. Under s 7 of the Constitutional Reform Act 2005 the Lord Chief Justice has became President of the Courts of England and Wales as well as Head of the Judiciary and responsible, *inter alia*, for representing the views of the judiciary in England and Wales (s 5).

■ **The law lords** (an overlap of the judiciary and legislature).

Part 3 of the Constitutional Reform Act 2005 (which came into effect in 2009) barred serving law lords from the upper chamber of Parliament and reconstituted them in a constitutionally and physically separate Supreme Court (see section 5.7.4).

In terms of the judicial function, although historically the judges have performed this function exclusively, the following points need to be noted:

■ **Tribunals** – The strict, formalised court system is supplemented by a system of tribunals (see section 21.1). These tribunals were historically not staffed by judges *per se* (although some were), but they did perform an essentially judicial function in applying legal rules to factual disputes (sometimes highly specialised and technical, eg Employment Tribunals). The Tribunals, Courts and Enforcement Act 2007 which reformed the tribunal system provides that legal members of tribunals (ie legally qualified members) are designated as Tribunal Judges.

■ **The executive performing judicial functions** – The executive, in the form of the Home Secretary, historically enjoyed powers to determine sentences (a judicial function) to be served by certain categories of prisoners (see section 5.7.6). In modern times, under the European Convention and the Human Rights Act 1998, the Home Secretary's powers have been circumscribed, thereby realigning the constitution so as to accord with a stricter separation of powers:

CASE EXAMPLE

R (Anderson) v Secretary of State for Home Department [2002] UKHL 46

Section 29 of the Crime (Sentences) Act 1997 empowered the Home Secretary to determine the tariff (for punitive purposes) to be served by persons convicted of murder. Anderson sought judicial review of the tariff set by the minister under the Human Rights Act 1998.

The House of Lords made a declaration of incompatibility that s 29 of the 1997 Act was incompatible with Art 6 (the right to a fair trial). In brief, the determination of a prison sentence was a judicial function and Art 6 required such a sentence to be decided by an independent and impartial tribunal. The Home Secretary was not independent of the executive (in fact, he was a key member of the Cabinet). Referring to the jurisprudence of the European Court of Human Rights, Lord Bingham observed that:

JUDGMENT

'The European Court was right to describe the complete functional separation of the judiciary from the executive as "fundamental", since the rule of law depends on it.'

As a result of the declaration, the Criminal Justice Act 2003 now provides for the tariff (minimum) term for those sentenced to life imprisonment by a judge to be exercised by the judiciary, and not the Home Secretary.

In discharging their judicial function, as indicated at section 5.7.10, inevitably judges will also exercise a *de facto* legislative function when they:

i) develop the common law (which is after all *judge made* law); and
ii) construe ambiguous and unclear statutory provisions.

13.2.2 Parliamentary sovereignty

As noted in Chapter 7, it is a central element of the British constitution that the Queen in Parliament is the sovereign law-making body and that the judiciary are subordinate to the will of the legislature. In short, in interpreting and applying legislation, the judiciary must simply give effect to the will of Parliament. Indeed, Lord Diplock in *Duport Steels Ltd and others v Sirs and others* [1980] 1 All ER 529 (for the facts of the case, see section 5.8.3), has made it very clear what the constitutional role of the courts is in relation to the provisions of a statute:

JUDGMENT

'Where the meaning of the statutory words is plain and unambiguous it is not for the judges to invent fancied ambiguities as an excuse for failing to give effect to its plain meaning because they themselves consider that the consequences of doing so would be inexpedient, or even unjust or immoral … It endangers continued public confidence in the political impartiality of the judiciary, which is essential to the continuance of the rule of law, if judges, under the guise of interpretation, provide their own preferred amendments to statutes…'

....
**Student
mentor tip**
....

"Try to get to
grips with what
the judges say
re Parliamentary
sovereignty, eg
Dicey."

*Audrie, University of
Dundee*
....

It has been a hallmark of the British constitution that, unlike in other countries such as the United States of America and Ireland, the United Kingdom judiciary is constitutionally limited. In other words, historically they have been unable to invalidate or challenge Acts of Parliament (but see section 7.7). Indeed, even with the advent of the new United Kingdom Supreme Court which came into operation in October 2009, this court is not the constitutional equivalent of the United States Supreme Court which can invalidate legislation which is inconsistent with the codified constitution (*Marbury v Madison* (1803) 1 Cranch 137). In recent years, however, the traditional judicial deference towards Acts of Parliament had to be revisited in light of European law:

■ European Union law

As we shall see at section 15.6.2, the European Court of Justice has developed the principle of the primacy of European Union law which states that Union law has primacy over, and is superior to, inconsistent national law. As a result, in *ex parte Factortame* (1991), the House of Lords disapplied provisions of an Act of Parliament as being in conflict with overriding European law (see section 15.6.4). The requirements of European law have also altered statutory interpretation in the United Kingdom with the British judiciary adopting the legal reasoning applied by the judges in the European Court in Luxembourg (eg the telelogical approach to interpreting legislation – see section 15.4.1).

■ European Convention law

In strict legal terms the Human Rights Act 1998 preserves parliamentary sovereignty. Section 4 does, however, authorise a court to issue a declaration of incompatibility (see section 17.7) which, at least in a moral sense, could be viewed as the courts *questioning* an Act of Parliament for being inconsistent with the provisions of European Convention law. The point must be remembered, however, that Parliament itself has specifically empowered the courts to make such a declaration. In any event, although there may be political pressure to reform the law as a result of a declaration, in law, Parliament is free to accept or ignore such a declaration.

13.2.3 The rule of law and the protection of the individual

QUOTATION

'I think the independence of the judiciary and the rule of law are very difficult to sever. It is the role of the judiciary, in practice, to uphold the rule of law, to apply the rule of law, to enforce the rule of law, and to do that they have to be independent of outside influence.'

Lord Phillips (Lord Chief Justice), The House of Lords Select Committee on the Constitution, Fourteenth Report of Session 2005–06, *Meeting with the Lord Chief Justice* HL 213 (2006), Q7.

JUDGMENT

'… the function of independent judges charged to interpret and apply the law is universally recognised as a cardinal feature of the modern democratic state, a cornerstone of the rule of law itself.'

Lord Bingham in *A and others v Secretary of State for the Home Department* [2004] UKHL 56.

The judicial arm of the constitution must be independent, because, as they ensure that state bodies act under the law (thereby enforcing the rule of law), inevitably they will come into constitutional conflict with the executive (see section 6.7.10). The independence and impartiality of the judiciary is also linked inextricably to the efficient administration of justice and public confidence in the judicial system to resolve disputes fairly and impartially.

One aspect of the rule of law requires the judiciary to protect the individual. In the absence of a written codified constitution, historically the courts have done so by:

- developing common law remedies such as trespass (see *Entick v Carrington* (1765) at section 4.8.2); and
- interpreting statutory provisions in the light of certain constitutional principles which protect the individual (eg their access to the courts *Chester v Bateson* (1920) at section 5.7.2).

Under the Human Rights Act 1998, the courts are charged specifically with applying and upholding the Convention rights of individuals (see Chapter 17).

13.2.4 Judicial review

Judicial review is linked inextricably with the principles of the rule of law (the courts holding the executive legally to account) and the separation of powers (the courts checking and balancing the actions of the executive – see section 19.2.3). It is of paramount importance, therefore, that the judiciary are independent of the executive. In the absence of a codified constitution limiting the actions of the executive, judicial review helps to fill the void by requiring government officials to exercise their executive powers legally, rationally and fairly (see Chapter 20).

QUOTATION

'The claim that the courts stand between the executive and the citizen, and control all abuse of executive power, has been reinvigorated and become a foundation of our modern democracy.'

J Steyn, 'The case for a Supreme Court' [2002] 118 LQR 382.

Constitutional principle	Role of the judiciary
The separation of powers	To interpret the law and resolve legal disputes.
Parliamentary sovereignty	To uphold the will of Parliament and give effect to its intention.
Rule of law	To uphold and enforce the rule of law, (particularly against the executive).
Protection of the individual	To protect the individual from state interference.
Judicial review	To hold the executive legally to account for the use of its powers.

13.3 The appointment of the judiciary

13.3.1 Judicial appointments

In historic terms, a member of the executive (whether the Lord Chancellor or the Prime Minister) has traditionally been involved in the appointment of the judiciary with the appointment thereafter being confirmed officially by the monarch. Under the Constitutional Reform Act 2005 (s 61 and Sched 12) a new Judicial Appointments Commission has been established (operational since 2006) to carry out the responsibility of recruiting and selecting candidates for judicial appointments in England and Wales. Whenever a vacancy occurs in the Supreme Court, a Supreme Court Selection Commission will be convened by the Lord Chancellor. Although the process of appointment is somewhat complex (it can comprise three stages), both the above commissions will consider the suitability of individuals and put forward an appropriate candidate for the Lord Chancellor to accept, reject, or request that they are reconsidered. It is of interest to note that there are no parliamentary affirmations of judges as the legislature does not take part in the appointment process. In 2008 the government in its White Paper on Constitutional Renewal (Cm 7342–I, (Crown Copyright, 2008), p 30), argued that the role of the executive in judicial appointments should be reduced. Thereafter, the 2010 Constitutional Reform and Governance Bill proposed to remove the (albeit formal) role of the Prime Minister in appointments to the Supreme Court. However, this provision was removed from the Bill before the measure became the Constitutional Reform and Governance Act 2010.

13.3.2 Arguments against executive involvement in judicial appointments

The system of appointing judges is of immense constitutional importance because the individuals appointed must be considered to be constitutionally acceptable and legitimate. In fact, it is arguable as to whether the executive should have any involvement in this process at all. The arguments against executive participation include the fact that some of the judges appointed will inevitably be involved in reviewing the actions of government ministers at some point in the future (eg in the context of judicial review claims and actions under the Human Rights Act 1998). As a result, it could be suggested that conferring a member of the executive (here the Lord Chancellor who is a Cabinet minister) with the power to determine who is appointed to the judiciary is manifestly inconsistent with the separation of powers.

In 2003 a Bar Working Party noted, in the context of the appointment of High Court Judges, that if the judiciary were 'to perform its proper role':

QUOTATION

'It must be protected by constitutional safeguards from the risk or even the perception that its independence might be threatened by the Executive. Put simply, it has become constitutionally unacceptable in our view that the judges should be appointed by the government of the day. We will stress that this is not an attack on the present or any past or future Lord Chancellor. It is a matter of public perception.'

Bar Council Working Party on Judicial Appointments and Silk Consultation Document
(The Bar Council (2003)), p 66.

13.3.3 Arguments in favour of executive involvement in judicial appointments

The arguments in favour of executive involvement include the following:

■ It has been commonly argued that if the judiciary were to appoint itself, this could amount to a self-appointing (and therefore constitutionally unaccountable) 'judicial oligarchy'.

■ The executive (Lord Chancellor) is ultimately accountable to Parliament for any appointments made.

■ The Commissions established under the Constitutional Reform Act 2005 necessarily fetter the discretion of the Lord Chancellor to that of accepting, requiring a reconsideration of, or rejecting the candidate put forward by each Commission. Indeed, in respect of the Supreme Court, the original version of the Constitutional Reform Bill envisaged the minister selecting a judge from a choice of between two and five candidates. The Bill was amended as it was felt that this conferred excessive discretion onto the minister/executive.

■ Other democracies have executive involvement. For example, in the United States the President selects proposed Supreme Court Justices (although these must be confirmed by the upper chamber of Congress: the Senate). In 2009 the President proposed, and the Senate confirmed, the appointment of Justice Sonia Sotomayor.

ACTIVITY

Self-test question

Do you think that the executive should be involved in any way with the appointment of the judiciary? If so, why?

13.4 The independence of the judiciary

In the absence of a codified constitutional provision explicitly safeguarding and protecting the judiciary, judicial independence in the British constitution is protected in the following ways:

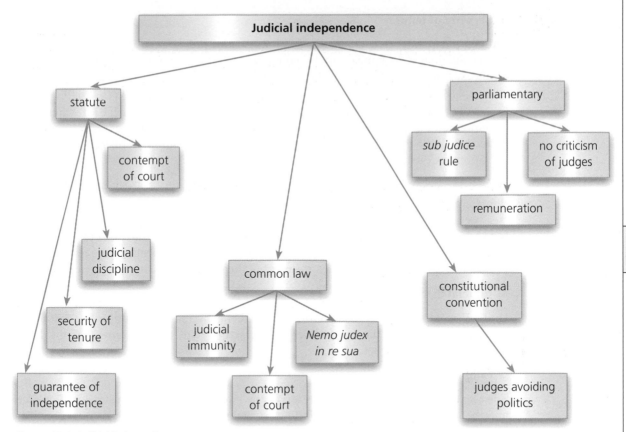

Figure 13.1 Judicial independence

13.4.1 Statutory protection

■ Guaranteed independence

Section 3(1) of the Constitutional Reform Act 2005 makes specific provision guaranteeing the independence of the judiciary:

SECTION

....

s3

'**Guarantee of continued judicial independence** (1) The Lord Chancellor, other Ministers of the Crown and all with responsibility for matters relating to the judiciary or otherwise to the administration of justice must uphold the continued independence of the judiciary.'

(Section 1 of the Tribunals, Courts and Enforcement Act 2007 extends this protection to the tribunal judiciary.) This provision presupposes the existence of judicial independence in the British constitution as it refers explicitly to its 'continued independence'. Section 17 stipulates that the oath to be taken by a Lord Chancellor charges him to defend the independence of the judiciary (see section 5.7.9). In addition, s 3(5) aims to protect judicial decision-making from the influence of the executive as it states that:

SECTION

....

s3(5)

'The Lord Chancellor and other Ministers of the Crown must not seek to influence particular judicial decisions through any special access to the judiciary.'

■ **Security of tenure**

Judicial independence is enhanced by giving senior judges security of tenure (during good behaviour) which means that their continued office is not dependent on the favour of the executive. In short, the political executive does not remove senior judges as this is achieved by the monarch following an address from both Houses of Parliament:

■ Act of Settlement 1700 as amended by s 11 of the Senior Courts Act 1981 (formerly the Supreme Court Act) in terms of Court of Appeal/High Court Judges.

■ Section 33 of the Constitutional Reform Act 2005 in relation to Justices of the new Supreme Court.

Moreover, as both Houses must act in concert, this serves to emphasise the constitutional significance of the modern House of Lords acting as a constitutional safeguard (see section 10.9.9) by protecting the senior judiciary from the executive. It should be noted, however, that although the senior judiciary are protected, the lower ranks, such as circuit judges are not, as they can be removed by the Lord Chancellor (due to incapacity or misbehaviour), albeit with the agreement of the Lord Chief Justice.

■ **Judicial discipline**

Under Pt 4 of the Constitutional Reform Act 2005, the disciplining of judges (eg warnings, reprimands) involves the Lord Chief Justice acting with the agreement of the Lord Chancellor.

■ **Contempt of court**

The Contempt of Court Act 1981 preserves the integrity of the administration of justice and the right to a fair trial by prohibiting words which would prejudice court proceedings. For example, a newspaper revealing the previous criminal convictions of a defendant so as to prejudice the jury against him.

13.4.2 Common law protection

■ **Judicial immunity**

In order for judges and the administration of justice to perform effectively, it is a common law principle that judges are immune from legal liability for things said during the course of a trial in their judicial capacity (*Anderson v Gorries* [1895] 1 QB 668). If this were not the case, the judiciary would be unable to ensure that the administration of justice was carried out. As pointed out by Lord Denning MR in *Sirros v Moore* [1975] 1 QB 118:

JUDGMENT

'If the reason underlying this immunity is to ensure "that they may be free in thought and independent in judgment", it applies to every judge, whatever his rank. Each should be protected from liability to damages when he is acting judicially. Each should be able to do his work in complete independence and free from fear. He should not have to turn the pages of his books with trembling fingers, asking himself: "If I do this, shall I be liable in damages?" So long as he does his work in the honest belief that it is within his jurisdiction, then he is not liable to an action … What he does may be outside his jurisdiction – in fact or in law – but so long as he honestly believes it to be within his jurisdiction, he should not be liable.'

Although the House of Lords subsequently overruled this majority decision in relation to magistrates (ie 'it applies to every judge') in *Re McC (A minor)* [1985] AC 528, the Courts Act 2003 now protects them in terms of acting in or out of their jurisdiction (unless bad faith is shown in the latter).

■ Common law contempt

Contempt laws protect the administration of justice and the integrity of court proceedings. It includes, for example, contempt in the face of the court which could involve a refusal to answer questions in court.

■ *Nemo judex in re sua*

This common law legal maxim means that no man can be a judge in his own cause (see section 20.5.3). It ensures that when the judiciary are hearing cases they remain independent and impartial so that people have confidence in the administration of justice. In modern times the most important case concerning judicial independence is *ex parte Pinochet*:

CASE EXAMPLE

R v Bow Street Metropolitan Stipendiary Magistrate, ex parte Pinochet Ugarte (No 2) [2000] 1 AC 119

In *R v Bow Street Metropolitan Stipendiary Magistrate, ex parte Pinochet Ugarte* [2000] 1 AC 61, the House of Lords held that Pinochet (as the former Head of State of Chile) did not enjoy immunity from extradition proceedings in respect of crimes against humanity allegedly committed during his period of office as Head of State. The judgment was a three to two decision with Lord Hoffmann in the majority. Following the decision, Pinochet discovered that Lord Hoffmann was an unpaid director and chairman of a charity which was controlled by Amnesty International who had joined the action in order to seek Pinochet's extradition. As a result, it was alleged that this link gave the appearance that Hoffmann may have been biased against Pinochet.

In the ensuing hearing in the House of Lords, the court set aside their previous decision on the basis that the principle that a man should not be a judge in his own cause applied to the situation where a judge's decision would lead to promoting a cause in which he was involved together with one of the parties to the case. As with the *Dimes* case (see section 20.5.3), there was no suggestion that Hoffmann was actually biased, but instead it concerned an *appearance* of bias.

JUDGMENT

'If the absolute impartiality of the judiciary is to be maintained, there must be a rule which automatically disqualifies a judge who is involved, whether personally or as a director of a company, in promoting the same causes in the same organisation as is a party to the suit' (Lord Browne-Wilkinson).

'One of the cornerstones of our legal system is the impartiality of the trials by which justice is administered … everyone whom the prosecutor seeks to bring to justice is entitled to the protection of the law, however grave the offence or offences with which he is being prosecuted. Senator Pinochet is entitled to the judgment of an impartial and independent tribunal on the question which has been raised here as to his immunity' (Lord Hope).

Thereafter, a differently constituted House of Lords decided that Pinochet could be extradited, albeit on narrower grounds (*R v Bow Street Metropolitan Stipendiary Magistrate, ex parte Pinochet Ugarte (No 3)* [2000] 1 AC 147).

As a postscript to *ex parte Pinochet*, in *Meerabux v Attorney General of Belize* [2005] UKPC 12, the Privy Council distinguished *ex parte Pinochet* and held that the *mere* membership of a professional body did not require automatic disqualification. In this case the chairman of the Belize Advisory Council who was also a member of the Bar Association (which was compulsory in this case) considered a complaint against a judge, but automatic disqualification did not apply as the chairman had no financial or personal interest in the outcome of the case. Moreover, he had not taken part in the processing of the Bar Association's complaints against Meerabux.

In *Locabail (UK) Ltd v Bayfield Properties Ltd* [2000] QB 451 the Court of Appeal (Lord Bingham CJ, Lord Woolf MR and Sir Richard Scott VC) joined together five cases alleging bias and requesting the disqualification of judges. It made clear that:

JUDGMENT

'It would be dangerous and futile to attempt to define or list the factors which may or may not give rise to a real danger of bias. Everything will depend on the facts, which may include the nature of the issue to be decided. We cannot, however, conceive of circumstances in which an objection could be soundly based on the religion, ethnic or national origin, gender, age, class, means or sexual orientation of the judge. Nor, at any rate ordinarily, could an objection be soundly based on the judge's social or educational or service or employment background or history, nor that of any member of the judge's family; or previous political associations or membership of social or sporting or charitable bodies; or Masonic associations; or previous judicial decisions; or extra-curricular utterances … By contrast, a real danger of bias might well be thought to arise if there were personal friendship or animosity between the judge and any member of the public involved in the case, or if the judge were closely acquainted with any member of the public involved in the case.'

It should be noted that today the test for bias is as follows:

JUDGMENT

'The question is whether the fair-minded and informed observer, having considered the facts, would conclude that there was a real possibility that the tribunal was biased.'

Lord Hope in *Porter v Magill* [2001] UKHL 67.

Three other cases are also worth noting:

CASE EXAMPLE

Taylor v Lawrence [2002] EWCA Civ 90

The Court of Appeal held that no observer would consider it conceivable that a judge would favour a party to the case (where no relationship existed), simply because this party was represented in the case by solicitors whom the judge was using on a personal matter concerning a will.

CASE EXAMPLE

Lawal v Northern Spirit Ltd [2003] UKHL 35

The House of Lords held that an informed observer would conclude that there was a real possibility that a lay member of an Employment Appeal Tribunal might be biased (subconsciously) where counsel appearing before them had previously sat with them as a part-time judge. As a result, the court noted that this practice should be discontinued.

CASE EXAMPLE

AWG Group Ltd and another v Morrison and another [2006] EWCA Civ 6

The Court of Appeal held that a judge should have disqualified himself from presiding over a case where on the eve of the trial he discovered that he was a long-standing family acquaintance of a witness which the claimant wished to call. The judge accepted the claimant's proposal not to call the witness but to call other witnesses instead and he was concerned about the disruption and cost in recusing himself from the case at this late stage. He had concluded that there was too small a risk that the case would change during the trial which would require him not to continue hearing it. In the Court of Appeal Mummery LJ, however, pointed out that:

JUDGMENT

'Inconvenience, costs and delay do not, however, count in a case where the principle of judicial impartiality is properly invoked. This is because it is *the* fundamental principle of justice, both at common law and under article 6 of the Convention for the Protection of Human Rights. If, on an assessment of all the relevant circumstances, the conclusion is that the principle either has been, or will be, breached, the judge is automatically disqualified from hearing the case. It is not a discretionary case management decision reached by weighing various relevant factors in the balance.'

A recent interesting case in relation to judicial bias is: *El Farargy v El Farargy* [2007] EWCA Civ 1149.

13.4.3 Parliamentary protection

■ **The *sub judice* resolution**

It is a rule of Parliament that members of either House do not discuss or comment on matters which are 'active' in the court system (this includes both civil and criminal matters). This is known as the *sub judice* resolution which was reaffirmed in 2001 in the House of Commons and 2000 in the Lords. This rule protects the integrity of the administration of justice and the independence of the judiciary.

■ **Remuneration**

Judicial salaries are relatively high, which ensures that appropriate candidates will apply (it also discourages bribery of judges). In addition, judicial salaries are drawn from the Consolidated Fund Services which means that there is constant provision for them and so they are not subject to political debate. They are also not subject to reduction by the government, acting unilaterally.

■ **No criticism of judges**

By parliamentary practice the judiciary are not criticised individually in Parliament as this could lead to an erosion in public respect for, and confidence in, judges. In short, there should be no reflection on the character or motive of a judge. An exception applies where the criticism of conduct is on a substantive motion for dismissal of a judge.

13.4.4 Protection through constitutional convention

By constitutional convention judges (though obviously having private political views) do not become overtly involved in politics.

ACTIVITY

Self-test question

Explain the different ways in which the independence of the judiciary is secured. Do you think that these methods achieve true independence?

13.5 Judicial accountability

Although judges are independent and impartial in our constitution, this does not mean that they are constitutionally unaccountable (this in itself would violate the rule of law). As indicated above, the senior judiciary can be removed by an address from both Houses of

Parliament (the lower ranks by the Lord Chancellor with the agreement of the Lord Chief Justice) and they can be subject to disciplinary proceedings. In addition, judicial advancement is dependent upon merit and ability rather than favour. Moreover, as pointed out by Bradley ('The constitutional position of the judiciary' in D Feldman (ed), *English Public Law*, p 291), judges are accountable in the following ways:

- The court process is in public and is typically adversarial (in general).
- Judges must take cognisance of the submissions made to them during the course of a case.
- In general, their decisions can be appealed against to a higher court (or possibly be subject to judicial review – see section 19.3.2).
- Judges give reasons for their decisions and deliver individual judgments which are a matter of public record.

13.6 The perception of judicial independence, neutrality and impartiality

13.6.1 The composition of the judiciary

The current composition of the judiciary is dominated by a socio-economic group largely comprising white men from a narrow social and educational background (a description provided by the Commission for Judicial Appointments – the precursor to the Judicial Appointments Commission at section 13.3.1). Indeed, according to judiciary.gov.uk, in April 2010, the only women in the senior judiciary were: one female member of the Supreme Court, three Lord Justices of Appeal and 16 High Court Judges. Furthermore, there were only three High Court judges from an ethnic minority (two men, one woman) and none at all above this judicial rank. As a consequence, for some commentators this raises concerns about the actual and perceived neutrality of the judiciary. The argument is that owing to their narrow composition there is an inevitability that sub-consciously their judgments will favour the state and the status quo/establishment.

Some counter arguments to this are that:

- As professionals, when judges perform their judicial functions they leave behind them any bias/influences.
- A significant proportion of the judiciary is female if Justices of the Peace (magistrates) are included within the term (around half of magistrates are female). Moreover, Magistrates' Courts process virtually all criminal cases in the legal system.
- The case law detailed in 13.6.2 indicates that the judiciary are prepared rigorously to hold the 'state' and executive to account.

Nonetheless, concern has been raised about composition of the judiciary:

- In 2003 a Bar Council Working Party report made clear the desirability of ensuring that there was greater diversity in the judiciary (*Bar Council Working Party on Judicial Appointments and Silk Consultation Document* (The Bar Council, 2003), pp 12–15).
- In 2003 the government indicated the need to do more to make the judiciary more reflective of the society it serves (*Constitutional reform: a new way of appointing judges* CP 10/03 (2003), p 45).
- In 2004 the Department for Constitutional Affairs issued a consultation paper into the current lack of diversity in the judiciary as a whole (*Increasing Diversity in the Judiciary* CP 25/04 (2004)).
- The first and only female member of the Supreme Court has consistently argued for a more diverse judiciary (Lady Hale, 'Making a difference? Why we need a more diverse judiciary' [2005] 56 NILQ 281).
- The Constitutional Reform Bill was amended so that (although selection would continue to be on merit) the Judicial Appointments Commission would be required to:

SECTION

s 64 of the Constitutional Reform Act 2005
'... have regard to the need to encourage diversity in the range of persons available for selection for appointments'.

Pt 2 of the Tribunals, Courts and Enforcement Act 2007 amended the eligibility requirements for judicial appointments in an effort to increase the diversity of the judiciary.

In 2009 an Advisory Panel on Judicial Diversity was established with the remit of making recommendations on how to make progress towards the goal of a more diverse judiciary.

For others, however, there is no obligation to appoint judges reflective of the community; Sir Thomas Legg KCB, QC noted that:

QUOTATION

'It is no part of the professional judiciary's function to represent anybody or reflect anything. It is different for the lay magistrates, for whom one qualification is, and should be, to reflect the make-up of their local communities. The professional judges, on the other hand, have the unique property of being at once a powerful branch of government and at the same time a highly-skilled professional elite, whose contribution depends essentially on their learning, detachment and wisdom, and not who they are or where they come from in the community. We do not choose brain surgeons to reflect the community. They are chosen on professional merit ... It is, and should continue to be, the same with judges. "Reflection" should not in itself be an aim of the appointments system. Nor do I accept the view that public confidence is undermined by the present composition of the judiciary, or that it could be improved by intervening in appointments policy to change it.'

House of Commons Select Committee on Constitutional Affairs, First Report, *Written Evidence – Volume II* HC 48-II (2004), *Supplementary Written Evidence*, para 6.

ACTIVITY

Self-test question

Do you think that from a constitutional perspective the judiciary should be reflective of society or do you agree with the view of Sir Thomas Legg?

13.6.2 Judges and civil liberties

Historically, the record of the judges in protecting civil liberties and holding the government to account has been variable at times (for example, see the historic cases of *ex parte Hosenball* (1977) and *Liversidge v Anderson* (1942) both at section 6.7.10). In recent years, however, there has been a measure of tension between the judiciary and the executive precisely because the courts have held government ministers to account, principally through judicial review proceedings (eg see *Anderson* (2002) at section 13.2.1, *ex parte Venables and Thompson* (1997) at section 5.7.6, *ex parte Fire Brigades* (1995) at 6.7.10 and *M v Home Office* (1994) at section 6.7.6).

These decisions indicate the judiciary are prepared to subject the executive to rigorous scrutiny and protect individual rights. In addition to the case of *A and others v Secretary of State* (2004) already considered at section 6.7.4, two other recent examples in the controversial area of terrorism further illustrate this point:

A and others v Secretary of State for the Home Department (No 2) [2005] UKHL 71

This case concerned the Special Immigration Appeals Commission (SIAC) which was established under the Anti-terrorism, Crime and Security Act 2001. It processed appeals made by individuals against certification (and detention) by the Home Secretary who, reasonably, believed them to be a risk to national security and reasonably suspected them of being terrorists. The House of Lords held that in hearing such appeals the SIAC could not receive evidence against these individuals where it had been obtained by torture.

CASE EXAMPLE

Secretary of State for the Home Department v JJ and others [2007] UKHL 45

This case concerned the Home Secretary making (non-derogating) control orders under the Prevention of Terrorism Act 2005, in respect of six individuals suspected of being involved in terrorism-related activity. The orders, *inter alia*, permitted them to leave their residences (a one bedroom flat) for six hours a day and restricted their movement to specified areas. The judge at first instance held that the cumulative effect of the orders was that they were contrary to Art 5 of the European Convention as being a deprivation of liberty and therefore these orders should be quashed. The Court of Appeal confirmed this decision and the House of Lords then dismissed an appeal by the Secretary of State.

KEY FACTS

Method of protection	Type of protection
Statute	• Constitutional Reform Act 2005 requires government ministers to protect judicial independence. • Act of Settlement 1700/Constitutional Reform Act 2005 provide security of tenure for senior judges. • Contempt of Court Act 1981 protects the administration of justice and the right to a fair trial.
Common law	• Judicial immunity for things said in a judicial capacity (*Anderson* (1895) and *Sirros* (1975)). • Contempt of court protects the administration of justice. • *Nemo judex in re sua* – no man should be a judge in his own cause.
Parliament	• *Sub judice* resolution ensures active court cases are not commented on. • Character and motives of individual judges are not commented on. • Salaries drawn from the Consolidated Fund Services.
Constitutional convention	• Judges are not overtly involved in politics.

SUMMARY

■ The independence and impartiality of the judiciary is a key aspect of Britain's uncodified constitution.

■ The independence of the judiciary is a fundamental principle as judges uphold the rule of law and protect the rights of individuals.

- In the context of the separation of powers the role of the judiciary is to interpret the law and resolve legal disputes.
- Judicial independence is secured through both law and constitutional convention.
- Judges are themselves accountable as proceedings exist to allow them to be removed and they can be subject to disciplinary proceedings.
- The current composition of the judiciary does not accurately reflect society at large (eg only one Supreme Court Justice is female).

 ## Further reading

Books

Bradley, A, and Ewing, K, *Constitutional and Administrative Law* (14th edn, Pearson/ Longman, 2007), Chapter 18.

Bradley, A, 'The constitutional position of the judiciary' in Feldman, D (ed), *English Public Law* (2nd edn, Oxford University Press, 2009), p 281.

Griffith, J, *The Politics of the Judiciary* (5th edn, Fontana, 1997).

Lord Nolan, 'The Judiciary' in Nolan, Lord and Sedley, S, *The Making and Remaking of the British Constitution* (Blackstone Press Limited, 1997), p 67.

Lord Woolf, *The Pursuit of Justice* (Oxford University Press, 2008).

Articles

Dickson, B, 'Safe in their hands? Britain's Law Lords and human rights' (2006) 26 LS 329.

Flannery, L, 'In the eye of the beholder?' (2006) 156 NLJ 278.

Griffith, J, 'Judicial decision-making in public law' [1985] PL 564.

Lady Hale, 'Making a difference? Why we need a more diverse judiciary' [2005] 56 NILQ 281.

Lord Woolf, 'Judicial review – the tensions between the executive and the judiciary' [1998] 114 LQR 579.

Internet links

www.judiciary.gov.uk

www.supremecourt.gov.uk

14

The decentralisation of public power

AIMS AND OBJECTIVES

At the end of this chapter you should be able to:

■ Understand the nature and constitutional significance of local government
■ Understand the nature, type and constitutional significance of the devolved arrangements in Scotland, Wales and Northern Ireland
■ Appreciate the position of England in terms of the overall devolution settlement

14.1 Introduction

QUOTATION

'… unity is not uniformity. The different parts of the UK have different histories, distinctive cultures and differing aspirations. That is why the Government believes in devolution and decentralisation throughout the UK. In each part of the country that can and should take different forms.'

Scotland's Future in the United Kingdom, Building on ten years of Scottish Devolution
Cm 7738 (Scotland Office, 2009) para 2.3.

The United Kingdom has a unitary state. In constitutional terms this means that power is focused and centralised in the apex of Parliament (which is generally controlled by central government). Historically, however, power has been *decentralised* to local government (local authorities) to carry out governmental functions at a local level. Further, in recent years power has also been *devolved* to regional bodies in Scotland, Wales and Northern Ireland and London. These different levels of government can be illustrated by the following diagram:

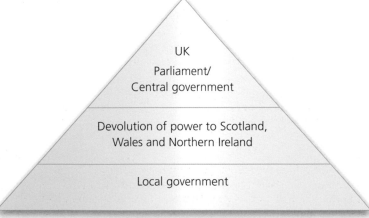

Figure 14.1 Tiers of government in the British constitution

14.2 Local government

14.2.1 Introduction and structure

QUOTATION

'Local government is a vital part of our democracy. The vast majority of interactions between citizens and the state take place through local government. It provides leadership for local areas and communities; democratic accountability for a wide range of public services; and is the key to effective partnership working at local level.'

Tony Blair: *Strong and prosperous communities, the Local Government White Paper*,
Volume 1Cm 6939-I (2006), Foreword p 2.

Local government is public power which has been decentralised and delegated to directly elected local authorities which administer governmental functions at a local level. Local government has existed for centuries (and certainly precedes modern democracy in Britain). For example, during the nineteenth century local government boroughs exercised responsibility for the sanitation and education of their local inhabitants.

In modern times local government (now in the form of statutory local authorities, which being creatures of statute, are at the mercy of Parliament) has been re-organised a number of times in the past few decades. Indeed, the result is that today the structure of local government is highly complex (not to say confusing for the public) and asymmetrical (ie some areas have different layers of government than others). Indeed, further restructuring took place in England in April 2009 with the establishment of more single tier unitary authorities in place of a number of two-tiered county/district councils (under the aegis of the Local Government and Public Involvement in Health Act 2007). This chapter provides a very basic outline of local government in England and Wales.

England				Wales	Scotland	Northern Ireland
In England there is a layer of strategic administration in the form of Regional Development Agencies (see section 14.6.2) London also has a tier of government called The Greater London Authority (see section 14.6.3)				Power has been devolved to the National Assembly for Wales and the Welsh Assembly Government (see section 14.5)	Power has been devolved to the Scottish Parliament and the Scottish Executive/ Government (see section 14.3)	Power has been devolved to the Northern Ireland Assembly and the Executive Committee (see section 14.4)
Outside London			**London**			
Non-metropolitan county councils *27 county councils* ↓ *201 district councils*	Metropolitan borough councils (in major urban areas) *36 metropolitan borough councils*	Unitary authorities/ councils *55 unitary authorities/ councils*	Borough councils *32 borough councils and the City of London Corporation*	Unitary authorities *22 unitary authorities*	Unitary authorities *29 unitary authorities and 3 Island councils*	Single tier district councils *26 single tier councils*
A tier exists below known as parish/ town councils	Some parish/ town councils exist as a tier below	Some parish/ town councils exist as a tier below		A tier below of Welsh community councils	A tier below of Scottish community councils	

Figure 14.2 The structure of local and regional government in the UK in 2009

D Wilson and C Game, *Local Government in the United Kingdom*, (4th edn, Palgrave Macmillan, 2006), p 78 and subsequently updated from *Whitaker's Almanac 2010* (142nd edn, A&C Black Publishers Ltd, London) pp 270–78

14.2.2 The functions of local government

What do local authorities do?

■ The provision of services

Local authorities, historically, have provided a wide range of different services. For example:

Housing – providing housing in the form of council housing and making provision for the homeless.

Licensing – regulating taxis, cinemas etc.

Planning – making decisions in respect of planning applications.

Environmental health – refuse collection, pollution control, food safety (through inspectors) and consumer protection (trading standards).

Highways – maintaining public roads, traffic management and the provision of street lighting.

Social services – care for the elderly/disabled and provision for the protection of children.

Education – providing and maintaining schools.

Leisure – providing libraries and museums.

ACTIVITY

Applying the law

Find out the type of local government that exists in your area and the various functions that it performs.

■ An administrative role

As indicated at section 5.3.2, local authorities are constitutionally part of the executive function of government (in a very broad sense of the term) and so therefore carry out government policy as expressed in primary legislation which has been passed at Westminster. In providing certain services, therefore, local authorities will be implementing government policy determined at the centre. For example, as a result of the National Curriculum introduced in the Education Reform Act 1988, local education authorities were required to publish a general policy statement on the National Curriculum being adhered to by the schools in their area.

In terms of an administrative function, local authorities have to make executive/administrative decisions, for example in the context of land planning or licensing (see *R v Liverpool Corporation, ex parte Liverpool Taxi Fleet Operators' Association* [1972] 2 QB 299).

■ A discretionary role

Local government has been traditionally characterised by the exercise of an element of discretion which allows them to adapt the provision of services to local needs. For example, the needs of an inner city area will not be the same as the requirements of that of a largely rural area. Moreover, in this way local authorities can be innovative as schemes can be tested. For example, under the aegis of the Representation of the People Act 2000, pilot schemes were introduced by various authorities to test strategies aimed at combating voter apathy (eg all postal ballots, extended polling times, touch-screen voting). Further, s 2(1) of the Local Government Act 2000 empowers a local authority 'to do anything which they consider is likely to achieve any one or more of the following objects': the promotion or improvement of the economic, social or environmental well-being of their area.

A legislative role

In order to carry out their roles, local authorities (like government ministers) are empowered by statute to enact a form of delegated legislation in the form of by-laws which apply to local areas (eg a local by-law concerned with banning alcohol consumption in a specified area). As local authorities are part of the executive, the enactment of such legislation is theoretically a breach of the separation of powers. However, the following controls do exist on their use:

(i) They will be subject to ministerial approval (however, s 129 of the Local Government and Public Involvement in Health Act 2007 provides that local authorities will be able to make certain by-laws to deal with local problems without confirmation by the Secretary of State).

(ii) If the by-law is *ultra vires* it can be challenged in the courts by way of judical review proceedings (see Chapters 19 and 20).

Raising of revenue

Local authorities acquire some of their revenue through taxation (formerly the rates, in modern times: the council tax). Councils also raise money through charges for certain activities (car parks, swimming baths, etc).

KEY FACTS

The role of local government	
Role	**Examples**
The provision of services	• Social services. • Street lighting.
Making legislation	• By-laws.
A discretionary role	• Piloting schemes (eg improving voter apathy).
Administrating government functions	• Education.
Raising taxes	• The council tax. • Charges for local services.

14.2.3 The advantages of local government

■ In constitutional terms it represents a decentralisation of power from the centre to local areas. In this way it acts as a constitutional counterbalance to central government and ensures that public power is not simply focused in central government departments.

■ Local government is an efficient way of administering government functions. Local authorities exist because central government could not operate without them. It would simply be impracticable for all services to be provided from the centre. As a result, local government prevents central government from being overburdened.

■ It allows governmental functions to be specifically tailored to purely local needs and requirements.

■ It promotes the constitutional principle of 'participatory democracy' whereby individuals can actively engage in the governmental process. Firstly, local authorities are directly elected and so they will be held directly accountable to local people for the public decisions that they make. This is equivalent to the European Union principle of 'subsidiarity' which is concerned with ensuring that decisions which affect people are taken at the lowest level nearest the people (this ensures greater accountability). Secondly, local government makes the democratic process and government in general more accessible to people in the sense that they have a far higher chance of becoming a local councillor than they ever would have of becoming a member of the government in Whitehall (or even an MP for that matter). It therefore provides an opportunity for groups which are currently under-represented (eg women, ethnic minorities) to become involved in political decision-making. It is certainly the case that, at least in terms of gender, for example, councillors are more representative of the population than MPs are, as almost a third of English councillors are female (contrast MPs at section 9.2.2). Nevertheless, even with 29 per cent of English Councillors in 2004 being female and 3.5 per cent from a non-white background, the 2006 White Paper (*Strong and Prosperous Communities, The Local Government White Paper*, Volume 1, Cm 6939-I (2006), p 50) stressed that 'councillors are not representative of the population as a whole'.

■ It allows a wider spread of political opinion to be represented, as some elected local councillors will not belong to the main political parties (eg the Green Party).

14.2.4 The disadvantages of local government

■ The public appear to lack interest in voting at local government elections. Wilson and Game have stated that:

QUOTATION

'The one thing that everyone thinks they know about local elections is that most people don't vote in them. They are right. Britain's 61.4 per cent in the 2005 General Election put us last among the "original" fifteen EU countries in a listing of turnouts in most recent parliamentary elections ... But that figure was roughly double the recent average for English local elections, and in that league table we are and have long been indisputably at the bottom.'

Local Government in the United Kingdom (4th edn, Palgrave Macmillan, 2006), p 233.

One reason for a poor turnout could be that people are not interested in local affairs or that there is a perception that voting makes no real difference. Another explanation is that as local authorities have been stripped of a number of their powers in recent decades this has led to a misconception that local councils lack real powers. Finally, the cycles of elections can cause confusion with some councils being elected as a whole, whereas other councils are elected one half or one third at a time. As a result of the very poor turnouts at local elections (although turnouts are higher in Scotland, Wales and Northern Ireland), it is possible to argue that local authorities may lack the constitutional or political legitimacy to make decisions. Indeed, a similar argument is used in respect of the European Parliament (see section 15.2.3). In the June 2009 elections (for all County Councils and seven English unitary authorities) the turnout was estimated to be 35 per cent ('Local elections 2009' Research paper 09/54 (House of Commons Library, 2009), p 1).

■ Local government results in a variation in the provision of services around the country. This could lead to a perception of unfairness.

■ Local government may actively encourage narrow local attitudes as well as providing a platform for political representatives with extreme political views.

■ Local authorities may be viewed as wasteful public bodies. For example, in the 1980s the incumbent Conservative government perceived local government as not providing value for money.

■ Where the political colour of central government is different from that of local government (this will always be the case in terms of a number of councils at any one time) political friction may result. In particular, in the 1980s there was a clear ideological divide between the Conservative central government and a number of Labour-held councils which led to a deterioration in the constitutional relationship between the two arms of the executive (see section 14.2.6).

ACTIVITY

Exercise

Do you think that the advantages of local government outweigh the disadvantages?

14.2.5 The control of local government

Local authorities are controlled in the following ways:

■ **Democratically**

Local councillors are subject to re-election and so the actions, decisions and policies of local authorities are accountable directly to the local electorate. The electoral systems used for local government elections in the UK vary and can cause confusion (for example, England and Wales uses the 'first past the post' system whereas Scotland and Northern Ireland use the Single Transferable Vote).

■ **Legally**

Local authorities, as public bodies, are subject to the law for their actions. They can be held to account in both public law (judicial review) and private law (contract, tort, etc). For example, in *Infolines Public Networks Ltd v Nottingham City Council* [2009] EWCA Civ 708 the Court of Appeal held that the council's disposal of Infolines' telephone kiosks was a wrongful interference with their goods. According to John Lambe (Senior Solicitor at DWF) who acted as Infolines' solicitor in this case:

'The case serves as a cautionary tale for local authorities and others who seek to exercise emergency powers and the restrictive interpretation which is likely to be adopted and applied when those powers concern dealing with the potential deprivation of another's property.'

For the purposes of s 6 of the Human Rights Act 1998, local authorities are public authorities and so must not act in a way which is incompatible with the articles of the European Convention. In addition, when a local authority enacts delegated legislation which is beyond its legal powers, it can be held accountable in the courts:

CASE EXAMPLE

Arlidge v Mayor, Aldermen, and Councillors of the Metropolitan Borough of Islington [1909] 2 KB 127

A by-law made by the council under the aegis of the Public Health (London) Act 1891, was held to be unreasonable as it would have required a landlord to commit an act of trespass in order to comply with it (ie to clean every part of a lodging house three months a year).

See also *Nicholls v Tavistock Urban District Council* [1923] 2 Ch 18.

■ **From the centre**

Local government is ultimately at the mercy of central government. In short, it is central government (via its control of Parliament) which can set the legal, political and financial context and parameters in which local government must work (as well as providing advice in the form of circulars as to how their delegated powers should be exercised). A government minister will also approve and confirm by-laws made by local government. Moreover, a government minister may well enjoy a 'default power' which authorises him to step in and exercise the decentralised power instead, or transfer it (see *R v Secretary of State for the Environment, ex parte Norwich City Council* [1982] 1 QB 808).

It must be remembered that local government, unlike in other countries with a codified constitution, does not have any legally protected or 'constitutional status'. Instead, local authorities are statutory bodies which owe their existence to Acts of Parliament and therefore, in constitutional theory, could be extinguished by an Act of Parliament which has been pushed through by a dominant executive.

Central government (by virtue of legislation being pushed through Parliament) can re-model local government as it sees fit. For example:

(a) In the 1980s the Conservative government reformed radically the nature of local government whereby, *inter alia*:
- Local government taxation was reformed (the poll tax – Local Government Finance Act 1988).
- Local government became 'enabling authorities' regulating services provided by private bodies, rather than directly themselves. This involved CCT (Compulsive Competitive Tendering) whereby councils which had traditionally provided services would have to compete with private contractors in order to deliver that service in an effort to secure more efficient services. For example, it applied to:
  - Highways (Local Government Planning and Land Act 1980)
  - Refuse collection (Local Government Act 1988).

The subsequent Labour government under the Local Government Act 1999 replaced CCT with a 'best value duty'.

(b) In terms of the constitutional arrangements of councils, the Labour government introduced new executive arrangements in relation to how councillors operated (Local Government Act 2000). Historically, the committee system within councils made many decisions, but the new executive arrangements involved making a clear separation between executive councillors (who would make executive policy decisions) and non-executive councillors (who would supervise the executive councillors). The main councils in England were required to adopt one of the following types of executive models
  - Council Constitutions (following consultation with the local population, another example of participatory government):
  - Leader and Cabinet (after an election a Leader is drawn from the council and a Cabinet would either be appointed by the Leader or the Council).
  - Mayor (directly elected by local people) and Cabinet (appointed by the Mayor).
  - Mayor (directly elected by local people) and Council Manager (appointed by the council).

Further reforms followed with the Local Government and Public Involvement in Health Act 2007 which provided for the discontinuance of the first and third executive models set out above. Section 62 of the Act requires English councils to operate either a (new style) Leader and Cabinet Executive or the Mayor and Cabinet Executive. According to the government:

QUOTATION

'The 2007 Act strengthens leadership models with a choice for councils between a directly elected mayor with a four year term and an indirectly elected leader with a four year term.'

Strong and Prosperous Communities, The Local Government White Paper Implementation Plan: One Year On (Crown Copyright, 2007), para 49.

Control is also exercised financially as a significant proportion of revenue which local government receives is, ultimately, determined by central government.

◼ Audits

Local authorities will be audited (by the Audit Commission) in terms of their financial efficiency.

◼ Ombudsman

maladministration
poor administration

Maladministration by English local authorities which result in injustice for individuals can be subject to investigation by the Commissioner for Local Administration (see section 21.3.7). Wilson and Game (*Local Government in the United Kingdom* (4th edn, Palgrave Macmillan, 2006), p 163), point out that the local government Ombudsman does valuable work (the office received 18,700 complaints in 2004/05). The major complaints related to the following areas: housing, planning, highways, parking and social services.

14.2.6 The relationship between central and local government

Relations between the two arms of the executive have historically been characterised by co-operation and an informal partnership (albeit with central government clearly being the dominant partner). Between the 1970s and the 1990s, however, this generally consensual relationship broke down. For example:

CASE EXAMPLE

Secretary of State for Education and Science v Tameside Metropolitan Borough Council [1976] 3 WLR 641

A Labour Secretary of State for Education and Science using powers under the Education Act 1944, tried to direct a Conservative council to introduce plans (already approved by their Labour predecessors) for the implementation of comprehensive schooling. Thereafter, he unsuccessfully sought an order to compel the authority to comply with his direction.

Loughlin has referred to central-local relations since 1979 as having become 'politicised' and 'juridified' (ie legalised) with the courts being resorted to in order to determine the legal boundary between them (M Loughlin, 'Restructuring of central-local government relations' in J Jowell and D Oliver (eds) *The Changing Constitution* (4th edn, Oxford University Press, 2000), p 137). An example is detailed below:

CASE EXAMPLE

Nottinghamshire County Council v Secretary of State for the Environment [1986] 1 AC 240

Nottinghamshire County Council and the City of Bradford Metropolitan Council unsuccessfully sought judicial review of the Secretary of State's guidance determining expenditure targets for local authorities. The councils had contended that the expenditure targets were unfairly low. The House of Lords held that the courts would not intervene on a matter of 'unreasonableness' (in the absence of, for example, bad faith) in respect of public financial administration which had been approved by the House of Commons.

In December 2007 a *Central-Local Concordat* was agreed between central government and the Local Government Association which established 'a framework of principles for how central and local government work together to serve the public'.

KEY FACTS

Controls on local government	
Control	**Example**
Democratic	• Local electors voting at local elections.
Legal	• Private law. • Public law (including under the Human Rights Act 1998).
Central government/Parliament	• Setting the legal and political parameters in which local government must operate. • Financial control as significant revenue is secured from the centre. • Ministerial approval for by-laws, etc.
Audit	• The auditing of local authority accounts.
Ombudsman	• Maladministration causing injustice to local individuals.

In May 2009 the House of Commons Communities and Local Government Select Committee issued a report analysing the relationship between local and central government (Sixth Report of Session 2008–09, *The Balance of Power: Central and Local Government*, HC 33-I (2009)). The conclusion it reached was that 'the balance of power between central and local government in England is currently in need of a tilt towards localities' (sic) (para 146).

ACTIVITY

Quick quiz
1. What is the constitutional function of local government?
2. Give examples of what it does.
3. How is local government controlled?
4. Explain how central and local government relate to each other.

14.3 Scottish devolution

14.3.1 History

Until 1707 England and Scotland had their own separate Parliaments. The Union with Scotland Act 1706 (passed by the then English Parliament) and the Union with England Act 1707 (passed by the then Scottish Parliament) united the two Parliaments into one single one in Westminster (thereafter the Parliament of Great Britain). After this date the Westminster Parliament legislated for both England (Wales) and Scotland.

Over the course of time, Scotland remained distinctive from the rest of the Union (England, Wales and Northern Ireland), in particular in terms of its different systems of education and law. During the latter half of the twentieth century there was an increasing call from Scottish nationalist politicians for Scotland to be able to direct and govern its own affairs through the re-establishment of a Scottish Parliament. Indeed, in 1978 a Scotland Act was passed which would have provided Scotland with its own elected assembly. The Act, however, did not come into effect (and was repealed) because the Scots voting in the referendum to support devolution did not meet the threshold stipulated in the Act.

The election of the 1997 Labour government placed devolution back on the political agenda. In July 1997 the Labour government issued a White Paper which stated at the outset:

QUOTATION

'The Government are determined that the people of Scotland should have a greater say over their own affairs. With their agreement we will change the way Scotland is governed by legislating to create a Scottish Parliament with devolved powers within the United Kingdom.'

Scotland's Parliament, Cm 3658 (The Scottish Office, 1997), p 1.

Following this, a referendum was held in Scotland in September 1997 for the Scots to either endorse or reject the government's proposals. In constitutional theory this is an example of participatory democracy whereby individuals are given direct influence over proposals which will affect them. At the referendum the Scots were asked two questions:

■ Do the Scottish people want a Scottish Parliament? (74 per cent voted Yes).
■ Should it have tax-raising powers? (64 per cent voted Yes).

As a result of this endorsement, Parliament duly passed the Scotland Act 1998.

The Scotland Act 1998

This Act devolved powers to Scotland so that for the first time in almost 300 years Scotland had its own Parliament to oversee its own affairs. In fact, the Scotland Act (like the corresponding legislation for Wales and Northern Ireland) can be seen as a type of constitution for Scotland. It should be remembered that the purpose of a constitution (see Chapter 2) is to:

- Establish governmental institutions (eg the Scottish Parliament and Executive).
- Allocate them powers (eg the Parliament is empowered to legislate on health and criminal law, etc).
- Limit their powers (eg the Scottish Parliament cannot pass legislation for independence).

14.3.2 Arguments for and against Scottish devolution

(It should be noted that some of the arguments from 1997 set out below can, to a greater or lesser extent, apply equally to the other devolved settlements in Wales and Northern Ireland).

Arguments for Scottish devolution

- As Scotland was hallmarked by distinct characteristics (particularly its law), it required a local Parliament to oversee its affairs, rather than a distant Parliament hundreds of miles away.
- In political terms, devolution intensified between 1979 and 1997 when the majority of Scotland consistently returned non-Conservative MPs (largely Labour) to Westminster, but was governed by an 'English Conservative government'. In particular, it must be remembered that the controversial community charge (colloquially known as the poll tax) was first introduced in Scotland, *before* England.
- In constitutional terms, too much power was centralised in London and so devolution to Scotland (and elsewhere) was healthy in a democracy as a way of decentralising and dispersing power.

Arguments against Scottish devolution

- Devolving power would lead to the constitutional anomaly of the 'West Lothian question', whereby Scottish MPs would be able to vote on English matters in legislation such as education and crime, but that English MPs would not be able to vote on corresponding Scottish matters as these would be devolved to the Scottish Parliament to decide (see section 14.3.12).
- Devolving power to Scotland (and Wales and Northern Ireland for that matter), but not simultaneously establishing an 'English Parliament' to oversee and legislate on specifically English affairs, would lead to an imbalance in the constitution.
- Devolving power would inevitably widen the differences between Scotland and the rest of the Union. This would, therefore, lead to the eventual break-up of the Union of the United Kingdom. In essence, once established, a Scottish Parliament would inevitably want more powers ceded to it from Westminster, eventually leading to Scotland becoming a completely separate and independent country. In response to this last point it has been argued that providing the Scottish people with devolution with the ability to a large extent to regulate their own affairs, would actually stave off political support for complete independence. Indeed, according to the government in its White Paper:

QUOTATION

'The Government want a United Kingdom which everyone feels part of, can contribute to, and in whose future all have a stake. The Union will be strengthened by recognising the claims of Scotland, Wales and the regions with strong identities of their own. The Government's devolution proposals, by meeting these aspirations, will not only safeguard but also enhance the Union.'

Scotland's Parliament, Cm 3658 (The Scottish Office, 1997), p 10.

More recently, in 2009 the government reiterated that, by giving expression to diversity, devolution strengthened the Union (*Scotland's Future in the United Kingdom, Building on ten years of Scottish Devolution*, Cm 7738 (Scotland Office, 2009), para 2.3). However, in 2007, the Scottish Executive/Government issued a paper aimed at initiating a 'national conversation' about Scotland's constitutional future, including Scottish independence and other constitutional possibilities (*Scotland's Future, A National Conversation: Independence and responsibility in the modern world*, (Crown Copyright, 2007)). In February 2010 a consultation paper setting out the proposals for a Referendum Bill were published (*Scotland's Future: Draft Referendum (Scotland) Bill Consultation Paper* (Crown Copyright, 2010)). The plan was that the Bill would be introduced in 2010.

ACTIVITY

Self-test question

Do you think that the advantages of Scottish devolution (or devolution in general) outweigh the disadvantages?

14.3.3 The Scottish Parliament

Section 1 of the Scotland Act 1998 established a Scottish Parliament (it sits at Holyrood in Edinburgh). The Parliament is unicameral consisting of one elected chamber.

Composition and elections

The Scottish Parliament consists of 129 members known as Members of the Scottish Parliament (MSPs). They are elected on the following basis:

- 73 Constituency MSPs elected under the simple majority system (s 1(2) – known as the constituency vote).
- 56 Regional MSPs 'additional members' elected under the Additional Member system of proportional representation (s 1(3)– known as the regional vote).

Unlike the House of Commons, the Scottish Parliament is not elected solely on the basis of the 'first past the post' system. This is because this system can distort the wishes of the electorate (see section 9.4.4) and the government's White Paper made it clear that the 'electoral arrangements for the Scottish Parliament should reflect the will of the Scottish people'. Instead, there is a combination of MSPs elected by different systems with the majority being elected under the 'first past the post' system, thereby ensuring that there is a constituency link between the MSPs and the Scottish people. These are supplemented by additional members (seven members elected from eight electoral regions, eg North East Scotland). According to the White Paper this will 'bring a closer relationship between votes cast and seats won', thereby injecting greater proportionality which, in turn, builds stability into the overall devolution settlement. These new electoral arrangements indicate a willingness to move away in our constitution from the traditional 'first past the post' system.

Section 2 states that elections take place every four years and so in this sense (unlike the Westminster Parliament) the Scottish Parliament is a fixed-term Parliament with elections at set intervals. Section 3, however, does make provision for extraordinary elections to take place (for example, if following an election a First Minister has not been nominated).

The first elections took place in 1999 and the second in 2003. The third set of elections took place in May 2007, the results of which are detailed below. It produced a Parliament in which no party held a majority of seats (the SNP as the largest party formed the minority Scottish Executive/Government). Voters are given two votes: one for a constituency MSP and one for a Regional MSP (cast for a party).

The Scottish Parliament 2007				
Elections May 2007				
Main Political Parties	**Constituency MSPs**	**Regional MSPs**	**TOTAL**	
Scottish Labour Party	37	9	46	
Scottish National Party (SNP)	21	26	47	
Scottish Liberal Democrats	11	5	16	
Scottish Conservative and Unionist Party	4	13	17	
Scottish Green Party	0	2	2	
Independent	0	1	1	
TOTAL	73	56	129	

Compiled from www.scottish.parliament.uk

Table 14.1

The role of MSPs is similar to that of MPs in the Westminster Parliament:

- Representing constituents.
- Resolving complaints from constituents.
- Holding the Scottish Executive/Government to account.
- Raising issues of public concern.
- Asking questions.
- Participating in debates and the committee system.

The Presiding Officer

Section 19 provides for a Presiding Officer together with two deputies to be elected from the MSPs. In effect the Presiding Officer is the equivalent of the Speaker of the House of Commons as he chairs proceedings in the parliamentary chamber and is required to be impartial. MSPs are also governed by *The Code of Conduct for MSPs* and under the Scottish Parliamentary Standards Commissioner Act 2002 an independent Scottish Parliamentary Standards Commissioner was created to process complaints concerning MSPs.

The committee system

As in Westminster, the Scottish Parliament has a sophisticated committee system. These committees include:

- Subject committees allocated in respect of government departmental areas (analogous to departmental select committees). For example, the Local Government and Communities Committee monitors the responsibilities falling within the remit of the Minister for Housing and Communities.
- Mandatory committees for the parliamentary term (eg the Equal Opportunities Committee).
- Committees which consider Bills.

14.3.4 The Scottish administration

Section 44 established the office of a Scottish Executive known collectively as 'the Scottish Ministers'. In 2007 the Scottish Executive renamed itself the *Scottish Government*; however, its technical and legal name still remains the Scottish Executive.

The executive consists of the following:

- The First Minister (analogous to the office of the Prime Minister).

- Ministers appointed by the First Minister (analogous to Cabinet ministers), but with the approval of Parliament.
- Lord Advocate and Solicitor-General for Scotland (these law officers, *inter alia*, provide legal advice).

The Executive is the 'Scottish Government/Cabinet'. It is responsible for implementing and developing policies and assumes responsibility in devolved matters (it is governed by the principles of collective responsibility – see section 12.2). Scottish ministers are also governed by a code: *The Scottish Ministerial Code* (2008). Ministers can also, like British Cabinet ministers, introduce Bills.

The constitutional arrangements in Scotland, therefore, involve a parliamentary executive (as in Westminster) whereby the Scottish Executive is held to account by the Scottish Parliament. For example, as in Westminster, Scottish ministers can be asked oral or written questions with the First Minister having a separate First Minister's Question Time (analogous to PMQs: see section 12.4.2). Furthermore, ss 45 and 47 require the resignation of the First Minister and individual ministers if it is resolved that the Scottish Executive/Government no longer enjoys the confidence of the Scottish Parliament (analogous with the Westminster vote of no confidence: see section 12.2.1).

In February 2010 the Scottish Executive/Government comprised the following:

- the First Minister (Alex Salmond, MSP)
- the Deputy First Minister and Cabinet Secretary for Health and Well being (Nicola Sturgeon, MSP)
- four other Cabinet Secretaries (eg Cabinet Secretary for Justice)
- ten ministers (eg Minister for Parliamentary Business)
- Law Officers (Lord Advocate and Solicitor-General).

Source: www.scotland.gov.uk

KEY FACTS

Composition of the Scottish devolved institutions	
Parliament	129 MSPs • 73 Constituency MSPs ('first past the post' system). • 56 Regional MSPs (Additional Member system).
Executive/Government	• The First Minister/Deputy First Minister. • other Scottish ministers. • Lord Advocate and Solicitor-General for Scotland.

14.3.5 Legislation

Primary legislation

Scottish devolution involved legislative devolution whereby the Scottish Parliament was empowered to pass primary legislation. Section 28 states that the Scottish Parliament can make laws which are to be known as Acts of the Scottish Parliament. After a Bill has passed through the Scottish Parliament and has obtained the Royal Assent, it becomes an Act of the Scottish Parliament (s 28(2)).

The constitutional standing of these Acts, however, is worth noting as, although these Acts are analogous to primary legislation:

- For the purpose of the Human Rights Act 1998 (s 21) such legislation is treated as having the standing of, and classed as, subordinate legislation and so amenable to challenge and invalidation under the Human Rights Act 1998 (see Chapter 17).
- Under the Scotland Act, if the Scottish Parliament passes an Act of Parliament outside its legal jurisdiction (eg in respect of the British constitution), under s 29 it can be

challenged as not being valid law. Contrast the position in respect of Westminster Acts (see Chapter 7).

Secondary legislation

The Scottish Executive/Government can pass delegated/secondary legislation (which is similar to Cabinet ministers enacting Statutory Instruments).

14.3.6 Devolved and reserved matters

Devolution involves devolving powers and responsibility from the centre (Westminster) to the regions (Scotland). The Scotland Act 1998 devolves powers to Scotland (devolved matters), while retaining specific powers in the centre (reserved matters).

Reserved matters

These are set out in Sched 5 of the Act and include for example:

- International relations.
- National security.
- Matters affecting the United Kingdom constitution.

The government argued in its White Paper that these sorts of issues 'can be more effectively and beneficially handled on a United Kingdom basis', thereby safeguarding the United Kingdom's integrity and the benefits of a consistent approach in such areas.

Devolved matters

The following are some of the matters over which the Scottish Parliament has legislative competence:

- Education (primary, secondary, further and higher).
- Health.
- Local government.
- Housing.
- Criminal law.
- Criminal justice and prosecution system.
- Civil and criminal courts.
- Economic development.

Since devolution the Scottish Parliament has not been reticent about exercising its legislative powers. Indeed, in its first parliamentary term (1999–2003, called Session 1) the Scottish Parliament passed 62 Bills:

- 50 were executive Bills (ie introduced by the Scottish Executive – similar to a Cabinet minister introducing a Bill in the Westminster Parliament).
- 8 were members' Bills (introduced by an MSP, analogous to Westminster Private Members' Bills).
- 3 were committee Bills (introduced by a parliamentary committee).
- 1 was a private Bill (analogous to a Westminster private Bill).

Source: www.scottish.parliament.uk

Some of these Bills proved to be controversial (for varying reasons) and actually served to widen the difference between Scotland and England. For example:

- The Protection of Wild Mammals (Scotland) Act 2002 (a members' Bill) ended mounted foxhunting and hare coursing in Scotland. This was two years before the Westminster Parliament passed the 2004 Hunting Act (see section 10.10.3).
- The Community Care and Health (Scotland) Act 2002 (an executive Bill). This Act set out the framework for providing, *inter alia*, free personal and nursing care for older people.

In Session 2 (2003–2007) 66 Acts were made ('Scottish Parliament Factsheet, Scottish Parliament Legislation, Session 2' (Scottish Parliament, 2008), p 8). More recently, in 2008, the Scottish Parliament passed seven Bills including the Judiciary and Courts (Scotland) Act 2008 which provided for a statutory guarantee for the continued independence of the Scottish judiciary.

14.3.7 Tax-varying powers

In the 1997 referendum the Scottish people endorsed the proposition that the Scottish Parliament should enjoy tax-raising powers. As a result, Pt IV of the Scotland Act 1998 permits the Scottish Parliament to vary central government taxation in Scotland (ie to alter the basic rate of income tax by up to 3 pence in the pound). To date this financial power has not been used; however, this provision sets Scottish devolution apart from the devolution arrangements in both Wales and Northern Ireland.

KEY FACTS

Scottish devolution powers	
Legislative	• Can pass primary legislation (Acts of the Scottish Parliament). • Can pass subordinate legislation.
Financial	• Tax-varying powers.

14.3.8 Legislative competence

In essence, the Scottish Parliament can legislate in respect of devolved matters and such Acts can modify existing primary legislation relating to Scotland. The Scottish Parliament, however, like other legislatures is a *limited* legislature (contrast the Westminster Parliament). It cannot pass laws outside of its legislative competence (ie outside of its devolved powers):

SECTION

> s 29(1) Scotland Act 1998
> 'An Act of the Scottish Parliament is not law so far as any provision of the Act is outside the legislative competence of the Parliament.'

Section 29(2) states that a provision will be outside Parliament's legislative competence if it:

(a) Would form part of the law of another country/territory (eg England).
(b) Related to reserved matters (eg national security).
(c) Breaches the restrictions in Sched 4 – this sets out certain legislation which is protected from being altered by an Act of the Scottish Parliament: (eg the Human Rights Act 1998, etc).
(d) Is incompatible with the following:
  • European Convention rights (under the Human Rights Act 1998)
  • European Community (now Union) law (under the European Communities Act 1972).
(e) Removed the Lord Advocate as the head of the systems of criminal prosecution and the investigation of deaths.

In this way the Scottish Parliament is not legislatively omnicompent, as its Acts can be challenged as *ultra vires* if it legislates outside of its competence.

14.3.9 Ensuring the Scottish Parliament legislates within its powers

Scottish primary legislation can in effect be challenged at two stages to ensure that it is within its legislative competence:

■ **The parliamentary stage**

Section 31 states that a member of the Scottish Executive in charge of a Bill shall at the outset state that in his view the Bill is within Parliament's legislative competence. In addition, the Presiding Officer must also decide whether or not the Bill is within Parliament's legislative competence (ie whether it is *ultra vires* the Scotland Act 1998).

Under s 33 the Advocate General for Scotland, the Lord Advocate or the Attorney-General may refer to the new Supreme Court the question as to whether a Bill which has been passed by Parliament, but before Royal Assent has been granted, is within the chamber's legislative competence. Under s 32 if the court determines that such a Bill is outside its powers, the Presiding Officer is unable to submit it for Royal Assent in an unamended form.

Under s 35 the Secretary of State is empowered to prohibit the Presiding Officer from submitting a Bill for Royal Assent if, for example, he has reasonable grounds for believing it would be incompatible with international obligations, etc.

■ **The court stage**

The legal validity of a Scottish Act of Parliament can be challenged in the courts if it is argued that the Act is outside the legal competence of the Scottish Parliament (*ultra vires* – contrast the Westminster Parliament in Chapter 7). This is known as *a devolution issue* and Scottish inferior courts may refer it to the Court of Session or the High Court of Justiciary. Ultimately, the issue may be determined by the new Supreme Court.

Few attempts have been made to challenge Acts of the Scottish Parliament. In *Anderson v Scottish Ministers* [2002] SC (PC) 1, s 1 of the Mental Health (Public Safety and Appeals) (Scotland) Act 1999 was unsuccessfully challenged as being contrary to Art 5 of the European Convention.

14.3.10 Challenging the actions of the Scottish Executive

In relation to actions of members of the Scottish Executive/Government, s 58 author-ises the Secretary of State to direct that such action is not taken if he has reasonable grounds to believe that it would be incompatible, for example, with any international obligations. Similarly, by order he can revoke subordinate legislation made by a member of the Scottish Executive which contains provisions which he has reasonable grounds to believe are incompatible with, for example, the interests of defence. Moreover, s 57 prohibits a member of the Scottish Executive from acting or making subordinate legisla-tion which is incompatible with European Convention rights or European Community (now Union) law.

14.3.11 The European Convention and devolution

The following three cases raised devolution issues concerning claims that Convention rights had been violated in Scottish criminal proceedings.

CASE EXAMPLE

Starrs v Ruxton 2000 SLT 42

The High Court of Justiciary declared that temporary Sheriffs were incompatible with the right to a fair trial (Art 6) as their appointments lacked security of tenure. As they held office at the pleasure, in effect, of the Lord Advocate (who was part of the Scottish Executive), the appearance of independence was absent.

Following this case, the Scottish Parliament enacted the Bail, Judicial Appointments etc (Scotland) Act 2000 abolishing the office of temporary sheriffs.

CASE EXAMPLE

Brown v Stott (Procurator Fiscal) [2003] 1 AC 681

The Privy Council held that the prosecution could use evidence of Brown's compulsory admission to the police under the 1988 Road Traffic Act (that she had been the driver of a car) against her. Brown unsuccessfully argued that this infringed her right not to incriminate herself under Art 6 of the European Convention (the right to a fair trial).

In *Alvin Lee Sinclair v Her Majesty's Advocate* [2005] UKPC D2, the Privy Council quashed a conviction on the basis that a failure to disclose evidence to the defence violated Art 6 (the right to a fair hearing).

14.3.12 The relationship with Westminster

Even though Scotland has its own Parliament, this does not mean that it loses its MPs at Westminster (although the recent Scottish Parliament (Constituencies) Act 2004 did reduce the number of Scottish MPs from 72 to 59). Scottish MPs are still needed in Westminster to represent the people of Scotland in respect of reserved matters (ie issues which affect the whole of the United Kingdom). These MPs are entitled (and do) vote on English matters such as English criminal law which has resulted in the 'West Lothian question' (raised in the 1970s by Tam Dalyell MP for the constituency of West Lothian). In short, Dalyell made reference to the anomaly that in the context of Scottish devolution, whereas Scottish MPs could not vote on devolved matters affecting Scotland (and their constituents) such as education and health, they *could* vote on purely English legislative matters of education and health. Indeed, even the Prime Minister in 2009, Gordon Brown (representing Kirkcaldy and Cowdenbeath), could not vote on those Scottish issues which had been devolved to the Scottish Parliament. One possible solution put forward to the 'West Lothian question' was proposed by Lord Baker's Private Members' Bill: The Parliament (Participation of Members of the House of Commons) Bill 2006 which would have enabled the Speaker of the House of Commons to certify the territorial extent of a Bill (eg a Bill affecting only England) on which only designated MPs could vote (ie English MPs voting on English legislation). Another solution is of course the creation of an 'English Parliament' (a parallel of the Scottish Parliament). According to the Justice Select Committee:

QUOTATION

'There is no consensus about solutions to the "English question", or the range of questions which arise under that heading. Each suggested answer has its own problems and limitations …'
Devolution: A Decade On, Fifth Report of Session 2008–09, HC 529-I (The Stationery Office, 2009), p 69.

Scotland is still represented in Cabinet by a Secretary of State and he represents a link between the Scottish Parliament, Westminster, Whitehall and the other devolved areas. In addition, a House of Commons Scottish Affairs Committee examines the administration and policy of the Scotland Office (including relations with the Scottish Parliament) and a Scottish Grand Committee (composed of Scottish MPs) discusses and debates Scottish matters in general (although it has not met recently).

14.3.13 Parliamentary sovereignty and the Scottish Parliament

In strict constitutional theory, parliamentary sovereignty has not been affected by the establishment of the Scottish Parliament. Indeed, on this point the government in its White Paper made it very clear that:

> 'The UK Parliament is and will remain sovereign in all matters … Westminster will be choosing to exercise that sovereignty by devolving legislative responsibilities to a Scottish Parliament without in any way diminishing its own powers'.
>
> *Scotland's Parliament*, Cm 3658 (The Scottish Office, 1997), p 12.

As a result, the United Kingdom Parliament (in legal theory) could choose if it wanted:

■ To legislate for Scotland in respect of devolved matters without the consent of the Scottish Parliament:

SECTION

> s 28(7) Scotland Act 1998
> 'This section does not affect the power of the Parliament of the United Kingdom to make laws for Scotland.'

■ To revoke the Scotland Act 1998 itself, although according to Laws LJ this would have to be done expressly (see section 4.4.5).

As indicated at sections 7.6.2 and 7.11, however, it would appear to be the case that politically it would be very difficult for the Westminster Parliament to repeal this legislation in practice. Indeed, in its White Paper the government noted that popular support for the Parliament would ensure that its place in our constitution was secure (albeit politically).

Furthermore, a constitutional convention has arisen recently known as the Sewel Convention (named after Lord Sewel who piloted the Scotland Bill through the upper House) which regulates the relationship between the two Parliaments. In essence the convention states that the United Kingdom Parliament will not legislate for Scotland on a devolved matter (or where the competence of the Parliament or the responsibilities of the Executive will be altered) without first obtaining the express consent of the Scottish Parliament. This consent is given in the form of a legislative consent motion (eg one was passed endorsing the principle of the putative Supreme Court, which of course would affect Scotland – Official Report, Session 2, 19th January 2005). Legally of course, the Westminster Parliament could simply pass any legislation without consulting the Scottish Parliament, but that action clearly would be regarded as 'unconstitutional' (see section 4.15).

Finally, there has been some debate over whether parliamentary sovereignty has historically been fully accepted in Scotland in any event. This is on the basis that the principle was a purely English notion associated with the English, but not the Scottish Parliament, prior to the Union with Scotland Act 1706 (see Lord Cooper in *MacCormick v Lord Advocate* (1953) SC 396).

14.3.14 Further reform

In June 2009 the Calman Commission issued its report (*Serving Scotland Better: Scotland and the United Kingdom in the 21st century, An Executive Summary of the Final Report – June 2009*, (Commission on Scottish Devolution, 2009)). Following this report, in November 2009 the British government unveiled its White Paper on its response to the Commission (*Scotland's Future in the United Kingdom, Building on ten years of Scottish devolution*, Cm 7738 (Scotland Office, 2009)). Its proposals included devolving further powers to the Scottish Parliament in the following areas, for example, the power to set Scottish speed limits, drink-driving limits and regulating air weapons. In financial matters, a new Scottish rate of income tax would replace the Scottish Variable Rate which the Scottish Parliament would be able to set. It was envisaged that this package of reforms would be implemented in the next Parliament. These reforms, if passed, illustrate the principle that devolution is not a fixed state of affairs, rather it is a (rolling) process.

ACTIVITY

Quick quiz

1. What do the Scottish Parliament and executive/government do?
2. What is the difference between devolved and reserved matters?
3. How can the actions of the Scottish Parliament and executive/government be challenged?
4. What is the relationship between the Scottish and the Westminster Parliaments?

14.4 Northern Irish devolution

14.4.1 History

England had exerted control over Ireland for centuries before the 1800 Act of Union unified the Parliaments of Great Britain with that of Ireland. This Union created the Parliament of the United Kingdom of Great Britain (England, Wales and Scotland) and Ireland. By the beginning of the twentieth century the pressure from Irish nationalist politicians for home rule to govern themselves led to the Government of Ireland Act 1914 which aimed to establish an Irish Parliament (it never came into effect owing to the First World War).

In 1920 the Government of Ireland Act was passed which recognised the reality that two separate Parliaments were needed:

■ One for the South (overwhelmingly Roman Catholic); and
■ One for the North (majority Protestant).

Although the Northern Irish Parliament (Stormont) was established and operated until the 1970s, in contrast, the Southern Irish Parliament was repudiated by Sinn Fein. This in effect led to the creation of the Irish Free State (with Dominion status) in 1922 which thereafter became a Republic (1937) and left the Commonwealth (1949). Northern Ireland with its Stormont Parliament remained part of the United Kingdom (now the United Kingdom of Great Britain and Northern Ireland).

Stormont

The Northern Irish Parliament functioned for five decades and was a bicameral legislature consisting of two chambers:

■ House of Commons (directly elected).
■ Senate (which was indirectly elected by the lower House).

The executive aspect of the arrangements involved a parliamentary executive comprising a Prime Minister together with a Northern Irish Cabinet. The Parliament was a limited legislature with certain areas (eg defence) excepted from its legislative competence.

The major problem with the Parliament was that in this divided community it continually had a Unionist majority. Civil unrest in the province, fuelled by the grievances of the Catholic minority led eventually in the 1970s to the suspension of Stormont (s 31 of the Northern Ireland Constitution Act 1973 abolished the Parliament of Northern Ireland) and direct rule being imposed by the United Kingdom government. Thereafter, a Secretary of State for Northern Ireland would make decisions for Northern Ireland and the legislative powers enjoyed by the defunct Stormont would be exercised through Orders in Council.

The 1998 Good Friday Agreement

During the period of direct rule there were various unsuccessful attempts at securing a solution to the 'Northern Ireland problem', but in 1998 in the aftermath of an IRA ceasefire, the Belfast Agreement was signed by all parties ('the Good Friday Agreement'). It endorsed the resumption of devolution of power to Ulster and the establishment of new institutional relationships between the United Kingdom, the Republic of Ireland and Ulster.

The Good Friday Agreement was subsequently endorsed in May 1998 by a vote north and south of the Irish border. Following this, the United Kingdom Parliament passed:

■ The Northern Ireland (Elections) Act 1998 – to enable elections to take place for the new Northern Ireland Assembly.
■ The Northern Ireland Act 1998 – to establish the institutional framework of devolution.

Subsequent developments

Unfortunately, the actual operation of the devolved arrangements proved to be very problematic as it was not until December 1999 that power was finally devolved to the institutions, and in October 2002 the Assembly was suspended. Notwithstanding the resumption of direct rule (with the Northern Ireland Office and Secretary of State exercising powers instead via Orders in Council), elections took place in November 2003 for a new Northern Ireland Assembly to revive devolution. Three years later, a 'transitional assembly' sat and was dissolved to pave the way for fresh elections to take place in March 2007. These elections were preceded by the *St Andrews Agreement* made by the Prime Minister and the Irish Taoiseach – subsequently given effect by the Northern Ireland (St Andrews Agreement) Act 2006 which set out a timetable to revive devolution. Thereafter, devolution in Northern Ireland resumed in May 2007 with a functioning Executive Committee and Assembly.

14.4.2 The Northern Ireland Assembly

The Northern Ireland Assembly is a unicameral legislature which is elected on a four-yearly term (it is interesting to remember that Stormont had been bicameral).

Northern Irish devolution is distinctive in that certain decisions, for example standing orders and the election of First and Deputy First Minister have to be made on a cross-community basis. This involves obtaining the support of the majority of both community representatives (known as parallel consent). Such parallel consent is seen as essential in a divided community.

Composition and elections

The Northern Ireland Assembly consists of 108 Members (MLAs), who are elected on the basis of STV (Single Transferable Vote) with 18 constituencies returning 6 members each. STV allows voters to indicate their varying preferences for different candidates, thereby maximising consensus among voters. The first elections took place in June 1998 and a second set took place in 2003. As a result of the second election the largest unionist party became the Democratic Unionist Party, while Sinn Fein became the largest nationalist party. A third election was held in March 2007 and the results are detailed below.

The Northern Ireland Assembly 2007	
Northern Ireland Assembly Election 2007	
Political Party	**Seats**
Ulster Unionist Party (UUP)	18
Democratic Unionist Party (DUP)	36
Social Democratic and Labour Party (SDLP)	16
Sinn Fein (SF)	28
Alliance	7
Others	3

Source: Electoral Office for Northern Ireland.

Table 14.2

All MLAs are governed by *The Code of Conduct of the Northern Ireland Assembly*, which details the standard of conduct expected of members.

Presiding Officer and committee system

Northern Irish devolution provides for the election from among its membership of a Presiding Officer (the Speaker) and three Deputies (analogous with the Scottish Parliament). As in Scotland, there is a committee system with committees shadowing the different Northern Irish government departmental portfolios (eg the Education Committee scrutinises the Department of Education).

14.4.3 The Northern Ireland Executive Committee

Part III of the 1998 Act provides for the establishment of the following ministerial offices (the Executive Committee):

■ First Minister and Deputy First Minister (one from the unionist and one from the nationalist community) – under the 1998 Act they are elected jointly by the Assembly through a majority of designated nationalists and a majority of designated unionists. In this way Northern Irish devolution differs from both Scotland and Wales in that it requires 'parallel consent' from both communities for these two officers to assume their ministerial positions. In February 2010 Peter Robinson MLA (DUP) was the First Minister with Martin McGuinness MLA (Sinn Fein) as the Deputy First Minister.

■ Northern Ireland ministers – these are determined using the *d'Handt* political system (s 18) based on the proportion of Assembly seats each party has acquired. In this way Northern Ireland devolution is distinctive as its executive reflects the balance of opinion within the Assembly. In short, its *raison d'etre* is power-sharing between the two communities and the various political parties (all of whom will be represented in the Executive Committee). Each minister will head a government department (eg Department of the Environment). All ministers are governed by *The Northern Ireland Executive Ministerial Code*.

KEY FACTS

Composition of the Northern Irish devolved institutions	
Assembly	• 108 Members (Single Transferable Vote system).
Executive	• First Minister and Deputy First Minister. • Northern Ireland ministers. In 2010 the Executive comprised the First and Deputy First Ministers, together with 12 other ministers (including two junior ministers): 5 DUP, 4 SF, 2 UUP and 1 SDLP.

14.4.4 Legislation and legislative competence

Section 5 empowers the Assembly to make primary legislation known as Acts of the Northern Ireland Assembly. In 2008 the Assembly passed 13 Acts. For example, the Public Authorities (Reform) Act (Northern Ireland) 2009 abolished specified public authorities such as the Fisheries Conservancy Board for Northern Ireland. As with Scotland, for the purposes of the Human Rights Act 1998 (s 21) such legislation is regarded as secondary and so subject to challenge.

The Northern Ireland Assembly (like its predecessor and the Scottish Parliament) is a limited and subordinate legislature:

SECTION

s 6(1) Northern Ireland Act 1998

'A provision of an Act is not law if it is outside the legislative competence of the Assembly.'

Section 6(2) sets out the circumstances which will be outside of the Assembly's legislative competence. These are very similar to those already set out in relation to the Scottish Parliament (see section 14.3.8); however, one additional circumstance which applies specifically to the Northern Ireland Assembly is if its Acts discriminate on the ground of religious belief or political opinion (s 6(2)(e)).

14.4.5 Reserved, excepted and transferred matters

▪ Reserved matters

The Assembly cannot legislate in respect of reserved matters (Sched 3) unless they are allocated the specific responsibility to do so by converting a reserved matter into a transferred one (under s 2 this would require an Order in Council). These areas include, for example, the Post Office.

▪ Excepted matters

The Assembly cannot legislate in respect of excepted matters (Sched 2). Excepted matters include, for example, the defence of the realm.

▪ Transferred matters

The Assembly can legislate in respect of transferred matters and these include, for example:

- The Arts.
- Education.
- Agriculture.

NB The Northern Ireland Act 2009 paved the way for the future transfer of policing and justice powers and following the *Hillsborough Castle Agreement* in February 2010 these powers were then devolved in April 2010.

14.4.6 Ensuring the Northern Ireland Assembly legislates within its powers

The Northern Ireland Assembly can be challenged at two stages:

▪ The parliamentary (Assembly) stage

(i) Section 9 requires that a minister in charge of a Bill makes a statement at the outset that in his view it is compatible with the Assembly's legislative competence.

(ii) Section 10 states that a Bill will not be introduced if the Presiding Officer considers that it is not within the Assembly's legislative competence.

(iii) Section 11 empowers the Attorney General for Northern Ireland to refer a Bill (which has been passed by the Assembly) to the new Supreme Court to determine whether it is within the Assembly's legislative competence. If it is not, the Secretary State (not the Presiding Officer) cannot submit the Bill for Royal Assent in an unamended form (s 14). In addition, the Secretary of State may refuse to submit a Bill which he considers would breach international obligations.

(iv) Under s 13 the Human Rights Commission (see section 14.4.9) may be asked by the Assembly whether a Bill is compatible with human rights.

▪ The court stage

The legal validity of an Act of the Northern Ireland Assembly can be challenged in the courts – ultimately before the new Supreme Court – on the basis of a devolution issue (ie has the devolved institution acted within its powers?).

14.4.7 Challenging the actions of the Northern Ireland Executive Committee

Under s 24, a Northern Ireland minister or Northern Ireland department has no power to act or to make subordinate legislation which, *inter alia*:

- Is incompatible with European Convention rights.
- Is incompatible with European Community (now Union) law.
- Discriminates on the ground of religious belief or political opinion.
- Modifies an entrenched enactment (eg modifies the Human Rights Act 1998 or European Communities Act 1972).

Moreover, if such legislation deals with an excepted or reserved matter the Secretary of State may revoke it by order (s 25). Similarly, he may do so where such legislation is incompatible, *inter alia*, with any international obligations (s 26).

KEY FACTS

Northern Irish devolution powers	
Legislative	• Pass primary legislation (Acts of the Northern Ireland Assembly). • Pass subordinate legislation.
Financial	• No tax-varying powers.

14.4.8 The relationship with Westminster and parliamentary sovereignty

As with Scotland, Northern Ireland returns MPs to Westminster. Northern Ireland also retains its Secretary of State. At Westminster, like Scotland at section 14.3.12, Northern Ireland has a House of Commons Northern Ireland Affairs Committee (in respect of the Northern Ireland Office) and a Northern Ireland Grand Committee (to debate and discuss the general affairs of Ulster).

As with Scotland, the existence of a Northern Ireland Assembly does not in strict constitutional theory affect parliamentary sovereignty.

SECTION

> s 5(6) Northern Ireland Act 1998
> 'This section does not affect the power of the Parliament of the United Kingdom to make laws for Northern Ireland.'

Further, the United Kingdom Parliament legally could revoke the Assembly. Indeed, as we have already seen, the previous Stormont Parliament was revoked by the Westminster Parliament in the 1970s.

In terms of sovereignty, however, the Act does make the following declaration at the outset:

SECTION

> s 1(1) Northern Ireland Act 1998
> 'It is hereby declared that Northern Ireland in its entirety remains part of the United Kingdom and shall not cease to be so without the consent of a majority of the people of Northern Ireland voting in a poll held for the purposes of this section.'

ACTIVITY

Applying the law

Does s 1 of the Northern Ireland Act 1998 mean that the United Kingdom Parliament could not:
(a) legally
and/or
(b) politically
legislate to sever Northern Ireland from the rest of the United Kingdom without first obtaining the consent of the Northern Irish people? (See also section 7.10.2.)

14.4.9 Other strands to the Belfast Agreement

These included the following:

- **The North-South Ministerial Council** – composed of ministers from the Irish government (Republic of Ireland) and the Northern Ireland Executive Committee to consider matters of mutual interest.
- **The British-Irish Council** – composed of representatives from the British and Irish governments, together with those from the devolved institutions to agree common policies.

Human Rights Commission

Section 68 of the Northern Ireland Act 1998 established a Northern Ireland Human Rights Commission. Its functions include, for example:

- Keeping under review Northern Ireland's law and practice in respect of protecting human rights.
- Advising the Secretary of State and Executive Committee of legislative (and other) measures which ought to be taken to protect human rights.
- Advising the Assembly whether a Bill is compatible with human rights.

ACTIVITY

Quick quiz
1. What do the Northern Ireland Assembly and Executive Committee do?
2. What is the difference between transferred, reserved and excepted matters?
3. How can the actions of the Assembly and the Executive Committee be challenged?
4. How does Northern Irish devolution differ from that in Scotland?

14.5 Welsh devolution

14.5.1 History

For centuries Wales has been closely connected with England as indicated by the 1536 Act of Union between the two countries. Today England and Wales are one single legal jurisdiction. By the second part of the twentieth century, however, there was a growing nationalist call in Wales for it to be able to govern itself. In 1978 the Wales Act was passed which conferred a diluted form of devolution on Wales, but the legislation did not come into effect because only 12 per cent voted in favour of it in a referendum. The Labour Party election manifesto of 1997 was committed to the establishment of Welsh devolution and in July 1997 the government issued its White Paper detailing its proposals (*A Voice for Wales* Cm 3718 (The Stationery Office, 1997)).

As in Scotland, these proposals were endorsed subsequently in a referendum in September 1997 (but only by the narrowest of margins: 50.3 per cent voted yes). Following this the Government of Wales Act 1998 was passed which devolved power to Wales. This Act has been superseded by the Government of Wales Act 2006 which re-enacts many of its provisions. The 2006 Act was enacted so as to strengthen and deepen the devolved arrangements in Wales and had been preceded by a White Paper, *Better Governance for Wales* Cm 6582 (Wales Office, 2005).

14.5.2 The National Assembly for Wales

Section 1 of the Government of Wales Act 2006 states that there is to be an Assembly known as the National Assembly for Wales (Cynulliad Cenedlaethol Cymru). Under s 1 of the 1998 Act the Assembly was a corporate body (with executive and legislative arms united) but this is no longer the case under the 2006 Act.

Composition and elections

The Assembly is composed of 60 Assembly Members (AMs). They are elected on the following basis:

- 40 Assembly constituency members – elected by the 'first past the post' system.
- 20 Assembly regional members – elected by the Additional Member system of proportional representation (four from each of the five regional electoral regions).

Section 7 of the 2006 Act prevents a person standing as both a regional and constituency candidate at the same time. As in Scotland, the combination of electoral systems is designed to offset the disproportionate nature of the 'first past the post' system. Elections took place in 1999 and 2003. The third set of elections took place in May 2007:

The National Assembly for Wales 2007			
2007 Assembly election			
Political Party	Constituency Seats	Regional Seats	Total
Labour Party	24	2	26
Welsh Conservative Party	5	7	12
Plaid Cymru (Welsh Nationalist)	7	8	15
Welsh Liberal Democrats	3	3	6
Other	1	0	1
TOTAL	40	20	60

Source: www.assemblywales.org.

Table 14.3

Section 6 provides that voters have two votes:

- A constituency vote – a vote cast for a candidate in their constituency.
- An electoral regional vote – a vote cast for a political party or for an individual candidate.

Elections are on a fixed-term basis of every four years (s 3), although s 5 permits an extraordinary election to be held, as is the case in Scotland. All Assembly Members are required to adhere to the standards of conduct set out in the *National Assembly for Wales: Code of Conduct for Assembly Members*.

Presiding Officer and committees

Section 25 of the 2006 Act provides for the election by the Assembly of a Presiding Officer together with a Deputy Presiding Officer, similar to the Scottish Parliament. The Assembly operates through a variety of different committees. These include:

- Scrutiny committees (eg the Health, Well being and Local Government Committee)
- Legislative committees (ie permanent committees which scrutinise legislative proposals)
- Other committees (eg Public Accounts Committee which scrutinises the expenditure of the Welsh Assembly Government).

14.5.3 The Welsh Assembly Government

Following the 2007 election, the Welsh Assembly Government comprised a Labour-Plaid Cymru coalition.

Section 45 of the 2006 Act established a Welsh Assembly Government (Llywodraeth Cynulliad Cymru) which comprises the following:

- The First Minister – nominated by the Assembly (in February 2010 this was Carwyn Jones AM).
- The remaining Welsh Ministers – appointed by the First Minister from among the Assembly members (the arrangements therefore are those of a parliamentary executive and under s 45 of the Act, the First Minister and Welsh Ministers are collectively known as the 'Welsh Ministers').
- The Counsel General to the Welsh Assembly Government – the government's legal adviser (a new office created by the 2006 Act).
- The Deputy Welsh Ministers – appointed by the First Minister to assist any of the above.

Ministers are governed by the following code: *The Ministerial Code (A Code of Ethics and Procedural Guidance for Ministers and Deputy Ministers* (Welsh Assembly Government, 2007)), which is issued by the First Minister.

Each minister will be allocated a particular governmental portfolio. For example in 2010 they included, *inter alia*, the following departments:

- Children, Education, Lifelong Learning and Skills.
- Social Justice and Local Government.
- Economy and Transport.

One key change brought about by the 2006 Act was to formally separate the Welsh executive from the Welsh legislature. The 1998 legislation (unlike in Scotland or Northern Ireland) did not separate these constitutional functions as the Assembly was a corporate body exercising both functions. In 2005 the government's White Paper had proposed separating the legislative and executive aspects of the Assembly and this had followed a Commission Report by Lord Richard (*The Report of the Commission on the Powers and Electoral Arrangements of the National Assembly for Wales* (March 2004)) who had recommended that the *status quo* was no longer sustainable. As pointed out in the White Paper:

QUOTATION

'Often, decisions are made in the name of the Assembly which are in fact, quite properly, the responsibility of one Minster or official, making it hard to know who should be accountable to the public for them.'

Better Governance for Wales, Cm 6582 (Wales Office, 2005), p 3.

Under the 2006 Act the Welsh Assembly government is a separate constitutional entity (although it sits in the Assembly and is directly accountable to it), thereby ensuring more transparent accountability for the use of its powers. In fact, under s 48 Welsh Ministers must resign if the Assembly resolves that they no longer enjoy the confidence of the Assembly (similar to a vote of no confidence in the House of Commons). Even before the 2006 Act, however, members of the executive were held accountable to the rest of the Assembly through the committee system, debates and questioning.

KEY FACTS

Composition of the Welsh devolved institutions	

Assembly	• 60 Assembly Members (AMs), comprising:
	   • 40 Assembly constituency members (the 'first past the post' system).
	   • 20 Assembly regional members (the Additional Member system).

Executive	• The First Minister. • Welsh Ministers (including Deputies). • The Counsel General to the Welsh Assembly Government.

14.5.4 Powers and responsibilities

■ Under the aegis of the 1998 Act devolved powers included, for example, housing, environment, education and training, sport, transport and culture. Powers were conferred on the Assembly, which in turn in practice were typically delegated to the executive which acted as the delegate of the Assembly. Today under the 2006 Act, s 58 permits the transfer of functions directly onto the Welsh Ministers by way of an Order in Council. In this way, the Welsh Ministers exercise functions in their own constitutional right rather than as delegates of the Assembly. They will, therefore, make executive decisions, subordinate/secondary legislation, etc, albeit they will be scrutinised by the Assembly.

■ Under the 1998 Act, the scheme of devolution as applied to Wales was termed *'executive devolution'* as the Assembly was not given powers to make primary legislation (contrast Scotland and Northern Ireland). It was commonly argued that Wales did not need legislative devolution because its arrangements were not sufficiently distinctive (unlike Scotland). Indeed, it was partly the diluted form of devolution offered to the Welsh which explained the disappointing support for it at the 1997 referendum.

The Assembly could, however, make subordinate legislation (which the executive could propose for the Assembly to endorse).

■ Today, under Pt 3 of the 2006 Act, the Assembly may make laws known as Measures of the National Assembly for Wales within its specified legislative competence (ie in relation to a 'matter' in respect of one of 20 broad 'Fields' in sch 5 of the Act). According to the explanatory notes to the 2006 Act (Crown Copyright, 2006, p 51) this instrument is 'a type of subordinate legislation' although such Assembly Measures 'have the same effect as an Act of Parliament' as according to s 94(1) they *'may make any provision that could be made by an Act of Parliament'*. Amendments can be made to the content of sch 5 by way of either:
  – a 'framework provision' in a Westminster Bill, or
  – a Legislative Competence Order (LCO). An LCO has to be approved in draft form by both the Assembly and both Houses of Parliament before an Order in Council is made by Her Majesty. For an example, see The National Assembly for Wales (Legislative Competence) (Social Welfare) Order 2008 SI 2008/1785 which extended the legislative competence of the Assembly in relation to Field 15 (Social Welfare).

■ In addition, the 2006 Act paves the way in the future for further legislative powers (to be known as Acts of the National Assembly for Wales) to be conferred subsequently onto the Assembly following the support of the Welsh people in a referendum (pt 4 of the 2006 Act). Pt 4 would then supersede pt 3 and enable the Assembly to pass laws (Acts) on a broad range of subjects without having to have recourse to Parliament on an *ad hoc* basis as now through the LCO procedure above.

■ In 2007 the Welsh Assembly Government established the *All Wales Convention* to assess the law-making powers that the Assembly should enjoy. It reported in 2009 (*All Wales Convention Report* (Crown Copyright, 2009)) and concluded that there was solid support among the Welsh people for devolution (para 6.2.9). The Convention was convinced that pt 4 of the Act offered 'substantial advantage' over the current arrangements of pt 3. According to the Convention, a 'yes' vote in a referendum on p 4 powers was obtainable (with 47 per cent declared voting intentions being in favour with 37 per cent against, p 98–100).

14.5.5 The competence of the institutions

The National Assembly for Wales

SECTION
....

s 94(2) Government of Wales Act 2006

'An Assembly Measure is not law so far as any provision of the Assembly Measure is outside the Assembly's legislative competence.'

Under s 94 a provision will be outside the Assembly's legislative competence if, *inter alia*:

■ It extends to a legal jurisdiction other than England and Wales (although England and Wales are a single jurisdiction, the Measures will invariably apply only in Wales).

■ It is incompatible with European Convention rights or European Community (now Union) law.

In addition, the person in charge of a proposed Assembly Measure must state at the outset that in their view it was within the competence of the Assembly, and the Presiding Officer must also decide if it is and state his decision (s 97). Further, under s 99 the Counsel General or the Attorney-General can seek a decision of the Supreme Court as to whether a proposed Measure is within the Assembly's legislative competence. Under s 101 the Secretary of State also has the power to intervene to prohibit a Measure from being approved by the Crown where, for example, he had reasonable grounds that the measure would have a serious impact on, for example, water resources in England.

The actions of the Welsh Ministers

■ Under the 2006 Act, Welsh Ministers have no power to make subordinate legislation or any other Act if it is incompatible with European Community (now Union) law (s 80) or European Convention rights (s 81).

■ In addition, s 82 empowers the Secretary of State to direct that the Welsh Ministers do not take proposed action if it would be incompatible with any international obligation. Similarly, he can revoke subordinate legislation on the same basis.

A devolution issue

Schedule 9 of the 2006 Act states that a devolution issue means:

1(1)(a) a question whether an Assembly Measure/Act of the Assembly is within the Assembly's legislative competence,

(b) a question whether any function is exercisable by the Welsh Ministers, First Minister or Counsel General,

(c) a question whether an exercise of a function by the above (in b) is within their powers (including ss 80 and 81 – see above),

(d) a question whether the above (in b) have failed to comply with a duty imposed on them (including any obligation under European Community (now Union) law under s 80),

(e) a question whether a failure to act by the above (in b) is incompatible with European Convention rights.

The court of last resort in relation to devolution issues, as with Scotland and Northern Ireland, is the Supreme Court.

KEY FACTS

Welsh devolution powers	
Legislative	• Passes laws (Assembly Measures) – Pt 3 of the Government of Wales Act 2006. • Provision is made in pt 4 of the Government of Wales Act 2006 for the Assembly to pass Assembly Acts in the future following approval by the Welsh people in a referendum.
Financial	• No tax-varying powers.

14.5.6 The relationship with Westminster and parliamentary sovereignty

Wales returns 40 MPs to Westminster and the country is represented by a Secretary of State. At Westminster, like Scotland and Northern Ireland, Wales has a House of

Commons Welsh Affairs Committee (which considers matters within the Secretary of State for Wales' responsibility) and a Welsh Grand Committee. According to the Justice Select Committee in 2009:

QUOTATION

'To date, the West Lothian question has not been such a "political hot potato" in Anglo-Welsh relations as it has been in Anglo-Scottish relations. There are fewer Welsh than Scottish MPs serving as ministers in the UK Government, and with fewer powers devolved to Wales than to Scotland, there are fewer policy areas where Welsh MPs cannot legitimately legislate.'

Devolution: A Decade On, Fifth Report of Session 2008–09, vol 1, HC 529-I (2009), para 156.

As with the other devolution settlements, in legal theory parliamentary sovereignty is unaffected by Welsh devolution as these arrangements could simply be repealed by a Westminster statute. Moreover, the 2006 Act makes it clear that notwithstanding the devolved arrangements, ultimately Parliament can legislate for Wales if it chooses to do so:

SECTION

s 93(5) Government of Wales Act 2006

'This Part does not affect the power of the Parliament of the United Kingdom to make laws for Wales.'

ACTIVITY

Quick quiz

1. What is the difference between the two Government of Wales Acts?
2. What powers and responsibilities do the National Assembly and Assembly Government have?
3. How can the actions of the National Assembly and the Assembly Government be challenged?
4. How does Welsh devolution differ from that in Scotland?

KEY FACTS

Links between the devolved settlements
• **The British-Irish Council** contains representatives from each of the devolved institutions together with the British and Irish governments.
• **The Joint Ministerial Council** which contains representatives of all three executive administrations together with the British government.
• A ***Memorandum of Understanding*** has been agreed which promotes cooperation and communication between the devolved administrations and the United Kingdom government (see *Devolution, Memorandum of Understanding and Supplementary Agreements*, Cm 7864 (Crown Copyright, 2010)).

14.6 The position of England

14.6.1 No English Parliament

The devolution arrangements in the British constitution are not symmetrical because while Scotland, Wales and Northern Ireland have a tier of government between local government and central government/Parliament, there is no corresponding tier in

England. In short, there is no English Parliament to regulate purely English affairs which means that the vast majority of people in the United Kingdom, who are English, are not regulated by any form of devolved infrastructure (but see below). Instead, England is regulated by the United Kingdom Parliament in Westminster which, of course, includes MP's who are not English (the 'West Lothian question'). It appears, however, that there is little public call or enthusiasm for the establishment of an English Parliament. In recent years, however, the constitutional arrangements of England have seen two changes:

14.6.2 Regional Development Agencies

Although no English Parliament has been created, a new level of strategic administration has been inserted: the Regional Development Agencies (RDAs). These were created under the Regional Development Agencies Act 1998. According to the Prime Minister in 2002:

QUOTATION

'We have already done a lot to decentralise decision-making to the English regions. Regional Development Agencies (RDAs) have been established to help strengthen the building blocks for economic growth in all regions, with a network of regional chambers to scrutinise them.'

Your Region, Your Choice: Revitalising the English Regions, Cm 5511 (The Stationery Office, 2002), Preface.

In 2009, there were nine RDAs (West Midlands, North West, etc). In essence they are strategic bodies whose remit includes, *inter alia*:

- improving economic performance, development and regeneration
- promoting employment (and developing employment skills)
- assisting sustainable development.

In this way they provide a strategic and regional approach to these issues, which is specifically tailored for each particular region. It is pertinent to note that the eight Regional Assemblies (voluntary bodies comprising representatives of local government, business and the wider community) were scheduled to be abolished by mid-2010.

In terms of parliamentary supervision by Westminster, in 2009 eight Regional Committees (eg East Midlands Committee) were established until the 2010 general election to examine regional strategies and regional bodies.

14.6.3 The London Mayor and Assembly

In 1985 Parliament revoked the Greater London Council (Local Government Act 1985) which meant that London as a large capital city lacked an overall strategic body. The Labour government elected in 1997 implemented plans for a democratic city government for London by establishing the Greater London Authority under the Greater London Authority Act 1999 which comprises the following:

- A directly elected Mayor of London.
- An elected London Assembly.

As in Scotland, Wales and Northern Ireland, this legislation followed an endorsement of the government's proposals in a referendum held in 1998.

The London Mayor

The office of Mayor (currently held by Boris Johnson) represents London. He has an executive role to, *inter alia*, develop transport, environment and planning strategies for London. He also sets a Budget for the Greater London Authority. He is supported by a mayoral team which includes a statutory Deputy Mayor (a member of the Assembly).

The London Assembly

This is composed of 25 elected Assembly Members (AMs) whose role, *inter alia*, is to hold the Mayor to account by monitoring, debating and questioning his activities and decisions (eg the *Mayor's Question Time* – analogous to PMQs at section 12.4.2). In addition, they investigate matters which are of significance to people living in London. The Assembly makes use of an investigative committee system (eg the Budget and Performance Committee) in carrying out its responsibilities. Both the Mayor and the Assembly members are asked questions by Londoners in a bi-annual '*People's Question Time*'.

Elections

As a result of the last election in May 2008 the political makeup of the Assembly was as follows:

The London Assembly 2008	
Political Party	**Number of AMs**
Labour Party	8
Conservative Party	11
Liberal Democrats	3
Green Party	2
British National Party	1
TOTAL	25

Source: Whitaker's Almanack 2010 (142nd edn, A & C Black Publishers Ltd, 2009), p 238.

Table 14.3

At the same time Boris Johnson was elected as Mayor of London. The Mayor and each AM are elected for a term of four years. The Greater London Authority Act 2007 provided the Mayor and Assembly with additional powers.

KEY FACTS

Key facts on the nomenclature, size and powers of the devolved institutions

	Scotland	Wales	Northern Ireland
Legislature	Scottish Parliament	National Assembly	Northern Ireland Assembly
Executive	Scottish Executive/ Government	Welsh Assembly Government	Executive Committee
Size of chamber and electoral systems	129 members in total • 73 Constituency MSPs (simple majority system) • 56 Regional MSPs (Additional Member system)	60 members in total • 40 Constituency AMs (simple majority system) • 20 Regional AMs (Additional Member system)	108 Members (MLAs) (Single Transferable Vote system)
Primary legislative powers	Yes	Assembly Measures can have the same effect as an Act of Parliament	Yes
Subordinate legislative powers	Yes	Yes	Yes
Tax-varying powers	Yes	No	No

SUMMARY

- Although the British constitution is hallmarked by being a unitary state, power has been decentralised to local government and to regional bodies in Scotland, Wales, Northern Ireland and London.
- Local government is public power which has been delegated to directly elected local authorities which administer governmental functions at a local level and tailored to local needs.
- Local government performs a wide range of functions ranging from the delivery of services to passing byelaws. It also has the power to raise revenue through taxation.
- The Scotland Act 1998 devolved power to Scotland and established the Scottish Parliament and Scottish Executive/Government.
- The Scottish Parliament is elected every four years and has the power to pass Acts of the Scottish Parliament and also enjoys a tax-varying power.
- The Scottish Executive/Government is composed of the First Minister, Scottish Ministers together with the Lord Advocate and Solicitor-General.
- Both the Scottish Parliament and Executive/Government must act within their powers as conferred by the Scotland Act 1998.
- As a consequence of the 1998 Good Friday Agreement power was devolved to Northern Ireland (it had previously enjoyed devolved powers earlier in the 20th century until being revoked in the 1970s).
- The Northern Ireland Assembly is elected every four years and has the power to pass Acts of the Northern Ireland Assembly.
- The Northern Ireland Executive Committee comprises the First Minister, Deputy First Minister and remaining ministers. It is unique in the devolution settlements in the United Kingdom as it includes the principle of power-sharing whereby ministers are determined using the *d'Handt* political system of representation.
- Both the Northern Ireland Assembly and Executive Committee must act within their powers as conferred by the Northern Ireland Act 1998.
- The Government of Wales Act 1998 devolved power to Wales. Today under the Government of Wales Act 2006, Wales has a National Assembly for Wales and a Welsh Assembly Government (the latter comprising the First Minister, Welsh Ministers and the Counsel General to the Welsh Assembly Government).
- The National Assembly for Wales is elected every four years and has the power to make laws known as Measures of the National Assembly for Wales. The competence of the Assembly can be expanded by a Legislative Competence Order or by a Westminster Act of Parliament.
- Both the National Assembly and Welsh Assembly Government must act within the powers conferred on them.
- Scotland, Northern Ireland and Wales all still send MPs to Westminster.
- England has no devolved equivalent of the Scottish Parliament, Northern Ireland Assembly or National Assembly for Wales, although the Greater London Authority Act 1999 established the Greater London Authority for London (including a directly elected Mayor).

SAMPLE ESSAY QUESTION

What is local government, what are its functions and why is it considered an important aspect of the British constitution?

Introduction:
- Define the term local government (ie decentralised governmental powers)

Nature of local government:
- The UK is broken down into areas managed by local authorities
- Local authorities/councils are statutory bodies
- The structure and arrangement of local government varies across the four countries of the UK and within England itself (eg some areas have county councils, others have metropolitan borough councils)

Functions and powers of local government:
- Providers of the delivery of services (eg environmental health)
- Administers policies expressed in primary (Westminster) legislation (ie in relation to schools)
  - Legislates on local issues
  - Raises local revenue
  - Has a limited element of discretion in performing its functions (see s 2(1) Local Government Act 2000)

Constitutional importance of local government:
- It disperses state power away from the centre so that public power is not all focused and centralised in the centre (ie Westminster/Whitehall)
- It gives expression to the constitutional and democratic principle of 'participatory government' which enables individuals to engage in the governmental process (eg by being elected as councillors). It allows local individuals to affect local decision-making (see the principle of subsidiarity)
- It is part of the executive, although the political complexion of local authorities may be different to that of central government (see the tension between the two and *juridification*)

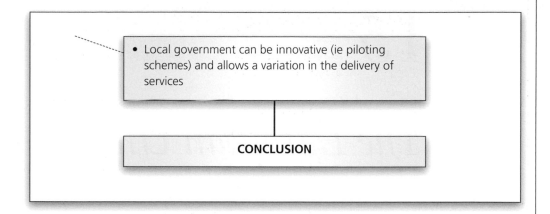

 # Further reading

Books

Bogdanor, V, *The New British Constitution* (Hart Publishing, 2009) Chapter 4.

Dalyell, T, 'Devolution: The End of Britain' in Sutherland, K (ed), *The Rape of the Constitution?* (Imprint Academic, 2000), p 257.

Wilson, D, and Game, C, *Local Government in the United Kingdom* (4th edn, Palgrave Macmillan, 2006), Chapters 3, 5, 9, 11 and 12.

Articles

Ryan, M, 'Central-local government relations' (2009) 14 *Coventry Law Journal* 18 (available at www.westlaw.com).

Papers

A Voice for Wales Cm 3718 (The Stationery Office, 1997).

Better Governance for Wales Cm 6582 (Welsh Office, 2005).

Devolution Monitoring Programme (The Constitution Unit). These publications are produced continuously by the Constitution Unit (University of London) and cover all aspects of devolution.

House of Commons Justice Committee, Fifth Report of Session 2008-09, *Devolution: A Decade On*, Vol 1, HC 529-I (2009).

Leeke, M, Sear, C and Gay, O, 'An introduction to devolution in the UK', 03/84, (House of Commons Library, 2003).

Scotland's Parliament Cm 3658 (The Scottish Office, 1997).

Your Region, Your Choice: Revitalising the English Regions Cm 5511 (The Stationery Office, 2002).

Internet links

www.scottish.parliament.uk
www.london.gov.uk
www.wales.gov.uk
www.niassembly.gov.uk

15

The European Union

AIMS AND OBJECTIVES

At the end of this chapter you should be able to:

■ Understand the constitutional features of the European Union
■ Appreciate the impact the European Union has had on Britain's uncodified constitutional arrangements

Introduction

In *Bulmer v Bollinger* [1974] Ch 401 Lord Denning MR observed that:

JUDGMENT

'… The Treaty is like an incoming tide. It flows into the estuaries and up the rivers. It cannot be held back.'

The United Kingdom has been a member of the European Union (formerly the European Community) since January 1973 (European law became part of our legal system via the European Communities Act 1972). As a result, it is impossible to examine the modern British constitution without considering the impact of European Union law. In fact, membership of the Union has had a profound and wide-ranging effect on various different aspects of our constitutional arrangements. In particular, it has altered our understanding of the lynchpin of the constitution: parliamentary sovereignty. In addition, it has also affected:

■ Individuals (by conferring rights on them).
■ Judges (by altering their approach to interpreting legislation).
■ Politicians/parliamentarians (who must now work within the constraints of European law).
■ The sources of law (the sources of the British constitution now embrace European Treaties, secondary legislation and case law decided by the European Court of Justice).

As European Union law is considered in detail in *Unlocking EU Law*, this chapter will simply highlight the key constitutional aspects raised by joining the European Union.

15.1 The Treaties

15.1.1 A *de facto* constitution?

The Treaty of Rome 1957 (technically the Treaty Establishing the European Economic Community) established the European Economic Community (called the European Community since 1993) and can be viewed as a *de facto* constitution. It should be remembered that in general terms a constitution will establish the apparatus of the state by creating institutions, allocating them specific responsibilities/powers and providing limitations on them (see Chapter 2). In this way the Treaty of Rome has many parallels with the constitution of a state. In particular, the Treaty:

■ Set out aims and objectives which included, *inter alia*, to establish a common market in goods, persons, capital and labour as well as to raise the standard of living. Similarly, state constitutions will set out their objectives (eg the protection of human rights). In fact, subsequent Treaties (eg the Amsterdam Treaty of 1997) do refer to the protection of human rights, democracy and the rule of law.

■ Established institutions (see section 15.2) – although it made use of the European Court and Assembly (later to be renamed the European Parliament) which already existed having been established under the Treaty of Paris 1951 for the European Coal and Steel Community.

■ Allocated these institutions specific roles. For example, one of the constitutional functions of the European Commission is to enforce European law by ensuring that Member States adhere to it (now Art 258). In addition, each institution is equipped with particular powers. For example, under Art 263 (as it is now) the European Court of Justice is authorised to review legislation which has been enacted by the other institutions. In this respect the European Court is acting in a way which is analogous to a Supreme or Constitutional Court in a state constitution.

■ Provided for the European Court of Justice to issue the definitive interpretation of European law (now Art 267). This is also similar to state constitutions whereby a Constitutional or Supreme Court (eg the US Supreme Court) will act as the final arbiter as to the meaning of the provisions of the written/codified constitution.

■ Has been interpreted by the European Court to be regarded as a form of higher and fundamental law which is superior to the law of Member States (see section 15.6.2). This is comparable with state constitutions where the law of the constitution has a special and fundamental legal status.

As indicated in Chapter 2, a codified constitution will usually set out the methods and procedures used to alter the content of the constitution. Similarly, in the context of Europe, the Treaty of Rome has periodically been revised by the enactment of subsequent Treaties:

■ 1986 Single European Act.
■ 1992 Treaty on European Union (TEU).
■ 1997 Treaty of Amsterdam.
■ 2000 Treaty of Nice.

In particular, the 1992 Treaty created the European Union which incorporated the (renamed) European Community as one of its three pillars. Moreover, each of the above Treaties has incrementally increased the powers of the European Parliament *vis-à-vis* the other institutions. The procedure used to amend the original Treaty of Rome involved the unanimous agreement at a summit of the European Council (containing the respective Presidents/Prime Ministers of the Member States) and thereafter being ratified by each Member State.

15.1.2 The European Constitution/Treaty of Lisbon

Although historically the British constitution has been described as unwritten or uncodified, by virtue of our membership of the European Community/Union, one part of our constitution *is* now written and codified (namely, European law and principles). Moreover, European law is a fundamental law with a higher status than any other Member State law (including the UK). In this sense, so long as we remain a member of the Union, European law will continue to have a special status in our constitutional arrangements.

In 2004 at a European Summit the Heads of State/Government agreed a European Constitution (technically called the Treaty Establishing a Constitution for Europe) which was scheduled to be ratified by all Member States. However, in 2005 both France and the Netherlands rejected the Treaty in separate referenda. In any event, the term *European Constitution* is somewhat of a misnomer. The term European Constitution appears to suggest or presuppose that Europe does not *already* have a constitution of some description, whereas as noted above, the original, founding European Treaty of Rome performs many of the functions of a state constitution. Following the rejection of the European Constitution, in December 2007 the European Council signed the Treaty of Lisbon. Although the term 'constitution' is not used in the Treaty, much of its content is similar to the rejected Constitution. After ratification by all 27 Member States, the Treaty of Lisbon came into force in December 2009 and its most interesting constitutional changes are as follows:

- References to the European Community were replaced with the European Union thereby removing the technical distinction between the Community and the Union. This meant that the Treaty of Rome was renamed the Treaty on the Functioning of the European Union (TFEU).
- The European Union now has a legal personality.
- Member States can now voluntarily withdraw from the Union.
- The posts of President of the European Council and the High Representative of the Union for Foreign Affairs and Security Policy were created.
- The powers of national parliaments were increased in relation to the creation of European legislation.

The United Kingdom incorporated the Treaty via the European Union (Amendment) Act 2008. Although the government had committed itself to holding a referendum in relation to the (aborted) European Constitution, it did not however give a similar commitment in respect of the Lisbon Treaty on the basis that it was significantly different to the European Constitution. In *R (Wheeler) v Office of the PM* [2008] EWHC 1409 (Admin) the court held that the government had not acted unlawfully in not holding a referendum on the Lisbon Treaty.

ACTIVITY

Applying the law

Revisit Chapter 2 and then consider whether the European Treaties represent a constitution for Europe, its institutions and citizens.

15.2 The institutions

15.2.1 An outline of the institutions

The European Union is a supranational body which comprises an institutional structure with each body having a designated role:

- **The European Council** – is composed of the Heads of State/Government which make important decisions concerning the direction of the Union. They also agree new Treaties.
- **The Council (formerly known as the Council of Ministers)** – is composed of a government minister representing each Member State. It co-ordinates the economic policies of Member States and adopts secondary legislation.
- **The European Commission** – is composed of one nominee from each Member State, but once appointed, they are independent of their respective Member State. The Commission has many roles which include drafting legislative proposals and enforcing European Union law.
- **The European Parliament** – is composed of elected MEPs (Members of the European Parliament) and, *inter alia*, is involved in the process of adopting legislation and acts in concert with the Council to agree the Union Budget.
- **The European Court of Justice** – is composed of one judge from each Member State. The court interprets European Union law (providing definitive interpretations under Art 267) and ensures both Member States and the other institutions follow Union law.

15.2.2 The separation of powers in Europe

We saw earlier in Chapter 5 that the British constitution is characterised by the fact that it does not adhere to a strict separation of powers. This is also true in relation to the institutional structure of the European Union as the three government functions are distributed between the various institutions:

The legislative function is performed by:
- The Council in adopting secondary legislation (see section 15.3.2).
- The European Parliament in adopting legislation when the *ordinary legislative procedure* (formerly co-decision) is in use.
- The European Court (in a *de facto* sense) when it develops principles of European Union law (eg the doctrine of direct effect – see section 15.5).
- The European Council when it agrees Treaty revisions (here it is performing effectively a *de facto* legislative role).

The executive function is performed by:
- The European Council in determining the direction of European policy.
- The Council in co-ordinating the national economies of Member States and making executive decisions.

The judicial function is performed by:
- The European Court of Justice in providing definitive interpretations of European law and resolving legal disputes
- The European Commission under Art 258 in determining that a Member State has breached European law and issuing a *reasoned* opinion (a non-binding opinion which sets out how the Commission believes that European Union law has been violated). In effect, it is performing a *de facto* quasi-judicial function.

Although there is no clear separation of powers in Europe, the institutional infrastructure has the following distinct checks and balances:

- Although the Council adopts legislation, under the *ordinary legislative procedure*, it has to work in concert (joint adoption) with the European Parliament.
- Although the Council adopts legislation (analogous to the UK Parliament) it is dependent on the European Commission to draft proposals to put before it (analogous to the British government drafting a Bill).

- While the European Commission has a degree of discretion in drafting legislative proposals, ultimately it has to make them acceptable to the Council/European Parliament who agree to them.
- The European Parliament can dismiss the Commission *en bloc*.
- The European Parliament can block the Budget which has been drafted by the European Commission and approved by the Council.
- The European Court of Justice can review the actions/legislation of the Council, Parliament and Commission. Under the Treaty of Lisbon the European Council is now included within the remit of the court.
- The European Council can amend the Treaty to increase or decrease the power or responsibilities of any institution (including the European Court of Justice).

15.2.3 Democracy and the European institutions

One charge which has historically been levelled at the European Community/Union has been its 'democratic deficit'. In other words, there was a deficit of democracy in its institutional framework as most of the institutions were not directly elected, and so lacked democratic legitimacy. Indeed, the body with the most democratic legitimacy (the European Parliament), historically had the least power.

- The European Council is composed of the various Presidents and Prime Ministers who may or may not be directly elected. For example, although the French President is elected by the people of France, neither the British Prime Minister nor the Irish Taoiseach are directly elected *per se*. Instead, they are drawn from their respective legislatures (United Kingdom Parliament, Irish Oireachtas), albeit they are drawn from the dominant political party within it.
- British ministers who sit in the Council (they vary depending on the subject-matter) are not directly elected *per se*, but rather they are drawn from the two Houses of Parliament, one of which is not elected at all (see section 11.6.2). Similarly, in the Republic of Ireland government ministers are drawn from the Oireachtas. Both the European Council and the Council represent the interests of the Member States.
- The European Commission is composed of Commissioners who have been, in effect, nominated by their respective national governments and approved by the (elected) European Parliament. The European Commission represents the interests of the European Union which is why once appointed, Commissioners must be independent of their respective Member State.
- The European Parliament is the only wholly directly elected body in the European Union (although it has only been elected since 1979; prior to that representatives of each national Parliament would sit). The European Parliament represents the interests of the people of Europe. In order to address the 'democratic deficit', each revision of the Treaty of Rome has provided the European Parliament with more powers. The point must be made, however, that the democratic legitimacy of the European Parliament itself has to be questioned when the turnout at European elections (which take place every five years) is poor. For example, at the 2004 election the average turnout for European countries was less than 50 per cent with the United Kingdom registering a turnout of 39 per cent, a British record high for European elections (A Mellows-Facer, R Cracknell and J Yonwin, 'European Parliament elections 2004' 04/50 (House of Commons Library, 2004), p 56). In the latest round of elections in June 2009, the average European turnout was 43 per cent with the UK registering only 35 per cent (source: TNS opinion in collaboration with the EP).
- The European Court of Justice is composed of a judge being nominated from each Member State.

Institution	Composition	Role	Represents
European Council	Heads of State/Government (composed of 27 Heads of State/Government and headed by the newly created office of the President of the European Council. The President of the European Commission also attends – the High Representative (see below) is also involved in the European Council's work.	• Provides general direction and impetus to the EU. • Makes political decisions. • Revises the Treaty.	Member States.
Council	Minister from each Member State (Council composed of 27 ministers).	• Adopts legislative proposals. • Makes executive decisions. • Co-ordinates national economies. • Confers powers on the Commission to make legislation. • Adopts the Budget.	Member States.
European Commission	Nominated from each Member State and approved (and removed) by the European Parliament (27 Commissioners headed by the President of the European Commission and now includes the newly created office of the High Representative of the Union for Foreign Affairs and Security Policy).	• Initiates and drafts legislative proposals. • Enforces EU law as a watchdog. • Exercises powers conferred by the Council. • Acts as a mediator. • Drafts the Budget.	European Union.
European Parliament	MEPs directly elected by the electorate in each Member State (736 MEPs). Parliament is headed by a President.	• Supervises the other institutions. • Involved in the legislative process. • Adopts the Budget with the Council.	European citizens.

ACTIVITY

Essay writing

To what extent does the institutional structure of the European Union depart from the separation of powers and do you consider that it is democratic?

15.3 Sources of law

Membership of the European Union has widened the legal sources of the British constitution. In broad terms, European Union law can be divided into primary and secondary sources:

15.3.1 Primary sources

These comprise the founding Treaty (Treaty of Rome 1957) together with its subsequent amendment over the years (eg Single European Act 1986).

15.3.2 Secondary sources

These comprise the legislation known as legal Acts of the Union (see section 4.7.2) made by the Union institutions.

ARTICLE

....

'The institutions shall adopt regulations, directives, decisions, recommendations and opinions.'

Art 288, TFEU.

- **Regulations** – these are self-executing and of general application (applying to all Member States). They ensure absolute uniformity and exactitude in all Member States. In constitutional terms they by-pass the legislatures of each Member State (including the UK Parliament) as they apply *automatically* in every Member State without the national legislature having to endorse it.
- **Directives** – these are more flexible than regulations and are addressed to specific Member States in order to ensure a harmonisation of national laws. For example, it may well be that the laws of three Member States are out of kilter with the rest of the Union and so a directive is addressed to them to bring their laws into line. Directives are binding as to the result to be achieved, but leave the Member State with a measure of discretion as to how to implement them.
- **Decisions** – these are binding on those to whom they are addressed (Member States or companies).

These secondary sources enter United Kingdom law via s 2 of the European Communities Act 1972. In addition to the sources above, case law and preliminary rulings of the European Court of Justice also represent a form of secondary source of law (see below).

15.4 The European Court of Justice

The European Court (technically known as the Court of Justice of the European Union) is the judicial arm of the European Union.

15.4.1 The distinctive nature of the court

The European Court is distinctive in constitutional terms (at least from the perspective of a British public lawyer) in the following ways:

- **Composition** – the court (like the European Court of Human Rights in Strasbourg) includes judges who are academics with no direct judicial experience.
- **No public dissent** – the court (unlike the European Court of Human Rights) does not issue dissenting/minority judgments. All judges, whether or not they agreed with the decision, must sign the judgment.
- **Advocate Generals** – the court is assisted by Advocate Generals which have no parallel in the British court system. In brief, after the parties have delivered their submissions, an Advocate General will summarise the legal points in the case (even adding some that have been overlooked so that the court is fully conversant with all relevant information) and put forward a non-binding submission. The court often adopts these submissions.
- **No *stare decisis*** – the court is, technically, not bound by precedent and so does not have to follow its own previous decisions. In practice, however, for legal certainty and practical reasons, the court generally follows its previous rulings.

- **Legal reasoning** – the court's method of interpreting legislation is different from the traditional approach used by the British judiciary (ie a literal/historical method). In contrast, the European Court judges have adopted a more teleological/purposive technique. As a result of the inception of Union law into our constitution and legal system, the United Kingdom judiciary in applying European law must adopt the legal reasoning employed by the European Court in Luxembourg. As indicated by Lord Denning MR in *Bulmer v Bollinger* [1974] Ch 401:

JUDGMENT

'Beyond doubt the English courts must follow the same principles as the European court. Otherwise there would be differences between the countries … They must follow the European pattern. No longer must they examine the words in meticulous detail. No longer must they argue about the precise grammatical sense. They must look to the purpose or intent. To quote the words of the European Court in the *Da Costa* case … they must deduce "from the wording and the spirit of the Treaty the meaning of the community rules".'

15.4.2 The role of the European Court of Justice

Application of European law

The European Court ensures that the application of European Union law is observed by Member States (Arts 258 and 259 where enforcement proceedings are brought by the European Commission or another Member State, respectively) and the political institutions of the Union (under Arts 263 and 265).

Interpretation of European law

Article 267 provides that the European Court shall have the jurisdiction to give preliminary rulings concerning, *inter alia*,

(a) the interpretation of the Treaties and
(b) the validity and interpretation of acts of the institutions of the Union (eg regulations, directives see section 15.3.2)

In brief, where a national/domestic court or tribunal is faced with a provision of either a primary or secondary source of law which is unclear and requires interpretation, Art 267 provides a mechanism whereby that court/tribunal can make a reference to the European Court which requests it to interpret and clarify the point of European law (a preliminary ruling). National courts against which there is no appeal/review *must* make such a reference. The ruling issued by the European Court is binding on the national court and represents *the* definitive interpretation of European law. In this way the European Court is the final arbiter as to the meaning of European Union law.

The Art 267 procedure provides a direct link between the European Court in Luxembourg and the national/domestic courts and tribunals of the Member States. It can be likened to a wheel, with the ECJ as the hub and the national courts and tribunals on the rim. In this way, all domestic courts and tribunals are directly connected to the European Court and it links these European judges with the judges of the Member States.

Article 267 is not an appellate system whereby national courts appeal to the European Court. Instead, it is a reference system which involves a partnership between the judges of the European Court and the respective judges of the Member States. In terms of the British constitution, the preliminary ruling procedure means that the UK Supreme Court is not the ultimate arbiter in respect of European law. This has been specifically authorised by s 3 of the European Communities Act 1972. Indeed, as a court of last resort, our Supreme Court Justices *must* refer ambiguous/unclear points of Union law to the judges in Luxembourg.

Student mentor tip

"Remember that all of the topics overlap and look for the links."

Adil, Queen Mary University

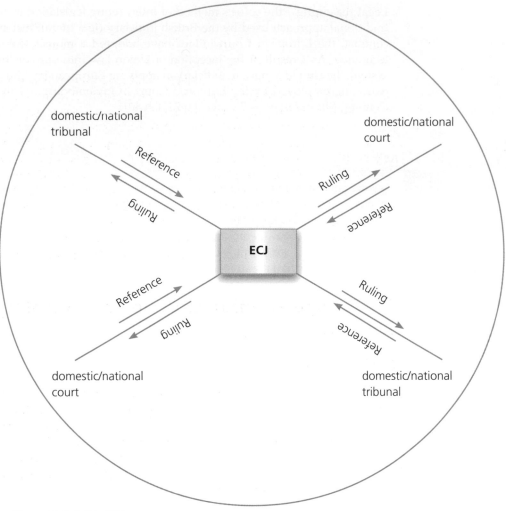

Figure 15.1 Article 267

KEY FACTS

Institution	Composition	Role
European Court	One judge from each Member State.	• Interprets Union law (Art 267). • Applies and enforces Union law against Union institutions (Arts 263 and 265) and Member States (Arts 258 and 259).

15.5 Individuals

Membership of the European Union has had a direct impact on individuals. Firstly, the Maastricht Treaty of 1992 conferred citizenship of the European Union on individuals in Member States. Secondly Union law has conferred rights on individuals (eg not to be discriminated against on the grounds of sex) which can be enforced in their own domestic courts. This principle is known as the doctrine of direct effect and it has been developed by the European Court (not having been explicitly set out in the original founding European Treaty).

Marshall v Southampton and South-West Hampshire AHA (No 1)
Case 152/84 [1986] ECR 723

Ms Marshall was employed by Southampton and South-West Area Health Authority and was forced to retire at 62 (the authority had a policy which required women to retire earlier than men – 60 rather than 65). She contended that the Sex Discrimination Act 1975 (which did not apply to retirement) contravened Directive 76/207 on the equal treatment of men and women.

The Court of Appeal made a reference to the European Court as to whether Marshall could rely on the directive (the doctrine of direct effect). The European Court issued its preliminary ruling that a policy of different retirement ages contravened the directive and that Marshall could rely on the rights set out in the directive. Thereafter, the Court of Appeal applied the ruling to the facts of the case and held that Marshall had been unlawfully discriminated against in being dismissed and she subsequently obtained compensation. This case illustrates an individual using European law rights (eg the right not to be discriminated against) in a domestic court against a public body (the Area Health Authority being treated as a public body as an emanation of the state).

15.6 European Union law and parliamentary sovereignty

15.6.1 Introduction

Membership of the European Union has had a profound effect on parliamentary sovereignty. As noted in Chapter 7, the classic and historic doctrine of parliamentary sovereignty is that the Crown in Parliament can pass any law it chooses. This absolute principle, however, is in direct opposition to the principle of the primacy of European Union law as developed and espoused by the European Court of Justice. In short, according to the European Court, where provisions of Union law and national/domestic law conflict, the former *must* prevail (see *Costa* (1964) below).

15.6.2 The primacy of European law

The doctrine of the primacy (or supremacy) of European Union law, like the doctrine of direct effect, was not expressly set out in the original founding Treaty of Rome. Instead, it has been developed by the European Court of Justice, thereby illustrating its quasi-legislative role in practice. The principle was first indicated in *Van Gend & Loos v Nederlandse administratie der belastingen* Case 26/62 [1963] ECR1 where the European Court stated:

JUDGMENT

'... the Community constitutes a new legal order of international law for the benefit of which the states have limited their sovereign rights, albeit within limited fields, and the subjects of which comprise not only Member States but also their nationals.'

In the subsequent case of *Costa v ENEL* Case 6/64 [1964] ECR 585 the European Court noted that:

JUDGMENT

'... the law stemming from the Treaty, an independent source of law, could not, because of its special and original nature, be overridden by domestic legal provisions, however framed, without being deprived of its character as Community law and without the legal basis of the Community itself being called into question.'

In short, if a provision of domestic law contravenes European law, the latter must prevail, thereby indicating the supreme and fundamental nature of Union law. In the later case of *Internationale Handelsgesellschaft mbH v EVGF* Case 11/70 [1970] ECR 1125 the court made it clear that the principle included secondary sources of European law (eg a regulation) and that it prevailed over the constitutional rules of a Member State (ie its constitutional law):

JUDGMENT

'… the law stemming from the Treaty, an independent source of law, cannot because of its very nature be overriden by rules of national law … Therefore the validity of a Community measure or its effect within a Member State cannot be affected by allegations that it runs counter to either fundamental rights as formulated by the constitution of that State or the principles of a national constitutional structure.'

See also *Simmenthal SpA v Amministrazione delle Finanze dello Stato* Case 70/77 [1978] ECR 1453 and *Commission v (French Republic)* Case 167/73 [1974] ECR 359. It is now pertinent to note that a Declaration (No 17) in the Treaty of Lisbon states explicitly that the 'well settled case law of the Court of Justice of the European Union, the Treaties and the law adopted by the Union on the basis of the Treaties have primacy over the law of Member States'.

ACTIVITY

Self-test question

What is the nature and constitutional significance of the principle of the primacy of directly effective European Union law?

15.6.3 The reception of European Union law in the British constitution

The United Kingdom has a dualist constitution which means that even if a Treaty is agreed to in international law, its provisions do not become legally enforceable in our domestic law unless an Act of Parliament has formally incorporated the Treaty. In 1972 Parliament passed the European Communities Act which provided for the reception of European law into our constitution and legal system. In constitutional terms, it is worth noting that this Act, in spite of its profound constitutional consequences, was passed in the ordinary manner, in the sense that no special majority was needed (although the committee stage was taken on the Floor of the House). In fact, the Bill only narrowly passed its third reading in the House of Commons. This indicates the flexibility of the British constitution as the Republic of Ireland, who joined the EEC (as it was then) at the same time, was required by its written constitution to hold a referendum.

By virtue of s 2(1) of the European Communities Act 1972, from 1st January 1973, Union law (as it is called today) formally became part of the law of the United Kingdom. Section 2(4) is the most controversial aspect of the Act as it deals with the impact of European law on domestic law:

SECTION

Any such provision (of any such extent) as might be made by Act of Parliament, and any enactment passed or to be passed, other than one contained in this part of this Act, shall be construed and have effect subject to the foregoing provisions of this section.

In constitutional terms s 2(4) means that United Kingdom statutes passed before and after 1972 must be construed and be held subject to European law:

CASE EXAMPLE

Macarthys Ltd v Smith [1981] 1 QB 180

Mrs Smith replaced a man to manage Macarthys' stockroom but was paid £10 a week less than he had been paid. She claimed equal pay under s 1 of the Equal Pay Act 1970 (although this appeared to be confined to contemporaneous employment) and this raised the issue of whether Art 119 (now Art 157 TFEU) of the Treaty of Rome (equal pay for equal work) applied to the situation where a woman replaced a man but who had not worked contemporaneously alongside him. The Court of Appeal was uncertain on this point of European law and sent a reference to the European Court asking whether Art 119 was confined to men and women working contemporaneously. The subsequent ruling stated that the principle of equal pay was not so confined but also applied where a woman replaced a man. The Court of Appeal then applied this ruling to the case and held for Mrs Smith. Lord Denning MR stated that:

JUDGMENT

'It is important now to declare – and it must be made plain – that the provisions of article 119 of the EEC Treaty take priority over anything in our English statute on equal pay which is inconsistent with article 119. That priority is given by our own law. It is given by the European Communities Act 1972 itself. Community law is now part of our law: and, whenever there is any inconsistency, Community law has priority.'

Similarly, in *Garland v British Rail Engineering Ltd* [1983] 2 AC 751, the House of Lords, following a preliminary ruling by the European Court of Justice, construed the Sex Discrimination Act 1975 in line with Art 119 (now Art 157) prohibiting discrimination. As a result the court held that British Rail had discriminated against Garland when it provided special travel facilities for the families of retired male employees, but not female ones. The words of the 1975 Act could (without being unnecessarily strained) be interpreted so as to be consistent with Art 119.

In terms of United Kingdom secondary legislation, in *Lister and others v Forth Dry Dock and Engineering Co Ltd and another* [1989] 1 All ER 1134, the House of Lords read and construed a domestic regulation (delegated legislation) so as to conform with a European directive which protected the rights of employees in circumstances when their employer changed. See also *Pickstone v Freemans plc* [1988] 2 All ER 803.

In terms of a conflict between Union law and an Act of Parliament, Lord Denning MR, prior to the reference to the European Court in *Macarthys Ltd v Smith* [1979] 3 All ER 325 (see above), made the following point concerning the constitutional impact of European law on United Kingdom statutes:

JUDGMENT

'Thus far I have assumed that our Parliament, whenever it passes legislation, intends to fulfill its obligations under the Treaty. If the time should come when our Parliament deliberately passes an Act with the intention of repudiating the Treaty or any provision in it or intention-ally of acting inconsistently with it and says so in express terms then I should have thought that it would be the duty of our courts to follow the statute of our Parliament … Unless there is such an intentional and express repudiation of the Treaty, it is our duty to give priority to the Treaty.'

In essence, Lord Denning was indicating that the domestic doctrine of implied repeal (see section 7.9.3) does not operate whenever European law applies. In other words, if domestic legislation passed after 1972 is inconsistent with European law (which forms part of our law through the European Communities Act 1972), European law (and so the 1972 Act) will prevail *unless* the later domestic legislation expressly and clearly intends to repudiate European law. If the legislation violates European law, but does not do so intentionally, then the courts will apply European law over the statute. This appears to have been the approach taken by the courts in *ex parte Factortame* which involved a statute which was passed *after* 1972 (ie after the European Communities Act), but which was inconsistent with European law (ie which forms part of our law through s 2 of the 1972 Act).

15.6.4 The *Factortame* litigation

CASE EXAMPLE

R v Secretary of State for Transport, ex parte Factortame Ltd and others (No 2) [1991] 1 AC 603

Part II of the Merchant Shipping Act 1988 restricted the number of fishing vessels whose catch could form part of the United Kingdom fishing quota (the EEC – as it was then – had a policy to prevent over fishing of depleted fishing stocks). Under the authority of the Act, the Transport Secretary issued the Merchant Shipping (Registration of Fishing Vessels) Regulations 1988 requiring vessels registered as British to re-register. Vessels would only qualify if their owners (or 75 per cent of their company shareholders) were British citizens or lived in Britain. Factortame and others were companies who before the Act had been registered as British, but most of whose directors/shareholders were Spanish. As they could not meet the new registration requirements, they sought judicial review of the Act and regulations on the basis that they breached European law, *inter alia*, in terms of discrimination.

The Divisional Court faced with a provision of European law which required interpretation made a reference to the European Court (the first reference) and pending the receipt of this ruling, provided Factortame with interim relief (thereby protecting their putative European law rights which had not yet been established) by disapplying pt II of the Act and preventing the minister from enforcing the legislation against Factortame. The Court of Appeal set aside the order on the basis that the court had no jurisdiction to issue it. The House of Lords confirmed that the court had no power to issue the interim injunction in terms of either granting an injunction against the Crown, or disapplying a statute prior to a ruling of the European Court on a point of European law. Nevertheless, the House of Lords did refer to the European Court the question (the second reference) as to whether it was a requirement of European law that a national court should provide an interim remedy in order to protect a party's putative European law rights while waiting for the European Court to issue a ruling on the point.

In June 1990, in response to the second reference, the European Court issued its ruling to the effect that a national court must set aside a rule of domestic law which impeded a national court from granting interim relief to protect European law rights (otherwise European law would be undermined).

Thereafter the House of Lords applied the ruling to the facts of the case and reinstated the interim injunction protecting Factortame's putative European law rights which had not yet been definitely established (ie in advance of the European Court's ruling in respect of the first reference). Lord Bridge noted that:

JUDGMENT

'Some public comments on the decision of the European Court of Justice, affirming the jurisdiction of the courts of member states to override national legislation if necessary to enable interim relief to be granted in protection of rights under Community law, have suggested that this was a novel and dangerous invasion by a Community institution of the sovereignty of the United Kingdom Parliament. But such comments are based on a misconception. If the supremacy within the European Community of Community law over the national law of member states was not always inherent in the EEC Treaty … it was certainly well established in the jurisprudence of the European Court of Justice long before the United Kingdom joined the Community. Thus, whatever limitation of its sovereignty Parliament accepted when it enacted the European Communities Act 1972 was entirely voluntary. Under the terms of the Act of 1972 it has always been clear that it was the duty of a United Kingdom court, when delivering final judgment, to override any rule of national law found to be in conflict with any directly enforceable rule of Community law.'

Following the ruling of the European Court in July 1991 in respect of the first reference (*R v Secretary of State for Transport, ex parte Factortame Ltd (No 3)* [1992] 1 QB 680), the Divisional Court applied it and declared that the Merchant Shipping Act breached European law. Thereafter, Parliament passed the Merchant Shipping (Registration) Act 1993, which amended and restated the law relating to the registering of shipping, and in *R v Secretary of State for Transport, ex parte Factortame Ltd (No 5)* [2000] 1 AC 524 Factortame obtained compensation for the loss and expenses incurred by the 1988 Act.

Similarly, in the later case of *Equal Opportunities Commission and another v Secretary of State for Employment* [1994] 1 All ER 910, the House of Lords issued a declaration that provisions of the Employment Protection (Consolidation) Act 1978 were contrary to European law (see section 19.4.2).

Also, in *Thoburn v Sunderland City Council* [2002] EWHC 195 (Admin), Laws LJ commented that the European Communities Act 1972 was one of a number of 'constitutional statutes' which were not subject to implied repeal (see section 4.4.5). On the facts of the case, however, the court held that there was no inconsistency between s 1 Weights and Measures Act 1985 and the earlier s 2(2) European Communities Act 1972.

KEY FACTS

Key facts on European Union Law and sovereignty

- Section 2(1) of the European Communities Act 1972 formally incorporated Community (now Union) law into the United Kingdom's legal system.
- Section 2(4) of the Act requires the courts to interpret all statutes passed before and after the 1972 Act in line with and subject to European law.
- In *Garland* (1983) the House of Lords interpreted the Sex Discrimination Act 1975 in line with Art 119, now Art 157 (prohibiting discrimination in retirement).
- In *Lister and others* (1989) the House of Lords interpreted domestic delegated legislation in line with a European directive.
- In *Factortame* (1991) the House of Lords suspended the operation of the Merchant Shipping Act 1988 as it conflicted with the putative European law rights of Factortame.
- In *EOC* (1994) the House of Lords issued a declaration that the Employment Protection (Consolidation) Act 1978 violated European law on the basis that it indirectly discriminated against women.

15.6.5 The constitutional impact of *Factortame*

The precise constitutional significance and impact of *Factortame* is not universally agreed upon by academics. Craig, however, has rather usefully summarised how the judgments in *Factortame* (1991), *EOC* (1994) and *Thoburn* (2002) can be conceptualised into three broad themes (P Craig, 'Britain in the European Union' in J Jowell and D Oliver (eds), *The Changing Constitution* (6th edn, Oxford University Press, 2007), pp 97–99):

(i) 'statutory construction':

This approach is a rule of construction which requires any inconsistency between European law and a United Kingdom statute to be resolved in favour of the former. This is subject to the United Kingdom Parliament passing legislation which is clearly meant to depart from European law.

(ii) 'a technical legal revolution':

This approach regards the jurisprudence of the courts as revolutionary in the sense that it affected the traditional view of parliamentary sovereignty. In short, in *Factortame* the courts altered the rule of recognition in respect of statutes with the result that the 1972 Parliament did something which Dicey (see section 7.9) had argued was not possible: it bound its successor. In other words, the 1972 Parliament (which passed the European Communities Act which gave European law overriding force in our law) bound the later Parliament of 1988, because the legislation that it had passed (the Merchant Shipping Act 1988) had to be disapplied as being inconsistent with European law (see H Wade, 'Sovereignty – Revolution or Evolution?' [1996] 112 LQR 568).

(iii) 'normative arguments of legal principle':

Craig argues that the third conceptualisation (and his favoured view) of the above judgments concerning supremacy/sovereignty can be regarded 'as being based on normative arguments of legal principle the content of which can and will vary across time'. (*sic*) In other words, the 'principled consequences' of membership of the European Union entail the United Kingdom being bound by European law (and so are reasoned constraints on Parliament's legislative omnipotence).

In any event, the following points are worth noting:

- It has been suggested that in the *Factortame* case the courts did something which Dicey had argued was impossible, namely the courts challenged and disapplied an Act of Parliament – the Merchant Shipping Act 1988. The constitutional/legal (and moral) authority for the courts to do this came from s 2(4) of the European Communities Act 1972. Indeed, as noted by Lord Bridge, it was Parliament which had voluntarily passed the 1972 Act. Moreover, by virtue of the jurisprudence of the European Court (*Van Gend* (1963) and *Costa* (1964) – see section 15.6.2), in 1972 the United Kingdom would have been fully conversant with the principle of the primacy of European law as indicated in the Labour government's 1967 White Paper (*Legal and Constitutional implications of United Kingdom membership of the European Communities* Cmnd 3301 (1967)).

- It has also been suggested that the doctrine of implied repeal does not apply where European Union law operates. In other words if, as a result of, for example, a parliamentary oversight or misunderstanding of the requirements of European law, an Act of Parliament is passed which is inconsistent with European law, the UK courts will ensure that European law prevails over the statute. However, this would not be the case where the violation of European law is deliberate (see below).

  Notwithstanding the above, Tomkins (*Public Law*, (Oxford University Press, 2003), pp 118–119), along with others, has argued that the *Factortame* case did *not* engage the doctrine of implied repeal as, for one thing, there was no conflict in terms of substance between the Merchant Shipping Act 1988 (dealing with fishing registration) and the earlier European Communities Act 1972 (dealing with the relationship between European law and domestic law). In short, they were different statutes dealing with different subject-matters.

- In *Factortame* although the House of Lords (and the Divisional Court in the earlier stage of the litigation) issued an interim injunction restraining the operation of the 1988 Act, it did not strike it down *per se*. This is not the same, therefore, as a Supreme or Constitutional Court striking down and permanently invalidating legislation.

- It must be remembered that whatever the impact of the decision on parliamentary sovereignty, European law does not govern every aspect of our lives and so in these contexts the full force of parliamentary sovereignty will continue.

Finally, it seems that if Parliament should decide to do so (although it is highly unlikely that it would do so in the near future), it could legislate to expressly repeal the

European Communities Act 1972. In this way it would repudiate European Union law and the jurisdiction and principles of the European Court of Justice. Having said this, we are not exactly sure how the British courts would react to such legislation, although it is highly probable that they would accept that Parliament had decided to leave the Union and give effect to the Act repudiating it. Short of this, however, it appears that the courts will continue to construe United Kingdom statutes in the light of Union law (and suspend them if necessary as in *Factortame*) until Parliament makes it clear that it no longer wishes to be governed by European Union law and principles (see Lord Denning MR at section 15.6.3).

In the event of the United Kingdom passing legislation which violated or repudiated European Union law, it is inevitable that an investigation would be mounted by the European Commission. It is not without significance to point out that now under the Treaty of Lisbon, Member States can withdraw formally from the European Union. Moreover, in 2009 Lord Willoughby introduced a Private Members' Bill (Constitutional Reform Bill – HL Bill 14) which proposed to repeal the 1972 Act and withdraw from the European Union. Although it did not become law, the Bill did presuppose that under parliamentary sovereignty the 1972 Act could be repealed.

In conclusion, Hoffmann J in *Stoke-on-Trent City Council v B & Q* [1991] Ch 48 has provided a useful summary of the constitutional impact of our membership of the European Community/Union:

JUDGMENT

'The EEC Treaty is the supreme law of this country, taking precedence over Acts of Parliament. Our entry into the European Economic Community meant that (subject to our undoubted but probably theoretical right to withdraw from the Community altogether) Parliament surrendered its sovereign right to legislate contrary to the provisions of the Treaty on the matters of social and economic policy which it regulated. The entry into the Community was in itself a high act of social and economic policy, by which the partial surrender of sovereignty was seen as more than compensated by the advantages of membership.'

ACTIVITY

Exercise

Explain the *Factortame* litigation. What impact has this case had on the nature of the British constitution?

SUMMARY

- European law became part of the United Kingdom's legal system via the European Communities Act 1972.
- Europe comprises a number of institutions (eg European Parliament) each of which have specified constitutional roles.
- European law is a source of the British constitution and comprises primary sources (Treaties) and secondary sources (eg Regulations).
- The European Court of Justice ensures that the application of European law is observed by Member States and European institutions and also provides definitive interpretations of EU law.
- Individuals in the United Kingdom enjoy rights under EU law which they can enforce in domestic courts.
- The European Court has developed the constitutional principle that European law takes primacy over inconsistent national law.
- Section 2(4) of the ECA 1972 requires that British courts interpret all statutes passed before and after 1972 in line with, and subject to, European law.

■ In *Factortame* the House of Lords disapplied the operation of the Merchant Shipping Act 1988 on the basis that it was inconsistent with the putative rights of Factortame under European law.

 ## Further reading

Books

Barnett, H, *Britain Unwrapped* (Penguin, 2002), Chapter 4.

Craig, P, 'Britain in the European Union' in Jowell, J and Oliver, D (eds), *The Changing Constitution* (6th edn, Oxford University Press, 2007), p 84.

Ellis, E, 'The Legislative Supremacy of Parliament and its Limits' in Feldman, D (ed), *English Public Law* (2nd edn, Oxford University Press, 2009), p 127.

Jenkins, R, 'Britain and Europe: The problem with being half pregnant' in Sutherland, K (ed), *The Rape of the Constitution?* (Imprint Academic, 2000), p 277.

Tebbit, N, 'Britain and Europe: The issue of sovereignty' in Sutherland, K (ed), *The Rape of the Constitution?* (Imprint Academic, 2000), p 291.

Tomkins, A, *Public Law* (Oxford University Press, 2003), pp 108–120.

Articles

Phillipson, G, 'Parliamentary sovereignty, European Community law and Parliament's ability to bind future parliaments', (2003) 39 *Student Law Review* 11.

Wade, H, 'Sovereignty – Revolution or Evolution?' [1996] 112 LQR 568.

Internet links

http://europa.eu.

16

The European Convention on Human Rights

AIMS AND OBJECTIVES

At the end of this chapter you should be able to:

- Appreciate the significance of the European Convention on Human Rights both with respect to its contribution to the international protection of human rights and its effect on human rights in the United Kingdom
- Understand the machinery for the enforcement of human rights laid down in the Convention and administered by the European Court of Human Rights
- Be aware of the central rights contained in the Convention and how they have been interpreted and enforced by the European Court of Human Rights
- Appreciate the central principles applied by the European Court which determine the enforcement and restriction of human rights
- Appreciate the potential effect of the Convention and its case law on the protection of human rights in the United Kingdom

16.1 Introduction and background

The European Convention on Human Rights (1950) is central to the understanding and study of human rights and civil liberties. It is an international treaty for the protection of individual human rights, containing such rights as the right to life (Art 2), freedom from torture (Art 3), liberty and security of the person (Art 5), the right to a fair trial (Art 6), the right to private life (Art 8) and freedom of expression (Art 10). The rights will be discussed in detail later in this chapter (see below).

1. The Convention has its own machinery for enforcing human rights and this machinery has been used on numerous occasions against the United Kingdom government, resulting in changes to domestic law and practice.
2. The Convention and its case law has informed the domestic law of human rights in the United Kingdom, being applied by the domestic courts as an indirect and persuasive source (see below).
3. More specifically, the Convention and its principles are now given effect by the Human Rights Act 1998, allowing the domestic courts to apply Convention principles and case law (see below).

The European Convention on Human Rights was devised by the Council of Europe, which was set up after the Second World War to achieve unity in matters such as the protection of fundamental human rights. It was drafted in the light of the atrocities that took place before and during the Second World War and was signed by the High

Contracting Parties in 1950, entering into force in 1953. The United Kingdom ratified the treaty in 1957, and in 1966 it accepted both the compulsory jurisdiction of the European Court and the power of the European Commission (now the Court) of Human Rights to receive alleged violations of Convention rights.

The Convention should not be confused with European Community (Union) law:

- The Council of Europe is separate from the European Communities and has a larger composition than the latter. In 2010 there were 47 member states of the Council of Europe.
- The Convention is enforced by the European Court of Human Rights (ECtHR), while union law is enforced by the European Court of Justice (ECJ).
- Whereas European Union law was incorporated via the European Communities Act 1972, the European Convention was given 'further effect' by the Human Rights Act 1998.
- European Union law has supremacy over domestic law via s 2 of the European Communities Act, while the Convention is still subordinate to clear contrary domestic law.
- Decisions of the ECJ have direct effect under s 3 of the 1972 Act, while the decisions of the ECtHR are binding in international law and can be taken into account by the domestic courts (under s 2 of the 1998 Act).
- The European Convention is not an EU Treaty, but the ECJ can take into consideration the decisions of the ECtHR, and *vice versa*.
- The European Convention on Human Rights should not be confused with the EC Charter of Fundamental Rights 2000, which, when adopted, will seek to protect a wide range of civil and political and social and economic rights within union law.

16.2 The enforcement machinery

The Convention has its own machinery for enforcement in the form of a European Court of Human Rights possessing the power to make judicial decisions, which are then binding on the Member States (High Contracting Parties).

Although the Convention is now given effect to by the Human Rights Act 1998, this machinery remains important:

- individuals can still petition the European Court of Human Rights if they do not receive a satisfactory remedy in domestic law;
- the domestic courts will apply the same principles and norms used by the European Court of Human Rights when adjudicating on human rights disputes;
- the case law (both former and current) will inform the domestic courts and law.

It should be noted that, under the Convention, the main obligation to protect human rights is placed on the Member States.

ARTICLE

Art 1
The High Contracting Parties shall secure to everyone within their jurisdiction the rights and freedoms defined in Section I of this Convention.

- This imposes an obligation on the Member State to provide an effective procedure and remedy for protecting human rights, although it is not mandatory to formally incorporate the Convention.
- Article 1 applies so as to impose a duty towards anyone within the state's jurisdiction, whether a citizen of that state or not.
- The Convention machinery is regarded as subsidiary to the national system for protecting rights and will only be used as a last resort.
- Individuals can only make a claim under the Convention machinery if they have exhausted all effective domestic remedies (Art 35).

■ The European Court affords each Member State a certain discretion (A 'margin of appreciation') as to how they protect Convention rights (*Handyside v United Kingdom* (1976) 1 EHRR 737).

16.3 The European Court of Human Rights

Article 19 establishes a European Court of Human Rights to 'ensure the observance of the engagements undertaken by the High Contracting Parties in the Convention and the Protocols thereto'.

Before Protocol 11, the European Commission of Human Rights considered the admissibility of applications, secured friendly settlements and considered the merits of the applications. These roles are now performed by the full-time European Court of Human Rights, although its decisions will still continue to influence the case law of the Convention, and under s 2 of the Human Rights Act 1998 domestic courts are required to take such decisions into account when determining cases raising Convention arguments (see below).

After the ratification of Protocol 11, the Court now functions on a permanent basis and has taken over any adjudicative role formerly carried out by the European Commission of Human Rights and the Committee of Ministers. The former body is now abolished, but their decisions are persuasive authority for both the European Court and the domestic courts under s 2 of the Human Rights Act 1998. The Committee of Ministers (the foreign secretaries of each state) carry out a diplomatic role and ensure that the European Court's judgments are fully and effectively executed (Art 46).

16.3.1 The Composition of the European Court of Human Rights

Under Art 20 the court consists of a number of judges equal to that of the High Contracting Parties, who are elected by the Parliamentary Assembly of the Council of Europe. The procedure of the court is regulated by the Rules of the European Court of Human Rights.

The European Court of Human Rights comprises of

■ Committees, consisting of three judges who consider the admissibility of applications (Art 27(1)) and who possess the power (Art 28) to strike out cases from its list;
■ Chambers of seven judges who decide on the admissibility and merits of the application (Art 27(2)) combining the roles formerly carried out respectively by the Commission and the old European Court;
■ The Grand Chamber, consisting of 17 judges who hear cases referred to them (Art 27(3)).

16.3.2 The Grand Chamber of the European Court

The Grand Chamber of the Court of Human Rights fulfils a number of roles

■ Under Art 31 it has the power to determine applications which, under Art 30, have been relinquished by a Chamber of the Court because the case raises a serious issue of interpretation of the Convention (for example, *A v United Kingdom* (2009) 49 EHRR 29 on the issue of detention in times of terrorist threats).
■ It can act as an appeal court by considering referrals by the parties under Art 43 of the Convention (for example, *Hatton v United Kingdom* (2003) 37 EHRR 28, overruling the Chamber's decision on whether night flights violated the right to home and private life).
■ It can consider requests for an advisory opinion under Art 47.

Decisions of the Grand Chamber are final and binding.

16.4 The Role of the European Court of Human Rights

The European Court of Human Rights is the judicial arm of the Convention. In addition to considering the admissibility of claims under the Convention and striking out cases (below), the main role of the European Court of Human Rights is to interpret and apply the European Convention with respect to alleged violations brought before it and to make binding judgments. The court is bound to give reasons for its decisions, including its decisions on admissibility (Art 45).

In practice it must decide whether there has been a violation of one of the substantive rights in the Convention and whether there is any justification for any such violation. It will interpret and apply the Convention in the light of both the intention of the drafters and current philosophy on human rights protection (*Selmouni v France* (1999) 29 EHRR 403), and will use various human rights norms during that process – democracy, the rule of law, equality, the protection of human dignity etc.

16.4.1 The effect of the European Court of Human Rights' judgments and their effect

Under Art 46 the decisions of the European Court (subject to any appeal to the Grand Chamber), are binding in international law against that state provided it has accepted the compulsory jurisdiction of the court. The judgment imposes an obligation on that state to comply with the judgment (including paying any 'just satisfaction') and to make any necessary changes to domestic law. For example, following the decision in *Malone v United Kingdom* (1984) 7 EHRR 14 Parliament passed the Interception of Communications Act 1985 to regulate telephone tapping.

However, unlike the decisions of the European Court of Justice, the decisions of the Court of Human Rights do not have an overriding force and do not automatically take precedence over inconsistent domestic law.

- The effect of the decision in domestic law will depend on how the Convention and its case law has been incorporated into that system.
- Under s 2 of the Human Rights Act 1998 domestic courts may take the decisions of the European Court into account, but any relevant domestic law remains in force until amended by Parliament.
- The courts can interpret and apply domestic law in the light of the Convention but decisions of the Court of Human Rights cannot override domestic law.

CASE EXAMPLE

R v Lyons and others [2002] UKHL 44

Following the decision of the European Court in *Saunders v United Kingdom* (1996) 23 EHRR 313, a number of individuals sought to have their convictions quashed as violating the rule against self-incrimination and thus in breach of Art 6 of the Convention.

The House of Lords held that at the time the convictions were lawful under domestic law and that the decision of the European Court could not retrospectively overrule such convictions. Any remedy provided in *Saunders* imposed an obligation in international law and did not overturn domestic law. As the convictions took place before the Human Rights Act 1998 came into force the Act could not be applied to that case and the applicants needed to petition the European Court (*Lyons v United Kingdom* (2003) 37 EHRR 183 CD).

16.4.2 The power to award just satisfaction

Where the European Court finds a violation of the Convention it may under Art 41 award 'just satisfaction' to the injured party. The Member State then has an obligation under the

Convention to abide by such a ruling and, for example, pay any compensation awarded by the court.

■ The phrase 'just satisfaction' is also used in s 8 of the Human Rights Act 1998 and the domestic courts must ensure that any remedies awarded by them reflect the principles in Art 41 (see below).

■ The European Court can award pecuniary damage to compensate for any direct financial loss, including loss, or depreciation of property (*Lopez Ostra v Spain* (1994) 20 EHRR 277), or recovery of any fines or compensation (*Jersild v Denmark* (1994) 19 EHRR 1).

■ The court may also award damages for non-pecuniary damage where the applicant has suffered things such as loss of liberty (*A v United Kingdom* (2009) 49 EHRR 29), or physical and/or mental distress from a violation of the European Convention (see *Smith and Grady v United Kingdom* (2000) 29 EHRR 493).

■ The court can compensate for legal costs and expenses actually, necessarily and reasonably incurred by the applicant (*McCann v United Kingdom* (1996) 21 EHRR 97).

■ In appropriate cases the court has the power to award no compensation other than costs and expenses (*McCann v United Kingdom* (above)) where no compensation awarded for unlawful deaths of suspected terrorists (contrast *A v United King*dom (above) where limited compensation was granted).

ACTIVITY

Self-test questions

1. Why was the European Convention on Human Rights devised and what does it generally contain?
2. How is the European Convention different from, and related to European Union law?
3. How do the Convention and its case law affect United Kingdom law and its practice?
4. How has the Convention been incorporated into domestic law? (Check your answer once you have studied Chapter 17)
5. What is the role of the European Court of Human Rights, and what powers does the court have?

16.5 State and individual applications

The European Court has the power to receive applications from either Member States or from individual applicants claiming to be victims of a violation of the Convention.

16.5.1 Inter-state applications

Under Art 33 any High Contracting Party may refer to the court any alleged breach of the provisions of the Convention or the protocols by another High Contracting Party, including claims with respect to victims other than the state's own nationals.

CASE EXAMPLE

Ireland v United Kingdom (1978) 2 EHRR 25

The Irish government brought an inter-state case against the United Kingdom in relation to the treatment of suspected terrorists by British authorities detained in army barracks in Northern Ireland. The government claimed that such treatment constituted a violation of, *inter alia*, Art 3 of the European Convention, guaranteeing freedom from torture and inhuman and degrading treatment (the European Court held that there had been a violation of Art 3 in that the interrogation techniques constituted inhuman and degrading treatment, but not torture).

State applications must comply with Art 35, which requires the exhaustion of all domestic remedies and for claims to be brought within six months of the final decision

16.5.2 Individual applications

Under Art 34 the court may receive applications from 'any person, non-governmental organisation or group of individuals' who claims to be a victim of a violation by one of the High Contracting Parties of the rights set forth in the Convention. The individual may bring an application against a state provided he or she was within that state's jurisdiction at the time (Art 1). Applications cannot be brought against another individual or a public authority, although the state can be liable for violations committed by state actors and individuals (*A v United Kingdom* (1999) 27 EHRR 611) and for the violations of another state if it exposes an individual to a risk of violation (*Soering v United Kingdom* (1989) 11 EHRR 439).

Individual applications are made to the Court Registry who will register the complaint and the case will then be referred to the European Court for a determination on admissibility, below. High Contracting Parties must not hinder any individual petition (*McShane v United Kingdom* (2002) 35 EHRR 23).

16.5.3 The requirement to be a victim

Applications under Art 34 may only be brought by persons claiming to be a 'victim' of a breach of the Convention.

■ The applicant must normally be directly affected by the alleged violation (*Klass v Germany* (1978) 2 EHRR 214).

■ The law or practice must normally be applied to the applicant's disadvantage, although an individual might be directly affected by the mere existence of incompatible law or practice (*Dudgeon v United Kingdom* (1982) 4 EHRR 149 – existence of discriminatory law against homosexuals made the applicant a victim, even though he was never prosecuted).

■ The court is also prepared to accept applications from family representatives of the actual victim, particularly in cases of potentially unlawful deaths (*McCann v United Kingdom* (1996) 21 EHRR 97).

The court thus takes a flexible approach to the issue where the applicant is a victim. In *Fairfield v United Kingdom* (Application No 24790/04) it held that the family of a person convicted for using insulting words and behaviour, and who subsequently died, were not victims under Art 34. The court noted that a different, more flexible, test applied in cases under Art 2 of the Convention, because of the importance of that right.

16.5.4 Admissibility of applications

Articles 34 and 35 of the Convention subject applications to an admissibility criteria and the initial role of the European Court is to rule on admissibility of the claim. This will filter out hopeless claims, or claims made in bad faith, and will ensure that the Convention machinery is only used as a last resort.

16.5.5 The admissibility criteria

Art 35, which applies to both inter-state and individual applications, provides that the court may only deal with the matter after all domestic remedies have been exhausted and within a period of six months from the date on which the final decision was taken.

■ The six month rule does not apply to continuing breaches of the Convention, or where the violation shows that there is no effective domestic remedy (*De Becker v Belgium* (1979–80)).

- The applicant is expected to exhaust all *effective* domestic remedies before applying to the court (*Spencer v United Kingdom* [1998] EHRLR 348 – failure to bring confidentiality proceedings for an alleged breach of Art 8).
- Since the passing of the Human Rights Act 1998, applicants would be expected to make full use of that Act in resolving their human rights dispute.
- The exhaustion rule does not apply to inter-state cases where the applicant state alleges widespread breaches (*Ireland v United Kingdom* (1978) 2 EHRR 25) or in individual applications where an administrative practice has rendered remedies ineffective (*Akdivar v Turkey* (1996) 1 BHRC 137).
- An applicant should normally pursue any effective appeal against an initial decision, unless such an appeal would be futile (*Handyside v United Kingdom* (1976) 1 EHRR 737, where the court held that appeal proceedings did not have to be exhausted when the initial court's finding was clearly within domestic law).

In addition to the above rules on time limits and exhaustion of remedies, the court may declare a case inadmissible under Art 35 on the following grounds:

- Where the application is anonymous.
- Where it is substantially the same as a matter that has already been examined by the court, or has already been submitted to another procedure of international investigation or settlement and contains no new information.
- Where the application is incompatible with the provisions of the Convention. In other words, where the claim does not engage a right protected by the Convention – *Bertrand Russell Peace Foundation v United Kingdom* 14 DR 117(1978), no right to diplomatic protection under the Convention.
- Where the application constitutes an abuse of the right of application. For example, where it is brought in bad faith for purely political or personal reasons (*M v United Kingdom* 54 DR 214 (1987)).
- Where the claim is manifestly ill-founded. In other words, where the applicant has failed to show a *prima facie* case against the respondent state, either because the relevant article is not engaged or where the violation is clearly justified (*Friend v United Kingdom*; *Countryside Alliance v United Kingdom* (2010) 50 EHRR SE6).

In addition, under Protocol No 14 (now finally ratified and coming into force in April 2010) cases can be declared inadmissible where the applicant has not suffered a serious disadvantage, and where respect for human rights does not require the court to examine the merits of the case (excluding cases where the dispute has not been considered by a domestic tribunal). Under that protocol, single judges may hear clear cut applications and three person committees cases where the case law is settled.

16.5.6 Friendly settlements and striking out

Article 38 permits the European Court of Human Rights to effect a friendly settlement between the applicant and the defendant state after deciding on its admissibility. In such a situation the case will be struck out of the court's list (Art 40).

- Some settlements are effected on the basis that the state admits the violation and promises to change its law (*Sutherland v United Kingdom, The Times*, 13th April 2001 – friendly settlement agreed when the UK government agreed to amend incompatible legislation and to equalise the age of consent for heterosexual and homosexual sex (The Sexual Offences (Amendment) Act 2000).
- Other settlements do not involve an admission of liability, and are affected by a payment of compensation to the applicant (*Amekrane v United Kingdom* (1974) 44 CD 101 – payment of £30,000 compensation to a relative of a member of the Moroccan Armed Forces who had been sent back to his country to face the death penalty).

16.6 Lawful and permissible interferences with Convention rights

Many Convention rights may be interfered with in particular circumstances, provided that interference has certain qualities. In particular, the 'conditional rights' contained in Arts 8–11 of the Convention, contain a particular mechanism for testing the legality of any interference:

■ any such interference must be prescribed by, or in accordance with the law;
■ it must relate to a legitimate aim listed in the qualifying part of the Article;
■ it must be necessary in a democratic society for the protection of one of a number of those aims.

This mechanism can also be used to test the legality of interferences with other rights, such as the right to a fair trial under Art 6 (*Osman v United Kingdom* (2000) 29 EHRR 245), the right to liberty of the person under Art 5 (*Steel v United Kingdom* (1998) 28 EHRR 603), and freedom from discrimination under Art 14 (*Pretty v United Kingdom* (2002) 35 EHRR 1).
The Human Rights Act 1998 adopts these principles and thus the domestic courts must subject any interference under domestic law to an equivalent test when adjudicating upon Convention rights.

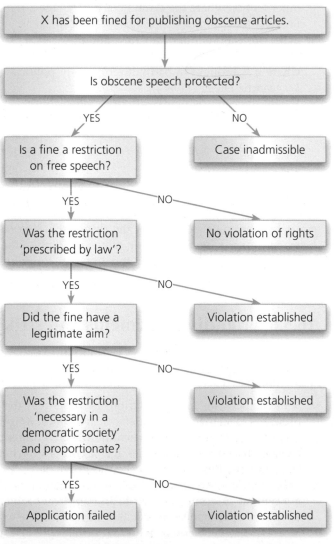

Figure 16.1 Conditional right – freedom of expression

16.6.1 Prescribed by law/in accordance with law

Any interference of Convention rights must comply with the rule of law and thus must derive from some legal provision.

- For example, under Art 2 of the Convention the death penalty is provided for, but only for a crime for which the penalty is *prescribed by law*.
- Art 5 of the Convention allows interference with a person's liberty, but only in accordance with a procedure *prescribed by law*.
- The 'conditional rights' contained in Arts 8 to 11 provide that any interference with those rights are *'prescribed by law'* or *'in accordance with law'*.

The meaning of 'in accordance with law' was considered in *Malone*, below, and the phrase 'prescribed by law' (used in Arts 9, 10 and 11), is interpreted and applied identically (*Silver v United Kingdom* (1983) 5 EHRR 347).

CASE EXAMPLE

Malone v United Kingdom (1984) 7 EHRR 14

The applicant's telephone had been tapped in the course of criminal investigation and the applicant claimed that the tapping was not authorised by law as the rules for interception were contained in administrative guidance.

The European Court held that for a measure to be prescribed by law it had to have a legal basis (in other words the law must be identified and established), the rule had to be accessible, and such a rule should be formulated with sufficient certainty to enable people to understand it and to regulate their conduct by it.

The court concluded that it could not be said what elements of the power to intercept communications were incorporated in legal rules and what elements remained within the discretion of the executive. Accordingly the tapping was not in accordance with law and was thus in violation of Art 8.

In *Malone* the European Court insisted that there is a measure of legal protection against arbitrary interference by public authorities and that provisions must exist which are sufficiently independent of those who administer them. This law can be either in statutory or common law form (*Sunday Times v United Kingdom* (1979) 2 EHRR 245).

In addition, the rule has to be accessible, so that those who are likely to be affected by it can access and understand it (*Silver v United Kingdom* (1983) 5 EHRR 347 – the regulation of prisoners' correspondence via administrative guidance produced by the Secretary of State was not prescribed by law because such guidance was only available to the prison authorities).

Finally, the provision should be sufficiently clear to allow individuals to govern their future behaviour. This was explained by the European Court of Human Rights in *Sunday Times v United Kingdom* (1979) 2 EHRR 245:

JUDGMENT

'A law has to be formulated with sufficient precision to enable the citizen to regulate his conduct: that person must be able – if need be with appropriate advice – to foresee, to a degree that is reasonable in the circumstances, the consequences which a given action may entail. Those consequences need not, however, be foreseeable with absolute certainty. Whilst the Court noted that certainty is desirable, it also accepted that excessive rigidity should be avoided and that laws are inevitably couched in terms which, to some extent, are vague and whose interpretation and application are questions of practice. Similarly, although the law itself may be vague, its meaning and scope may become apparent after it has been construed and applied by the courts.'

The law's meaning and extent must, therefore, be capable of reasonable prediction, even though the European Court accepts that many laws are inevitably vague and open to flexible interpretation. For example, in *Hashman and Harrap v United Kingdom* (1999) 30 EHRR 241 when the applicants were ordered to desist in conduct that was *contra bones mores* (conduct which is seen as wrong in the eyes of the majority of contemporary citizens) the court held that the offence failed to give sufficient guidance to the applicants as to what conduct they were not allowed to carry out in the future. See also *Gillan v United Kingdom*, (2010) (Application No 4158/05), where it was held that stop and search powers under s 44 of the Terrorism Act 2000 were too arbitrary and uncertain to be prescribed by law.

16.6.2 Legitimate aims

Not only should any restriction of a Convention right be based in law, it must pursue a legitimate aim. These aims are expressly mentioned in the qualifying paragraphs of Arts 8–11 of the Convention, but also constitute implied restrictions of other Articles, such as freedom from discrimination (Art 14), the right to marry (Art 12) and the right to vote (Art 3, Protocol 1).

For example, Art 10, guaranteeing the right to freedom of speech and expression, refers to a host of legitimate aims.

ARTICLE

Art 10(2)

'The exercise of these freedoms … may be subject to such … restrictions, conditions and formalities as are prescribed by law and necessary in a democratic society, in the interests of national security, territorial integrity, public safety, the prevention of disorder or crime, the protection of health or morals, the protection of the reputation and or rights of others, the prevention of the disclosure of information received in confidence and the maintenance of the authority and impartiality of the judiciary.'

The Member State must then satisfy the court that the restriction pursued one of those aims and was genuinely applied to the applicant in a particular case. Thus, in *Handyside v United Kingdom* (1976) 1 EHRR 737 the court accepted that the applicant had been prosecuted and convicted under the Obscene Publications Act 1959 for the legitimate purpose of protecting health and morals and the rights of others (the right of young, vulnerable individuals not to be corrupted).

16.6.3 Necessary in a democratic society

In addition to the restricting being legal and related to a legitimate aim, the Convention (and now the Human Rights Act 1998) guards against excessive or unnecessary interferences by insisting that a restriction is 'necessary in a democratic society' for achieving its legitimate aim.

The phrase 'necessary in a democratic society' was defined in *Handyside v United Kingdom* (1976) 1 EHRR 737:

JUDGMENT

'The word "necessary" does not mean "absolutely necessary" or "indispensable", but neither does it have the flexibility of terms such as "useful" or "convenient". Instead there must be a "pressing social need" for the interference. The Court must ask whether is there a pressing social need for some restriction of the Convention and whether the particular restriction corresponds to that need, including whether it is a proportionate response to that need, and whether the reasons advanced by the authorities are relevant and sufficient.'

The court has also stressed that it is not faced with a choice between two conflicting principles, but with a principle of, for example, freedom of expression subject to a number of exceptions, which must be narrowly interpreted (*Sunday Times v United Kingdom* (1979) 2 EHRR 245). However, the principle of necessity, and proportionality, are linked to the doctrine of the margin of appreciation (see directly below).

16.6.4 The doctrine of proportionality

The doctrine of proportionality (now part of domestic law after the Human Rights Act 1998 was passed – see Chapter 17) ensures that there is a fair balance between pursuing a legitimate aim and the protection of Convention rights.

Thus the European Court insists that any restriction should be strictly proportionate to the legitimate aim being pursued and that the authorities can show that it does not go beyond what is strictly required to achieve that purpose (*Barthold v Germany* (1985) 7 EHRR 383). In doing so the court can consider the following factors:

- The importance of the right that has been interfered with.
- The extent to which the right was violated, including the level of the sanction or penalty.
- The nature and importance of the legitimate aim (*Handyside v United Kingdom* (1976) 1 EHRR 737 – protection of morals best decided by national authorities).
- Whether there was a less restrictive alternative available to the domestic authorities (*Goodwin v United Kingdom* (1996) 22 EHRR 123 – disclosure of press source not necessary in addition to an injunction to prohibit disclosure of confidential information).
- Whether the restriction destroys the very essence of the Convention right in question (*Hirst v United Kingdom* (2006) 42 EHRR 41 – blanket prohibition of the prisoner's right to vote disproportionate).

margin of appreciation

a concept created by the European Court of Human Rights to allow a certain amount of freedom for each signatory state to regulate its own activities and its application of the European Convention on Human Rights

16.6.5 The margin of appreciation

In deciding whether there has been a violation of the Convention, and in determining whether the Member State has achieved a correct balance, the European Court is prepared to give the state a level of discretion - a '**margin of appreciation**'.

The doctrine was first used in the context of Art 15, allowing derogation in times of war or other emergency, and where the European Court gives the state a margin of error in deciding how to compromise Convention rights in such circumstances. The margin is offered by the European Court because it recognises that its role under the Convention is subsidiary to the system of rights protection adopted by each Member State (Art 1 of the Convention):

JUDGMENT

'The machinery of the Convention is subsidiary to the national systems safeguarding human rights, and consequently the Convention leaves to each state a margin of appreciation, given both to the domestic legislature and to the bodies called upon to interpret and apply the laws. This margin of appreciation goes hand in hand with the Court's power to give the final meaning on whether a restriction is compatible with the Convention right in question.' (*Handyside v United Kingdom* (1976) 1 EHRR 737)

The doctrine is flexible, and the court will offer a wide or narrow margin depending on the circumstances. A wide margin will be offered in cases where free speech conflicts with public morality. Thus, in *Handyside v United Kingdom* (above) the European Court stated that it was not possible to find a uniform conception of morals within the Council of Europe, and that states were in a better position than the international judge to give an opinion on the exact content of the requirements of morals.

However, a narrower margin may be offered where the restriction in question impinges on the enjoyment of the individual's right to *private* life (*Dudgeon v United Kingdom* (1982) 4 EHRR 149).

CASE EXAMPLE

Smith and Grady v United Kingdom (2000) 29 EHRR 493

The applicants had been dismissed from the armed forces because of their homosexuality and claimed that their right to private life had been violated.

The court held that the restriction placed on homosexuals from remaining in the armed forces was not necessary for the purpose of achieving national security and public order. The negative attitudes of heterosexuals towards homosexuals could not, of themselves, justify the interferences in question.

A similarly narrow margin may be offered in cases where the restriction impinges on press freedom. Thus, in *Sunday Times v United Kingdom* (1979) 2 EHRR 245 the court held that the laws of contempt of court displayed a much more common European approach, allowing the court to more easily judge the necessity of any particular interference. In addition, the publication in question (an article on the ongoing Thalidomide disaster) reported on a matter of great public interest, and an injunction should not be granted unless it was *absolutely certain* that the publication would hinder the due administration of justice.

The doctrine of margin of appreciation does not, theoretically, apply to domestic proceedings under the Human Rights Act 1998. However, it is clear that the domestic courts will show Parliament and public authorities a good deal of deference in cases where human rights have to be balanced with other rights and interests (see Chapter 17).

ACTIVITY

Problem Solving

Consider the following hypothetical case and answer the questions that follow it.

In November 2012 Parliament passed the (imaginary) Public Offices Act 2012, which regulated the conduct of those who hold public office and which encouraged responsible government. Under s 60 of the Act it is an offence for any person to use grossly offensive words either in describing a person who holds a public office, or to criticise such a person with respect either to the performance of his public duties or to the conducting of his or her private life; under s 60(4) 'grossly offensive words' are defined as those which relate to an individual's reputation or integrity and which a reasonable person would regard as highly indecent or improper'. The maximum fine for committing an offence under the Act is £2,000.

ACTIVITY

Applying the law

In March 2013, Lionel, a local councillor, was convicted under s 60 of the Act by Birdchester Magistrates when he distributed leaflets in Birdchester city centre which criticised the local Member of Parliament for his recent speech on immigration and asylum seekers. In the leaflet Lionel described the MP as 'a bloody Nazi and a hypocrite' stating that the MP and those who subscribed to his views were as dangerous as sex offenders. Lionel was fined £1,000 and the conviction and fine were upheld by the Court of Appeal.

Lionel now brings an application under the European Convention.

1. Have any of L's Convention rights been interfered with?
2. If so, is that restriction 'prescribed by law'?
3. Do the Act and the conviction pursue a legitimate aim?
4. In your view, was the conviction and fine necessary in a democratic society?
5. What level of margin of appreciation would the European Court give to the UK authorities in such a case?

16.7 Derogations and reservations

The Convention recognises that a state might not always be able to fully comply with its obligations under the Convention and allows it to compromise those rights in certain cases. Accordingly, Art 15 allows derogation in times of war or other emergency, and Art 57 permits the state to make a reservation with respect to a particular Convention right and its application within that jurisdiction.

16.7.1 Derogation in times of war or other public emergency

Article 15 of the Convention provides as follows:

ARTICLE

> Art 5
> In times of war or other public emergency threatening the life of the nation any High Contracting Party may take measures derogating from its obligations under this Convention to the extent strictly required by the exigencies of the situation, provided that such measures are not inconsistent with its other obligations under international law.

student mentor tip

"Remember the terrorist cases."

Holly, University of Southampton

The right to derogate under Art 15 is qualified in a number of respects:

- ■ The High Contracting Party can only take such measures as are *strictly required* by the exigencies of the situation.
- ■ The measures must not be inconsistent with the state's other obligations under other Treaties.
- ■ Article 15(2) provides that no derogation is allowed in respect of certain Convention rights: no derogation is possible in relation to Art 2 (the right to life), (excluding deaths resulting from lawful acts of war), Art 3 (prohibition of torture etc), Art 4(1) (prohibition of slavery or servitude) or Art 7 (prohibition of retrospective criminal law).
- ■ The High Contracting Party must keep the Secretary General of the Council of Europe informed of the measures which it has taken and when such measures have ceased to operate, including the reasons for such action.

Derogation measures can be challenged under the European Convention and the court can adjudicate on their compatibility. In doing so, the Court will provide the state with a wide margin of error.

CASE EXAMPLE

Lawless v Ireland (No 3) (1961) 1 EHRR 15

Although the court found that the detention of the applicant without trial for a period of five months was in violation of Art 5(3) of the Convention, it held that the Irish government was entitled to derogate from its obligations by virtue of the existence of a public emergency.

The court stressed that the measures governments can take when derogating are strictly limited to what is required by the exigencies of the situation and must not be in conflict with other international law obligations. However, the court was satisfied that those strict limitations were met in the present case. The court held that the respondent government should be afforded a certain margin of error or appreciation in deciding what measures were required by the situation, and it was not the court's function to substitute for the government's assessment any other assessment of what might be the most prudent or most expedient policy to combat terrorism.

Moreover, the court must arrive at its decision in the light of the conditions that existed at the time that the original decision was taken, rather than reviewing the matter retrospectively.

A similarly wide discretion had been given to the UK government with respect to provisions intended to deal with terrorism in Northern Ireland.

CASE EXAMPLE

Brannigan and McBride v United Kingdom (1993) 17 EHRR 539

The United Kingdom government lodged a derogation after the European Court's decision in *Brogan v United Kingdom* (1989) 11 EHRR 117, where it was held that detention provisions in the Prevention of Terrorism (Temporary Provisions) Act 1984 were in contravention of Art 5(3) of the Convention, guaranteeing the right to be brought promptly before a judge or other officer.

The European Court held that the derogation was lawful. The derogation was not invalid merely because the government had decided to keep open the possibility of finding a means in the future of ensuring greater conformity with Convention obligations. In addition there were effective measures in domestic law to challenge the use of the provisions and thus to safeguard against arbitrary action.

Note, the *domestic* courts have shown less deference with respect to the compatibility of recent anti-terrorism measures: *A and others v Secretary of State* (see 17.11.1). That decision on derogation was subsequently upheld by the European Court of Human Rights (*A v United Kingdom* (2009) 49 EHRR 29).

16.7.2 Reservations

Article 57 of the Convention allows a state to make reservations to specific provisions of the Convention when ratifying the Convention. The reservation must be in respect of laws in existence at the time of ratification and the article does not allow reservations of a general character. For example it would not be possible to make a reservation of an entire Convention right.

The United Kingdom made a reservation with regard to Art 2 of the First Protocol to the Convention, which imposes a duty on each state to respect the rights of parents to ensure education and teaching in conformity with their own religious and philosophical convictions. This duty is only accepted in so far as it is compatible with the provision of efficient instruction and training and the avoidance of unreasonable public expenditure. The reservation is contained in Sched 3 of the Human Rights Act 1998 and thus has effect in domestic law.

KEY FACTS

Principle	Legal Authority
The European Convention imposes an obligation on each state to ensure the observance of Convention rights within its own jurisdiction.	Art 1, ECHR
The UK has given effect to the Convention via the Human Rights Act 1998 and thus the principles of the Convention and the court can be used in domestic proceedings.	s 2, HRA 1998
In addition, the Convention machinery can be used by victims who have exhausted all effective domestic remedies.	Art 34, ECHR
The European Court was set up to ensure the observance of the Convention and can receive inter-state or individual applications.	Arts 19, 33 and 34, ECHR
A full-time European Court decides on the admissibility of all applications, which must be received within 6 months of the act and the applicant must have exhausted all effective domestic remedies.	Art 34, ECHR

Principle ctd	Legal Authority ctd
A Grand Chamber of the European Court hears appeals and referrals from the European Court of Human Rights and its decisions are final.	Arts 43 and 44, ECHR
Individual applications are subject to further tests of admissibility and must not be manifestly ill-founded.	Art 35, ECHR
The court has the power to strike out cases and to secure friendly settlements between the parties.	Art 38, ECHR
The court has the power to make awards of 'just satisfaction', including granting pecuniary and non-pecuniary loss and costs and expenses.	Art 41, ECHR
Certain Convention rights can be interfered with provided the restriction is in accordance with or prescribed by law and necessary in a democratic society for the pursuance of a legitimate aim.	*Malone v United Kingdom* (1984) and *Handyside v United Kingdom* (1976)
The European Court adopts the concept of proportionality to judge the necessity of restrictions but also offers the state a margin of appreciation when they pass and maintain laws that interfere with Convention rights.	*Barthold v Germany* (1985) and *Handyside v United Kingdom* (1976)
The standard of review, and the width of the margin of appreciation, depends on the nature of the legitimate aim and the importance of the right.	*Handyside v United Kingdom* (1976) and *Smith and Grady v United Kingdom* (1999)
States can derogate from their Convention obligations and can make reservations under Art 57. Derogations are subject to regulation by the Council of Europe and the European Court, but the court offers a wide margin of error to the states.	Arts 15 and 57, ECHR and *Brannigan and McBride v United Kingdom* (1993)

16.8 The rights guaranteed under the European Convention on Human Rights

The substantive rights guaranteed under the European Convention are contained in Section One of the Convention, in Arts 2–14 and a number of optional protocols. Most of these rights (excluding Art 13, guaranteeing an effective remedy in domestic law for violation of these rights) are contained in s 1 of the Human Rights Act 1998.

16.8.1 Absolute and conditional rights

Some Convention rights are absolute rights, while some are conditional. An absolute right is not capable of derogation under Art 15, and their violation cannot generally be justified. A conditional right, however, can be violated provided that interference is lawful and necessary.

For example, Art 2 (the right to life), Art 3 (prohibition of torture etc), Art 4(1) (freedom from slavery), and Art 7 (no punishment without law) cannot be derogated from under Art 15. Additionally, in the case of an absolute right such as freedom from torture, there can be no justification for a violation, whereas for conditional rights (such as freedom of expression), interference is allowed provided the restriction was prescribed by law and was necessary for the purpose of achieving a legitimate aim (see 16.6 above).

The Convention also makes certain rights subject to express restrictions:

- Article 4 excludes work done in the course of detention from the term 'forced or compulsory labour'.
- Article 5 lays down a number of specific circumstances where it is permissible to interfere with liberty of the person.
- Article 2 provides that deprivation of life will not be unlawful where it results from the use of absolutely necessary force during, for example, a lawful arrest.
- Article 7(2) states that prohibition against retrospective criminal law does not apply to behaviour that is criminal according to the general principles of international law.

16.9 Article 2 – The Right to Life

The fundamental right to life is protected by Art 2 of the Convention, which seeks to protect a person's right to life under the law.

ARTICLE

Art 2

Law shall protect everyone's right to life. No one shall be deprived of his life intentionally save in the execution of a sentence of a court following his conviction of a crime for which the penalty is provided by law.

16.9.1 The scope of Article 2

The right to life cannot be derogated from even in times of war and other public emergency (apart from lawful acts of war), but intentional deprivation of life is allowed in exceptional cases listed in Art 2(2) (see 16.9.3 below).

Article 2 imposes an obligation on the state to preserve life, but does not extend to the right to die (*Pretty v United Kingdom,* (2002) 35 EHRR 1). Neither does Art 2 extend to protect the right to life of the unborn child (*Vo v France* (2005) 40 EHRR 12).

Article 2 imposes a negative duty not to interfere with a person's right to life, but also places a positive duty on the state to ensure that an individual's life is not taken unnecessarily. The duty applies where the act is one of a state official (*McCann v United Kingdom* (1996) 21 EHRR 97), and the state can also be responsible where the death is caused by a private individual and the state has not taken due care to safeguard the victim's life.

CASE EXAMPLE

Osman v United Kingdom (2000) 29 EHRR 245

The applicants, the wife and son of the deceased, brought a claim under Art 2 after one of the son's teachers had killed the husband after forming an attachment to the son.

The European Court held that under Art 2 the state must take appropriate steps to safeguard the lives of those within its jurisdiction, including the duty to put into place effective criminal law provisions backed up by law-enforcement machinery for preventing and sanctioning such deaths. This would also include a positive (although not an impossible or disproportionate) obligation on the authorities to take preventive operational measures to protect an individual whose life is at risk from the criminal acts of another individual. (On the facts, the court held the police could not be criticised for attaching greater weight to the presumption of the teacher's innocence, and accordingly there had been no violation of Art 2.)

That decision was followed in a recent domestic decision in *Van Colle v Chief Constable of Hertfordshire* [2008] UKHL 50 where the House of Lords held that there had been no violation of Art 2 when the police had in the circumstances taken adequate steps to safeguard the life of a prosecution witness from a real risk of attacks by suspects in a forthcoming trial.

The state will owe a specific positive duty to safeguard the lives of those in detention, either from the actions of fellow inmates, or themselves (*Edwards v United Kingdom* (2002) 35 EHRR 19 – a cellmate posed a real and serious risk to the applicant's son and the prison authorities had not been properly informed of the cellmate's medical history and perceived dangerousness). Article 2 might also be engaged where the individual has taken his or her own life, provided there was a *clear risk* of such – *Keenan v United Kingdom* (2001) 33 EHRR 38, no breach of Art 2 when a vulnerable prisoner had committed suicide while under supervision by the prison authorities.

16.9.2 The duty to carry out an effective investigation

In addition to the substantive duty under Art 2, the article imposes a procedural duty on every Member State to carry out a proper investigation into any death that may be in violation of Art 2. In the case below, the court established some guidelines for establishing a violation of this procedural duty.

CASE EXAMPLE

Jordan and others v United Kingdom (2003) 37 EHRR 2
The court held that Art 2 required that there had to be some form of effective official investigation when individuals had been killed as a result of the use of force. The state must take the initiative in conducting the investigation and it should be carried out by someone independent from those involved in the events. It should lead to a determination of whether the force used in such circumstances was justified, and to the identification and punishment of those responsible. The authorities must take reasonable steps to secure the necessary evidence and the investigation should be carried out with reasonable promptness.

Article 2 also gives the victim's relatives the right to effectively participate in the investigation (*Edwards v United Kingdom* (above)) and, in conjunction with Art 13 of the Convention, the right to effective compensation, where appropriate (*Keenan v United Kingdom* (above)).

The procedural right has also been upheld by the domestic courts under the Human Rights Act 1998. In *R (Amin) v Secretary of State for the Home Department* [2003] UKHL 51 the House of Lords held that an internal investigation into the killing of a prisoner by his racist cellmate did not fulfil the requirements of Art 2, and that a full independent public investigation had to be held.

16.9.3 The exceptions under Article 2.2

Article 2(2) provides exceptions to the general right to life where the intentional deprivation of life will not constitute a violation of that right.

ARTICLE

Art 2(2)
The deprivation of life shall not be regarded as inflicted in contravention of Art 2 when it results from the use of force which is no more than absolutely necessary … in defence of any person from unlawful violence, in order to effect a lawful arrest or to prevent the escape of a person lawfully detained, or in action lawfully taken for the purpose of quelling a riot or insurrection.

For the exceptions in Art 2(2) to come into play the force used must be no more than absolutely necessary.

CASE EXAMPLE

McCann v United Kingdom (1996) 21 EHRR 97

Three suspected IRA terrorists were seen near a car. Members of the SAS, believing that the car contained a bomb and that it was to be detonated, shot them dead. The families brought a claim under Art 2 of the Convention.

The European Court held that although the SAS members had used no more force than was necessary in the circumstances, there had been a violation of the right to life through the careless planning of the operation by the administrative authorities. The authorities had been negligent in the planning of the operation and the soldiers had been provided with misinformation.

Despite this decision, the court will normally afford the authorities and individual officers a wide area of discretion where they have acted in good faith and with reasonable diligence (*Bubbins v United Kingdom* (2005) 41 EHRR 24).

16.9.4 Article 2 and the death penalty

The first sentence of Art 2 provides for the death penalty, provided it takes the form of an execution of a sentence of a court following a person's conviction of a crime for which the penalty is provided by law. However the death penalty may be unlawful in a number of cases.

- Optional Protocol No 6 of the Convention provides that the death penalty shall be abolished in peacetime and that no one shall be condemned to such penalty or executed. In addition optional Protocol No 13 abolishes it in all circumstances. The UK has ratified both protocols and thus any execution within its jurisdiction would be contrary to its Convention obligations. This would include executions in other jurisdictions where there was a real risk of such a penalty (*Soering v United Kingdom* (1989) 11 EHRR 439).
- In *Al-Saadoon and Mufhdi v United Kingdom, The Times*, 10th March, 2010 the European Court held that the second sentence in Art 2 should now be amended by state practice and that accordingly states would now regard it as an unacceptable form of punishment in violation of Art 3.
- In any case, the circumstances of a death penalty may constitute a violation of Art 3 of the Convention (*Soering v United Kingdom* (1989) 11 EHRR 439), and any execution not proceeded by a fair trial would breach Art 2(1).

16.10 Article 3 – Prohibition of torture and inhuman and degrading treatment and punishment

ARTICLE

Art 3

No one shall be subject to torture or to inhuman or degrading treatment or punishment.

16.10.1 The scope of Article 3

The Article imposes an absolute prohibition on such treatment, even in times of war or other public emergency (see above). Thus once a violation of Art 3 has been found, there can be no justification for that breach (*Chahal v United Kingdom* (1997) 23 EHRR 413).

The role of the European Court of Human Rights in such cases is, thus, to define the terms 'torture' and 'inhuman and degrading treatment or punishment' and to assess whether the applicant has been subjected to treatment in violation of the article.

Under Art 3 Member States owe a positive, yet limited, duty to ensure that a person does not suffer ill treatment at the hands of others, whether state actors or public or private individuals.

CASE EXAMPLE

A v United Kingdom (1999) 27 EHRR 611

The applicant, a young boy, had been beaten with a cane by his step-father, who was then acquitted after relying on the defence of reasonable chastisement.

The European Court held that the United Kingdom government was held liable for the ill treatment of the applicant because domestic law provided him with inadequate protection against treatment which was contrary to Art 3 (see now s 58 of the Children Act 2004).

Also in *Z v United Kingdom* (2002) 34 EHRR 3 the European Court held that the state (via social services) had a duty to take such measures to provide effective protection against long-term abuse and neglect in the home.

16.10.2 Definition of torture, inhuman and degrading treatment or punishment

The terms used in Art 3 were explored in the inter-state case of *Ireland v United Kingdom*.

CASE EXAMPLE

Ireland v United Kingdom (1978) 2 EHRR 25

The applicants had been the victims of the 'Five Techniques' interrogation measures, involving being subjected to intense noise, wall-standing, and deprivation of food and sleep.

The European Court defined torture as treatment constituting deliberate inhuman treatment causing very serious and cruel suffering; inhuman treatment as causing if not bodily injury, at least intense physical and mental or psychiatric suffering; and degrading treatment as that which would arouse in victims feelings of fear, anguish and inferiority capable of humiliation, or taking away one's physical or moral resistance.

On the facts the court found that the techniques were inhuman and degrading, but were not severe enough to constitute torture.

A finding of torture is, therefore, reserved for treatment constituting an aggravated and deliberate form of inhuman treatment or punishment; although the court has stressed that Art 3 must be interpreted in the light of present-day conditions. As a result certain acts (in this case, the deliberate, serious and prolonged assault of a detainee) which in the past were classified as inhuman and degrading as opposed to torture, might now be classified as torture (*Selmouni v France* (1999) 29 EHRR 403).

For a breach to take place the treatment or punishment must cross the threshold set by Art 3. Accordingly the humiliation or debasement must reach a particular level, and the European Court has stressed that such an assessment is relative and depends on all the circumstances of the case, including the victim's age (*Tyrer v United Kingdom* (1978) 2 EHRR 1).

16.10.3 Article 3 and corporal punishment

Not all forms of corporal punishment will necessarily be in violation of Art 3, although judicial corporal punishment appears to be outlawed by the European Court.

CASE EXAMPLE

Tyrer v United Kingdom (1978) 2 EHRR 1

A 15-year-old boy in the Isle of Man had been found guilty of assault and birched on his bare buttocks in accordance with Isle of Man law. The government argued that the punishment was an effective deterrent and that in all the circumstances was not inhuman or degrading.

The European Court described the punishment as institutionalised violence and held that the applicant had been subjected to an assault on his dignity and physical integrity and that it was immaterial that the punishment was an effective deterrent, or that the majority of society in the Isle of Man approved it as a punishment.

Corporal punishment in schools was abolished in the United Kingdom by the Schools Standard and Framework Act 1998, although the European Court has never outlawed the practice *per se* (*Costello-Roberts v United Kingdom* (1993) 19 EHRR 112). However, corporal punishment of a child against the parents' wishes would be in breach of Art 2 of the First Protocol, which gives them the right to have their children educated in conformity with their philosophical and religious convictions (*Campbell and Cosans v United Kingdom* (1982) 4 EHRR 293).

Whether parental chastisement is in breach of Art 3 depends on all the circumstances and the severity of the punishment. Thus, in *A v United Kingdom* (1999) 27 EHRR 611, when a nine-year-old boy had been repeatedly and severely beaten by his stepfather with a garden cane it was held that the threshold in Art 3 of the Convention had been satisfied.

16.10.4 Article 3 and deportation and extradition

Deportation or extradition may expose a person to a real risk that they will face treatment or punishment in breach of Art 3. In such a case the state which deports or extradites may be liable for the violation committed by the receiving state.

CASE EXAMPLE

Soering v United Kingdom (1989) 11 EHRR 439

A young German national was to stand trial in the USA for the murder of his girlfriend's parents. The UK government agreed to his extradition having been assured that the prosecutors would argue that he should not face the death penalty.

The European Court held that the UK government could be liable for a violation by the USA if it exposed the applicant to a real risk of a violation of Art 3. In this case, the death row phenomenon constituted a breach of Art 3 and extradition would constitute a violation of that article by the UK government as there was a real risk that he would be exposed to those conditions.

The *Soering* principle applies even though there may be good national or other security reasons for deportation. Thus, in *Chahal v United Kingdom* (1997) 23 EHRR 413 the European Court held that the prohibition under Art 3 is absolute and the activities of the person, however undesirable, cannot be a material consideration in deciding whether Art 3 has been breached. This was upheld more recently in *Saadi v Italy* (2009) 49 EHRR 30.

However, the court must be satisfied that the facts reveal a real risk of ill treatment in violation of Art 3, as opposed to a *mere possibility* (*Vilvarajah v United Kingdom* (1991) 14 EHRR 248).

The *Soering* principle can also apply even where the receiving state would not be in violation of Art 3, but nevertheless the applicant would be subjected to inhuman or degrading treatment (*D v United Kingdom* (1997) 24 EHRR 423 – return of applicant to the West Indies where there would be inadequate medical treatment to deal with his condition (he had contracted AIDS) constituted a violation of Art 3 by the UK). However, the court stressed that the decision was based on the very exceptional facts of the case (see now *N v United Kingdom* (2008) 47 EHRR 39 on not allowing the claim unless the suffering is intense).

Self-test questions

1. What obligation does Art 2 impose on states with respect to the right to life?
2. Is the death penalty now in violation of Articles 2 and 3?
3. When is it lawful under Art 2 for life to be intentionally taken away?
4. How has the European Court defined the terms 'torture' and 'inhuman and degrading treatment'?
5. What is the '*Soering*' principle and what is its importance with respect to the protection of human rights?

16.11 Article 4 – Prohibition of slavery and forced labour

ARTICLE

Art 4(1)
No one shall be held in slavery or servitude.

Art 4(2)
No one shall be required to perform forced or compulsory labour.

Article 4(1) prohibits slavery and servitude in absolute terms and no derogation is allowed under Art 15.

16.11.1 The prohibition of slavery and servitude

CASE EXAMPLE

Siliadin v France (2006) 43 EHRR 16

The applicant had been used as unpaid help by a French couple for four years. She claimed that this constituted slavery and servitude under Art 4.

The European Court held that this did not amount to 'slavery'; although she had lost her autonomy, there was insufficient evidence that her employers had exercised a genuine right of ownership over her. However, the court found that as she was a vulnerable and unofficial immigrant entirely dependent on her employers for all assistance, she had been held in servitude. The failure of domestic law to create a specific criminal offence against slavery, and the failure to secure a criminal conviction against her abusers for wrongfully using the services of a dependent person, meant that the state was in violation of its positive duty under Art 4.

16.11.2 Prohibition of forced or compulsory labour

Article 4(2) then guarantees freedom from forced or compulsory labour, which has been defined as unjust or oppressive work done against the will of the person causing avoidable hardship (*X v FRG* (1974) 46 CD 22). This aspect of Art 4 can be derogated from and is subject to a number of exceptions listed in Art 4(3):

■ 'forced or compulsory labour' does not include work required to be done in the ordinary course of detention or during conditional release from such detention.

■ Article 4(3) excludes any service of a military character, or in the case of conscientious objectors, service instead of such service (*Johansen v Norway* (44 DR 155 (1985))).

■ Article 4(3) exempts service exacted in the case of an emergency or calamity threatening the life or well-being of the community, and any work or service which forms part of normal civic obligations.

Note s 71 of the Coroners and Justice Act 2009 makes it a criminal offence to hold someone in slavery or servitude or to require them to carry out forced labour.

16.12 Article 5 – Liberty and security of the person

Art 5(1)
Everyone has the right to liberty and security of the person. No one shall be deprived of his liberty save in ... accordance with a procedure prescribed by law.

16.12.1 Scope of the article

Article 5 is concerned with the protection of an individual's liberty as opposed to a right of free movement, guaranteed under Art 2 of the Fourth Protocol (not ratified by the UK). However, a curfew or house arrest may amount to a deprivation of liberty (*Secretary of State for the Home Department v JJ and others* [2007] UKHL 45). Also Art 5 is not engaged by a claim relating to the conditions of lawful detention (*Winterwerp v Germany* (1979) 2 EHRR 387).

The right under Art 5 is subject to a number of exceptions contained in Art 1(a)–(f), below. Under Art 5(1) any interference will only be lawful if it is 'in accordance with a procedure prescribed by law' so must comply with principles of fairness and legality (see 16.6.1 above).

16.12.2 Lawful detention after conviction

Art 5(1)(a) provides for the lawful detention of a person after conviction by a competent court. Under this provision, any conviction must have a sufficient basis under domestic law (*Tsirlis and Kouloumpas v Greece* (1997) 25 EHRR 198) and there must be a sufficient connection between a finding of guilt by a competent *court* and any subsequent detention.

The European Court allows some exercise of administrative involvement in the detention process (*Van Droogenbroek v Belgium* (1982) 4 EHRR 443) provided there is a sufficient link with the original sentence.

Stafford v United Kingdom (2002) 35 EHRR 32

The applicant had been sentenced to life imprisonment for murder and after release committed a number of property offences. The Home Secretary refused to release him on the grounds that there was a risk of him committing property offences in the future.

The European Court held that there was an insufficient connection between imposing a mandatory life sentence for murder, and the subsequent recall and detention of that prisoner on the basis of perceived fears that he would commit crimes of a non-violent nature. Accordingly, there was a violation of Art 5(1).

Such executive involvement may also constitute a violation of Arts 5(4) and 6, below.

16.12.3 Lawful arrest or detention for non-compliance of a lawful court order

Article 5(1)(b) permits the arrest or detention of a person who has not complied with a court order when such arrest or detention is required for the fulfilment of an obligation that is prescribed by law.

This normally requires that a specific legal obligation has been, or is danger of being, breached (*Engel v Netherlands* (1976) 1 EHRR 647), although in *Steel v United Kingdom* (1998) 28 EHRR 603, the European Court held that the power to bind over an individual in order to keep the peace was compatible with Art 5, provided the applicant's conduct displayed some threat to the peace.

A detention by a court will not be unlawful simply because the decision to detain is overruled on appeal provided the initial court acted in good faith (*Benham v United Kingdom* (1996) 22 EHRR 293), unless it did not properly consider the law (*Beets and others v United Kingdom, The Times*, 10th March 2005).

16.12.4 Lawful detention following arrest

Article 5(1)(c) allows for the lawful arrest or detention of a person for bringing them before a competent legal authority, either on reasonable suspicion of them having committed an offence, or when it is necessary to prevent them committing an offence or fleeing after having done so.

Any arrest or detention must be in accordance with clear domestic law (*K-F v Germany* (1997) 26 EHRR 390), and in particular any arrest must be made on *reasonable* suspicion. This does not require evidence that would justify a conviction at trial or the bringing of a criminal charge (*O'Hara v United Kingdom* (2002) 34 EHRR 32), but the European Court has laid down strict requirements in order to justify deprivation of liberty on such grounds.

CASE EXAMPLE

Fox, Campbell and Hartley v United Kingdom (1990) 13 EHRR 157

The applicants were arrested under s 1 of the Northern Ireland (Emergency Provisions) Act 1978 on suspicion of being terrorists and then released without charge.

The European Court held that 'reasonable suspicion' under Art 5(1)(c) presupposes the existence of facts that would satisfy an objective observer that the person might have committed the offence. However, in respect of terrorism the test differs from that involved in conventional crime, provided the essence of reasonableness is not impaired. The government must provide at least some facts or information which were capable of showing that the arrested person was reasonably suspected of having committed the offence. (In this case the only evidence was that they had committed offences seven years previously, which was insufficient for the purposes of Art 5.)

16.12.5 Other lawful restrictions

Article 5 also provides for lawful detention in the following cases:

- The detention of a minor for the purpose of educational supervision or for the purpose of bringing him before a competent legal authority (Art 5(1)(d)).
- For the prevention of the spreading of infectious diseases, of persons of unsound mind, alcoholics or drug addicts or vagrants (Art 5(1)(e) and *Winterwerp v Germany* (1979) 2 EHRR 387).
- For the lawful arrest or detention of a person to prevent him from effecting an unauthorised entry into the country or to facilitate a person's deportation or extradition (Art 5(1)(f) and *Chahal v United Kingdom* (1997) 23 EHRR 413). In *A v United Kingdom* (2009) 49 EHRR 29 the European Court held that the detention of foreign terrorist suspects was not done for the purpose of eventual deportation and thus was in breach of article 5.

16.12.6 Right to be informed of reasons for arrest and charge

Article 5(2) provides that everyone who is arrested shall be informed properly, in a language which he understands, of the reasons for his arrest and of any charge against him. An individual need not be supplied with full reasons for arrest at the actual time of that arrest provided it is done promptly in all the circumstances.

Murray (Margaret) v United Kingdom (1994) 19 EHRR 193

The applicant was arrested under s 14 of the Northern Ireland (Emergency Provisions) Act 1978 on suspicion of having committed a terrorist offence and informed of the fact and reasons of arrest after two hours.

It was held that although the reasons for her arrest had not been brought to her attention at the time of her arrest, she had been sufficiently notified during her subsequent interrogation and an interval of a few hours did not fall outside the definition of promptness as required by Art 5(2).

16.12.7 The right to be brought promptly before a judge for trial or release

Article 5(3) provides that everyone arrested or detained under Art 5 must be brought *promptly* before a judge or other officer authorised by law to exercise judicial power, that person then being entitled either to trial within a reasonable time, or to release (either absolutely or on conditions) pending trial.

The relevant 'officer' must be independent of the executive and of any parties to the action (*Assenov v Bulgaria* (1999) 28 EHRR 652), and the person must, in all the circumstances, be brought before the relevant judicial authority 'promptly'.

CASE EXAMPLE

Brogan v United Kingdom (1989) 11 EHRR 117

The applicants had been arrested on suspicion of terrorism and had been detained for periods between four and a half days and six days and eventually released without charge.

The European Court held that even the shortest of the periods in this case was inconsistent with the notion of promptness as required by Art 5(3). Even in the context of terrorism, such a period seriously weakened the essence of the procedural right guaranteed by that provision.

Article 5(3) does not preclude pre-trial detention provided there are sufficient safeguards (*Caballero v United Kingdom* (2000) 30 EHRR 643).

16.12.8 Right to challenge lawfulness of detention

Article 5(4) of the Convention provides that everyone deprived of their liberty by arrest or detention shall be entitled to take proceedings by which the lawfulness of their detention shall be decided speedily by a court and their release ordered if the detention is not lawful. This is the case even if the original detention was lawful, and for Art 5(4) to be complied with the original court order must be linked sufficiently with any subsequent detention (*De Wilde, Ooms and Versyp v Belgium* (1971) 1 EHRR 373).

Where a person is deprived of their liberty by the executive that person has a right of access to a court or court-like body in order to question the legality of that detention, including the evidence on which the decision was made (*Chahal v United Kingdom* (1997) 23 EHRR 413). Further, any review must not be limited to judging simple legality, and must assess the necessity and proportionality of the detention (*Winterwerp v Netherlands* (1979) 2 EHRR 387).

Article 5(4) has been used to challenge the legality of domestic law allowing the Home Secretary to determine the release of life sentence prisoners and the European Court has held that such powers were incompatible with both the separation of powers and the Convention (*Thynne, Wilson and Gunnell v United Kingdom* (1990) 13 EHRR 666 (discretionary lifers) and *Stafford v United Kingdom* (2002) 35 EHRR 32 (mandatory lifers)). In addition, such prisoners are entitled to a review of their detention by a court-like body at reasonably regular intervals (*Oldham v United Kingdom* (2001) 31 EHRR 34).

In *A v United Kingdom* (2009) 49 EHRR 29 the European Court held that there had been a violation of article 5(4) because the detainees had been deprived of their right to effectively challenge the legality of their detention because the closed evidence relied upon by the Secretary of State had not been made available to them.

16.12.9 Right to compensation for breach of Article 5

Article 5(5) provides that everyone who has been the victim of an arrest or detention in contravention of Art 5 shall have an enforceable right to compensation. The provision is contained within s 9(3) of the Human Rights Act 1998 (see Chapter 17).

The provision guarantees compensation whether the detention was lawful or otherwise under domestic law (*Brogan v United Kingdom* (1989) 11 EHRR 117 and *A v United Kingdom* (above)) and is supplemented by Art 13, which guarantees an effective remedy for violation of Convention rights (see below).

16.13 Article 6 – The right to a fair and public hearing

ARTICLE

Art 6(1)
In the determination of his civil rights and obligations or of any criminal charge against him, everyone is entitled to a fair and public hearing within a reasonable time by an independent and impartial tribunal established by law.

16.13.1 The scope of Article 6

Article 6 guarantees the right to a hearing before an impartial and unbiased court or tribunal, and specifically a number of procedural rights before and during the trial.

Article 6 applies to all proceedings where the applicant is either facing a 'criminal charge', or where that person's 'civil rights and obligations' are subject to determination.

With respect to the term 'civil rights and obligations' it is not necessary that both parties to the proceedings are private individuals (or that the proceedings are classed as public – for example judicial review proceedings), provided the result of the proceedings were decisive of private rights and obligations (*Ringeisen v Austria* (1971) 1 EHRR 455). For example, in *Tinnelly v United Kingdom* (1998) 27 EHRR 249 the European Court held that a right not to be discriminated against in the provision of contracts under domestic legislation was a 'civil right' even though the source of the right was statutory.

Whether the proceedings constitute a criminal charge will depend on how the offence has been classified in domestic law, the nature of the offence, and the severity of the punishment (*Engel v Netherlands* (1976) 1 EHRR 647). Prison disciplinary proceedings amount to a criminal charge where the penalty is sufficiently serious and the offence sufficiently criminal in nature (*Ezeh and Connors v United Kingdom* (2004) 39 EHRR 691).

16.13.2 The right of access to the courts

The European Court held in *Golder v United Kingdom* (1976) 1 EHRR 524 that the right of access to the courts is implicit in Art 6:

JUDGMENT

'Article 6(1) of the Convention was not limited to guaranteeing the right to a fair trial in legal proceedings that are already pending, but secures in addition a right of access to the courts to every person wishing to commence an action in order to have his civil rights and obligations determined … the Court could scarcely conceive of the rule of law without there being a possibility of having access to the courts.'

This includes the obligation of the state to provide facilities so to allow individuals to seek legal redress, for example legal aid (*Airey v Ireland* (1979) 2 EHRR 305). The right may be restricted to certain persons and on grounds of security (*Campbell v United Kingdom* (1992) 15 EHRR 137).

In addition, domestic law must not place procedural obstacles in the way of the parties, precluding claims irrespective of their merits.

CASE EXAMPLE

Osman v United Kingdom (2000) 29 EHRR 245

The applicants brought civil proceedings against the police in negligence but the domestic courts held that no action could lie against the police with respect to the investigation and suppression of crime.

It was The European Court held that the blanket application of that rule unjustifiably deprived the applicants of their right to have the merits of her civil action tried before a court. The application of the rule in this case constituted a disproportionate restriction on the applicant's rights under Art 6.

However, that case is now regarded as misguided and it is not now regarded as unlawful for *substantive* domestic law to limit the success of a particular legal action (*Z and others v United Kingdom* (2002) 34 EHRR 3 and *Smith v Chief Constable of Sussex* [2008] UKHL 50), although such a rule might violate Art 13 (see below).

16.13.3 The right to a public hearing before an impartial court or tribunal

Under Art 6 an individual is entitled to a trial before an impartial and unbiased court and this means a court that is free from the *appearance* of bias (*Findlay v United Kingdom* (1997) 24 EHRR 221). This includes freedom from the appearance of executive and political bias.

CASE EXAMPLE

McGonnnel v United Kingdom (2000) 30 EHRR 289

The Deputy Bailiff of Guernsey, a senior judge and President of a number of state committees, adjudicated on the applicant's planning permission application.

It was held that there had been a violation of Art 6. That person's direct involvement in the passage of legislation or of executive rules was capable of casting doubt on his impartiality and thus was in violation of Art 6.

- ■ Executive adjudication is not incompatible with Art 6 provided such decisions are subject to appropriate judicial review (*Bryan v United Kingdom* (1995) 21 EHRR 342).
- ■ Article 6 can be violated where there is evidence of bias from a jury (*Sander v United Kingdom* (2001) 31 EHRR 44).
- ■ Article 6 guarantees the right to a fair sentence (*V and T v United Kingdom* (2000) 30 EHRR 121 and *R (Anderson) v Secretary of State for the Home Department* [2002] UKHL 46).
- ■ Article 6 states that everyone is entitled to a fair and *public* hearing and that judgment shall be pronounced publicly, although it is lawful to limit the open and public nature of the proceedings in order to protect the rights of the participants, or justice in general (*V and T v United Kingdom* (2000) 30 EHRR 121).
- ■ Article 6(1) guarantees that an individual receives a fair trial within a *reasonable time*. This applies to the length of the judicial proceedings, including appeals, and what amounts to a reasonable time depends on all the circumstances of the case (*Robins v United Kingdom* (1997) 26 EHRR 527).

16.13.4 The right to effective participation in the trial

Article 6(1) implicitly guarantees the right to put legal arguments before the court in support of one's case. This right is supplemented by the right of legal assistance, contained in Art 6(3)(c) (see 16.13.6 below).

Any restriction of this right must be proportionate and necessary and ensure a basic right to a fair trial.

CASE EXAMPLE

P, C and S v United Kingdom (2002) 35 EHRR 31

The applicants (a mother and father of a child who was felt to be in danger from the mother) were not legally represented in the relevant care order or adoption proceedings.

The European Court held that although courts had to strike a balance between the interests of the parents and the welfare of the child, the refusal of the domestic courts to defer the proceedings and to allow the applicants to obtain legal representation prevented the applicants from putting forward their case in a proper and effective manner.

Equally, *both* parties should be able to present any relevant evidence before the court in an equal manner (*Rowe and Davis v United Kingdom* (2000) 30 EHRR 1 – refusal to order disclosure of a document that the prosecution had provided to the court during a murder trial was in violation of Art 6). However, exclusionary rules are not unlawful provided they do not interfere with the basic right to a fair trial (*Jasper and Fitt v United Kingdom* (2000) 30 EHRR 97).

The use of unlawfully obtained evidence may lead to a violation of Art 6, but will not do so in all cases. Accordingly, in *Khan v United Kingdom* (2001) 31 EHRR 45 the European Court held that the admission of evidence obtained in breach of Art 8 did not violate the applicant's right to a fair trial within Art 6 because the applicant had been given an opportunity to question the admissibility of the evidence and the domestic courts had considered whether its inclusion would cause substantive unfairness.

For Art 6 to be complied with the individual should be aware of the nature of the charge or other proceedings and must be allowed to participate constructively in them (*V and T v United Kingdom* (2000) 30 EHRR 121 – subjection of 11-year-old defendants to an adult trial violated Art 6). Specifically, Art 6(3)(a) provides that every person has the right to be informed promptly, in a language which he understands and in detail, of the nature and cause of the accusation made against him (*Broziek v Italy* (1989) 12 EHRR 371), and Art 6(3)(e) guarantees right to have the free legal assistance of an interpreter if he cannot understand or speak the language used in court.

16.13.5 The presumption of innocence and the rule against self-incrimination

Article 6(2) states that everyone charged with a criminal offence shall be presumed innocent until proved guilty according to law and in conjunction with Art 6(1) protects an individual from self-incrimination.

CASE EXAMPLE

Saunders v United Kingdom (1996) 23 EHRR 313

The applicant had been required to answer questions put to him by the Department of Trade and Industry in the course of their administrative investigations. The answers were used as evidence in a subsequent criminal trial where he was found guilty.

The European Court held that the use of such evidence by the prosecution infringed the applicant's right against self-incrimination. In this case the prosecution had made use of these statements to question the applicant's honesty and integrity and it was irrelevant that the statements were not self-incriminating.

Although Art 6(2) implicitly recognises the right to silence, that right is not absolute (*Murray v United Kingdom* (1996) 22 EHRR 29), provided the applicant receives a fair hearing in all the circumstances (*Condron v United Kingdom* (2001) 31 EHRR 1 – violation of Art 6 when the trial judge had impliedly directed the jury to draw an adverse inference from the applicant's silence).

16.13.6 The right to legal assistance

Article 6(3)(c) states that everyone has the right to defend themselves against any criminal charge in person or through legal assistance of one's own choosing. In addition, if the defendant has not got sufficient means to pay for such assistance, he has the right to be given it free where the interests of justice demand it. Whether the defendant is entitled to free legal assistance depends on all the circumstances, including the complexity of the case (*Steel and Morris v United Kingdom* (2005) 41 EHRR 22 – breach of Art 6 when protestors not able to effectively defend a lengthy defamation case brought by multi-national coroporation).

CASE EXAMPLE

Granger v United Kingdom (1990) 12 EHRR 469

The applicant, a man of limited intelligence, had been charged with a criminal offence and had been refused legal aid and thus not provided with counsel on appeal. The applicant had notes from his solicitor but he clearly did not understand them when he read them out in court.

The European Court held that Art 6(1) and 6(3)(c) should be read together, and where it was apparent that a fair hearing could not take place without legal advice, then both provisions would be violated. In the present case, having regard to the applicant's intelligence and the complexity of the case he should have been given legal aid.

Article 6(3)(c) also guarantees the right to legal assistance during detention and interrogation where justice so requires (*Brennan v United Kingdom* (2002) 34 EHRR 18).

16.13.7 The right to call and question witnesses

Article 6(3)(d) gives an individual the right to examine, or have examined, witnesses against him and to obtain the attendance and examination of witnesses on his behalf. This includes the right to confront witnesses (*Saidi v United Kingdom* (1993) 17 EHRR 251).

Article 6 does not guarantee an unlimited right to call and examine witnesses, the number of which remains within the discretion of the domestic courts provided the applicant receives a fair trial in the round (*Van Mechelen v The Netherlands* (1997) 25 EHRR 647).

16.14 Article 7 – Prohibition of retrospective criminal law and penalties

ARTICLE

Art 7(1)

No one shall be held guilty of any criminal offence on account of any act or omission which did not constitute a criminal offence under national or international law at the time when it was committed. Nor shall a heavier penalty be imposed than the one that was applicable at the time that the criminal offence was committed.

16.14.1 The scope of Article 7

Article 7 prohibits retrospective criminal law and penalties, and is fundamental to the rule of law and due process. Accordingly, under Art 15(2) a state cannot derogate from Art 7.

The article only applies where the applicant is found guilty of a criminal offence (see *Engel v Netherlands* (1976) 1 EHRR 706, discussed above), and lays down two basic principles:

- No person shall be guilty of an offence for an act which at the time of its commission was not an offence in domestic or international law.
- No person should be subjected to a heavier penalty than the one which existed at that time.

CASE EXAMPLE

Welch v United Kingdom (1995) 20 EHRR 247

The applicant was convicted of drug offences and as part of the sentence the trial judge imposed a confiscation order under the Drug Trafficking Act 1986, which came into force after the applicant's arrest but before his conviction.

The European Court held that the confiscation was clearly retrospective as it was made in respect of offences committed before the relevant provision came into force. Whether the confiscation proceedings constituted a 'penalty' depended on whether the measure was imposed following conviction for a criminal offence, the nature and purpose of the measure, its characterisation, and its severity. Taking into account a combination of punitive elements involved in this measure, the proceedings came within Art 7.

16.14.2 The exceptions to Article 7

Article 7 will not be violated where the relevant law has been developed in a foreseeable manner and then applied to the detriment of the defendant.

CASE EXAMPLE

SW and CR v United Kingdom (1995) 21 EHRR 404

The applicants had been convicted of rape as a result of the domestic courts' ruling that a husband could no longer rely on the defence of 'marital rape' (*R v R* [1991] 4 All ER 481).

The European Court held that there had been no violation of Art 7. The development of the law in this case, whereby such immunity was lost, had been foreseeable and consistent and the applicants must have foreseen that their act was unlawful at the time they committed it.

In addition, Art 7(2) states that Art 7 does not prejudice the trial and punishment of any person for any act or omission which, at the time it was committed, was criminal according to the general principles of law recognised by civilised nations (for example torture or 'war crimes').

ACTIVITY

Self-test questions

1. What rights does Art 5 of the Convention provide to the individual and what is the importance of those rights?
2. What exceptions to the right to liberty does Art 5 allow, and what are the restrictions on those exceptions?
3. What values does Art 6 of the Convention seek to uphold?
4. Name five specific rights that Art 6 bestows on the individual.
5. What does Art 7 of the Convention prohibit, and why?

16.15 Article 8 – Right to private and family life

ARTICLE

Art 8(1)

Everyone has the right to respect for his private and family life, his home and his correspondence.

16.15.1 The scope of Article 8

Article 8 provides the right to *respect* for private and family life, home and correspondence, including freedom from interference with those rights by both state actors and, in certain cases, private individuals (*X and Y v Netherlands* (1985) 8 EHRR 235). Thus, Art 8 can have a 'horizontal' effect, and the domestic courts have adopted this approach in developing the private law of confidentiality (*Douglas v Hello! Ltd* [2001] 2 WLR 992).

- Article 8 imposes a positive obligation on the state to ensure the enjoyment of those rights (*Marckx v Belgium* (1979) 2 EHRR 330).
- The right to private life includes the right to physical integrity, to private space, to communicate privately with others, to access personal information, and the right to private sexual life.
- In particular Art 8 provides freedom from press and other intrusions into privacy (*Von Hannover v Germany* (2005) 40 EHRR 1 and *Peck v United Kingdom* (2003) 36 EHRR 31).
- Article 8 is a conditional right and interferences are permitted under Art 8(2) provided they are in accordance with law and necessary in a democratic society in the interests of national security, public safety or the economic well-being of the country, for the prevention of disorder or crime, for the protection of health or morals, or for the protection of the rights and freedoms of others.
- Such restrictions will be invalid if they lack a proper legal basis (*Malone v United Kingdom* (1984) 7 EHRR 14).

16.15.2 The right to respect for private life

Article 8 covers privacy and confidentiality and the right to be let alone, but the European Court has also recognised the right to develop and establish relationships with others (*Niemietz v Germany* (1992) 16 EHRR 97). The court has also accepted that a private life can be enjoyed in the employment sphere (*Halford v United Kingdom* (1997) 24 EHRR 523).

Article 8 protects a person's right to physical and moral integrity, and a state owes a positive duty to protect those interests from attack from both state officials and other individuals (*X and Y v The Netherlands* (1985) 8 EHRR 235). Equally, the European Court has also held that the term private life protects an individual's health (*McGinley and Egan v United Kingdom* (1998) 27 EHRR 1).

The European Court will be reluctant to allow interference with private sexual life on the grounds of public morality or disapproval (*Dudgeon v United Kingdom* (1982) 4 EHRR 149 and *Smith and Grady v United Kingdom* (2000) 29 EHRR 493), but will permit it in cases where there is a sound reason for enforcing morality and protecting the rights of others (*Laskey, Jaggard and Brown v United Kingdom* (1997) 24 EHRR 39 – conviction of voluntary sado-masochistic acts permitted by Art 8(2)).

The court has also used Art 8 (and Art 12) to recognise the private rights of transsexuals (*Goodwin v United Kingdom* (2002) 35 EHRR 18), leading to the passing of the Gender Recognition Act 2004.

16.15.3 The right to respect for family life

Along with Art 12, guaranteeing the right to marry, Art 8 protects the right to *family* life and the European Court has extended the meaning of family beyond the marriage relationship (*X, Y and Z v United Kingdom* (1997) 24 EHRR 143 and *Goodwin v United Kingdom*, above). However, Art 8 does not guarantee the right to divorce (*Johnston v Ireland* (1986) 9 EHRR 203).

Although restrictions are permitted under Art 8(2), the European Court will have to be satisfied that there are pressing reasons for such interference and that such reasons are not arbitrary.

CASE EXAMPLE

Dickson v United Kingdom (2008) 46 EHRR 41

A prisoner had sought permission from the Home Secretary to allow his wife to be artificially inseminated by his sperm so as to found a family. The request was refused on policy reasons (that the interests of the child would not be furthered by such a birth as the relationship with his wife had not been tested outside prison).

The Grand Chamber held that the Home Secretary's policy did not give sufficient weight to the right to family life of the prisoner and his wife and that it placed too much onus on the applicant to justify his request.

16.15.4 The right to respect for the home

Article 8 guarantees the right to respect for the home, protecting that right from intrusions by the state (*Akdivar v Turkey* (1996) 1 BHRC 137). The right is also related to Art 1 of the First Protocol (see 16.20 below) protecting the right to property.

Such a right can be breached in the public interest, although the European Court will require a strong justification for any violation (*Gillow v United Kingdom* (1986) 11 EHRR 335). Thus any planning laws must strike a correct balance between the public interest and the enjoyment of private and family life (*Buckley v United Kingdom* (1996) 23 EHRR 101).

Despite the fundamental character of this right, the European Court will offer each state a wide margin of appreciation in balancing these respective rights.

CASE EXAMPLE

Hatton v United Kingdom (2003) 37 EHRR 28

Residents living on the flight path of Heathrow airport complained that the introduction of a scheme to regulate flights had increased night-time noise and interfered with their private and family lives and their homes.

The Grand Chamber of the European Court held that the authorities had achieved a proper balance between the rights of the residents to peaceful enjoyment of their homes and their family lives in allocating the number of night flights at Heathrow. Only a limited number of people were affected by the noise and house prices had not devalued, thus giving those people the opportunity to move.

16.15.5 The right to respect for correspondence

Article 8 protects the right to communicate with others, including correspondence with friends and family (*Silver v United Kingdom* (1983) 5 EHRR 347) and in a business context (*Halford v United Kingdom* (1997) 24 EHRR 523).

The European Court has afforded special protection with respect to legal correspondence, which also engages the right of access to the courts (*Golder v United Kingdom* (1976) 1 EHRR 524 – refusal of permission for prisoner to contact a solicitor for the purpose of bringing a civil action against a prison officer constituted a disproportionate interference with the prisoner's Art 8 rights and also constituted an impermissible breach of his right of access to the courts under Art 6).

16.16 Article 9 – Freedom of thought, conscience and religion

ARTICLE

Art 9(1)

Everyone has the right to freedom of thought, conscience and religion; this right includes freedom to change his religion or belief and freedom, either alone or in community with others and in public or private, to manifest his religion or belief, in worship, teaching, practice and observance.

16.16.1 The scope of Article 9

The right to freedom of thought, conscience and religion is an absolute right in the sense that it is not subject to the restrictions laid down in para 2 of the article, which only apply to the manifestation of those beliefs.

Article 9 protects an individual from persecution on grounds of his beliefs and is not limited to religious beliefs or convictions (*Arrowsmith v United Kingdom* (1978) 3 EHRR 218 – pacifism was protected by Art 9). However Art 9 does not apply to every individually held opinion or conviction.

CASE EXAMPLE

Pretty v United Kingdom (2002) 35 EHRR 1

The applicant claimed that the state had interfered with her beliefs under Art 9 by denying her the right to die with the assistance of her husband.

The European Court held that the applicant's views on euthanasia did not involve a manifestation of a 'religion or belief, through worship, teaching, practice or observance'. The term 'practice' did not cover each act that was motivated or influenced by a religion or belief. (The applicant's views engaged her ideas of personal autonomy, under Art 8, but such a right was overtaken by the need to protect the rights of others.) Note, in *Purdy v Director of Public Prosecutions* [2009] UKHL 45 the House of Lords held that clear guidelines should be published with respect to the prosecution policy under the Suicide Act 1961.

Article 9 imposes a positive obligation on the state to allow individuals to enjoy their beliefs peacefully and without interference (*Dubowska and Skup v Poland* (1997) 24 EHRR CD 75), including enjoying these rights in employment, subject to necessary restrictions on the manifestation of such rights (*Ahmed v United Kingdom* (1981) 4 EHRR 126).

The European Court has not insisted that domestic law pass and maintain a law of blasphemy (*Choudhury v United Kingdom* (1991) 12 HRLJ 172). The English law of blasphemy was abolished by s 79 of the Criminal Justice and Immigration Act 2008.

16.16.2 Permissible restrictions

The right to manifest one's religion or beliefs is subject to limitations that are prescribed by law and necessary in a democratic society in the interests of public safety, for the protection of public order, health or morals, or for the protection of the rights and freedoms of others.

CASE EXAMPLE

Sahin v Turkey (2004) 19 BHRC 590

The applicant had been refused permission to wear a Muslim headscarf and was suspended from University for non-compliance of that order.

The Grand Chamber of the European Court held that the ban was proportionate to the protection of the rights of others and of public order, being necessary to preserve secularism in the country's educational institutions. Article 9 did not always guarantee the right to behave in a manner governed by religious beliefs and did not confer a right to disregard justifiable rules.

See also *(R) Begum v Denbigh High School* [2006] UKHL 15 (see below), where the House of Lords held that a school uniform policy banning full Muslim dress was not in breach of a schoolgirl's Convention rights.

16.17 Article 10 – Freedom of expression

ARTICLE

> Art 10(1)
> Everyone has the right to freedom of expression. This right shall include freedom to hold opinions and to receive and impart information and ideas without interference by public authority and regardless of frontiers ...

16.17.1 The scope of Article 10

Article 10 guarantees the right to impart information and ideas, and the right of others to receive them. It is viewed as fundamental to both democracy and individual freedom by the European Court of Human Rights (*Handyside v United Kingdom* (1976) 1 EHRR 737).

Article 10 covers both commercial speech (*Markt Intern Velag Gmbh and Klaus Beermann v Germany* (1989) 12 EHRR 161) and obscene and indecent speech (*Handyside* (above)), although the European Court has accepted that the state will be given a wider margin of appreciation to regulate such speech.

In contrast, the European Court places greater significance on the dissemination of information and ideas in the public interest (*Sunday Times v United Kingdom* (1979) 2 EHRR 245, protecting such speech in particular from prior restraint (*Observer and Guardian v United Kingdom* (1991) 14 EHRR 153)).

The European Court has also given greater weight to press and media freedom.

CASE EXAMPLE

Jersild v Denmark (1994) 19 EHRR 1

A broadcasting company had been fined for aiding and abetting the dissemination of unlawful racist speech by broadcasting their views as part of a documentary.

The European Court held that although the views of the group were not protected by Art 10, punishing the applicant for statements made by that group during an interview was a serious restriction on the duty of the press to discuss matters of public interest.

Article 10 applies to restrictions on freedom of expression and does not provide a general right of freedom of information (*Leander v Sweden* (1987) 9 EHRR 343). However, refusal of access to private information could constitute a violation of Art 8.

16.17.2 Restrictions on freedom of expression – Article 10(2)

Article 10(2) provides that the exercise of the rights contained in para 1 carry with it duties and responsibilities and is therefore subject to restrictions and penalties that are 'prescribed by law,' and necessary in a democratic society for the furtherance of a number of listed legitimate aims.

In such cases, therefore, the court has to consider whether the need for the legal restriction is sufficiently pressing and whether any penalty or condition is reasonable and proportionate.

CASE EXAMPLE

Von Hannover v Germany (2005) 40 EHRR 1

The former Princess Caroline of Monaco complained that persistent photographs taken of her by the 'paparazzi' was in violation of her rights under Art 8.

The European Court held that there had been an interference with the applicant's privacy rights and that there was no overriding public interest in the photographs so as to justify that violation on grounds of freedom of expression and the public right to know.

16.18 Article 11 – Freedom of assembly and association

ARTICLE

Art 11(1)
Everyone has the right to freedom of peaceful assembly and to freedom of association with others, including the right to form and to join trade unions for the protection of his interests.

16.18.1 The scope of Article 11

Article 11 of the European Convention provides that everyone has the right of association with others (including the right to join a trade union) and of *peaceful* assembly. The Article is conditional and subject to restrictions provided they are prescribed by law and necessary in a democratic society in the interests of national security or public safety, for the prevention of disorder or crime, for the protection of health or morals or for the protection of the rights and freedoms of others (Art 11(2)).

In addition, Art 11(2) allows lawful restrictions on members of the armed forces, of the police or of the administration of the state (*Council of Civil Service Unions and others v United Kingdom* (1987) 50 DR 228).

16.18.2 Freedom of association

The right of association specifically includes the right to form trade unions and the state has an obligation to ensure that this right is enjoyed by individuals even against private employers (*Swedish Engine Drivers' Union v Sweden* (1976) 1 EHRR 617). Although there is no right to insist on collective bargaining with employers, union members are entitled not to be discriminated against on grounds of their membership (*Wilson and others v United Kingdom* (2002) 35 EHRR 20).

Article 11, together with Art 9, also provides the negative right not to join a trade union (*Young Webster and James v United Kingdom* (1982) 4 EHRR 38), thus protecting non-unionists from discriminatory treatment.

The European Court has also held that the term 'association' covers various groups, including political parties (*United Communist Party of Turkey v Turkey* (1998) 26 EHRR 121). However, it does not include gatherings for entirely social purposes (*Anderson v United Kingdom* (1998) 25 EHRR CD 172).

The right of association is conditional and subject to lawful and necessary restrictions. However, proscription of a group would only be allowed in the most exceptional cases (*United Communist Party of Turkey v Turkey* (1998) 26 EHRR 121) – the banning of a group merely because it used the word communist in its name could not be justified in relation to any legitimate aim.

CASE EXAMPLE

Refha Partisi Erbakan Kazan and Tekdal v Turkey (2003) 37 EHRR 1

The applicant's party had been dissolved by the Turkish Constitutional Court on the ground that it had become a centre of activities against the principles of secularism.

The European Court held that political parties who incite others to use violence or support political aims that were inconsistent with democracy and the rights and freedoms of democracy could not rely on Art 11. In this case the measure was necessary and proportionate.

Such a finding may be strengthened by the state's reliance on Art 17 of the Convention, which provides that nothing in the Convention gives any person or group any right to engage in any activity or perform any act aimed at the destruction of any of the rights and freedoms in the Convention.

16.18.3 Freedom of peaceful assembly

Article 11 of the European Convention contains both a negative right not to have one's peaceful assembly interfered with, but also imposes a positive obligation on the state to ensure that everyone can enjoy that right (*Platform Arzte fur dan Laeben v Austria* (1988) 13 EHRR 204).

The Convention protects the right to *peaceful* assembly, excluding assemblies that use, advocate or incite violence. Such assemblies would also conflict with Art 17 of the Convention, above. Moreover, the alleged restriction must actually interfere with the right of assembly, as opposed to curtailing one of its activities (*R (Countryside Alliance) v Attorney-General* [2007] UKHL 52 – the ban on hunting did not stop the group assembling, but simply outlawed a particular activity of that assembly).

As Art 11 is a conditional right, Art 11(2) also allows restrictions on peaceful assemblies, provided those restrictions are legal, necessary and proportionate to legitimate aims such as the preservation of public order, the protection of the rights of others and the prevention of crime. In this respect the European Court has given the domestic law and authorities a wide margin of appreciation in balancing the right of peaceful assembly with those aims, and may even permit the banning of meeting in advance (*Rai, Allmond and Negotiate Now v United Kingdom* (1995) 19 EHRR CD 93).

The European Court will give the police authorities a wide discretion when dealing with alleged breaches of the peace (*Chorherr v Austria* (1993) 17 EHRR 358), although interferences must not be disproportionate to achieving any legitimate aim (*Ollinger v Austria* (2008) 46 EHRR 38).

CASE EXAMPLE

Steel v United Kingdom (1998) 28 EHRR 603

Two demonstrators had been arrested and bound over for breach of the peace when handing out leaflets outside a conference.

The European Court held that on the evidence the police had no grounds for believing that the applicant's conduct would cause a breach of the peace. Consequently their arrest and subsequent restraint was an unlawful and disproportionate interference with their right to liberty and freedom of expression and assembly.

16.19 Article 12 – The right to marry

ARTICLE

Art 12
Men and women of marriageable age have the right to marry and found a family, according to the national laws governing the exercise of that right.

16.19.1 The scope of Article 12

Article 12 complements Art 8 of the Convention (the right to private and family life), and imposes a negative duty on the state not to interfere with the enjoyment of the right to marry. It does not guarantee the right to divorce (*Johnston v Ireland* (1986) 9 EHRR 203), but if national law does allow divorce, it must not place unreasonable restrictions on a person's right to remarry (*F v Switzerland* (1987) 10 EHRR 411).

Although Art 12 leaves the right to marry and found a family at the discretion of national law, any conditions or restrictions on such a right must be necessary and proportionate (see below).

16.19.2 Restrictions on the right to marry

The European Court will offer Member States a reasonably wide margin of appreciation with respect to an individual's right to marry, although any restriction must not be arbitrary or destroy the essence of that right (*F v Switzerland* (1987) 10 EHRR 411).

CASE EXAMPLE

B and L v United Kingdom (2006) 42 EHRR 11

The applicants – former father and daughter-in law – were prohibited by domestic law from marrying unless both former spouses were deceased and claimed that this contravened Art 12.

The European Court held that the legal prohibition of such marriages was a disproportionate interference with the right to marry. Although there was a legitimate aim – the protection of family life and of children's interests – the fact that such relationships did not establish criminal liability suggested that there was no pressing need for such prohibition.

Domestic law prohibiting prisoners from marrying while incarcerated was held to destroy the essence of Art 12 (*Hamer v United Kingdom* (1982) 4 EHRR 139) and in *Goodwin v United Kingdom* (2002) 35 EHRR 18 the European Court recognised the right of transsexuals to marry in accordance with their new gender.

16.20 Article 1 of the First Protocol – the right to property

ARTICLE

Art 1

Every natural or legal person is entitled to the peaceful enjoyment of his possessions. No one shall be deprived of his possessions except in the public interest and subject to the conditions provided for by law and by the general principles of international law.

16.20.1 The scope of the right to property

This article guarantees the right to peaceful enjoyment of possessions (both real and personal property), and complements Art 8 of the Convention, guaranteeing respect for family life and the home.

The article makes the enjoyment of this right subject to the rules of domestic law and further states that it does not impair the right of a state to enforce such laws as it deems necessary to control the use of property in accordance with the general interest or to secure the payment of taxes or other contributions or penalties.

16.20.2 Lawful restrictions on the right to property

Any such restriction must be in accordance with law and constitute a necessary and proportionate measure, and the court will attempt to strike a fair balance between the interests of the community in general and the protection of the individual's property rights (*Sporrong and Lonnroth v Sweden* (1982) 5 EHRR 35).

The court will provide each state with a wide margin of appreciation in this respect (*James v United Kingdom* (1986) 6 EHRR 123; *National and Provincial Building Society v United Kingdom* (1997) 25 EHRR 127), but will protect the individual from arbitrary or unfair interferences.

CASE EXAMPLE

Pye (Oxford) Ltd v United Kingdom (2006) 46 EHRR 45 (Grand Chamber)

Landowners had lost possession of their land by virtue of the domestic rules on adverse possession.

The European Court (2008) 43 EHRR 3 held that the law at that time provided inadequate protection to the true owners, particularly as there was no statutory right for them to be notified of the possessor's intention to claim those rights. However, the Grand Chamber reversed that decision stating that the law achieved a proportionate balance between the conflicting interests.

16.21 Article 2 of the First Protocol – the right to education

ARTICLE

Art 2

No person shall be denied the right to education. In the exercise of any functions which it assumes in relation to education and to teaching, the State shall respect the right of parents to ensure such education and teaching in conformity with their own religious and philosophical convictions.

Article 2 of the first protocol provides the individual with the right to enjoy the means of instruction that is provided by the state at any given time. The right is limited and there is no obligation on the part of the state to establish or fund any particular type of educational institution (*The Belgian Linguistic Case* (1968) 1 EHRR 252). The UK government has made a reservation with respect to guaranteeing parents' rights, restricting its obligations to the provision of efficient instruction and training and the avoidance of unreasonable public expenditure.

In addition, the Article complements the rights to private and family life (under Art 8) and the right to religion (under Art 9) by providing parents with the right to have their children taught in conformity with their religious and philosophical convictions.

CASE EXAMPLE

Campbell and Cosans v United Kingdom (1982) 4 EHRR 293

The applicants claimed that the threat of corporal punishment to their children constituted a violation of their Convention right to respect for their philosophical convictions.

The European Court held that although there had been no breach of Art 3 (because the children had not been punished or threatened with punishment), there had been a violation of Art 2 of the First Protocol by subjecting the children to the regime of corporal punishment against the wishes of the parents.

(Note, there is no corresponding right to insist that one's child is subjected to corporal punishment *(R (Williamson) v Secretary of State for Employment* [2005] UKHL 15), see section 17.10.)

16.22 Article 3 – the right to free elections

ARTICLE

Art 3

The High Contracting Parties undertake to hold free elections at reasonable intervals by secret ballot, under conditions which will ensure the free expression of the people in the choice of the legislature.

16.22.1 The scope of the right to vote

The article imposes an obligation on each Member State to hold free elections, and thus provides a right to the general public to have such elections. Also, the European Court has held that the article provides individuals with the right to vote and the right to stand for election to the legislature (*Mathieu-Mohin and Clerfast v Belgium* (1988) 10 EHRR 1).

An individual also has the right to vote in non-national elections (*Matthews v United Kingdom* (1999) 28 EHRR 361 – exclusion from voting in the elections to the European Parliament violated Art 3).

16.22.2 Limitations on the right to vote

The right to vote and stand for election is subject to implied limitations and domestic law can restrict it provided the very essence of the right to free elections is not undermined (*Mathieu-Mohin v Belgium* (1988)). The European Court has considered the legality of depriving prisoners of the right to vote (*Hirst v United Kingdom* (No 2) (2006) 42 EHRR 41(see section 9.6.3)), and the government is considering reforming the law to allow certain prisoners with shorter sentences the right to vote.

16.23 Articles 13 and 14 – the right to an effective remedy and freedom from discrimination

To facilitate the enjoyment of the above rights the European Convention guarantees the right to an effective remedy for their breach (Art 13) and that the rights are enjoyed free from discrimination (Art 14).

16.23.1 The right to an effective remedy – Article 13

ARTICLE

Art 13
Everyone whose rights and freedoms as set forth in this Convention are violated shall have an effective remedy before a national authority notwithstanding that the violation has been committed by persons acting in an official capacity.

Article 13 complements Art 1 of the Convention, which places a duty on Member States to secure the rights and freedoms laid down in the Convention. Article 13 does not place a duty on the state to incorporate the Convention into domestic law, but domestic law should ensure that a person can enjoy his or Convention rights in reality rather than theory. Article 13 is not 'incorporated' by the Human Rights Act 1998, but the government argue that the passing of the Act in itself satisfies Art 13.

In *Silver v United Kingdom* (1983) 5 EHRR 347 the European Court laid down the following principles with respect to Art 13:

- Where individuals have an arguable claim of a violation of their Convention rights, they should have a remedy before a national authority to have the claim decided and to obtain redress.
- The authority should normally be a judicial one, and if it is not then its powers and the guarantees should be as effective.
- The aggregate of remedies provided under domestic law must provide effective redress for the individual.

There will be a violation of Art 13 if domestic law fails to recognise a Convention right (*Malone v United Kingdom* (1984) 7 EHRR 14), or if proceedings are struck out, precluding the court from determining whether there has been a violation, and if so what compensation should be granted (*Z v United Kingdom* (2002) 34 EHRR 3).

Domestic law should allow individuals to argue their case in accordance with principles such as proportionality (*Smith and Grady v United Kingdom* (2000) 29 EHRR 493), to air their complaint before a sufficiently independent body (*Khan v United Kingdom* (2001) 31 EHRR 45), and to be awarded compensation for breach of Convention rights in appropriate cases (*Edwards v United Kingdom* (2002) 35 EHRR 19).

16.23.2 Prohibition of discrimination – Article 14

ARTICLE

Art 14
The enjoyment of the rights and freedoms set forth the in this Convention shall be secured without discrimination on any ground such as sex, race, colour, language, religion, political or other opinion, national or social origin, association with a national minority, property, birth or other status.

As with Art 13, above, Art 14 complements the substantive Convention rights and prohibits discrimination in the enjoyment of such rights.

16.23.3 The scope of Article 14

Unlike Art 26 of the International Covenant on Civil and Political Rights 1966 – which ensures equality under the law – Art 14 does not provide a 'free-standing' right against discrimination. Thus, any complaint under Art 14 must be related to a violation of another Convention right. Note, Protocol No 12, as yet not ratified by the United Kingdom Government, imposes a general prohibition on discrimination, thus establishing a general right of freedom from discrimination.

Thus, Art 14 is used in addition to (or in conjunction with) a claim under another article of the Convention (*Smith and Grady v United Kingdom* (2000) 29 EHRR 493 – dismissal from the armed forces on grounds of sexual orientation a breach of Arts 8 and 14; and *ADT v United Kingdom* (2001) 31 EHRR 33 – conviction of homosexual men for gross indecency a violation of Arts 8 and 14 as the law discriminated against homosexuals). Accordingly the court cannot find a violation of Art 14 unless it establishes first that the Convention right in question is engaged.

CASE EXAMPLE

Choudhury v United Kingdom (1991) 12 HRLJ 172
The applicants complained that the absence of a law of blasphemy to protect the Muslim faith was in breach of Art 9 and was discriminatory under Art 14.

The European Commission held that freedom to manifest one's religion under Art 9 of the Convention did not include a duty on the state to pass specific blasphemy laws. Accordingly, even though the domestic law discriminated in favour of the Anglican faith, the claim under Art 14 failed as Art 9 was not engaged.

However, the court may find a breach of a Convention right on the facts because of the evidence of discrimination (*Abdulaziz Cabales and Balkandali v United Kingdom* (1985) 7 EHRR 471).

16.23.4 Justifiable discrimination

Article 14 is not an absolute right and the European Court recognises that discrimination in the enjoyment of Convention rights is legitimate where there is objective or reasonable justification for such treatment. In such a case any difference must not only pursue a legitimate aim, but the measure must also be reasonably proportionate (*'Belgian Linguistic' case* (1968) 1 EHRR 252).

CASE EXAMPLE

Willis v United Kingdom (2002) 35 EHRR 21

The applicant applied for the equivalent of a widow's payment and Widowed Mother's Allowance when he was forced to leave his employment to care for his children after his wife died. No such payments were available to him as a widower.

The European Court held that there had been a violation of Art 14 taken in conjunction with Art 1 of the First Protocol to the Convention; the only reason for being refused the benefits was that he was a man; a female in the same position would have had a right to such payments, and the difference in treatment between men and women was not based on any objective and reasonable justification.

Similarly, in *PM v United Kingdom* (2006) 42 EHRR 45, where the applicant had been denied tax relief in respect of maintenance payments made to his daughter because he had not been married to the girl's mother the European Court held that there was no justifiable reason to treat him differently from a married father, who would have been eligible for relief.

However, the European Court might be prepared to offer a wide margin of appreciation in some cases (*Pretty v United Kingdom* (2002), see section 16.16.1 – subjection of the applicant to a uniform law prohibiting assisted suicide was reasonably justifiable).

KEY FACTS

Key facts on the European convention on Human Rights

The substantive Convention rights are contained in both Part One of the Convention and various protocols	Arts 2–14 and Arts 1, 2 and 3 of the First Protocol, ECHR
The rights (apart from Art 13) are 'incorporated' into domestic law via the Human Rights Act 1998	s 1 and Sched 1, HRA
Some rights are absolute (for example, freedom from torture) and cannot be compromised, while others (for example, freedom of expression) are conditional and can be interfered with under specific conditions	Arts 3 and 10, ECHR
Under the Convention a state must protect life and must conduct effective investigations into deaths	Art 2, ECHR, *Osman v United Kingdom* (2000) and *Jordan v United Kingdom* (2003)
The Convention prohibits torture and inhuman and degrading treatment or punishment in absolute terms and irrespective of any public good	Art 3, ECHR and *Chahal v United Kingdom* (1997)
States can be liable under Art 3 for violations committed by other states	*Soering v United Kingdom* (1989)
The Convention guarantees due process by safeguarding liberty of the person and the right to a fair trial	Arts 5 and 6, ECHR
The Convention complements the above rights by prohibiting retrospective criminal law or penalties	Art 7, ECHR
The Convention rights of private and family life, freedom of religion, free speech, freedom of association and assembly, and the right to marry are conditional rights and can be restricted provided the interference is prescribed by law, has a legitimate aim, and is necessary in a democratic society	Arts 8–12, ECHR

The Convention protects the rights to property, education and the duty to hold free elections. These rights can be interfered with by legitimate and proportionate measures	Arts 1, 2 and 3 of the First Protocol, ECHR (ratified by the UK and included in the 1998 Act)
The Convention guarantees access to an effective remedy when Convention rights have been violated	Art 13, ECHR and *Silver v United Kingdom* (1983)
The Convention guarantees the enjoyment of all Convention rights free from discrimination	Art 14, ECHR
Article 14 does not provide a 'free-standing' right against discrimination	*Choudhury v United Kingdom* (1991)

SUMMARY

- The Convention is a product of the Council of Europe and was passed in order to enhance human rights and to achieve peace and stability in Europe
- It contains a list of civil and political rights which are the basis of human dignity, individual liberty and the rule of law
- The Convention contains its own enforcement machinery – the European Court of Human Rights – which hears state and individual applications and which has the power to make decisions which are binding on the states
- Decisions of the European Court of Human Rights do not automatically alter UK domestic law, but can be followed by our courts and will generally be accepted by the government who will change relevant laws and practices
- The Convention (in Article 1) encourages states to protect these rights via its own domestic law and the European Court's role is to supervise such enforcement
- The Convention is 'given effect' in the United Kingdom via the Human Rights Act 1998 where domestic courts must take into account Convention rights and interpret domestic law in line with such rights (see Chapter 17)
- The European Court uses principles of legality (prescribed by law) and reasonableness (legitimate aim, necessary in a democratic society, proportionality) to resolve applications and to achieve an appropriate balance. It also applies a 'margin of appreciation' to each state to allow them a discretion in protecting Convention rights within their own jurisdiction
- The Convention rights are contained in Articles 2–14 of the Convention and in its additional protocols
- Some of these rights are absolute (freedom from torture) and others conditional (freedom of expression)
- The Convention allows derogations of these rights during times of war or other emergencies (Article 15)

SAMPLE ESSAY QUESTION

What impact has the European Convention on Human Rights (1950) had on the protection of human rights, and, specifically, in the UK?

Explain (briefly) the history of the Convention's passing and ratification, its central aims, and the nature of the rights contained in the Convention

Explain the 'dual' role of the Convention – to encourage domestic protection of human rights via 'incorporation' of the Convention, and to offer an international machinery for the resolution of human rights disputes brought by Member States or individuals

Explain (briefly) the enforcement machinery of the Convention (the European Court) and the application process contained in Articles 34 and 35

By the use of claims, illustrate how the European Court has decided cases under the Convention and what impact those cases have had on specific rights and domestic law: *Golder v UK, Hirst v UK* (prisoners' rights); *Goodwin v UK* (transsexual rights); *Sunday Times v UK* (freedom of the press); *A v United Kingdom* (detention without trial)

Explain the effect of European Court judgments on domestic case law and the 'incorporation' of the Convention via the Human Rights Act 1998

CONCLUSION (summarising effect of the Convention in both international and domestic law)

Further reading

Books

Amos, M, *Human Rights Law* (Hart 2006), Pt II.

Foster, S, *Human Rights and Civil Liberties* (2nd edn, Longman, 2008), Chapter 2.

Harris, D, O'Boyle, M and Warbrick, C, *The Law of the European Convention on Human Rights* (2nd edn, Oxford University Press, 2009).

Mowbray, A, *Cases and Materials on the European Convention on Human Rights* (2nd edn, Butterworths, 2007).

Articles

Cavanaugh, K, 'Policing the Margins: Rights Protection under the European Court of Human Rights' [2006] EHRLR 422.

O'Boyle, K, 'On Reforming the Operation of the European Court of Human Rights' [2008] EHRLR 1.

17

The Human Rights Act 1998

AIMS AND OBJECTIVES

At the end of this chapter you should be able to:

- Appreciate the constitutional and legal significance of the Human Rights Act 1998 and why it was passed
- Appreciate the role of the law in protecting human rights before the Act was passed and how the Act has impacted on that role
- Understand the central provisions of the Act and appreciate how the Act impacts on the protection of human rights in the United Kingdom
- Be aware of the essential case law decided under the Act and appreciate whether and how such case law has achieved the Act's purpose

17.1 Introduction

The Human Rights Act 1998 came into effect on 2nd October 2000 and while it does not strictly *incorporate* the European Convention into domestic law, it allows the courts to give 'further effect' to the Convention and to take Convention rights and case law into account when interpreting and developing domestic law. As a consequence individuals can now rely *directly* on Convention rights in the domestic courts.

Before the Act the courts could only give indirect effect to the Convention (eg where an Act of Parliament was ambiguous (*R v Home Secretary, ex parte Brind* [1991] 1 AC 696), and they could not apply Convention rights where the domestic law did not recognise that right (*Malone v Metropolitan Police Commissioner* [1979] Ch 344 – an individual could not claim that telephone tapping was in violation of Art 8 of the Convention, guaranteeing the right to private life).

The Act builds on and enhances the traditional method of protecting civil liberties (see section 17.2). Thus, the courts can still apply traditional constitutional principles such as the presumption of innocence, the control of arbitrary power and the rules of natural justice. However, the doctrine of parliamentary sovereignty is retained – the courts still cannot refuse to recognise an Act of Parliament and Parliament retains the right to pass incompatible legislation.

17.2 Pre-Human Rights Act 1998 position

In the absence of a written constitution and a Bill of Rights, individual human rights were protected by the courts, Parliament and the democratic process, including public support and opinion.

Dicey distinguished the British method from other countries by stating that our constitution was not the *source* but the *consequence* of the rights of individuals, as expounded by the common law courts (see Chapter 6). Thus individual rights resulted from court decisions, applying the traditional private law to which all, including the government, were subject. For example in *Entick v Carrington* (1765) 19 St Tr 1030 the court upheld the individual's right to property and person by applying the traditional law of trespass against government officials.

17.2.1 The role of the courts in protecting civil liberties

By the above methods and through the formal procedure of judicial review (see Chapters 18 and 19) the courts could safeguard against arbitrary and unreasonable interference with human rights. Thus the courts could:

- Interpret legislation in the light of constitutional fundamentals, ensuring a human rights friendly interpretation (*Waddington v Miah* [1974] 2 All ER 377).
- Assume Parliament did not intend to interfere with fundamental rights (*Raymond v Honey* [1984] AC 1). Even in the post-Human Rights Act era the courts can have regard to these constitutional values in declaring secondary legislation *ultra vires*, and in *Ahmed v HM Treasury* [2010] UKSC 2 the Supreme Court held that the Terrorism Order 2006, which allowed for freezing orders to be placed on the funds of those who were reasonably suspected of committing an act of or facilitating terrorism were *ultra vires* s 1 of the United Nations Act 1946.
- Subject executive decisions to stricter review where human rights were violated (*R v Ministry of Defence, ex parte Smith* [1996] 1 All ER 257).
- Apply the principles of natural justice to ensure a fair and impartial hearing (*Ridge v Baldwin* [1964] AC 40 and *R v Bow Street Metropolitan Stipendary Magistrate, ex parte Pinochet Ugarte (No 2)* [2000] 1 AC 119).

17.2.2 The role of Parliament in protecting civil liberties

In addition, Parliament could pass legislation securing the rights and freedoms of its citizens.

- Statutes such as the Equality Act 2010 protect individuals from unlawful discrimination and safeguard the right to equality.
- The Police and Criminal Evidence Act 1984 provides safeguards against arbitrary police powers with respect to arrest, detention and search and entry.
- The Data Protection Acts 1984 and 1998 safeguard the right to privacy with respect to personal information.

However, Acts of Parliament could take away or interfere with rights without challenge from the courts on human rights grounds.

- The War Damage Act 1965 retrospectively took away the individual's right to compensation for war damage.
- The Public Order Act 1986 contained restrictions on the right to peaceful protest.
- Anti-terrorism legislation (for example the Terrorism Acts 2000 and 2006) provided wide powers to the authorities to control terrorist activities and association.

17.2.3 The criticisms of the traditional system

The 'common law' method was subject to a number of criticisms:

- The common law courts did not recognise all rights, for example the right of privacy (*Malone v Metropolitan Police Commissioner* [1979] Ch 344).
- The courts were powerless to challenge primary legislation which clearly violated individual rights (*Rossminster Ltd* (1980) – see section 6.7.5).

- The courts were not willing to apply 'European' principles of necessity and proportionality when challenging executive actions (*R v Home Secretary, ex parte Brind* [1991] 1 AC 696).
- The courts could not take the European Convention on Human Rights into account as a direct source of rights (*Brind* (1991) and *Malone* (1979)).
- Acts of Parliament enjoyed sovereignty and could not be questioned by the courts.

As a consequence of these defects individuals very often had to take direct cases under the European Convention on Human Rights 1950. This resulted in a number of high-profile (and dozens of other) defeats for the United Kingdom government before the European Court of Human Rights:

- *Malone v United Kingdom* (1984) 7 EHRR 14 – where the European Court held that unregulated telephone tapping was contrary to the right to private life and correspondence under Art 8 of the Convention.
- *Sunday Times v United Kingdom* (1979) 2 EHRR 245 – where domestic contempt laws were held in violation of Art 10, guaranteeing freedom of expression and press freedom.
- *Smith and Grady v United Kingdom* (2000) 29 EHRR 493 – where the European Court held that the dismissal of homosexual armed forces personnel was both contrary to Art 8 and discriminatory under Art 14.
- *Chahal v United Kingdom* (1997) 23 EHRR 413 – where it was held that the deportation of the applicant on grounds of national security violated Arts 3 and 5 of the Convention (freedom from inhuman treatment and liberty of the person).

17.3 The passing of the Human Rights Act 1998

The passing of the Human Rights Act 1998 was intended to rectify these deficiencies and to allow the domestic courts to directly apply Convention principles and case law, thus improving our human rights record in Strasbourg and reducing the need for citizens to seek the assistance of the European Court.

17.3.1 Central aims and provisions of the Act

- To give effect to the rights contained in Part 1 of the European Convention (s 1).
- To allow victims of violations of human rights to rely on their Convention rights in domestic proceedings (ss 7–9).
- To make it unlawful for public authorities to violate Convention rights (s 6).
- To allow the domestic courts to take into account Convention case law when determining human rights cases (s 2).
- To give the courts greater powers to interpret legislation in line with the Convention (s 3).
- To allow the courts to declare domestic legislation incompatible with the Convention (s 4).
- To make provision for the government to initiate legislation repealing or amending incompatible legislative provisions (s 10).
- To make special provision for the protection of freedom of expression and freedom of religion (ss 12 and 13).
- To require the government to make statements of compatibility with respect to new legislation (s 19).

The basic aim of the Act is to bring the European Convention rights 'home' to domestic law and allow its provisions to be applied in the domestic courts. This will mean that individuals will not in most cases be required to use the Convention machinery in Strasbourg, although the individual is still entitled to petition the European Court after exhausting domestic remedies (s 11).

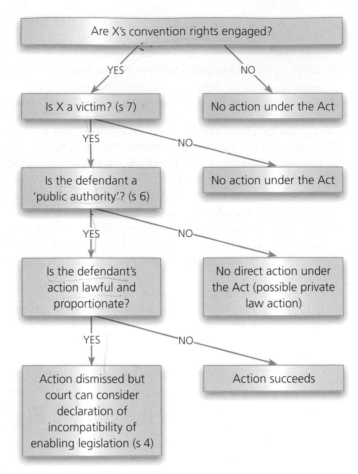

Figure 17.1 Actions under the Human Rights Act

17.3.2 Retrospective effect of the Act

The provisions of the Act generally only apply to acts or decisions of public authorities taking place after the coming into operation of the Act. Thus violations taking place
before this time are subject to the general principles of judicial review and legality.

CASE EXAMPLE

Secretary of State for the Home Department v Wainwright [2003] UKHL 53

The claimants brought a case against the Prison Service alleging that they had been subjected
to unlawful searches. Part of their claim was that this had violated their right to privacy under
Art 8 of the Convention.

The House of Lords held that as the alleged violation took place before the Act came into
force the claimants could not rely on the Act and the right to private life under Art 8.

CASE EXAMPLE

Wilson v First County Trust Ltd (No 2) [2003] UKHL 40

The Court of Appeal had held that provisions of the Consumer Credit Act 1974 were incompatible with Article 6 of the Convention because they prevented credit companies from
enforcing agreements unless specific procedures had been followed in the making of such
agreements.

The House of Lords held that the Court of Appeal had been wrong in making a declaration of incompatibility in respect of a cause of action that arose before the Act came into operation; the Court of Appeal were wrong to find that the original court's order in refusing to enforce the agreement was the relevant act for the purpose of s 6 of the Act.

Neither does the Act apply to appeals against criminal convictions that took place before the Act, even where the appeal takes place after the Act's operation. Thus, in *R v Lambert, Ali and Jordan* [2001] UKHL 37 the House of Lords held that the Act does not have such retrospective effect and that such effect only applied to proceedings brought by a public authority. An unsuccessful appeal, brought by the defendant, was not to be treated as proceedings brought by or at the instigation of a public authority.

The decision in *Lambert* was reluctantly accepted by the House of Lords in *R v Kansal* [2001] UKHL 62, and the individual in such a case would need to petition the European Court: see now *Kansal v United Kingdom* (2004) 39 EHRR 31, finding a violation of Art 6.

Neither can the domestic courts overrule a court decision made before the Act, which has now become inconsistent with a decision of the European Court: see *R v Lyons and others* [2002] UKHL 44, explained at section 16.4.1 The individual in such a case would need to petition the European Court.

Also, the courts have not allowed the Act to have retrospective effect with respect to their powers of statutory interpretation.

CASE EXAMPLE

R (Hurst) v HM Coroner for Northern District Council [2007] UKHL 13

The applicants claimed that a coroner was bound to construe the Coroners Act 1988 so as to order the resumption of an inquest into a death, even though the death had taken place before the Human Rights Act came into force.

The Court of Appeal held that in appropriate circumstances a court could give a Convention compliant interpretation to any legislation even though the dispute in the case related to an act committed before the Act came into effect. Whether an Act could be interpreted in such a way as to bestow individual rights and public duties with respect to pre-Act actions depended on the circumstances, and in this case public policy dictated that Art 2 should inform the duty of the coroner and that would not cause unfairness to the public body. The House of Lords overturned this decision and held that Art 2 could not be employed retrospectively.

17.3.3 The rights guaranteed under the Act

Section 1(1) of the Human Rights Act 1998 gives effect to the Convention rights contained in Arts 2 to 12 and 14 of the main Convention, Arts 1 to 3 of the First Protocol and Arts 1 and 2 of the Sixth Protocol (see Chapter 16 for details on the individual rights).

The rights that can be relied on are as follows:

- Article 2 – The Right to Life.
- Article 3 – Freedom from Torture and Inhuman and Degrading Treatment and Punishment.
- Article 4 – Freedom from Slavery and Forced Labour.
- Article 5 – Liberty and Security of the Person.
- Article 6 – The Right to a Fair Trial.
- Article 7 – Prohibition on Retrospective Criminal Law and Penalties.
- Article 8 – The Right to Private and Family Life, Home and Correspondence.
- Article 9 – Freedom of Religion, Thought and Conscience.
- Article 10 – Freedom of Expression.
- Article 11 – Freedom of Association and Peaceful Assembly.
- Article 12 – The Right to Marry.
- Article 1 of the First Protocol – The Right to Peaceful Enjoyment of Possessions.
- Article 2 of the First Protocol – The Right to Education.
- Article 3 of the First Protocol – The Duty to Hold Free Elections and the Right to Vote.

The Act omits Art 1 of the European Convention (Member States must ensure that the rights laid down in Part One of the Convention are guaranteed to everyone within the state's jurisdiction) and Art 13 of the Convention (which guarantees an effective remedy for breach of a person's Convention rights). This was because the government felt that the passing of the Human Rights Act 1998 in itself would provide the individual with a satisfactory remedy and thus comply with its obligations under the Convention.

These rights are subject to any designated derogation or reservation made under ss 14 and 15 of the Act (see section 17.11).

17.4 Use of Convention case law by the domestic courts

Section 2 of the Act allows domestic courts to consider the relevant case law of the European Convention when determining disputes that raise Convention rights.

SECTION

S2

When a court or tribunal is determining a question involving any Convention right, it must take into account any judgment, decision, declaratory or advisory opinion of the European Court of Human Rights, any opinion of the European Commission given in a report, any decision of the European Commission, and any decision of the Committee of Ministers whenever made or given, so far as, in the opinion of the court and tribunal, it is relevant to the proceedings in which that question has arisen.

The section does not state that the courts have to *apply* such decisions, but as the main aim of the Act is to avoid individuals having to petition the European Court, the domestic courts are unlikely to refuse to apply any case law favourable to the claimant. In addition the courts are unlikely to depart from such case law and replace it by a more generous interpretation of the Convention, as seen in *Anderson and Taylor* (2001), below.

CASE EXAMPLE

R v Secretary of State for the Home Department, ex parte Taylor and Anderson [2001] EWCA Civ 1698

The Court of Appeal was asked to declare the Home Secretary's power to set tariffs for mandatory life sentence prisoners incompatible with Art 6, even though the European Court had stated that such powers were not in breach of the Convention.

The Court of Appeal held that it would be improper for the domestic courts to decide a case in a way that was contrary to the application currently being applied by the European Court of Human Rights. The Home Secretary's power to set tariffs for mandatory life sentence prisoners had clearly been accepted by the European Court of Human Rights *(Wynne v United Kingdom* (1995) 12 EHRR 333) and thus it would not be proper to act in a manner which was inconsistent with that approach.

NB When the European Court overruled *Wynne* in the later case of *Stafford v United Kingdom* (2002) 35 EHRR 32, the House of Lords in *Anderson and Taylor* (2002) declared the Home Secretary's powers as incompatible with Art 6 and the government accordingly introduced new legislation in this area (see section 13.2.1).

Also, the courts may choose to follow binding domestic law, where the European Court has not ruled directly on the legal issue.

CASE EXAMPLE

Kay v Lambeth LBC; Price v Leeds County Council [2006] UKHL 10

Here the Court of Appeal ([2004] EWCA Civ 926) held that when faced with a House of Lords' decision that was inconsistent with a decision of the European Court of Human Rights

it should follow the decision of the House of Lords and r[...]
Lords. As the domestic decision was on a particular statutory [...]
certainty if the European decision was followed.

In the House of Lords it was held that the European Court a[...]
appreciation to the national authorities, attaching much import[...]
Thus, it was for the courts to decide how in the first instance [...]
Strasbourg should be applied in the special context of national le[...]
and other considerations.

In contrast, in *R (Purdy) v Director of Public Prosecutions* [200[...]
Lords followed the decision of the European Court in *Pretty* [...]*guom* (2002)
35 EHRR 1 in preference to the decision of the House of Lords in *R (Pretty) v DPP* [2002]
1 AC 800 with respect to whether Article 8 was engaged in decisions on the termina-
tion of life. Further in *AF v Secretary of State for the Home Department* [2009] UKHL 28 the
House of Lords chose to follow the decision of the European Court in *A v United Kingdom*
(2009) 49 EHRR 29 rather than its own judgment in *MB v Secretary of State for the Home
Department* [2007] UKHL 46 with respect to the use of closed evidence in control order
proceedings.

See also *Re P and others* [2008] UKHL 38, where the House of Lords held that where the
European Court has not laid down a definitive interpretation of the legal position the
domestic courts were not bound to follow those decisions – the rights in the Human
Rights Act were domestic and not international human rights and the domestic courts
could give their own interpretation to them and could apply the division between the
decision-making powers of the courts and Parliament in a way which appeared appropriate for the UK.

17.5 The doctrine of proportionality

Section 2 allows the courts to employ the doctrine of proportionality, which had been
rejected by the domestic courts before the Act (*R v Home Secretary, ex parte Brind* [1991]
1 AC 696). Interference with a Convention right, such as freedom of expression, must
correspond to a pressing social need and be proportionate to the aim that the restriction
was seeking to achieve.

The effect of the doctrine on the court's review powers, and the distinction between
proportionality and the traditional *Wednesbury* unreasonableness principles, were
explained by Lord Steyn in *R v Secretary of State for the Home Department, ex parte Daly*
[2001] UKHL 26:

JUDGMENT

'There is a material difference between the *Wednesbury* and *Smith* grounds of review and
the approach of proportionality applicable in respect of review where Convention rights
were at stake. Most cases would be decided in the same way whichever approach were
adopted. But the intensity of review is somewhat greater under the proportionality approach
… First, the doctrine of proportionality may require the reviewing court to assess the balance
which the decision-maker has struck, not merely whether it is within the range of rational
or reasonable decisions. Secondly … it may require attention to be directed to the relevant
weight accorded to interests and considerations. Thirdly, even the heightened scrutiny test
developed in *R v Ministry of Defence, ex parte Smith* [1996] 1 All ER 257 is not necessarily
appropriate to the protection of human rights … The intensity of the review … is guaranteed by the twin requirements that the limitation of the right was necessary in a democratic
society, in the sense of meeting a pressing social need, and the question whether the interference was really proportionate to the legitimate aim being pursued.'

after the Human Rights Act 1998 the courts do not have to show that the decision affecting the enjoyment of a Convention right was outrageous or irrational, but can conduct a balancing exercise to see whether the interference was necessary and proportionate. This new power has been used in a number of high-profile cases.

CASE EXAMPLE

R (A and others) v Lord Saville of Newdigate and another [2001] EWCA Civ 408

The chairman of the 'Bloody Sunday' inquiry had refused requests from a number of soldiers to give their evidence at a venue other than Londonderry, believing that this would increase public confidence in the inquiry and concluding that there was no real and immediate risk to the soldiers' lives.

Held – the decision-maker had to consider whether interference with fundamental human rights was a serious or real possibility and it was for him to find compelling justification for any interference. The tribunal should have asked whether it had exposed any of the soldiers to the real possibility of a risk to life. In this case the tribunal had used public confidence as the determinative factor, and accordingly its decision was wrong.

See also *A and others v Secretary of State for the Home Department* [2004] UKHL 56. In that case the House of Lords had to decide whether the detention of foreign nationals suspected of terrorism under s 23 of the Anti-terrorism, Crime and Security Act 2001 was a disproportionate response to the threat of terrorism and strictly required by the exigencies of the situation so as to allow the government's derogation under Art 15 of the Convention.

The House of Lords held that while any decision of a representative democratic body commanded respect, the degree of respect would be conditioned by the nature of the decision made. The traditional *Wednesbury* approach was no longer appropriate and the domestic courts themselves had to form a judgment whether a Convention right was breached. Even in terrorist situations the Convention organs were not willing to relax their supervisory role. Given the importance of Art 5, judicial control of the executive's interference with individual liberty was essential; although the judiciary must keep to their proper limits, the courts possessed an express role under the Act to interpret legislation compatibly with Convention rights. On the facts, the House of Lords held that the detention provisions contravened Arts 5 and 14 of the Convention (see section 17.11.1). This decision was upheld by the European Court of Human Rights in *A v United Kingdom* (2009) 49 EHRR 29.

The doctrine of proportionality increases the review powers of the courts (see *Huang v Secretary of State for the Home Department* [2007] UKHL 1) and raises concerns about whether it is proper for the courts to interfere with the decisions of government, or Parliament. In response the courts often show deference towards the executive and, in particular, to Parliament and in *Edore v Secretary of State for the Home Department* [2003] EWCA Civ 716, the Court of Appeal held that given the margin of discretion available to decision-makers, there was often room for two possible proportionate outcomes in a particular situation. Within that margin, a decision-maker may, in some circumstances, fairly reach one of two opposite conclusions. However, both decisions would strike a fair balance between the competing claims and be proportionate.

In some cases, therefore, the courts will show deference to the decision-maker and offer a wide margin of discretion to government and Parliament, either because the decision-maker has an area of expertise or because the issue is policy-based and sensitive.

CASE EXAMPLE

R (British American Tobacco and others) v Secretary of State for Health [2004] EWHC 2493 (Admin)

The High Court had to consider the proportionality of regulations banning the advertising of tobacco products and their compatibility with Art 10 of the European Convention and the applicant's right to commercial speech. It was held that although any restriction on freedom of expression had to be proportionate, there were areas in which the courts had to be particularly wary of imposing their own value judgments upon a legislative scheme. The protection of health was a far-reaching aim and the objective of the regulations was much wider than the protection of children and was sufficiently important to justify limiting a fundamental right. Thus, the measures were rationally connected and were proportionate to promoting health by restricting advertising at the point of sale.

See also *R (Countryside Alliance) v Attorney General* [2007] UKHL 52 where the House of Lords held that the courts should show deference to Parliament with respect to its reasons to ban fox-hunting because the matter had been subject to great parliamentary and public debate. A subsequent application to the European Court of Human Rights was dismissed on similar grounds (*Countryside Alliance v United Kingdom* (2010) 50 EHRR SE6).

See further *Re E (A Child)* [2008] UKHL 66, where the House of Lords held that the police authorities had not broken their obligation under Article 3 of the Convention in protecting parents and children from violence when walking to and from school. The police were uniquely placed to make a judgment by reason of their experience and intelligence.

CASE EXAMPLE

R v Secretary of State for the Home Department, ex parte Farrakhan [2002] EWCA Civ 606

The Home Secretary had excluded F from entering the country because the claimant's presence would not be conducive to the public good and that he was likely to threaten public order and commit offences of racial hatred. The High Court held that the Home Secretary had failed to produce any evidence so as to justify his decision. The Court of Appeal held that the Secretary of State had struck a proportionate balance between the legitimate aim of the prevention of disorder and freedom of expression. The fact that the decision was personal to the Secretary, who was far better placed to reach an informed decision than the court, and that the Secretary was democratically accountable for his decision, made it appropriate to give him a particularly wide margin of discretion.

ACTIVITY

Self-test questions
1. Why was the Human Rights Act 1998 passed?
2. What were the deficiencies of the traditional method of protecting human rights in the UK and how does the Act address those issues?
3. What is the importance of s 2 of the Human Rights Act 1998?
4. What is the doctrine of proportionality and how important is it to the resolution of human rights disputes?
5. Do you think the decision in *A and others v Secretary of State* (2004) (above) displayed too much judicial power?

17.6 Interpreting statutory provisions in the light of the Convention

Under the Act the courts are given increased powers of statutory interpretation to allow them to reach a Convention-friendly result wherever that is possible. Even before, the courts could interpret legislation in the light of the European Convention when the statute was ambiguous (*Waddington v Miah* [1974] 2 All ER 377).

Section 3 of the Act provides as follows:

(1) So far as it is possible to do so, primary legislation and subordinate legislation must be read and given effect in a way which is compatible with … Convention rights

(2) This section – does not affect … (b) the validity, continuing operation or enforcement of any incompatible primary legislation; and (c) does not affect the validity, continuing operation and enforcement of any incompatible subordinate legislation if … primary legislation prevents removal of the incompatibility.

■ Courts are now allowed to adopt a different interpretation to statutory provisions than applied by the courts before the Act and to disregard any previous interpretation of a higher court.

■ The doctrine of parliamentary sovereignty is preserved because the section does not affect the validity etc of any incompatible primary legislation or any incompatible subordinate legislation where the parent Act clearly allows interference with Convention rights.

■ Thus, the courts have no power to set aside an Act of Parliament and must follow it even where it is not possible to interpret it in a Convention-friendly manner.

■ Under section 3 the court does not have to find a true ambiguity in the statute, provided the Convention interpretation is 'possible'.

In addition, in *Wilson v First County Trust Ltd (No 2)* [2003] UKHL 40 the House of Lords held that courts were entitled to have regard to the policy objectives behind the legislation by looking at ministerial statements at the time the Bill was proceeding through Parliament.

17.6.1 The scope of section 3

The scope of s 3 depends on the extent to which the courts are prepared to interpret legislation in the light of Convention rights – in other words what the courts regard as a 'possible' interpretation.

CASE EXAMPLE

R v Offen [2001] 1 WLR 253

Section 2 of the Crime (Sentences) Act 1997 imposed a duty on the courts to grant an automatic life sentence to defendants who have committed two serious offences, unless there were 'exceptional circumstances'. The defendant was sentenced to life imprisonment despite the fact that the trial judge conceded that the offences were at the lower end of the scale and had been committed using a toy gun.

The Court of Appeal held that a court was entitled to decide that there existed exceptional circumstances if an offender did not constitute a significant risk to the public. An alternative interpretation would have made the sentence arbitrary and thus in violation of Art 5 of the European Convention on Human Rights. The word 'exceptional' must be given its ordinary meaning and Parliament could not have intended that the section apply to someone who did not pose a future risk.

A more radical approach was taken by the House of Lords in *R v A* (2001), below, and thus the courts were accused of legislating rather than interpreting existing legislation passed by the democratically elected Parliament.

CASE EXAMPLE

R v A (Complainant's sexual history) [2001] UKHL 25

Section 41 of the Youth Justice and Criminal Evidence Act 1999 provides that evidence of the complainant's sexual behaviour can only be allowed with leave of the court in express circumstances. The defendant wished to use the section in circumstances that appeared outside its terms.

The House of Lords held that the interpretative obligation placed on the courts under s 3 of the Human Rights Act 1998 applied even where there was no ambiguity and the court must strive to find a possible interpretation compatible with Convention rights. Section 3 required the courts to proceed on the basis that the legislature would not, if alerted to the problem, have wished to deny the right of an accused to put forward a full and complete defence by advancing truly probative evidence. Thus, the section should be read as being subject to the implied exclusion that evidence required to secure a fair trial under Art 6 of the Convention should not be inadmissible.

Section 3 thus allows the courts to depart from traditional principles of statutory interpretation and to assume, wherever possible, that legislation is not intended to conflict with the 1998 Act.

CASE EXAMPLE

Sheldrake v DPP: Attorney-General's Reference (No 4) [2004] UKHL 43

The House of Lords interpreted s 11(2) of the Terrorism Act 2000 as imposing an evidential rather than legal burden on the defendant so as to make that provision compatible with Art 6 of the Convention and to avoid a finding that that provision was disproportionate and incompatible.

The House of Lords held that even though Parliament had intended to impose a legal burden in such cases when passing the 2000 Act, having regard to its intention in passing s 3 of the Human Rights Act 1998 it was possible to read s 11(2) down in such a way as to avoid a legal burden.

However, s 3 does not allow the courts to read words into a statute that are clearly not there, and in *Poplar Housing and Regeneration Community Association Ltd v Donoghue* [2001] EWCA Civ 595 Lord Woolf CJ stressed that the courts must not radically alter a statute in order to achieve compatibility.

The House of Lords sounded a clear warning against 'judicial legislation' in the case below:

CASE EXAMPLE

In Re W and B (Children: Care Plan); In Re W (Child: Care Plan) [2002] UKHL 10

The Court of Appeal ([2001] EWCA Civ 757) had authorised a system under the Children Act 1989 which allowed courts to star essential milestones in the care plan of a child so that action had to be taken by a local authority if they were not achieved within a reasonable time.

The House of Lords held that the 1998 Act maintained the constitutional boundary between the interpretation of statutes and the passing and repeal of legislation, and that a meaning that departed substantially from a fundamental feature of an Act of Parliament was likely to have crossed the boundary. Further, in using their powers of interpretation under s 3 the courts should be able to identify clearly the particular statutory provision or provisions whose interpretation led to that result.

The distinction between robust interpretation and judicial legislation is often difficult to make and will often depend on whether the courts are prepared to leave Parliament with the task of amending incompatible legislation. Thus, in *Bellinger v Bellinger* [2003] UKHL 21 the House of Lords held that it was not possible to use s 3 to interpret the words 'man and woman' to include a person who had undergone gender reassignment. However, in *Mendoza v Ghaidan* [2004] UKHL 40 the House of Lords held the words 'living together as husband and wife' could be interpreted to mean as if they were living together as husband and wife. In *Mendoza* Lord Millett dissented on the grounds that it was for Parliament to change a law that was quite clearly not intended to cover same-sex relationships.

In some cases (such as *Bellinger*) the courts might feel that certain changes in the law should be carried out by Parliament rather than the courts: the decision in *Bellinger* was followed by the passing of the Gender Recognition Act 2004.

ACTIVITY

Self-test questions

1. How does s 3 of the Act change the courts' role with respect to statutory interpretation?
2. Does the Act threaten parliamentary sovereignty in any respect?
3. What is the difference between statutory interpretation and judicial legislation?
4. Do you think the House of Lords was guilty of judicial legislation in *R v A* (2001), above?
5. Should the courts use s 3 to 'change' incompatible law, or should it make a declaration of incompatibility (below) instead?

17.7 Declarations of incompatibility

Under s 4 of the Act courts are allowed to declare both primary and secondary legislation incompatible with the substantive rights of the European Convention.

SECTION

> S 4(2) 'If the court is satisfied that the provision (of primary legislation) is incompatible with a Convention right, it may make a declaration of incompatibility.'
>
> S 4(4) 'If the court is satisfied that the provision (of secondary legislation) is incompatible with a Convention right and that the primary legislation concerned prevents removal of the incompatibility it may make a declaration of incompatibility.'
>
> S 4(6) 'A declaration … does not affect the validity, continuing operation or enforcement of the provision in respect of which it is given and is not binding on the parties to the proceedings in which it is made.'

■ Section 4 applies where the court has not been able to use its powers of interpretation under s 3 of the Act.
■ Section 4 restricts the power to issue such declarations to courts including the High Court and above.
■ Section 5 of the Act gives the Crown the power to intervene where a court is considering making a declaration of incompatibility.
■ Section 4 does not include the right to strike down incompatible, but clear legislation.
■ Incompatible legislation must be addressed and amended by Parliament, see s 10 of the Act, below.

Declarations cannot be granted in respect of violations of human rights caused by the application of incompatible legislation that took place before the Act came into operation: *Wilson v First County Trust Ltd (No 2)* [2003] UKHL 40 (see section 17.3.1).

It is not possible to use the powers under s 4 where the relevant legislation has not, or is not likely to, personally affect any particular person. Thus, the claimant must prove that they are a 'victim' of the violation.

CASE EXAMPLE

R v Attorney-General, ex parte Rushbridger and another [2003] UKHL 38

The House of Lords was asked to declare s 3 of the Treason Felony Act 1848 as incompatible with Art 10 of the European Convention.

It was held that the courts would refuse to make such a declaration without proof that there was any victim of the legislation. In this case there was no real risk of anyone being prosecuted under the legislation for non-violent conduct and thus no real risk of any interference with free speech. It was for the legislature and not the courts to keep the statute book up to date.

See also *R (Chester) v Secretary of State for Justice*, [2009] EWHC 2923 (Admin), where the domestic court refused to grant a declaration of incompatibility with respect to the Representation of the People Act 1983 and the government's decision not to allow post–tariff life sentence prisoners the right to vote. The court would not consider granting a declaration until the statutory provision was in place; otherwise the parliamentary process would be interfered with.

Courts will not issue a declaration of incompatibility merely because a statute contains a gap, which, if included, would make it compatible with the Convention; *In Re S; Re W* (section 17.6.1). The relevant 'victim' would then have to pursue an action in Strasbourg. Following the decision of the House of Lords in *Re S; Re W* an application was lodged before the European Court of Human Rights, alleging a violation of Arts 6 and 8 of the Convention: *S v UK* (Application No 34407/02, 31st August 2004).

In *Wilson v First County Trust Ltd (No 2)* [2003] UKHL 40 (section 17.3.1 above) the House of Lords held that in assessing the compatibility of primary legislation, a court was entitled to have regard to the policy objectives behind the legislation by looking at ministerial statements at the time the Bill was proceeding through Parliament. However, the content of parliamentary debates had no direct relevance to the issues the court was called upon to decide in compatibility matters and those matters were not a matter for investigation or consideration by the courts.

17.7.1 Declarations of incompatibility in practice

Since the Act has come into force, the courts have issued a number of declarations, some of which have resulted in legislative change. For example, in *R v Mental Health Tribunal ex parte H* [2001] EWCA Civ 415 the Court of Appeal held that ss 72 and 73 of the Mental Health Act 1983 were incompatible with Art 5 of the European Convention because they placed the burden of proof on a restricted patient to show that he no longer warranted detention. Following this decision the Mental Health Act 1983 (Remedial) Order 2001 amended the offending legislation.

The courts will declare legislation incompatible if it imposes excessive or unfair penalties.

CASE EXAMPLE

International Transport Roth GMBH and others v Secretary of State for the Home Department [2002] EWCA Civ 158

Drivers and owners of vehicles had all been subjected to penalties for effecting clandestine entrants to the United Kingdom contrary to s 32 of the Immigration and Asylum Act 1999. They claimed that the penalties were contrary to Arts 5 and 6 of the Convention and to the right of property under Art 1 of the first protocol.

Held – the penalty regime did not adequately protect the rights of those alleged to be responsible for clandestine entrants. The scheme was unfair in imposing strict liability and in imposing so high a fixed penalty without the possibility of mitigation.

Also, a court is likely to declare legislation as incompatible if it is clearly out of line with the case law of the European Court of Human Rights.

CASE EXAMPLE

Bellinger v Bellinger [2003] UKHL 21

Here the House of Lords held that the refusal of domestic law to recognise a marriage celebrated between a man and a transsexual born a male was contrary to Arts 8 and 12 of the European Convention and in particular, the decision of the European Court of Human Rights in *Goodwin v United Kingdom* (2002) 35 EHRR 18.

Similarly, in *Anderson* (2002) (see section 13.2.1), the House of Lords declared the Home Secretary's sentencing powers incompatible with both Art 6 of the Convention and the decision of the European Court in *Stafford v United Kingdom* (2002) 35 EHRR 32.

The courts have issued a number of declarations of incompatibility where the relevant provisions are discriminatory:

CASE EXAMPLE

Re P and others [2008] UKHL 38

Here the House of Lords granted a declaration that a rule, contained in article 14 of the Adoption (Northern Ireland) Order 1987 exempting unmarried couples from adopting, unjustifiably discriminated against unmarried couples. European Court case law pointed to the conclusion that such discrimination would be unlawful under Art 14 of the Convention (*EB v France* (2008) 47 EHRR 21) and favoured the view that discrimination against persons on the grounds of marital status in this area was not acceptable.

See also the decision of the House of Lords in *A and others v Secretary of State* (2004) (see section 17.5) with respect to the detention without trial of foreign terrorist suspects. The decision in *A* also shows the courts' insistence that individual liberty and due process are not unduly interfered with. See also the case of *Re MB*, below.

CASE EXAMPLE

Re MB [2007] UKHL 46

Here the House of Lords held that the procedures in s 3 of the Prevention of Terrorism Act 2005 relating to the admissibility of closed evidence for supervision orders under that Act were compatible with Art 6 of the Convention, *provided* that the words 'except where to admit such evidence would be incompatible with the right of the controlled person to a fair trial' were added.

On the other hand, the domestic courts are unlikely to interfere with legislation that appears consistent with European Convention case law and principles.

CASE EXAMPLE

R v Secretary of State for the Environment, Transport and the Regions, ex parte Barnes [2001] UKHL 23

The courts considered the compatibility with Art 6 of the Secretary of State's statutory power to determine planning applications that had not been determined by the local authority and to determine appeals against refusal of planning permission. The High Court held that such powers were incompatible as interfering with the claimants' right to an independent and impartial tribunal.

The House of Lords held that the planning laws were not incompatible with Article 6. Although the Secretary of State was not an independent and impartial tribunal, the power of the High Court in judicial review proceedings to review the legality of the decision and the procedures followed was sufficient to ensure compatibility with Art 6(1). Where the decision at issue was a matter of administrative policy, the European Court of Human Rights in *Bryan v United Kingdom* (1995) 21 EHRR 342 had accepted that the court's powers of appeal and review were sufficient to ensure that the decision-making process, as a whole, complied with Art 6.

The courts have also shown a good deal of deference to Parliament in deciding whether to grant a declaration of incompatibility.

CASE EXAMPLE

Brown v Stott (Procurator Fiscal) [2003] 1 AC 681

The Privy Council had to consider whether s 172(2)(a) of the Road Traffic Act 1988, which compelled a person to answer the question whether he or she had been driving a car, was compatible with the rule against self-incrimination as guaranteed by Art 6 of the Convention.

It was held that although the right to a fair trial is an absolute right that cannot be compromised, there might be exceptional cases in which the defendant's procedural rights have to give way to the greater interests of the public that justice be done. Consequently national courts should give weight to the decisions of the representative legislature and the democratic government within the discretionary area of judgment accorded to such bodies. In this case, therefore, it was held that the provision was proportionate and compatible with Art 6. The reasoning behind this case was applied and upheld by the European Court of Human Rights in *O'Halloran and Francis v United Kingdom* (2008) 46 EHRR 21.

See also *R v Shayler* [2002] UKHL 11 where the House of Lords held that ss 1 and 4 of the Official Secrets Act 1989 were compatible with Art 10 of the European Convention. See section 18.3.6.

CASE EXAMPLE

R v DPP, ex parte Pretty and another [2001] UKHL 61

The House of Lords had to decide whether the DPP had the power to give an undertaking that the applicant's husband would not be prosecuted under s 2(1) of the Suicide Act 1961 if he assisted her in taking her own life, and whether that provision was incompatible with her rights under the European Convention.

The House of Lords held the right to life under Art 2 did not include the right to die. Further, although the case engaged the claimant's right to private and home life, and her right to enjoy her Convention rights free from discrimination, any interference with those rights was necessary and proportionate to meet the aims of the Suicide Act 1961. This decision was upheld by the European Court of Human Rights in *Pretty v United Kingdom* (2002) 35 EHRR 1 where it was held that it was within the state's discretion to impose a blanket ban on assisting suicide. However, in *Purdy v Director of Public Prosecutions* [2009] UKHL 45 the House of Lords held that as Article 8 rights were engaged the DPP must give sufficient guidance on his prosecution policies under the Suicide Act 1961.

17.7.2 Statements of compatibility

Under s 19(1) a Minister of the Crown in charge of a Bill in either House must, before the second reading of the Bill, either make a statement of compatibility to the effect that in his view the provisions of the Bill are compatible with the Convention rights, or make a statement to the effect that the government nevertheless wishes the House to proceed with the Bill.

- Because an Act of Parliament cannot bind future Parliaments as to the manner in which legislation is passed, a Bill that did not contain such a declaration could not be invalidated by the courts.
- A declaration that a Bill is Convention-compliant would not bind the courts and prevent them from subsequently declaring legislation incompatible with Convention rights.

Thus far, only one statement of incompatibility has been made. This was in respect of s 321(2) of the Communications Act 2003, which makes political advertising unlawful. As the provision may be inconsistent with the European Court's decision in *VgT Verein gegen Tierfabriken v Switzerland* (2002) 34 EHRR 4 the responsible minister made a declaration under s 19(1) that he intended to proceed with the Bill. Subsequently the provision was declared compatible with Art 10: *R (Animal Defenders International) v Secretary of State for Culture and Media and Sport* [2008] UKHL 15.

17.7.3 Remedial action

The Act leaves the ultimate power of deciding the compatibility of domestic legislation with Convention rights with the democratically elected legislature. Thus, where a court had declared a statutory provision as incompatible with the Convention, it has no power to disapply the provision and the ultimate decision of whether the provision remains on the statute books rests with the law-makers. Thus, Parliament can either leave the provision on the statute books, risking an application under the European Convention by a relevant victim, or alter that provision in line with the court's finding.

Specifically, s 10 of the Human Rights Act 1998 provides that where legislation has been declared incompatible under s 4 of the Act (or it appears to a minister of the Crown that a finding of the European Court of Human Rights against the United Kingdom makes such legislation appear to be incompatible with the Convention) the minister may make such amendments to the legislation as he considers necessary to amend that incompatibility.

Under s 10(3) a similar power is created in the case of subordinate legislation, where a minister considers it necessary to amend the primary legislation under which the subordinate legislation was made. This will allow an incompatibility between the provision and the Convention right to be removed. In such a case he may order such amendments to that primary legislation, as he considers necessary.

- Under Sched 2, para 2 of the Act no remedial order can normally be made unless a draft of the order has been approved by a resolution of each House of Parliament made after the end of the period of 60 days beginning on the day that the draft was laid.
- Under para 3(1) of the Schedule no draft can be laid unless the person proposing to make the order has laid a document before Parliament containing a draft of the proposed order and the required information, explaining the reasons for the order, and a period of no less than 60 days has expired.
- In emergency cases where the order is made without being approved in draft, para 4 provides that the person making the order must lay it before Parliament, accompanied by the required information, after it is made.

KEY FACTS

Issue	Effect	Provision
European case law	Domestic courts can now have direct reference to the Articles, principles and case law of the European Convention on Human Rights	s 2, HRA
Convention principles	Domestic courts must now inquire whether domestic law and decisions are prescribed by law, have a legitimate aim, and are necessary in a democratic society (including whether the measure is proportionate)	ss 2 and 6, HRA
Following precedent	The courts must merely take the case law of the European Convention into account when determining disputes raising Convention rights; it is not bound to follow it	s 2, HRA
Statutory Interpretation	Courts must interpret all legislation, wherever possible, in a way that is compatible with Convention rights	s 3, HRA
Parliamentary sovereignty	Courts are not able to legislate or to strike down incompatible legislation	ss 3 and 4, HRA
Declarations of incompatibility	Where it is not possible to achieve a Convention-friendly result, the higher courts can declare inconsistent legislation as incompatible, leaving the government to initiate any relevant legislative changes	s 4, HRA

Issue	Effect	Provision
Amending incompatible legislation	Minister empowered to make remedial orders, amending incompatible legislation	s 19, HRA
Ministerial declarations of incompatibility	Relevant minister to make a statement of compatibility or incompatibility when introducing legislation before Parliament	s 10, HRA

ACTIVITY

Problem Solving

In 2012 Parliament passed the (imaginary) Public Order Act 2012. Section 1 of that Act allows the Home Secretary to pass such regulations as he thinks fit to secure public order. Acting under that provision, the Home Secretary passed a regulation in June 2012 that provided that if the Secretary of State is of the opinion that the formation of any group or society poses a serious threat to public order, he may order the proscription of that group, in which case it will be unlawful to join or take part in the activities of that group or society.

1. What Convention rights does s 1 potentially threaten?
2. Could the courts interpret s 1 in such a way that it would not conflict with any Convention rights?
3. In particular, could the courts interpret 'group or society' to exclude groups or societies who have a political message or mandate?
4. Do you think that the power of the Home Secretary under that section is compatible with those Convention rights?
5. How could the doctrine of proportionality be used to ensure that the section, and its use by the minister, is not excessive?

17.8 Liability of public authorities under the Act

The Act applies principally with respect to violations committed by public authorities, although the act can also operate in a 'horizontal' fashion and be applied in private proceedings.

Section 6 of the Act imposes an obligation on public authorities not to violate Convention rights.

SECTION

S6(1) It is unlawful for a public authority to act in a way that is inconsistent with a Convention right.

(2) Subsection 6(1) does not apply …

(a) if as the result of one or more provisions of primary legislation, it could not have acted differently; or

(b) in the case of a provision of, or made under, primary legislation which cannot be read or given effect in a way which is compatible with Convention rights, the authority was acting so as to give effect to or enforce those provisions.

▪ Section 7 then provides a remedy to a person who claims that a public authority has acted (or proposes to act) in a way that is unlawful under s 6 (see section 17.9).

▪ An act includes a failure to act but does not include a failure to introduce in, or lay before, Parliament a proposal for legislation, or make any primary legislation or remedial order (s 6(6)).

- Section 6 retains parliamentary sovereignty by providing that the duty does not apply where the authority could not have acted differently having regard to the power granted by Parliament.
- In such a case the court is limited to making a declaration of incompatibility under s 4 (see section 17.7).

17.8.1 Definition of 'public authority'

The term public authority is not defined under s 6, however:

- it includes a court or tribunal, and does not include either House of Parliament or a person exercising functions in connection with proceedings in Parliament (s 6(3));
- 'public authority' includes any person whose functions are functions of a public nature (s 6(3)(b));
- in relation to a particular act a person is not a public authority if the nature of the Act is private (s 6(5));
- thus the act preserves the distinction between public and private bodies, and public and private law issues, employed formerly in judicial review proceedings (see Chapter 19).

In the post-HRA era the courts have had to distinguish between public and private bodies and acts. Contrast the cases of *Heather* and *Poplar*, below.

CASE EXAMPLE

Heather, Ward and Callin v Leonard Cheshire Foundation [2002] EWCA Civ 366

A housing foundation had closed a care home, allegedly in violation of Article 8 of the Convention.

The Court of Appeal held that the housing foundation was not a public authority and did not exercise a public law function within the meaning of s 6. Before the 1998 Act it had been established that such bodies were not susceptible to judicial review, and the Human Rights Act had not done anything to alter that. The foundation was essentially private and carrying out private functions, despite the fact that it received public funding, was state regulated, and, had it not existed, its functions would have been provided by the state.

However, note:

CASE EXAMPLE

Poplar Housing and Regeneration Community Association Ltd v Donoghue [2001] EWCA Civ 595

The applicant argued that a possession order executed by the defendants, an association set up by the local authority to take over its housing stock, was in breach of her Convention rights.

The Court of Appeal held that the defendant housing association was a public authority under s 6. The court held that the fact that the association provided a public service and was regulated by the local authority, which would have exercised its powers had the association not existed, were relevant, yet not decisive, factors. However, in this case the role of the association was so closely connected to that of the local authority that *in this case* it was performing public rather than private functions.

The decision in *Heather* was followed in *YL v Birmingham City Council* [2007] UKHL 27, but see now s 145 of the Health and Social Care Act 2008, which extends the protection of the Human Rights Act to people receiving publicly arranged care in independent sector homes.

The body in question thus has to have *sufficient* governmental links and public status.

CASE EXAMPLE

Parochial Church Council of the Parish of Aston Cantlow and others v Wallbank [2003] UKHL 37

The applicants had been required by the defendants to pay for the repair of the chancel of a church they had bought and claimed this was in violation of their right to property. The Court of Appeal held that the Parochial Church Council was a public authority because it was created and empowered by the law and its notice to repair had statutory force.

On appeal the House of Lords held that a parochial church council was essentially a religious body and not a governmental one. It was not a 'core' public authority under the Act and its duty in this case was private rather than a public function. (The House also agreed that there was no violation of Article 1 of the first protocol to the Convention simply because the owners of the property acquired a very expensive duty to repair.)

A Bill to clarify the meaning of public authorities under s 6 is was introduced to Parliament: the Human Rights Act 1998 (Meaning of Public Authorities) Bill 2009.

17.8.2 The 'horizontal' effect of the Human Rights Act 1998

Although the Act applies directly to public authorities, it can, to a limited extent, impose obligations on private persons and thus be used in private proceedings. As courts are public authorities under s 6, and it is unlawful for them to act in a way that is incompatible with Convention rights, they will have a duty to develop the law, including the private law, consistently with Convention rights.

The Act will, therefore, have a 'horizontal' effect. This has been most evident in the area of the law of confidentiality, where that law has been applied and expanded so as to afford an individual a right of privacy consistent with Art 8 of the European Convention (see *Douglas and others v Hello! and others* [2001] 2 WLR 992 and *Venables and Thompson v Associated Newspapers* [2001] 1 WLR 1038 – where the courts accepted that confidentiality could be expanded to accommodate the claimants' Art 8 privacy rights).

The Act can also be applied to other areas of private law, such as the law of defamation (*Reynolds v Times Newspapers* [2001] 2 AC 127) and the law of employment, below:

CASE EXAMPLE

In X v Y [2004] EWCA Civ 662

An employee claimed that his dismissal for receiving a caution for an indecency offence committed in a public toilet with another man was in breach of his Convention rights under Arts 8 and 14 of the Convention and that the test of unfairness should be interpreted in the light of those rights.

The Court of Appeal held that the 1998 Act might have an effect on unfair dismissals in the private sector in appropriate cases. It would not normally be fair to dismiss an employee in violation of the enjoyment of his Convention rights, although if there was a justifiable reason for his dismissal under the Employment Rights Act 1996 the tribunal should consider (Art 8) in the context of the application of s 3 of the 1998 Act to the provisions of the 1996 Act. On the facts Arts 8 and 14 were not engaged because the act in question was not part of his private life and that the real reason for the dismissal was his failure to disclose the criminal caution.

The 1998 Act is thus used as a guiding principle for the main substantive law and the case below illustrates the courts' reluctance to give the Act full horizontal effect.

Wainwright v Home Office [2003] UKHL 53

The applicants claimed that their search by a prison officer violated their right to privacy, even though it occurred before the 1998 Act came into force.

The House of Lords confirmed that there was no common law tort of invasion of privacy and that it was not necessary to develop such a general tort: the gap in the law had been filled by the passing of the Human Rights Act 1998, and it was not necessary to develop a law of privacy to apply to actions which occurred before the passing of the Act. The development of the law of privacy in accordance with Art 8 has been realised through the law of confidence and not by creating a separate tort of privacy: see *Campbell v Mirror Group Newspapers* [2004] UKHL 22.

17.9 Remedies under the Act

As we have seen, s 6 makes it unlawful for public authorities to act in a way that is incompatible with a person's convention rights. Further, under s 7(1) a person who claims that a public authority has acted (or proposes to act) in a way which is made unlawful by s 6 may either bring proceedings against the authority under this Act in an appropriate court or tribunal, or may rely on the Convention right or rights concerned in *any legal proceedings* – such as during a criminal trial or in judicial review proceedings.

In the case of judicial review proceedings, the applicant may now take advantage of the 1998 Act where he is, or would be, a victim under that Act (s 7(3)). Thus, such an applicant could use the grounds of proportionality and breach of a Convention right, established under the 1998 Act. Other affected persons, such as representative groups, would bring proceedings on traditional grounds of review (*R v Secretary of State for the Environment, ex parte Greenpeace Ltd* [1994] 4 All ER 352).

Section 7(5) imposes a time limit and provides that proceedings must be brought before the end of the period of one year from the date on which the act complained of took place, or such longer period as the court or tribunal considers equitable having regard to all the circumstances. This provision is made subject to any rule imposing a stricter time limit in relation to the procedure in question, such as the time limit imposed under the Civil Procedure Rules 1998, where an application for judicial review must normally be brought within three months of the decision against which review is sought.

17.9.1 Victims of a Convention violation

Section 7(1) limits the Act to those who are 'victims' of a violation of Convention rights. Further, a person is only a victim of an unlawful act if he would be regarded as such for the purposes of Art 34 of the European Convention (s 7(7)) (see Chapter 16). This will cover anyone directly or potentially affected by the act as well as relatives and dependants of such persons (*R (Holub and another) v Secretary of State for the Home Department* [2002] EWHC 2388, and *R (Amin) v Home Secretary* [2003] UKHL 51).

However for the person to be a victim there must be a real risk that the relevant legal provision be applied against them (*Rusbridger v Attorney-General* [2003] UKHL 38). The court will not thus decide a hypothetical case and will *generally* wait for a substantive decision.

R (Hirst) v Parole Board [2002] EWHC 1592 (Admin)

Here it was held that a prisoner could not bring an application for a declaration that the Crime (Sentences) Act 1997 was incompatible with Art 5 of the European Convention until the Parole Board had considered his case for release. It would not be proper for it to rule on the question of compatibility until the Board had considered the claim, because until that time it would not be apparent that the statutory power was capable of impacting on the prisoner's case.

The Convention accepts that a person can be a victim if the individual is affected by the mere existence of the restriction (*Dudgeon v United Kingdom* (1982) 4 EHRR 149), and where there is an anticipated and real risk of a breach (*Soering v United Kingdom* (1989) 11 EHRR 439).

17.9.2 Power to award an appropriate remedy

Section 8 of the Act bestows on the courts the power to grant remedies for breach of the victim's Convention rights:

SECTION

Where a court finds that an act (or proposed act) of a public authority is (or would be) unlawful, it might grant such relief or remedy, or make such order, within its powers as it considers just and equitable.

Section 8 applies directly to violations committed by public authorities, but as that term includes courts and tribunals, victims will be able to rely on the principles and case law of the European Convention in all types of legal proceedings, including those taken against private individuals (see, for example, *Campbell v MGN Ltd* [2004] UKHL 22, where damages for breach of confidence included a claim for breach of the right to private life).

The courts' liability for violating Convention rights is limited and s 9(1) provides that the remedy for such a breach will be via judicial review or by appeal. Under s 9(3) of the Act damages are not generally awarded in respect of a judicial act done in good faith, although s 9(3) makes an exception in cases where there is a violation of Art 5(5) of the European Convention. This provision guarantees an effective remedy when a person's right to liberty has been violated.

17.9.3 Damages and the Human Rights Act 1998

The courts' power under s 8 includes the power to award damages, although only where the court has a power to award damages or order the payment of compensation in civil proceedings (s 8(2)).

Under s 8(3) no award of damages shall be made unless the court is satisfied in the circumstances that the award is necessary to afford 'just satisfaction' to the person in whose favour it is made. In deciding whether to award damages, or in deciding the amount of any award, the court must take into account the principles applied by the European Court of Human Rights in relation to the award of compensation under Art 41 of the Convention (s 8(4)) (see Chapter 16).

The domestic courts have taken a flexible approach to the award of damages under the Act, taking into account factors such as the type of right that has been violated, the effect of the violation on the victim and the conduct of the public authority.

CASE EXAMPLE

R (Bernard and others) v Enfield LBC [2002] EWHC 2282 (Admin)

The local authority had failed to find suitable accommodation for the claimant (who was disabled) and her husband and six children.

The High Court held that damages for breach of human rights under the Act should be no lower than for a comparable tort and should, as far as possible, reflect the English level of damages. Also, awards recommended by the Local Government Ombudsman were a helpful guide. Awards should not be so minimal so as to diminish the policy that public authorities should respect Convention rights. Given the conduct of the authority and the humiliation suffered by the victim the award should be at the top end of the scale, in this case £10,000 (£8,000 to the wife and £2,000 to the husband).

CASE EXAMPLE

R (KB) v Mental Health Review Tribunal [2003] EWHC 193 (Admin)

The court held that damages would not be granted automatically for violation of Art 5, and that the courts should follow the principle of just satisfaction as practised by the European Court. Mental patients should not automatically receive damages for a violation of their rights, but the courts should recognise their vulnerability in assessing any damages. In this case the court awarded damages of between £750 and £1,000 to patients whose release had been delayed in breach of Art 5(4) of the Convention.

However, some cases have taken a more cautious approach and have limited the right to claim damages for breach of Convention rights.

CASE EXAMPLE

R (N) v Secretary of State for the Home Department; Anufrijeva v London Borough of Southwark [2003] EWCA Civ 1406

The High Court in *N* had granted damages when the Home Office had mishandled the claimant's asylum application, thus depriving him of income support and related benefits. On appeal the Court of Appeal held that although Art 8 of the Convention was capable of imposing a positive obligation to provide such support, maladministration on the part of an authority would only infringe Art 8 where the consequences were serious.

The Court of Appeal also held (in *Anufrijeva v London Borough of Southwark*) that damages for breach of Art 8 of the Convention were not recoverable automatically, and would only be awarded when necessary to give just satisfaction. Breach of a public law duty would not be sufficient on its own and for an award to be made there would have to be a degree of culpability together with foreseeable harm.

Also, in *Secretary of State for the Home Department v Wainwright* [2003] UKHL 53 the House of Lords held that it was doubtful whether damages could be claimed under the Human Rights Act 1998 for invasion of privacy by a public authority which had caused distress to a person, where that act was merely negligent.

In some cases a finding of a violation in itself is just satisfaction, especially if there is insufficient causal connection between any violation and the victim's loss.

CASE EXAMPLE

R (Greenfield) v Home Secretary [2005] UKHL 14

A prisoner had been refused legal representation during prison disciplinary proceedings, in violation of Art 6 of the European Convention.

The House of Lords held that when domestic courts are considering awarding compensation under s 8 of the Human Rights Act 1998 they should take into account the case law of the European Court, although they are not bound to follow such decisions. In particular, the courts should apply the principle applied by the European Court in cases where there has been held to be a breach of Art 6, to the effect that a finding of a violation of Art 6 is normally just satisfaction in itself, and that it was not appropriate for such awards to be comparable to tortious awards.

In the present case it would not be appropriate to speculate whether the procedural defect would have influenced the outcome of the proceedings and the prisoner's guilt or sanction.

Issue	Effect	Authority
Application to private law	The Act has a limited horizontal effect, allowing the principles of the Act to be applied in proceedings of a private nature	*Douglas v Hello!* (2001)
Who can use the Act and where?	The Act can be used in any proceedings by anyone who is a 'victim' of any alleged violation	s 7, HRA
Time limit for bringing proceedings	Proceedings under the Act must be brought within one year, or via other proceedings in line with the appropriate time limit for such proceedings	s 7, HRA
Remedies	The courts have the power to grant appropriate remedies to those whose Convention rights have been violated	s 8, HRA
Just satisfaction, including damages	The courts may award 'just satisfaction' to the victim, in line with the principles applied by the European Court of Human Rights. 'Just satisfaction' includes the power to award damages to compensate for pecuniary and non-pecuniary loss suffered by the victim	s 8, HRA
Availability of damages	The courts will not automatically grant damages for breach of Convention	*Greenfield v Home Secretary* (2005)

17.10 Freedom of expression and freedom of religion

Because of fears that the Act might interfere unduly with free speech, press freedom and freedom of religious organisations, it makes specific provision to protect freedom of expression (s 12) and freedom of religion (s 13).

Section 12 applies whenever a court is considering granting relief which might affect the right of freedom of expression. The section then lays down three rules:

■ Any such relief should not normally be granted where the respondent is neither present or represented (s 12(2)).
■ Where such relief would have the effect of restraining publication before trial, no such order should be given unless the applicant is likely to establish that publication should not be allowed (s 12(3) – see *Cream Holdings v Banerjee* [2004] UKHL 44).
■ Where the proceedings relate to material which is journalistic, literary or artistic, the court must have regard to the extent to which the material has, or is about to become available to the public, whether it is, or would be, in the public interest for the material to be published, and any relevant privacy code (s 12(4)).

However the courts must not give added weight to Article 10 when it is in conflict with other rights (*Re S (A Child)* [2005] UKHL 47) and must balance each right proportionately.

During the passage of the Human Rights Bill church organisations were concerned that the right to employ suitable teachers in religious schools and to impose requirements for religious marriages would be threatened by actions under the 1998 Act. Under s 13, if a court's determination of any question arising under the Act might affect the exercise by a religious organisation of its right to freedom of thought, conscience and religion, it must have particular regard to the importance of that right. Thus, the courts will be obliged to take this right into account in developing the law in favour of the enjoyment of the rights contained in Art 9, including allowing interferences with other Convention rights.

Despite s 13, the right to religion may be outweighed by other interests and rights.

CASE EXAMPLE

R (Williamson) v Secretary of State for Employment [2005] UKHL 15

Teachers and parents claimed that the prohibition of corporal punishment in schools interfered with their Convention rights to have their children educated in conformity with their
religious convictions (under Art 2 of the First Protocol) and was in violation of Art 9 of the
European Convention, guaranteeing freedom to manifest religion.

The House of Lords held that although the Articles were engaged, Parliament was entitled
to make an exception to those rights on the basis that they interfered with the child's rights
not to be subject to inhuman and degrading treatment under Art 3. Parliament was entitled
to have a broad blanket rule on prohibition and the domestic legislation was thus not
incompatible.

CASE EXAMPLE

R (Begum) v Denbigh High School [2006] UKHL 15

A school had insisted that a student wear school uniform, which precluded the wearing of
the full Muslim 'jilbab'. The student claimed that she had been excluded from the school in
breach of her Convention rights to manifest her religion.

The House of Lords held that there had been no interference with her right to manifest her
religion as she had chosen a school where such a policy existed; the two-year disruption to
her schooling was the result of her unwillingness to comply with a rule to which the school
was entitled to adhere. In any case the school was fully justified in acting in that manner as
it had, after full consultation with parents and religious bodies, designed a flexible and fair
uniform policy.

17.11 Derogations and reservations

Article 15 of the European Convention allows Member States to lodge a formal derogation in respect of a state of war or other public emergency. Article 16 also allows a state to
place a reservation on its commitment to a specific Convention right.

17.11.1 Derogations

Article 15 allows a Member State to 'derogate' from its obligations under the Convention in times of war or other public emergency threatening the life of the nation (see
Chapter 16), and under s 14 of the Human Rights Act United Kingdom derogations
existing at the time of the Act's implementation are contained in Sched 3.

This included the government's derogation notices of 1988 and 1989, which were made
after the European Court's decision in *Brogan v United Kingdom* (1989) 11 EHRR 117, where
the court found that domestic provisions allowing extended detention of suspected
terrorists were in violation of Art 5 of the Convention.

This derogation was withdrawn by an order made under the Human Rights Act
(Human Rights Act (Amendment) Order 2001 SI 2001/1216) when the relevant statutory
provisions were replaced by the Terrorism Act 2000. The Secretary of State then made The
Human Rights Act 1998 (Amendment No 2) Order 2001, derogating from Art 5(1) of the
European Convention and providing for an extended power to arrest and detain foreign
nationals, whom it is intended to remove or deport from the United Kingdom, but where
such removal would be in violation of the Convention if a person was returned to that
particular country (*Chahal v United Kingdom* (1997) 23 EHRR 413).

These powers were challenged in *A and others v Secretary of State for the Home Department* [2004] UKHL 56 where it was alleged that the detention provisions contained in
s 23 of the Anti-terrorism, Crime and Security Act 2001 were in violation of Arts 5 and
14 of the Convention. The House of Lords held that the detention of foreign nationals
suspected of terrorism under s 23 of the Anti-terrorism, Crime and Security Act 2001

was a disproportionate response to the threat of terrorism and not 'strictly required by the exigencies of the situation'. The fact that the provisions did not apply to British terrorists and failed to adequately safeguard against the threats from foreign terrorists (deported suspects could be deported and continue their activities) made those provisions discriminatory under Art 14, and a disproportionate interference with liberty of the person. The decision in *A* was upheld by the Grand Chamber of the European Court of Human Rights: *A v United Kingdom* (2009) 49 EHRR 29.

17.11.2 Reservations

Article 57 of the European Convention on Human Rights allows each Member State to make reservations in connection with its obligations under the Convention (see Chapter 16) and s 15 of the Human Rights Act 1998 incorporates any designated reservation that has been lodged under the Convention. If a designated reservation is withdrawn wholly or in part it ceases to have effect (s 15(3)), and reservations cease to have effect five years after the Act came into force, or five years after the designation order (s 16(1)). The Secretary may extend that period by a further five years, under s 16(2).

ACTIVITY

Self-test questions

1. What constitutes a 'public authority' under the Act, and how have the courts interpreted that term?
2. Who can claim to be a 'victim' under the Act? Give real and hypothetical examples.
3. Explain the term 'just satisfaction' with respect to the courts' powers to grant remedies under the 1998 Act.
4. In what circumstances may damages be granted by the courts and on what basis are they assessed?
5. How are freedom of expression and freedom of religion given specific protection under the 1998 Act?
6. Explain the powers of derogation under s 14 of the Act and explain how the government's derogation was successfully challenged in *A and others v Secretary of State* (2004)?

SUMMARY

- Civil liberty is traditionally protected in the UK by the common law and by Parliament and the common law courts.
- Common law rights are subject to parliamentary sovereignty and the limited constitutional powers of the courts.
- Inconsistency of domestic law and protection with the European Convention on Human Rights, and a desire to strengthen human rights domestically, led to the passing of the Human Rights Act 1998.
- The Act came into force in October 2000, did not have retrospective effect for breaches before that date, and gave further effect to the rights contained in the Convention (Articles 2–12, 14 and subsequent protocols).
- The Act allows courts to employ Convention case law (including proportionality) when resolving Convention disputes (s 2), to interpret all legislation compatibly with such rights (wherever possible) (s 3), and to declare legislation incompatible with Convention rights (s 4).
- The Act does not affect the right of individual petition to the European Court of Human Rights (see Chapter 16).
- The Act does not allow the courts to question the validity of primary legislation, or secondary legislation that is consistent with clear primary legislation: thus parliamentary sovereignty is preserved.

- All public authorities must act compatibly with Convention rights, unless authorised otherwise clearly by primary legislation (s 6) Courts are public authorities and must apply all law (public and private) compatibly with Convention rights.
- The Act, thus, has some 'horizontal' effect (*Campbell v MGN*).
- Victims of Convention violations can bring actions (under s 7) in any legal proceedings against public authorities (and can use Convention rights 'horizontally' in private law against private individuals).
- Domestic courts can award just satisfaction to the victim against public authorities if they find a violation of their Convention rights (s 8).
- Ministers can fast-track legislative change when alerted to incompatibility of legislation (s 10), and must make a declaration of compatibility or otherwise of a Bill when introducing it to Parliament.
- The Act makes special provision for the protection of freedom of expression (s 12) and freedom of religion (s 13), although neither provision allows the courts to give added weight to those rights when in conflict with other Convention rights (*Re S (A Child)* and *R (Williamson)*).
- The Act allows ministers to make Article 15 derogations of Convention rights (s 14) and Article 16 reservations (s 15).

SAMPLE ESSAY QUESTION

How has the Human Rights Act 1998 changed the constitutional method of protecting human rights and civil liberties in the United Kingdom?

> Explain the particular features of the British constitution with respect to the protection of fundamental human rights: no formal constitution or Bill of rights, protection by the courts via the common law, parliamentary sovereignty and the limited role of the courts and the rule of law

> Explain the advantages and defects of the 'traditional' method of rights protection, drawing on examples of protection (*Entick v Carrington*) and its limitations (*ex parte Brind*). In particular, give examples of defeats before the European Court of Human Rights as a result of inconsistency with the Convention (*Golder v UK; Sunday Times v UK; Malone v UK* etc)

> Explain the purpose of passing the Human Rights Act 1998 and its effects: to give effect to Convention rights within domestic law; to allow domestic courts to achieve consistency of domestic law with Convention law by the process of interpretation and declarations of incompatibility; to provide a statutory list of positive fundamental rights as opposed to residual liberties

Explain and analyse the central provisions of the Act with respect to the courts' new powers (ss 2–4 and 6–8), together with provisions allowing Parliament and the government to achieve compatibility (ss 10 and 19)

Critical explanation of relevant case law to examine whether the Act has, in practice, changed the constitutional method of protecting rights: Has it provided the courts with greater powers of review and interpretation (*A, Daly, R v A*), and specifically has it changed the constitutional role of the courts and the British constitutional arrangements? Have we now got a Bill of rights with a constitutional court? (assess the significance of the new Supreme Court in this respect)

CONCLUSION

(Summarise the effect of the Act on the protection of human rights in the UK and the effect on the constitutional arrangements for their protection)

Further reading

Books

Amos, M, *Human Rights Law* (Hart 2006), Pt I.

Fenwick, H *Civil Liberties and Human Rights* (4th edn, Routledge 2007), Chapters 3 and 4

Foster, S, *Human Rights and Civil Liberties* (2nd edn, Longman, 2008), Chapter 3.

Wadham, J and Mountfield, H, *Blackstone's Guide to the Human Rights Act 1998* (5th edn, Oxford University Press, 2009).

Articles

Clayton, R, 'The Human Rights Act six years on: where are we now?' [2007] EHRLR 11.

Feldman, D, 'The Human Rights Act and Constitutional Principles' (1999) 19 *Legal Studies* 165.

Klug, F 'A Bill of Rights, do we need one or do we already have one?' [2007] PL 701.

Masterman, 'Interpretations, declarations and dialogues: rights protection under the Human Rights Act' [2009] PL 112.

18

Freedom of speech

AIMS AND OBJECTIVES

At the end of this chapter you should be able to:
- Appreciate the constitutional importance of freedom of expression and its position within the British constitution
- Appreciate the impact of the Human Rights Act 1998 on this right
- Explain some of the circumstances in which the criminal law can interfere with freedom of expression
- Explain some of the circumstances in which the civil law can interfere with freedom of expression

18.1 The constitutional importance of free speech

18.1.1 Introduction

Freedom of expression is a central aspect of all democratic states. In most countries this right is constitutionally ring-fenced and protected by being incorporated into a Bill or Charter of Rights. For example, the First Amendment of the United States constitution (ie the 1791 Bill of Rights) declares that:

ARTICLE

Congress shall make no law … abridging the freedom of speech, or of the press.

Similarly, Pt III, Art 19 of the Indian constitution states that:

ARTICLE

All citizens have the right to freedom of speech.

Freedom of speech, therefore, is one of the most important constitutional rights that an individual enjoys. The overriding constitutional significance of freedom of expression has been re-affirmed by the European Court of Human Rights in *Handyside v United Kingdom* (1976) 1 EHRR 737:

JUDGMENT

'… The Court's supervisory functions oblige it to pay the utmost attention to the principles characterising a "democratic society". Freedom of expression constitutes one of the essential foundations of such a society, one of the basic conditions for its progress and for the development of every man. Subject to paragraph 2 of Article 10 [see section 18.2.4], it is applicable not only to "information" or "ideas" that are favourably received or regarded as inoffensive or as a matter of indifference, but also to those that offend, shock or disturb the State or any sector of the population. Such are the demands of that pluralism, tolerance and broadmindedness without which there is no "democratic society".'

Finally, two further points need to be made:

Firstly, although the terms freedom of expression and free speech are used interchangeably, the former is more inclusive than the latter. In short, whereas speech is typically associated with the written and spoken word, expression can be broader and includes artistic expression (eg a sculpture in an art gallery).

Secondly, the media have a particular role to play in a democracy in advancing freedom of expression interests and this function has been recognised by the European Court of Human Rights (*Lingens v Austria* (1986) 8 EHRR 407). In particular, the media can impart information which informs political debate and the political decision-making process.

18.1.2 The justification for the principle of free expression

Fenwick has drawn attention to four main justifications widely advanced in favour of free speech (H Fenwick, *Civil Liberties and Human Rights* (4th edn, Cavendish, 2007) at pp 300–06):

▪ Moral autonomy

The argument under this heading is that freedom of expression supports an individual's moral autonomy by permitting him to make choices for himself as to what he reads, sees or hears. In other words, the individual chooses the information which he receives, rather than this being decided by the state.

▪ Self-fulfilment

The argument in relation to self-fulfilment is based on the notion that freedom of expression advances the growth of an individual. In short, free access to information can stimulate and foster an individual's intellectual and moral growth.

▪ Democracy

This argument is based on the inherent connection between free speech and the democratic process. In order for a democracy to function and flourish, it necessitates that individuals (and in particular the press) have the freedom to disseminate information concerning governmental and public affairs. In this way free speech informs political debate, discussion and the electoral process. Indeed, the European Court of Human Rights has repeatedly emphasised the importance of political speech. In *Castells v Spain* (1992) 14 EHRR 445:

JUDGMENT

'The limits of permissible criticism are wider with regard to the government than in relation to a private citizen, or even a politician. In the democratic system the actions or omissions of the government must be subject to the close scrutiny not only of the legislative and judicial authorities but also of the press and public opinion.'

■ **Truth**

The argument under this heading is that freedom of speech leads ultimately to the discovery of the truth. In other words, the danger with limiting free speech is the possibility that the truth is being suppressed.

ACTIVITY

Self-test question

Why do you think that freedom of expression is considered to be one of the most important human rights enjoyed by an individual?

18.2 Freedom of expression in the British constitution

18.2.1 The residual liberty of expression

Prior to the enactment of the Human Rights Act 1998, the British constitution was hallmarked by providing negative, residual liberties, rather than positive human rights (see at section 6.7.8 Dicey's views on the role of the judiciary being to protect the liberties of the individual). Historically, in the United Kingdom individuals did not (as in the United States) enjoy a positive right to free speech *per se*; instead they had the residual liberty of expression. In other words, an individual could write or say whatever they liked provided they did not infringe a law (statutory or common law). See Sir Robert McGarry VC in *Malone v Metropolitan Police Commissioner* (1979) at section 6.7.7.

In this sense, therefore, provided an individual did not violate the laws of defamation, obscenity, indecency, contempt of court, etc, everything else was permitted (ie the residue left when all the laws have been identified). This is illustrated by the figure below:

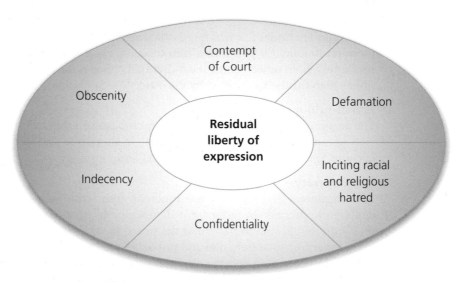

Figure 18.1 The residual liberty of expression

There were a number of difficulties with residual liberties:

■ Firstly, it presupposed that an individual was aware of the laws (and their parameters) which restricted their liberty of expression.

■ Secondly, Parliament (through the enactment of statutes), the executive (through the enactment of delegated legislation) and the courts (through the development of the common law) could incrementally reduce the residue of liberty. In this sense, residual liberties were vulnerable in a way that positive rights were not.

18.2.2 The interplay of freedom of speech with other competing interests

Notwithstanding the above, historically the courts, indirectly, have tried to protect residual liberties (such as the liberty of expression) from unnecessary interference. In other words, in interpreting, applying and determining the parameters of laws such as defamation and confidentiality, the courts could (indirectly) determine the extent to which these laws impinged on the residue of freedom of expression.

For example, in the context of the law of libel, the wider the defences to this tort are drawn the more difficult it will be for an individual to sue for libel. This in turn gives greater protection to freedom of expression. For example, in *Reynolds v Times Newspapers* [2001] 2 AC 127 the House of Lords developed the common law defence of qualified privilege to provide the press, in appropriate circumstances, with a defence (albeit restricted) of qualified privilege where the publication of information is in the public interest. This restricted defence depended on factors such as the seriousness of the allegation, public concern in respect of the subject-matter, together with whether the claimant had been given an opportunity to explain or comment on the allegations. On the facts, however, the allegations made by the press were not considered to be information which the public had a right to know (*The Sunday Times* had failed to mention Reynolds' explanation). On defamation see section 18.4.1.

Conversely, the narrower these defences are drawn, the easier it is to sue for libel, and this necessarily impacts on free speech. In this way, the courts, in determining the parameters of laws which aim to protect other interests (eg defamation serves to protect reputations, confidentiality aims to protect private information) can indirectly affect freedom of expression. In *R v Home Secretary, ex parte Brind* [1991] 1 AC 696 in the House of Lords, Lord Bridge stressed that there had to be a strong justification for interfering with free speech:

JUDGMENT

'… this surely does not mean that in deciding whether the Secretary of State, in the exercise of his discretion could reasonably impose the restriction he has imposed on the broadcasting organisations, we are not perfectly entitled to start from the premise that any restriction of the right to freedom of expression requires to be justified and that nothing less than an important competing public interest will be sufficient to justify it.'

At times, however, judges have disagreed with each other over the weight that should be attached to competing interests (eg the conflicting interests of protecting an individual's reputation with the principle of freedom of speech of the press). Another set of competing interests involve the freedom of speech of the press and the administration of justice/national security.

CASE EXAMPLE

Harman v Secretary of State for the Home Department [1983] 1 AC 280

Harman, a solicitor (legal officer of the National Council for Civil Liberties – now called LIBERTY), was acting for a person taking legal action against the Home Office. In the context of the litigation the latter disclosed documents and after the court hearing Harman allowed a journalist access to documents which had already been read out in court. The journalist then wrote an article and the Home Office sought an order against Harman for contempt of court. The House of Lords (dismissing Harman's appeal) held by three to two that a solicitor gave an implied undertaking not to use the information obtained on discovery during the course of litigation for a purpose other than for her client's action. The court confirmed that Harman had been guilty of a (civil) contempt of court.

Their Lordships, however, opined different views over whether the case engaged freedom of expression. Lord Diplock (in the majority) stated that:

JUDGMENT

'I start by saying what the case is *not* about. It is *not* about freedom of speech, freedom of the press, openness of justice or documents coming into "the public domain".'

Conversely, Lord Scarman (in the dissenting minority) commented that:

JUDGMENT

'A balance has to be struck between two interests of the law – on the one hand, the protection of a litigant's private right to keep his documents to himself notwithstanding his duty to disclose them to the other side in the litigation, and, on the other, the protection of the right, which the law recognises, subject to certain exceptions, as the right of everyone, to speak freely, and to impart information and ideas, upon matters of public knowledge.'

Similarly, see the different judicial attitudes exhibited by the majority on the one hand, and Lords Scarman and Fraser (in the minority) on the other, in relation to the issue of national security impinging upon the freedom of the press and compelling journalists to disclose their sources in *Secretary of State for Defence v Guardian Newspapers* [1985] 1 AC 339.

Fenwick has stated that before the Human Rights Act 1998 'the judiciary did not seem to be united around a clear conception of their role' and 'that common practice as regards fundamental freedoms did not emerge'. In effect, the British courts, unlike in other countries, lacked a Bill or Charter of Rights to 'anchor', and so help shape, their decisions (H Fenwick, *Civil Liberties and Human Rights* (4th edn, Cavendish, 2007) p 113). The existence, however, of such a Charter or Bill of Rights which protects freedom of expression has not prevented judicial inconsistency in, for example, the Supreme Court of the United States.

Finally, it should be noted that the balancing of freedoms/rights/liberties is achieved sometimes by Parliament in enacting legislation. For example, the Obscene Publications Act 1959 makes it a criminal offence to publish an obscene article; however, s 4 of the Act protects freedom of expression where the article is in the interests of the public good (eg literature) (see section 18.3.3).

18.2.3 The Human Rights Act 1998

The passing of the Human Rights Act 1998 resulted in negative residual liberties being converted into positive rights which can be directly asserted in domestic courts. Moreover, the Human Rights Act 1998, together with the European Convention on Human Rights with its voluminous European Court of Human Rights case law, provide the modern judiciary with an established set of principles concerning the protection of human rights and how they interrelate with other competing rights and interests. Indeed, s 2 of the Human Rights Act 1998 places a statutory obligation on our judges to have regard for the jurisprudence of the European Court in Strasbourg.

18.2.4 Article 10

Article 10 of the European Convention states that:

ARTICLE

Art 10(1)
'Everyone has the right to freedom of expression. This right shall include freedom to hold opinions and to receive and impart information and ideas without interference by public authority and regardless of frontiers ...'

Article 10 is a conditional right and can be legitimately interfered with by other competing interests. This right also carries with it certain responsibilities and duties. The primary right of freedom of expression is thus not an absolute right (as it conflicts with other interests and carries with it responsibilities) and therefore can be restricted by the following wide range of interests as set out in Art 10(2):

ARTICLE

> 'national security, territorial integrity or public safety, for the prevention of disorder or crime, for the protection of health or morals, for the protection of the reputation or rights of others, for preventing the disclosure of information received in confidence, or for maintaining the authority and impartiality of the judiciary'.

Under the Human Rights Act 1998, if individuals contend that the state (public authority) has, without lawful justification, interfered with their right to freedom of expression, they can petition a domestic court and seek a remedy. In such circumstances the court must follow the legal reasoning adopted by Strasbourg and will, therefore, have to determine:

- Whether there has been an interference with the primary right under Art 10.
- Whether the interference (ie the restriction) can be justified as:
    - (i) being prescribed by law (ie being sufficiently clear and certain – see the case of *Sunday Times v United Kingdom* (1979) 2 EHRR 245 at section 16.6.1),
    - (ii) having a legitimate aim (ie seeking to achieve one of the objectives set out in Art 10(2) above),
    - (iii) being necessary in a democratic society (ie there is a pressing social need for it and it is not disproportionate).

In this way the courts will balance competing interests, but will have the advantage of the jurisprudence of the European Court to assist them in determining this. In domestic law the Human Rights Act 1998 makes particular provision for Art 10 and freedom of expression: s 12 of the Act applies to a situation where a court is considering to grant relief that will impact on Art 10. In particular, a temporary injunction which restrains an article from being published pending the full trial on the matter will only be granted if the court is satisfied that the applicant (at the full trial) is likely to prove that the article should not be published. Section 12(2) also prevents *ex parte* applications (ie those where the other party is not present) being made, although they could be made in exceptional circumstances.

It should be noted that s 12 is peculiar to the Human Rights Act 1998 (ie the provision is not drawn from a corresponding European Convention Article) and it is clear that the domestic judges have differed over its requirements (ie whether Art 10 should be given an elevated weighting – see *Re S (a child)* [2004] UKHL 47). In *Cream Holdings v Banerjee* [2004] UKHL 44, the House of Lords held that in applying s 12(3), when an applicant sought an interim injunction (which if granted would infringe Art 10), the test which the court should employ was to consider whether the applicant's prospect of success at the full trial was sufficiently favourable to justify the granting of the interim injunction.

ACTIVITY

Essay writing

Compare and contrast how freedom of expression was protected by the British courts before and after the passing of the Human Rights Act 1998.

KEY FACTS

Key facts on freedom of expression in the British constitution

> Freedom of expression is one of the most important constitutional rights that an individual enjoys and it is recognised by all democratic states.

Article 10 of the European Convention states that: Everyone has the right to freedom of expression. This is, however, a conditional right which can be legitimately interfered with to secure a wide range of competing interests.

Under the Human Rights Act 1998 individuals can now raise Art 10 directly in domestic courts and the judiciary are required to take cognisance of the case law of the European Court of Human Rights and adopt the legal reasoning that it employs in determining whether Art 10 can be legitimately interfered with.

18.3 Free speech and the criminal law

Introduction

Although freedom of expression is of fundamental constitutional importance, as indicated above, it is not (and cannot be) an absolute right. As free speech comes into conflict with other competing interests (eg national security, public decency and the administration of justice), it is necessarily a conditional right which can be legitimately interfered with to protect these other interests. There are a wide variety of ways in which the criminal law (whether statutory or common law) can legitimately interfere with an individual's freedom of expression.

18.3.1 Protecting religious sensibilities (now historic)

Blasphemy was a common law criminal offence which in effect outlawed the scurrilous treatment and vilification of matters sacred to Christians which were likely to outrage and shock their feelings. A number of points should be noted about this offence. Firstly, it was confined to the Anglican version of Christianity. Secondly, it criminalised the publication of matters (blasphemous libel if in written form) for which a convicted person could (in theory) endure life imprisonment. Thirdly, blasphemy did not apply to other religions (*R v Chief Metropolitan Stipendiary Magistrate, ex parte Choudhury* [1991] 1 All ER 306). Fourthly, there was no 'public good' defence available to a defendant (contrast obscenity at section 18.3.3). Fifthly, in modern times prosecutions for blasphemy were very rare. The only prosecution since the early twentieth century was *Lemon* and this was a private prosecution instigated by Mary Whitehouse:

CASE EXAMPLE

Whitehouse v Lemon [1979] AC 617

Lemon was the editor of *Gay News* which in 1976 published a poem (together with a drawing) which, among other things, purported to describe acts of sodomy with Christ following his death as well as attributing homosexual practices to him with his Apostles. Mary Whitehouse successfully instituted a private prosecution against Lemon and Gay News Ltd for blasphemous libel. The House of Lords upheld the conviction by a majority on the basis that it was not necessary for the prosecution to prove an intention to blaspheme, merely an intention to publish a matter which *was* blasphemous.

Gay News Ltd subsequently unsuccessfully petitioned the European Commission of Human Rights on the basis that blasphemy violated freedom of expression (*Gay News Ltd and Lemon v United Kingdom* (1982) 5 EHRR 123). In any event, the offence of blasphemy was abolished by s 79 of the Criminal Justice and Immigration Act 2008.

Any law of blasphemy could be justified under Art 10(2) of the European Convention as a legitimate interference with free speech as protecting the *rights of others* (ie Christian believers not to be outraged, see *Wingrove v United Kingdom* (1996) 24 EHRR 1).

18.3.2 Protecting the public from indecent material

▪ Common law indecency

It is a common law offence to commit an act to outrage public decency (this is to protect the public from outrage). As with blasphemy above, there is no public good defence to this offence.

CASE EXAMPLE

R v Gibson and another [1991] 1 All ER 439

Sylveire ran an art gallery. In the gallery's catalogue was an exhibition entitled 'Human Earrings' which was a work (made by Gibson) which consisted of a model's head to which a freeze-dried human foetus had been attached to each ear lobe. Both Gibson and Sylveire were convicted of outraging public decency. The Court of Appeal dismissed their appeals against conviction on the ground, *inter alia*, that the prosecution did not have to prove that the appellants had intended to outrage public decency.

▪ Statutory indecency

A number of statutory offences outlaw indecency. For example, s 1 of the Indecent Displays (Control) Act 1981 makes it a criminal offence (punishable by up to two years' imprisonment) publicly to display an indecent matter. The Act is essentially designed to deal with nuisance public displays and there is no public good defence.

The laws of indecency could be justified under Art 10(2) of the European Convention as a legitimate interference with free speech as serving the legitimate objective of protecting the rights of others (ie individuals not be offended by, or subject to, nuisance material) and the protection of health or morals.

18.3.3 Controlling material which depraves and corrupts

The Obscene Publications Act 1959 (as amended in 1964) makes it a criminal offence, punishable by up to three years' imprisonment, for a person to publish an obscene article (or to have such an article in his possession for publication for gain).

The definition of obscenity is set out in s 1 namely that the effect of the article is such as (taken as a whole) to tend to deprave and corrupt those persons who are likely to see, read or hear the matter. In this context, therefore, the Act is not concerned with articles which shock or offend, but instead with something more pernicious: corruption. It should be recalled that Handyside (a publisher) was convicted under the Act for having in his possession for publication for gain an obscene article: copies of a reference book called *The Little Red Schoolbook* (see section 6.6.2). He was convicted and a forfeiture order was issued which resulted in the destruction of these books. Handyside subsequently unsuccessfully petitioned the European Court of Human Rights contending that this violated Art 10; however, the court held that it was a legitimate and proportionate interference with Handyside's right to freedom of expression.

The Obscene Publications Act 1959 aims to strike a balance between protecting the public from being depraved and corrupted and freedom of expression. Section 4 states that a person has a defence (the defence of public good):

SECTION

s 4(1)
'... if it is proved that publication of the article in question is justified as being for the public good on the ground that it is in the interests of science, literature, art or learning, or of other objects of general concern'.

In this context, it is of interest to note that Penguin Books were unsuccessfully prosecuted under the Act in relation to the publication of DH Lawrence's *Lady Chatterley's Lover* (*R v Penguin Books* [1961] Crim LR 176). The defence made use of expert witnesses to testify to the literary importance of the book and the jury acquitted, evidently on the basis that the book fell within s 4 as being justified in the interests of literature.

The law of obscenity could be justified under Art 10(2) of the European Convention as a legitimate interference with free speech as serving the legitimate objective of *the protection of health or morals* (ie preventing the corruption of individuals) – see *Handyside* (1976).

ACTIVITY

Exercise

Do you think that the laws of indecency and obscenity are necessary in a democratic society and achieve a proper balance between free speech and public morality?

18.3.4 Protecting public order

There are a number of offences which restrict free speech in order to preserve public order. For example, s 18 of the Public Order Act 1986 makes it a criminal offence for a person to use threatening, abusive or insulting words and behaviour in order to intend to stir up racial hatred (or where it is likely to be stirred up). The Racial and Religious Hatred Act 2006 amended the Public Order Act 1986 and made it unlawful to stir up religious hatred. However, as a concession to free speech s 29J (as incorporated into the 1986 Act) provides that:

SECTION

S 29J

'Nothing in this part shall be read or given effect in a way which prohibits or restricts discussion, criticism or expressions of antipathy, dislike, ridicule, insult or abuse of particular religions or the beliefs or practices of their adherents, or of any other belief system or the beliefs or practices of its adherents, or proselytising or urging adherents of a different religion or belief system to cease practising their religion or belief system.'

The law of inciting racial hatred could be justified under Art 10(2) of the European Convention as a legitimate interference with free speech as serving to prevent disorder or crime.

18.3.5 Protecting the administration of justice

Under s 1 of the Perjury Act 1911 it is an offence for a person sworn in as a witness to make a statement during judicial proceedings which he knows to be false (or does not believe to be true). The law of perjury could be justified under Art 10(2) of the European Convention as a legitimate interference with free speech as serving to maintain the authority and impartiality of the judiciary. In addition, the Contempt of Court Act 1981 is designed to protect the integrity of court proceedings.

18.3.6 Protecting national security

Section 1 of the Official Secrets Act 1989 makes it a criminal offence for a member of the security and intelligence services to disclose information (without lawful authority) relating to security or intelligence:

R v Shayler [2002] UKHL 11

Shayler had been charged with unlawfully disclosing information contrary to ss 1 and 4 of the 1989 Act. As the Human Rights Act 1998 was in force, he contended that the 1989 Act should be interpreted with a public interest defence (ie that Shayler was acting in the public interest in disclosing such information). The House of Lords dismissed Shayler's appeal and held that the Official Secrets Act 1989 was consistent with the requirements of Art 10 of the Convention. It was noted that Shayler could have sought internal authorisation for the disclosure of the information.

The Official Secrets Act could, therefore, be justified under Art 10(2) of the European Convention as a legitimate interference with free speech as serving the interests of *national security*.

18.4 Free speech and the civil law

In addition to the restrictions imposed by the criminal law, free speech can be legitimately interfered with by the civil law with the intention of protecting private interests such as reputation and confidential information.

18.4.1 The protection of reputation

The law of defamation serves to provide protection for a person's reputation from false statements which damage it, or which are capable of doing so. There are a number of defences to an action for defamation which serve to protect free speech. These are:

- **Justification** – that the impugned statement was true (or substantially true).
- **Fair comment** – that the statement was simply a fair comment on an issue of public interest.
- **Absolute privilege** – this provides immunity from legal liability for things said during the proceedings in court (see section 13.4.2) or Parliament (see section 8.6).
- **Qualified privilege** – this defence (providing there is no malice) is available in certain situations, for example, where one party has a duty to inform another who has a corresponding interest/duty to receive such information. In *Reynolds v Times Newspapers* (2001) (see section 18.2.2), the House of Lords held that although the press did not have a defence of public interest *per se*, in certain circumstances the defence of qualified privilege might be available to the press to justify information published in the public interest. See also *Jameel v Wall Street Journal Europe Sprl* [2006] UKHL 44.
- **Innocent dissemination** – this is particularly relevant to broadcasters.

As noted above, the judges in interpreting and applying the law of defamation and its defences determine its impact on freedom of expression. For example, in *Derbyshire County Council v Times Newspapers Ltd* (1993) (for the facts see section 4.8.2) the House of Lords held that under the common law a local authority could not sue in defamation. Lord Keith stated that:

JUDGMENT

'It is of the highest public importance that a democratically elected governmental body, or indeed any governmental body, should be open to uninhibited public criticism … I regard it as right for this House to lay down that not only is there no public interest favouring the right of organs of government, whether central or local, to sue for libel, but that it is contrary to the public interest that they should have it. It is contrary to the public interest because to admit such actions would place an undesirable fetter on freedom of speech.'

The law of the defamation could be justified under Art 10(2) of the European Convention as a legitimate interference with free speech as serving to protect the reputation of others.

18.4.2 The protection of confidential information

The law of confidentiality seeks to protect the confidentiality of private/secret information (including information held by the state).There are a number of defences to an action for confidentiality which serve to protect free speech. One such defence is that such information is already in the public domain as demonstrated in the *'Spycatcher'* case:

CASE EXAMPLE

Attorney General v Observer Ltd and others [1988] 3 WLR 776

Peter Wright (a former member of MI5) wrote *Spycatcher*, a book which detailed alleged unlawful activities of members of MI5. In 1985 in Australia, the Attorney General sought to prevent the book being published on the ground of confidentiality (ie a duty to the Crown not to disclose information).

Thereafter, the Attorney General obtained interlocutory (temporary) injunctions against *The Guardian* and the *Observer* until trial from publishing any information from Peter Wright in his role as a member of MI5. The Attorney General also subsequently secured an interlocutory injunction restraining *The Sunday Times* from publishing further extracts from its serialisation of *Spycatcher*.

The House of Lords held that the world-wide publication of *Spycatcher* (it had been published in the United States) had destroyed the secrecy of its contents (hence its confidentiality) and as a consequence, the injunctions against the newspapers were not necessary and should be discharged. In essence, for a public body to override freedom of expression in the context of confidentiality, a clear public interest of non-disclosure must be demonstrated.

The newspapers subsequently successfully petitioned the European Court of Human Rights on the basis that the continuation of the injunctions after the book was freely available (having been published in America) violated Art 10 (*Observer and Guardian v United Kingdom* (1991) 14 EHRR 153).

The law of confidentiality could be justified under Art 10(2) of the European Convention as a legitimate interference with free speech as serving to protect the *rights of others* (ie a private life/privacy). This is illustrated by the following case which involves a balance between privacy (private life) and the exercise of freedom of expression by the press:

CASE EXAMPLE

Campbell v MGN Ltd [2004] UKHL 22

Naomi Campbell (a model) sued MGN Ltd for breach of confidentiality for publishing details of her therapy for drug addiction at a self-help group meeting, together with photographs of her leaving a meeting.

The House of Lords held that the Convention right of Art 8 (the right of Campbell to a private life – including details of her therapy which was private and confidential information) outweighed the competing right under Art 10, the freedom of expression of the press. As a consequence Campbell was entitled to damages.

KEY FACTS

Key facts on free speech

| As a conditional right, freedom of expression can be legitimately interfered with by both the criminal and civil law. |

The criminal law

Free speech can be infringed in order to secure the following legitimate objectives:

- The protection of national security (Official Secrets Act 1989).
- The protection of public order (Public Order Act 1986).
- The protection of the administration of justice (Perjury Act 1911/Contempt of Court Act 1981).
- The protection of the public from indecent material (common law and statutory indecency).
- The prevention of corruption (Obscene Publications Acts 1959 and 1964).

The civil law

Free speech can be infringed in order to secure the following legitimate objectives:

- The protection of reputation (defamation).
- The protection of confidential information (confidentiality).

SUMMARY

- Freedom of expression/speech is a central aspect of all democratic states.
- In the United Kingdom, individuals historically enjoyed the residual liberty of expression, however, this was overtaken with the advent of the Human Rights Act 1998 which allows individuals to raise Article 10 (the right to freedom of expression) directly before a British court.
- Freedom of expression is not an absolute right as it conflicts with other interests and so can be legitimately interfered with in specified situations. Article 10(2) sets out the wide range of circumstances when the primary right of expression (set out in Article 10(1)) can be lawfully restricted.
- Free speech can be legitimately interfered with by both the criminal law (eg to protect national security) as well as the civil law (eg to protect confidential information).

SAMPLE ESSAY QUESTION

How is it possible to balance the fundamental right of freedom of expression with other rights and interests it comes into conflict with?

> Explain (briefly) the fundamental importance of freedom of expression in a democratic society and the values that it upholds – moral autonomy, freedom of the press, democracy, the discovery of the truth etc.

> Explain the 'conditional' status of freedom of expression under Art 10 of the European Convention – that it is subject to duties and responsibilities and legal and necessary restrictions. Give examples of legitimate aims listed in Art 10(2) and try to link those aims to relevant laws – for example, 'the reputation or rights of others' refers to the laws of defamation and confidentiality.

Explain the strict rules of legitimacy and necessity that any interference with free speech has to satisfy – that restrictions must be prescribed by law, have a legitimate aim and be necessary in a democratic society. Use cases such as *Sunday Times v United Kingdom* (1979) and *Observer and Guardian v United Kingdom* (1991) to illustrate. Also explain the constitutional status of free speech in the UK ('Spycatcher', *Attorney General v Observer Ltd* (1988) and *ex parte Brind* (1991).

Explain and analyse s 12 of the Human Rights Act 1998 with respect to the protection of free speech and the courts' role in upholding it.

Critically analyse a number of domestic laws, for example obscenity, racial hatred, defamation, confidentiality, contempt etc to consider the compatibility of such laws with Art 10 and the constitutional right of free speech in the UK.

CONCLUSION
Summarise the current position of free speech protection with respect to the balance of free speech and other rights and interests.

 ## Further reading

Books

Barendt, E, *Freedom of Speech* (2nd edn, Oxford University Press, 2005).

Bradley, A and Ewing, K, *Constitutional and Administrative Law* (14th edn, Pearson/ Longman, 2007), Chapter 23.

Fenwick, H, *Civil liberties and Human Rights* (4th edn, Cavendish, 2007) Pt II, pp 299–315 and Chapters 5–7.

Klug, F, Starmer, K and Weir, S, *The Three Pillars of Liberty* (Routledge, 1996), Chapter 9.

Foster, S, *Human Rights and Civil Liberties* (2nd edn, Longman, 2008), Chapters 9 and 10.

Articles

Amos, M, 'Can we speak freely now?' [2002] EHRLR 750.

19

Judicial review I (rationale and procedure)

AIMS AND OBJECTIVES

At the end of this chapter you should be able to:

■ Define and understand the nature of administrative law
■ Understand the nature and constitutional significance of judicial review
■ Understand who can seek judicial review and which bodies are subject to it
■ Appreciate the general public law procedure of judicial review

19.1 Administrative law

19.1.1 Introduction

As noted earlier at section 1.2.2, in broad terms administrative law concerns the principles relating to executive/governmental powers. Government officials and agencies are conferred with extensive powers (typically by statute) to provide public services (social security, housing, etc). Administrative law focuses specifically on the powers and responsibilities exercised by governmental bodies and how they are regulated and controlled by both legal and extra-judicial means. Although there is no clear demarcation between constitutional and administrative law (due largely to the absence of a codified constitution), the latter is particularly concerned with how the executive/administration uses and misuses its public law powers. In short, administrative law is concerned with ensuring that government and public law decision-makers are accountable for their actions.

Public lawyers are particularly interested in the following:

■ The methods by which the exercise of public powers and duties may be controlled by the courts or by other extra-judicial bodies (eg the Ombudsman).
■ The ways in which the government/administration in exercising its public law powers and duties facilitates the following constitutional principles: justice, participation in public affairs, open government.

An overview of the regulation of governmental power

Although administrative law primarily concerns the legal regulation of the exercise of public power by governmental bodies, it also embraces non-legal controls outside the strict court system. In general terms, government power is regulated in the following ways:

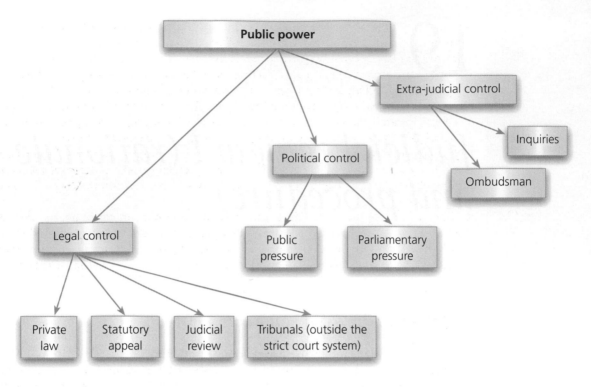

Figure 19.1 The regulation of public power

19.1.2 Political control

The government is politically controlled in the following ways:

i) **Public pressure** – Government is influenced by public pressure and may therefore react to public opinion (for example, the replacement of the controversial community charge 'the poll tax' with the council tax by virtue of the Local Government Finance Act 1992). Sometimes by reacting to public opinion, the government may act illegally (see *ex parte Venables and Thompson* (1997) at section 5.7.6 where the Home Secretary acted unlawfully in taking into account public concern regarding the length of Venables and Thompson's detention for killing James Bulger). Ultimately, of course, governments (or more accurately, MPs in the government) need to seek re-election at least every five years and obtain the support of the electorate (see the notion of political sovereignty at section 7.2.2).

ii) **Parliamentary pressure** – In constitutional theory, government ministers are controlled and regulated in Parliament through the following devices:

■ Parliamentary questions (see section 12.4).
■ Parliamentary debates (see section 12.5).
■ Parliamentary committees (see section 12.6).

In fact, two of the most fundamental constitutional conventions underpinning our constitution are the conventions of collective and individual responsibility (see sections 12.2 to 12.3).

19.1.3 Legal control

The government is legally controlled in the following ways:

■ **Private law remedies** – In general terms, government bodies, like private individuals, are subject to the private laws of tort and contract, etc. In other words, should a local authority fail to fulfill its obligations under a contract made with a private citizen, the latter may sue for breach of contract. In private law, however, public bodies are treated differently in two respects. Firstly, for public interest reasons they may have defences to private law actions which private individuals do not. Secondly, the courts may apply constitutional principles of acting fairly (and not capriciously) to public bodies when they act in a purely private way, for example in contract law.

- **Statutory appeal** – Appeals are statutory mechanisms which Parliament has specifically legislated for and so it may be possible, for example, to appeal against the decision of an administrative officer (in particular, see tribunals below).
- **Judicial review** – This is the cornerstone of administrative law and will be considered in detail here and in Chapter 20. In essence, judicial review is the legal mechanism whereby a claimant can seek to judicially review the decision-making process of a public body.
- **Tribunals** – In essence, tribunals are a grievance mechanism which are an alternative to the strict formal court system. For example, an appeal concerning a social security officer's decision to refuse eligibility in respect of a particular benefit would proceed not to a court, but instead to a more informal (and cheaper) specialist tribunal (see section 21.1).

19.1.4 Extra-judicial remedies

The government is also regulated by a number of supplementary non-judicial remedies:

- **Ombudsmen** – There are a number of different Ombudsmen who supervise and regulate the activities of the administration (see section 21.3). The first, and most constitutionally significant, is the Parliamentary Commissioner for Administration who investigates complaints that government departments have engaged in maladministration (in effect, faulty administration) which has caused injustice to the complainant.
- **Inquiries** – There are a number of different types of inquiry which include, for example, a land inquiry concerning the decision of a local authority to refuse planning permission. Further, a public inquiry can be held in respect of, for example, the siting of a new motorway. From a constitutional perspective, this permits individuals to influence the decision-making process of a public official.

19.2 Judicial review

19.2.1 Definition

QUOTATION

'Judicial review represents the means by which the courts control the exercise of governmental power. Government departments, local authorities, tribunals, state agencies and agencies exercising powers which are governmental in nature must exercise their powers in a lawful manner.'

H Barnett, *Constitutional and Administrative Law* (7th edn, Routledge–Cavendish, 2009) p 685.

The High Court historically has exercised an inherent power to supervise the actions of public bodies, as well as inferior courts, to ensure that these bodies act strictly within their legal powers and thus act legally. For the purposes of judicial review, the part of the High Court which processes these cases is now known as the Administrative Court (see section 19.2.5). In addition, as a result of the Tribunals, Courts and Enforcement Act 2007, the Upper Tribunal has been conferred with a power of judicial review in relation to the First-tier Tribunal. The following examples illustrate the nature of judicial review acting as a check on the following bodies:

- **Government ministers** – In *R v Secretary of State for Foreign and Commonwealth Affairs, ex parte World Development Movement Ltd* [1995] 1 WLR 386 the pressure group WDM successfully challenged the Foreign Secretary's decision to grant funding for the construction of a Malaysian hydro-electric power station on the Pergau river under the Overseas Development and Co-operation Act 1980 on the basis of it being economically unsound.

In relation to delegated legislation, in *R v Secretary of State for Health, ex parte United States Tobacco International Inc* [1992] 1 QB 353 the court quashed the Oral Snuff (Safety) Regulations 1989 made by the Secretary of State for Health, on the basis that the claimants had not been given the opportunity to make representations before they were enacted.

- **Local authorities** – In *R v Wear Valley District Council, ex parte Binks* [1985] 2 All ER 699, a street trader successfully sought judicial review of the Wear Valley District Council's decision (made without prior notification or reasons) to give her notice to quit her hot food take-away caravan.
- **Parole Board** – In *R (West) v Parole Board* [2005] UKHL 1, prisoners successfully challenged the procedural fairness of the Parole Board in respect of revoking their licences (they had been released on licence) as they had not been offered oral hearings (see section 20.5.4).
- **Inferior courts** – In *R (DPP) v South East Surrey Youth Court* [2005] EWHC 2929 (Admin) the Director of Public Prosecutions sought judicial review of the decision of the South East Surrey Youth Court not to commit a defendant for trial at Crown Court. On the facts the court did not quash the decision of the Youth Court, but noted that its approach had been flawed when it had declined to consider certain statutory provisions.

These cases illustrate a number of points concerning judicial review:

i) Firstly, judicial review can be brought against a disparate number of different public bodies (from a Secretary of State to a Parole Board). In fact, judicial review can be used against bodies which are not, in a strict sense, part of the government at all (see the *Panel on Take-overs and Mergers* case at section 19.3.3).

ii) Judicial review can be sought by a number of different claimants (from individual street traders and pressure groups through to the DPP acting in the public interest).

iii) Judicial review is not confined to supervising the actions of government bodies, as it can include reviewing the decision-making process of judicial bodies (eg inferior courts, which are those ranking lower than the High/Administrative Court).

iv) Judicial review is technically brought in the name of the Crown and as stated by Keene J in *R v Commissioner of Customs and Excise, ex parte Kay* [1996] STC 1500 '… it reflects the fact that this court is dealing with what are essentially issues of public law …'.

19.2.2 A review and not an appellate jurisdiction

In *Chief Constable of the North Wales Police v Evans* [1982] 1 WLR 1155, Lord Brightman stated that:

JUDGMENT

'Judicial review is concerned, not with the decision, but with the decision-making process. Unless that restriction on the power of the court is observed, the court will in my view under the guise of preventing the abuse of power, be itself guilty of usurping power.'

The constitutional function behind judicial review is to supervise the decision-making process of public bodies and not to act as an appellate court which questions the decision itself. In short, the Administrative Court is concerned with the legality and lawfulness of the actions taken by a public authority, rather than the merits of its decisions. Judicial review, therefore, is concerned with the nature of the decision-making process and with asking, for example, the following questions:

In reaching its decision (as part of the decision-making process) did the public body:

- Misinterpret its legal powers?
- Take into account an irrelevant matter?
- Ignore a relevant matter?
- Act for an improper purpose?
- Act in a procedurally unfair way by either ignoring a statutory requirement or by failing to follow the common law rules of natural justice?

By asking these sorts of questions, in constitutional theory, the court is in effect questioning the *process* of making the decision and not the *decision* itself. In other words, the reviewing court is not questioning the merits or quality of the decision made (eg was it qualitatively a good or bad decision?), which is an exercise carried out by an appellate court, but rather was the process lawful? It is in this way that judicial review can be constitutionally justified. It must be noted that this is an inherent remedy which the courts themselves have developed rather than Parliament. Appeals, on the other hand are statutory, whereby Parliament has decided that in a particular set of circumstances where a person disagrees with the decision made by a public body, it can be appealed against. As Lord Greene MR has made clear in *Associated Provincial Picture Houses Ltd v Wednesbury Corporation* [1948] 1 KB 223, the role of the court in judicial review proceedings (in the context of a local authority):

JUDGMENT

'is not as an appellate authority to override a decision of the local authority, but as a judicial authority which is concerned, and concerned only, to see whether the local authority have contravened the law by acting in excess of the powers which Parliament has confided in them'.

The following points need to be noted in this context:

i) The constitutional theory set out above is more readily applicable to some grounds of judicial review than to others. For example, in relation to the ground of **irrationality**, the courts are, in effect, questioning the quality of the decision made (albeit, for the court to intervene the decision must be so irrational that no reasonable decision-maker could have arrived at it). Moreover, today in the context of the Human Rights Act 1998, the courts may have to consider whether an interference with human rights is proportionate.

ii) The traditional view that a reviewing court has a supervisory role only (ie it does not *substitute* a decision for the decision in question) is now subject to Pt 54.19(2) of the Civil Procedure Rules.

19.2.3 The constitutional dimension of judicial review

Judicial review is a central component of Britain's uncodified constitution and is inextricably linked with the following constitutional principles:

The rule of law

Judicial review can be viewed as the rule of law in operation (see Chapter 6). In short, it ensures that public bodies act strictly within their legal powers and do not exceed them. As indicated earlier, the rule of law necessities that government acts within the law and judicial review can provide a remedy if a public body misuses or exceeds its public law powers. In particular, the court will ensure that public decision-makers do not abuse their public law discretion. There is a clear public policy case for conferring discretion on government officials and administrators (see section 6.7.5) and the process of judicial review aims to control and regulate the use of that discretion. In essence, judicial review underpins the rule of law in our uncodified constitution.

irrationality
a decision in law which no reasonable person could have come to

The separation of powers

As noted at section 5.8.4, from one perspective judicial review can be seen as an illustration of the separation of powers with the judicial arm of the constitution (the Administrative Court) checking and balancing the actions of the executive (the government/administration). In this way the executive is held legally to account. Moreover, the courts have used the principle of the separation of powers as justifying their somewhat limited constitutional role as a reviewing court. Thus, in constitutional theory the judges confine themselves simply to reviewing the decision-making process of public bodies, while leaving the latter to make the actual decision themselves. After all, it is the public bodies which have been specifically charged with the responsibility to make the decision (a specialist executive/administrative role). In this way, the courts avoid trespassing on the constitutional role of the executive, which is to administer the law and take decisions. The courts will intervene via judicial review proceedings only when, for example, a public body misunderstands or misuses its powers, or adopts a faulty decision-making process.

Parliamentary sovereignty

As government derives many of its public law powers from Parliament, judicial review can be viewed as simply upholding parliamentary sovereignty by ensuring that public bodies act strictly within their allocated statutory powers. If these authorities were permitted to exceed their legal powers as conferred by Parliament, they would undermine the legal authority and status of Acts of Parliament. Judicial review ensures that public decision-makers act within the legal parameters set by Parliament.

One difficulty with this point is that government also enjoys substantial common law powers in the form of the royal prerogative and some uses of this power have been held subject to judicial review (see section 11.9.6). Clearly in these cases, the justification for judicial review in this context *cannot* be to uphold the will of Parliament. A second problem concerns the judicial attitude to ouster clauses (see section 19.2.4).

The protection of human rights

Judicial review is a procedural remedy in the sense that it challenges the decision-making process, and in this way it is a somewhat limited remedy. In recent decades, however, the human rights context of a judicial review application has assumed increasing significance. In other words, the more a decision has impacted adversely on human rights, the more justification would be required by the court for the public body to be able to make it (see *ex parte Smith* (1996) at section 20.3.2). Today the Human Rights Act 1998 is in operation and the Convention rights can be upheld through an action in judicial review. Under s 6 of the Act, public authorities must act in accordance with the rights set out in the European Convention and if they do not, their actions can now be subject to judicial review.

The control of the exercise of public law powers

Judicial review can be constitutionally justified as a legal control on the misuse of public law powers (including both statutory and common law prerogative powers). In the absence of a formal codified constitution which constitutionally constrains the actions of the executive, judicial review provides a mechanism whereby the abuse of public law powers (which can affect millions of people) can be legally constrained. In fact, it could be observed that the dramatic growth of judicial review in the past 30 years has coincided with the overwhelming dominance of the executive in the legislature and so has, therefore to some extent, re-balanced the constitution. It is true to say that although in the past 30 years there has been less *political* control over the executive, there has, however, been a significant increase in the *legal* control over it via judicial review proceedings.

19.2.4 The controversial nature of judicial review

Judicial review has a number of controversial and/or disputed elements.

An inherent and unelected jurisdiction

Judicial review is in effect a judge-driven process as it stems from the common law. In other words, it is the courts themselves which have developed, expanded and refined the principles, grounds and remedies available in judicial review proceedings. In effect, the courts determine who can seek judicial review, against whom and on what grounds. The judges are, of course, unelected and largely unrepresentative of society (see Chapter 13) and therefore would appear to lack a democratic mandate for their actions in supervising the executive.

This common law basis of judicial review can, however, be justified as upholding the constitutional principles set out in section 19.2.3 and, in particular, controlling the abuse of public law powers. Moreover, it should also be remembered that the executive itself is not elected *per se*; it is merely drawn (largely, though not exclusively) from the elected House of Commons. In *ex parte Witham* (1997), for example, the courts declared secondary legislation passed by the *unelected* Lord Chancellor to be unlawful and *ultra vires* (see section 4.8.3). In a democracy it is paramount that the executive does not exceed its legal powers; therefore judicial review upholds the rule of law.

Controlling ultra vires action?

There is debate concerning the constitutional justification for judicial review, namely whether it is, in essence, concerned with questioning actions which are *ultra vires* (beyond the powers conferred). On the one hand, it has been argued that traditionally the courts are simply upholding the will of Parliament as by challenging *ultra vires* action they ensure that public bodies act *intra vires* (within the powers conferred). As noted earlier, however, judicial review also regulates the exercise of the royal prerogative which is a common law power. In addition, the courts imply certain principles (eg the need to use powers rationally and fairly) into the statutory powers conferred on public bodies.

According to Barnett:

QUOTATION

'… the concept of *ultra vires* is nowadays regarded by many as an inadequate rationale for judicial review. The preferred view is that the courts need not resort to fictions such as the "intention of Parliament" or the technicalities of "jurisdictional facts" and "errors of law" … but that rather the courts will intervene wherever there has been an unlawful exercise of power.'

H Barnett, *Constitutional and Administrative Law* (7th edn, Routledge–Cavendish, 2009), p 719.

The ground of irrationality

As will be indicated below, irrationality (historically) is the second ground on which judicial review can be sought (see section 20.3). The difficulty with this ground is that it is difficult to reconcile with the principle that judicial review is concerned simply with review rather than appeal. When a court decides that a decision is irrational, in practice it is in effect questioning the *quality* of the decision made.

Red light/green light theories

Leyland and Anthony, *Textbook on Administrative Law* (6th edn, Oxford University Press, 2009), pp 4–9) have drawn attention to the following theories (the so-called red/green light models as set out by C Harlow and R Rawlings in *Law and Administration* (Weidenfeld & Nicolson, 1984)) which have been associated with judicial review:

■ The red light theory is that the function of the courts in judicial review is to act as a clear brake on the administration (hence the red light). This places restrictions on the executive and limits its impact on individuals and society. In effect, it limits state interference.

■ The green light theory, in contrast, facilitates administrative action by limiting judicial intervention with it on the basis that it is in the public interest that public decision-makers make decisions which benefit the public. In short, administrators should be enabled to engage in administrative tasks without fearing that every action will be legally challenged (which in itself causes administrative paralysis in decision-making).

■ Leyland and Anthony note that the amber light theory is a compromise between the two opposed views above. In other words, this essentially balances the need to control public bodies so that public power is not abused (red), with the recognition that the state must be permitted to make decisions for the benefit of society (green).

Ouster clauses

Ouster clauses are provisions in legislation which specifically exclude the jurisdiction of the courts. The judiciary have historically resisted such clauses, and it could be argued therefore, that in these circumstances, strictly speaking, the courts are not really upholding the plain will of Parliament. For example, in *Anisminic Ltd* (1969) at section 20.2.6, the relevant statutory provision stated explicitly that the determination of the Commission 'shall not be called in question in any court of law'. The court nevertheless held that this provision did not apply where the Commission had acted beyond its jurisdiction and so had not made a determination at all.

The controversial nature of total ouster clauses (which are arguably contrary to the principles underpinning the rule of law, as they aim specifically to exclude the supervisory remedy of judicial review) was demonstrated when the government was persuaded to drop such a clause from the Asylum and Immigration Bill in 2004. This episode also raises the issue of the role of the Lord Chancellor whose function is to defend rigorously the rule of law (including within the Cabinet) and in doing so, prevent such legislative provisions from being put forward (see section 5.7.9).

The courts are, however, willing to accept provisions which restrict court jurisdiction to a limited time period (*Smith v East Elloe RDC* [1956] AC 736 and *R v Secretary of State for the Environment, ex parte Ostler* [1977] 1 QB 122). An example of such a provision is s 38 of the Inquiries Act 2005 which states that:

SECTION

S 38

An application for judicial review of a decision made –

(a) by the Minister in relation to an inquiry, or

(b) by a member of an inquiry panel,

must be brought within 14 days after the day on which the applicant became aware of the decision, unless that time limit is extended by the court. (The rationale behind this provision is to prevent delays to inquiries).

An uneven remedy?

In some respects judicial review can be seen as lacking a clear overall uniform pattern. This is partly due to the fact that the court is a *reactive* body simply processing judicial review claims as and when they are brought before them. Thus, their ability to develop overarching judicial review principles is dependent upon the type and nature of the case brought before them at any one time.

In addition, as indicated at section 18.2.2, the courts historically have lacked an authoritative set of clear and agreed constitutional guidelines and so judicial review has developed in an *ad hoc* fashion. The modern courts do at least now enjoy the benefit of the principles espoused in the European Convention when processing human rights cases (see s 2 of the Human Rights Act 1998 at section 17.4).

The following points suggest judicial review lacks uniformity:

■ The courts will determine, on a case by case basis, which bodies will be subject to judicial review. For example, in terms of two non-governmental bodies: the Panel on Take-overs and Mergers and the Jockey Club, the former (in principle) was subject to judicial review while the latter was not (see section 19.3.3).

■ Claimants seeking judicial review need to demonstrate that they have sufficient interest in the matter. For example, in terms of organisations/groups seeking review, Greenpeace was permitted to do so, while *Rose Theatre Trust Co (1990)* was not (see section 19.4.2).

■ The courts will deem certain executive actions to be *non-justiciable* (ie owing to its subject-matter, unsuitable for judicial resolution) and so not subject to judicial review. Historically, *non-justiciable* subjects have included national security and national finance (for example, on the latter see *Nottinghamshire County Council* (1986) at section 14.2.6).

■ The remedies in judicial review are discretionary and so even though an individual may succeed in demonstrating that a public body has acted illegally, the court may nevertheless decline to give a remedy on the basis that if, for example, it quashed the decision in question, it could cause administrative chaos.

Conflict between the judicial and executive arms of the constitution

Judicial review has inevitably increased constitutional tension between the judiciary and government ministers (see for example, D Blunkett, 'I won't give in to the judges', *Evening Standard*, 12th May 2003). In recent years, this tension has been further heightened with the passage of the Human Rights Act 1998 which has provided a further ground of review, namely that a minister has breached the European Convention. This is particularly ironic given that it was a Labour government that drafted and oversaw the passage of the Human Rights Bill through Parliament.

ACTIVITY

Self-test questions

1. What is the constitutional distinction between a review and an appeal?
2. To what extent do you think that judicial review is controversial? Revisit this question after you have completed Chapter 20.

19.2.5 A special 'administrative court'?

In the context of the rule of law (see section 6.7.6), it was pointed out that Dicey contrasted our constitution with that of France where disputes between French citizens and government officials were processed in special tribunals (*tribunaux administratifs*) which were separate from the main court system. Instead, Dicey preferred our constitutional arrangements whereby state officials were held to account before the ordinary courts like any other individual. This view, however, must be revised in the light of the modern development and nature of judicial review proceedings which in the following respects is similar to the French system of administrative law (*droit administratif*):

■ In 2000, for the purposes of processing applications for judicial review proceedings, the Crown Office List was renamed the Administrative Court as it was recognised by Sir Jeffrey Bowman (Chairman of the Review of the Crown Court Office List) that there was a need for a specialist court to process public and administrative law cases. This court is staffed by specialist judges conversant with the principles of judicial review and administrative law. Judicial review is a highly specialist field of law.

■ Under the '**exclusivity**' principle (see section 19.5.2) if a claimant wishes to challenge the misuse of public law powers by a public body, they must use the exclusive judicial review procedure set out in the Civil Procedure Rules and the Senior Courts Act 1981 (formerly the Supreme Court Act). In other words, an individual will not be permitted to use the ordinary court system in order to assert public law rights.

■ In judicial review proceedings judges apply special administrative principles (eg the responsibility of the public body to act rationally and to follow the precepts of natural justice). These are principles which purely private bodies and individuals do not generally have to follow (but note section 19.3.4).

exclusivity

the principle that the enforcement of public law rights should be via the judicial review procedure

Constitutional concept	The connection with judicial review
The rule of law	It upholds the rule of law by ensuring that public bodies do not exceed their legal powers.
The separation of powers	It forms part of the checks and balances on the actions of the executive.
Parliamentary sovereignty	It upholds parliamentary sovereignty by ensuring that public bodies act within the powers allocated to them by Parliament.
The protection of human rights	Under the Human Rights Act 1998 public authorities can be subject to judicial review if they disregard Convention rights.
The control of the exercise of public law powers	It is a legal control on the misuse of public law powers.

19.2.6 The mechanics of judicial review

The basic mechanics of judicial review are illustrated by the following diagram:

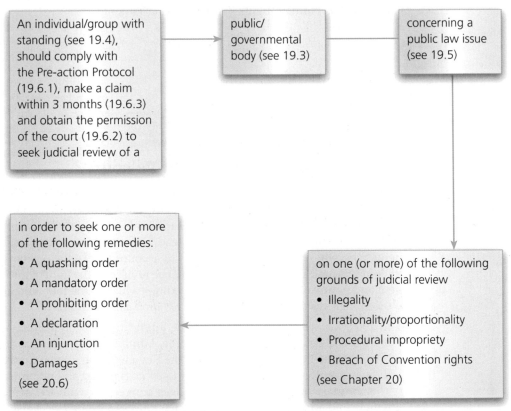

Figure 19.2 The mechanics of judicial review

19.3 Bodies subject to judicial review

Which bodies are subject to judicial review? In essence, judicial review is aimed chiefly at controlling government bodies/public authorities (public law bodies), although both non-governmental bodies and inferior courts are also subject to judicial review proceedings.

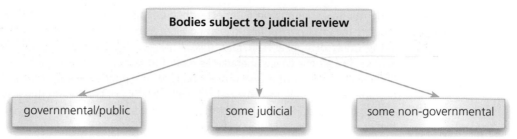

Figure 19.3 Bodies subject to judicial review

19.3.1 Government/public bodies

The following governmental/public bodies are subject to judicial review:

- **Government ministers/departments:** In *ex parte Venables and Thompson* (1997) (see section 5.7.6) the House of Lords held that the Home Secretary had acted illegally by abusing his public law discretion. In fact, government ministers are regularly subject to challenges in judicial review.
- **Local authorities:** In *ex parte Times Newspapers Ltd* (1986) (see section 20.2.4) the court held that the banning of *The Times* newspaper from the libraries of three councils was unlawful.
- **Parole Board:** For an example, see section 19.2.1.
- **Devolved institutions/bodies**: The devolved institutions set up under the various devolution settlements are subject to judicial review proceedings – see Chapter 14.

19.3.2 Judicial bodies

The following inferior courts and tribunals are also subject to judicial review by the higher Administrative Court:

- **The Crown Court:** providing the issue is unconnected with a trial on indictment.
- **Magistrates' Court:** (*R v Hereford Magistrates' Court, ex parte Rowlands* [1998] 1 QB 110).
- **The Coroners' Court:** (*R v Greater Manchester Coroner, ex parte Tal* [1985] 1 QB 67).
- **Tribunals**: (*R (Nottingham Healthcare NHS Trust) v Mental Health Review Tribunal* [2008] EWHC 2445 (Admin)). It is important to remember that as a result of the Tribunals, Courts and Enforcement Act 2007, the Upper Tribunal has been conferred with a power of judicial review.

NB The High/Administrative Court and above are not subject to judicial review.

19.3.3 Non-governmental bodies

Judicial review is also available to challenge certain non-governmental bodies. These are bodies which are not part of the government/administration *per se*, but which exercise *de facto* public law powers. In practice, therefore, although these bodies have not been established by the government or Parliament, they do nevertheless exercise powers which are analogous to governmental powers. The courts, therefore, in determining who is subject to review do not merely confine themselves to looking at the source of power (statutory or royal prerogative), but also consider the nature of it (ie is the power *de facto* governmental in nature?).

CASE EXAMPLE

R v Panel on Take-overs and Mergers, ex parte Datafin plc [1987] 1 QB 815

Datafin plc sought judicial review of the actions of the Panel on Take-overs and Mergers. The panel was not a government body and had not been established by an Act of Parliament or under the royal prerogative. In effect, it had been set up in the City of London in order to regulate the City Code on Take-overs and Mergers of companies (a system of self-regulation).

The Court of Appeal held that judicial review was adaptable. Its jurisdiction could be extended to a body which operated as part of a system which performed public law duties. The panel, though not a government body, was a powerful body which made important decisions in regulating the financial activity in the City of London. In this way the panel was treated as a *de facto* public body, although on the facts, however, there were no grounds in this case to judicially review its actions.

Contrast *ex parte Datafin* with the following case:

CASE EXAMPLE

R v Disciplinary Committee of the Jockey Club, ex parte Aga Khan [1993] 2 All ER 853

The Disciplinary Committee of the Jockey Club disqualified the Aga Khan's horse which had won a major race. The latter sought judicial review of the Committee's decision.

The Court of Appeal held that although the Jockey Club regulated horse racing in Britain which affected the public (eg race meetings had to be licensed by the Jockey Club and people connected to racing had to be licensed by, or registered with it), nevertheless, it was not subject to judicial review. According to the court the club was not a public body (in terms of its history, constitution or membership) and the powers it exercised were not governmental in nature. In this case the powers of the Jockey Club derived from the agreement between the parties (ie with the Aga Khan) which gave rise to private rights which were enforceable by private law remedies. It should be noted that judicial review is a remedy of last resort, so the courts may decline judicial review where another legal remedy exists.

See also *R v Football Association Ltd, ex parte Football League Ltd* [1993] 2 All ER 833.

CASE EXAMPLE

R v Chief Rabbi of the United Hebrew Congregations of Great Britain and the Commonwealth, ex parte Wachmann [1993] 2 All ER 249

The High Court refused to subject the functions of the Chief Rabbi to the jurisdiction of judicial review. The court indicated that his functions were in essence spiritual and religious and were such that the government would not seek to discharge them in his absence.

A case in the context of the Human Rights Act 1998 is:

CASE EXAMPLE

R (West) v Lloyd's of London [2004] EWCA Civ 506

The Court of Appeal held that the actions of the Business Conduct Committee of Lloyd's were not amenable to judicial review. The decisions made by Lloyds were of a private nature and in terms of s 6 of the Human Rights Act 1998 it was not exercising public or governmental functions (contrast *ex parte Datafin* (1987) above).

In short, if a non-governmental body exercises powers which are of a public nature and which are sufficiently governmental in nature (ie the government would have to exercise those powers if the body did not exist), then the court is more likely to declare that that body is susceptible to judicial review. Where, however, the relationship between the claimant and the non-governmental body is essentially a commercial one governed, for example, by contract law, the court may decline the claim for judicial review on the basis that an alternative remedy in private law is open to the claimant.

19.3.4 Private bodies and administrative principles

Even if a (powerful) private non-governmental body is not held to be subject to judicial review, there appears to be some evidence that the courts in the context of private law proceedings may nevertheless subject these bodies to certain administrative principles (eg to act fairly and not capriciously). This appears to be the case in the context of some sporting activities: *Nagle v Feilden* [1966] 2 QB 633.

KEY FACTS

Bodies subject to judicial review
• **Government bodies** Government ministers, government departments, local authorities, devolved institutions, etc are subject in principle to judicial review.
• **Non-governmental bodies** These may be subject to judicial review providing their *de facto* powers are essentially governmental in nature and no other reasonable alternative remedy is available to the claimant (*ex parte Datafin* (1987)).
• **Purely private bodies/individuals** These are not subject to judicial review; however, some powerful private bodies *may* be subject to the administrative principles of acting fairly and not capriciously even in an area of private law (*Nagle v Feilden* (1966)).

19.4 Standing in judicial review

Who or what can seek judicial review? For a claimant (individual or group) to claim judicial review they must have sufficient interest (formerly known as *locus standi*) in the matter. In other words, there must be a connection between the claimant and the contested action of the public law body. From a constitutional perspective this ensures that those not affected by the action (ie 'mere busybodies') cannot seek judicial review as such claims would necessarily inflate the volume of claims before the Administrative Court and in doing so unnecessarily interfere with the process of administration.

The following have standing (ie sufficient interest) to seek judicial review:

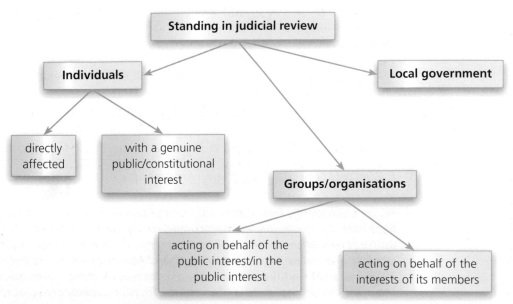

Figure 19.4 Standing in judicial review

The following categories of standing draw upon and adapt those used in M Supperstone, J Goudie and Sir P Walker (eds) *Judicial Review* (3rd edn, LexisNexis Butterworths, 2005), Ch 17.

19.4.1 Individuals

■ Individuals directly affected by a public law decision

Individuals have standing to seek judicial review where they have been directly affected (financially or otherwise) by the actions of a public law body. For example, in *ex parte Binks* (1985) (see section 19.2.1), Binks was directly affected by the decision of the Wear Valley District Council to issue her with a notice to quit her take-away food caravan without prior notice or any accompanying reasons. In contrast, individual 'busybodies' (for example, a well-meaning citizen who is upset on Binks's behalf) would not be able to apply for judicial review to challenge the District Council as they had not been directly affected.

■ Individuals with a genuine public/constitutional interest

An exception to the 'mere busybody' rule above is that individuals who have a genuine constitutional interest in the actions of a public body may have standing to challenge it in judicial review:

CASE EXAMPLE

R v Secretary of State for Foreign and Commonwealth Affairs, ex parte Rees-Mogg [1994] QB 552

Lord Rees-Mogg (a peer in the House of Lords) unsuccessfully sought judicial review of the Foreign Secretary's decision to ratify the Maastricht Treaty. Although on the facts his claim failed, Lloyd LJ noted that there was no dispute as to standing: 'we accept without question that Lord Rees-Mogg brings the proceedings because of his sincere concern for constitutional issues'.

In the context of a public interest see the case of *R (Feakins) v Secretary of State for the Environment, Food and Rural Affairs* [2003] EWCA Civ 1546.

19.4.2 Groups/organisations

■ Acting on behalf of the public interest/in the public interest

Groups/pressure groups or organisations may seek judicial review if they are a recognised body acting in the interests of the wider public (analogous to *ex parte Rees-Mogg* (1994) above). In essence, they are not acting in their own interest *per se*, but rather for the general public interest. As indicated at section 19.2.1, the pressure group World Development Movement Ltd successfully challenged the Foreign Secretary's decision to issue a grant to fund the Pergau Dam.

An early (rather restrictive) case is the following:

CASE EXAMPLE

R v Secretary of State for the Environment, ex parte Rose Theatre Trust Co [1990] 2 WLR 186

A trust company (the Rose Theatre Trust Company) was established to preserve the remains of an historical theatre which were discovered during a development in London. They sought judicial review of the Secretary of State who had declined to register the theatre in the schedule of monuments pursuant to the Ancient Monuments and Archaeological Areas Act 1979. The court held that the company did not have standing, as members of the public had insufficient interest to be entitled to apply for judicial review in respect of this particular matter (ie not to schedule the theatre).

The case of *ex parte Rose Theatre Trust Co* (1990) should be contrasted with the following two later cases:

CASE EXAMPLE

Equal Opportunities Commission and another v Secretary of State for Employment [1994] 1 All ER 910

The Equal Opportunities Commission (a body established by statute) was successful in obtaining a declaration that provisions of the Employment Protection (Consolidation) Act 1978 were contrary to European Community law (as it was then known) as they indirectly discriminated against women. The House of Lords (by a majority) accepted that the EOC had standing as its statutory responsibility was to work towards eradicating sex discrimination.

CASE EXAMPLE

R v Inspectorate of Pollution and another, ex parte Greenpeace Ltd (No 2) [1994] 4 All ER 329

Greenpeace (a pressure group on environmental issues) was granted standing to challenge the Inspectorate of Pollution's decision to vary authorisations concerning radioactive waste (although on the facts their claim failed). The court recognised that Greenpeace was a well-established and respected pressure group with concern for the environment. It is important to remember that a number of Greenpeace members lived in the Sellafield area.

■ **Acting on behalf of the interests of its members**

These groups would include professional bodies and trade unions etc. See for example *R (Montpeliers and Trevors Association and another) v Westminster City Council* [2005] EWHC 16 (Admin), where an association representing the residents of two squares in London successfully challenged a traffic order made by Westminster City Council which affected their residential areas.

19.4.3 Local government

It must be remembered that judicial review can also be used by one branch of the executive against another. For example, in *Nottinghamshire County Council v Secretary of State for the Environment* (1986), Nottinghamshire County Council sought (albeit unsuccessfully on the facts) judicial review of the Secretary of State's guidance in respect of local authority expenditure targets (see section 14.2.6).

19.4.4 When should standing be determined?

CASE EXAMPLE

IRC v National Federation of Self-Employed and Small Businesses Ltd [1982] AC 617

The National Federation (representing small businesses and the self-employed) sought judicial review of the Inland Revenue in respect of its treatment of casual workers in Fleet Street (ie giving them an amnesty in terms of past tax which had not been paid). The National Federation sought a declaration that this was unlawful (as it differentiated between taxpayers) and an order of mandamus to compel the Inland Revenue to assess and collect this outstanding income tax.

The House of Lords held that the National Federation did not have standing (the Court of Appeal had said that they did) as it was merely a body of taxpayers. One taxpayer (or group of taxpayers like the Federation) did not have sufficient interest in asking the court to investigate the tax affairs of another.

The above case is notable as the House of Lords made clear that although in obvious ('simple') cases the issue of standing could be definitively decided at the leave stage (ie when permission is being sought from the court to bring a claim for judicial review – see section 19.6.2), in other more complex cases standing should be decided at the substantive hearing where full (factual and legal) information would be available. As a result, although standing may be initially granted, it may be subsequently reconsidered and refused at the main hearing in the context of the merits of the case as a whole.

ACTIVITY

Quick quiz
1. Who is subject to judicial review?
2. Who can seek judicial review?

19.5 A public law issue

19.5.1 Public law issues

Judicial review is concerned with public law issues and the enforcement of public law rights. It is not concerned with private matters and private law rights (eg contract and tort).

Not every action of a public body falls within the ambit of judicial review. In order to seek judicial review a claimant must raise an issue of public law. In essence, this will relate to how public law powers have been misused, misunderstood or misapplied. The Civil Procedure Rules, Pt 54.1(2)(a) states that judicial review is concerned with the lawfulness of:

i) an enactment; or
ii) a decision, action or failure to act in relation to the exercise of a public function.

For example, should a local authority breach its contract with an individual (eg it fails to pay a supplier for the supply of certain goods), the remedy lies in private contract law (a *private law* matter). Should the local authority, however, by statute revoke a market licence without any prior notification or reasons etc, then the remedy lies in asserting a public law right (namely that of the requirement in natural justice to be treated fairly) in judicial review proceedings (a *public law* matter). In other words, the mere fact that the defendant is a public body is not sufficient on its own to bring the matter within the ambit of judicial review. The issue at stake has to involve a public law issue.

19.5.2 Exclusive proceedings

If a claimant can demonstrate that a public law issue is at stake, in general terms he must use the special judicial review procedure (formerly under Order 53 and now governed by Pt 54 of the Civil Procedure Rules) to enforce this public law right. This procedure (see section 19.6) is hallmarked by certain characteristics, for example:

■ The requirement to obtain permission in order to bring an action for judicial review.
■ A short time limit to bring a claim.

These requirements *protect* public law bodies by limiting the number of judicial review claims made and also prevents 'busybodies' from engaging in this process.

CASE EXAMPLE

O'Reilly v Mackman [1983] 2 AC 237

Four prisoners were charged with disciplinary offences in Hull Prison. The Board of Visitors found the charges proved and imposed penalties. The prisoners sought to challenge the Board alleging that it had breached the rules of natural justice; the fourth prisoner alleged bias. The prisoners did not use the judicial review procedure, but instead used private law proceedings (writ and originating summons).

The House of Lords confirmed the order to strike out these proceedings as the prisoners had used the wrong procedure. It would be contrary to public policy as well as an abuse of the court process for an individual to seek redress by ordinary private law action when it was contended that his public law rights (eg a breach of natural justice) had been violated. Lord Diplock stated:

JUDGMENT

'My Lords, I have described this as a general rule … there may be exceptions, particularly where the invalidity of the decision arises as a collateral issue in a claim for infringement of a right of the plaintiff arising under private law, or where none of the parties objects to the adoption of the procedure by writ or originating summons.'

In essence, *O'Reilly* stands for the principle that the enforcement of public law rights (ie a grievance in public law) should be through the judicial review procedure which, of course, protects the administration. This is known as the *exclusivity* principle. There are, however, some exceptions which are illustrated in the diagram below:

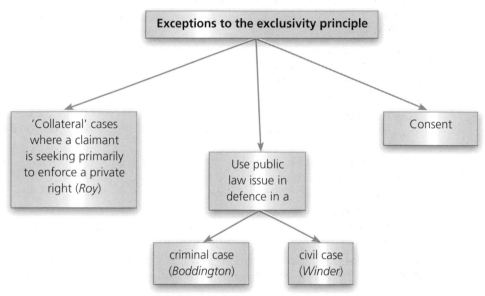

Figure 19.5 Exceptions to the exclusivity principle

19.5.3 Collateral cases

The judicial review procedure need not be used where the questioning of a public law decision is a collateral issue (ie incidental) to the enforcement of a private right.

CASE EXAMPLE

Roy v Kensington and Chelsea and Westminster Family Practitioner Committee [1992] 1 AC 624

Roy was a general practitioner who brought a private action against the Family Practitioner Committee for withholding payment of part of his basic practice allowance. The Committee sought to have the action struck out as an abuse of process on the basis that the challenge should have been made by way of judicial review. The House of Lords held that the bringing of an ordinary action to enforce a private law right was not an abuse of the court, even though it would involve a challenge to a public law decision.

In this case, Roy's purpose was to enforce a private law right to compensation and it was merely collateral that this also involved considering the validity of a public law decision (eg the Committee's finding that Roy had failed to devote a substantial amount of his time to general practice).

It is important to point out that, as recognised by the Court of Appeal in *Clark v University of Lincolnshire and Humberside* [2000] 1 WLR 1988, today the Civil Procedure Rules have diminished in practice the differences between bringing an action under the 'ordinary' court process as opposed to the judicial review procedure.

19.5.4 The use of a public law issue in an individual's defence

In *Roy* (1992) above, the claimant had initiated legal action. Sometimes, however, an individual will be the defendant in legal proceedings commenced by another body. In these circumstances it appears that the questioning of the validity of a public law decision/act (a public law issue) can be used in defence.

■ **A criminal prosecution**

CASE EXAMPLE

Boddington v British Transport Police [1999] 2 AC 143

Boddington was prosecuted under by-law 20 of the Railways Byelaws 1965 (made under the Transport Act 1962) for smoking in a train carriage. The House of Lords stated that he was not prevented from raising in his defence the contention that the by-law was *ultra vires* and unlawful (on the facts it was held that the railway company had not acted unlawfully in bringing into operation the by-law as it did).

■ **A civil case**

CASE EXAMPLE

Wandsworth London Borough Council v Winder [1985] 1 AC 461

Wandsworth Council commenced legal proceedings in the County Court against Winder (a council tenant) for arrears of rent and possession of his flat. Winder had considered recent rent increases excessive and refused to pay them. In his defence he argued that the resolutions to increase these rents were *ultra vires* and void.

The House of Lords stated that (in the absence of clear words to the contrary) an individual had a right to challenge a local authority's decision in their defence. Winder had not, after all, initiated the action.

19.5.5 Consent

This is where the parties to the case (ie the public body and the claimant) agree that a remedy can be sought via the 'ordinary' court procedure.

ACTIVITY

Quick quiz

1. What is a public law issue?
2. What is meant by the principle of exclusivity?
3. What is the purpose of this rule?

19.6 Procedure

In seeking judicial review special rules and principles apply. Formerly, judicial review was regulated by Order 53 Rules of the Supreme Court and the Senior Courts Act 1981 (formerly the Supreme Court Act). Order 53 has now been superseded by Part 54 of the Civil Procedure Rules 1998 which came into force in 2000 and were added to in 2002 by the Pre-action Protocol.

The basic outline of the procedure for a claim for judicial review is as follows:

19.6.1 The Pre-action Protocol and claim

Before commencing proceedings the claimant (formerly the applicant) should write to the public body identifying the issues at stake to which the defendant should reply. The purpose of the Pre-action Protocol is to avoid litigation and achieve a settlement. One of the problems with judicial review in recent years has been its popularity, which in turn has lengthened the time the court takes to process a claim. For example, in 2007 there were 6,690 applications for permission to apply for judicial review (*Judicial and Court Statistics 2007*, Cm 7467 (Crown Copyright, 2008), p 16). In this context, in *R (Cowl) v Plymouth City Council* [2001] EWCA Civ 1935, the Court of Appeal emphasised the importance of avoiding litigation whenever possible. Judicial review claims are brought before the Administrative Court. The claim form should state the action being challenged and the remedy sought.

19.6.2 Permission to apply for judicial review

Judicial review is not available as of right to a claimant, as the permission of the court (Pt 54.4) is required to commence the action (formerly known as seeking leave to apply). This is one way in which judicial review differs from private law actions. This acts as a filter system whereby the courts can weed out vexatious claims with no foundation. This protects public bodies and facilitates good administration whereby the government is not unnecessarily hampered by unarguable/unrealistic claims. Judicial review is also a remedy of last resort which means that if a claimant has an alternative remedy (eg a statutory appeal), he should avail himself of it instead. For example, in relation to judicial review by the Administrative Court of a decision by the First-tier Tribunal, Craig points out that the court may decide that the claimant should exercise his statutory appeal rights to the Upper Tribunal (P Craig, *Administrative Law* (6th edn, Sweet & Maxwell, 2008), p 273).

Permission was formerly sought *ex parte* (in the absence of the other side), but today it is dealt with on a more *inter parties* (both sides present) basis. This enables the court to be better informed about the whole nature of the matter.

QUOTATION

'The precise test as to when permission should be granted has been variously stated but there is no doubt that at bottom the question is as to whether there is an arguable case, which merits full consideration at a substantive hearing.'

R Drabble and T Buley in M Supperstone, J Goudie, Sir P Walker (eds),
Judicial Review (3rd edn, LexisNexis Butterworths, 2005), p 551.

19.6.3 The time limit

Claims for judicial review must be made '*promptly*' (Pt 54.5(1)(a)). In any event, they must be made 'not later than three months after the grounds to make the claim first arose' (Pt 54.5(1)(b)). However, statute may specify a shorter time period for making a claim (see s 38 of the Inquiries Act 2005 at section 19.2.4). This is another hallmark of judicial review which distinguishes it from private law actions as the time to make a claim is very short. The purpose of this is twofold:

■ It protects public bodies (and the administrative process) as such bodies know that three months after their action/decision it will not ordinarily be subject to judicial review.

■ If a public body is acting illegally (which has consequences for the public), then in accordance with the rule of law it is of paramount importance that it is legally constrained from doing so as soon as is possible.

The case of *R v Warwickshire CC, ex parte Collymore* [1995] ELR 217 is an example of a court accepting an out of time application for good reasons (ie the circumstances of the case).

19.6.4 The substantive hearing

At the substantive hearing (ie a full hearing of the claim for judicial review) the court will determine whether or not the defendant has infringed one or more of the grounds of judicial review (see Chapter 20 for the grounds). At this stage it can also reconsider whether the claimant has standing. The substantive hearing typically involves the consideration of documentary evidence, and the burden (civil burden of proof) rests on the claimant to prove unlawful action (cross-examination is rare in judicial review). If proven, the court may or may not issue a remedy (see section 20.6.2).

KEY FACTS

An overview of the judicial review procedure	
Pre-action Protocol	This should be complied with before a claim is made.
The claim	Is brought before the Administrative Court.
Permission required	Judicial review is not a remedy as of right.
Time limit	The claim must be made promptly (within three months).
Standing	The claimant must have sufficient interest in the matter.
Public body	The claim must be sought against a public body.
Public law issue	The claim must concern a public law issue (public law rights).
Substantive hearing	The Administrative Court will determine whether a public body has acted unlawfully and if so, may provide a remedy (see Chapter 20).

SUMMARY

■ Judicial review is the process whereby the Administrative Court supervises the actions of public bodies (and inferior courts) to ensure that they act strictly within their legal powers.

■ Judicial review is a key aspect of the British constitution as it enables the executive to be held to account thereby upholding the rule of law.

■ Both individuals and groups can seek judicial review of a public body providing they have standing to do so and the claim involves a public law issue.

■ Claimants must overcome certain procedural obstacles (eg a claim must be made promptly) in order to seek judicial review.

Further reading

Books

Barnett, H, *Constitutional and Administrative Law* (7th edn, Routledge–Cavendish, 2009), Chapter 26.

Budge, I, Crewe, I, McKay, D and Newton, K, *The New British Politics* (Addison Wesley Longman, 1998), Chapter 11.

Craig, P, 'Access to mechanisms of Administrative Law' in Feldman, D (ed) *English Public Law* (2nd edn, Oxford University Press, 2009), p 757.

Leyland, P and Anthony, G, *Textbook on Administrative Law* (6th edn, Oxford University Press, 2009), Chapters 9 and 18.

Weir, S and Beetham, D, *Political Power and Democratic Control in Britain* (Routledge, 1999), Chapter 15.

Articles

Forsyth, C, 'Of fig leaves and fairy tales: The ultra vires doctrine, the sovereignty of parliament and judicial review' [1996] CLJ 122.

Laws, Sir J, 'Is the High Court the Guardian of Fundamental Constitutional Rights?' [1993] PL 59.

Oliver, D, 'Is the ultra vires rule the basis of judicial review?' [1987] PL 543.

Woolf, Lord 'Judicial review – the tensions between the executive and the judiciary' [1998] 114 LQR 579.

Paper

Horne, A and Berman, G, 'Judicial Review: A short guide to claims in the Administrative Court', 06/44, (House of Commons Library, 2006).

20

Judicial review II (grounds of review and remedies)

AIMS AND OBJECTIVES

At the end of this chapter you should be able to

■ Identify and explain the different grounds of judicial review
■ Distinguish between those grounds
■ Identify those remedies that are available for a successful judicial review claim
■ Assess the effectiveness of judicial review as a public law remedy

20.1 Grounds for judicial review

Judicial review can be sought on a number of different grounds. In *Council of Civil Service Unions v Minister for the Civil Service* [1985] 1 AC 374 (commonly known as the *GCHQ* case) Lord Diplock took the opportunity to reclassify the existing grounds of review in the following terms (in doing so he, in effect, provided a codification of them):

JUDGMENT

'Judicial review has I think developed to a stage today when without reiterating any analysis of the steps by which the development has come about, one can conveniently classify under three heads the grounds upon which administrative action is subject to control by judicial review. The first ground I would call "illegality", the second "irrationality" and the third "procedural impropriety".'

According to Lord Diplock although there were essentially three different grounds of judicial review, he noted that proportionality may be developed at a later date (this has now occurred with the advent of the Human Rights Act 1998 – see section 20.4). It must be emphasised that these three grounds should not be viewed as rigid categories which are mutually exclusive from each other as it is possible for a claimant to argue that the actions of a public law body involve more than one ground of review.

In 2010, the different grounds of judicial review can be illustrated as follows:

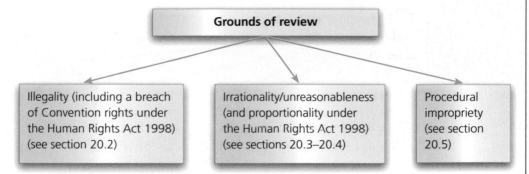

Figure 20.1 Grounds of review

20.2 The ground of illegality

20.2.1 Definition and classification

The ground of illegality has a number of different aspects to it and was defined by Lord Diplock in *Council of Civil Service Unions v Minister for the Civil Service* [1985] 1 AC 374 in the following way.

JUDGMENT

'By "illegality" as a ground for judicial review I mean that the decision-maker must understand correctly the law that regulates his decision-making power and must give effect to it.'

Illegality can be further broken down into the following elements – the decision-maker has acted illegally because he has:

- Acted in an *ultra vires* way, that is beyond his powers (simple *ultra vires*).
- Misinterpreted his public law powers (excess of jurisdiction).
- Wrongly delegated his legal powers (wrongful delegation).
- Acted for an improper purpose (improper/ulterior purpose).
- Abused his discretion by failing to exercise it at all, or he has considered irrelevant factors and/or ignored relevant ones (an abuse of discretion).
- Acted in a way which is incompatible with the rights in the European Convention on Human Rights (the Human Rights Act 1998).

In essence, the ground of illegality is concerned with the misinterpretation or wrongful application of public law powers. These categories are not rigidly demarcated however; for example, a public body which takes into account an irrelevant factor may also act for an improper purpose at the same time.

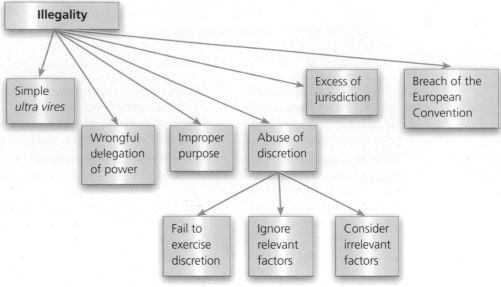

Figure 20.2 Illegality

20.2.2 Simple *ultra vires*

The principle of *ultra vires* means acting beyond and exceeding legal powers. For example, if A has been conferred with the legal power to do X, when he does X he acts *intra vires* (within his powers), but if he does Y instead, he acts *ultra vires*. The concept of *ultra vires* is associated with the intention of Parliament and so an action not authorised by the statute (eg Y above) is unlawful. As indicated previously (see section 19.2.4), however, the concept of *ultra vires* alone cannot explain the ambit and nature of judicial review.

CASE EXAMPLE

R v Secretary of State for the Home Department, ex parte Leech [1993] 4 All ER 539

Under s 47(1) Prison Act 1952 the Secretary of State could make rules in order to regulate and manage prisons. Leech (a prisoner) successfully sought judicial review of r 33(3) of the Prison Rules 1964 which enabled a prison governor to read letters to and from a prisoner and stop any letter which was of inordinate length or objectionable. Leech argued that this rule allowed the reading and stopping of correspondence between a prisoner and his legal adviser where no legal proceedings were pending.

The Court of Appeal granted a declaration that r 33(3) was *ultra vires* the enabling Act (s 47(1) of the Prison Act 1952). It could not have been Parliament's intention to impede a prisoner's right of access to the courts (via his legal adviser).

CASE EXAMPLE

Attorney General v Fulham Corporation [1921] 1 Ch 440

Fulham Corporation, purporting to act under powers under the Baths and Wash-houses Acts 1846–78, established a laundry which involved customers bringing their clothes to the wash-house to be washed. These clothes were then washed by the employees of the Corporation and returned to the customers.

It was held that this scheme was *ultra vires* as it was not authorised by the Baths and Wash-houses Acts 1846–78. These Acts authorised the establishment of wash-houses whereby people could use the facilities to wash their own clothes. Instead, Fulham Corporation had created a laundry which was an entirely different enterprise and not authorised by the 1846–78 legislation.

See also *London County Council v Attorney General* [1902] AC 165.

In addition, earlier examples of the use of *ultra vires* which we have already encountered in the text include the following:

- *Chester v Bateson* (1920) – where reg 2A(2) was held *ultra vires* the Defence of the Realm (Consolidation) Act 1914 for obstructing access to the courts (see section 5.7.2).
- *Commissioners of Customs and Excise v Cure & Deeley Ltd* (1962) – where reg 12 was held *ultra vires* the Finance (No 2) Act 1940 as it, in effect, purported to confer onto the Commissioners of Customs and Excise the powers of a judge and which ousted the jurisdiction of the courts (see section 6.7.5).
- *R v Lord Chancellor, ex parte Witham* (1997) – where the Supreme Court Fees (Amendment) Order 1996 was held *ultra vires* the Supreme Court Act 1981 (now known as the Senior Courts Act 1981) for precluding a person's access to the courts (see section 4.8.3).

More recently in *Ahmed v HM Treasury* [2010] UKSC 2 the Supreme Court quashed the Terrorism (United Nations Measures) Order 2006 as being *ultra vires* s 1 of the United Nations Act 1946. In *HM Treasury v Ahmed* [2010] UKSC 5 the Supreme Court refused the Treasury's application to suspend the judgment of the court. Thereafter, the Terrorist Asset-Freezing (Temporary Provisions) Act 2010 was passed which specifies that the 2006 Order is deemed to have been validly made under the 1946 Act.

The 'fairly incidental rule'

Although the *ultra vires* principle states that a public body may not do that which is not *expressly* authorised, in practice the courts have also permitted actions which are 'fairly incidental' to these expressly authorised powers.

CASE EXAMPLE

Attorney-General v Crayford Urban District Council [1962] 2 All ER 147

Crayford UDC made arrangements with an insurance company for council tenants to be able to insure their effects. This sum was collected at the same time as the council rent.

The Court of Appeal upheld the scheme as *intra vires* as acts of general management within s 111 of the Housing Act 1957. In short, if council tenants were uninsured, should they suffer loss (ie by virtue of fire or storm) then they were more likely to default on their council rent to make up the loss, than if they were insured against such loss. As a result, the council was helping to ensure the payment of council rents and so by implication were allowed to act as they did.

Furthermore, Parliament has recognised that local authorities should not be confined strictly to only those actions explicitly authorised – s 111 Local Government Act 1972 states that local authorities shall be empowered to do anything:

SECTION

S 111

… which is calculated to facilitate, or is conducive or incidental to, the discharge of any of their functions.

McCarthy & Stone Ltd v Richmond Upon Thames London Borough Council
[1992] 2 AC 48

Richmond Borough Council levied a charge on developers in respect of inquiries concerning speculative development proposals.

The House of Lords held that the above charge for pre-application advice was unlawful. In terms of s 111 of the Local Government Act 1972, the charge for such advice did not facilitate (nor was it conducive or incidental to) the council's functions of considering and determining applications for planning.

See also *Hazell v Hammersmith and Fulham London Borough Council* [1992] 2 AC 1.

20.2.3 Wrongful delegation of power

As a general constitutional principle, if public law powers are conferred on A (eg delegated to A by Parliament), they should not be delegated (or sub-delegated) to B.

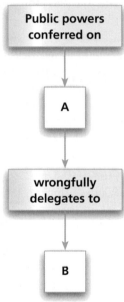

Figure 20.3 Wrongful delegation of power

The constitutional consequences of this are twofold:

- A does not fulfill his public law obligation to exercise the power conferred on him (he may well have been delegated that power because of his expertise).
- The wrong person in law (ie B) is exercising public law powers.

This principle is encapsulated in the legal maxim: *'delegatus non potest delegare'* (the delegate is not permitted to delegate).

CASE EXAMPLE

Allingham and another v Minister of Agriculture and Fisheries [1948] 1 KB 780

A county war agricultural executive committee (which itself had been lawfully delegated powers by the Minister of Agriculture and Fisheries) decided that a number of acres of sugar beet should be grown by the owners of certain land. The committee, however, delegated to its executive officer the selection of the exact field on which to grow the sugar beet. It was held that the committee could not delegate its power to determine the land to be used and cultivated.

Whether a body can delegate powers is a matter of statutory construction for the court to determine. For example, the Act may expressly authorise delegation. Where, however, the Act is silent as to delegation, the courts will consider the nature, purpose and context of the powers. For example:

- Is the power a judicial or quasi-judicial one?
- Is the power purely administrative (eg involving simply the collation of information)?
- Has the power been conferred on a government minister?
- Would delegation be in the public interest and would it cause injustice?

Judicial/quasi-judicial powers (including disciplinary powers)

Where the power is essentially a judicial or quasi-judicial power, the courts are reluctant to allow delegation. Lord Parker CJ, in *R v Governor of Brixton Prison, ex parte Enahoro* [1963] 2 QB 455 stated that:

JUDGMENT

'It is well settled that certainly no person made responsible for a judicial decision can delegate his responsibility.'

In relation to disciplinary powers examine the following case:

CASE EXAMPLE

Barnard and Others v National Dock Labour Board and Another [1953] 1 All ER 1113

The Dock Workers (Regulation of Employment) Order 1947 established the National Dock Labour Board which in turn was authorised to delegate specified disciplinary functions, including the power of suspension, to local dock boards (an example of an express author-isation to delegate). The secretary of a local board suspended Barnard and others with the power to do so being purportedly delegated by the local board. The Court of Appeal held that the power of suspension was a judicial/quasi-judicial function (it affected a person's rights) which could not be delegated by the local board. The suspensions were declared a nullity.

See also *Vine v National Dock Labour Board* [1957] AC 488, where a local dock labour board wrongfully delegated their disciplinary powers to a disciplinary committee which had terminated Vine's employment. This dismissal was therefore invalid due to the delega-tion of a quasi-judicial function.

Administrative powers

Where a power is not judicial, but merely consists of, for example, the collection of evidence or a preliminary investigation, then the courts have held delegation to be permissible (in this context see: *Jeffs v New Zealand Dairy Production and Marketing Board* [1967] AC 551 and *R v Race Relations Board, ex parte Selvarajan* [1975] 1 WLR 1686).

Government ministers

The courts have recognised the practical reality of government administration, that it is not practically possible for a government minister to exercise every single power conferred on him. Lord Greene MR, in *Carltona Ltd v Commissioners of Works* [1943] 2 All ER 560 (see section 4.13.12), stated that:

JUDGMENT

'The functions which are given to ministers … are functions so multifarious that no minister could ever personally attend to them … The duties imposed upon ministers and the powers given to ministers are normally exercised under the authority of the ministers by responsible officials of the department. Public business could not be carried on if that were not the case.'

In fact, for the purposes of the decision the official becomes the *alter ego* of the minister and therefore in reality there is no real delegation (on this point see Widgery LJ in *R v Skinner* [1968] 2 QB 700). Moreover, the minister must select an appropriate official of sufficient experience and expertise:

CASE EXAMPLE

R v Secretary of State for the Home Department, ex parte Oladehinde [1991] 1 AC 254

The Home Secretary delegated to officials (of not less than inspector level) the power to make decisions, on his behalf, to deport persons under the Immigration Act 1971. Oladehinde was served with a notice of an intention to deport and he sought judicial review to quash the decision on the basis that the Home Secretary had wrongfully delegated his power under the Act to immigration inspectors.

The House of Lords held that the minister was entitled to authorise responsible officials to exercise his powers. The officials (immigration inspectors) were of suitable grading and experience to exercise these powers.

It should also be remembered that the minister will remain constitutionally accountable to Parliament for his decisions (whether or not he took them personally). Furthermore, in some cases delegation may be prohibited where a statute specifically requires the minister personally (and no other person) to take the decision. For example, s 13(5) of the Immigration Act 1971 refers to directions having 'been given by the Secretary of State (and not by a person acting under his authority)'.

ACTIVITY

Self-test questions

1. What is meant by action which is *ultra vires*?
2. What is meant by unlawful delegation of power?
3. When is it permissible to delegate a power?

20.2.4 Improper purpose

A public law power should be exercised for the purpose for which it has been conferred. If a power has been conferred in order for a public body to achieve purpose X, it will be unlawful for that power to be used to achieve purpose Y. In short, public power should not be used with an ulterior motive/purpose in mind, as this is an abuse of power (this area, therefore, could arguably also fall under section 20.2.5).

CASE EXAMPLE

Congreve v Home Office [1976] 1 All ER 697

In 1975 the cost of a colour television licence was increased from £12 to £18. In order to avoid paying this increase Congreve (along with others) renewed his licence early. The Home Office became aware of this and with the anticipated loss of revenue, Congreve and others were informed that unless they paid the £6 difference, their licences would be revoked.

The Court of Appeal held that the licence which Congreve had obtained lawfully was valid and the demand for payment was an unlawful exercise of power. Lord Denning MR held that the Home Secretary must use his statutory power to revoke licences under the Wireless Telegraphy Act 1949 in accordance with the law, that is to say not being influenced by ulterior/improper motives (eg want of money). It would be different if an individual had breached the conditions of the licence (a proper purpose).

Similarly, in *Porter v Magill* [2001] UKHL 67, the House of Lords held that a local authority could dispose of land under s 32 of the Housing Act 1985 to achieve proper housing objectives, but not for promoting an electoral advantage of a party on the council (an improper purpose). The case concerned the sale of council houses and the belief that owner-occupiers were more likely to vote Conservative as a result of these sales.

CASE EXAMPLE

R v Ealing London Borough Council, ex parte Times Newspapers Ltd and others (1986) 85 LGR 316

Under the Public Libraries and Museums Act 1964 it is the duty of a library authority to provide a comprehensive and efficient library service. As a result of an industrial dispute between *The Times* newspaper and their former employees, three councils banned copies of these newspapers in their library. *The Times* successfully sought judicial review of these decisions. The court held that the ban was imposed for an ulterior object (to be used as a weapon against *The Times* in their industrial dispute) and so declared it to be unlawful.

In *Wheeler v Leicester City Council* [1985] 1 AC 1054 Leicester City Council passed a resolution which prevented Leicester Football Club from using the council's recreational grounds for one year (the council considered that Leicester Football Club had failed to discourage three of its players from playing in an England Rugby tour of South Africa during the apartheid era and should have condemned the tour). The House of Lords held that the council had *inter alia*, misused its powers as, although under s 71 of the Race Relations Act 1976 it had a duty to make arrangements with a view to securing that its functions were carried out with due regard to the need to promote good race relations, Leicester Football Club had not acted improperly or broken any law. In this context also see *R v Lewisham London Borough Council, ex parte Shell UK Ltd* [1988] 1 All ER 938. One of the most significant cases in terms of improper purpose is the following case:

CASE EXAMPLE

Padfield v Minister of Agriculture, Fisheries and Food [1968] AC 997

Under the Agricultural Marketing Act 1958 the minister had a power/discretion to send (in any case he so directed) complaints arising out of the operation of the milk marketing scheme to a committee of investigation. Padfield (and others) asked the minister to appoint a committee to investigate their complaint (ie to refer their complaint to a committee of investigation) but the minister refused.

The House of Lords held that an order of *mandamus* should be made directing the minister to consider Padfield's complaint according to the law. The minister had argued that under the Act he had, in effect, a complete discretion in respect of whether or not to refer a complaint. The House of Lords held, however, that his discretion was not unlimited as it was conferred on him so that he could promote the object and policy of the Act (ie the investigation of substantial and genuine complaints).

This case illustrates that the courts will not recognise an absolute discretion. It should be remembered that public decision-makers are exercising public law powers which can directly or indirectly affect millions of people. The *Padfield* case was, however, a somewhat pyrrhic victory as although following the court case the complaint was referred, the minister subsequently decided that it would not be in the public interest to implement the conclusions of the committee.

20.2.5 Abuse of discretion

A public law discretion (the conferment of a power to act) should not be abused by a public law decision-maker. Abuse of discretion is a generic term which covers a number of unlawful actions which include:

■ Fettering a discretion.
■ Ignoring relevant factors.
■ Taking irrelevant factors into consideration.

In fact, it could also be argued that acting for an improper purpose (see section 20.2.4) is also an abuse of discretion. As indicated earlier, there are no rigid sub-categories within illegality. For example, it could be argued that by wrongfully delegating a power (section 20.2.3), a public decision-maker has failed to exercise his public law discretion because he has divested himself of it altogether.

Although a statute may provide that a public body can make a decision as it thinks fit the courts have adopted the approach that this does not mean that the public body can make literally any decision it thinks fit. Instead, the courts will imply certain limitations, as they do not accept the notion of an absolute or complete discretion. This is consistent with the rule of law (see section 6.7.5) as although public law discretion is a valuable tool in public administration, if the use of the discretion is not structured and controlled, it is akin to an arbitrary power.

Fettering a discretion

If a public decision-maker has been conferred with a public law discretion he should consider whether to exercise it.

Public law decision-makers can also abuse their discretion if they unnecessarily restrict the circumstances in which they will use it (eg they adopt an overly-rigid or blanket policy which affects an individual). In this way the decision-maker is fettering his discretion by refusing to exercise it when new or exceptional circumstances arise. Lord Reid, in *British Oxygen Co Ltd v Minister of Technology* [1971] AC 610 stated that:

JUDGMENT

'What the authority must not do is to refuse to listen at all. But a Ministry or large authority may have had to deal already with a multitude of similar applications and then they will almost certainly have evolved a policy so precise that it could well be called a rule. There can be no objection to that, provided the authority is always willing to listen to anyone with something new to say.'

The point here is that it is common in public administration for administrators to adopt general guidelines or policies to assist them in making decision-making more efficient (this is a 'structuring' of a discretion – see section 6.7.5). However, the adoption of an over-rigid policy, excluding any exceptions in any circumstances, could be challenged by a claimant affected by it.

Relevancy and irrelevancy

In making public law decisions a public decision-maker will necessarily have to consider a number of different factors. In public law a decision-maker must:

■ Consider *relevant* factors and
■ Disregard *irrelevant* factors.

Relevant factors

A decision-maker must consider relevant factors:

CASE EXAMPLE

R v Immigration Appeal Tribunal, ex parte Singh [1986] 1 WLR 910

The House of Lords held that an immigration adjudicator in deciding whether or not to deport Singh had ignored a relevant factor: that third party interests might be relevant. Singh was a talented musician who had performed the functions of a priest in the Sikh community and so his deportation would have had an impact upon the community.

Similarly, in *Bromley London Borough Council v GLC* [1983] AC 768 the House of Lords held *inter alia* that the Greater London Council (GLC) should have had regard to the interests of ratepayers (a fiduciary duty) in implementing its reduced fares scheme.

Irrelevant factors

In some respects the issue of a public body taking into account irrelevant factors can blur into the ground of acting for an improper purpose. For example, if a public decision-maker in exercising a discretion has an ulterior motive in mind, he is also necessarily taking into account an irrelevant factor (ie the ulterior motive).

Below are some examples involving the consideration of irrelevant factors:

CASE EXAMPLE

R v Somerset County Council, ex parte Fewings [1995] 3 All ER 20

The council passed a resolution banning deer hunting over its land as the majority of councillors viewed the activity as morally repulsive. In the Divisional Court Laws J held that the council could not ban hunting on the basis that it was morally repugnant, as this was a free-standing moral perception and not an objective judgment as to what would 'conduce to the better management of the estate' as required by s 120 (1)(b) of the Local Government Act 1972. According to Laws J, the councillors' moral view on hunting had 'nothing whatever to do with such questions' (ie it was an irrelevant factor).

The Court of Appeal affirmed this decision that the hunting ban was unlawful (albeit on other grounds). The court held by a majority that the council had not exercised its power in order to promote the benefit of its area as, for one thing, it had not considered the statutory provision of s 120(1)(b). It is of interest to note that Sir Thomas Bingham MR and Simon Brown LJ indicated that it could not be said that the 'cruelty' argument was necessarily irrelevant to the question as to what is for the benefit of the area.

In addition, as noted earlier in *ex parte Venables and Thompson* (1997) at section 5.7.6, the House of Lords held that the Home Secretary had misdirected himself in law by considering an irrelevant consideration (public protest concerning the sentences to be imposed in respect of these two particular individuals). Moreover, he had ignored relevant factors (ie the progress and development of Venables and Thompson while they were detained).

This aspect of judicial review can be somewhat controversial as the judges are, in effect, determining which factors are relevant. As noted by Forbes J, however, judges are not concerned with whether due or proper weight is given to any particular material consideration/factor (*Pickwell v Camden London Borough Council* [1983] 1 All ER 602) – although now see the impact of proportionality on this distinction. Nevertheless, the controversial nature of this ground is illustrated by the area of financial considerations concerning the 'duties' of local authorities to provide services:

CASE EXAMPLE

R v Gloucestershire County Council, ex parte Barry [1997] AC 584

Barry's cleaning and laundry services had been withdrawn because of financial resources. The House of Lords held (by a majority) that, in effect, financial considerations (ie the cost of care and the availability of resources) might be proper factors for a local authority to consider in assessing an individual's need for a service under the Chronically Sick and Disabled Persons Act 1970.

In contrast, however, see the following case: *R v East Sussex County Council, ex parte Tandy* [1998] 2 All ER 769. The House of Lords distinguished *ex parte Barry* above and held that the availability of resources was *not* a consideration in determining what constituted suitable education (in the case – special educational needs) under the Education Act 1993. In particular see Lord Browne-Wilkinson's insistence that the lack of financial resources will not result in the courts downgrading 'a statutory duty to a discretionary power'.

Finally, a case concerning the relevance of considerations in the context of the rule of law is the following case:

CASE EXAMPLE

R v Coventry City Council, ex parte Phoenix Aviation and others [1995] 3 All ER 37

Judicial review applications were sought against public authorities operating air and sea ports as to whether lawfully, they could ban the transportation of livestock so as to avoid the consequences of unlawful protests by animal rights protestors. It was held that the air and sea ports had to remain open to traffic and the trade in livestock.

In terms of their concern about the actions of the protestors, Simon Brown LJ commented:

JUDGMENT

'One thread runs consistently throughout all the case law; the recognition that public authorities must beware of surrendering to the dictates of unlawful pressure groups. The implications of such surrender for the rule of law can hardly be exaggerated … Tempting though it may sometimes be for public authorities to yield too readily to threats of disruption, they must expect the courts to review any such decision with particular rigour – this is not an area where they can be permitted a wide measure of discretion.'

20.2.6 Excess of jurisdiction

Jurisdiction refers to the power of a body to act, for example if a local authority is empowered to provide a service or exercise a discretion. In terms of jurisdiction it is possible for a public body to make either a:

- Mistake of fact or
- Mistake of law.

Mistake of fact

In broad terms the courts in judicial review proceedings will not interfere when a body makes a mistake of fact (ie they get factual details wrong). This is because

- They take the view that the specified public body has been conferred with the responsibility of determining facts.
- Judges are experts in law and not facts.
- Judicial review would become overwhelmed with cases involving public bodies that had made factual errors.

- The nature of judicial review proceedings is not particularly amenable to investigating disputed facts (eg there is a limited use of cross-examination).

There are, however, some mistakes of fact that the courts will subject to review:

- Precedent facts.
- Facts which have no supporting evidence.

Precedent facts

The courts will interfere where the fact is a 'precedent fact' or 'jurisdictional fact' in that its existence is necessary in order for the public body to act. In other words, certain facts must be correctly established before the body can act, as these facts are central to the decision-makers' power.

CASE EXAMPLE

R v Secretary of State for the Home Department, ex parte Khawaja [1984] 1 AC 74

The House of Lords held that the existence of the power to detain Khawaja (with a view to deportation) under the Immigration Act 1971 depended upon him being an 'illegal entrant'. This was a precedent fact which had to be satisfied and it was the duty of the court to inquire whether there had been sufficient/adequate evidence to justify and support the immigration officer's belief that entry into the United Kingdom had been illegal. The executive/government had to prove to the court the facts that the immigration officer had relied upon.

In other words, the existence of some facts are so fundamental that they trigger the public law power of a public body to act. Similarly, in *White and Collins v Minister of Health* [1939] 2 KB 838 a local authority was not permitted to compulsorily purchase land which was part of a park. In this case the land was factually held to be part of a park and so the compulsory purchase order was quashed. See also *R (Maiden Outdoor Advertising) v Lambeth LBC* [2004] JPL 820.

Facts which have no supporting evidence

This concerns the position whereby a public body makes a decision regarding a fact for which there is objectively no supporting evidence to support that factual finding. Lord Denning MR, in *Ashbridge Investments Ltd v Minister of Housing and Local Government* [1965] 3 All ER 371 stated that:

JUDGMENT

'The Minister must himself decide the question of "house or not a house", just as he must decide "fit or unfit". The legislature has entrusted it to the Minister for decision ... it seems to me that the court can interfere with the Minister's decision if he has acted on no evidence; or if he has come to a conclusion to which, on the evidence, he could not reasonably come.'

See also *Coleen Properties Ltd v Minister of Housing and Local Government* [1971] 1 WLF 433. Finally, in the context of errors of fact, note should be taken of the developing area of errors of material fact (causing unfairness to a person) – see P Leyland and G Anthony, *Textbook on Administrative Law*, (6th edn, Oxford University Press, 2009), p 276.

In this context see *E v Secretary of State for the Home Department* [2004] EWCA Civ 49 and the recent case of *Connolly and Havering LBC v Secretary of State for Communities and Local Government* [2009] EWCA Civ 1059 and the associated article of C Brasted and J Marlow, 'Matters of Fact' (2010) 160 NLJ 609.

Mistake of law

The courts are less reluctant to review errors of law. An error of law refers to a body misinterpreting its legal powers by misunderstanding the statutory provisions which enable it to act. It should be noted that not every interpretation of a word will involve an error of law. Lord Reid, in *Brutus v Cozens* [1973] AC 854 noted that:

JUDGMENT

'The meaning of an ordinary word of the English language is not a question of law. The proper construction of a statute is a question of law. If the context shows that a word is used in an unusual sense the court will determine in other words what that unusual sense is.'

According to Barnett (*Constitutional and Administrative Law*, 7th edn, Routledge–Cavendish, 2009, p 728) one example of an error of law is the wrongful interpretation of a word to which a legal meaning has been attached. Historically, the issue of the court reviewing errors of law has generated some highly complex case law with the seminal case being *Anisminic Ltd* (1969):

CASE EXAMPLE

Anisminic Ltd v Foreign Compensation Commission [1969] 2 AC 147

Under the Foreign Compensation Act 1950 the Foreign Compensation Commission was charged with the responsibility of determining claims of compensation in respect of British property which had been seized or destroyed during the Suez crisis in 1956. Anisminic was a British company (whose property had been sequestrated by the Egyptian authorities) which appeared to satisfy the criteria required to claim compensation. In 1957 Anisminic sold the sequestrated property to an Egyptian organisation. The Commission rejected Anisminic's claim for compensation. Section 4 of the Act stated that a determination of the Commission could not be called into question by a court of law. In other words, this was an 'ouster clause' (which ousted the jurisdiction of the courts) which left the final decision with the Commission.

The House of Lords, however, held that the Commission had, in determining Anisminic's claim, asked itself in law the wrong question by misconstruing its responsibilities. In short, the Commission had asked whether the successor in title to Anisminic's property was British (on the facts it was an Egyptian organisation), rather than simply: was the applicant (and original owner of Anisminic) British? Thus, the court held that the Commission had gone outside its jurisdiction and as a result the ouster clause of s 4 did not apply as the Commission had not made a 'determination', but had merely purported to do so.

The case indicates that the courts will intervene where a public decision-maker has misunderstood its legal powers. In addition, it indicates the resistance of the courts to 'ouster clauses' (see section 19.2.4).

Following *Anisminic Ltd* (1969) a number cases (eg *Pearlman v Keepers and Governors of Harrow School* [1979] 1 QB 56, *Re Racal Communications Ltd* [1981] AC 374 and *R v Lord President of the Privy Council, ex parte Page* [1992] 3 WLR 1112) clarified the position of the courts in respect of errors of law. Today the courts are concerned that public bodies properly interpret their public law powers. It may well be that a statutory appeal may be available where a body commits an error of law, but failing that, the courts will now review errors of law regarding them as 'jurisdictional errors of law'.

Craig (*Administrative Law* (6th edn, Sweet & Maxwell, 2008), p 461) helpfully has set out the modern position as follows:

- The courts will review an error of law although the error must be a relevant/material one.
- In relation to a tribunal/administrative body the courts adopt the presumption that Parliament did *not* intend that body to be the definitive arbiter in respect of an issue of law and so will subject it to review.

- In relation to an inferior court there is *no* presumption that Parliament did not intend the issue of law to be left to the inferior court.

It should be remembered that in terms of the higher courts, these are not subject to judicial review in any case. In respect of the Upper Tribunal see the recent case of *R(C) v Upper Tribunal* [2009] EWHC 3052 (QB).

Mistake of law and fact

In terms of a mistake of a mixture of law and fact, the courts will be unlikely to interfere unless it is an aberrant interpretation. For example, in *South Yorkshire Transport Ltd* (below) the House of Lords held that the Monopolies Commission's interpretation of the term 'in a substantial part of the United Kingdom' in the context of s 64 of the Fair Trading Act 1973 (a mixture of law and fact) would be upheld as it was within the permissible field of judgment open to it. Lord Mustill, in *South Yorkshire Transport Ltd and another v Monopolies and Mergers Commission and another* [1993] 1 All ER 289 noted that:

JUDGMENT

'The criterion so established may itself be so imprecise that different decision-makers, each acting rationally, might reach differing conclusions when applying it to the facts of a given case. In such a case the court is entitled to substitute its own opinion for that of the person to whom the decision has been entrusted only if the decision is so aberrant that it cannot be classed as rational.'

ACTIVITY

Self-test questions

1. What is meant by a decision-maker abusing his discretion?
2. What is the difference between a mistake of:
   - fact
   - law or
   - a mixed question of fact and law?

20.2.7 Breach of the European Convention on Human Rights

As a result of the Human Rights Act 1998, it is now possible for a claimant to seek judicial review of a public law body on the basis that they have violated the rights set out in the European Convention. Under s 6 of the Act, a new statutory obligation is placed on public bodies that they must act consistently with Convention rights. Any discretion a public decision-maker has must now be exercised in line with the Convention (see Chapter 17).

If a public body infringes the Convention, the claimant (as a victim under s 7) can seek judicial review on the ground of illegality: namely, that the public body has acted illegally by infringing the European Convention. Although in general terms the Human Rights Act 1998 has added a new aspect of illegality, where Art 6 and the right to a fair hearing is raised, this will be subsumed under the third ground of review: procedural impropriety. A recent case involving a violation of the Convention is *R (Purdy) v DPP* [2009] UKHL 45 in which the House of Lords held that Purdy's right to respect for private life under Art 8 had been breached by the DPP's failure to provide a specific policy as to the factors which would be taken into account in deciding whether a person would be prosecuted for aiding suicide contrary to s 2 of the Suicide Act 1961.

The ground of illegality	
Simple *ultra vires*	Acting beyond and exceeding legal powers (*Fulham Corporation* (1921), *ex parte Witham* (1997)).
Wrongful delegation of power	Public law powers should not be unlawfully delegated (*Vine* (1957)). Government ministers, however, typically confer power on officials to take decisions on their behalf (*Carltona Ltd* (1943)).
Improper purpose	Power should be used for their proper and lawful purpose (*Congreve* (1976)).
Abuse of discretion	A public law discretion should not be fettered (*British Oxygen Co Ltd* (1971)). Relevant factors must be considered (*ex parte Singh* (1986)). Irrelevant factors must not be taken into consideration (*ex parte Venables* (1997)).
Excess of jurisdiction	Generally the courts will not interfere with a mistake of fact unless it is a precedent fact (*White and Collins* (1939)) or lacks supporting evidence (*Ashbridge Investments Ltd* (1965)). Today the courts will intervene in order to rectify a mistake of law (*Anisminic Ltd* (1969)).
Breach of the European Convention on Human Rights	Section 6 of the Human Rights Act 1998 requires public bodies to act in line with the European Convention on Human Rights (*Purdy* (2009)).

20.3 The ground of irrationality

20.3.1 Origins and definition

In general terms, an Act of Parliament will not state expressly that a statutory power conferred on a public law body must be exercised 'rationally'. The courts, however, imply that Parliament never intended such a power to be used unreasonably or in an irrational way. The ground of irrationality, therefore, is concerned with a public body acting strictly within its legal powers (ie within the four corners of its powers), but arriving at a decision which is totally unreasonable. In his reclassification of the grounds of review, Lord Diplock, in *Council of Civil Service Unions v Minister for the Civil Service* [1985] 1 AC 374, described irrationality as follows:

JUDGMENT

'By "irrationality" I mean what can by now be succinctly referred to as "Wednesbury unreasonableness" … It applies to a decision which is so outrageous in its defiance of logic or of accepted moral standards that no sensible person who had applied his mind to the question to be decided could have arrived at it.'

Lord Diplock's reference to Wednesbury unreasonableness is derived from the following case:

CASE EXAMPLE

Associated Provincial Picture Houses Limited v Wednesbury Corporation [1948] 1 KB 223

Under s 1 of the Sunday Entertainments Act 1932 a local authority had the power to grant licences for cinema performances on a Sunday 'subject to such conditions as the authority thinks fit to impose'. Wednesbury Corporation granted Associated Provincial Picture Houses Ltd a licence to give Sunday performances subject to the condition that 'no children under the age of fifteen years shall be admitted to any entertainment whether accompanied by an adult or not'. The claimants sought a declaration that this condition was unreasonable and *ultra vires*.

The Court of Appeal held that Wednesbury Corporation had not acted *ultra vires* or unreasonably in setting this condition. Lord Greene MR noted that:

JUDGMENT

'It is true to say that, if a decision on a competent matter is so unreasonable that no reasonable authority could ever have come to it, then the courts can interfere. That, I think, is quite right; but to prove a case of that kind would require something overwhelming and, in this case, the facts do not come anywhere near anything of that kind.'

In other words, acting unreasonably (Wednesbury unreasonableness) means that a body has come to a decision which no reasonable body could have come to: 'be something so absurd that no sensible person could ever dream that it lay within the powers of the authority' (Lord Greene MR). It is often forgotten in this case that the court held that Wednesbury Corporation had imposed a condition which a reasonable corporation *could* have imposed. In *GCHQ*, Lord Diplock redefined this narrow form of unreasonableness (Wednesbury unreasonableness) as 'irrationality'.

ACTIVITY

Self-test question

Do you think that a modern court would hold the condition set by Wednesbury Corporation to be rational?

20.3.2 The controversial nature of irrationality

Irrationality is, historically, the most controversial ground of judicial review because, as indicated earlier at section 19.2.2, the nature of judicial review is that it concerns the decision-making process rather than the decision itself:

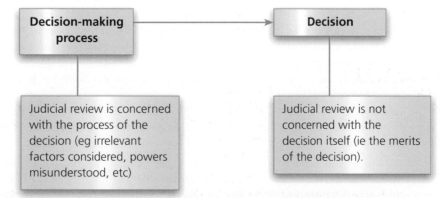

Figure 20.4 Judicial review and the decision-making process

The difficulty with irrationality, however, is that in essence it challenges the *decision* itself: namely *a decision which no reasonable decision-maker could have made*. Thus, it could be argued that this infringes the separation of powers as Parliament had conferred the power to make the final decision on the public body and not the courts.

The justification for irrationality is on the following basis:

i)   For a decision to be irrational, by definition, the decision-making process is likely to have been faulty.

ii) The courts set a very high threshold for irrationality. A court cannot interfere with a decision with which they simply disagree, but only if *no* reasonable body could have come to that decision. As an irrational decision needs to be, in effect, an absurd one, there are few examples of successful challenges on this ground.

iii) The courts, in interfering with an irrational decision are only exercising a secondary judgment. The public body exercises the primary judgment and is only subject to a 'second look' (secondary judgment) by the courts in the event that the decision is absurd.

■ It appears that historically the level of judicial intensity in looking at 'irrational decisions' depended on the context. For example, in the context of politically controversial policy areas such as national security or national economic considerations, the courts would be reluctant to interfere short of a minister taking leave of his political senses: *Nottinghamshire County Council v Secretary of State for the Environment* (1986) (see section 14.2.6). Indeed as noted by Sir Thomas Bingham MR in *R v Ministry of Defence, ex parte Smith* [1996] 1 All ER 257:

JUDGMENT

'The greater the policy content of a decision, and the more remote the subject matter of a decision from ordinary judicial experience, the more hesitant the court must necessarily be in holding a decision to be irrational … Where decisions of a policy-laden, esoteric or security-based nature are in issue even greater caution than normal must be shown in applying the test, but the test itself is sufficiently flexible to cover all situations.'

In contrast, in respect of human rights, the courts provided a more intensive look. Lord Bridge in *Bugdaycay v Secretary of State for the Home Department* [1987] 1 AC 514 pointed out:

JUDGMENT

'The most fundamental of all human rights is the individual's right to life and when an administrative decision under challenge is said to be one which may put the applicant's life at risk, the basis of the decision must surely call for the most anxious scrutiny.'

Similarly, in *ex parte Smith* (see above and section 20.4.2) the Court of Appeal stated that the human rights context of a judicial review application was important and that the greater the interference with human rights, the more justification the court would require on the part of the decision-maker (see also *R v Secretary of State for the Home Department, ex parte McQuillan* [1995] 4 All ER 400).

In either case, however, according to Sir Thomas Bingham MR in *ex parte Smith*, the test of irrationality was sufficiently flexible to adapt to the context of the application (whether this involved a policy matter or fundamental human rights).

■ Today in the light of the operation of the Human Rights Act 1998 there is some academic debate over whether the ground of irrationality still exists as a separate free-standing ground of review, or whether it has been subsumed under the doctrine of proportionality (see section 20.4.5).

20.3.3 Irrationality in practice

Although the ground of irrationality has historically been raised by claimants, it is not usually successful. This is because the threshold which needs to be crossed is set at a very high level by the courts. Indeed, Lord Greene MR in *Associated Provincial Picture Houses Ltd* (1948) made reference to the example provided by an earlier judge which indicates the level of absurdity required. Warrington LJ, in *Short v Poole Corporation* [1926] 1 Ch 66 commented that:

JUDGMENT

'I suppose that if the defendants were to dismiss a teacher because she had red hair, or for some equally frivolous and foolish reason, the Court would declare the attempted dismissal to be void.'

An unsuccessful example of the ground being raised is as follows:

CASE EXAMPLE

R v Home Secretary, ex parte Brind [1991] 1 AC 696

The House of Lords held that the minister's decision to direct broadcasters to refrain from broadcasting words spoken by individuals representing organisations proscribed under terrorism legislation was not unreasonable/irrational.

Similarly, the argument of irrationality failed in *ex parte Smith* (1996) (see section 20.4.2).

There are however, three recent cases where the ground of irrationality was successful. In *R (Rogers) v Swindon NHS Primary Care Trust* [2006] EWCA Civ 392, the Court of Appeal held that the Trust's policy in relation to the funding of a drug was irrational. Similarly, in *R (Technoprint Plc & ANOR) v Leeds City Council* [2007] EWHC 638 (Admin), the granting of retrospective planning permission relating to industrial filters subject to the implementation of noise attenuation measures was deemed irrational by the Administrative Court. An interesting case in relation to the findings of the Ombudsman is *Bradley* (2008) (see section 21.3.4) in which the Court of Appeal held that the Secretary of State for Work and Pensions had acted irrationally in rejecting a finding of maladministration by the Ombudsman.

20.4 The ground of proportionality

20.4.1 Origins and definition

In 1984 when Lord Diplock reclassified the grounds of judicial review he confined them to three grounds in *Council of Civil Service Unions v Minister for the Civil Service* [1985] 1 AC 374:

JUDGMENT

'That is not to say that further development on a case by case basis may not in course of time add further grounds. I have in mind particularly the possible adoption in the future of the principle of "proportionality".'

A test of proportionality is as follows:

QUOTATION

'Proportionality works on the assumption that administrative action ought not go beyond what is necessary to achieve its desired result (in everyday terms, that you should not use a sledge-hammer to crack a nut) and, in contrast to irrationality, is often understood to bring courts much closer to reviewing the merits of a decision.'

P Leyland and G Anthony, *Textbook on Administrative Law*
(6th edn, Oxford University Press, 2009), p 295.

In other words, proportionality considers the aim of the decision-maker and whether the means to achieve that objective are proportionate.

For example, suppose with the aim of maintaining public order under the (imaginary) Public Order Act 2013, the Home Secretary chooses to ban *all* public demonstrations for two years. Although the government would inevitably succeed in securing the mainten-ance of public order (the objective), at what cost to human rights (eg the right to protest) has this been achieved? In short, the Home Secretary would be acting disproportionately (ie using a hammer to crack a nut).

Although historically proportionality has not been a ground of judicial review, it is a principle well known in other European countries (eg Germany) as well as in international law (both European Union and Convention laws – see Chapters 15 and 16, respectively).

20.4.2 Proportionality and irrationality compared

The tests of proportionality and irrationality are different legal tests. This is neatly illus-trated in the *ex parte Smith* litigation:

CASE EXAMPLE

R v Ministry of Defence, ex parte Smith [1996] 1 All ER 257

The Ministry of Defence had a policy which prevented homosexual men and women from serving in the armed forces. This policy required the discharge of those of homosexual orien-tation. As a result three gay men and a lesbian were discharged and they sought judicial review of the policy on, *inter alia*, the ground that it was irrational.

The Court of Appeal held that in terms of irrationality the greater the interference with human rights, the more justification would be required. Nevertheless, it could not be said that the policy was irrational – for one thing Parliament had supported the policy.

Although the claimants were unsuccessful domestically, subsequently they petitioned the European Court of Human Rights:

CASE EXAMPLE

Smith and Grady v United Kingdom (2000) 29 EHRR 493
Lustig-Prean and Beckett v United Kingdom (2000) 29 EHRR 548

The claimants successfully contended that the MOD policy violated Art 8 – the right to a private sexual life. The European Court held in both cases that the blanket policy which required automatic discharge on the basis of sexual orientation could not be justified as it was a disproportionate interference with their right to private life.

In short, the domestic and international tests were different:

- In the Court of Appeal the issue was one of irrationality:
  Could a reasonable body have devised that policy?
- In the European Court of Human Rights the issue was one of proportionality:
  Was the interference with the claimants' right of private life justified and in proportion?

Thus, the proportionality test is much stricter and more exacting than the irrationality test. It is easier for a public body to show that their decision was not irrational (as such a decision needed to be perverse), rather than to show that their decision was in proportion (ie it was a balanced one which was a proportionate method of achieving a lawful objective).

The test of proportionality, therefore, has a controversial element to it as it requires the court, in effect, to *assess the quality* of the decision made and to determine if the appropriate balance between means and objective has been achieved. It is for this reason, that Lords Ackner and Roskill were particularly averse to the introduction of proportionality as a ground of review in *ex parte Brind* (1991) (see section 20.3.3). Nevertheless, as a result of the Human Rights Act the principle of proportionality is now a part of judicial review.

20.4.3 Proportionality pre-Human Rights Act?

Although historically the courts were unwilling to establish a separate ground of review labelled proportionality, to some extent the concept was not unknown in our law *before* the advent of the Human Rights Act 1998.

■ European Community law (now called European Union law) used the principle and so our judges were required to apply it in the context of European law:

CASE EXAMPLE

R v Chief Constable of Sussex, ex parte International Trader's Ferry Ltd [1999] 2 AC 418

Animal rights groups protested against ferry operators carrying livestock cargo on their ferries. Due to resource implications, the Chief Constable of Sussex Police decided to reduce the level of policing provided. International Trader's Ferry Ltd sought judicial review on the ground, *inter alia*, that it violated European law (Art 34 of the Treaty of Rome – as it was then – as being a quantitative restriction on exports between Member States).

The House of Lords held that assuming Art 34 could be enforced by the claimant, the actions of the Chief Constable were not disproportionate to the restrictions which they imposed. The actions were therefore within the public policy exemption of Art 36 (as it was known then).

It is interesting to note that a claim that the Chief Constable had acted irrationally also failed.

■ It was accepted that if a decision was lacking any proportionality at all, it was likely to be irrational in any event. Furthermore, in *R v Barnsley Metropolitan Borough Council, ex parte Hook* [1976] 3 All ER 452, the majority of the Court of Appeal held that the punishment imposed on a market trader (the loss of his licence) was altogether excessive and out of proportion.

■ In *ex parte Leech* (1993) (see section 20.2.2) the Court of Appeal held that the more fundamental the right interfered with by a rule (in this case r 33) and the more drastic that interference, the stronger the justification would have to be. This is, in effect, a kind of proportionality in practice. Similarly, see *ex parte Smith* (1996) (section 20.4.2).

20.4.4 Proportionality and the Human Rights Act 1998

The Human Rights Act 1998 gave further effect to the rights of the European Convention in domestic law. This meant that the domestic courts must follow the legal reasoning adopted in Strasbourg which includes the principle of proportionality. For example, as indicated earlier (sections 6.7.4, 17.5 and 17.11.1), in *A and others v Secretary of State for the Home Department* (2004), the House of Lords held that s 23 of the Anti-terrorism, Crime and Security Act 2001 was a disproportionate response and not strictly required by the exigencies of the situation.

In *R v Secretary of State for the Home Department ex parte Daly* [2001] UKHL 26 Lord Steyn made the following comments concerning proportionality:

JUDGMENT

'First, the doctrine of proportionality may require the reviewing court to assess the balance which the decision maker has struck, not merely whether it is within the range of rational or reasonable decisions. Secondly, the proportionality test may go further than the traditional grounds of review inasmuch as it may require attention to be directed to the relative weight accorded to interests and considerations.'

NB For the full quotation see section 17.5.

ACTIVITY

Exercise

Define the terms irrationality and proportionality and explain the difference between them.

20.4.5 The demise of irrationality?

There is currently a debate over whether irrationality continues to exist as a ground of review, or whether with the establishment of the Human Rights Act 1998, it has been overtaken by (and subsumed under) proportionality. In *R (Association of British Civilian Internees: Far East Region) v Secretary of State for Defence* [2003] EWCA Civ 473 the Court of Appeal held that the principle of proportionality had not replaced irrationality where no European Community (now Union) or Convention issues were raised. In this context, however, Dyson LJ giving judgment for the court made the following comments:

JUDGMENT

'The *Wednesbury* test is moving closer to proportionality and in some cases it is not possible to see any daylight between the two tests … Although we did not hear argument on the point, we have difficulty in seeing what justification there now is for retaining the *Wednesbury* test. But we consider that it is not for this court to perform its burial rites. The continuing existence of the *Wednesbury* test has been acknowledged by the House of Lords on more than one occasion.'

In conclusion, although it appears that irrationality is still a free-standing ground of review, to what extent this will be the case in future is debatable. According to Craig, writing in 2009:

QUOTATION

'It remains to be seen whether the *Wednesbury* test continues to exist together with proportionality, or whether the latter takes over as a general, independent head of review. It may be that the *Wednesbury* test will survive and continue to be used in cases where there is no link with EC law, and where this is no claim under the HRA. *Wednesbury* may however cease to operate as an independent test in its own right. It will be increasingly difficult, or impractical, for courts to apply different tests to different allegations made in an application for judicial review.'

'Grounds for Judical Review: Substantive Control Over Discretion' in D Feldman (ed) *English Public Law* (2nd edn, Oxford University Press, 2009), p 729.

The ground of irrationality/proportionality	
Irrationality	A decision which no reasonable body could have come to: *Associated Provincial Picture Houses Limited* (1948). Historically, the test was flexible to involve: • a less intense review in the context of politically controversial policy areas (*Nottinghamshire County Council v Secretary of State for the Environment* (1986)) • a more intensive review in the context of human rights (*ex parte Smith* (1996)).
Proportionality	Proportionality considers the aim of the decision-maker and whether the means to achieve that objective are proportionate (the Human Rights Act 1998).

20.5 The ground of procedural impropriety

20.5.1 Definition

Lord Diplock in *Council of Civil Service Unions v Minister for the Civil Service* [1985] 1 AC 374 stated:

JUDGMENT

'I have described the third head as "procedural impropriety" rather than failure to observe basic rules of natural justice or failure to act with procedural fairness towards the person who will be affected by the decision. This is because susceptibility to judicial review under this head covers also failure by an administrative tribunal to observe procedural rules that are expressly laid down in the legislative instrument by which its jurisdiction is conferred, even where such failure does not involve any denial of natural justice.'

Procedural impropriety can be sub-divided into the following:

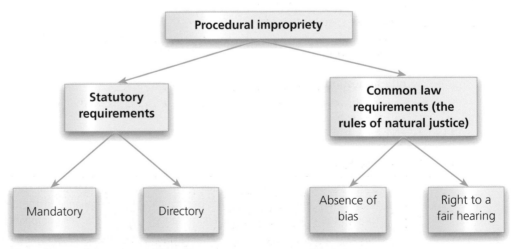

Figure 20.5 Procedural impropriety

In other words, a public decision-maker will breach this ground of review if he ignores either the requirements of a statute or the principles of natural justice.

20.5.2 Statutory requirements

The courts can subject a public body to review if it has failed to comply with statutory procedural requirements (eg before X can take a decision, X must consult A, B and C). The point must be made at the outset, however, that not all breaches of statutory requirements are the same. Historically, therefore, the courts have distinguished between two types of statutory requirements:

■ a mandatory requirement (an essential requirement which will invalidate the action if not followed).

■ a directory requirement (a less important requirement which is not fatal, as it is a minor technical defect or a minor detail).

In a sense this is analogous to the classification of contractual terms into conditions (very important) and warranties (less important).

The above dichotomy begs the question as to which statutory requirements are mandatory and which are directory? This is essentially a question of statutory interpretation for the courts to determine using the following factors:

■ The Act itself (rather unusually) may expressly state the consequences of a breach of a statutory requirement.

■ In the absence of the above, what did Parliament intend to be the result in the event of a failure to follow a procedural requirement?

■ Were obligatory terms such as 'must' used?

■ What is the purpose of the Act/requirement? Who or what is it intended to protect and for what reason?

■ Does the requirement affect individual rights?

In *London & Clydeside Estates Ltd v Aberdeen District Council* [1980] 1 WLR 182 Lord Hailsham LC stated that although the terms mandatory and directory may be helpful, he emphasised that the courts should not adopt an overly rigid set of legal categories in this regard.

JUDGMENT

'It may be that what the courts are faced with is not so much a stark choice of alternatives but a spectrum of possibilities in which one compartment or description fades gradually into another.'

In recent years, Lord Woolf MR has noted that the question of whether a requirement was mandatory or directory was only at most a first step before, in the majority of cases, other questions have to be asked:

JUDGMENT

'The questions which are likely to arise are as follows.

1. Is the statutory requirement fulfilled if there has been substantial compliance with the requirement and, if so, has there been substantial compliance in the case in issue even though there has not been strict compliance? (The substantial compliance question).

2. Is the non-compliance capable of being waived, and if so, has it, or can it and should it be waived in this particular case? (The discretionary question).

3. If it is not capable of being waived or is not waived then what is the consequence of the non-compliance? (The consequences question).

Which questions arise will depend upon the facts of the case and the nature of the particular requirement.' (*R v Secretary of State for the Home Department, ex parte Jeyeanthan* [2000] 1 WLR 354.)

More recently in this context see *R v Soneji* [2005] UKHL 49.

Historically the case law has indicated the following principles:

■ **A requirement to consult**
This is generally viewed as a mandatory and important requirement:

CASE EXAMPLE

Agricultural, Horticultural and Forestry Industry Training Board v Aylesbury Mushrooms Ltd [1972] 1 WLR 190

As the Industrial Training Act 1964 provided for prior consultation by the Ministry of Labour with interested organisations, and the Mushroom Growers' Association had not actually been consulted, a 1966 Order (establishing a training board imposing a levy) had no application to them. Consultation was treated as a mandatory requirement in relation to the Mushroom Growers' Association.

■ **A requirement to notify of the right to appeal**

CASE EXAMPLE

Agricultural, Horticultural and Forestry Industry Training Board v Kent [1970] 1 All 340

The Court of Appeal held that the provisions of the Industrial Training Levy (Agricultural, Horticultural and Forestry) Order 1967 were mandatory. As a consequence an assessment notice (indicating a levy to be paid) must state clearly the address of the training board in order that an individual (employer) may serve a notice of appeal.

■ **Time limits**
According to Wade and Forsyth (*Administrative Law* (10th edn, Oxford University Press, 2009), p 190), 'It has often been held that an act may be validly done after the expiry of a statutory time limit'. However, time limits may be mandatory if they have special importance or 'the rights of other persons depend on them'.

20.5.3 Common law requirements: *Nemo judex in re sua*

The rules of natural justice (also known as the duty to act fairly) can be sub-divided into the following:

■ *Nemo judex in re sua* (directly below).
■ *Audi alteram partem* (see section 20.5.4).

Natural justice is a substantial area in its own right and accordingly below is a very basic outline of the subject.

Nemo judex in re sua

(No man should be a judge in his own cause/the decision-maker must be unbiased)
In essence, the rule against bias can be sub-divided in the following way:

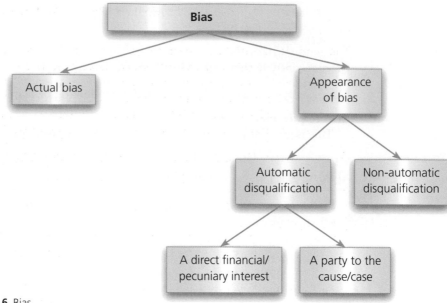

Figure 20.6 Bias

Adapted from the categorisation used by J Goudie QC in M Supperstone, J Goudie, Sir P Walker (eds), *Judicial Review* (3rd edn, LexisNexis Butterworths, 2005, p 355).

Actual bias

It is self-evidently a breach of natural justice if the decision-maker is actually biased. For example, an immigration official deports X because he has taken a personal dislike to him. Cases of actual bias are, for obvious reasons, rare. Actual bias will result in automatic disqualification.

Appearance of bias – automatic disqualification: A direct financial interest

As no man should be a judge in his own cause, a direct financial/pecuniary interest in the outcome of the proceedings leads to automatic disqualification of the decision maker:

CASE EXAMPLE

Dimes v The Proprietors of the Grand Junction Canal (1852) 3 HLC 759

In this case the Lord Chancellor (Lord Cottenham) affirmed on appeal the Vice-Chancellor's decree that Dimes could not obstruct the Grand Junction Canal's land. It transpired that the Lord Chancellor held shares in the Grand Junction Canal, and so had a financial interest in it. The House of Lords reversed the Lord Chancellor's decree and Lord Campbell stated that:

JUDGMENT

'No one can suppose that Lord Cottenham could be, in the remotest degree, influenced by the interest that he had in this concern; but, my Lords, it is of the last importance that the maxim that no man is to be a judge in his own cause should be held sacred.'

The courts have more recently reaffirmed this principle. Slade J in *R v Camborne Justices, ex parte Pearce* [1955] 1 QB 41 stated that:

JUDGMENT

'It is, of course, clear that any direct pecuniary or proprietary interest in the subject-matter of a proceeding, however small, operates as an automatic disqualification. In such a case the law assumes bias.'

Appearance of bias – automatic disqualification: A party to the cause/case

The seminal case in this respect (though now since refined through a later decision) is *ex parte Pinochet Ugarte* (2000) (see section 13.4.2). This case concerned the connection between one of the judges in the case (Lord Hoffmann) and Amnesty International which had joined the case as a party seeking Pinochet's extradition for alleged human rights violations. The House of Lords held that Lord Hoffmann was automatically disqualified from the case and so set aside its own decision and re-heard the matter.

Appearance of bias – non-automatic disqualification

According to James Goudie QC this category of case:

QUOTATION

'is where any financial or proprietary interest is indirect, or where there is no financial or proprietary interest at all, but nonetheless the surrounding circumstances give rise to a real possibility of lack of impartiality. In such a case disqualification is not automatic.'

M Supperstone, J Goudie, Sir P Walker (eds), *Judicial Review* (3rd edn, LexisNexis Butterworths, 2005), p 355.

This category involves various forms of interest and below are three cases in which bias was successfully raised:

■ **A family link**

CASE EXAMPLE

Metropolitan Properties Co (FGC) v Lannon [1969] 1 QB 577

In this case, landlords, Metropolitan Properties Co contended that the chairman of a rent assessment committee should be disqualified on the ground of bias. In short, the chairman had acted for and advised Regency Lodge tenants in dispute with their landlords (who were a company in the same group as Metropolitan Properties). He had also advised his father, a Regency Lodge tenant, about a fair rent.

The Court of Appeal held that the decision of the committee must be quashed (and remitted to another committee) because of the connection between the chairman and Regency Lodge tenants. This connection was such as to give the reasonable impression that the chairman was biased – though this was an appearance of bias as there was no actual bias.

■ **An intermingling of functions**

CASE EXAMPLE

Hannam v Bradford City Council [1970] 2 All ER 690

Hannam was a schoolmaster who absented himself and refused to return to work. In December 1967 his employment was terminated by a meeting of the school governors. In January 1968 a council staff sub-committee met to consider whether the council should prohibit the dismissal. It decided not to do so. Three of the members of the sub-committee were governors, although they had not attended the meeting in December 1967.

The Court of Appeal held that as the three governors had sat on the staff sub-committee this gave rise to the possibility of bias. They did not cease to be part of the school governors when they sat on the sub-committee and it did not matter that they had not personally attended the meeting of the governors.

JUDGMENT

'No man can be a judge of his own cause. The governors did not, on donning their sub-committee hats, cease to be an integral part of the body whose action was being impugned, and it made no difference that they did not personally attend the governors' meeting.'

Sachs LJ

CASE EXAMPLE

R v Barnsley Metropolitan Borough Council, ex parte Hook [1976] 3 All ER 452

The court held that the rules of natural justice had been breached when a local authority committee considered a complaint about Hook's (a market trader) behaviour in allegedly urinating in a side street. The committee heard the oral evidence (of the market manager) in the absence of Hook. He could not therefore challenge or orally cross-examine this evidence. The market manager (in the position of prosecutor) was also present during the deliberations of the committee. The court quashed the decision of the committee.

For the modern test for apparent bias see Lord Hope in *Porter* (2001) at section 13.4.2. However, in relation to the application of bias and predetermination to planning permission/policy of local authorities see *R (Lewis) v Persimmon Homes Teeside Ltd* [2008] EWCA Civ 746 and the following related article, N Dobson 'Bias revisited' (2008) 158 NLJ 1173.

ACTIVITY

Self-test questions

1. What is the consequence of failing to follow the procedural requirements of a statute?
2. Explain the different ways in which a decision-maker could be biased.

20.5.4 Common law requirements: *Audi alteram partem*

Audi alteram partem

(Hear the other side/the right to a fair hearing.)

Natural justice (and now Art 6 of the European Convention) provides minimum standards of fairness in respect of public decision-making. Historically, *Ridge v Baldwin* (below) and the subsequent case of *In re HK (An Infant)* [1967] 2 QB 617 acted as a watershed in the development of the right to a fair hearing.

CASE EXAMPLE

Ridge v Baldwin [1964] AC 40

Ridge, a Chief Constable, had been dismissed from his office by a watch committee. The House of Lords held that this decision was null and void as the committee had not followed the rules of natural justice. They had not informed Ridge of the charges against him nor had they given him the opportunity to be heard.

It has been argued that this decision:

QUOTATION

'liberated natural justice from the constraints which had been imposed upon it by earlier cases, placing a renewed emphasis on the impact of administrative decisions on individuals' rights and interests'.

M Elliot, *Beatson, Matthews and Elliott's Administrative Law*
(3rd edn, Oxford University Press, 2005), p 355.

The exact requirements of natural justice (in modern parlance – the duty to act fairly/in fairness) will vary according to the context:

- the body involved
- the nature of the decision and
- the issue at stake.

NB Art 6 of the Convention applies only to 'criminal charges' or 'the determination of civil rights'.

In essence, the requirements of a fair hearing embody the following elements:

- The knowledge of the charge/allegations.
- An indication of adverse evidence.
- Notice of the hearing.
- The right to submit a defence (in writing or orally).
- The right to challenge adverse evidence (in writing or orally).
- The right to submit evidence.
- The right to legal representation.
- The right to reasons for a decision.

The right to a fair hearing (or fairness/the duty to act fairly) is variable depending upon the context and so its requirements may include all or a number of the features set out directly above. Sir Robert Megarry VC in *McInnes v Onslow-Fane* [1978] 1 WLR 1520 rather usefully identified the following categories:

- **Forfeiture cases** – where a decision takes away an existing position or right (eg a person is expelled from an organisation or a licence is revoked).
- **Application cases** – where the decision refuses to grant the position or right that the applicant seeks (eg admission to an organisation or application for a licence).
- **Expectation cases** – where the applicant has a legitimate expectation (see below)that his application will be accepted (on the basis of what has already happened). For example, Megarry referred to an existing licence-holder seeking renewal of it.

Megarry made the point that in forfeiture cases the following features can be expected in terms of natural justice (the right to an unbiased tribunal, notice of charges and to be heard in respect of them). In contrast, in mere application cases where 'nothing is being taken away' (as in the actual case at hand where the British Board of Boxing Control should act 'under a duty to reach an honest conclusion without bias and not in pursuance of any capricious policy') there was no expectation of a hearing. In other words, there is a sliding scale of fairness: the nearer the case is towards the forfeiture scenario, the more rights can be expected (akin to the characteristics of a criminal court hearing). In contrast, the nearer to the mere application scenario, the less can be expected (in effect the obligation/duty to be fair). Megarry noted that legitimate expectation cases would fall nearer the scenario of a forfeiture case.

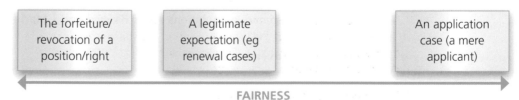

Figure 20.7 The sliding scale of fairness (Sir Robert Megarry VC)

It has been pointed out that although the *McInnes* case 'should not be read as establishing rigid categories to which different templates of fairness apply, it usefully indicates some of the factors which help determine where on the scale particular cases will be located' (M Elliott, *Administrative Law, Text and Materials* (3rd edn, Oxford University Press, 2005), pp 365–366). Indeed, as noted by Lord Bridge in *Lloyd v McMahon* [1987] 1 AC 625:

JUDGMENT

'… the so-called rules of natural justice are not engraved on tablets of stone. To use the phrase which better expresses the underlying concept, what the requirements of fairness demand when any body, domestic, administrative or judicial, has to make a decision which will affect the rights of individuals depends on the character of the decision-making body, the kind of decision it has to make and the statutory or other framework in which it operates.'

The case law of natural justice is voluminous and below is a selection of some examples to suggest an outline of this area:

■ Legitimate expectation

According to Endicott, a legitimate exception is:

QUOTATION

'An expectation that deserves legal protection. The form of protection can vary. The reason for giving legal protection may be that it is procedurally unfair for an administrative authority to disappoint your expectation without giving you a hearing, or that disappointing your expectation would involve substantive unfairness that a court ought to prevent.'

T Endicott, *Administrative Law*, (Oxford University Press, 2009), p 611.

There are various ways in which a legitimate expectation can arise. Below are a number of cases in which it was raised:

- *ex parte Liverpool Taxi Fleet Operators' Association* (1972) – taxi drivers had a legitimate expectation – based on past history and an undertaking given on behalf of the council – to make representations before more licences were issued (see section 20.6.1).
- *GCHQ* (1985) (see section 11.9.6) – civil service unions had a legitimate expectation based on previous practice to be consulted prior to their terms and conditions of service being changed (in the event trumped by national security).
- *R v North and East Devon Health Authority, ex parte Coughlan* [2001] 1 QB 213 – a number of disabled people had a legitimate expectation that a Heath Authority would keep the assurance that it had given to them that their move to an NHS facility would be for life.
- *Attorney General of Hong Kong v Ng Yuen Shiu* [1983] 2 All ER 346 – the Privy Council held that the Hong Kong government's announcement that the case of each illegal immigrant would be treated on its merits created a legitimate expectation of a hearing before removal.
- *R (Bancoult) v Secretary of State for Foreign and Commonwealth Affairs* [2008] UKHL 61 – the House of Lords held that no legitimate expectation had been created by the government (no unambiguous and clear promise) that former inhabitants of the Chagos Islands would be allowed to return.

In the context of legitimate expectations see C Brasted and J Marlow 'Great expectations' (2008) 158 NLJ 1441.

■ The right to know adverse evidence

Lord Denning in the Privy Council in *Kanda v Government of the Federation of Malaya* [1962] AC 322 commented that:

JUDGMENT

'If the right to be heard is to be a real right which is worth anything, it must carry with it a right in the accused man to know the case which is made against him. He must know what evidence has been given and what statements have been made affecting him.'

Although it may appear axiomatic that a person should know the exact particulars of the case against them, this principle has in the past been modified by national security. In *ex parte Hosenball* (1977) at section 6.7.10, Hosenball had a deportation order issued against him under the Immigration Act 1971. The Court of Appeal held there had been no breach of natural justice as the Secretary of State had considered personally Hosenball's request for further particulars of the allegations. Hosenball's request had been denied as it was not in the interests of national security to provide further information. The court noted that on occasions natural justice had to give way to considerations of national security. See also *R v Secretary of State for the Home Department, ex parte Cheblak* [1991] 1 WLR 890. More recently, however, now see the case of *Secretary of State for the Home Department v AF* (2009) at section 6.8.

■ **The right to have sufficient time to prepare a defence/answer the case against him**
In order for an individual to defend himself, he must be given a reasonable time to defend himself in answer to a charge:

CASE EXAMPLE

R v Thames Magistrates' Court, ex parte Polemis [1974] 2 All ER 1219

Polemis was served with a summons at 10.30am concerning an alleged breach of the Prevention of Oil Pollution Act 1971. At 4.00pm that day a stipendiary magistrate heard the case and convicted him. Polemis's conviction was quashed by an order of *certiorari* on the basis that natural justice required that a party should have a reasonable opportunity to prepare his case. Lord Widgery CJ stated that:

JUDGMENT

'Nothing is clearer today than that a breach of the rules of natural justice is said to occur if a party to proceedings, and more especially the defendant in a criminal case, is not given a reasonable chance to present his case … it necessarily extends to a reasonable opportunity to prepare your case before you are called on to present it.'

■ **The right to make representations**
In *ex parte Binks* (1985) (see section 19.2.1) the council's decision to issue Binks with a notice to quit was quashed. It was held that as her livelihood was at stake (a street trader selling hot food under an informal arrangement), the council had denied her natural justice because:

1. she had not been given prior notification before the issuing of its decision giving her notice to quit;
2. she had not been given an opportunity to be heard;
3. it had not given any reasons for its decision.

In *ex parte Doody* (1994) (see below) the House of Lords held that the Home Secretary was required to provide a mandatory life sentence prisoner with the opportunity to make written representations concerning the period he should serve (to satisfy deterrence and retribution) before the date was set by the Home Secretary for the first review of that prisoner's sentence.

■ **The right to an oral hearing**
The right to a hearing does not necessarily mean the right to an oral hearing, as (depending on the circumstances and what is at stake) the right to a hearing may only mean that written representations can be put forward. In any event, in a written hearing an individual can still submit evidence which he wishes the decision-making body to see.

CASE EXAMPLE

R (West) v Parole Board [2005] UKHL 1

The House of Lords held that an oral hearing before a Parole Board, in respect of prisoners who had had their licences revoked, might be necessary where, for example, facts were at issue (ie were in dispute) which could affect the outcome (such issues, of course, could be better resolved in person than on paper). Although the court held that whether an oral hearing was necessary depended on the circumstances of each particular case, on the facts it was held that the Parole Board had breached their common law duty of procedural fairness by failing to offer the prisoners an oral hearing.

Also see *Hopkins v Parole Board* [2008] EWHC 2312 (Admin) where the Parole Board had acted unfairly in not giving the prisoner an oral hearing allowing him to state his side of the case in relation to a parole application.

In *R v Army Board of the Defence Council, ex parte Anderson* [1992] 1 QB 169, the court held that the Army Board had been wrong to adopt an inflexible policy where it did not permit oral hearings before it.

The disadvantage of oral hearings is that they are much more time-consuming than paper hearings. The advantage of an oral hearing is, of course, the possibility of cross-examining evidence and witnesses (thereby allowing adverse evidence to be tested orally). Cross-examination is also another important aspect of the principles of natural justice. In *R v Hull Prison Board of Visitors, ex parte St Germain and others (No 2)* [1979] 3 All ER 545 the court noted that in terms of hearsay evidence, a fair hearing might involve the prison board informing prisoners (accused of breaching Prison Rules) of the hearsay evidence against them and of allowing them the opportunity to cross-examine witnesses whose evidence was before the decision-maker as hearsay. In addition, the board had improperly failed to allow witnesses to be called in defence (ie the right to submit evidence).

■ The right to legal representation

When appearing before a criminal court a person will expect to enjoy legal representation; however, whether lawyers will be available/permitted in other circumstances will depend on the facts/issue. The advantage of legal representation is that it enables individuals lacking specialist knowledge or competence to present their case. The disadvantage of legal representation is that lawyers inevitably lengthen and complicate proceedings. Indeed, Lord Denning MR in *Enderby Town Football Club Ltd v Football Association Ltd* [1971] 1 Ch 591 noted that:

JUDGMENT

'In many cases it may be a good thing for the proceedings of a domestic tribunal to be conducted informally without legal representation. Justice can often be done in them better by a good layman than by a bad lawyer.'

In the context of prisoners see the following case:

CASE EXAMPLE

R v Secretary of State for the Home Department, ex parte Tarrant [1985] 1 QB 251

The court held that the Board of Visitors had a discretion as to whether prisoners should be granted legal representation. In this case the two prisoners should have been allowed to have been legally represented (here the charge of mutiny was an especially grave offence).

See also Art 6 of the European Convention on Human Rights which specifically states that everyone charged with a criminal offence has, *inter alia*, the following rights:

ARTICLE

Art 6(3)(c)

To defend himself in person or through legal assistance of his own choosing or, if he has not sufficient means to pay for legal assistance, to be given it free when the interests of justice so require.

In *Ezeh and Connors v United Kingdom* (2004) 39 EHRR 691 the European Court of Human Rights held that the right to a fair trial had been breached when prisoners (who had been sentenced to additional days under Prison Rules) had been denied legal representation. For the purposes of Art 6, the court considered the charges against the prisoners under the Prison Rules as criminal.

■ The duty to give reasons for a decision?

Although there is in law no general duty for a decision-maker to provide reasons for a decision (in contrast, the judiciary give reasons in court as well as in tribunals), in modern times it is the hallmark of good administrative practice. Lord Mustill in *R v Secretary of State for the Home Department, ex parte Doody* [1994] 1 AC 531 stated that:

JUDGMENT

'The law does not at present recognise a general duty to give reasons for an administrative decision. Nevertheless, it is equally beyond question that such a duty may in appropriate circumstances be implied.'

In this context see *R (Hasan) v Secretary of State for Trade and Industry (now Business, Enterprise and Regulatory Reform)* [2008] EWCA Civ 1311.

The following case is interesting as it concerns the provision of information during the decision-making process.

CASE EXAMPLE

R v Secretary of State for the Home Department, ex parte Al Fayed and another [1997] 1 All ER 228

The Fayed brothers applied for naturalisation as British citizens under the British Nationality Act 1981. Their applications were refused and no reasons were given for this refusal. They sought judicial review of the Home Secretary's failure to give reasons and claimed that there had been a breach of natural justice.

The Court of Appeal held that although the Home Secretary was not (owing to s 44 of the 1981 Act) required to give reasons when an application was refused, he still had to act fairly in arriving at a decision. As a result, the Home Secretary should have given the Fayeds information (ie the right to notice/adequate disclosure) in respect of the area of his concern. This in turn, would then have allowed them to make representations on this issue to the Home Secretary before he made his decision. In the case, the decision of the Home Secretary was quashed. Lord Woolf MR, stated that:

JUDGMENT

'I appreciate that there is also anxiety as to the administrative burden involved in giving notice of areas of concern. Administrative convenience cannot justify unfairness but I would emphasise that my remarks are limited to cases where an applicant would be in real difficulty in doing himself justice unless the area of concern is identified by notice.'

This case illustrates an example of Parliament legislating to exclude a requirement to give a reason for a decision.

ACTIVITY

Exercise

Explain the different aspects of *audi alteram partem*. Why do such rules exist?

The ground of procedural impropriety	
Statutory requirements	A failure to comply with statutory procedural requirements: • A mandatory requirement is an essential requirement which will invalidate an action if not followed (*Aylesbury Mushrooms Ltd* (1972)). • A directory requirement is a minor technical defect. See now Lord Woolf's analysis (*ex parte Jeyeanthan* (2000)).
Nemo judex in re sua	• Actual bias where a decision-maker is actually biased. • Automatic disqualification where there is direct financial interest (*Dimes* (1852) or the judge is a party to the cause/case (*ex parte Pinochet Ugarte* (2000)) • Non-automatic bias (eg a family link, *Lannon* (1969))
Audi alteram partem	Decision-makers must respect all or most of the following requirements which protect the right to a fair hearing: • An awareness of the charge/allegations and notice of the hearing. • The right to submit a defence and evidence (in writing and/or orally). • An indication of adverse evidence and the right to challenge it (in writing and/or orally). • The right to legal representation. • The right to reasons for a decision.

20.6 Remedies

20.6.1 The different remedies available

If a claimant can demonstrate that a public body has breached one of the grounds of judicial review, he *may* obtain a remedy. There are six remedies available:

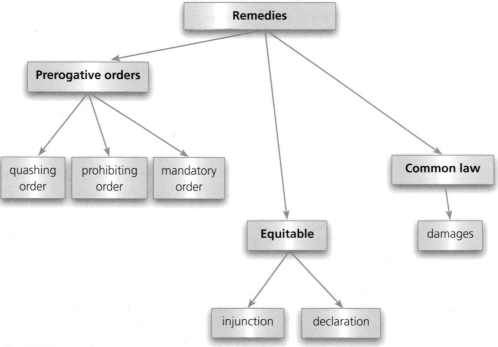

Figure 20.8 Remedies

It should be noted that a combination of remedies may be appropriate. For example, a quashing order combined with a mandatory order would compel a public body to take the decision again (after the original decision had been quashed by a quashing order), but this time in accordance with the law.

■ **A quashing order**

This order (formerly known as *certiorari*) quashes an unlawful decision. For example, in *ex parte Binks* (1985) (see sections 19.2.1 and 20.5.4), Binks successfully obtained an order to quash an unlawful decision of Wear Valley District Council that she should cease trading. Similarly, in the context of delegated legislation see *R v Secretary of State for Health, ex parte United States Tobacco International Inc* [1992] 1 QB 353 at section 19.2.1.

■ **A prohibiting order**

This order (formerly known as *prohibition*) is pre-emptive in the sense that it prevents a body from acting unlawfully in the future (see *R v Liverpool Corporation, ex parte Liverpool Taxi Fleet Operators' Association* [1972] 2 QB 299 – preventing a council from granting further taxi licences without first hearing the representations of interested parties).

■ **A mandatory order**

This order (formerly known as *mandamus*) compels a body to act (eg to perform a statutory function). In *Padfield* (1968) (see section 20.2.4) the court directed the Minister of Agriculture to consider a complaint submitted to him according to the law.

■ **An injunction**

This equitable remedy can compel a body to perform an act or restrain it from doing so. In *ex parte Factortame* (1991) at section 15.6.4 the House of Lords issued an interim injunction which prevented the Secretary of State from enforcing provisions of the Merchant Shipping Act 1988. An injunction is a useful remedy because it can be obtained in a temporary form as in the *Factortame* litigation.

■ **A declaration**

This equitable remedy is non-coercive as it represents a formal statement of the law by the courts. For example, in *Equal Opportunities Commission* (1994) (see section 19.4.2) a declaration was issued stating that provisions of domestic law indirectly discriminated against women and so were contrary to European law. This is also a remedy which can be obtained on an interim basis.

■ **Damages**

This common law remedy has historically not been a free-standing remedy as it had to be combined with another remedy. In practice, to claim damages a claimant was required to show that the unlawful public decision was also, for example, negligent.

Today a breach of the European Convention by a public body may result in damages; however, the awards will usually be relatively modest as they will be in line with awards in the European Court in Strasbourg (see section 17.9.3).

20.6.2 The discretionary nature of remedies

The above remedies are discretionary. Even though a claimant can demonstrate that a public body has acted unlawfully, the court may nevertheless decide to provide no remedy at all (or may provide a different one from the one sought). A remedy may be refused on, *inter alia*, the following bases:

■ The behaviour of the claimant in the case (eg an ulterior motive in seeking judicial review).
■ If the claimant has delayed in processing a claim (see section 19.6.3).
■ A remedy would result in an adverse effect on either (a) general administration or (b) third parties.
■ The remedy would provide no tangible benefit/use in practice.

20.7 The effectiveness of judicial review

How effective is judicial review?

20.7.1 Factors which support its effectiveness

Lord Scarman in *Nottinghamshire County Council v Secretary of State for the Environment* [1986] 1 AC 240 stated that:

JUDGMENT

'Judicial review is a great weapon in the hands of the judges: but the judges must observe the constitutional limits set by our parliamentary system upon their exercise of this beneficial power.'

■ The existence of judicial review necessarily improves good administration. It encourages administrators and public decision-makers to exercise their powers in accordance with the law as they are aware that otherwise they will be subject to review. Indeed, government officials have been issued with the booklet 'The Judge Over Your Shoulder' (4th edn, Crown Copyright, 2006) which has been revised to take into account the Human Rights Act and which reminds officials of their public law responsibilities. As a preventative measure, we will never know how many illegal public law decisions judicial review has prevented.

■ Judicial review has caused friction between the courts and the executive in the past two decades, as successive ministers, of whatever political colour, have been subject to judicial review. In fact, it is arguable that it is actually healthy in a democracy for there to be some friction between the two arms of the constitution as it suggests that the courts are successfully holding the executive to account and restraining their actions. This is particularly important in the light of the modern executive's domination of the legislature.

■ Judicial review claims can be used to highlight a particular issue (homelessness, prisoners' rights, etc). A recent example of this concerned the settlement of Gurkhas in the United Kingdom (*R (Limbu) v Secretary of State for the Home Department* [2008] EWHC 2261 (Admin)).

■ An example of a successful case is *R (Brooke) v Parole Board* [2008] EWCA Civ 29 in which the Court of Appeal held that the Parole Board was insufficiently independent of the executive (for the purposes of Art 5 of the European Convention) owing to its sponsorship arrangements. Two months after this decision, the Secretary of State for Justice announced a change in its sponsorship, transferring it to the Access to Justice Group within the Ministry of Justice.

20.7.2 Factors which question its effectiveness

■ It must be remembered that judicial review is in essence a procedural remedy whereby the courts have historically confined themselves to questioning the decision-making process, rather than the decision itself. The result of this is that judicial review may be in some cases a rather pyrrhic victory. Although the court may quash the offending decision of a public body, it will not replace it with another one, but instead may require the body to take the decision again, but this time in accordance with the law (eg this time by considering relevant considerations that were previously ignored). This could still result in the decision-maker making the same decision, and provided it was taken legally, rationally and fairly, it will stand. In *R (Ali) v Secretary of State for the Home Department* [2003] EWHC 899 (Admin) Goldring J granted judicial review of the Secretary of State's decision refusing the claimant leave to remain in the country. He stated, however, that: 'Of course, dependent upon reconsideration on sufficient and proper evidence, the Secretary of State may reach exactly the same decision'.

■ Some areas of public law decision-making such as national security and national economic considerations are not susceptible to judicial review (ie they are *non-justiciable*).

- The remedies available are discretionary and may be denied even though it has been demonstrated that a public body has acted unlawfully.
- Judicial review is necessarily a reactive jurisdiction in which the ability of the courts to develop administrative principles is subject to claimants initiating actions.
- As noted by the Democratic Audit of the United Kingdom, in terms of the effectiveness of judicial review, it is clear that the few thousand of judicial review claims made each year 'are infinitesimal when compared with the millions of decisions taken every year by public bodies'. (S Weir and D Beetham, *Political Power and Democratic Control in Britain* (Routledge, 1999), p 446). Indeed, in 2007 a total of 6,690 applications were made for permission to apply for judicial review (847 of the total applications considered in 2007 were granted) and of the 336 substantive applications for judicial review decided that year, 48 per cent were allowed (*Judicial and Court Statistics 2007*, Cm 7467 (Crown Copyright, 2008), p 16).
- Judicial review is a remedy of last resort to be used when there are no other (or reasonable) remedies available.

ACTIVITY

Exercise

Do you think that judicial review is effective?

20.8 Judicial review checklist

Judicial review examination questions are particularly amenable to problem-solving questions. One useful way of approaching such questions is to list each ground (and sub-division) of judicial review and work down this checklist in order to determine which issues are raised by the scenario:

Judicial review checklist
Procedural issues:
Is the decision-maker a public body (or one which the courts would regard as performing governmental functions)?
Is the decision/action complained about a public law issue?
Does the claimant have standing?
Has the claimant complied with the public law procedure?
Grounds of review:
Has the decision-maker acted illegally? Have they:
• Acted *ultra vires* the parent Act?
• Wrongfully delegated public law powers?
• Acted for an improper purpose?
• Abused their discretion by (a) fettering their discretion (b) ignoring relevant factors (c) considering irrelevant factors?
• Acted in excess of their jurisdiction by misinterpreting their legal powers?
• Breached a European Convention right (and acted disproportionately)?
Has the decision-maker acted irrationally?
• Has the decision-maker made a decision which no reasonable decision-maker would have made?
Has the decision-maker acted in a procedurally unfair manner? Have they:
• Breached a statutory requirement?
• Demonstrated bias or an appearance of bias?
• Ignored the rules concerning the right to a fair hearing?

Table 20.1 Judicial review checklist

SUMMARY

■ In *GCHQ* (1985)Lord Diplock reclassified the grounds of judicial review into illegality, irrationality and procedural impropriety.

■ Illegality includes the following:
- Simple *ultra vires* – exceeding specified legal powers.
- Wrongful delegation – delegating power to another body.
- Improper purpose – power is used for an improper purpose.
- Abuse of discretion – discretion is fettered and/or relevant factors are ignored/irrelevant factors are considered.
- Excess of jurisdiction – a mistake of law/fact.
- Breach of the European Convention – a public body acts inconsistently with the Convention's articles.

■ Irrationality is a decision which no reasonable body could have arrived at.

■ In recent years the ground of proportionality has been developed which considers the aim of the decision-maker and whether the means to achieve that objective are proportional.

■ Procedural impropriety includes a failure to follow specified procedural requirements as laid out in statute.

■ Procedural impropriety also includes the common law requirements of fairness/natural justice:
- The absence of bias (*nemo judex in re sua*).
- The right to a fair hearing (*audi alteram partem*).

■ There are a range of remedies available in judicial review, although they are issued at the discretion of the court.

 # Further reading

Books

Bailey, S, 'Grounds for Judicial Review: Due Process, Natural Justice, and Fairness' in Feldman, D (ed), *English Public Law* (2nd edn, Oxford University Press, 2009), p 667.

Barnett, H, *Constitutional and Administrative Law* (7th edn, Routledge–Cavendish, 2009), Chapter 26.

Bradley, A and Ewing, K, *Constitutional and Administrative Law* (14th edn, Pearson/Longman, 2007), Chapter 30.

Craig, P, 'Grounds for Judicial Review: Substantive Control Over Discretion' in Feldman, D (ed), *English Public Law* (2nd edn, Oxford University Press, 2009), p 719.

Leyland, P and Anthony, G, *Textbook on Administrative Law* (6th edn, Oxford University Press, 2009), Chapters 10–16.

Parpworth, N, *Constitutional and Administrative Law* (5th edn, Oxford University Press, 2008), Chapters 13 and 14.

Sunkin, M, 'Grounds for Judicial Review: Illegality in the Strict Sense' in Feldman, D (ed), *English Public Law* (2nd edn, Oxford University Press, 2009), p 615.

Weir, S and Beetham, D, *Political Power and Democratic Control in Britain* (Routledge, 1999), Chapter 15.

Articles

Turner, I, 'Judicial Review, Irrationality and the Review of Merits' (2006) 15(2) *Nottingham Law Journal* 37.

Walker, P, 'What's Wrong with Irrationality?' [1995] PL 556.

Papers

Horne, A and Berman, G, 'Judicial Review: A short guide to claims in the Administrative Court' 06/44 (House of Commons Library, 2006).

21

Grievance mechanisms

AIMS AND OBJECTIVES

At the end of this chapter you should be able to:

■ Appreciate the role of grievance mechanisms (other than the courts) in the British constitution
■ Understand the nature and constitutional role of the tribunal system
■ Understand the nature and constitutional role of inquiries
■ Appreciate the role, workings and constitutional importance of the system of Ombudsmen

Introduction

As government officials and agencies exercise disparate and wide-ranging powers to provide services and discharge responsibilities, it is inevitable that the actions and decisions of state officials will come into conflict with individuals. As a result, a number of different grievance mechanisms are available to individuals who feel aggrieved by the actions of the state. In brief, tribunals provide individuals with a legal form of redress which is an alternative to the strict formal court system. In contrast, inquiries are an extra-judicial grievance mechanism which permit individuals to challenge, for example, the decision of a local planning authority to refuse an application for planning permission. A further (extra-judicial) form of redress is the Ombudsman which investigates an injustice caused to an individual by maladministration (ie faulty administration) by the state. This chapter will provide a very general overview of all three grievance mechanisms against the state.

21.1 Tribunals

21.1.1 Definition and history

In historical terms, the powers and responsibilities of the state have increasingly impacted on the lives of individuals (for example, whether it was the collection of taxes or the entitlement to a social security benefit). In the light of the volume of millions of decisions made by state officials and administrators each year, mistakes and discrepancies are inevitably going to cause injustice to particular individuals. As a consequence, tribunals have been established on an *ad hoc* basis (mainly by Parliament, although some under the royal prerogative) to enable individuals to challenge the decisions of state officials in these areas in a forum which is outside the formal court system. In essence, tribunals are adjudicative bodies which apply laws and rules to a case in order to resolve disputes between the individual and the state.

In 1957 the Franks Committee (*Report of the Committee on Administrative Tribunals and Inquiries* Cmnd 218 (1957)) examined the network of tribunals. This in turn led to the passing of the Tribunals and Inquiries Act 1958 (as subsequently consolidated in the Tribunals and Inquiries Acts 1971 and 1992) which, among other things, established the Council on Tribunals whose responsibility was to oversee and report on the operation and workings of tribunals (as well as inquiries). A further review of tribunals was undertaken by Sir Andrew Leggatt whose report in 2001 (*Tribunals for Users: One System, One Service* (The Stationery Office, 2001)) indicated that at this point in time (and for the purposes of the report's terms of reference) there were 70 different types of administrative tribunals in England and Wales which processed one million cases between them. The network of these tribunals, however, lacked co-ordination and needed to be rationalised. The government has now implemented reforms to the organisation and system of tribunals (see section 21.1.6).

21.1.2 Types of tribunals

Today there are various different types of tribunals ranging from tax (the Tax Chamber), mental health (the Mental Health Tribunal) and education (the Special Educational Needs and Disability Tribunal). In broad terms, however, a clear distinction can be drawn between:

- those which resolve disputes between the individual and the state (eg the Asylum Support Tribunal); and
- those which regulate disputes between private parties (eg employee and employer in the context of employment law issues such as redundancy (Employment Tribunals)).

Below are three brief examples of tribunals in operation:

- A has a dispute with the state concerning his entitlement to social security payments and to which social security officials have decided that he is no longer entitled. A can appeal against this decision to the Social Security and Child Support Tribunal (part of the Social Entitlement Chamber).
- B has made a claim under the Criminal Injuries Compensation Scheme but it was rejected by the Criminal Injuries Compensation Authority as being insufficiently serious. B can appeal against this review/decision to the Criminal Injuries Compensation Tribunal (part of the Social Entitlement Chamber).
- C claims that he has been unfairly dismissed by his employer. He can seek redress in an Employment Tribunal.

(Examples adapted from the Tribunals Service website: www.tribunals.gov.uk.)

21.1.3 The constitutional position of tribunals

Tribunals are fact-finding bodies which apply legal principles and administrative rules in order to adjudicate on legal disputes (largely between an aggrieved individual and the state). In constitutional terms tribunals are impartial grievance mechanisms which are distinct from both the government as well as the ordinary court system.

Independent of the government/state

The existence of tribunals necessarily raises the constitutional question as to whether such bodies are part of the administration (executive) or the judicial arm of the state. In countries such as Australia, the tribunal system is considered to be part of the administration because as noted by Leggatt, they are specifically charged with administrative duties and 'putting themselves in the shoes of the relevant Government official'. In Britain, however, the 1957 Franks Committee plainly refuted the view that tribunals were part of the administration:

QUOTATION

'Tribunals are not ordinary courts, but neither are they appendages of Government Departments ... We consider that tribunals should properly be regarded as machinery provided by Parliament for adjudication rather than as part of the machinery for administration.'

Report of the Committee on Administrative Tribunals and Inquiries
Cmnd 218 (1957) para 40.

Notwithstanding this, historically there has always been a necessarily close connection between the tribunal and the arm of the state which it regulates. This is due to the fact that the government department invariably provided the former with support. As a result, there has been concern that in terms of 'appearance', tribunals were not independent of the administration. Indeed, the Leggatt Report noted that there were significant doubts as to whether the (then) current arrangements of tribunals provided individuals with 'the necessary confidence in their independence and effectiveness'.

Moreover, the report commented that:

QUOTATION

'There is no question of the Government improperly attempting to influence individual decisions. In that sense, tribunal decisions seem to us clearly impartial. But it cannot be said with confidence that they are demonstrably independent. Indeed, the evidence is to the contrary. For most tribunals, the departments provide administrative support, pay the salaries of members, pay their expenses, provide accommodation, provide IT support ... are responsible for some appointments, and promote the legislation which prescribes procedures to be followed. At best, such arrangements result in tribunals and their departments being, or appearing to be, common enterprises.'

Tribunals for Users: One System, One Service, (The Stationery Office, 2001), para 2.20.

As a result of the Leggatt Report and the subsequent 2004 government White Paper, the government, in an effort to enhance the independence of tribunals, implemented reforms in terms of their organisation (see section 21.1.6).

Distinct from the court system

Tribunals are part of the justice system, but are outside the formal court structure. They are similar to courts in the sense that they act fairly, impartially, decide facts and apply legal rules to resolve legal disputes. Sometimes these are highly complex rules; for example, Employment Tribunals will apply convoluted European and employment law and principles. Tribunals, however, are broadly speaking less formal, less adversarial and less concerned with procedural/evidential rules than the courts. Tribunals and courts are nevertheless connected in the sense that both are governed by an appellate system. In fact, appeals from tribunals can ultimately end up being resolved in a court. For example, an appeal can progressively be made from the Employment Tribunal to the Employment Appeal Tribunal through to the Court of Appeal and the Supreme Court. The government has now implemented reforms to rationalise the tribunal appellate system (see section 21.1.7). For example, under the Tribunals, Courts and Enforcement Act 2007, an appeal on a point of law can be made from the First-tier Tribunal to the Upper Tribunal and thereafter to the Court of Appeal.

21.1.4 Advantages of tribunals

There are a number of distinct advantages to tribunals:

■ **Volume of cases**
State officials take millions of decisions annually and it is not practicable to process all challenges to official decisions in a court as this would inevitably overload the court

system. For example, in 2003–04 the Appeals Service received 235,657 appeals and the Mental Health Review Tribunals 20,408 (*Transforming Public Services: Complaints, Redress and Tribunals*, Cm 6243 (DCA, 2004), para 3.28). As the Leggatt Report pointed out, in terms of their experience of the justice system, an individual is more likely to appear before a tribunal than a court.

■ **Cost and efficiency**

The court system involves lawyers and so is necessarily expensive. In contrast, tribunals are more efficient and cost effective as typically, they operate without paid legal representation and the awarding of costs (although the 2007 Act confers a discretion on tribunals to order costs and expenses). It should be noted, however, that in some tribunals such as Mental Health Tribunals, parties do use lawyers with publicly funded legal assistance being available. Tribunals provide swifter resolution of disputes which is consistent with the principle that *justice delayed is justice denied*.

■ **Specialism**

Tribunals are subject specific so that they process cases involving a highly specialist aspect of the administration (eg social security benefits) and they are accordingly staffed by experts in that particular area. For example, Mental Health Tribunals will include a medical expert. Similarly, whenever a Social Security and Child Support Tribunal is processing an appeal involving a disability living allowance, in determining the case, the Tribunal Judge will be supplemented by a medical practitioner and a disability expert. In contrast, where specialist knowledge is required in the court system, an expert witness will be called. In a number of cases the tribunal will be composed of a single Tribunal Judge acting alone.

■ **Formalism and accessibility**

Tribunals are intended to be more accessible and user-friendly than courts and so do not necessarily follow strict procedural (eg evidential) rules. As noted by the Leggatt Report, the procedure in tribunals (both pre and during hearings) is generally simpler and more informal than the court system. In fact, the government in its 2004 White Paper (see section 21.1.6) has commented that, in general terms, individuals should be able to deal with public officials without the need to study voluminous information or seek professional/legal help. Not only are tribunals less formal than courts, they also tend to be less adversarial and so more inquisitorial.

■ **Good governance**

As pointed out in the Leggatt Report, in the light of the volume and variety of cases that they process, tribunals are in the invaluable position of being able to identify and highlight systematic administrative problems in departmental decision-making. In terms of good governance/administration, see the Ombudsman at section 21.3.5.

21.1.5 Disadvantages of tribunals

A number of problems are associated with tribunals:

■ **Historically, the organisation of tribunals was haphazard.**

The Leggatt Report described the then existing network of tribunals as incoherent and ineffectual with different procedures and rules applying to different tribunals. This was due to tribunals having being established in an *ad hoc* fashion responding to specific needs at the time. In fact, the report argued that in view of this lack of coherence: 'It is obvious that the term "tribunal system" is a misnomer' (but now see the reforms at section 21.1.7).

■ **Independence**

As indicated at section 21.1.3, historically there has been concern that tribunals were not necessarily seen to be independent, however impartial they were. The Leggatt

Report stated that: 'plainly they are not independent. Even in tribunals which are no longer paid for by "their" departments, there can be an unhealthy closeness' (para 1.10). (Now see the reforms detailed below at section 21.1.6.)

■ **Legal representation**

Research conducted in this area has indicated that individuals are likely to be more successful in a tribunal if they are represented. The Leggatt Report recognised that although legal representation can be beneficial, such representation inevitably drives up costs and works against tribunals being accessible. In any event, as suggested by the report, individuals could be better informed through the provision of more advice and assistance from the tribunal itself.

■ **Delay**

The Leggatt Report identified some unacceptable delays in processing cases, thereby mirroring the problems associated with the modern and overloaded court system.

ACTIVITY

Essay writing

Explain the constitutional and practical advantages and disadvantages of tribunals. Do the former outweigh the latter?

21.1.6 Reform

In 2001 the Leggatt Report made a number of recommendations which included:

■ Rationalising the structure of the network of tribunals (bringing them together under one system) and its appellate system, thereby ensuring common structural arrangements.

■ Enhancing the position of 'users' of the tribunal system.

Following the report the government issued its White Paper (*Transforming Public Services: Complaints, Redress and Tribunals* Cm 6243 (DCA, 2004) in which it stated, *inter alia*, that it intended to:

■ Place the system of tribunals on a unified and cohesive basis (including appeals).

■ Rename the legal members of a tribunal 'Tribunal Judges'.

■ Create the post of a Senior President of Tribunals.

In April 2006 the Tribunals Service became operational as an executive agency (now under the aegis of the Ministry of Justice), providing common administrative support to the major tribunals of central government. At this time the Tribunals Service included the tribunals for which the then Department for Constitutional Affairs was responsible (eg asylum) and these were added to with other major central government tribunals such as (the then named) Social Security and Child Support Appeals Tribunal, the Criminal Injuries Compensation Appeals Panel and the Special Educational Needs and Disability Tribunal (others were scheduled to be added periodically). In this way, the independence of tribunals would be enhanced by removing them from their associated departments (eg the Mental Health Review Tribunals was transferred from the Department of Health, and the Social Security and Child Support Appeals Tribunal was moved from the Department for Work and Pensions).

Further reforms to the organisation of tribunals were achieved by the Tribunals, Courts and Enforcement Act 2007 (see below) which created a two-tier (flexible) system of tribunals which would allow other tribunals to be transferred in as well as enable new jurisdictional areas to be included. According to the Tribunals Service website (www.tribunals.gov.uk) in 2010, the aim of these changes was to improve the service provided to customers by:

- 'Making clear the complete independence of the judiciary, and their decision making, from Government;
- Speeding up the delivery of justice;
- Making processes easier for the public to understand;
- Bringing together the expertise from each Tribunal.'

21.1.7 The Tribunals, Courts and Enforcement Act 2007

The two-tiered tribunal system

The Act created a simplified two-tiered statutory framework of tribunals (composed of a First-tier Tribunal and an Upper Tribunal) to which tribunals would be periodically transferred. The two generic tribunals (ie First-tier and Upper) are organised into 'Chambers', each headed by a Chamber President so that similar jurisdictional areas can be grouped together. This allows for a more efficient organisational use of tribunal members and resources.

According to the Tribunals Service website, in 2010 the First-tier Tribunal included, among others, the following Chambers:

- Social Entitlement Chamber (Asylum Support, Social Security and Child Support and Criminal Injuries Compensation)
- Health, Education and Social Care Chamber (Care Standards, Mental Health, Special Educational Needs and Disability and Primary Health Lists)

The Upper Tribunal contained the following Chambers:

- Administrative Appeals
- Lands
- Tax and Chancery
- Immigration and Asylum

In general terms, the Upper Tribunal acts as an appellate tribunal (on a point of law) from the First-tier Tribunal, thereby rationalising the appeals process. Thereafter appeals are possible from the Upper Tribunal to the courts. It is of interest to note that the Act conferred on the Upper Tribunal a power of judicial review in respect of the First-tier Tribunal in specified circumstances (s 18). In this jurisdiction, the Upper Tribunal will have similar powers to those exercised by the existing Administrative Court.

Personnel

Under the Act the legal members of tribunals (ie those legally qualified) are designated as Tribunal Judges and the Constitutional Reform Act 2005 has been amended so as to provide for the independence of the tribunal judiciary (see section 13.4.1). In addition, a new statutory judicial office was created (the Senior President of Tribunals) to provide leadership to the tribunal judiciary and oversee the system of tribunals.

The Administrative Justice and Tribunals Council

The Act replaced the Council on Tribunals (which oversaw tribunals and inquiries and made appropriate recommendations) with an Administrative Justice and Tribunals Council. This body will not only oversee and report on the new tribunal system, but it also has a wider remit to review the whole *Administrative Justice System* (including how government departments, the Ombudsman, etc, relate to the public).

Procedures and rules

The rules and procedures which historically governed tribunals were generally composed by the Lord Chancellor or the relevant government minister. The Act created the Tribunal

Procedure Committee which has assumed responsibility for making these rules (Tribunal Procedure Rules), thereby providing greater consistency in the rules used in the tribunal system. In addition, the Senior President of Tribunals is able to issue Practice Directions (analogous to those in court).

KEY FACTS

Tribunals
1. Tribunals are a grievance remedy which enables individuals to challenge decisions made by state officials in a forum which is outside the formal court system.
2. Tribunals can be divided into those which resolve disputes between the individual and the state (eg the Mental Health Tribunal), and those which regulate legal disputes between individuals and, for example, companies (eg Employment Tribunals).
3. Tribunals are impartial decision-making bodies which are not part of the government department which it oversees.
4. They are also separate and distinct from the formal court system.
5. They are intended to be more accessible and user-friendly than the courts.
6. They do not necessarily follow strict procedural rules.
7. They typically do not involve paid legal representatives.

21.2 Inquiries

Introduction

In very broad terms inquiries can be divided into two types:

■ Those which investigate and report on local land issues (eg the refusal of a local planning authority to grant planning permission). This concerns an individual's dispute with the state.

■ Those which investigate and report on specific events/scandals (eg the Bloody Sunday inquiry into the shooting of civilians in Londonderry).

21.2.1 Land inquiries

When a local planning authority refuses to grant planning permission, an individual may seek to challenge such a decision by way of an appeal to the Planning Inspectorate. The determination of this appeal can be processed in three different ways (all involving an Inspector from the Planning Inspectorate – an executive agency of the Department for Communities and Local Government).

■ **The written representations procedure** – this is the most basic of appeals and is appropriate for minor issues/works or alterations. The vast majority of appeals are dealt with by this procedure which involves the Inspector considering the appeal on the basis of written representations.

■ **The hearing procedure** – this is presided over by an Inspector and is appropriate for more complicated cases than those discussed above, or where questions need to be asked. It is less formal than the inquiry procedure (below).

■ **The local inquiry procedure** – this is the most formal of all the appeals (although it only occurs in a minority of cases) and considers the most complicated or largest appeals. The interested parties (ie the individual and the local planning authority) can call evidence and cross-examine witnesses and will usually involve legal representation (this is analogous to a court; however, the inquiry is *not* a court of law). The Inspector will thereafter issue a report.

According to statistics for England, during 2007–08, in respect of planning appeals:

- 16,875 written representations were decided (of which 34 per cent were allowed)
- 2,252 hearings were held (39 per cent allowed)
- 889 inquiries were conducted (54 per cent allowed)

The Planning Inspectorate, Statistical Report: England 2007–2008 (2008),
Table 1.4 'Decisions by procedure type'.

In the overwhelming majority of cases, appeals in practice are determined by an Inspector (the decision having been delegated to him) with a few being determined by the Secretary of State themselves. On the powers of the Secretary of State in this context and their compatibility with Art 6 of the European Convention see *R (Alconbury Developments Ltd) v Secretary of State for the Environment, Transport and the Regions* [2001] UKHL 23.

In addition, inquiries can also involve major infrastructure projects such as, for example, the site of a motorway.

21.2.2 Inquiries into national events/scandals

The second type of inquiry investigates and makes recommendations in respect of a national event (eg the Scarman Report into the riots and disorder in Brixton in the early 1980s) or a public scandal (eg the Denning report into the Profumo affair). There are two categories of these types of inquiry:

- A statutory inquiry.
- A non-statutory inquiry.

In both cases these inquiries are not courts and their findings do not have legal effect:

QUOTATION

'Inquiries are designed to establish facts through an inquisitorial, investigatory process … inquiries are not courts and are not designed to determine criminal or civil liability or to settle disputes between parties.'

Department for Constitutional Affairs Consultation Paper,
Effective Inquiries (DCA, 2004), para 81.

In the context of statutory inquiries this point is reaffirmed by s 2 of the Inquiries Act 2005.

The constitutional purpose of both types of inquiry is to investigate issues of national concern, evaluate the evidence and make recommendations. In doing so, as noted by the government's consultation paper, these inquiries can restore public confidence, provide some benefit for those affected by the event in question and identify lessons that can be learnt.

21.2.3 Statutory inquiries into national events

Historically, there have been two types of statutory inquiry:

- A statutory inquiry under subject specific legislation, for example, the Stephen Lawrence Inquiry established under s 49 of the Police Act 1996.
- A statutory inquiry under the Tribunals of Inquiry (Evidence) Act 1921, for example, the (first) Bloody Sunday Inquiry under Lord Widgery.

Today, statutory inquiries are held under the Inquiries Act 2005. This Act repealed the Tribunals of Inquiry (Evidence) Act 1921 together with other statutory provisions authorising inquiries (eg s 49 of the Police Act 1996). Under s 1 of the 2005 Act a government minister can establish an inquiry and set out its terms of reference:

SECTION

S 1(1)

… where it appears to him that –

(a) particular events have caused, or are capable of causing, public concern, or

(b) there is public concern that particular events may have occurred.

Formerly, under the 1921 Act such inquiries were relatively rare, with less than 25 in total, with the last two being the Shipman Inquiry (into the deaths of a number of elderly women) and the (second) Bloody Sunday Inquiry under Lord Saville which was established in 1998 and reported in 2010. Section 21 of the 2005 Act empowers the Chairman of the inquiry to compel evidence (witnesses or documents) and under s 35 it is a criminal offence not to comply with a notice issued by the Chairman under the Act.

The Act enables a minister to appoint a judicial figure to act as a panel member or Chairman (though there would be consultation with, for example, the Lord Chief Justice). In constitutional terms the involvement of the judiciary in high-profile inquiries can raise questions as to whether it (ultimately) undermines their constitutional independence. In other words, as the subject-matter of such inquiries can be overtly politically charged (eg into the events of Bloody Sunday), and as the government set out the terms of the inquiry, it can be argued that whatever recommendations are made, the judge involved inevitably will be subject to criticism. The government, however, has defended the use of judges:

QUOTATION

'The Government believes that it can be appropriate for judges to chair inquiries, because their experience and position make them particularly well suited to the role. The judiciary has a great deal of experience in analysing evidence, determining facts and reaching conclusions … The judiciary also has a long tradition of independence from politics, and judges are widely accepted to be free from any party political bias.'

Department for Constitutional Affairs Consultation Paper,
Effective Inquiries (DCA, 2004), para 46.

Under the 2005 Act a number of inquiries have been established, including:

■ An inquiry into an explosion at a Glasgow factory – announced by the Secretary of State for Work and Pensions and the Lord Advocate in 2007.

■ An inquiry into the death of Baha Mousa (an Iraqi citizen in British custody in Iraq) – set up by the Secretary of State for Defence in 2008.

21.2.4 Non-statutory inquiries into national events

The government has regularly established non-statutory inquires to consider major national events. For example:

■ The Hutton Inquiry into the circumstances surrounding the death of Dr David Kelly.

■ The Scott Inquiry into the export of equipment to Iraq (see section 12.3.5).

Student mentor tip

"Keep up-to-date with current affairs – it really helps if you can mention hot topics in your exam."

Adil, Queen Mary University

Such inquiries are more flexible than statutory inquiries, although they lack enforcement powers to compel evidence (witnesses or documents). Under s 15 of the 2005 Act, however, a government minister can convert such an inquiry into a statutory one, for example where it was considered that enforcement powers were required. Two recent inquiries involving a committee of Privy Councillors (a variant of the non-statutory inquiry) were:

■ The 2004 Butler Inquiry concerning the intelligence on WMD (Weapons of Mass Destruction).

■ The 2009 Iraq Inquiry. This was set up to establish what happened in Iraq and identify the lessons that can be learned from the Iraq conflict. Sir John Chilcot (an ex-civil servant) is the Chairman of the inquiry that began hearing evidence in late 2009. In respect of this inquiry, the Public Administration Select Committee made the following constitutional observation:

QUOTATION

'It is wrong in principle that the executive alone should determine the terms of this inquiry, when the conduct of the executive is a central part of what the inquiry will have to consider.'

Ninth Report of Session 2008–09, *The Iraq Inquiry*, HC 721 (2009), para 18.

Finally, in respect of Iraq, see the case of *R (Gentle) v Prime Minister* [2008] UKHL 20.

KEY FACTS

Inquiries
Inquiries are an extra-judicial grievance mechanism which permit individuals to challenge, for example, the decision of a local authority to compulsorily purchase land or to refuse planning permission.
A second type of inquiry investigates and reports on major public events. Such inquiries are either: **Statutory inquiries** – historically these were established under statute: • Stephen Lawrence Inquiry under the aegis of the Police Act 1996. • Bloody Sunday Inquiry under the aegis of the Tribunals of Inquiry (Evidence) Act 1921. These have now been replaced by the Inquiries Act 2005. Under the 2005 Act a government minister can establish an inquiry into events which have, or are capable of, causing public concern. • The Gage Inquiry into the death of Baha Mousa.
Non-statutory inquiries • Hutton Inquiry.

ACTIVITY

Essay writing

In terms of their nature and constitutional role, compare and contrast inquiries with tribunals.

21.3 Ombudsmen

Introduction

QUOTATION

'The activities of the Ombudsmen are concerned with holding public bodies to account and exposing maladministration where it has occurred. In so doing, part of their function is to encourage best practice in public administration.'

Reform of Public Sector Ombudsmen Services in England
(Cabinet Office, 2005), para 45.

The British constitution has a number of different public sector Ombudsmen which cover central and local government, the National Health Service and the devolved administrations in Wales, Scotland and Northern Ireland. The function of these Ombudsmen is to investigate complaints relating to maladministration – in other words, faulty government/administration. This part of the Chapter will focus on arguably the most constitutionally significant of the Ombudsmen: the Parliamentary Commissioner for Administration (hereafter the Ombudsman).

21.3.1 Origins

Prior to the creation of the Ombudsman, there were essentially two main remedies available to an individual who was aggrieved by the actions of the officials of government departments:

- **The parliamentary remedy** – individuals could consult their constituency MP in order to resolve their grievance. The effectiveness of this remedy depended upon the tenacity and ability of the MP to access governmental information.
- **The legal/judicial remedy** – individuals could seek justice before the courts by suing the government department concerned in public or private law. This was (as it is today) necessarily expensive and in any event, the action causing the grievance may not even be illegal as not falling within a recognised legal category (eg negligence, breach of contract).

The *Whyatt* Report (The Citizen and the Administration: the Redress of Grievances (JUSTICE, 1961)) noted the limitations of the then 'existing means of seeking redress' and recommended the creation of an independent officer of Parliament to investigate such grievances against the state. There was concern that the creation of the Ombudsman independently examining departmental issues, would undermine the constitutional convention of ministerial responsibility. It is clear, however, that the office has enhanced the operation of the convention by requiring ministers to explain publicly and account for maladministration found in their department. In 1967 Parliament established the Parliamentary Commissioner for Administration under the Parliamentary Commissioner Act 1967 (as amended). Under s 1 the Ombudsman (currently Ann Abraham) is appointed by the Crown. The constitutional function of the Ombudsman is to independently investigate complaints of injustice caused by maladministration by government and public bodies.

21.3.2 Maladministration

Maladministration is referred to in the 1967 Act, but it is not specifically defined. As a consequence, historically it has been apposite to refer to the famous *'Crossman Catalogue'* to indicate the type of behaviour that maladministration covers:

QUOTATION

'bias, neglect, inattention, delay, incompetence, inaptitude, perversity, turpitude, arbitrariness and so on. It would be a long and interesting list.'

Hansard HC Vol 734, col 51.

Latterly the Ombudsman's website has indicated that maladministration also embraces, *inter alia*, the following types of behaviour:

- A faulty procedure.
- Rudeness.
- Avoidable delay.
- A refusal to answer reasonable questions.
- A failure to indicate a right of appeal.

Three points can be made in relation to maladministration:

Firstly, maladministration is concerned essentially with the procedure (behaviour) of state officials as opposed to the actual decision itself. In other words, it is concerned, for example, with how a person's claim for a social security benefit was processed by the department (eg was there an avoidable delay? Were forms lost? Were officials rude?), rather than whether they are legally entitled to a particular benefit (which is a legal question). In this way maladministration focuses on the decision-making process rather than the actual decision itself. However, the select committee supporting the Ombudsman has urged the office to infer maladministration where a decision is *bad* (as this presupposes an element of maladministration).

Secondly, although maladministration is broader than illegality, the precise dividing line between maladministration and illegality may well on occasions be a very fine one. For example, avoidable delay or the provision of inadequate advice could well be considered to be legally actionable in negligence.

Thirdly, although the lists above suggest behaviour which to an objective observer may appear to be somewhat trivial and unimportant (eg discourtesy by a public official), nonetheless, to the individual concerned, such behaviour will inevitably leave them feeling that they have a grievance against the state.

Under s 5 of the Act individuals must claim 'to have sustained injustice in consequence of maladministration in connection with the action so taken'. The cases indicate that injustice can embrace financial hardship/loss or even distress.

21.3.3 Jurisdiction

The bodies subject to the investigations of the Ombudsman are set out in Sched 2 of the Act and include:

- Central government departments of state (eg the Home Office).
- Bodies performing a public function and quangos (eg the Arts Council of England).

In terms of complaints received, the 2008–09 Annual Report identified the following five government departments against which most complaints were made:

- Department for Work and Pensions (2,692)
- HM Revenue and Customs (2,159)
- Home Office (818)
- Ministry of Justice (743)
- Department for Transport (337)

Annual Report 2008–09, Every Complaint Matters, HC 786 (2009), Figure 12.

It is not altogether surprising that these types of bodies should have the most complaints registered against them given that the public have regular contact with them. A number of matters are excluded from the Ombudsman's remit and these are detailed in Sched 3 and include, *inter alia*, investigations relating to:

- Foreign relations.
- Contractual/commercial matters.
- The investigation of crime.

In addition, the Ombudsman is precluded from investigating where the individual has a legal remedy available to them in a court or tribunal. This is subject to the proviso (s 5) that the Ombudsman *can* investigate such a compliant if satisfied that it would be unreasonable for that person to resort to such a remedy (eg it is too expensive or the law is unclear on the point). In the context of the *Debt of Honour case* (see below), the House of Commons Public Administration Select Committee made the following point:

QUOTATION

'The entire basis of the 1967 Parliamentary Commissioner for Administration Act is that it is possible for a measure to be legal, and yet to be maladministered. The fact that legality has been established through Judicial Review may be irrelevant to maladministration. There may even be circumstances where the Ombudsman feels it is appropriate to conduct an investigation while Judicial Review proceedings are taking place, so that she can subsequently report without delay.'

First Report of Session 2005–06, *A Debt of Honour*, HC 735 (2006), para 20.

In fact, the overlap between the Ombudsman and the courts can be illustrated by the *Congreve* case (see section 20.2.4) in which the court decided that the Home Secretary had acted illegally by threatening to revoke television licences purchased early in order to avoid paying an increased licence fee. This court ruling followed an earlier investigation by the Ombudsman which had held that maladministration had occurred, but had not recommended a remedy. According to the Law Commission:

QUOTATION

'Through the notion of maladministration, the ombudsmen are able to conduct a broad-brush assessment of the overall manner in which a public body has conducted itself, including instances of institutional failure. In this respect, it is a more holistic inquiry than judicial scrutiny, which tends to focus on isolated acts or omissions as being negligent or unlawful.'

Administrative Redress: Public Bodies and the Citizen, A Consultation Paper,
Law Commission, No 187, para 3.65.

21.3.4 The investigation process

In broad terms the three stages are as follows:

■ **The first/screening stage**

This is known as the filter or screening stage whereby an aggrieved person must first send their complaint to an MP (generally their own, but other MPs can deal with it) who in turn may pass it on to the Ombudsman. The complaint must be given to the MP within 12 months of the individual having notice of the grievance; however, although the Ombudsman has a discretion to accept a complaint outside the time limit, the limit is usually applied. In short, complainants cannot complain directly to the Ombudsman; instead the MP referral system operates, which has proved controversial.

In fact, this filter system is unusual among the different public sector Ombudsmen and it can be seen to act as a barrier preventing access to the Ombudsman. On the other hand, the rationale behind the referral system was to protect the constitutional position of the MP, one of whose functions is to resolve the problems of constituents. A further problem with removing the filter is the argument that direct access would overwhelm the Ombudsman with complaints. In any event, over the years there have been attempts at removing this filter. In fact, in July 2001, the government indicated that it supported its removal. More recently, in 2009 the Public Administration Select Committee recommended the abolition of the filter as 'long overdue' (*Parliament and the Ombudsman*, Fourth Report of Session 2009–10, HC, 107 (2009), p 4).

In terms of figures, the *Annual Report 2008–09, Every Complaint Matters*, HC 786 (Crown Copyright, 2009), Chapter 2, revealed that during this period, the Parliamentary and Health Service Ombudsman received 16,317 enquiries. According to the report, 713 investigations were carried out by the office that year (for more on this process, see below).

■ **The investigation stage**

On receipt of a referral by an MP, under the Act the Ombudsman has discretion as to whether or not to investigate a complaint (s 5) and how an investigation is conducted (s 7). Moreover, the Ombudsman can also discontinue an investigation once commenced. She has wide-ranging powers of investigation which enable her to require any government minister, officer or member of the department (or other person) to furnish information or documents apposite to the investigation. The Act states that for the purpose of the investigation the Ombudsman:

SECTION

s 8(2)
'shall have the same powers as the Court in respect of the attendance and examination of witnesses … and in respect of the production of documents.'

Furthermore, it will amount to contempt to obstruct the work of the Ombudsman (s 9). Although the Ombudsman has powerful investigatory powers, she operates in a more inquisitorial way than the courts, which employ an adversarial approach. Investigations are carried out in private and she can go directly to the heart of the government department or public body and obtain information. On completion of the investigation, a report will be issued.

■ The report stage

Under s 10 of the Act, a report of the investigation is sent to the MP who referred the complaint, and to the principal officer of the government department. Where the report indicates a finding of maladministration resulting in injustice, generally speaking the department/authority concerned will comply with the recommendations for remedial action. Below are the percentages of complaints which were upheld (in full or part) against some of the bodies investigated during the 2008–09 session:

- Department for Transport – Driver & Vehicle Licensing Agency (67 per cent partly upheld).
- Department for Work and Pensions – Child Support Agency (50 per cent fully upheld, 45 per cent partly upheld).
- HM Revenue and Customs (27 per cent fully upheld, 35 per cent partly upheld).
- HM Revenue and Customs – the Adjudicator's Office (7 per cent fully upheld).
- Ministry of Justice – HM Courts Service (80 per cent partly upheld).

Annual Report 2008–09, Every Complaint Matters, HC 786 (Crown Copyright 2009), Figure 14.

It should be noted, however, that despite the Ombudsman's wide-ranging investigatory powers, her recommendations are not legally binding. In other words, although she can invite a department to, for example, award compensation, alter its administrative procedures or offer an apology, she cannot legally insist on it. Having said this, in general terms (although see below) the Ombudsman's recommendations are accepted as indicated by the Barlow Clowes affair, where the government paid out *ex gratia* payments even though they did not accept the findings of maladministration. The work of the Ombudsman is overseen (but also supported) by a select committee: the House of Commons Public Administration Select Committee.

Under s 10(3) of the Act, if after conducting an investigation the Ombudsman believes that the injustice she has identified will not be remedied, a special report can be issued which will draw the attention of Parliament (and the wider public) to this deficiency. The second of these reports to be issued occurred in relation to the Channel Tunnel Link which resulted in the 'blighting' of houses which could not be sold while the exact route was being determined and in the event, the government proposed compensation. More recent examples of two special reports being issued are detailed below (these represent the third and fourth special reports issued by the Ombudsman in four decades):

CASE STUDY

'A Debt of Honour: The ex-gratia scheme for British groups interned by the Japanese during the Second World War', HC 324 (July 2005).

The Ombudsman held that injustice had been caused as a result of maladministration by the Ministry of Defence in respect of the operation of its *ex-gratia* payments for British internees held by the Japanese during the Second World War. The government refused (at least initially) to accept two of the recommendations made: (i) to review the operation of the scheme and (ii) to reconsider the position of those denied payment under the scheme. In January 2006 the Public Administration Select Committee published a report which was critical of the Ministry of Defence: First Report of Session 2005–06, *A Debt of Honour*, HC 735 (2006). In a written answer in May 2006, Lord Drayson the Parliamentary Under-Secretary of State, Minister of Defence confirmed that the Ministry of Defence had now in effect implemented all of the Ombudsman's recommendations (ie eligibility under the scheme would be extended with the expectation of Professor Hayward thereby qualifying). *Hansard*, HL Vol 681, col WA 87.

One interesting point to note about this case was that there was a delay in processing this complaint because the Association of British Internees Far Eastern Region challenged the Secretary of State in judicial review proceedings. They contended that the civilian eligibility criterion which meant that for the purposes of the scheme being British meant being a civilian who had been born in Britain or whose parent or grandparent had been, was disproportionate and or/ irrational and defeated a legitimate expectation. The Court of Appeal dismissed their appeal and held, *inter alia*, that it was not irrational for the Secretary of State to limit the application of the scheme to those individuals with close links to the United Kingdom at the time of their detention as an internee or to introduce the birth criteria (*R (Association of British Civilian Internees: Far East Region) v Secretary of State for Defence* [2003] EWCA Civ 473).

CASE STUDY

'Trusting in the pensions promise: Government bodies and the security of final salary occupational pensions', HC 984 (March 2006)

The Ombudsman found injustice caused by maladministration *inter alia* in terms of official information provided by the government in respect of the security of members' final salary occupational pension schemes (the 'first' finding of maladministration). The government rejected the findings that maladministration had occurred and most of the Ombudsman's recommendations. In July 2006 the Public Administration Select Committee in support of the Ombudsman made the following constitutional point:

QUOTATION

'This system will only work if the Parliamentary Ombudsman, the Government and Parliament share a broad common understanding of what maladministration might be and who should properly identify it (para 76) … We share the Ombudsman's concern that the Government has been far too ready to dismiss her findings of maladministration … It would be extremely damaging if Government became accustomed simply to reject findings of maladministration, especially if an investigation by this Committee proved there was indeed a case to answer. It would raise fundamental constitutional issues about the position of the Ombudsman and the relationship between Parliament and the Executive (para 78). We trust that this Report will act as a warning to the Government … The Parliamentary Commissioner is Parliament's Ombudsman: Government must respect her' (para 79).

Sixth Report of Session 2005–06, *The Ombudsman in Question: the Ombudsman's report on pensions and its constitutional implications*, HC 1081 (2006).

As an interesting postscript to this case, in *R (Bradley and others) v Secretary of State for Work and Pensions* [2008] EWCA Civ 36, although the Court of Appeal made it clear that the Secretary of State was not required to accept findings of maladministration by virtue of the 1967 Act, the Secretary of State had, however, acted irrationally in rejecting the Ombudsman's first finding of maladministration and confirmed that this rejection should be quashed.

More recently, a fifth report was issued in May 2009:

CASE STUDY

'Injustice unremedied: The Government's response on Equitable Life' HC 435 (Crown Copyright, 2009)

In this report the Ombudsman stated that she was:

'… satisfied that the injustice I found in my report [ie *Equitable Life: A Decade of Regulatory Failure*, HC 815 (Crown Copyright 2008)], to have resulted from maladministration on the part of the public bodies responsible for the prudential regulation of the Society has not so far been remedied' (para 72).

In October 2009, the Administrative Court heard an action: *R (Equitable Members Action Group) v HM Treasury* [2009] EWHC 2495 (Admin), for (a partly successful) judicial review brought by the Equitable Members' Action Group, of HM Treasury's rejection of certain findings of the Ombudsman (the government had accepted a number of them). The court held, *inter alia*, that the government had failed to provide a cogent reason for rejecting certain of the Ombudsman's findings.

In addition to the periodic special reports above, the Ombudsman is required to provide an annual report detailing her activities.

21.3.5 Ombudsman or Ombudsmouse?

There has always been academic debate over the effectiveness of the Ombudsman. On the one hand the Ombudsman has wide-ranging investigatory powers, but on the other, she has no legal powers of enforcement. As noted by the Public Administration Select Committee in the context of the report on pensions (see above), however, historically even when government departments have denied maladministration found by the Ombudsman, 'they have ultimately been willing to offer some recompense out of respect for the Ombudsman's office' (para 67). In addition, in her speech to the Constitution Unit in December 2006 the Ombudsman made it clear that in relation to the vast majority of complaints where maladministration is found, the government accept these findings and then comply with her recommendations. As a consequence, she noted that she could not see the need for legal enforcement powers, although she added that this was subject to a proviso that if government departments systematically ignored her findings then she 'might begin to see some role for legal enforceability'.

In addition, it must be remembered that the Ombudsman also performs a *de facto* preventative role in that the very existence of the office acts to some extent as a deterrent to government departments to avoid engaging in behaviour which could be deemed as maladministration. In this way the Ombudsman promotes good governance. Indeed, according to her 2005–06 annual report one of the aims for the 2006–09 period was: 'To contribute to improvements in public service delivery by being an influential organisation, sharing our knowledge and expertise' (p 59). Indeed, in 2007 the Ombudsman, after consultation, produced a document on developing '*Principles of Good Administration*'. It set out in broad terms the Ombudsman's view as to what the organisations and bodies subject to her jurisdiction should be doing in order to deliver good administration/customer service. The 2009 annual report stated that part of the aim and vision of the Ombudsman was to drive 'improvements in public services'. The following two case studies illustrate the effectiveness of the Ombudsman:

CASE STUDY

Mr M (2008-09)

The Ombudsman found maladministration when the Service Personnel and Veterans Agency (an MOD agency) had effectively excluded M (who lived in Australia) from the enjoyment of its services (they had refused to correspond mainly or solely via email). As a result, the Agency thereafter agreed: to conduct email correspondence with M, apologise, pay him £250 for inconvenience and consider its guidance on the email of personal data.

Source: *Annual Report 2008–09*, p 14

Child Support Agency (2001–02) Case No C.1685/00

The Ombudsman found injustice caused by maladministration by the Child Support Agency when they unreasonably demanded payment of arrears as well as failing to reply to correspondence. This indicated that the CSA had consistently failed to handle this case in a satisfactory fashion. The complainant was awarded £900 by the Child Support Agency.

Kirkham's report *The Parliamentary Ombudsman: Withstanding the Test of Time* (HC 421, (2007)) was published on the 40th anniversary of the 1967 Act. Richard Kirkham, who wrote the report, commented that the Parliamentary Ombudsman 'has proved to be an effective addition to the system of administrative justice in the UK' (p 18) and concluded that: 'As well as improving the power of the citizen to gain redress, as was originally intended, Parliament itself has gained a valuable tool in the ongoing process of calling the government to account' (p 20).

21.3.6 Accountability

Under the rule of law all bodies are subject to the law. Although the Ombudsman is an independent officer of Parliament she is still accountable to:

■ **The courts** – in *R v Parliamentary Commissioner for Administration, ex parte Dyer* [1994] 1 All ER 375 the court held that the Ombudsman was not outside the ambit of judicial review; however, she did enjoy a broad discretion under the 1967 Act. In December 2006 in her speech to the Constitution Unit, the Ombudsman noted that although the number of applications for judicial review of the Ombudsman was increasing, they were generally rejected by the courts. The *2008–09 Annual Report* noted that of seven cases of judicial review issued against the Ombudsman during this period, six were refused permission to proceed, with one awaiting a decision. However, in a series of cases involving Balchin, the courts did review and quash the decisions of the Ombudsman: *R v Parliamentary Commissioner for Administration, ex parte Balchin* [1997] COD 146; *R v Parliamentary Commissioner for Administration, ex parte Balchin (No 2)* [2000] JPL 267; *R (Balchin) v Parliamentary Commissioner for Administration (No 3)* [2002] EWHC 1876 (Admin).

■ **Parliament** – under s 1 of the 1967 Act, the Ombudsman is removable by both Houses of Parliament (analogous to senior judges – see section 13.4.1). In addition, the Ombudsman also provides Parliament with an annual report of her workload.

KEY FACTS

The Ombudsman
The Ombudsman is an extra-judicial form of redress who investigates complaints of maladministration (eg poor government) against: • Central government departments of state (eg Department for Work and Pensions). • Bodies performing a public function and quangos (eg the Arts Council of England).
Individuals must have sustained injustice in consequence of maladministration and this can take the form of financial hardship or distress.
The Ombudsman (after being contacted by an MP) works in an inquisitorial manner and has wide investigatory powers to ascertain whether maladministration has occurred.
On conclusion of the investigation a report will be issued detailing the maladministration found (or otherwise) together with recommendations for remedial action.
Although the Ombudsman cannot legally enforce her recommendations, she can issue a special report where she considers that the maladministration will go unremedied.

21.3.7 Other ombudsmen

The system of public sector Ombudsmen embraces the following:

◼ **Health Commissioner** – This Ombudsman was established under the National Health Service Reorganisation Act 1973 (as amended), and investigates complaints concerning a failure in services provided by the NHS in England. Traditionally the office holder also operates as the Parliamentary Commissioner for Administration, hence references to the Parliamentary and Health Service Commissioner (PHSO).

◼ **Local government** – The three local government Ombudsmen covering different geographical areas of England (established under the Local Government Act 1974 as amended) investigate complaints of maladministration in the context of local councils. It should be noted that in 2005 the government recommended streamlining the constitutional relationship of the parliamentary, health and local commissioners (*Reform of Public Sector Ombudsmen Services in England* (Cabinet Office: 2005). In 2007 the Regulatory Reform (Collaboration etc between Ombudsmen) Order 2007/1889 was passed in order to increase the collaboration between the local government Ombudsmen and the PHSO (ie in undertaking a joint investigation).

◼ **Scotland** – The Scottish Public Services Ombudsman Act 2002 (a Scottish statute) rationalised the different Ombudsmen under one organisation. The Scottish Public Services Ombudsman considers complaints in relation to, among others, the:
  • Scottish Executive/Government.
  • NHS in Scotland.
  • Councils and housing associations in Scotland.

◼ **Wales** – The Public Services Ombudsman for Wales was established under the Public Services Ombudsman (Wales) Act 2005. It considers complaints in the context of, for example:
  • Local government.
  • NHS in Wales.
  • Welsh Assembly Government/National Assembly for Wales Commission.

◼ **Northern Ireland** – The Northern Ireland Ombudsman considers complaints in respect of:
  • Northern Ireland government departments and agencies (as *The Assembly Ombudsman for Northern Ireland*).
  • Local councils and Health and Social Services Boards/Councils/Trusts (as The Northern Ireland Commissioner for Complaints).

◼ **Europe** – Under the Maastricht Treaty a European Ombudsman was established to investigate maladministration by the institutions of the EU (except the judicial bodies acting in their judicial capacity).

◼ **Judges** – Under s 62 of the Constitutional Reform Act 2005 a Judicial Appointments and Conduct Ombudsman has been created to investigate complaints in the context of the judicial appointments process and the handling of issues involving judicial conduct/discipline.

SUMMARY

◼ There are a number of grievance mechanisms available to individuals who feel aggrieved by the actions of the state.

◼ Tribunals enable individuals to challenge decisions made by state officials in a forum which is outside the formal court system.

◼ Tribunals are more accessible and user-friendly than courts.

◼ Major structural reforms have taken place in recent years with the Tribunals, Courts and Enforcement Act 2007 which created a two-tiered system of tribunals (the First-tier Tribunal and the Upper Tribunal).

◼ Inquiries come in different forms:

- A local land inquiry into, for example, the refusal of a local planning authority to grant planning permission.
- An inquiry into a major infrastructure project such as the citing of a new motorway.
- An inquiry into a national event or scandal. These can either be in the form of a non-statutory inquiry or a statutory inquiry under the Inquiries Act 2005.

■ The Ombudsman is an officer who investigates injustice caused to individuals as a result of maladministration (faulty administration) by departments of state or bodies performing a public function.

■ Complaints are referred by MPs. Thereafter the Ombudsman has wide-ranging powers of investigation in order to determine whether maladministration has occurred. On completion of the investigation a report will be issued.

■ The finding of maladministration and any recommendations made are not legally binding, although (with some recent exceptions) they are generally accepted and followed.

SAMPLE ESSAY QUESTION

The Ombudsman is, in reality, an 'Ombudsmouse' and is in need of reform. Discuss.

Introduction:

- Definition – Parliamentary Commissioner for Administration (the Ombudsman) investigates complaints concerning maladministration
- Established under the Parliamentary Commissioner Act 1967

Purpose:

- Rationale for establishing the Ombudsman (see the *Whyatt* Report 1961) and the limitations of the existing parliamentary and legal avenues of redress for an aggrieved individual suffering at the hands of the administration
- Investigates complaints of injustice owing to maladministration caused by the government and bodies performing a public function (sch 2)

An Ombudsmouse:

- Jurisdiction is limited thereby excluding certain issues (eg commercial matters – sch 3)
- In essence, concerned with the process of decision-making rather than the actual decision itself (analogous to judicial review)
- Findings of maladministration and recommendations not legally enforceable which government can disregard (Trusting in the Pensions Promise, Equitable Life), but note *Bradley* (2008)
- Most complaints she initially receives are not investigated

An Ombudsman:

- Provides a remedy (which is free) when there is typically no other available.
- Considerable number of bodies subject to her jurisdiction
- Strong powers of investigation – it is contempt to obstruct her work
- Generally speaking the government accepts her findings and recommendations
- In cases where the government does not accept maladministration they may nevertheless provide a remedy (Barlow Clowes)
- In *A Debt of Honour* although the government initially did not implement all her recommendations, eventually they did
- She acts in a *de facto* preventative capacity
- She improves public administration/government (see *Principles of Good Administration*)
- The Ombudsman model has been extended to other contexts (eg local government)

Reform?

- Removal of the MP filter
- Enforceable legal powers
- Extended jurisdiction
- Power to initiate an investigation
- More publicity concerning her role

CONCLUSION

Further reading

Books

Craig, P, *Administrative Law* (6th edn, Sweet & Maxwell, 2008), Chapter 9.

Leyland, P and Anthony, G, *Textbook on Administrative Law* (6th edn, Oxford University Press, 2009), Chapters 6 and 7.

Purdue, M, 'Investigations by the Public Sector Ombudsmen' in Feldman, D (ed), *English Public Law* (2nd edn, Oxford University Press, 2009), p 881.

Purdue, M, 'Public Inquiries as a Part of Public Administration' in Feldman, D (ed), *English Public Law* (2nd edn, Oxford University Press, 2009), p 919.

Richardson, G, 'Tribunals' in Feldman, D (ed), *English Public Law* (2nd edn, Oxford University Press, 2009), p 849.

Wade, H and Forsyth, C, *Administrative Law* (10th edn, Oxford University Press, 2009), Chapters 23 and 24.

Articles

Beatson, J, 'Should judges conduct public inquiries?' [2005] 121 LQR 221.

Scorer, R, 'Modern Inquiries and the public purse' (2005) NLJ 61.

Papers

Gay, O, 'Investigatory inquiries and the Inquiries Act 2005', SN/PC/02599 (House of Commons Library, 2009).

Internet links

www.ombudsman.org.uk

www.tribunals.gov.uk

Glossary

Administrative Court
that part of the High Court which processes judicial review cases

Bill of rights
document containing a list of basic and fundamental human rights

bicameralism
a legislature composed of two chambers

by-law
subordinate legislation made by local authorities

by-election
an election which takes place in a constituency when an MP's seat becomes vacant

Cabinet
the collection of the most senior government ministers

Civil Service
the personnel who carry out and implement policies as determined by government ministers

constitution
the rules which govern the government which can be found in either a codified or uncodified form

constitutional convention
a binding political rule of the constitution

constitutionalism
the principle which requires a constitution to provide sufficient restraints on government/state power

declaration of incompatibility
a declaration by the courts under the Human Rights Act 1998 that legislation is inconsistent with the European Convention

delegated legislation
legislation made by the executive

devolution
power which has been delegated to regional bodies in Scotland, Wales and Northern Ireland

EU law
law and legal practices emanating from the European Union

electorate
individuals eligible to vote in an election

European Convention on Human Rights
originally formulated in 1950, this document aims to protect the human rights of all people in the member states of the Council of Europe

exclusivity
the principle that the enforcement of public law rights should be via the judicial review procedure

'first past the post'
the electoral system used to elect MPs in which the candidate with the most votes in a constituency wins the seat

freedom of expression
a right set out in Article 10 of the European Convention on Human Rights and now part of UK law as a consequence of the Human Rights Act 1998

human rights
rights and freedoms to which every human being is entitled

Human Rights Act
legislation enacted in 1998 that brought the European Convention on Human Rights into domestic law for the whole of the UK on 2 October 2000

irrationality
a decision in law which no reasonable person could have come to

judicial independence
the principle that judges are independent of the other arms of the state

judicial review
the process whereby the courts review the legality of governmental actions

legislature
the law-making body in a constitution

life peers
persons appointed to the upper chamber of Parliament

local authorities
directly elected layer of government which administers functions at a local level and tailored to local needs

maladministration
poor administration

margin of appreciation
a concept created by the European Court of Human Rights to allow a certain amount of freedom for each signatory state to regulate its own activities and its application of the European Convention on Human Rights

Ministerial Code
a code of conduct issued by the Prime Minister which government ministers are required to follow

MP

a member of Parliament, specifically in the House of Commons

natural justice / duty to act fairly

common law rules developed by the judiciary to ensure that public bodies exercise their powers and functions fairly

non-justiciable

an issue not suitable for resolution by the courts

Ombudsman

an officer who investigates complaints of maladministration

parliament

composed of the House of Commons and the House of Lords

parliamentary executive

the constitutional arrangement whereby the executive/government is drawn from, and accountable to, the legislature/Parliament

parliamentary sovereignty

the legal principle that the Crown in Parliament can pass any law it chooses

peer

a person conferred with a peerage and a member of the upper chamber of Parliament, the House of Lords

private law

the law regulating the relationship between individuals

proportionality

the legal principle whereby the court considers the aims of the decision-maker and whether the means to achieve that objective is proportionate (ie the means used are not excessive)

public law

the law regulating the powers of the institutions of the state, how they relate to each other and how they relate to individuals

Royal Assent

the consent conferred on a Bill by the monarch in order to convert into an Act of Parliament

royal prerogative

powers which the government draws from the common law

sub judice

the principle that there should be no discussion of matters proceeding through the courts

Supreme Court

the highest domestic court

ultra vires

acting beyond specified legal powers

Index

access to courts
  human rights, and, 375–376
accountable government
  British constitution, and, 27
  judiciary, and, 295–296
  separation of powers, and, 68–69
acts of parliament
  parliamentary sovereignty, and, 129–131
administrative law
  extra-judicial remedies, 435
  inquiries, 435
  introduction, 433
  judicial review
    and see **judicial review**
    bodies subject to, 442–445
    checklist, 489
    constitutional dimension, 437–438
    definition, 435–436
    effectiveness, 488–489
    generally, 435
    grounds, 454–486
    jurisdiction, 436–437
    mechanics, 442
    nature, 438–441
    procedure, 451–452
    public law issue, 448–450
    remedies, 486–487
    standing, 445–448
    summary, 490
  legal control, 434–435
  Ombudsmen, 435
  overview, 5
  political control, 434
  private law remedies, 434–435
  regulation of government power, 433–434
  statutory appeal, 435
  tribunals, 435
administrative tribunals
  rule of law, and, 111
  separation of powers, and, 82–83
Appellate Committee of the House of Lords
  separation of powers, and, 72–74
applications
  human rights, and
    admissibility, 356
    criteria for admissibility, 356–357
    friendly settlements, 357
    individual, 356
    inter-state, 355–356
    introduction, 355
    striking out, 357
    victim requirement, 356
armed forces
  royal prerogative, and
    deployment abroad, 245–246

    deployment domestically, 246
association and assembly
  generally, 384–385
  introduction, 384
  scope, 384
Attorney-General
  separation of powers, and, 76–77
audi alteram partem
  generally, 480–482
  knowledge of adverse evidence, 482–483
  legal representation, 484–485
  legitimate expectation, 482
  meaning, 480
  oral hearing, 483–484
  reasons for decisions, 485
  representations, 483
  time to prepare defence or answer case, 483
audits
  local government, and, 306
authoritative writers
  sources of constitution, and, 55
bicameral legislature
  British constitution, and, 27

Bill of Rights 1689
  sources of constitution, and, 35
British constitution
  absence of codified document, 18–19
  accountable government, 27
  bicameral legislature, 27
  case law, 23
  conclusion, 28–29
  development, 22
  executive, 26
  features, 22–27
  five tenets, 20
  flexibility, 24–25
  human rights protection, 27
  independent and impartial judiciary, 26
  indicative factors, 19
  international treaties, 23
  introduction, 18
  legal sources, 23
  limited monarchy, 25–26
  membership of international bodies, 20
  nature, 21–22
  non-legal sources, 23
  parliamentary executive, 26
  parliamentary sovereignty
    generally, 134–135
    introduction, 20
  political practices, 23
  principles, 28
  representative democracy, 27
  responsible government, 27

rule of law
  Dicey, 103–122
  introduction, 102–103
  overview, 27
separation of powers
  generally, 66–89
  introduction, 26
sources
  authoritative writers, 55
  classification, 34
  constitutional conventions, 48–54
  domestic case law, 41–44
  domestic legislation, 34–40
  EU case law, 45–47
  EU legislation, 40–41
  international law, 47
  introduction, 30
  law and custom of Parliament, 47
  location, 30–33
  overview, 23
  royal prerogative, 45
  summary, 57–59
  treaties, 47
sovereignty of Parliament
  generally, 134–135
  introduction, 20
status, 23–24
supremacy of Parliament, 23
system of government, as, 20–21
terminology, 18
uncodified, 21–22
unconstitutional acts, 55–57
Union of the United Kingdom, 20
unitary, 25
unwritten, 22–23

by-elections
House of Commons, and, 186

cabinet
executive, and, 231–232
calling and questioning witnesses
human rights, and, 378
carrying out effective investigation
human rights, and, 367
case law
British constitution, and, 23
central government departments
executive, and, 233–234
civil liberties
judiciary, and, 297–298
introduction, 285
civil service
anonymity, 236
constitutional characteristics, 236
impartiality, 236
introduction, 234–235
lower-ranking civil servants, 235
management, 236–237
permanence, 236
senior civil servants, 235
codified constitutions
generally, 13–14
Commissioner for Local Administration
local government, and, 306
committee stage
constitutional Bills, 278

generally, 277–278
committee system
advantages, 275
classification, 271
disadvantages, 275–276
framework, 271
House of Lords, in, 274
joint committees, 274
Northern Irish devolution, and, 320
reforms, 276
Scottish devolution, and, 311
select committees, 271–274
Welsh devolution, and, 324
common law
judges, and, 80–82
parliamentary sovereignty, and, 132
rule of law, and, 113–116
sources of constitution, and, 42–43
compensation
right to liberty and security of person, 375
compulsory purchase
rule of law, and, 106
constituency boundaries
House of Commons, and, 190–191
constitutional conventions
conversion into laws, 53–54
definition, 48
distinction from laws, 52
executive, and, 49
flexibility, 51
introduction, 48
judicial recognition, 52–53
judiciary, and
  generally, 50
  independence, 295
ministerial responsibility, and
  classification, 255–256
  collective responsibility, 256–258
  individual responsibility, 258–263
  Ministerial Code, 256
monarchy, and, 49
obligations, as, 51
origins, 51
Parliament, and, 49
parliamentary sovereignty, and, 139–140
preliminary points, 48–49
purpose, 50
significance, 50
summary, 54
constitutional law
generally, 4–5
introduction, 4
Constitutional Reform Act 2005
sources of constitution, and, 36–37
constitutionalism
basic principles, 16–17
introduction, 15–16
constitutions
alteration, 9
British constitution
  and see **British constitution**
  generally, 18–29
codified constitutions, 13–14
constitutionalism
  basic principles, 16–17
  introduction, 15–16

constitutions – *contd*
contents
alteration of constitution, 9
institutions of government, 7–8
introduction, 7
relationship between institutions, 8
relationship between institutions and the
individual, 8–9
definition, 6–7
entrenching, 9–10
establishment of institutions of government
generally, 7–8
relationship with other institutions, and, 8
relationship with the individual, and, 8–9
federal constitutions, 14–15
flexible constitutions, 14
institutions of government
generally, 7–8
relationship with other institutions, 8
relationship with the individual, 8–9
methods of alteration, 9
procedures for alteration, 9
purpose
act as limit and control on governmental
power, 12
affirm particular values and goals, 12–13
ensure moral legitimacy, 11–12
ensure operation of government by consent,
11–12
ensure stability and order, 10–11
introduction, 10
represent a watershed, 12
rigid constitutions, 14
types
codified constitutions, 13–14
federal constitutions, 14–15
flexible constitutions, 14
introduction, 13
rigid constitutions, 14
uncodified constitutions, 13–14
unitary constitutions, 14–15
unwritten constitutions, 13–14
written constitutions, 13–14
uncodified constitutions, 13–14
unitary constitutions, 14–15
unwritten constitutions, 13–14
written constitutions, 13–14
contempt of court
judiciary, and
common law protection, 292
statutory protection, 292
corporal punishment
human rights, and, 369–370
Council (of Ministers)
democracy, 338–339
generally, 337
separation of powers, 337–338
criminal law
public law, and, 3
crossbench peers
appointment, 205–206
generally, 211–212
Crown
executive, and, 229–230
separation of powers, and
executive function, and, 71–72
introduction, 71
judicial function, and, 72
legislative function, and, 71

death penalty
human rights, and, 368
debates
advantages, 270
disadvantages, 270
House of Commons
Budget, 268
Early Day Motion, 269
introduction, 267
opposition day, 268–269
other, 269
Queen's speech, 268
vote of no confidence, 268
House of Lords, 269
introduction, 267–271
decentralisation of public power
devolution
England, 328–32
Northern Ireland, 317–323
Scotland, 308–317
Wales, 323–328
England, and
generally, 328–329
London Mayor and Assembly, 329–330
regional development agencies, 329
introduction, 300
local government
advantages, 303–304
control, 305–306
disadvantages, 304
functions, 302–303
introduction, 301
relationship with central government,
307–308
structure, 301
Northern Irish devolution
challenging actions of Executive, 321–322
excepted matters, 321
historical background, 318–319
legislation, 320
legislative competence, 320
Northern Ireland Assembly, 319–320
Northern Ireland Executive Committee, 320
other bodies, 323
parliamentary sovereignty, 322
relationship with Westminster, 322
reserved matters, 321
scrutiny, 321
transferred matters, 321
Scottish devolution
arguments for and against, 309–310
challenging actions of Executive, 315
devolved matters, 313–314
ECHR, and, 315–316
historical background, 308–309
legislation, 312–313
legislative competence, 314–315
parliamentary sovereignty, 316–317
primary legislation, 313
reform proposals, 317–318
relationship with Westminster, 316
reserved matters, 313

Scottish administration, 311–312
Scottish Executive, 311–312
Scottish Parliament, 310–311
scrutiny, 315
secondary legislation, 313
tax-varying powers, 314
summary, 331
Welsh devolution
devolution issues, 327
historical background, 323
institutional competence, 326–327
National Assembly for Wales, 323–324
powers and responsibilities, 326
parliamentary sovereignty, 328
relationship with Westminster, 327–328
Welsh Assembly Government, 324–325
decisions
EU law, and, and, 40
Declaration of Delhi
rule of law, and, 102
declaration of war
royal prerogative, and, 245
declarations of incompatibility
generally, 404–405
practice, in, 405–407
remedial action, 408–409
statements of compatibility, 407
delegated legislation
examples, 39
legislative process
constitutional issues, 280–281
generally, 279–280
local authorities, and, 39
nature, 39
separation of powers, and
introduction, 69
legal control, 70–71
other countries, in, 71
parliamentary control, 70
rationale, 70
democracy
British constitution, and, 27
European Union, and, 338–339
local government, and, 305
deportation
human rights, and, 370–371
derogations
human rights, and, 363–364
devolved institutions
parliamentary sovereignty, and, 154–155
separation of powers, and, 69
sources of constitution, and, 40
devolution
and see under individual headings
England, and
generally, 328–329
London Mayor and Assembly, 329–330
regional development agencies, 329
executive, and, 238
introduction, 300
Northern Irish devolution
challenging actions of Executive, 321–322
excepted matters, 321
historical background, 318–319
legislation, 320
legislative competence, 320

Northern Ireland Assembly, 319–320
Northern Ireland Executive Committee, 320
other bodies, 323
parliamentary sovereignty, 322
relationship with Westminster, 322
reserved matters, 321
scrutiny, 321
transferred matters, 321
parliamentary sovereignty, and, 154–155
Scottish devolution
arguments for and against, 309–310
challenging actions of Executive, 315
devolved matters, 313–314
ECHR, and, 315–316
historical background, 308–309
legislation, 312–313
legislative competence, 314–315
parliamentary sovereignty, 316–317
primary legislation, 313
reform proposals, 317–318
relationship with Westminster, 316
reserved matters, 313
Scottish administration, 311–312
Scottish Executive, 311–312
Scottish Parliament, 310–311
scrutiny, 315
secondary legislation, 313
tax-varying powers, 314
summary, 331
Welsh devolution
devolution issues, 327
historical background, 323
institutional competence, 326–327
National Assembly for Wales, 323–324
powers and responsibilities, 326
parliamentary sovereignty, 328
relationship with Westminster, 327–328
Welsh Assembly Government, 324–325
directives
generally, 39–40
introduction, 340
discretionary powers
parliamentary sovereignty, and, 136–137
rule of law, and, 106–109
dissolution of Parliament
royal prerogative, and, 243
domestic case law
common law, 42–43
role of courts, 41–42
statutory interpretation, 43–44
domestic legislation
delegated legislation
examples, 39
local authorities, and, 39
nature, 39
devolved institutions, and, 40
local authorities, and, 39
primary legislation, 34–39
draft legislation
legislative scrutiny, and, 277

effective participation in the trial
human rights, and, 377
election broadcasts
generally, 196–197

Electoral Commission
generally, 196
electoral system
constituency boundaries, 190–191
electorate
constitutional significance of voting, 193
persons disqualified from voting, 194–196
persons entitled to vote, 193–196
'first past the post'
advantages, 188–189
constitutional significance, 197–198
disadvantages, 189–190
generally, 186–187
reforms, 199
supervision and conduct of elections
broadcasts, 196–197
Electoral Commission, 196
turnouts, 187–188
voters
disqualified persons, 194–196
entitled persons, 193–194
voting system, 186–187
enforcement
human rights, and, 352–353
enrolled Bill rule
parliamentary sovereignty, and, 140
equality before the law
rule of law, and, 109–113
EU case law
European Court of Human Rights, 46–47
European Court of Justice, 45–46
introduction, 45
EU law
case law
European Court of Human Rights, 46–47
European Court of Justice, 45–46
introduction, 45
legislation
decisions, 40
directives, 39–40
introduction, 39
opinions, 40
primary sources, 39
recommendations, 40
regulations, 39
secondary sources, 40–41
parliamentary sovereignty, and
Factortame litigation, 346–349
introduction, 343
primacy of EU law, 343–344
reception of EU Law in British constitution, 344–346
public law, and, 4
EU legislation
decisions, 40
directives, 39–40
introduction, 39
legislative scrutiny, and, 282
opinions, 40
primary sources, 39
recommendations, 40
regulations, 39
secondary sources, 40–41
European Commission
democracy, 338–339
generally, 337

separation of powers, 337–338
European Communities Act 1972
sources of constitution, and, 36
European Convention on Human Rights
See also **Human rights**
absolute rights, 365–366
access to courts, 375–376
applications
admissibility, 356
criteria for admissibility, 356–357
friendly settlements, 357
individual, 356
inter-state, 355–356
introduction, 355
striking out, 357
victim requirement, 356
association
generally, 384–385
introduction, 384
scope, 384
background, 351–352
bringing promptly before judge, 374
call and question witnesses, 378
carrying out effective investigation, 367
challenging lawfulness of detention, 374–375
compensation
right to liberty and security of person, 375
conditional rights, 365–366
Convention rights
absolute rights, 365–366
conditional rights, 365–366
derogations, 363–364
freedom of assembly and association, 384–385
freedom of expression, 383–384
freedom of thought, conscience and religion, 382–383
inhuman and degrading treatment and punishment, 368–371
introduction, 365
lawful and permissible interferences, 358–362
prohibition of discrimination, 389–390
prohibition of forced labour, 371
prohibition of retrospective criminal law and penalties, 378–379
prohibition of slavery, 371
prohibition of torture, 368–371
reservations, 364–365
right to education, 387
right to effective remedy, 388–389
right to fair and public hearing, 375–378
right to free elections, 387–388
right to liberty and security of person, 372–375
right to life, 366–368
right to marry, 385–386
right to private and family life, 380–381
right to property, 386–387
corporal punishment, 369–370
death penalty, and, 368
deportation, 370–371
derogations, 363–364
duty to carry out effective investigation, 367
effective participation in the trial, 377
enforcement machinery, 352–353

European Court of Human Rights
  applications, 355–357
  composition, 353
  effect of judgments, 354
  establishment, 353
  Grand Chamber, 353–354
  individual applications, 355–357
  introduction, 353
  just satisfaction awards, 354–355
  role, 354–355
  state applications, 355–357
extradition, 370–371
freedom of association
  generally, 384–385
  introduction, 384
  scope, 384
freedom of peaceful assembly
  generally, 385
  introduction, 384
  scope, 384
freedom of expression
  introduction, 383
  restrictions, 383–384
  scope, 383
freedom of thought, conscience and religion
  introduction, 382
  restrictions, 382–383
  scope, 382
Grand Chamber of the European Court,
  353–354
impartial court or tribunal, 376
in accordance with law, 359–360
individual applications
  admissibility, 356
  criteria for admissibility, 356–357
  friendly settlements, 357
  generally, 356
  introduction, 355
  striking out, 357
  victim requirement, 356
information as to reasons for arrest and charge,
  373–374
inhuman and degrading treatment and
  punishment
  corporal punishment, 369–370
  definition, 369
  deportation, 370–371
  extradition, 370–371
  introduction, 368
  scope, 368–369
inter-state applications
  admissibility, 356
  criteria for admissibility, 356–357
  friendly settlements, 357
  generally, 355–356
  introduction, 355
  striking out, 357
  victim requirement, 356
introduction, 351–352
lawful and permissible interferences with rights
  generally, 358
  in accordance with law, 359–360
  legitimate aims, 360
  margin of appreciation, 361–362
  necessary in a democratic society, 360–361
  prescribed by law, 359–360

  proportionality, 361
lawfulness of detention, 374–375
legal assistance, 378
legitimate aims, 360
margin of appreciation, 361–362
necessary in a democratic society, 360–361
parliamentary sovereignty, and, 135
peaceful assembly
  generally, 385
  introduction, 384
  scope, 384
prescribed by law, 359–360
presumption of innocence, 377–378
private and family life
  correspondence, 381
  family life, 380–381
  home, 381
  introduction, 380
  private life, 380
  scope, 380
prohibition of compulsory labour, 371
prohibition of discrimination
  introduction, 389
  justifiable discrimination, 389–390
  scope, 389
prohibition of forced labour, 371
prohibition of retrospective criminal law and
  penalties
  exceptions, 379
  introduction, 378
  scope, 379
prohibition of slavery and servitude, 371
prohibition of torture
  corporal punishment, 369–370
  definition of 'torture', 369
  deportation, 370–371
  extradition, 370–371
  introduction, 368
  scope, 368–369
proportionality, 361
public emergency, and, 363–364
questioning witnesses, 378
reservations, 364–365
retrospective criminal law and penalties
  exceptions, 379
  introduction, 378
  scope, 379
right to access to courts, 375–376
right to be brought promptly before judge for
  trial or release, 374
right to be informed as to reasons for arrest and
  charge, 373–374
right to challenge lawfulness of detention,
  374–375
right to education, 387
right to effective remedy, 388–389
right to fair and public hearing
  access to courts, 375–376
  call and question witnesses, 378
  effective participation in the trial, 377
  impartial court or tribunal, before, 376
  introduction, 375
  legal assistance, 378
  presumption of innocence, 377–378
  scope, 375
  self-incrimination, 377–378

European Convention on Human Rights – *contd*
  right to free elections
    introduction, 387
    limitations on right to vote, 388
    scope of right to vote, 388
  right to liberty and security of person
    bringing promptly before judge, 374
    challenging lawfulness of detention, 374–375
    compensation, 375
    information as to reasons for arrest and
      charge, 373–374
    introduction, 372
    lawful arrest for non-compliance of court
      order, 372–373
    lawful detention after arrest, 373
    lawful detention after conviction, 372
    other lawful restrictions, 373
    scope, 372
  right to life
    death penalty, and, 368
    duty to carry out effective investigation, 367
    exceptions, 367–368
    introduction, 366
    scope, 366–367
  right to marry, 385–386
  right to property
    introduction, 386
    restrictions, 386–387
    scope, 386
  right to respect for private and family life
    correspondence, 381
    family life, 380–381
    home, 381
    introduction, 380
    private life, 380
    scope, 380
  right to vote in elections
    introduction, 387
    limitations, 388
    scope, 388
  rule of law, and, 101–102
  Scottish devolution, and, 315–316
  self-incrimination, 377–378
  summary, 391
  thought, conscience and religion
    introduction, 382
    restrictions, 382–383
    scope, 382
  victim requirement, 356
  war, and, 363–364
European Council
  democracy, 338–339
  generally, 337
  separation of powers, 337–338
European Court of Human Rights
  applications, 355–357
  composition, 353
  effect of judgments, 354
  establishment, 353
  generally, 46–47
  Grand Chamber, 353–354
  individual applications, 355–357
  introduction, 353
  just satisfaction awards, 354–355
  role, 354–355
  state applications, 355–357

European Court of Justice
  application of law, 341
  democracy, 338–339
  generally, 337
  interpretation of law, 341
  introduction, 340
  overview, 45–46
  role, 341–342
  separation of powers, 337–338
  structure, 340–341
European legislation
  introduction, 339
  legislative scrutiny in the UK, and, 282
  primary sources, 340
  secondary sources, 340
European Parliament
  democracy, 338–339
  generally, 337
  separation of powers, 337–338
European Union
  Council (of Ministers)
    democracy, 338–339
    generally, 337
    separation of powers, 337–338
  decisions, 340
  democracy, 338–339
  directives, 340
  European Commission
    democracy, 338–339
    generally, 337
    separation of powers, 337–338
  European Council
    democracy, 338–339
    generally, 337
    separation of powers, 337–338
  European Court of Justice
    application of law, 341
    democracy, 338–339
    generally, 337
    interpretation of law, 341
    introduction, 340
    role, 341–342
    separation of powers, 337 338
    structure, 340–341
  European Parliament
    democracy, 338–339
    generally, 337
    separation of powers, 337–338
  executive, and, 238–239
  executive function, and, 337
  Factortame litigation
    constitutional importance, 347–349
    generally, 346–347
  individuals' role, 342–343
  institutions
    democracy, 338–339
    outline, 336–337
    separation of powers, 337–338
  introduction, 334
  judicial function, 337
  legislative function, 337
  parliamentary sovereignty, and
    Factortame litigation, 346–349
    introduction, 343
    primacy of EU law, 343–344
    reception of EU Law, 344–346

primacy of EU law, 343–344
primary legislation, 340
reception of EU Law in British constitution,
    344–346
regulations, 340
rule of law, and, 102
secondary legislation, 340
separation of powers, 337–338
sources of law
    introduction, 339
    primary sources, 340
    secondary sources, 340
summary, 349
treaties
    de facto constitution, as, 335
    European constitution, 336
Treaty of Lisbon, 336
Treaty of Rome (1957), 335
Treaty on European Union, 335
Treaty on the Functioning of the European
    Union, 336
executive
    British constitution, and, 26
    bureaucratic executive, 234–238
    Cabinet, 231–232
    central government departments, 233–234
    civil service
        anonymity, 236
        constitutional characteristics, 236
        impartiality, 236
        introduction, 234–235
        lower-ranking civil servants, 235
        management, 236–237
        permanence, 236
        senior civil servants, 235
    common law powers, 242
    constitutional conventions, and, 49
    Crown, 229–230
    devolution, and, 238
    European Union, and, 238–239
    executive agencies, 237
    forms
        bureaucratic executive, 234–238
        generally, 230
        non-political executive, 234–238
        other bodies, 238–239
        political executive, 231–234
        practical terms, in, 238
    functions, 240–241
    'government', 229
    government ministers
        generally, 233–234
        House of Lords, in, 239
        parliamentary executive, 239
        statistical breakdown, 239–240
    Her Majesty's Government
        Cabinet, 231–232
        central government departments, 233–234
        junior ministers, 233
        ministers, 233–234
        monarch, 231
        Prime Minister, 231
        Privy Council, 235
    junior ministers, 233
    local authorities, 238
    ministerial responsibility

and see ministerial responsibility
    collective responsibility, 256–258
    committee system, 271–276
    constitutional convention, 255–256
    individual ministerial responsibility, 258–263
    introduction, 255
    Parliamentary debates, 267–271
    Parliamentary questions, 263–267
    summary, 282–283
ministers
    government ministers, 233–234
    House of Lords, in, 239
    junior ministers, 233
    statistical breakdown, 239–240
monarch, 231
monarchy, 229–230
'Next Step Agencies', 236
non-departmental public bodies, 237–238
non-political executive
    Civil Service, 234–236
    executive agencies, 237
    'Next Step Agencies', 236
    non-departmental public bodies, 237–238
other bodies, 238–239
parliamentary executive, 239
political executive
    Cabinet, 231–232
    central government departments, 233–234
    junior ministers, 233
    ministers, 233–234
    monarch, 231
    Prime Minister, 231
    Privy Council, 235
powers
    common law, 242
    introduction, 241
    statutory, 241–242
practical terms, in, 238
Prime Minister, 231
Privy Council, 235
royal prerogative
    and see royal prerogative
    classification, 243–247
    definition, 242–243
    executive powers, 245–247
    government review (2009), 247–248
    legal prerogatives of the Crown, 244
    Queen's constitutional prerogatives, 243–244
    reform proposals, 243
    relationship with judiciary, 249–250
    relationship with Parliament, 248–249
    significance, 251–252
    types, 243
scrutiny of legislative process
    committee stage, 277–278
    delegated legislation, 279–281
    draft legislation, 277
    European matters, 282
    financial matters, 281–282
    introduction, 276
    procedural matters, 279
    report stage, 278
    second reading, 277
    summary, 282–283
    third reading, 278
senior civil servants, 235

executive – *contd*
    separation of powers, and, 240
    statutory powers, 241–242
    summary, 252
executive agencies
    executive, and, 237
executive function
    separation of powers, and
    generally, 61–62
    introduction, 61
    law officers, and, 76–77
    Lord Chancellor, and, 77–80
    monarchy, and, 71–72
    Privy Council, and, 75–76
    relationship with other powers, 63–64
executive powers
    parliamentary sovereignty, and, 136–137
extradition
    human rights, and, 370–371
extra-territorial jurisdiction
    parliamentary sovereignty, and, 136

federal constitutions
    generally, 14–15
financial matters
    legislative scrutiny, and, 281–282
'first past the post' electoral system
    advantages, 188–189
    constitutional significance, 197–198
    disadvantages, 189–190
    generally, 186–187
flexible constitutions
    British constitution, and, 24–25
    generally, 14
freedom of association
    generally, 384–385
    introduction, 384
    scope, 384
freedom of expression
    administration of justice, 428
    blasphemy, 426
    British constitution, in
        ECHR Article 10, 424–426
        Human Rights Act 1998, 424
        other competing interests, and, 423–424
        residual liberty, 422
    civil law, and
        confidential information, 430–431
        introduction, 429
        reputation, 429–430
    common law indecency, 427
    competing interests, and, 423–424
    confidential information, 430–431
    constitutional importance
        introduction, 420–421
        justification, 421–422
    criminal law, and
        administration of justice, 428
        indecent material, 427
        introduction, 426
        material which depraves and corrupts, 427–428
        national security, 428–429
        public order, 428
        religious sensibilities, 426–427
    defamation, and, 429

democracy, 421
depraved material, 427–428
ECHR, under
    generally, 424–426
    introduction, 383
    restrictions, 383–384
    scope, 383
generally, 415–416
Human Rights Act 1998, under
    British constitution, in, 422–426
    civil law, and, 429–431
    constitutional importance, 420–422
    criminal law, and, 426–429
    generally, 415–416
    summary, 431
indecent material, 427
justification, 421–422
material which depraves and corrupts, 427–428
moral autonomy, 421
national security, 428–429
other competing interests, and, 423–424
public order, 428
religious sensibilities, 426–427
reputation, 429–430
self-fulfilment, 421
statutory indecency, 427
summary, 431
freedom of peaceful assembly
    generally, 385
    introduction, 384
    scope, 384
freedom of speech
    and see **freedom of expression**
    Convention right, 383–384
    generally, 415–431
freedom of thought, conscience and religion
    introduction, 382
    restrictions, 382–383
    scope, 382

government ministers
    generally, 233–234
    House of Lords, in
        generally, 239
        introduction, 211
    parliamentary executive, 239
    statistical breakdown, 239–240
Government of Wales Act 1998
    sources of constitution, and, 36
Grand Chamber of the European Court
    generally, 353–354
grievance mechanisms
    inquiries
        introduction, 497
        land inquiries, 497–498
        national events or scandals, 498–500
    introduction, 491
    Ombudsmen
        accountability, 507
        effectiveness, 506–507
        introduction, 500
        investigation process, 503–504
        jurisdiction, 502–503
        maladministration, 501–502
        origins, 501
        report stage, 504–506

screening stage, 503
  types, 508
summary, 508–509
tribunals
  advantages, 493–494
  background, 491–492
  constitutional position, 492–493
  definition, 491
  disadvantages, 494–495
  independence, 492–493
  reforms, 495–497
  types, 492

Her Majesty's Government
  Cabinet, 231–232
  central government departments, 233–234
  junior ministers, 233
  ministers, 233–234
  monarch, 231
  Prime Minister, 231
  Privy Council, 235
hereditary peers
  background, 207
  death, 209
  overview, 210
  removal, 207–208
  renouncing peerage, 209
  statutory basis, 208
High Court of Parliament
  separation of powers, and, 74
House of Commons
  broadcasts, 196–197
  by-elections, 186
  composition
    generally, 181–183
    overview, 198–199
  constituency boundaries, 190–191
  election broadcasts, 196–197
  Electoral Commission, 196
  electoral system
    constituency boundaries, 190–191
    first past the post, 188–190
    reforms, 199
    turnouts, 187–188
    voting system, 186–187
  electorate
    constitutional significance of voting, 193
    persons disqualified from voting, 194–196
    persons entitled to vote, 193–196
  elements, 198–199
  'first past the post' electoral system
    advantages, 188–189
    constitutional significance, 197–198
    disadvantages, 189–190
    generally, 186–187
  functions
    Bagehot, and, 179
    introduction, 179
    judicial, 181
    legitimise government actions, 181
    maintain government, 180–181
    make laws, 180
    provide Official Opposition, 180
    provide personnel of government, 180
    represent and reflect will of the people,
      179–180

    scrutinise executive, 180
  members of parliament
    disqualification, 184–186
    qualifications, 184
    role, 183–184
  number of seats, 181–182
  political composition, 191–192
  reforms, 199
  representative body, as, 182–183
  size, 181–182
  summary, 199–200
  supervision and conduct of elections
    broadcasts, 196–197
    Electoral Commission, 196
  voters
    disqualified persons, 194–196
    entitled persons, 193–194
  voting system, 186–187
House of Commons Disqualification Act 1911
  sources of constitution, and, 36
House of Lords
  composition
    generally, 203
    political breakdown, 210–211
  constitutional conventions, 220–222
  crossbench peers
    appointment, 205–206
    generally, 211–212
  disqualification of membership, 212–213
  functions
    consideration of subordinate legislation, 215
    debate, 214
    guardian of constitution, 216–217
    initiation of public legislation, 215
    introduction, 213–214
    judicial, 214
    revision of public Bills, 214–215
    scrutiny, 215–216
    watchdog of civil liberties, 216–217
  gender of members, 203
  government ministers, 211
  hereditary peers
    background, 207
    death, 209
    overview, 210
    removal, 207–208
    renouncing peerage, 209
    statutory basis, 208
  independent peers
    appointment, 205–206
    generally, 211–212
  introduction, 202
  judicial function, 214
  judicial peers
    generally, 204
    overview, 210
  Leader of the House, 212
  legal powers
    convention limitations, 220–222
    introduction, 217
    legal limitations, 218
    legality of statutes, 219–220
    use of Parliament Acts, 218–219
  life peers
    Appointments Commission, 206
    creation, 205

House of Lords – *contd*
  life peers – *contd*
    non-political appointments, 205–206
    overview, 210
    political appointments, 205
    statutory basis, 204–205
  limitations on power, 220–222
  Lords Spiritual
    generally, 203–204
    overview, 210
  party political composition, 210–211
  reforms, 224–226
  relationship with the Commons, 222–224
  scrutiny function
    activities of executive, 215–216
    European legislation, 216
    private legislation, 216
  size, 202
  Speaker of the House, 212
  summary, 226
House of Lords Act 1999
  sources of constitution, and, 36
human rights
  and see **European Convention of Human Rights**
  British constitution, and, 27
  Northern Irish devolution, and, 323
  statutory interpretation, and, 44
Human Rights Act 1998
  and see **European Convention of Human Rights**
  aims, 395–396
  damages, 413–415
  declarations of incompatibility
    generally, 404–405
    practice, in, 405–407
    remedial action, 408–409
    statements of compatibility, 407
  derogations, 416–417
  freedom of expression
    and see **freedom of expression**
    British constitution, in, 422–426
    civil law, and, 429–431
    constitutional importance, 420–422
    criminal law, and, 426–429
    generally, 415–416
    summary, 431
  freedom of religion, 415–416
  guaranteed rights, 397–398
  horizontal effect, 411–412
  introduction, 393
  parliamentary sovereignty, and
    generally, 155–156
    introduction, 135
  pre-Act position
    criticisms, 394–395
    generally, 393–394
    role of courts, 394
    role of Parliament, 394
  proportionality, 399–401
  provisions, 395
  public authorities' liability
    introduction, 409–410
    'public authority', 410–411
  purpose, 395
  remedies

    damages, 413–415
    generally, 412
    power to award, 413
    victims of Convention violation, 412–413
  reservations, 417
  retrospective effect, 396–397
  sources of constitution, and, 37
  statements of compatibility, 407
  statutory interpretation
    generally, 401–402
    introduction, 44
    scope or provisions, 402–404
  summary, 417–418
  use of Convention case law by domestic courts, 398–399
  victims of Convention violation, 412–413

illegality
  see also **judicial review**
  abuse of discretion, 462–464
  breach of the ECHR, 467–468
  classification, 455–456
  definition, 455–456
  excess of jurisdiction, 464–467
  'fairly incidental rule', 457–458
  improper purpose, 460–462
  ulterior purpose, 460–462
  ultra vires, 456–458
  wrongful delegation, 458–460
immunity
  judiciary, and, 292
impartiality of judiciary
  human rights, and, 376
  overview, 26
in accordance with law
  human rights, and, 359–360
indefinite detention
  rule of law, and, 105
independence of judiciary
  British constitution, and, 26
  common law protection, 292–295
  constitutional convention, 295
  generally, 290–291
  introduction, 285
  overview, 26
  parliamentary protection, 295
  statutory protection, 291–292
independent peers
  appointment, 205–206
  generally, 211–212
information as to reasons for arrest and charge
  human rights, and, 373–374
inhuman and degrading treatment and punishment
  corporal punishment, 369–370
  definition, 369
  deportation, 370–371
  extradition, 370–371
  introduction, 368
  scope, 368–369
innocence
  rule of law, and, 121
inquiries
  introduction, 497
  land inquiries, 497–498
  national events or scandals, 498–500

institutions of government
  generally, 7–8
  relationship with other institutions, 8
  relationship with the individual, 8–9
international bodies
  British constitution, and, 20
International Convention on Civil and Political Rights 1966
  sources of constitution, and, 47
international law
  parliamentary sovereignty, and, 135–136
  sources of constitution, and, 47
international treaties
  British constitution, and, 23
  royal prerogative, and, 246
  sources of constitution, and, 47
interpretation of statutes
  Duport Steels Ltd v Sirs, 85–86
  generally, 43–44
  Human Rights Act 1998, and, 44
  judges, and, 80
  parliamentary sovereignty, and, 133
irrationality
  see also **judicial review**
  compared with proportionality, 472–473
  definition, 468–469
  introduction, 439
  nature, 469–470
  origins of ground, 468–469
  practice, in, 471

judge-made law
  rule of law, and, 113–116
judges
  and see **judiciary**
  appointments, 85
  disqualification, 85
  rule of law, and
    control of de facto arbitrary powers, 116–118
    defence of fundamental constitutional principles, 119–121
    introduction, 116
    judicial deference, 118–119
    presumption of innocence, 121
    retrospective legislation, 119–120
  separation of powers, and
    appointments, 85
    common law, 80–82
    disqualification, 85
    introduction, 80
    other countries, in, 82
    statutory interpretation, 80
judicial appointments
  separation of powers, and, 85
judicial deference
  rule of law, and, 118–119
judicial disqualification
  separation of powers, and, 85
judicial peers
  generally, 204
  overview, 210
judicial recognition
  constitutional conventions, and, 52–53
judicial review
  abuse of discretion, 462–464

actual bias, 478–480
administrative law, and
  extra-judicial remedies, 435
  introduction, 433
  legal control, 434–435
  political control, 434
  regulation of government power, 433–434
audi alteram partem
  generally, 480–482
  knowledge of adverse evidence, 482–483
  legal representation, 484–485
  legitimate expectation, 482
  meaning, 480
  oral hearing, 483–484
  reasons for decisions, 485
  representations, 483
  time to prepare defence or answer case, 483
bodies subject to
  government bodies, 443
  introduction, 442–443
  judicial bodies, 443
  non-governmental bodies, 443–444
  private bodies, 445
  public bodies, 443
breach of the ECHR, 467–468
checklist, 489
claims, 451
collateral cases, 449–450
consent, 450
constitutional dimension
  human rights, and, 438
  parliamentary sovereignty, 438
  rule of law, 437
  separation of powers, 438
damages, 487
declarations, 487
definition, 435–436
effectiveness, 488–489
excess of jurisdiction, 464–467
exclusive proceedings, 448–449
'fairly incidental rule', 457–458
generally, 435
government bodies, 443
government ministers, 435–436
grounds
  illegality, 455–468
  introduction, 454–455
  irrationality, 468–471
  procedural impropriety, 475–485
  proportionality, 471–475
groups or organisations, 446–447
human rights, and, 438
illegality
  abuse of discretion, 462–464
  breach of the ECHR, 467–468
  classification, 455–456
  definition, 455–456
  excess of jurisdiction, 464–467
  'fairly incidental rule', 457–458
  improper purpose, 460–462
  ulterior purpose, 460–462
  ultra vires, 456–458
  wrongful delegation, 458–460
improper purpose, 460–462
injunctions, 487

judicial review – *contd*
  irrationality
    compared with proportionality, 472–473
    definition, 468–469
    nature, 469–470
    origins of ground, 468–469
    practice, in, 471
  irrationality, 439
  judicial bodies, 443
  judiciary's role, 288–289
  jurisdiction, 436–437
  local authorities, 436
  local government, 447
  mandatory orders, 487
  mechanics, 442
  nature, 438–441
  nemo judex in re sua
    actual bias, 478–480
    appearance of bias, 478–480
    family link, 479
    intermingling of functions, 479
    introduction, 477
    meaning, 477–478
  non-governmental bodies, 443–444
  ouster clauses, 440
  parliamentary sovereignty, 438
  Parole Board, 436
  permission to apply, 451
  pre-action protocol, 451
  prerogative orders, 486–487
  pressure groups, 446–447
  private bodies, 445
  procedural impropriety
    actual bias, 478–480
    audi alteram partem, 480–486
    common law requirements, 477–486
    definition, 475
    nemo judex in re sua, 477–480
    statutory requirements, 476–477
  procedure
    claims, 451
    introduction, 451
    permission to apply, 451
    pre-action protocol, 451
    substantive hearing, 452
    time limits, 451–452
  prohibiting orders, 487
  proportionality
    compared with irrationality, 472–473
    definition, 471–472
    effect, 474–475
    HRA 1998, and, 473–474
    origins of ground, 471–472
    prior to HRA 1998, 473
  public bodies, 443
  public law issue
    collateral cases, 449–450
    consent, 450
    exclusive proceedings, 448–449
    generally, 448
    use in individual's defence, 450
  quashing orders, 487
  red light/green light theories, 439–440
  remedies
    discretion, and, 487
    generally, 486–487
  rule of law
    generally, 437
    introduction, 111
  separation of powers, 438
  'special' administrative court, 441–442
  standing
    groups or organisations, 446–447
    individuals, 446
    introduction, 445–446
    local government, 447
    pressure groups, 446–447
    timing of determination, 447–448
  substantive hearing, 452
  summary, 490
  time limits, 451–452
  ulterior purpose, 460–462
  ultra vires, 456–458
  wrongful delegation, 458–460
judiciary
  accountability, 295–296
  appointment
    generally, 289
    involvement of executive, 289–290
    separation of powers, 85
  British constitution, and, 26
  civil liberties, and, 297–298
  common law protection
    contempt of court, 292
    immunity, 292
    nemo judex in re sua, 293–295
  composition, 296–297
  constitutional conventions, and
    generally, 50
    independence, 295
  constitutional dimension
    introduction, 285
    judicial review, 288–289
    parliamentary sovereignty, 287–288
    protection of the individual, 288
    rule of law, 288
    separation of powers, 286–287
  contempt of court
    common law protection, 292
    statutory protection, 292
  definition, 285
  discipline, 292
  disqualification, 85
  immunity, 292
  impartiality, 26
  independence
    common law protection, 292–295
    constitutional convention, 295
    generally, 290–291
    overview, 26
    parliamentary protection, 295
    statutory protection, 291–292
  introduction, 285
  judicial immunity, 292
  judicial review, 288–289
  law lords, 286
  Lord Chancellor, 286
  nemo judex in re sua, 293–295
  parliamentary protection
    no criticism of judges, 295
    remuneration, 295
    sub judice resolution, 295

parliamentary sovereignty, 287–288
protection of the individual, 288
remuneration, 295
royal prerogative, and, 249–250
rule of law, and
  constitutional dimension, 288
  control of de facto arbitrary powers, 116–118
  defence of fundamental constitutional
    principles, 119–121
  introduction, 116
  judicial deference, 118–119
  presumption of innocence, 121
  retrospective legislation, 119–120
security of tenure, 291–292
separation of powers, and
  appointments, 85
  common law, 80–82
  constitutional dimension, 286–287
  disqualification, 85
  interpretation of statutes, 80
  introduction, 80
  other countries, in, 82
statutory interpretation, 80
statutory protection
  contempt of court, 292
  discipline, 292
  generally, 291
  security of tenure, 291–292
sub judice resolution, 295
summary, 298–299
tribunals, and, 286
junior ministers
executive, and, 233

law and custom of Parliament
separation of powers, and, 74
sources of constitution, and, 47
law lords
generally, 204
introduction, 286
overview, 210
law officers
separation of powers, and, 76–77
lawfulness of detention
human rights, and, 374–375
Leader of the House
House of Lords, and, 212
legal assistance
human rights, and, 378
legal entrenchment
conclusion, 154
form of legislation, as to, 150–153
generally, 148
Jackson case, 153–154
manner of legislation, as to, 150–153
redefinition theory, 152–153
subject-matter, as to, 148–149
legal sovereignty
and see **parliamentary sovereignty**
acts of parliament, 129–131
generally, 127
introduction, 128
origins, 128–129
legislative function
generally, 61
House of Lords, and, 72–74

introduction, 61
law officers, and, 76–77
Lord Chancellor, and, 77–80
monarchy, and, 71
Parliament, and, 74
Privy Council, and, 75–76
relationship with other powers, 63–64
legislative process
committee stage
  constitutional Bills, 278
  generally, 277–278
delegated legislation
  constitutional issues, 280–281
  generally, 279–280
draft legislation, 277
European matters, 282
financial matters, 281–282
introduction, 276
procedural matters, 279
report stage, 278
second reading, 277
summary, 282–283
third reading, 278
legitimate aims
human rights, and, 360
life peers
Appointments Commission, 206
creation, 205
non-political appointments, 205–206
overview, 210
political appointments, 205
statutory basis, 204–205
local authorities
delegated legislation, and, 39
executive, and, 238
human rights, and
  introduction, 409–410
  'public authority', 410–411
local government
advantages, 303–304
audits, 306
control, 305–306
democracy, and, 305
disadvantages, 304
functions
  administrative, 302
  discretionary, 302
  legislative, 303
  revenue raising, 303
introduction, 301
judicial review, and, 447
Ombudsman, 306
relationship with central government, 307–308
structure, 301
London
decentralisation of public power, and
  Assembly, 330
  elections, 330
  introduction, 329
  Mayor, 329–330
Lord Chancellor
appointment of judges, 79
executive function, 79
government minister, as, 79
head of judiciary, 80
introduction, 77–78

Lord Chancellor – *contd*
judicial function, 79–80
judiciary, and, 286
legislative function, 78–79
peer, as, 79
reform of office, 88
Lords Spiritual
generally, 203–204
overview, 210

Magna Carta 1215
sources of constitution, and, 35
margin of appreciation
human rights, and, 361–362
members of parliament
disqualification, 184–186
qualifications, 184
role, 183–184
Ministerial Code
ministerial responsibility, and, 256
ministerial questions
advantages, 265
disadvantages, 265
generally, 265
ministerial responsibility
classification, 255–256
collective ministerial responsibility, 256–258
committee system
advantages, 275
classification, 271
disadvantages, 275–276
framework, 271
House of Lords, in, 274
joint committees, 274
reforms, 276
select committees, 271–274
constitutional convention
classification, 255–256
collective responsibility, 256–258
individual responsibility, 258–263
Ministerial Code, 256
debates in House of Commons
Budget, 268
Early Day Motion, 269
introduction, 267
opposition day, 268–269
other, 269
Queen's speech, 268
vote of no confidence, 268
debates in House of Lords, 269
individual ministerial responsibility
actions of departmental officials, 259–260
conduct in private life of minister, 260–261
decisions or actions of minister, 259
departmental activity, 258–259
introduction, 258
professional conduct, 258–259
introduction, 255
Ministerial Code, 256
ministerial questions
advantages, 265
disadvantages, 265
generally, 265
Next Step Agencies, and, 262
oral questions in House of Commons
generally, 263

government ministers, to, 265
Prime Minister, to, 264–265
urgent, 267
oral questions in House of Lords, 266–267
Parliamentary debates
advantages, 270
disadvantages, 270
House of Commons, in, 267–269
House of Lords, in, 269
introduction, 267–271
Parliamentary questions
House of Commons, in, 263–266
House of Lords, in, 266–267
introduction, 263
urgent, 267
Prime Minister's questions
advantages, 264–265
disadvantages, 264–265
generally, 264
resignation of ministers
actions of departmental officials, 259–260
conduct in own private life, 260–261
financial activity, 261
own decisions or actions, 259
sexual activity, 261
uncertain aspect, 262
secrecy of Cabinet discussions, 258
select committees
advantages, 275
composition, 273
disadvantages, 275–276
function, 272
generally, 271–272
other, 274
powers, 273
reports, 273–274
uncertain aspects, 262–263
urgent questions, 267
written questions in House of Commons
advantages, 266
disadvantages, 266
generally, 265–266
written questions in House of Lords, 266–267
ministers
government ministers, 233–234
House of Lords, in, 239
junior ministers, 233
statistical breakdown, 239–240
monarch
executive, and, 231
monarchy
British constitution, and, 25–26
constitutional conventions, and, 49
executive, and, 229–230
separation of powers, and
executive function, 71–72
introduction, 71
judicial function, 72
legislative function, 71

National Assembly for Wales
And see **Welsh devolution**
committee system, 324
competence, 326–327
composition, 324
elections, 324

introduction, 323
Presiding Officer, 324
necessary in a democratic society
human rights, and, 360–361
nemo judex in re sua
actual bias, 478–480
appearance of bias, 478–480
family link, 479
intermingling of functions, 479
introduction, 477
judiciary, and, 293–295
meaning, 477–478
Next Step Agencies
executive, and, 236
ministerial responsibility, and, 262
Northern Irish devolution
challenging actions
Assembly, of, 321
Executive Committee, of, 321–322
committee system, 320
elections, 319–320
excepted matters, 321
Good Friday Agreement (1998), 318–319
historical background, 318–319
Human Rights Commission, 323
legislation, 320
legislative competence, 320–321
Northern Ireland Assembly
committee system, 320
composition, 319–320
elections, 319–320
introduction, 319
Presiding Officer, 320
Northern Ireland Executive Committee, 320
other bodies, 323
parliamentary sovereignty, 322
Presiding Officer, 320
relationship with Westminster, 322
reserved matters, 321
scrutiny, 321
Stormont, 318
transferred matters, 321

ombudsmen
accountability, 507
effectiveness, 506–507
introduction, 500
investigation process, 503–504
judicial review, and, 435
jurisdiction, 502–503
local government, and, 306
maladministration, 501–502
origins, 501
report stage, 504–506
screening stage, 503
types, 508
opinions
EU law, and, 40
oral questions
House of Commons
generally, 263
government ministers, to, 265
Prime Minister, to, 264–265
House of Lords, 266–267
introduction, 263
Prime Minister's questions

advantages, 264–265
disadvantages, 264–265
generally, 264
urgent, 267
ouster clauses
judicial review, and, 440
pardons
royal prerogative, and, 247

Parliament
bicameralism
arguments in favour, 163
generally, 162
Code of Conduct for Members, 175–176
constitutional conventions, and, 49
construction placed upon proceedings, 167
contempt, 173–174
debate, 165
deliberative function
examination of proposed EU legislation,
165–166
forum for debate, 164
introduction, 164–165
safeguard rights of individuals, 165
tax and finance, 165
determination of own composition, 172
examination of proposals for law
EU legislation, 165–166
generally, 164
'four petitions', 167
forum for debate, 164
free access to the monarch, 167
freedom from arrest, 167
freedom of speech
Article 9 of Bill of Rights 1689, 168–169
introduction, 167
'ought not to be impeached or questioned in
any court', 171–172
'proceedings' in Parliament, 170–171
publication of proceedings outside
Parliament, 171–172
s 13 Defamation Act 1996, 169–170
functions
deliberative, 164 166
introduction, 164
judicial, 166
legislative, 164
House of Commons
And see **House of Commons**
constitutional significance of electoral
system, 187–198
electoral system, 186–191
electorate, 193–196
elements, 198–199
functions, 179–181
members of parliament, 183–186
political composition, 191–192
reforms, 199
size and composition, 181–183
summary, 199–200
supervision and conduct of elections,
196–197
House of Lords
And see **House of Lords**
composition, 203
constitutional conventions, 220–222

Parliament – *contd*
House of Lords – *contd*
crossbench peers, 211–212
disqualification of membership, 212–213
functions, 213–217
government ministers, 211
hereditary peers, 207–210
independent peers, 211–212
introduction, 202
judicial peers, 204
Leader of the House, 212
legal powers, 217–220
life peers, 204–207
limitations on power, 220–222
Lords Spiritual, 203–204
party political composition, 210–211
reforms, 224–226
relationship with the Commons, 222–224
size, 202
Speaker of the House, 212
summary, 226
introduction, 160–162
judicial function, 166
law and custom, 47
legislative function, 164
members' interests and standards
Parliamentary Standards Act 2009,
176–178
Register of Members' Financial Interests,
174–175
Standards in Public Life, 175–176
Parliamentary Commissioner for Standards,
175
Parliamentary Standards Act 2009, 176–178
passing proposals for law, 164
privilege
construction placed upon proceedings,
167
definition, 166–167
determination of own composition, 172
free access to the monarch, 167
freedom from arrest, 167
freedom of speech, 168–172
origins, 167–168
punishment of individuals for contempt,
173–174
rationale, 167–168
regulation of own internal proceedings,
172–173
sources, 167–168
types, 167
prorogation, 162
punishment of individuals for contempt,
173–174
Queen in Parliament, 163
Register of Members' Financial Interests,
174–175
regulation of internal proceedings, 172–173
royal prerogative, and, 248–249
safeguard rights of individuals, 165
scrutiny of executive policy and
administration, 164–165
Select Committee on Standards and
Privileges, 175
separation of powers, and, 74
sessions, 161–162

sovereignty
And see **Parliamentary sovereignty**
generally, 126–159
Standards in Public Life, 175–176
summary, 178
summoning, 161
tax and finance, 165
terminology, 160–162
terms, 160–161
unicameralism, 163
vote of no confidence, 161
Parliament Act 1911
sources of constitution, and, 36
Parliamentary Commissioner for Standards
generally, 175
parliamentary executive
British constitution, and, 26
constitutional conventions, and, 49
separation of powers, and
accountable government, and, 68–69
devolved institutions, and, 69
generally, 67–68
other countries, in, 69
parliamentary privilege
construction placed upon proceedings, 167
definition, 166–167
determination of own composition, 172
free access to the monarch, 167
freedom from arrest, 167
freedom of speech
Article 9 of Bill of Rights 1689, 168–169
introduction, 167
'ought not to be impeached or questioned in
any court', 171–172
'proceedings' in Parliament, 170–171
publication of proceedings outside
Parliament, 171–172
s 13 Defamation Act 1996, 169–170
origins, 167–168
punishment of individuals for contempt,
173–174
rationale, 167–168
regulation of own internal proceedings,
172–173
sources, 167–168
types, 167
parliamentary sessions
generally, 161–162
parliamentary sovereignty
acts of parliament, 129–131
British constitution, and
generally, 134–135
introduction, 20
common law, and, 132
constitutional conventions, 139–140
courts do not challenge authority of
statutes
assumption that Parliament did not intend
to act unconstitutionally, 143–144
introduction, 141–143
surrender of sovereignty, 144–145
devolution, and, 154–155
Dicey, and
courts do not challenge authority of statutes,
141–145
introduction, 131–132

Parliament cannot bind its successors,
145–147
Queen in Parliament can pass any law,
131–141
discretionary powers, and, 136–137
enrolled Bill rule, 140
European Convention on Human Rights, 135
European Union, and
Factortame litigation, 346–349
introduction, 343
primacy of EU law, 343–344
reception of EU Law, 344–346
executive powers, and, 136–137
extra-territorial jurisdiction, and, 136
Human Rights Act 1998
generally, 155–156
introduction, 135
international law, and, 135–136
introduction, 126–127
judicial review, and, 438
judiciary, and, 287–288
law-making process, and, 132
legal entrenchment
conclusion, 154
form of legislation, as to, 150–153
generally, 148
Jackson case, 153–154
manner of legislation, as to, 150–153
redefinition theory, 152–153
subject-matter, as to, 148–149
legal sovereignty
acts of parliament, 129–131
generally, 127
introduction, 128
origins, 128–129
limitation on the laws that can be passed,
140–141
non-legal restraints
constitutional conventions, 139–140
political entrenchment, 138
political restraints, 137–138
practical restraints, 138–139
Northern Irish devolution, and, 322
origins, 128–129
Parliament cannot bind its successors
express repeal, 146
implied repeal, 146–147
introduction, 145–146
political entrenchment, 138
political restraints, 137–138
political sovereignty, 127–128
practical restraints, 138–139
Queen in Parliament can pass any law
common law, 132
generally, 131
limitations, 140–141
non-legal restraints, 137–140
redefinition theory, 152–153
repeal of legislation
express, 146
implied, 146–147
introduction, 145–146
rule of law, and, 156–157
Scottish devolution, and, 316–317
statutory interpretation, and, 133
summary, 157

surrender of, 144–145
terminology, 127–128
Welsh devolution, and, 328
Parliamentary Standards Act 2009
generally, 176–178
parliamentary terms
generally, 160–161
passports
royal prerogative, and, 246–247
peaceful assembly
generally, 385
introduction, 384
scope, 384
political entrenchment
parliamentary sovereignty, and, 138
political practices
British constitution, and, 23
political restraints
parliamentary sovereignty, and, 137–138
political sovereignty
parliamentary sovereignty, and, 127–128
politics
public law, and, 3
powers of the state
executive function, 61–62
introduction, 61
judicial function, 62
legislative function, 61
relationship between powers, 63–64
prescribed by law
human rights, and, 359–360
Presiding Officer
National Assembly for Wales, and, 324
Northern Irish Assembly, and, 320
Scottish Parliament, and, 311
presumption of innocence
human rights, and, 377–378
rule of law, and, 121
primacy of EU law
generally, 343–344
primary legislation
affecting organs of the state, 35–37
conferring rights on the individual, 37–38
constitutional status, with, 38–39
European Union, and, 340
generally, 34–35
restricting freedoms of the individual, 38
Scottish devolution, and, 312–313
Prime Minister
executive, and, 231
royal prerogative, and, 244
Prime Minister's questions
advantages, 264–265
disadvantages, 264–265
generally, 264
private and family life
correspondence, 381
family life, 380–381
home, 381
introduction, 380
private life, 380
scope, 380
private law
generally, 1–2
introduction, 1
other than private individuals, and, 2

Privy Council
  executive, and, 235
  separation of powers, and, 75–76
procedural impropriety
  see also judicial review
  actual bias, 478–480
  audi alteram partem
    generally, 480–482
    knowledge of adverse evidence, 482 483
    legal representation, 484–485
    legitimate expectation, 482
    meaning, 480
    oral hearing, 483–484
    reasons for decisions, 485
    representations, 483
    time to prepare defence or answer case, 483
  common law requirements, 477–486
  definition, 475
  nemo judex in re sua
    actual bias, 478–480
    appearance of bias, 478–480
    family link, 479
    intermingling of functions, 479
    introduction, 477
    meaning, 477–478
  statutory requirements, 476–477
prohibition of compulsory labour
  generally, 371
prohibition of discrimination
  introduction, 389
  justifiable discrimination, 389–390
  scope, 389
prohibition of forced labour
  generally, 371
prohibition of retrospective criminal law and
  penalties
  exceptions, 379
  introduction, 378
  scope, 379
prohibition of slavery and servitude
  generally, 371
prohibition of torture
  corporal punishment, 369–370
  definition of 'torture', 369
  deportation, 370–371
  extradition, 370–371
  introduction, 368
  scope, 368–369
proportionality
  human rights, and, 361
  judicial review, and
    compared with irrationality, 472–473
    definition, 471–472
    effect, 474–475
    HRA 1998, and, 473–474
    origins of ground, 471–472
    prior to HRA 1998, 473
prorogation
  parliament, and, 162
prospective laws
  rule of law, and, 96–97
public emergency
  human rights, and, 363–364
public law
  administrative law, 5
  constitutional law, 4–5

criminal law, and, 3
EU law, and, 4
generally, 2–3
introduction, 1
politics, and, 3
punishment only for breach of law
  compulsory purchase, 106
  generally, 103–109
  indefinite detention of suspected terrorists,
    105
  remand, 104–105
  search powers, 105

Queen in Parliament
  generally, 163
  parliamentary sovereignty, and
    common law, 132
    generally, 131
    limitations, 140–141
    non-legal restraints, 137–140
questioning witnesses
  human rights, and, 378

Race Relations Act 1976
  sources of constitution, and, 37
recommendations
  EU law, and, 40
redefinition theory
  parliamentary sovereignty, and, 152–153
regional development agencies
  generally, 329
Register of Members' Financial Interests
  generally, 174–175
regulations
  generally, 39
  introduction, 340
remand
  rule of law, and, 104–105
removal of judges
  separation of powers, and, 87
repeal of legislation
  parliamentary sovereignty, and
  express, 146
  implied, 146–147
  introduction, 145–146
report stage
  legislative scrutiny, and, 278
Representation of the People Act 1983
  sources of constitution, and, 37
representative democracy
  British constitution, and, 27
reservations
  human rights, and, 364–365
responsible government
  British constitution, and, 27
retrospective criminal law and penalties
  exceptions, 379
  introduction, 378
  scope, 379
retrospective legislation
  rule of law, and, 119–120
right to access to courts
  generally, 375–376
right to be brought promptly before judge for
  trial or release
  generally, 374

right to be informed as to reasons for arrest and charge
  generally, 373–374
right to challenge lawfulness of detention
  generally, 374–375
right to education
  generally, 387
right to effective remedy
  generally, 388–389
right to fair and public hearing
  access to courts, 375–376
  call and question witnesses, 378
  effective participation in the trial, 377
  impartial court or tribunal, before, 376
  introduction, 375
  legal assistance, 378
  presumption of innocence, 377–378
  scope, 375
  self-incrimination, 377–378
right to free elections
  introduction, 387
  limitations on right to vote, 388
  scope of right to vote, 388
right to liberty and security of person
  bringing promptly before judge, 374
  challenging lawfulness of detention, 374–375
  compensation, 375
  information as to reasons for arrest and charge, 373–374
  introduction, 372
  lawful arrest for non-compliance of court order, 372–373
  lawful detention after arrest, 373
  lawful detention after conviction, 372
  other lawful restrictions, 373
  scope, 372
right to life
  death penalty, and, 368
  duty to carry out effective investigation, 367
  exceptions, 367–368
  introduction, 366
  scope, 366–367
right to marry
  generally, 385–386
right to property
  introduction, 386
  restrictions, 386–387
  scope, 386
right to respect for private and family life
  correspondence, 381
  family life, 380–381
  home, 381
  introduction, 380
  private life, 380
  scope, 380
right to vote in elections
  introduction, 387
  limitations, 388
  scope, 388
rigid constitutions
  generally, 14
Royal Assent
  royal prerogative, and, 244
royal prerogative
  appointments
    government ministers, 244

    Prime Minister, 244
  classification
    constitutional prerogatives, 243–244
    executive powers, 245–247
    introduction, 243
    legal prerogatives, 244
  constitutional significance, 251–252
  declaration of war, 245
  definition, 242–243
  deployment of armed forces
    abroad, 245–246
    domestically, 246
  dissolution of Parliament, 243
  encourage, warn and advise ministers, 244
  executive powers, 245–247
  government review (2009), 247–248
  grant of Royal Assent, 244
  legal prerogatives of the Crown, 244
  pardons, 247
  passports, 246–247
  prerogative executive powers, 245–247
  Queen's constitutional prerogatives, 243–244
  ratification of international treaties, 246
  reform proposals, 243
  relationship with judiciary, 249–250
  relationship with Parliament, 248–249
  significance, 251–252
  sources of constitution, and, 45
  types, 243
rule of law
  administrative tribunals, 111
  antithesis of anarchy and chaos, as, 100
  British constitution, and
    Dicey, 103–122
    introduction, 102–103
    overview, 27
  clear laws, 97
  common law, 113–116
  compulsory purchase, 106
  conclusion, 122–123
  control of de facto arbitrary powers, 116–118
  Declaration of Delhi, and, 102
  defence of fundamental constitutional principles, 119–121
  definition, 93–94
  Dicey, and
    administrative tribunals, 111
    common law, 113–116
    compulsory purchase, 106
    discretionary powers, 106–109
    equality before the law, 109–113
    excessive state power, 121–122
    first aspect, 103–109
    generally, 103
    indefinite detention of suspected terrorists, 105
    judge-made law, 113–116
    judicial review, 111
    predominance of regular law, 106–109
    punishment only for breach of law, 103–106
    remand, 104–105
    search powers, 105
    second aspect, 109–113
    third aspect, 113–116
  discretionary powers, 106–109
  equality before the law, 109–113

rule of law – *contd*
European Convention on Human Rights, and, 101–102
European Union, and, 102
excessive state power, 121–122
indefinite detention of suspected terrorists, 105
international terms, in
Declaration of Delhi, 102
ECHR, 101–102
European Union, 102
introduction, 100
UDHR, 100
judge-made law, 113–116
judicial deference, 118–119
judicial review
generally, 437
introduction, 111
judiciary, and
constitutional dimension, 288
control of de facto arbitrary powers, 116–118
defence of fundamental constitutional
principles, 119–121
introduction, 116
judicial deference, 118–119
presumption of innocence, 121
retrospective legislation, 119–120
legal principle, as
generally, 94–95
limitation, 95–96
open laws, 97
parliamentary sovereignty, and, 156–157
political ideal or theory, as
formal view, 96
J Raz, 96–98
presumption of innocence, 121
procedural mechanism
generally, 94–95
limitation, 95–96
prospective laws, 96–97
punishment only for breach of law
compulsory purchase, 106
generally, 103–109
indefinite detention of suspected terrorists,
105
remand, 104–105
search powers, 105
remand, 104–105
presumption of innocence, 121
retrospective legislation, 119–120
role of UK courts
control of de facto arbitrary powers, 116–118
defence of fundamental constitutional
principles, 119–121
introduction, 116
judicial deference, 118–119
presumption of innocence, 121
retrospective legislation, 119–120
search powers, 105
substantive concept, as, 99–100
summary, 123–124
Universal Declaration of Human Rights, and,
100

Scottish devolution
arguments for and against, 309–310
challenging actions of Executive, 315

committee system, 311
devolved matters, 313–314
ECHR, and, 315–316
historical background, 308–309
legislation, 312–313
legislative competence, 314–315
parliamentary sovereignty, 316–317
Presiding Officer, 311
primary legislation, 312–313
reform proposals, 317–318
relationship with Westminster, 316
reserved matters, 313
Scottish administration, 311–312
Scottish Executive, 311–312
Scottish Parliament
committee system, 311
composition, 310–311
elections, 310–311
introduction, 310
Presiding Officer, 311
scrutiny, 315
secondary legislation, 313
tax-varying powers, 314
search powers
rule of law, and, 105
second reading
legislative scrutiny, and, 277
**Select Committee on Standards and
Privileges**
generally, 175
select committees
advantages, 275
composition, 273
disadvantages, 275–276
function, 272
generally, 271–272
other, 274
powers, 273
reports, 273–274
self-incrimination
human rights, and, 377–378
separation of powers
accountable government, and, 68–69
administrative tribunals, 82–83
Appellate Committee of the House of Lords,
72–74
Attorney-General, 76–77
avoid concentration of public power, 65
British constitution, and
generally, 66–89
introduction, 26
conclusion, 89–90
Crown
executive function, and, 71–72
introduction, 71
judicial function, and, 72
legislative function, and, 71
definition
introduction, 60–61
less than pure separation, 61–62
pure separation, 61
delegated legislation
introduction, 69
legal control, 70–71
other countries, in, 71
parliamentary control, 70

rationale, 70
devolved institutions, and, 69
European Union, and, 337–338
executive function
  generally, 61–62
  introduction, 61
  law officers, and, 76–77
  Lord Chancellor, and, 77–80
  monarchy, and, 71–72
  Privy Council, and, 75–76
  relationship with other powers, 63–64
High Court of Parliament, 74
introduction, 60
judges
  appointments, 85
  common law, 80–82
  constitutional dimension, 286–287
  disqualification, 85
  introduction, 80
  other countries, in, 82
  statutory interpretation, 80
judicial appointments, 85
judicial disqualification, 85
judicial function
  executive, and, 74–75
  generally, 62
  House of Lords, and, 72–74
  introduction, 61
  law officers, and, 76–77
  Lord Chancellor, and, 77–80
  monarchy, and, 72
  Parliament, and, 74
  Privy Council, and, 75–76
  relationship with other powers, 63–64
judicial independence, 87
judicial review
  generally, 438
  introduction, 87–88
judiciary, and
  appointments, 85
  common law, 80–82
  constitutional dimension, 286–287
  disqualification, 85
  introduction, 80
  other countries, in, 82
  statutory interpretation, 80
law and custom of Parliament, 74
law officers, 76–77
legislative function
  generally, 61
  House of Lords, and, 72–74
  introduction, 61
  law officers, and, 76–77
  Lord Chancellor, and, 77–80
  monarchy, and, 71
  Parliament, and, 74
  Privy Council, and, 75–76
  relationship with other powers, 63–64
Lord Chancellor
  appointment of judges, 79
  executive function, 79
  government minister, as, 79
  head of judiciary, 80
  introduction, 77–78
  judicial function, 79–80
  legislative function, 78–79

  peer, as, 79
  reform of office, 88
monarchy
  executive function, 71–72
  introduction, 71
  judicial function, 72
  legislative function, 71
Parliament, 74
parliamentary executive
  accountable government, and, 68–69
  devolved institutions, and, 69
  generally, 67–68
  other countries, in, 69
powers of the state
  executive function, 61–62
  introduction, 61
  judicial function, 62
  legislative function, 61
  relationship between powers, 63–64
Privy Council, 75–76
provide efficient government, 65–66
provide system of checks and balances, 65
rationale, 64–66
removal of judges, 87
safeguard independence of judiciary, 66
Solicitor General, 76–77
Speaker of the House of Lords
  background, 78–79
  generally, 89
sub judice resolution, 84
summary, 90–91
Supreme Court, 72–74
Sex Discrimination Act 1975
  sources of constitution, and, 37
Solicitor General
  separation of powers, and, 76–77
sources of the British constitution
  authoritative writers, 55
  classification
    authoritative writers, 55
    constitutional conventions, 48–54
    domestic case law, 41–44
    domestic legislation, 34–40
    EU case law, 45–47
    EU legislation, 40–41
    international law, 47
    introduction, 34
    law and custom of Parliament, 47
    royal prerogative, 45
    treaties, 47
  common law, 42–43
  constitutional conventions
    conversion into laws, 53–54
    definition, 48
    distinction from laws, 52
    executive, and, 49
    flexibility, 51
    introduction, 48
    judicial recognition, 52–53
    judiciary, and, 50
    monarchy, and, 49
    obligations, as, 51
    origins, 51
    Parliament, and, 49
    preliminary points, 48–49
    purpose, 50

sources of the British constitution – *contd*
  constitutional conventions – *contd*
    significance, 50
    summary, 54
  decisions, 40
  delegated legislation
    examples, 39
    local authorities, and, 39
    nature, 39
  devolved institutions, 40
  directives, 39–40
  domestic case law
    common law, 42–43
    role of courts, 41–42
    statutory interpretation, 43–44
  domestic legislation
    delegated legislation, 39
    devolved institutions, and, 40
    local authorities, and, 39
    primary legislation, 34–39
  EU case law
    European Court of Human Rights, 46–47
    European Court of Justice, 45–46
    introduction, 45
  EU law
    case law, 45–47
    legislation, 40–41
  EU legislation
    decisions, 40
    directives, 39–40
    introduction, 39
    opinions, 40
    primary sources, 39
    recommendations, 40
    regulations, 39
    secondary sources, 40–41
  European Court of Human Rights, 46–47
  European Court of Justice, 45–46
  international law, 47
  introduction, 30
  law and custom of Parliament, 47
  local authorities, and, 39
  location difficulties
    lack of court to resolve constitutional issues, 33
    lack of demarcation between laws, 31–32
    lack of list of statutes of constitutional nature, 32
    meaning of constitutional issue, 30–31
    statutes passed in similar manner, 32
  opinions, 40
  overview, 23
  primary legislation
    affecting organs of the state, 35–37
    conferring rights on the individual, 37–38
    constitutional status, with, 38–39
    generally, 34–35
    restricting freedoms of the individual, 38
  recommendations, 40
  regulations, 39
  royal prerogative, 45
  statutory interpretation
    generally, 43–44
    Human Rights Act 1998, and, 44
  summary, 57–59
  treaties, 47

sovereignty of Parliament
  acts of parliament, 129–131
  British constitution, and
    generally, 134–135
    introduction, 20
  common law, and, 132
  constitutional conventions, 139–140
  courts do not challenge authority of statutes
    assumption that Parliament did not intend to act unconstitutionally, 143–144
    introduction, 141–143
    surrender of sovereignty, 144–145
  devolution, and, 154–155
  Dicey, and
    courts do not challenge authority of statutes, 141–145
    introduction, 131–132
    Parliament cannot bind its successors, 145–147
    Queen in Parliament can pass any law, 131–141
  discretionary powers, and, 136–137
  enrolled Bill rule, 140
  European Convention on Human Rights, 135
  executive powers, and, 136–137
  extra-territorial jurisdiction, and, 136
  Human Rights Act 1998
    generally, 155–156
    introduction, 135
  international law, and, 135–136
  introduction, 126–127
  law-making process, and, 132
  legal entrenchment
    conclusion, 154
    form of legislation, as to, 150–153
    generally, 148
    Jackson case, 153–154
    manner of legislation, as to, 150–153
    redefinition theory, 152–153
    subject-matter, as to, 148–149
  legal sovereignty
    acts of parliament, 129–131
    generally, 127
    introduction, 128
    origins, 128–129
  limitation on the laws that can be passed, 140–141
  non-legal restraints
    constitutional conventions, 139–140
    political entrenchment, 138
    political restraints, 137–138
    practical restraints, 138–139
  origins, 128–129
  Parliament cannot bind its successors
    express repeal, 146
    implied repeal, 146–147
    introduction, 145–146
  political entrenchment, 138
  political restraints, 137–138
  political sovereignty, 127–128
  practical restraints, 138–139
  Queen in Parliament can pass any law
    common law, 132
    generally, 131
    limitations, 140–141
    non-legal restraints, 137–140

redefinition theory, 152–153
repeal of legislation
  express, 146
  implied, 146–147
  introduction, 145–146
rule of law, and, 156–157
statutory interpretation, and, 133
summary, 157
surrender of, 144–145
terminology, 127–128
Speaker of the House of Lords
background, 78–79
generally, 89
introduction, 212
Standards in Public Life
generally, 175–176
statutory interpretation
Duport Steels Ltd v Sirs, 85–86
generally, 43–44
Human Rights Act 1998, and, 44
judges, and, 80
parliamentary sovereignty, and, 133
sub judice resolution
judiciary, and, 295
separation of powers, and, 84
supremacy of Parliament
British constitution, and, 23
Supreme Court
separation of powers, and, 72–74

taxation
functions of parliament, and, 165
Scottish devolution, and, 314
terrorists
rule of law, and, 105
third reading
legislative scrutiny, and, 278
thought, conscience and religion
introduction, 382
restrictions, 382–383
scope, 382
treaties
British constitution, and, 23
European Union, and
  de facto constitution, as, 335
  European constitution, 336
  Treaty of Lisbon, 336
  Treaty of Rome (1957), 335
  Treaty on European Union, 335
  Treaty on the Functioning of the European
    Union, 336
sources of constitution, and, 47
tribunals
advantages, 493–494
background, 491–492
constitutional position, 492–493
definition, 491
disadvantages, 494–495
independence, 492–493
judiciary, and, 286
reforms, 495–497
types, 492

uncodified constitutions
British constitution, and, 21–22
generally, 13–14
unconstitutional acts
examples, 55–57
generally, 55
unicameralism
parliament, and, 163
Union of the United Kingdom
British constitution, and, 20
Union with Ireland Act 1800
sources of constitution, and, 35
Union with Scotland Act 1706
sources of constitution, and, 35
unitary constitutions
British constitution, and, 25
generally, 14–15
Universal Declaration of Human Rights 1948
rule of law, and, 100
sources of constitution, and, 47
unwritten constitutions
British constitution, and, 22–23
generally, 13–14

victim requirement
human rights, and, 356
vote of no confidence
parliament, and, 161

war
human rights, and, 363–364
royal prerogative, and, 245
Welsh devolution
committee system, 324
devolution issues, 327
elections, 324
historical background, 323
institutional competence, 326–327
National Assembly for Wales
  committee system, 324
  competence, 326–327
  composition, 324
  elections, 324
  introduction, 323
  Presiding Officer, 324
powers and responsibilities, 326
parliamentary sovereignty, 328
Presiding Officer, 324
relationship with Westminster, 327–328
Welsh Assembly Government, 324–325
written constitutions
generally, 13–14
written questions
House of Commons
  advantages, 266
  disadvantages, 266
  generally, 265–266
House of Lords, 266–267